Notes for
The University of Toronto
A History

Martin L. Friedland

UNIVERSITY OF TORONTO PRESS
Toronto Buffalo London

© University of Toronto Press Incorporated 2002
Toronto Buffalo London

Reprinted 2014

ISBN 978-0-8020-8526-9 (paper)

National Library of Canada Cataloguing in Publication Data

Friedland, M.L. (Martin Lawrence), 1932–
Notes for The University of Toronto : a history

ISBN 978-0-8020-8526-9 (pbk.)

1. University of Toronto – History – Bibliography. I. Title.

LE3.T52F75 2002 Suppl. 378.7139'541 C2002-900419-5
978

University of Toronto Press acknowledges the financial assistance to its publishing program of the Canada Council for the Arts and the Ontario Arts Council.

This book has been published with the help of a grant from the Humanities and Social Sciences Federation of Canada, using funds provided by the Social Sciences and Humanities Research Council of Canada.

University of Toronto Press acknowledges the finacial support for its publishing activities of the Government of Canada, through the Book Publishing Industry Development Program (BPIDP).

Contents

CHAPTER 1 – 1826 – A CHARTER FOR KING'S COLLEGE

1. Page 3, para. 1 – "later called Toronto": York became the city of Toronto on March 6, 1834: Eric Arthur, *Toronto: No Mean City,* 3rd edition (University of Toronto Press, 1986) at 68.

2. Page 3, para. 1 – "a proposed university for Upper Canada": *Colonial Advocate,* March 23, 1826; *University of King's College, Toronto, Upper Canada – Proceedings at the Ceremony of Laying the Foundation Stone, April 23, 1842; and at the Opening of the University, June 8, 1843* (Toronto: H. & W. Rowsell, 1843) at 38; J. George Hodgins, *Documentary History of Education in Upper Canada,* v. 1 (Toronto: Warwick Bros. and Rutter, 1984) at 215; G. M. Craig, "John Strachan," *DCB,* v. 9 at 758.

3. Page 3, para. 2 – "until 1841": Craig, "John Strachan" at 755.

4. Page 3, para. 2 – "education for the province": Craig, "John Strachan" at 756; the Board did not go into operation until after Imperial approval had been received in 1823.

5. Page 3, para. 2 – "a charter for a university": W. Stewart Wallace, *A History of the University of Toronto, 1827-1927* (University of Toronto Press, 1927) at 10.

6. Page 3, para. 3 – "the eyebrows of his opponents over the years": *E.g.,* the *Colonial Advocate,* November 8, 1827 : "Such a man would turn Turk or Pagan if it answered his purpose, for he is the real atheist, being truly of no religion at all."

7. Page 3, para. 3 – "until his death in 1867 at the age of 90": Craig, "John Strachan" at 754, 755, and 764-5; John S. Moir, *Church and State in Canada West: Three Studies in the Relation of Denominationalism and Nationalism, 1841-1867* (University of Toronto Press, 1959) at 163; Elizabeth Helen Pearce, "King's College: Purpose and Accountability in Higher Education: The Dilemma of King's College, 1827-1853," (Ph.D. thesis, Ontario Institute for Studies in Education, 1998); John G. Slater, "Philosophy at Toronto" (unpublished manuscript) at 5.

8. Page 4, para. 1 – "Prime Minister Mackenzie King's grandfather": Frederick H. Armstrong and Ronald J. Stagg, "William Lyon Mackenzie," *DCB,* v. 9 at 497-508; William Kilbourn, *The Firebrand: William Lyon Mackenzie and the Rebellion in Upper Canada* (Toronto: Clarke, Irwin, 1956).

9. Page 4, para. 1– "'...with which you now obey the nod of a Colonial Governor": *Colonial Advocate,* March 9, 1826.

10. Page 4, para. 2 – "and was knighted later that year": Hartwell Bowsfield, "Sir Peregrine Maitland," *DCB,* v. 8 at 595-604; Wallace, *A History of the University of Toronto* at 5. While Wallace states the knighthood was for Maitland's services at Waterloo, Bowsfield identifies his responsibilities for administering occupied Paris after the victory as the motive for the honour. Maitland was a friend of Lord Bathurst, the colonial secretary, and this probably assisted in his selection as governor. It was also probably a factor that his father-in-law, the Duke of Richmond, had just been appointed Governor-General of British North America. Maitland served as lieutenant governor until 1828.

11. Page 5, para. 1 – "one-seventh of the public lands in the province": Aileen Dunham, *Political Unrest in Upper Canada, 1815-1836* (Toronto: McClelland and Stewart, 1965) at 84-85.

12. Page 5, para. 1 – "to build an Anglican institution": Bowsfield, " Sir Peregrine Maitland" at 601; F. M. Quealey, "The administration of Sir Peregrine Maitland, lieutenant-governor of Upper Canada, 1819-1828" (Ph.D. thesis, U of T, 1968) at 472, 479.

13. Page 5, para. 2 – "perhaps 25,000 Europeans": G. M. Craig, *Upper Canada; The Formative Years* (Toronto: McLelland and Stewart, 1963) at 8, 40. There were under 7,000 Loyalists on the rolls in 1784, and immigration

from the United States was just starting when Simcoe left. A. B. McKillop estimates the population at 35,000 at the end of the 18th century: see A.B. McKillop, *Matters of Mind: The University in Ontario, 1791-1951* (University of Toronto Press, 1994) at xvii. All population figures for this period are approximations.

14. Page 5, para. 2 – "throughout the new province had been set aside": Hodgins, *Documentary History,* v. 1 at 23.

15. Page 5, para. 2 – "the different branches of liberal knowledge.": Ibid. at 17.

16. Page 5, para. 3 – "a college of a higher class": Ibid. at 11, Governor Simcoe to Sir Joseph Banks, January 8, 1791.

17. Page 5, para. 3 – "what would later be called Upper Canada": *Proceedings at the Ceremony* at 33 (referring to a memorial of 1789 from Loyalists to Lord Dorchester).

18. Page 5, para. 3 – "of infinite support to government": Hodgins, *Documentary History,* v. 1 at 11, Governor Simcoe to Sir Joseph Banks, January 8, 1791.

19. Page 5, para. 3 – "will send their children": Ibid. at 11, Governor Simcoe to Henry Dundas, Secretary of State, April 28, 1792.

20. Page 5, para. 3 – "in the revolutionary war": Simcoe was seriously wounded as well: see S. R. Mealing, "Sir John Graves Simcoe," *DCB,* v. 5 at 754.

21. Page 5, para. 4 – "though I am daily confirmed in its necessity": E. A. Cruikshank, ed., *The Correspondence of Lieut. Governor John Graves Simcoe, with Allied Documents Relating to His Administration of the Government of Upper Canada* (Toronto : Ontario Historical Society, 1923-31), v. 5 (Supplement) at 264, Governor Simcoe to Bishop Mountain, February 27, 1796; McKillop, *Matters of Mind* at 6-7.

22. Page 5, para. 4 – "a lasting obedience to His Majesty's authority": Hodgins, *Documentary History,* v. 1 at 12, Governor Simcoe to the Bishop of Quebec, April 30, 1795; Elizabeth Helen Pearce, "King's College" at 27.

23. Page 5, para. 4 – "those who corrupt them": Hodgins, *Documentary History,* v. 1 at 12, Governor Simcoe to the Bishop of Quebec, April 30, 1795; Wallace, *History of the University of Toronto* at 2.

24. Page 5, para. 5 – "a university be established in the Town of York": Hodgins, *Documentary History,* v. 1 at 22.

25. Page 5, para. 5 – "half the education endowment be used for that purpose": Ibid. at 23.

26. Page 5, para. 5 – "until after Maitland arrived": Pearce, "King's College" at 41-2.

27. Page 5, para. 5 – "to his executive council": *Proceedings Held In the Legislature of Upper Canada During the years 1831-2 & 3* (Montreal: Desbarats & Derbishire, 1845) at 24-5 (Report of the Committee of the Executive Council, 7 January, 1819); Hodgins, *Documentary History of Education,* v. 1 at 152-3.

28. Page 5, para. 5 – "use of the endowment lands for a university": Hodgins, *Documentary History,* v. 1 at 204; Pearce, "King's College" at 47-8.

29. Page 5, para. 5 – "to serve both Upper and Lower Canada": Craig, *Upper Canada* at 183.

30. Page 6, para. 1 – "a welcome annuity of £300 a year": Craig, "John Strachan" at 753.

31. Page 6, para. 1 – "Strachan had lavish tastes": Roger Hall, "John Strachan – Sharpening the Focus" (unpublished manuscript) UTA B89-0003-02.

32. Page 6, para. 1 – "to found an educational institution": Stanley Brice Frost, *McGill University: For the Advancement of Learning* (Montreal: McGill-Queen's University Press, 1980) at 21 and 35. McGill died in 1813.

33. Page 6, para. 1 – "Strachan would be its first principal": Craig, "John Strachan" at 754.

34. Page 6, para. 2 – "is not of the first quality": Hodgins, *Documentary History,* v. 1 at 205.

35. Page 6, para. 2 – "waste lands": *Proceedings at the Ceremony* at 37.

36. Page 6, para. 2 – "the more valuable crown reserves": Hodgins, *Documentary History,* v. 1 at 205.

37. Page 6, para. 2 – "for the proposed change in the endowment": Pearce, "King's College" at 54.

38. Page 6, para. 3 – "outlining why a university was necessary": Hodgins, *Documentary History,* v. 1 at 211.

39. Page 6, para. 3 – "things of which Englishmen are proud": Ibid. at 212.

40. Page 6, para. 3 – "the advantage of a religious establishment": Ibid. at 213.

41. Page 7, para. 1 – "upon the petite theatre here": *Colonial Advocate,* March 23, 1826.

42. Page 7, para. 2 – "relating to the clergy reserves": Craig, "John Strachan" at 757-8; Hall, "John Strachan" at 12.

43. Page 7, para. 2 – "but shy and of feeble health": A. N. Bethune, *Memoir of the Right Reverend John Strachan* (Toronto: Henry Rowsell, 1870) at 118; Wallace, *History of the University of Toronto* at 11.

44. Page 7, para. 2 – "firmly in control of the university": *Proceedings at the Ceremony* at 39; Pearce, "King's College" at 55.

45. Page 8, para. 1 – "who likely took a more liberal position": Paul Knaplund, *James Stephen and the British Colonial System, 1813-1847* (University of Wisconsin Press, 1953) at 171-2.

46. Page 8, para. 1 – "a tory of the old school": *Dictionary of National Biography* (Oxford University Press), v. 1 at 1328; Wilmot-Horton, his under-secretary of state for the colonies from 1822 to 1827, commented in 1839 that "undoubtedly his general politics did not respond to movement of the latter days in which he lived": Sir Robert Wilmot-Horton, *Exposition and Defence of Earl Bathurst's Administration of the Affairs of Canada* (London: John Murray, 1839) at 39.

47. Page 8, para. 1 – "meeting objections raised": *Proceedings at the Ceremony* at 39.

48. Page 8, para. 2 – "hence the title 'Dr Strachan'": Strachan received the degree from Aberdeen in 1811: see Craig, "John Strachan" at 752-754; A. N. Bethune, *Memoir* at 114-6.

49. Page 8, para. 2 – "speaks very thick and through his nose": Bethune, *Memoir* at 117.

50. Page 8, para. 3 – "to be called 'King's College'": *Charter of the University of King's College,* University of Toronto Archives; Wallace, *History of the University of Toronto* at 11 (giving March 22 as the date of the seal). A copy of the charter with the royal seal is on display in the University of Toronto Archives. The picture of the charter in the text was found in the University of Toronto Development Office. It was taken in 1979 and clearly shows that the charter photographed is not identical with the one in the Archives. The Archives personnel do not know where it is located. They thought they had the only copy. I will leave it to the next historian of the University to determine where the other copy of the charter is located.

51. Page 8, para. 4 – "who at that time was Strachan": Hodgins, *Documentary History,* v. 1 at 222.

52. Page 8, para. 4 – "the Thirty Nine Articles of Religion of the Church of England": Ibid. at 223.

53. Page 8, para. 4 – "Students, however, could be of any faith": Ibid. at 225.

54. Page 8, para. 4 – "at Oxford or Cambridge": Pearce, "King's College" at 55.

55. Page 8, para. 4 – "the King's Colleges in Nova Scotia and New Brunswick": Stanley Brice Frost, *McGill University* at 60-61: King's of New Brunswick permitted non-Anglicans to graduate in January 1829. The original provincial charter of the College of New Brunswick, in 1800, had restricted attendance to Anglicans, but this was removed by the Royal charter for King's College, New Brunswick in 1828: see Alfred G. Bailey, ed., *The University of New Brunswick Memorial Volume* (Fredericton: The University of New Brunswick, 1950) at 18-21. King's College in Windsor, Nova Scotia was founded in 1789, and received a royal charter in 1802 which compelled students to keep terms of residence and to subscribe on graduation to the thirty-nine Articles. King's affiliated with Dalhousie in 1923, eventually relocating to Halifax: see P.B. Waite, *The Lives of Dalhousie University, Volume One, 1818-1925, Lord Dalhousie's College* (Montreal: McGill-Queen's University Press, 1994) at 11 and 274-275.

56. Page 8, para. 4 – "that had ever been granted": *Proceedings at the Ceremony* at 39.

57. Page 8, para. 4 – "did not restrict either students or professors to the Church of England": Frost, *McGill University* at 60.

58. Page 9, para. 1 – "was granted a charter as University College": Pearce, "King's College" at 13 and 66; Negley Harte, *The University of London, 1836-1986* (London: Athlone Press, 1986) at 61-76.

59. Page 9, para. 2 – "in the dying days of Lord Liverpool's ministry": Lord Liverpool effectively left office on March 25, 1827 after a serious stroke in February. He had been unwell for some time, and his resignation had been awaited. The Duke of Wellington in partnership with Robert Peel carried on the government until the Whig victory in 1830. Bathurst remained in office as Lord President of the Council until then. Cf. Norman Gash, *Lord Liverpool* (London: Weidenfield and Nicolson, 1984) at 249; *Dictionary of National Biography*, v. 1 at 1328; W. R. Brock, *Lord Liverpool and Liberal Toryism* (London: Francis Cass & Co., 1967) at 283.

60. Page 9, para. 2 – "far less valuable 'waste lands'": Hodgins, *Documentary History*, v. 1 at 205 (March 31, 1827); Pearce, "King's College" at 58.

61. Page 9, para. 2 – "transferred to King's College": Hodgins, *Documentary History*, v. 1 at 205, 238; Pearce, "King's College" at 98.

62. Page 9, para. 2 – "for building purposes": Hodgins, *Documentary History*, v. 1 at 226, 238; Pearce, "King's College" at 58.

63. Page 10, para. 1 – "returned to his large family": Craig, "John Strachan" at 753. There were six children born to the Strachans still alive in 1827.

64. Page 10, para. 1 – "at the north-west corner of the present Front Street and University Avenue": Craig, "John Strachan" at 755; Hall, "John Strachan" at 10; Arthur, *Toronto* at 44. The site was originally bounded by York, Simcoe, Wellington, and Front streets.

65. Page 10, para. 1 – "Judas like work": Cited in Pearce, "King's College" at 60.

66. Page 10, para. 1 – "without the consent of parliament?": The *Colonial Advocate*, October 11, 1827, citing the Kingston *Herald*. The original *Advocate* quote has "U.C."

67. Page 10, para. 1 – "in comparison with the total of members of other Christian faiths": Craig, *Upper Canada* at 173-5.

68. Page 10, para. 2 – "the civil and religious liberty of the people": Hodgins, *Documentary History*, v. 1 at 233. The actual inquiry was initiated by a request for papers on February 15, 1828: ibid. at 235.

69. Page 10, para. 2 – "a new one granted to meet the assembly's concerns": Hodgins, *Documentary History,* v. 1 at 242 (March 20, 1828).

70. Page 10, para. 3 – "would necessarily be created": Hodgins, *Documentary History,* v. 1 at 254.

71. Page 10, para. 3 – "no religious test whatever should be required": Ibid.

72. Page 10, para. 3 – "the professor's chair of political economy": Cited in Wallace, *History of the University of Toronto* at 15.

73. Page 10, para. 4 – "proceeding at a rapid pace": Pearce, "King's College" at 67-8.

74. Page 12, para. 1 – "the design of the buildings": Hodgins, *Documentary History of Education in Upper Canada,* v. 3 at 15-22; Wallace, *History of the University of Toronto* at 20.

75. Page 12, para. 1 – "Chief Justice William Campbell": R. J. Morgan and Robert Lochiel Fraser, "Sir William Campbell," *DCB,* v. 6 at 113-119.

76. Page 12, para. 1 – "perhaps his closest friend": Robert E. Saunders, " Sir John Beverley Robinson," *DCB,* v. 9 at 668, 674, and 677. Robinson became the Chief Justice in 1829.

77. Page 12, para. 2 – "many choices for a site": Hodgins, *Documentary History,* v. 3 at 20. The possible sites included farms owned by the Hon. James McGill and George Crookshank.

78. Page 12, para. 2 – "not far from an old Indian trading post": Arthur, *Toronto* at 5.

79. Page 12, para. 2 – "because of its swampy soil": Hodgins, *Documentary History,* v. 3 at 19 (Council meeting , May 5, 1828); Pearce, "King's College" at 67-8; Wallace, *History of the University of Toronto* at 24.

80. Page 12, para. 2 – "150 acres of land from the former chief justice John Elmsley": Henri Pilon, "John Elmsley," *DCB,* v. 9 at 239.

81. Page 12, para. 2 – "unanimously approved by the council": Hodgins, *Documentary History,* v. 3 at 20 (Council meeting, May 5, 1828); Pearce, "King's College" at 68.

82. Page 12, para. 2 – "the highest part of the property": Laurence K. Shook, *Catholic Education in English-speaking Canada : A History* (University of Toronto Press, 1971) at 133-4; Pilon, "John Elmsley" at 242. Elmsley had become a Catholic and donated the land.

83. Page 13, para. 1 – "50 acres from the Elmsley family": Hodgins, *Documentary History,* v. 3 at 20 (Council meetings of May 21 and 24, 1828); Pearce, "King's College" at 68.

84. Page 13, para. 1 – "about equal to the cost of John Strachan's home": Austin Seton Thompson, *Spadina: A Story of Old Toronto* (Toronto: Pagurian Press, 1975) at 79; Hall, "John Strachan" at 10. Hall cites Strachan's estimate of £2,250 as the cost of the house before its completion. In 1829, Chief Justice John Beverley Robinson's yearly salary from the government was £1,960: see Major-General C.W. Robinson, *Life of Sir John Beverley Robinson Bart. C.B. D.C.L.* (Edinburgh: William Blackwood and Sons, 1904), Appendix at 423-424.

85. Page 13, para. 2 – "sent to Upper Canada": Hodgins, *Documentary History,* v. 2 at 222; Douglas Richardson, *A Not Unsightly Building: University College and its History* (Toronto: Mosaic Press, 1990) at 27.

86. Page 13, para. 2 – "the site where the Parliament Buildings of Ontario now stand was purchased": Roger Hall, *A Century to Celebrate/Un Centenaire à fêter, 1893-1993* (Toronto: Dundurn Press, 1993) at 20.

87. Page 13, para. 2 – "from Yonge Street to the new site": Wallace, *History of the University of Toronto* at 25; Hall, *A Century to Celebrate* at 20.

88. Page 13, para. 3 – "a portion of the general design": J. L. Henderson, ed., *John Strachan: Documents and Opinions* (Toronto: McClelland and Stewart, 1969) at 123.

89. Page 13, para. 3 – "about to open its doors": Hodgins, *Documentary History*, v. 3 at 23-4; Pearce, "King's College" at 69.

CHAPTER 2 – 1842 – LAYING THE CORNERSTONE

1. Page 14, para. 1 – "an impressive ceremony on April 23, 1842": *University of King's College, Toronto, Upper Canada, Proceedings at the Ceremony of Laying the Foundation Stone, April 23, 1842; and at the Opening of the University, June 8, 1843* (Toronto: H. & W. Rowsell, 1843) at 1-27; Plinius Secundus, *Curiae Canadenses, or the Canadian Law Courts; being A Poem, describing the several courts of Law and Equity, which have been effected from time to time in the Canadas; with Copious Notes, explanatory and historical and an Appendix of much Useful Matter* (Toronto: H. & W. Rowsell, 1843) at n. 36, p. 31; Henry Scadding, *Toronto of Old* (Toronto: Oxford University Press, 1966) at 233-5; Eric Arthur, *Toronto: No Mean City*, 3rd edition (University of Toronto Press, 1986) at 98-100.

2. Page 14, para. 1 – "A civic holiday was observed in the City of Toronto": *Proceedings* at xv, p. 6, n. 2.

3. Page 14 para. 1 – "when Maitland left in 1828": Peter G. Goheen, *Victorian Toronto, 1850 to 1900: Pattern and Process of Growth* (University of Chicago Department of Geography Research paper No. 127, 1970) at 48-53; J. M. S. Careless, *The Union of the Canadas: The Growth of Canadian Institutions* (Toronto: McClelland & Stewart, 1967) at 58; Arthur, *Toronto* at 68; Alan Wilson, "Sir John Colborne," *DCB*, v. 9 at 139.

4. Page 14, para. 2 – "at the beginning of the year": John G. Slater, ed., "Letters from the Papers of Sir Charles Bagot Concerning the Opening of King's College in 1842-1843" (unpublished manuscript) at 16-17, Sir Charles Bagot to E.G. Stanley, 27 April, 1842. E.G. Stanley would later become Lord Stanley.

5. Page 14, para. 2 – "which controlled the number of naval vessels on the Great Lakes": He had also negotiated a treaty with Russia that had opened up navigation around Alaska: see Jacques Monet, "Sir Charles Bagot," *DCB*, v. 7 at 30-33.

6. Page 14, para. 2 – "it would be Bagot": Careless, *The Union of the Canadas* at 59-62; George Metcalf, "William Henry Draper" in J. M. S. Careless, ed., *The Pre-Confederation Premiers: Ontario Government Leaders, 1841-1867* (University of Toronto Press, 1980) at 43-4.

7. Page 14, para. 3 – "the new seat of government for the United Province": Slater, ed., "Letters" at 11, W. H. Draper to Sir Charles Bagot, 6 April, 1842; ibid. at 12, Sir Charles Bagot to Bishop Strachan, 8 April, 1842; ibid. at 16, Sir Charles Bagot to E.G. Stanley, 27 April, 1842.

8. Page 15, para. 1 – "who was leader of the legislative assembly": George Metcalf, "William Henry Draper," *DCB*, v. 10 at 254.

9. Page 15, para. 1 – "Strachan's invitation to stay at 'The Palace'": Slater, "Letters" at 13, W. H. Draper to Sir Charles Bagot, 11 April, 1842.

10. Page 15, para. 1 – "as little of an exclusive character as possible": Slater, "Letters" at 9, W. H. Draper to Sir Charles Bagot 2 April, 1842; Ibid. at 12, Sir Charles Bagot to W. H. Draper, 6 April, 1842. As chancellor of the university, Bagot could accept Strachan's invitation for dinner after the ceremony. Moreover, a University dinner conveniently avoided the political consequences of accepting an invitation to attend the annual dinner that night of the English St. George Society, see Slater, "Letters" at 9, W. H. Draper to Sir Charles Bagot, 2 April, 1842; Ibid. at 11, W. H. Draper to Sir Charles Bagot, 6 April, 1842; Ibid.. at 12, Sir Charles Bagot to W. H. Draper, 10 April, 1842. The university dinner was originally scheduled to be held at William Draper's house. After declining the invitation from the St. George's Society, Bagot, with Draper's consent, accepted Strachan's invitation to host the event because of what was "due to him and due to his position," Sir Charles Bagot to W.H. Draper, 13 April, 1842.

11. Page 15, para. 2 – "at the corner of the present Queen Street and University Avenue": Then called Lot Street and College Avenue, see *Proceedings* at xv, p. 6, n. 1.

12. Page 15, para. 2 – "tastefully decorated with ever-green boughs": *Proceedings* at 3.

13. Page 16, para. 1 – "the principal of Upper Canada College": G. M. Craig, "John McCaul," *DCB,* v. 11 at 540-2.

14. Page 16, para. 1 – "lined the route": *Proceedings* at 6; Scadding, *Toronto of Old* at 234. *Proceedings* identifies the regiment as the 93rd. Scadding says the regiment lining the street was the 43rd and that the 93rd was not on duty.

15. Page 16, para. 1 – "He went on": Scadding, *Toronto of Old* at 234, citing *Curiae Canadenses* at 31, n. 36.

16. Page 16, para. 2 – "who thus commanded a view of the whole ceremony": *Proceedings* at 7 and xv, p. 7, n. 1.

17. Page 16, para. 2 – "just south-east of the present Convocation Hall": J. George Hodgins, *Documentary History of Education in Upper Canada* (Toronto: Warwick Bros. & Rutter, 1895), v. 3 at 299-300; Elizabeth Helen Pearce, "King's College: Purpose and Accountability in Higher Education: The Dilemma of King's College, 1827-1853," (Ph.D. thesis, Ontario Institute for Studies in Education, 1998) at 117.

18. Page 16, para. 2 – "still standing today": *Toronto Star,* August 20, 1997; recent research by Harold Averill suggests that very few, if any, of the trees still standing were in existence in 1842: see Averill memo to Friedland, January 29, 2001.

19. Page 16, para. 3 – "of what a university should be": *Proceedings* at 8 (Bishop Strachan's speech) and 21 (Sir Charles Bagot's speech).

20. Page 16, para. 3 – "filled with coins, various bibles, the charter and other papers": *Proceedings* at 11 and xv-xvi, p. 11, n. 3.

21. Page 16, para.3 – "three cheers for Her Majesty": *Proceedings* at 17; cheers were also given for Sir Charles Bagot, John Strachan and John Beverley Robinson.

22. Page 16, para. 4 – "this hitherto imaginary college": Slater, "Letters" at 23, Sir Charles Bagot to Richard Bagot, Bishop of Oxford, 10 May, 1842.

23. Page 17 , para. 1 – "results of a very objectionable nature": Ibid. at 3, Sir Charles Bagot to E.G. Stanley, 21 February, 1842.

24. Page 17, para. 1 – "the influence of democratic associations and principles": Ibid. at 16, Sir Charles Bagot to E.G. Stanley, 27 April, 1842.

25. Page 17, para. 1 – "I verily believe that it has been this act": Ibid. at 23, Sir Charles Bagot to Richard Bagot, Bishop of Oxford, 10 May, 1842.

26. Page 17, para. 2 – "there were two parties in the town": Ibid. at 17, Sir Charles Bagot to E.G. Stanley, 28 April, 1842.

27. Page 17, para. 2 – "two in Upper Canada had been hanged": Ten more would be hanged after the Battle of the Windmill at Prescott in November, 1838: see G.M. Craig, *Upper Canada: The Formative Years* (Toronto: McClelland and Stewart, 1963) at 255 and 258.

28. Page 18, para. 1 – "arrived in York in late 1828": Some have credited his action with assuring British victory in that decisive battle: Wilson, "Sir John Colborne" at 138.

29. Page 18, para. 1 – "under seven colonial secretaries": J. C. Sainty, comp., *Office Holders in Modern Britain: VI Colonial Office Officials* (London: University of London Institute of Historical Research, 1976) at 8. The Colonial Secretaries listed are: Sir G. Murray (app. 30 May, 1828), Lord Goderich (app. 22 November, 1830), E.G.

Stanley (app. 3 April, 1833), T. Spring-Rice (app. 5 June, 1834), Duke of Wellington (app. 17 November, 1834), Earl of Aberdeen (app. 20 December, 1834), and C. Grant (app. 18 April, 1835). Elizabeth Helen Pearce, "King's College" at 71 mentions six.

30. Page 18, para. 1 – "he was head of the military in Canada": Wilson, "Sir John Colborne" at 142-3.

31. Page 18, para. 1 – "Upper Canada's ablest governor": Ibid. at 138.

32. Page 18, para. 1 – "particularly from Strachan": Ibid. at 139.

33. Page 18, para. 2– "the most prompt and serious attention": Hodgins, *Documentary History,* v. 1 at p. 258; Pearce, "King's College" at 72.

34. Page 18, para. 2 – "a strong preparatory school, Upper Canada College": *Proceedings at the Ceremony* at 41-2; Hodgins, *Documentary History,* v. 1 at 284-90; Pearce, "King's College" at 73-8; Wilson, "Sir John Colborne," at 141; W. S. Wallace, *A History of the University of Toronto* (University of Toronto Press, 1927) at 25-30.

35. Page 18, para. 3 – "elected to the legislative assembly in 1829": Michael S. Cross and Robert Lochiel Fraser, "Robert Baldwin," *DCB,* v. 8 at 47.

36. Page 18, para. 3 – "More than 10,000 persons signed the petition": Hodgins, *Documentary History,* v. 1 at 318-19.

37. Page 18, para. 3 – "his efforts to change the charter": Cross and Fraser, "Robert Baldwin" at 51 (1843 bill).

38. Page 18, para. 3 – "such as Egerton Ryerson": Ryerson was a convert from the Church of England: see R. D. Gidney, "Egerton Ryerson," *DCB,* v. 11 at 783-795; A. B. McKillop, *Matters of Mind: The University in Ontario 1791-1951* (University of Toronto Press, 1994) at 12-3.

39. Page 18, para. 4 – "approved by the British government": Hodgins, *Documentary History,* v. 2 at 55; Pearce, "King's College" at 85.

40. Page 18, para. 4 – "the dignity of a 'Royal Charter'": Hodgins, *Documentary History,* v. 2 at 77; Pearce, "King's College" at 88.

41. Page 18, para. 4 – "need not be the archdeacon": Hodgins, *Documentary History,* v. 2 at 34; Pearce, "King's College" at 100.

42. Page 18, para. 4 – "need not hold any ecclesiastical office": Hodgins, *Documentary History,* v. 2 at 84-91; Pearce, "King's College" at 105.

43. Page 18, para. 4 – "the Thirty-Nine Articles": Hodgins, *Documentary History,* v. 2 at 34; Pearce, "King's College" at 100.

44. Page 18, para. 5 – "rejected by the appointed legislative council": Hodgins, *Documentary History,* v. 2 at 209-13; Pearce, "King's College" at 92.

45. Page 18, para. 5 – "a new lieutenant governor, Sir Francis Bond Head": S. F. Wise, "Sir Francis Bond Head," *DCB,* v. 10 at 342-345; *Report of the Royal Commission on the University of Toronto* (Toronto: L. K. Cameron, Printer to the King's Most Excellent Majesty, 1906) at xii – Head "exerted his influence to prevent a more complete modification of the Charter, and was successful to the extent of securing to the authorities of one church the guidance and control of the University."

46. Page 18, para. 5 – "was passed by both houses": Hodgins, Documentary History, v. 2 at 88-9 (7 William IV, Chapter VI, *An Act to Amend the Charter of the University of King's College*); *Report of the Royal Commission on the*

University of Toronto at 203-208 (7 William IV, Chapter VI, *An Act to Amend the Charter of the University of King's College*); Wallace, *A History of the University of Toronto* at 29-30.

47. Page 19, para. 1 – "in the Doctrine of the Holy Trinity": Hodgins, *Documentary History*, v. 3 at 89 (*An Act To Amend the Charter*, s. 1); Pearce, "King's College" at 93; John G. Slater, "Philosophy at Toronto" (unpublished manuscript) at 7.

48. Page 19, para. 1 – "directly into the running of the university": Hodgins, *Documentary History*, v. 3 at 88-89 (*An Act To Amend the Charter*, s. 1); Pearce, "King's College" at 92-93.

49. Page 19, para. 2 – "The curriculum of the university was approved": Hodgins, *Documentary History*, v. 3 at 92-96 (College Council Meeting, 10 June, 1837); Slater, "Philosophy" at 10.

50. Page 19, para. 2 – "plans were made for the construction of the college": Hodgins, *Documentary History*, v. 3 at 95 (College Council Meeting, 10 June, 1837).

51. Page 19, para. 2 – "Thomas Young": Shirley G. Morriss, "Thomas Young," *DCB*, v. 8 at 959-961.

52. Page 19, para. 2 – "engaged to plan the building": Hodgins, *Documentary History*, v. 3 at 184 (Council Meetings of 26 July, 5 August, 1837; Morriss, "Thomas Young" at 959-960; Arthur, *Toronto* at 98; Douglas Richardson, *A Not Unsightly Building: University College and its History* (Toronto: Mosaic Press, 1990) at 32-37; Wallace, *History of the University of Toronto* at 33. John Howard, Young's perennial rival, also submitted a plan, but it was not adopted.

53. Page 19, para. 2 – "connected by a covered walkway": William Dendy, *Lost Toronto* (Toronto: Oxford University Press, 1978) at 134. Several sources of inspiration have been suggested for Young's design. Dendy says it was "probably influenced by William Wilkins' Downing College, Cambridge," but Henry Scadding in *Toronto of Old* at 233 says the inspiration was Girard College, Philadelphia: see Averill to Friedland, January 29, 2001.

54. Page 19, para. 3 – "found serious irregularities": Hodgins, *Documentary History*, v. 3 at 189 (Council meeting of July 11, 1839); Wallace, *A History of the University of Toronto* at 35.

55. Page 19, para. 3 – "censurable conduct": Hodgins, *Documentary History*, v. 3 at 193 (The Hon. Joseph Wells to the Council of the University of King's College, July 8, 1839).

56. Page 19, para. 3 – "of which £1,875 was outstanding": Hodgins, *Documentary History*, v. 3 at 301-2; Pearce, "King's College" at 110-11; Roger Hall, "John Strachan – Sharpening the Focus" (unpublished manuscript, UTAB89-3-2) at 19; *Final Report of the Commissioners of Inquiry into the Affairs of King's College* (Quebec: R. Campbell, 1852) at 121-3 .

57. Page 19, para. 3 – "new political problems": Careless, *The Union of the Canadas* at 1.

58. Page 19, para. 4 – "with Ryerson as principal": Hodgins, *Documentary History of Education*, v. 4 at 57-61 (*An Act to Incorporate the Upper Canada Academy Under the Name and Style of Victoria College*) and at 218 (Opening, 21 June, 1842); R. D. Gidney, "Egerton Ryerson" at 786; A. B. McKillop, *Matters of Mind* at 12-15; C. B. Sissons, *A History of Victoria University* (University of Toronto Press, 1952) at 43-48.

59. Page 19, para. 4 – "for Queen's College in Kingston in 1841": Hodgins, *Documentary History*, v. 4 at 84-88 (Royal Charter of Queen's College, Kingston, 16 October, 1841); McKillop, *Matters of Mind* at 15-16.

60. Page 19, para. 4 – "with two professors and eleven students": Hodgins, *Documentary History*, v. 4 at 215-6; Pearce, "King's College" at 139; Hilda Neatby, *Queen's University: and not to yield* (Kingston: McGill-Queen's University Press, 1978) at 3. Neatby gives the number of students as 15, but the sources she cites make it clear that there were only 11 registered students, as well as some unofficial attendants.

61. Page 19, para. 4 – "by the Roman Catholic Bishop of Kingston": Hodgins, *Documentary History*, v. 3 at 80-1 (*An Act to Incorporate Certain Persons Therein-named as a Board of Trustees for the Erection, Superintending and Management of a Roman Catholic College at Kingston, to be known by the Name of 'The College of Regiopolis.' And for other purposes therein-mentioned* March 4, 1837); Lawrence K. Shook, *Catholic Post-Secondary Education in English-speaking Canada* (University of Toronto Press, 1971) at 18-20; Pearce, "King's College" at 137.

62. Page 19, para. 5 – "the two wings of King's": Hodgins, *Documentary History*, v. 4 at 176 (Meeting of February 23 1842); Wallace, *A History of the University of Toronto* at 38.

63. Page 20, para. 1 – "until the new buildings were completed": John G. Slater, "Letters" at 17, Sir Charles Bagot to E.G. Stanley, April 27, 1842; Hodgins, *Documentary History*, v. 4 at 179; Roger Hall, *A Century to Celebrate/ Un Centenaire à fêter, 1893-1993* (Toronto: Dundurn Press, 1993) at 11; Wallace, *A History of the University of Toronto* at 38.

64. Page 20, para. 1– "the 62-year-old Bagot knew that he was dying": Slater, "Letters" at 83, Sir Charles Bagot to Sir Robert Peel, March 26, 1843.

65. Page 20, para. 2 – "Against the wishes of President Strachan": Slater, "Letters" at 22, Bishop Strachan to Sir Charles Bagot, May 6, 1842.

66. Page 20, para. 2 – "as vice-president of King's and professor of classics": Slater, "Letters" at 23-4, Sir Charles Bagot to Richard Bagot, Bishop of Oxford, May 10, 1842; Hodgins, *Documentary History*, v. 4 at 198-202 (College Council, meeting of November 29, 1842); Craig, "John McCaul" at 540-2; Ward W. Briggs, ed., *Biographical Dictionary of North American Classicists* (Westport: Greenwood Press, 1994) at 381-2; Wallace, *A History of the University of Toronto* at 42-3.

67. Page 20, para. 2 – "leading professors must without exception be from England": Slater, "Letters" at 7, Bishop Strachan to Sir Charles Bagot, March 14, 1842.

68. Page 21, para. 1 – "allow a visit to England": Ibid. at 37-8, W. H. Draper to Sir Charles Bagot, August 11, 1842.

69. Page 21, para. 1 – "filled that role in the finding of a chemistry professor": Ibid. at 29, Sir Charles Bagot to Michael Faraday, June 1, 1842.

70. Page 21, para. 1 – "under a number of distinguished professors": Ibid. at 33, Michael Faraday to Sir Charles Bagot, July 19, 1842.

71. Page 21, para. 1 – "until his retirement in 1880": G. M. Craig, "Henry Holmes Croft," *DCB*, v. 11 at 218-9.

72. Page 21, para. 1 – "is named after him": Richardson, *A Not Unsightly Building* at 124.

73. Page 22, para. 1 – "as the Mathematical Professor?": Slater, "Letters" at 27-28, Sir Charles Bagot to Lord Lyttleton, May 28, 1842.

74. Page 22, para. 1 – "but left after a year": Slater, "Philosophy" at 15.

75. Page 22, para. 1 – "James Sylvester": Karen Hunger Parshall, *James Joseph Sylvester: Life and Works in Letters* (Oxford: Clarendon Press, 1998) at 1; Lewis S. Feuer, "America's First Jewish Professor: James Joseph Sylvester at the University of Virginia," *American Jewish Archives*, vol. XXXVI, no. 2 (1984) at 188.

76. Page 22, para. 1 – "had actually applied for the job": Slater, "Letters" at 35, James J. Sylvester to Sir Charles Bagot, July 20, 1842. This is an inference because the issue is not raised in the correspondence.

77. Page 22, para. 1 – "the Copley Medal of the Royal Society": Parshall, *James Joseph Sylvester* at 235-9; Feuer, "America's First Jewish Professor" at 152.

78. Page 22, para. 2 – "had converted to Christianity": Hodgins, *Documentary History of Education in Upper Canada,* v. 5 at 132; Mel Starkman, "A Meshamud at the University of Toronto," *Canadian Jewish Historical Journal* (1981) at 70-90; Stephen Speisman, *The Jews of Toronto* (Toronto: McClelland & Stewart, 1979) at 15: Hirshfelder was appointed in 1844, after Bagot's death. Hirshfelder was the only member of the staff at the rank of tutor: see Averill to Friedland, January 29, 2001.

79. Page 23, para. 1 – "the crowded state of the ecclesiastical profession": Slater, "Letters" at 24, Sir Charles Bagot to Richard Bagot, Bishop of Oxford, May 10, 1842.

80. Page 23, para. 1 – "at least their third choice": T. R. Millman, "James Beaven," *DCB,* v. 10 at 39-40; Slater, "Philosophy" at 14.

81. Page 23, para. 2 – "After Attorney-General Draper had turned it down": Slater, "Letters" at 67, Sir Charles Bagot to W. H. Draper, December 9, 1842 (nomination) and at 70, W. H. Draper to Sir Charles Bagot, December 12, 1842 (refusal).

82. Page 23, para. 2 – "on a part-time basis to William Hume Blake": Donald Swainson, "William Hume Blake," *DCB,* v. 9 at 55-9.

83. Page 23, para. 2 – "during his fatal illness": Slater, "Letters" at 54, n. 53.

84. Page 23, para. 2 – "who became the professor of anatomy and physiology": *Proceedings* at xiii.

85. Page 23, para. 2 – "but very unwarrantably directed against us": Slater, "Letters" at 44, Sir Charles Bagot to Bishop Strachan, October 18, 1842.

86. Page 23, para. 3 – "on June 8, 1843": *Proceedings* at 28; Hodgins, *Documentary History,* v. 4 at 277.

87. Page 23, para. 3 – "with some degree of solemnity": Slater, "Letters" at 63, Bishop Strachan to Sir Charles Bagot, November 29, 1842.

88. Page 23, para. 3 – "Eight professors and twenty-six students took part": *Proceedings* at 30-32, and xviii, p. 31, n. 2.

89. Page 23, para. 3 – "to poison the minds of the people against the charter": Ibid. at 40.

90. Page 23, para. 3 – "as all such godless imitations of Babel ever must": Ibid. at 48.

CHAPTER 3 – 1849 – THE CREATION OF THE UNIVERSITY OF TORONTO AND TRINITY COLLEGE

1. Page 24, para. 1 – "into the University of Toronto": Elizabeth Gibbs, ed., *Debates of the Legislative Assembly of United Canada* (Montreal: Centre de recherche en histoire économique du Canada français, 1977), v. 8, pt. 2 at 1688, April 3, 1849; J. George Hodgins, *Documentary History of Education in Upper Canada* (Toronto: L. K. Cameron, 1901), v. 8 at 119 (Robert Baldwin's speech to the Legislative Assembly on a motion for leave to introduce his bill, April 2, 1849); Elizabeth Helen Pearce, "King's College: Purpose and Accountability in Higher Education: The Dilemma of King's College, 1827-1853" (Ph.D. thesis, Ontario Institute for Studies in Education, 1998) at 165; Michael Cross and Robert Lochiel Fraser, "Robert Baldwin," *DCB,* v. 8 at 55.

2. Page 24, para. 1 – "eliminating any publicly funded chairs of divinity": *An Act to Amend the Charter of the University of Toronto and Regulate the Upper Canada College and Royal Grammar School, 12 Victoria, Chapter 82* (Toronto: Henry Rowsell, 1852) at s. 12; Hodgins, Documentary History, v. 8 at 120; Pearce, "King's College" at 166.

3. Page 24, para. 1 – "whether student or professor": *An Act to Amend the Charter* at s. 29; Pearce, "King's College" at 166; A. B. McKillop, *Matters of Mind: The University in Ontario, 1791-1951* (University of Toronto Press, 1994) at 20.

4. Page 24, para. 1 – "perhaps as divinity halls": John S. Moir, *Church and State in Canada West: Three Studies in the Relation of Denominationalism and Nationalism,* 1841-1867 (University of Toronto Press, 1959) at 88; J. M. S. Careless, *The Union of the Canadas: The Growth of Canadian Institutions* (Toronto: McClelland & Stewart, 1967) at 123.

5. Page 24, para. 1 – "and centralism in Upper Canadian higher education": Careless, *The Union of the Canadas* at 123.

6. Page 24, para. 2 – "legislative building on Front Street": Austin Seton Thompson, *Spadina: a Story of Old Toronto* (Toronto: Pagurian Press Ltd., 1975) at 84.

7. Page 24, para. 2 – "with the Reverend James Beaven in charge": W. S. Wallace, *A History of the University of Toronto* (University of Toronto Press, 1927) at 50.

8. Page 24, para. 2 – "before the gates were closed at 9.30 in the evening": Hodgins, *Documentary History,* v. 5 at 209.

9. Page 24, para. 2 – "a certain number of chapel services": Wallace, *A History of the University of Toronto* at 49.

10. Page 24, para. 2 – "the same pies and puddings made their appearance": Ibid. at 50.

11. Page 24, para. 3 – "several others had graduated": Ibid. at 49.

12. Page 25, para. 1 – "shares in the Welland Canal Company for that purpose": Hodgins, *Documentary History,* v. 5 at 152-3 (Council meeting of December 23, 1844).

13. Page 25, para. 1 – "22 of the first 26 students": *University of King's College, Toronto, Upper Canada, Proceedings at the Ceremony of Laying the Foundation Stone, April 23, 1842; and at the Opening of the University, June 8, 1843* (Toronto: H. & W. Rowsell, 1843) at 31 and xviii, p. 31, n. 2; Wallace, A History of the University of Toronto at 47; Pearce, "King's College," at 155.

14. Page 25, para. 1 – "had much chance of admission": Hodgins, *Documentary History,* v. 15 at 179-180 (John Langton's testimony before the Select Committee of 1860); Wallace, *A History of the University of Toronto* at 49.

15. Page 25, para. 1 – "nearly all the chief classics of ancient times": Hodgins, *Documentary History,* v. 15 at 213 (Daniel Wilson's testimony before the Select Committee of 1860); Wallace, *A History of the University of Toronto* at 48-9.

16. Page 25, para. 2 – "a similar bill back in 1843": Hodgins, *Documentary History,* v. 5 at 67-87 (text of Bill); Careless, *The Union of the Canadas* at 82.

17. Page 26, para. 1 – "in the fall of 1842": Careless, *The Union of the Canadas* at 68-9; Cross and Fraser, "Robert Baldwin" at 50. Bagot had wanted only the adhesion of LaFontaine and his supporters, but LaFontaine honoured his agreement with Baldwin and refused to enter office without the Upper Canadian. The Assembly accepted Bagot's Great Measure on September 20, 1842.

18. Page 26, para. 1 – "more of a provincial character": John G. Slater, ed., "Letters from the Papers of Sir Charles Bagot Concerning the Opening of King's College in 1842-1843" (unpublished manuscript) at 76, Robert Baldwin to Captain Bagot, 16 March, 1843.

19. Page 26, para. 1 – "class favouritism": Cross and Fraser, "Robert Baldwin" at 55.

20. Page 26, para. 1 – "was continuing to decline": A. B. McKillop, *Matters of Mind* at 11; Careless, *The Union of the Canadas* at 113.

21. Page 26, para. 1 – "several theological chairs": Hodgins, *Documentary History,* v. 5 at 73-4, s. 31.

22. Page 26, para. 1 – "on other grounds in November 1843": Careless, *The Union of the Canadas* at 82-3. Sir Charles Metcalfe, Bagot's successor, objected to LaFontaine's and Baldwin's use of patronage to build up partisan support.

23. Page 26, para. 2 – "The new leader of the government, William Draper": Hodgins, *Documentary History,* v. 5 at 159-166; J. S. Moir, *Church and State in Canada West* at 91-94; Pearce, "King's College" at 147-8; George Metcalf, "William Henry Draper," *DCB,* v. 10 at 256.

24. Page 26, para. 2 – "according to the number of students it attracted": Hodgins, *Documentary History,* v. 5 at 163, s. 29.

25. Page 27, para. 1 – "that would not emerge again until the 1960s": Pearce, "King's College" at 148.

26. Page 27, para. 1 – "instead of large well endowed ones": Hodgins, *Documentary History,* v. 5 at 188; Pearce, "King's College" at 151.

27. Page 27, para. 1 – "opposed to this solution": Hodgins, *Documentary History,* v. 5 at 135-8 (Petition of the President of King's College University to the Governor General on the Proposed Draper University Bills of 1845); Pearce, "King's College" at 148-9; Donald Robert Beer, "Henry Sherwood," *DCB,* v. 7 at 799-800; Hereward Senior, "William Henry Boulton," *DCB,* v. 10 at 80.

28. Page 27, para. 1 – "complained that they were being shut out": Hodgins, *Documentary History,* v. 7 at 257 (5th Annual meeting of the Canada Baptist Church, endorsing Macdonald's partition proposal).

29. Page 27, para. 1 – "two defecting conservatives": Pearce, "King's College" at 161; Beer, "Henry Sherwood" at 800.

30. Page 27, para. 2 – "an important issue in the election": Careless, *The Union of the Canadas* at 117-118

31. Page 27, para. 2 – "under instructions from London to maintain political neutrality": Ibid. at 119; Cross and

Fraser, "Robert Baldwin" at 52. In private, Elgin exercised more influence than his official neutrality would suggest. W. L. Morton, "James Bruce," *DCB*, v. 9 at 90.

32. Page 28, para. 1 – "through which internal self-government was worked out for Canada": Careless, *The Union of the Canadas* at 119-120 .

33. Page 28, para. 1 – "the financial functioning of the college": Cross and Fraser, "Robert Baldwin" at 55; Hodgins, *Documentary History*, v. 8 at 3-4, (University Statute of 1848, Authorizing the Commissioners to Make the Inquiry). The Statute was passed on 20 March, 1848; the *Final Report of the Commissioners of Inquiry into the Affairs of King's College University* (Quebec: R. Campbell, 1852) was submitted to the Legislature in 1852.

34. Page 28, para. 2 – "St. Anne's Market building in Montreal": Careless, *The Union of the Canadas* at 96.

35. Page 28, para. 2 – "any portion of the students attending the University": Ibid.

36. Page 28, para. 2 – "the British minority in Canada East": Ibid. at 124-6; Cross and Fraser, "Robert Baldwin" at 54; W. L. Morton, "James Bruce," *DCB*, v. 9 at 91-2.

37. Page 28, para. 2 – "that boil and toss beneath our feet": Careless, *The Union of the Canadas* at 126.

38. Page 28, para. 3 – "the quickly refurbished Bonsecours Market": Ibid.

39. Page 28, para. 3 – "It was immediately attacked by William Boulton": Senior, "William Henry Boulton," *DCB*, v. 10 at 79-81.

40. Page 28, para. 3 – "owner of the stately Grange residence in Toronto": Eric Arthur, *Toronto: No Mean City*, 3rd edition (University of Toronto Press, 1986) at 54; Senior, "William Henry Boulton" at 79; The Grange Home Page at www.ago.net/information/grange.

41. Page 28, para. 3 – "Strachan's spokesman in the assembly": Senior, "William Henry Boulton," *DCB*, v. 10 at 79-80.

42. Page 28, para. 3 – "entirely infidel": Elizabeth Gibbs, ed., *Debates*, v. 8, pt. 3 at 2248, May 11, 1849.

43. Page 28, para. 3 – "without leaving one vestige of it remaining": Ibid. at 2249.

44. Page 28, para. 3 – "A Bill for the Spoliation and Robbery of the Church": Ibid. at 2250.

45. Page 28, para. 3 – "as other denominations also possessed one": Ibid.

46. Page 28, para. 3 – "he would be prepared to grant it": Ibid. at 2255.

47. Page 28, para. 4 – "that is, the 1849 bill": Ibid. at 2249.

48. Page 28, para. 4 – "Professors Croft and Gwynne": L. G. Thomas, "William Charles Gwynne," *DCB*, v. 10 at 325-6.

49. Page 28, para. 4 – "another medical professor, William Beaumont": W. G. Crosbie, "William Rawlins Beaumont," *DCB*, v. 10 at 38-9.

50. Page 28, para. 4 – "council members Robert Baldwin and William Hume Blake": Hodgins, *Documentary History*, v. 7 at 239-40 (Council meeting of 27 September, 1848); J. S. Moir, *Church and State in Canada West* at 88.

51. Page 28, para. 4 – "undue clerical influence": Moir, *Church and State in Canada West* at 88; Hodgins, *Documentary History*, v. 4 at 238-9, (Proceedings of the Legislative Assembly, 18 November, 1843).

52. Page 29, para. 1 – "were strongly opposed to the bill": Hodgins, *Documentary History*, v. 8 at 193-6 (Council meetings of 24 April, 9 May, 1849).

53. Page 29, para. 1 – "and McCaul was now its president": Hodgins, *Documentary History*, v. 7 at 258-61; John G. Slater, "Philosophy at Toronto" (unpublished manuscript) at 39; G. M. Craig, "John Strachan," *DCB*, v. 9 at 762.

54. Page 29, para. 2 – "became law on May 30, 1849": Gibbs, ed., *Debates* at 2259, May 11, 1849 (2nd reading by 42-2) and at 2326, May 18, 1849 (3rd reading by 44-14).

55. Page 29, para. 2 – "real charter of the institution": *Report of the Royal Commission on the University of Toronto* (Toronto: L. K. Cameron, Printer to the King's Most Excellent Majesty, 1906) at xiii.

56. Page 29, para. 2 – "to be described in the next chapter": See Chapter 4 (1850).

57. Page 29, para. 3 – "his proposed new Church of England institution, Trinity College": Craig, "John Strachan" at 763; Wallace, *A History of the University of Toronto* at 57.

58. Page 29, para. 3 – "if the Percy family would put up the money": J. L. H. Henderson, "The Founding of Trinity College, Toronto," *Ontario History*, vol. XLIV(1952), No. 1 at 7.

59. Page 29, para. 3 – "say, Trinity College": Ibid. at 8.

60. Page 29, para. 4 – "a calamity not easy to bear": Craig, "John Strachan" at 763; Henri Pilon, "The Founding of the University of Trinity College," *Trinity Convocation Bulletin* (vol. 14 no. 3, 1977) at 4.

61. Page 29, para. 4 – "He himself pledged £1,000 to the cause": Craig, "John Strachan" at 763; Pilon, "The Founding of the University of Trinity College" at 2 (Subscription List).

62. Page 29, para. 4 – "to take the steamer *Europa* to England": Henderson, "The Founding of Trinity College, Toronto" at 10; Arthur, *Toronto: No Mean City* at 125. Arthur identifies the vessel upon which Strachan left Toronto as the *America*; it may have been the steamer that took Strachan to New York.

63. Page 29, para. 4 – "this time without a Royal Charter": Henderson, "The Founding of Trinity College, Toronto" at 10-11.

64. Page 29, para. 4 – "Neither the government of the colony": Ibid. at 11-13; Pearce, "King's College" at 175-6.

65. Page 29, para. 4 – "nor the University of Toronto": Henderson, "The Founding of Trinity College, Toronto" at 13-14; Pearce, "King's College" at 174-5; John G. Slater, "Philosophy at Toronto" at 40; Hodgins, *Documentary History*, v. 9 at 51-54 (Correspondence between Hon. Peter de Blaquière, Chancellor of the University of Toronto and Bishop Strachan, 1851).

66. Page 30, para. 2 – "the emerging Catholic system of education in the province": William Westfall, "Constructing Public Religions at Private Sites: The Anglican Church in the Shadow of Disestablishment," in Marguerite Van Die, ed., *Religion and Public Life in Canada: Historical and Comparative Perspectives* (University of Toronto Press, forthcoming), draft at 41-43.

67. Page 30, para. 2 – "Encouraged by Robinson": Robert E. Saunders, "Sir John Beverley Robinson," *DCB*, v. 9 at 677.

68. Page 30, para. 2 – "even though it could not yet grant degrees": Henderson, "The Founding of Trinity College, Toronto" at 14.

69. Page 30, para. 2 – "near Church and Adelaide streets": Westfall, "The Divinity 150 Project" (unpublished draft), chap. 7 at 9; Henderson, "The Founding of Trinity College, Toronto" at 11; T. A. Reed, ed., *A History of the University of Trinity College, Toronto, 1852-1952* (University of Toronto Press, 1952) at 40.

70. Page 30, para. 3 – "for £2,000": Westfall, "The Divinity 150 Project," chap. 7 at 11-12; Henderson, "The Founding of Trinity College, Toronto" at 11; Reed, ed., *A History of the University of Trinity College* at 38; Henri Pilon, "The Founding of the University of Trinity College" at 4-5.

71. Page 30, para. 3 – "with many fine estates along it": Westfall, "The Divinity 150 Project," chap. 7 at 13-16.

72. Page 30, para. 3 – "a splendid view of the lake and the harbour": Henderson, "The Founding of Trinity College, Toronto" at 11.

73. Page 30, para. 3 – "A college council was formed at about the same time": Reed, ed., *A History of the University of Trinity College* at 41; Westfall, "The Divinity 150 Project," chap. 7 at 16.

74. Page 30, para. 3 – "Architect Kivas Tully": Stephen A. Otto, "Kivas Tully," *DCB,* v. 13 at 1037-1039.

75. Page 30, para. 3 – "which would later build University College": Arthur, *Toronto: No Mean City* at 130; Westfall, "The Divinity 150 Project," chap. 7 at 16-17. Cumberland and Ridout applied for the Trinity job, but it would be Cumberland and Storm who built U.C.: see Chapter 6 (1856).

76. Page 30, para. 3 – "at the corner of Yonge and Front streets": Otto, "Kivas Tully" at 1038; Eric Arthur, *Toronto: No Mean City* at 85.

77. Page 30, para. 3 – "Sod was turned in the spring of 1851": Westfall, "The Divinity 150 Project," chap. 7 at 17; Pilon, "The Founding of the University of Trinity College" at 5; Henderson, "The Founding of Trinity College, Toronto" at 11. The first sod was turned on 17 March, 1851.

78. Page 30, para. 3 – "took part in the laying of another corner stone": Craig, "John Strachan" at 763; Pilon, "The Founding of the University of Trinity College" at 6. The cornerstone was laid on 30 April, 1851.

79. Page 30, para. 3 – "about two years after the closing of King's": Pilon, "The Founding of the University of Trinity College" at 7 ; Henderson, "The Founding of Trinity College, Toronto" at 11; Westfall, "The Divinity 150 Project," chap. 7 at 10.

80. Page 30, para. 4 – "permitting it to grant degrees": *Statutes and Regulations of Trinity College and St. Hilda's College and Historical Documents* (Toronto: Trinity College Archives, 1996) at E1(Charter) and D1 (Act of Incorporation).

81. Page 30, para. 4 – "and join the University of Toronto": Henderson, "The Founding of Trinity College, Toronto" at 14.

82. Page 30, para. 4 – "it was hard to deny the Church of England the similar privilege of a charter": Hodgins, *Documentary History,* v. 10 at 203, February 3, 1852, John Strachan to Lord Elgin; Westfall, "The Divinity 150 Project," chap. 6 at 37; Henderson, "The Founding of Trinity College, Toronto" at 14.

83. Page 31, para. 1 – "students had to declare their allegiance to the Church of England": Westfall, "The Divinity 150 Project," chap. 7 at 51-2.

84. Page 31, para. 1 – "He had a wife and at least eight children": Christopher Fergus Headon, "George Whitaker," *DCB,* v. 11 at 916-8.

85. Page 31, para. 1 – "that the professors be celibate": McKillop, *Matters of Mind* at 89. McKillop states that this policy was in effect until 1859. The building on Queen Street was designed with living accommodations for the

provost's family. The other members of the faculty were expected to be in residence; William Westfall has written of the importance of this residential idea in the pedagogy of Trinity: see Westfall, "The Divinity 150 Project," chap. 7 at 53. Westfall also points out that there is no evidence of a requirement for celibacy, although there was no resident space for professors' wives other than for Whitaker: see e-mail from William Westfall to Charles Levi, February 9, 2001.

86. Page 31, para. 1 – "what others had put asunder": Henderson, "The Founding of Trinity College, Toronto" at 11.

87. Page 31, para. 2 – "in a very few years some change would be loudly called for": Gibbs, ed., *Debates*, v. 8, pt. 3 at 2325, May 18, 1849.

CHAPTER 4 – 1850 – STARTING OVER

1. Page 32, para. 1 – "When the University of Toronto officially came into existence on January 1, 1850": W.S. Wallace, *History of the University of Toronto* (Toronto: University of Toronto Press, 1927) at 60.

2. Page 32, para. 1 – "automatically became professors in the University of Toronto": *An Act to Amend the Charter of the University of Toronto and Regulate the Upper Canada College and Royal Grammar School, 12 Victoria, Chap. 82, together with An Act to Remove Certain Doubts Respecting the Intention of the Above, 13&14 Victoria, Chap. 49* (Toronto: Henry Rowsell, 1852) at s. 46. The professors were issued new commissions under s. 46 of the Act: *Report of the Caput for the Year 1850*, Canada, Legislative Assembly Journals, 1851, Appendix I.I.I. August 2. "The teaching staff was taken over, practically without change, from King's College": Wallace, *History of the University of Toronto* at 61.

3. Page 32, para. 1 – "In spite of his opposition to its founding": J.G. Hodgins, *Documentary History of Higher Education in Ontario*, v. 8 at 193-6 (Council meetings of April 24 and May 9, 1849).

4. Page 32, para. 1 – "for the next thirty years": G.M. Craig, "John McCaul," *DCB*, v. 9 at 541.

5. Page 32, para. 1– "He also continued his 'high scholarship'": Ward Briggs Jr., ed., *Biographical Dictionary of North American Classicists* (Westport: Greenwood Press, 1994) at 381.

6. Page 32, para. 6 – "Christian epitaphs of the first six centuries a few years later": Craig, "McCaul" at 541.

7. Page 32, para. 2 – "he became the professor of metaphysics and ethics": Wallace, *History of the University of Toronto* at 61; T.R. Millman, "James Beaven," *DCB*, v.10 at 39.

8. Page 32, para. 2 – "as the dean of arts": As per *An Act to Amend the Charter of the University of Toronto*, s. 13; *Report of the Caput for the Year 1850*, (Canada: Legislative Assembly Journals, 1851, Appendix I.I.I., August 2). Beaven was re-elected in December, 1851: Hodgins, *Documentary History of Higher Education in Ontario*, v. 9 at 79 (Report of the Caput of the University of Toronto for 1851).

9. Page 32, para. 2 – "an Institution which I abominate": Hodgins, *Documentary History*, v. 9 at 269-270; John G. Slater, "Philosophy at Toronto" (unpublished manuscript) at 41.

10. Page 32, para. 2 – "remain as one of its Professors": Hodgins, *Documentary History*, v. 9 at 270.

11. Page 32, para. 2 – "I cannot see my way clear to acting otherwise": Hodgins, *Documentary History*, v. 9 at 271; Slater, "Philosophy" at 42.

12. Page 33, para. 1 – "so he remained": Beaven had "four sons and three daughters": see Millman, "James Beaven" at 40.

13. Page 33, para. 1 – "Beaven apologised": Hodgins, *Documentary History*, v. 9 at 282; Slater, "Philosophy" at 43.

14. Page 33, para. 2 – "unsuccessfully tried to find Beaven a pulpit": William Westfall, "The Divinity 150 Project" (unpublished manuscript) at 74.

15. Page 33, para. 2 – "Beaven was neither a good scholar nor a good teacher": Slater, "Philosophy" at 39.

16. Page 33, para. 2 – "His real interest was in church work": Millman, "James Beaven" at 39-40.

17. Page 33, para. 2 – "as dry as his lectures": William James Loudon, *Sir William Mulock: A Short Biography* (Toronto: The Macmillan Company, 1932) at 39; Slater, "Philosophy" at 54.

18. Page 33, para. 2 – "incompetent for the chair": *Toronto World*, October 23, 1889; Slater, "Philosophy" at 56.

19. Page 34, para. 1 – "I wish you a very good morning": William H. Van Der Smissen, "More Reminiscences," *University of Toronto Monthly*, v. 21 at 248-9; John Campbell, "The Reverend Professor James Beaven, D.D., M.A.," *University of Toronto Monthly*, v. 3 at 71; Slater, "Philosophy" at 56.

20. Page 34, para. 2 – "where all professors had a place": *An Act to Amend the Charter of the University of Toronto*, s. 17.

21. Page 34, para. 2 – "Croft was elected vice-chancellor by the senate": *Report of the Caput for the Year 1850*.

22. Page 34, para. 2 – "who had been on the faculty of King's College since 1843": William Canniff, *The Medical Profession in Upper Canada 1783-1850* at 535.

23. Page 34, para. 2 – "was elected dean of medicine by his colleagues": As per *An Act to Amend the Charter of the University of Toronto*, s. 13; *Report of the Caput for the Year 1850*. Beaumont was elected in his place in December, 1851: Hodgins, *Documentary History*, v. 9, 79 (Report of the Caput of the University of Toronto for 1851).

24. Page 34, para. 2 – "The part-time professor and dean of law": Ibid.

25. Page 34, para. 2 – "George Skeffington Connor": R. Lynn Ogden, "Skeffington O'Connor," *DCB*, v. 9 at 151.

26. Page 34, para. 2 – "together with their families in 1832": Ibid.

27. Page 34, para. 2 – "where he had to rely entirely on student fees": Hodgins, *Documentary History*, v.9 at 133; Mel Starkman, "A Meshamud at the University of Toronto," *Canadian Jewish Historical Society Journal*, v.5, n.2 (1981) at 75.

28. Page 34, para. 3 – "parliament returned to Toronto for its sittings": R.M. and J. Baldwin, *The Baldwins and the Great Experiment* (Toronto: Longman's, 1969) at 221.

29. Page 34, para. 3 – "as well as Professor Croft's laboratory": *Report of the Caput for the Year 1850* at 1; Wallace, *History of the University of Toronto* at 62.

30. Page 34, para. 3 – "were transferred to Trinity College": *An Act to Amend the Charter of the University Established at Toronto*, s. 81 (requires the University to dispose of the books as the Society requests); Hodgins, *Documentary History*, v. 9 at 72 (Correspondence between the Society and the University of Toronto directing that the books be transferred to Trinity).

31. Page 34, para. 3 – "along with the Duke of Wellington Scholarship": T.A. Reed, *A History of the University of Trinity College, Toronto 1852-1952* (University of Toronto Press, 1952) at 55-56.

32. Page 34, para. 3 – "on the site of the present Medical Sciences Building": Wallace, *History of the University of Toronto* at 62; William Denby, *Lost Toronto: Images of the City's Past* (Toronto: McClelland and Stewart, 1993) at 181; Roger Hall, *A Century to Celebrate: The Ontario Legislative Building* (Toronto: Dundurn Press, 1993) at 21.

33. Page 34, para. 3 – "and other official university bodies": *Report of the Caput for the Year 1850*, at 1-2 (the property of Mr. George Ridout on Wellington Street); Wallace, *History of the University of Toronto* at 62 (1851 Report – property of Mr. Ridout).

34. Page 35, para. 1– "He produced an elegant design": Hall, *Century* at 22; Douglas Richardson, *A Not Unsightly Building: University College and Its History* (Toronto: Mosaic Press, 1990) at 42-46.

35. Page 35, para. 1 – "thinking that Toronto would become the capital": Wallace, *History of the University of Toronto*

at 70. Section 46 of the *University of Toronto Amendment Act, 1853*, placed all University land and property under the control of the Canadian government to be disposed of as it pleased: Hall, *Century* at 22. The University returned to the legislative buildings on Front street: see Wallace, *History of the University of Toronto* at 70.

36. Page 35, para. 1 – "The building was needed for a woman's mental hospital": Hall, *Century* at 23.

37. Page 35, para. 1 – "The University Lunatic Asylum": A.B. McKillop, *Matters of Mind: The University in Ontario 1791-1951* (University of Toronto Press, 1994) at 25.

38. Page 35, para. 2 – "roughly the same as had been at King's": *Report of the Caput for the Year 1850* at 6.5; *The University of Toronto and Its Colleges, 1827-1906*, Appendix H, "Attendance of Students at University College, Including Attendance on King's College, 1843-49 and on the University of Toronto, 1850-53."

39. Page 36, para. 1 – "but rose to 56 in 1857": *The University of Toronto and Its Colleges, 1827-1906*, Appendix H.

40. Page 36, para. 1 – "preparing for the Law Society and medical exams": *Report of the Caput for the Year 1850* at 6.5.

41. Page 36, para. 1 – "the Northern to Collingwood": George Kennedy, "Some Recollections of an Old Boy," *University of Toronto Monthly* (1907/08) at 103-104.

42. Page 36, para. 1 – "with first-prize medals in both classics and metaphysics": Robert M. Stamp, "Adam Crooks," *DCB*, v.11 at 221.

43. Page 36, para. 1 – "received the silver medal in classics": Ben Forster and Jonathan Swainger, "Edward Blake," *DCB*, v. 14 at 75; Joseph Schull, *Edward Blake: The Man of the Other Way* (Toronto: Macmillan of Canada, 1975) at 8.

44. Page 36, para. 1 – "probably the greatest intellectual in our history": R.D. Francis, *Frank H. Underhill, Intellectual Provocateur* (University of Toronto Press, 1986) at 59.

45. Page 36, para. 1 –"later as Ontario's first minister of education": Stamp, "Crooks" at 221

46. Page 36, para. 2 –"a bulwark against the Roman Catholicism of Lower Canada": Hilda Neatby, *Queen's University: And not to Yield, 1841-1917* (Kingston: McGill-Queens University Press, 1978) at 53. Queen's did not become a University until 1912, see ibid. at 265.

47. Page 36, para. 2 –"provided there was no cost to the university": *An Act to remove certain doubts respecting the intention of the Act of the last session of the Parliament of this province for amending the Charter of the University of Toronto, 13&14 Victoria, Chap. 49* at s. 1; C.B. Sissons, *A History of Victoria University* (University of Toronto Press, 1952) at 85.

48. Page 36, para. 2 –"might have joined the University of Toronto at that time": Sissons, *Victoria* at 86. Victoria College did not formally become "The University of Victoria College" until 1884: see ibid. at v.

49. Page 36, para. 3 –"a Lower Canadian colleague, Augustin-Norbert Morin": Michael S. Cross and Robert Lochiel Fraser, "Robert Baldwin," *DCB*, v. 8 at 56-7; William G. Ormsby, "Sir Francis Hincks," in J.M.S. Careless, ed., *The Pre-Confederation Premiers: Ontario Government Leaders, 1841-1867* (University of Toronto Press, 1980) at 161.

50. Page 36, para. 3 –"but there were also professional and personal reasons": R. D. Gidney and W.P.J. Millar, *Professional Gentlemen: The Professions in Nineteenth-Century Ontario* (University of Toronto Press, 1994) at 61-62.

51. Page 36, para. 3 –"his wife had died in childbirth in 1836": Cross and Fraser, "Robert Baldwin" at 50-51; R.M.

and J. Baldwin, *Great Experiment* at 245; Austin S. Thompson, *Spadina: A Story of Old Toronto* (Toronto: Pagurian Press, 1975) at 84.

52. Page 37, para. 1 –"from the disagreeable rumbling noise in my head": Cross and Fraser, "Robert Baldwin" at 57.

53. Page 37, para. 1 – "but was defeated": Ibid.

54. Page 37, para. 1 – "just east of the present Casa Loma": Thompson, *Spadina* at 92.

55. Page 37, para. 2 – "which were given representation on the senate": See Chapter 7 (1860).

56. Page 37, para. 2 – "the Queen's University, Belfast, model": Harold Averill and Gerald Keith, "A Railway to the Moon: Daniel Wilson and the University of Toronto," in Elizabeth Hulse, ed., *Thinking with Both Hands: Sir Daniel Wilson in the Old World and the New* (University of Toronto Press, 1999) at 140.

57. Page 37, para. 2 – "from the exclusive benefit of the University of Toronto": C.B. Sissons, *Egerton Ryerson: His Life and Letters* (Toronto: Clarke Irwin, 1947) at 260-263; Elizabeth H. Pearce, "King's College: Purpose and Accountability in Higher Education: The Dilemma of King's College, 1827-1853" (Ph.D. thesis, Ontario Institute for Studies in Education, 1998) at 185; Hodgins, *Documentary History of Education*, v. 10 at 147-148.

58. Page 37, para. 2 – "Hincks introduced a bill in September 1852": Elizabeth Gibbs, ed., *Debates of the Legislative Assembly of United Canada 1841-1867* (Montreal: Centre De Recherche en Histoire Economique du Canada Français), v. 9, pt. 1 at 626-8.

59. Page 37, para. 2 – "adopting the University of London model": Ibid., v. 9, pt. 3 at 1741-61 (2nd Reading, February 25, 1853). During the debate, Queen's of Ireland was also frequently mentioned. Cf. *University of Toronto Amendment Act, 1853*, section 1 (Preamble).

60. Page 38, para. 1 – "no religious test would be permitted": *University of Toronto Amendment Act, 1853*, ss. 27 and 34.

61. Page 38, para. 1 – "a set of little paltry colleges": Cited in McKillop, *Matters of Mind* at 24; Ormsby, "Hincks," in Careless, *Pre-Confederation Premiers* at 175. Brown forecast, "A multitude of small sectarian colleges, with chairs clubbed together and filled with inferior men, the youth educated as sectarians, and sent abroad with all the prejudices of narrow education": J.M.S. Careless, *Brown of the Globe*, v.1 (Toronto: Macmillan Company of Canada, 1959) at 170.

62. Page 38, para. 1 – "resigned in protest": G.M. Craig, "Peter Boyle De Blaquière," *DCB*, v. 8 at 206.

63. Page 38, para. 1 – "the course adopted by the present Government": Cross and Fraser, "Robert Baldwin" at 57; Baldwin and Baldwin, *Great Experiment* at 232.

64. Page 38, para. 1 – "The bill was given Royal Assent on April 22, 1853": Gibbs, ed., *Debates*, v. 9, pt. 3 at 2777; Hodgins, *Documentary History*, v. 11 at 3.

65. Page 38, para. 2 – "from the official Church of Scotland": Brian J. Fraser, *Church, College, and Clergy : A History of Theological Education at Knox College, Toronto, 1844-1944* (Montreal: McGill-Queen's University Press, 1995) at 4-6; Hodgins, *Documentary History*, v. 5 at 121-3; McKillop, *Matters of Mind* at 23. Knox was affiliated with the Free Church: see e-mail from Peter Richardson to author, January 19, 2001.

66. Page 38, para. 2 – "no other college joined": Hamilton College did affiliate in 1856, but this seems to have had no effect on the development of the University: Hodgins, *Documentary History*, v. 11 at 269 (Senate meeting, November 21, 1856).

67. Page 38, para. 2 – "but it was not": Wallace, *History of the University of Toronto* at 65.

68. Page 38, para. 2 – "it was only to be the 'surplus' income": *Toronto University Amendment Act, 1853*, s. 54.

69. Page 38, para. 2 – "to construct University College": Wallace, *History of the University of Toronto* at 65; McKillop, *Matters of Mind* at 24; Sissons, *Victoria* at 93.

70. Page 38, para. 3 – "but was turned down by the University": Hodgins, *Documentary History*, v.11 at 276 and 278.

71. Page 38, para. 3 – "so richly endowed": Leo D. Burns, "Reverend Jean Mathieu Soulerin 1807-1879: Founder of St. Michael's College" (M.A. Major Essay, University of Toronto, 1965) at 59.

72. Page 38, para. 3 – "to turn them away from it as far as possible": Ibid. at 58.

73. Page 38, para. 3 – "The senate politely said no": Hodgins, *Documentary History*, v.11 at 276 and 278.

74. Page 38, para. 3 – "strengthen the position of the university in its Toronto constituency": Lawrence Shook, *Catholic Post-Secondary Education in English-Speaking Canada – A History* (University of Toronto Press, 1971) at 136.

75. Page 38, para. 3 – "St. Michael's was largely a high school": Ibid. at 13.

76. Page 38, para. 3 – "had expressed such views": Slater, "Philosophy" at 34. George Brown added, "we oppose the Church of Rome, the most grasping and tyrannical of churches, the ally of despotism in every country in which it has a foothold": Burns, "Soulerin" at 55.

77. Page 39, para. 1 – "founded by the French Basilians in 1852": Shook, *Catholic Post-Secondary* at 129-30.

78. Page 39, para. 1 – "four members of the 30-member French-speaking community": James Hanrahan, *The Basilian Fathers: A Documentary Study of One Hundred and Fifty Years of the History of the Congregation of Priests of St. Basil* (Toronto: Basilian Press, 1973) at 32-33.

79. Page 39, para. 1 – "even the stairs of the houses are carpeted": Charles Roume, *A History of the Congregation of St. Basil to 1864*, Kevin J. Kirley and William J. Young, trans., (Toronto: Basilian Press, 1975) at 332.

80. Page 39, para. 1 – "had offered them some of his land": The Jesuits declined in part because they had no men available for an English-language college in Toronto, see Shook, *Catholic Post-Secondary* at 130.

81. Page 39, para. 1 – "a parish church along with a college": Ibid. at 133.

82. Page 39, para. 1 – "officially opened in 1856": Ibid. at 134. The church was expanded in 1876 and 1886: see J. Bernard Black, *Familiar Landmarks: Four Walks Through the Historic Campus of the University of St. Michael's College* (Toronto: University of St. Michael's College Archives, 1984) at 26-27.

83. Page 39, para. 1 – "its neighbour, the University of Toronto": Shook, *Catholic Post-Secondary* at 141-42.

84. Page 39, para. 2 – "which had repealed the 1849 act": *University of Toronto Amendment Act, 1853*, preamble, which lists the Acts "hereby repealed," including *An Act to Amend the Charter of the University Established at Toronto* (Baldwin's 1849 Act).

85. Page 39, para. 2 – "effectively controlled by the government": Sissons, *Victoria* at 92; *University of Toronto Amendment Act, 1853*, s. 4 (the Senate appointed by the government); s. 10 (all Statutes of the Senate to be approved by the government); s. 6 (appointment of Chancellor of the University of Toronto); s. 32 (President, Vice-President and faculty of University College appointed by the government to hold office at pleasure); s. 31 (statutes of University College require the government's approval); ss. 51, 52 (governmental control of the University and College budget). The government control of the budget was such that John Langton complained,

"We cannot even pay current expenses out of income without a statute to which the Governor considers he must give active consent." W. A. Langton, ed.; *Early days in Upper Canada; letters from the Backwoods of Upper Canada to the Audit Office of the Province of Ontario* (Toronto: Macmillan Company of Canada Ltd., 1926) at 279-280.

86. Page 39, para. 2 – "significant expenditures required government approval": McKillop, *Matters of Mind* at 24; *University of Toronto Amendment Act, 1853*, s. 4 (the Senate appointed by the government); s. 10 (all Statutes of the Senate to be approved by the government); s. 6 (appointment of Chancellor of the University of Toronto); s. 32 (President, Vice-President and faculty of University College appointed by the government to hold office at pleasure); s. 31 (statutes of University College require the government's approval); ss. 51, 52 (governmental control of the University and College budget).

87. Page 40, para. 1 – "by a chancellor and a vice-chancellor": *1853 Act*, ss. 5 and 15.

88. Page 40, para. 1 – "as had been provided under the 1849 legislation": As under *An Act to Amend the Charter of the University of Toronto*, s. 5.

89. Page 40, para. 2 – "which in turn would elect the vice-chancellor": *1853 Act*, s. 7.

90. Page 40, para. 2 – "about half the members of the former senate had been professors": Wallace, *History of the University of Toronto* at 69-70; Averill and Keith, "A Railway to the Moon" at 143.

91. Page 40, para. 2 – "who was elected as vice-chancellor": Wallace, *History of the University of Toronto* at 66.

92. Page 40, para. 2 – "had chosen not to affiliate with the University": Cross and Fraser, "Robert Baldwin" at 57; *University of Toronto Amendment Act, 1853*, s. 4 (the Senate appointed by the government). The government appears to have established a convention of naming the heads of the denominational colleges to the Senate; there is no statutory basis for it.

93. Page 40, para. 2 – "only to obstruct": John Langton, "The University of Toronto in 1856," *Canadian Historical Review*, v.5 (1924) at 134.

94. Page 40, para. 3 – "the elimination of the faculties of medicine and law": *University of Toronto Amendment Act, 1853*, ss. 18 and 32, especially 32, "after the first day of January one thousand eight hundred and fifty-four, there shall be no Professorship or Teachership of Law, or of any of the branches of Medicine or Surgery, except in so far as the same may form part of a general system of liberal Education"; Hodgins, *Documentary History*, v.11 at 141.

95. Page 40, para. 3 – "degrees in these fields": *University of Toronto Amendment Act, 1853*, s. 19.

96. Page 40, para. 3– "it would not offer instruction": Wallace, *History of the University of Toronto* at 65.

97. Page 40, para. 3 – "an additional year's pay": UTA/B72-0031/006(37), James H. Richardson to President [James] Loudon, June 27, 1899 at 9. This was given statutory form in the *University of Toronto Amendment Act*, s. 52.

98. Page 40, para. 3 – "a crucial role in the elimination of the medical faculty": G.M. Craig, "John Rolph," *DCB*, v. 9, at 689; Wallace, *History of the University of Toronto* at 66; Sandra Frances McRae, "The 'Scientific Spirit' in Medicine at the University of Toronto, 1880-1910" (Ph.D. thesis, University of Toronto, 1987) at 67, 326; Charles Godfrey, *John Rolph: Rebel With Causes* (Madoc: Codam Publishing, 1993) at 217.

99. Page 40, para. 3 – "a major commercial venture": Craig, "John Rolph" at 683, 685, and 687.

100. Page 40, para. 3 – "which was incorporated in 1851": Ibid. at 688.

101. Page 40, para. 3 – "he agreed to join Hincks' cabinet": Ibid.

102. Page 40, para. 3 – "increasing competition from the University of Toronto medical school": Ibid. at 689.

103. Page 41, para. 1 – "the Rolph Act": James H. Richardson to President [James] Loudon, June 27 at 8-9. Dr. J. H. Richardson, one of the ex-Professors of the Faculty of Medicine, recollected being informed by a confidant of Hincks that Rolph had demanded "control of the Toronto Gen Hospital. The Lunatic Asylum & the University of Toronto Question."

104. Page 41, para. 1 – "Rolph was behind the act": Gibbs, ed., Debates, v. 11, Part 3 at 2446; G. Mercer Adam, *Canada's Patriot Statesman: The Life and Career of the Right Honourable Sir John A. Macdonald Based on the Work of Edmund Collins, Revised, With Additions to Date* (Toronto: Rose Publishing Co., 1891) at 161.

105. Page 41, para. 1 – "the government fell": Craig, "Rolph" at 688-689.

106. Page 41, para. 2 – "with special grants from the government": Hodgins, *Documentary History of Education,* v. 10 at 153.

107. Page 41, para. 2 – "a very expensive and very bad medical school": Langton, "The University of Toronto in 1856" at 133.

108. Page 41, para. 2 – "for about 30 years": James H. Richardson to President [James] Loudon, June 27 at 6.

109. Page 41, para. 2 – "A faculty of medicine was not established again at the University until 1887": Wallace, *History of the University of Toronto* at 211; see also Chapter 12 (1887).

110. Page 41, para. 3 – "The story of Rolph's school is complex": Sandra Frances McRae, "The 'Scientific Spirit'" at 67-73; Charles Godfrey, *John Rolph* at 233-251; Gidney and Millar, *Professional Gentlemen* at 89.

111. Page 41, para. – "to be used for their library in Cobourg": Sissons, *Victoria* at 98.

112. Page 41, para. 3 – "using the name 'Toronto School of Medicine'": Ibid. at 102.

113. Page 41, para. 3 – "to prevent the use of the name of his old school": Ibid.

114. Page 41, para. 3 – "transferred to the Toronto School of Medicine": Ibid. at 141-42. See Chapter 12 (1887).

115. Page 42, para. 1 – "degrees could still be awarded": Wallace, *History of the University of Toronto* at 65.

116. Page 42, para. 1 – "the teaching of law in a serious manner": G. Blaine Baker, "Legal Education in Upper Canada 1785-1889: The Law Society as Educator," in David H. Flaherty, ed., *Essays in the History of Canadian Law* (Toronto: Osgoode Society, 1983), v.2 at 97.

117. Page 42, para. 1 – "almost without a clue to guide their steps": Christopher Moore, *The Law Society of Upper Canada and Ontario's Lawyers 1797-1997* (University of Toronto Press, 1997) at 115.

118. Page 42, para. 1 – "if it set up their own school": Hodgins, *Documentary History,* v. 10 at 153; J. McGregor Young, "The Faculty of Law", in *The University of Toronto and Its Colleges, 1827-1906* (Toronto: University Librarian, 1906) at 153.

119. Page 42, para. 1 – "the habitually cash-strapped society": Assuming they knew about the offer. There is no clear evidence that they did.

120. Page 42, para. 2 – "the incorporated Law Society of Upper Canada": Hodgins, *Documentary History,* v. 10 at 153.

121. Page 42, para. 2 – "the concurrence of the Law Society": Baker, "Legal Education" at 97, citing Minutes of Convocation, III at 397-8 and 416-17. Baldwin, as Treasurer of the Law Society, became a senator of the Univer-

sity but doesn't seem to have played an active role in either the University or the Law Society: see Moore, *Law Society* at 112.

122. Page 42, para. 2 – "then closed again in 1877": Baker, "Legal Education" at 99-103. As Gidney and Millar point out, "in the main, learning to be a lawyer in nineteenth-century Ontario took place outside classrooms": see Gidney and Millar, *Professional Gentlemen* at 164-165.

123. Page 42, para. 2 – "Osgoode Hall Law School – in 1889": C. Ian Kyer and Jerome E. Bickenbach, *The Fiercest Debate: Cecil A. Wright, the Benchers, and Legal Education in Ontario 1923-1957* (Toronto: Osgoode Society, 1987) at 35-36. In the nineteenth century, classes at Osgoode Hall were scheduled to allow law students to continue to carry on apprentice work in their law firms: see Gidney and Millar, *Professional Gentlemen* at 372-373.

124. Page 42, para. 2 – "as equivalent to the Law Society's Osgoode Hall Law School until 1957": Kyer and Bickenbach, *The Fiercest Debate* at 264.

CHAPTER 5 – 1853 – NEW PROFESSORS

1. Page 43, para. 1 – "at £350 a year": A.B. Macallum, "Huxley and Tyndall at the University of Toronto," *University of Toronto Monthly* (1901) at 71; Harold Averill and Gerald Keith, "Daniel Wilson and the University of Toronto," in Elizabeth Hulse, ed., *Thinking with Both Hands: Sir Daniel Wilson in the Old World and the New* (University of Toronto Press, 1999) at 139.

2. Page 43, para. 1 – "and was growing rapidly": "Sir Daniel Wilson's Journal", in UTA/Langton Family Papers/B65-0014/004 at 6 (September 21, 1853); Peter G. Goheen, *Victorian Toronto, 1850 to 1900: Pattern and Process of Growth* (University of Chicago Department of Geography Research paper No. 127, 1970) at 48-53.

3. Page 43, para. 2 – "the professor of English history and literature": W.S. Wallace, *History of the University of Toronto* (University of Toronto Press, 1927) at 68.

4. Page 43, para. 2 – "the first such professor in British North America": A.B. McKillop, *Matters of Mind: The University in Ontario 1791-1951* (University of Toronto Press, 1994) at 108.

5. Page 43, para. 2 – "from classics to literature and history": Ibid.

6. Page 43, para. 2 – "*The Archaeology and Prehistoric Annals of Scotland*": Carl Berger, "Sir Daniel Wilson," *DCB*, v. 12 at 1109.

7. Page 43, para. 2 – "having first used the word 'prehistory'": Ibid.

8. Page 43, para. 2 – "the first course in anthropology in the world": Bruce G. Trigger, "*Prehistoric man* and Daniel Wilson's later Canadian Ethnology" in Hulse, ed., *Thinking with Both Hands* at 86. Wilson started teaching his course "Ancient and Modern Ethnology" in 1857.

9. Page 43, para. 2 – "awarded him an honorary doctorate": Berger, "Sir Daniel Wilson" at 1109.

10. Page 43, para. 2 – "familiar with Wilson's work and career": Averill and Keith, "Daniel Wilson" at 141.

11. Page 44, para. 2 – "reveals his views of Toronto and the University": "Sir Daniel Wilson's Journal."

12. Page 44, para. 2 – "he need want for nothing here that he desires": Ibid. at 6 (September 21, 1853).

13. Page 44, para. 2 – "raised to £400 a year": Ibid. at 7.

14. Page 45, para. 1 – "very well fitted for his post": Ibid.

15. Page 45, para. 1 – "otherwise than in cap and gown": Ibid. at 9 (October 15, 1853).

16. Page 45, para. 1 – "to administer an exam to a single student": Ibid. at 9-10.

17. Page 45, para. 1 – "a confounded intriguer": Ibid. at 17 (January 20, 1854).

18. Page 45, para. 1 – "never out of some mean trick or another": Averill and Keith, "Daniel Wilson" at 143-44.

19. Page 47, para. 1 – "calling them 'clever fellows'": "Sir Daniel Wilson's Journal" at 10 (October 15, 1853).

20. Page 47, para. 1 – "a 'dreadfully dry stick'": Ibid.

21. Page 47, para. 2 – "a more respectful or gentlemanly set of students": Ibid. at 17 (January 20, 1854).

22. Page 47, para. 2 – "a thing greatly needed here": Ibid. at 18-19 (February 21, 1854); Charles Levi, "Where the Famous People Were? The Origins, Activities and Future Careers of Student Leaders at University College, Toronto, 1854-1973" (Ph.D. thesis, York University, 1998) at 52-3.

23. Page 47, para. 3 – "The Relative Merits of the Arts of War and the Arts of Peace": George Kennedy, "Some Recollections of an Old Boy," *University of Toronto Monthly* (1907/08) at 104-105; also cited in Levi, "Where the Famous People Were?" at 53.

24. Page 47, para. 3 – "to the University College Literary and Athletic Society": Levi, "Where the Famous People Were?" at 166.

25. Page 47, para. 4 – "'a Cambridge man whom I expect to like,' wrote Wilson": "Sir Daniel Wilson's Journal" at 10 (October 15, 1853).

26. Page 47, para. 4 – "only a 'sixth wrangler'": Suzanne Zeller, "John Cherriman," *DCB*, v. 13 at 192.

27. Page 47, para. 4 – "without reference to prior work in the field": Yves Gingras, *Physics and the Rise of Scientific Research in Canada*, Peter Keating, trans., (Montreal: McGill-Queen's University Press, 1991) at 19.

28. Page 48, para. 1 – "the first superintendent of insurance for the Dominion of Canada": Zeller, "Cherriman" at 192.

29. Page 48, para. 2 – "the 31-year-old John Tyndall": A.S. Eve and C.H. Creasey, *Life and Work of John Tyndall* (London: Macmillan & Co., 1945) at 35.

30. Page 48, para. 2 – "explained why the sky is blue": David Abbott, ed., *The Biographical Dictionary of Scientists: Physicists* (London: Frederick Muller Limited, 1984) at 161.

31. Page 48, para. 2 – "to inorganic compounds and even single atoms": Suzanne Zeller, "'Merchants of Light': The Culture of Science in Daniel Wilson's Ontario, 1853-1892," in Hulse, ed., *Thinking With Both Hands* at 127.

32. Page 48, para. – "the inventor of the Bunsen Burner": Abbott, *Physicists* at 162.

33. Page 48, para. 2 – "the great Michael Faraday": Ibid.; Eve and Creasey, *Life and Work of John Tyndall* at 37-41.

34. Page 48, para. 2 – "to the government for consideration": J.G. Hodgins, *Documentary History of Higher Education in Ontario*, v.10 at 219 (Proceedings of the Senate, November 30, 1852). Tyndall applied for the position in 1851 and was elected to the Royal Society June 3, 1852: see Eve and Creasey, *Life and Work of John Tyndall* at 35 and 38. The senate of the University made its recommendations at the meeting of November 30, 1852.

35. Page 49, para. 1 – "opened up the professorship": *Report of the Caput for the Year 1850*, (Canada: Legislative Assembly Journals, 1851, Appendix I.I.I. August 2) (Cherriman taking care of the responsibilities of the professor of mathematics and natural science); Zeller, "John Cherriman", v.13 at 192 (Cherriman's appointment after Murray's death).

36. Page 49, para. 2 – "in the philosophical transactions of the society": Macallum, "Huxley and Tyndall" at 71. The Medal was not in fact awarded until December 30, 1852, after Huxley's application: see Leonard Huxley, ed., *Life and Letters of Thomas Henry Huxley* (New York: S. Appleton and Company, 1900), v. 1 at 87, 111. The Senate considered Huxley's application on 14 July, 1852: see Hodgins, *Documentary History*, v. 10 at 213; *The Dictionary of National Biography* (Oxford University Press), v. 22 (Supplement) at 894-903.

37. Page 49, para. 2 – "a great future for the 27-year-old scientist": Macallum, "Huxley and Tyndall" at 71.

38. Page 49, para. 2 – "whatever private influence they may have": Macallum, "Huxley and Tyndall" at 73; Huxley, *Life and Letters of Thomas Henry Huxley,* v. 1 at 83-4.

39. Page 49, para. 3 – "most of his earlier career as a Unitarian minister": J. Donald Wilson, "William Hincks," *DCB,* v. 10 at 349-350; Jennifer Coggon, "'A Great Plan Running Through Nature': Reverend William Hincks and his Tendencies of Development Theory" (unpublished paper prepared for Professor P. Winsor, University of Toronto, 1998); Suzanne Zeller, *Inventing Canada: Early Victorian Science and the Idea of a Transcontinental Nation,* (University of Toronto Press, 1987) at 208-217. Coggon, at 3, points out that the identification of Hincks as a Presbyterian is misleading in that "most Irish Presbyterians in the year of Hincks' birth, 1794, were Unitarians."

40. Page 49, para. 3 – "older brother of Francis Hincks": Macallum, "Huxley and Tyndall" at 73; Huxley, *Life and Letters of Thomas Henry Huxley,* v. 1 at 83-4.

41. Page 49, para. 3 – "better than all the testimonials in the world": Macallum, "Huxley and Tyndall" at 73; Huxley, *Life and Letters of Thomas Henry Huxley,* v. 1 at 108.

42. Page 49, para. 3 – "more than rival the leading universities of this Continent": Macallum, "Huxley and Tyndall" at 75.

43. Page 49, para. 4 – "left much to be desired": Wilson, "Hincks" at 350.

44. Page 49, para. 4 – "memorize lists of classifications": Coggon, "'A Great Plan Running Through Nature'" at 1; Wilson, "Hincks" at 350.

45. Page 49, para. 4 – "in the amateur naturalist tradition": Zeller, "Culture of Science" at 122.

46. Page 50, para. 1 – "the so-called quinarian theory": Coggon, "'A Great Plan Running Through Nature'" at 2; Zeller, "Culture of Science" at 120-121.

47. Page 50, para. 1– "through a hole in the wall": McKillop, *Matters of Mind* at 93.

48. Page 50, para. 2 – "Supreme in Wisdom and Benevolence": William Hincks, "Grallatores: Waders or Stilted Birds," *The Canadian Journal: New Series,* v. 11, no. 53 (July, 1866) at 162, cited in Coggon, "'A Great Plan Running Through Nature'" at 28.

49. Page 50, para. 2 – "on the thinking and research of its professors": The impact of the idea of evolution may not have been visible. As Carl Berger comments, "most naturalists [in Canada] in the last four decades of the century maintained a puzzling reticence on the idea of evolution. After the flurry of reviews of the 1860s, they seldom wrote general appraisals of the theory and kept to themselves whatever spiritual anguish this new view of life may have caused them": see Carl Berger, *Science, God, and Nature in Victorian Canada* (University of Toronto Press, 1983) at 69. Similarly, Ramsay Cook has commented that "the Canadian scientific community gradually and quietly came to terms with the Darwinian hypothesis": see Ramsay Cook, *The Regenerators: Social Criticism in Late Victorian English Canada* (University of Toronto Press, 1985) at 11. See also Michael Gauvreau, *The Evangelical Century: College and Creed in English Canada from the Great Revival to the Great Depression* (Montreal: McGill-Queen's University Press, 1991).

50. Page 50, para. 3 – "where 'Social Darwinism' would be debated'": Robert Vipond and Georgina Feldberg, "The Law of Evolution and the Evolution of the Law: Mills, Darwin, and Late Nineteenth Century Legal Thought" (unpublished paper) at 2. The discussion of the social implications of Darwinism was a product of Late Victorian thought and more connected with the publication of *The Descent of Man* in 1871 than *On the Origin of Species* in 1859: see Cook, *The Regenerators* at 12 and 209.

51. Page 50, para. 4 – "The Reverend James Beaven obviously did": McKillop, *Matters of Mind* at 115-116.

52. Page 50, para. 4 – "a comment on Beaven's views about Darwin": Ibid. at 93.

53. Page 50, para. 4 – "who had come to Toronto in 1853 from University College, London": W. Hodgson Ellis, "The Late Professor E.J. Chapman," *University of Toronto Monthly*, v. 4 (1904) at 151.

54. Page 50, para. 4 – "our restricted powers of inquiry": E.J. Chapman, "Review of *On the Origins of Species by means of Natural Selection, or the Preservation of Favoured Races in the Struggle for Life* by Charles Darwin," The Canadian Journal, new series, no. XXVIII (July 1860) at 386.

55. Page 50, para. 4 – "some strong claims to consideration": McKillop, *Matters of Mind* at 119, citing Chapman review of *The Geological Evidences of the Antiquity of Man* in the *Canadian Journal*, 1863. McKillop points out the gradual nature of the change in Chapman's thought.

56. Page 50, para. 5 – "field work and study in American libraries": Bruce G. Trigger, "*Prehistoric man* and Daniel Wilson's later Canadian Ethnology" in Hulse, ed., *Thinking with Both Hands* at 86.

57. Page 51, para. 1 – "wholly inadequate for his purposes": "Sir Daniel Wilson's Journal" at 12 (November 12, 1853).

58. Page 51, para. 1 – "one of the great anthropological syntheses of the nineteenth century": Trigger, "*Prehistoric Man*" at 82 and 98.

59. Page 51, para. 1 – "many of whose predictions have been fulfilled": T.F. McIlwraith, "Sir Daniel Wilson: A Canadian Anthropologist of One Hundred Years Ago," *Transactions of the Royal Society of Canada*, 4th Series IV, v. 2, June, 1964, Section II at 129.

60. Page 51, para. 1 – "a surprise to at least one British reviewer": Berger, "Sir Daniel Wilson" at 1111; McIlwraith, "Daniel Wilson" at 129.

61. Page 52, para. 1 – "a soul had been infused into an animal body": Trigger, "*Prehistoric Man*" at 93.

62. Page 52, para. 2– "thus justifying the subjugation of blacks": Bennett McCardle, "Heart of Heart: Daniel Wilson's Human Biology," in Hulse, ed., *Thinking With Both Hands* at 105; Zeller, "Culture of Science" at 123-124.

63. Page 52, para. 2 – "produce a new North American people": Trigger, "Prehistoric Man" at 90.

64. Page 52, para. 3 – "such as the biologist Ramsay Wright": "Robert Ramsay Wright," Henry James Morgan, ed., *The Canadian Men and Women of the Time* (Toronto: William Briggs, 1912) 2nd ed. at 1189.

65. Page 52, para. 3 – "and the physicist James Loudon": James Greenlee, "James Loudon," *DCB*, v.14 at 664-66.

66. Page 52, para. 3 – "an explicit disentangling of science and religion": Zeller, "'Merchants of Light'," in *Thinking with Both Hands* at 128; see also Berger, *Science, God, and Nature in Victorian Canada* at 75-6. Berger dates the general acceptance of Darwinism among Canadian naturalists to the end of the century or later.

67. Page 52, para. 3 – "'definitely settled' by Darwin": Zeller, "'Merchants of Light'" at 128.

68. Page 52, para. 4 – "James Forneri": John King, *McCaul, Croft, Forneri* (Toronto: Macmillan, 1914) at 161-256.

69. Page 52, para. 4 – "had taught together in Belfast": John King, *McCaul* at 248; Maddalena Kuitunen, *A History of Italian Studies at the University of Toronto 1840-1990* (Toronto: Department of Italian Studies, 1991) at 8.

70. Page 52, para. 4 – "three years before I was born": "Sir Daniel Wilson's Journal" at 15 (November 25, 1853).

71. Page 52, para. 4 – "much in need of a course in English": Ibid. at 10 (October 15, 1853).

72. Page 52, para. 4 – “Dat it ees”: Kennedy, “Some Recollections” at 106.

73. Page 52, para. 4 – “an excellent teacher of French, German, Italian and Spanish”: William J. Loudon, *Sir William Mulock: A Short Biography* (Toronto: Macmillan Company, 1932) at 39.

74. Page 52, para. 4 – “until reaching the age of 77 in 1866”: Kuitunen, *Italian Studies* at 10.

75. Page 52, para. 5 – “received a diploma in agricultural science”: Loudon, *Mulock* at 39. Loudon says “one or two,” but Harold Averill suggests as many as seven: see Harold Averill comments to Friedland, January 29, 2001.

76. Page 52, para. 5 – “towards Bloor Street”: Hodgins, *Documentary History*, v.9 at 268 and 282; Douglas Richardson, *A Not Unsightly Building: University College and Its History* (Toronto: Mosaic Press, 1990) at 57.

77. Page 53, para. 1 – “when it became the University of Guelph”: Ann MacKenzie, “George Buckland,” *DCB*, v. 11 at 133; McKillop, *Matters of Mind* at 566.

78. Page 53, para. 2 – “the architect of Trinity College”: Stephen A. Otto, “Kivas Tully,” *DCB*, v. 13 at 1038; Richardson, *A Not Unsightly Building* at 121.

79. Page 53, para. 2 – “applied for the position after the deadline”: Hodgins, *Documentary History*, v. 10 at 210 and 214; Geoffrey Simmins, *Fred Cumberland: Building the Victorian Dream* (University of Toronto Press, 1997) at 16; F. H. Armstrong and Peter Baskerville, “Frederic William Cumberland,” *DCB*, v. 11 at 228 (Cumberland's membership in the Senate from 1853 until his death); C. R. Young, *Early Engineering Education at Toronto* (University of Toronto Press, 1958) at 10-13.

80. Page 53, para. 2 – “without indication of an order of preference”: Hodgins, *Documentary History*, v. 10 at 220.

81. Page 53, para. 2 – “never appointed anyone to the chair”: Young, *Early Engineering Education* at 13; Richardson, *A Not Unsightly Building* at 53.

82. Page 53, para. 2 – “physically located on university grounds”: Young, *Early Engineering Education* at 19; McKillop, *Matters of Mind* at 170.

CHAPTER 6 – 1856 – BUILDING UNIVERSITY COLLEGE

1. Page 54, para. 1 – "and professors Croft and Wilson": W.S. Wallace, *A History of the University of Toronto* (University of Toronto Press, 1927) at 75.

2. Page 54, para. 1 – "but also full of fear": Douglas Richardson, *A Not Unsightly Building: University College and Its History* (Toronto: Mosaic Press, 1990) at 69; Harold Averill and Gerald Keith, "Daniel Wilson and the University of Toronto" in Elizabeth Hulse, ed., *Thinking with Both Hands: Sir Daniel Wilson in the Old World and the New* (University of Toronto Press, 1999) at 148.

3. Page 54, para. 1 – "Perhaps it was well and wisely done": Wallace, *A History of the University of Toronto* at 75.

4. Page 54, para. 1 – "renewed opposition from the denominational colleges": Richardson, *A Not Unsightly Building* at 69.

5. Page 54, para. 1 – "so much less plunder to fight for": Wallace, *A History of the University of Toronto* at 72; John Langton, "The University of Toronto in 1856," *Canadian Historical Review*, v.5 (1924) at 145.

6. Page 54, para. 1 – "even Methodists can't steal bricks and mortar": Wallace, *A History of the University of Toronto* at 72; cf. Sissons, *A History of Victoria College*, (University of Toronto Press, 1952) at 123, who says that the quote was written down by Wilson. Sissons says, 'it represents less the sober judgment of Macdonald than the accumulated animus of Wilson.'

7. Page 54, para. 2 – "an engraving of one of J.M.W. Turner's works": Marinell Ash, "Daniel Wilson: The Early Years" in Hulse, ed., *Thinking With Both Hands* at 21; Carl Berger, "Sir Daniel Wilson," *DCB*, v. 12 at 1109.

8. Page 54, para. 2 – "a graduate of Cambridge": Cameron, "John Langton," *DCB*, v.12 at 527.

9. Page 56, para. 1 – "and its financial affairs": Wendy Cameron, "John Langton" at 528.

10. Page 56, para. 1– "for the position of vice-chancellor": John Langton to William Langton, May 24, 1856, in W. A. Langton, ed., *Early Days in Upper Canada: From the Backwoods of Upper Canada and the Audit Office of the Province of Canada* (Toronto: Macmillan Company of Canada Ltd., 1926) at 265.

11. Page 56, para. 2 – "Oxford for eight years": James A. Gibson, "Sir Edmund Walker Head," *DCB*, v. 9 at 381.

12. Page 56, para. 2 – "to borrow the title of a biography of Head": D.G.G Kerr, *Sir Edmund Head, a scholarly governor* (Toronto: 1954), as noted in Gibson, "Edmund Walker Head" at 386.

13. Page 56, para. 2 – "now that King's had become an asylum": Averill and Keith, "Daniel Wilson" at 147.

14. Page 56, para. 2 – "about the best friend we have": Richardson, *A Not Unsightly Building* at 52.

15. Page 56, para. 2 – "to include a library and a museum": J.G. Hodgins, *Documentary History of Education in Ontario*, v. 12 at 260; Langton, "University of Toronto" at 136.

16. Page 56, para. 2 – "subsequently added to the building committee": Langton became, in effect, the building committee. Chief Justice William Draper, a member of the committee, did not play a significant role in the design, and William Blake, the other member of the committee, had resigned as chancellor and was not replaced for some time: see Langton, "University of Toronto" at 142. R.E. Burns was appointed on December 12, 1856: see Hodgins, *Documentary History*, v. 12 at 271; Wallace, *A History of the University of Toronto* at 75.

17. Page 56, para. 3 – "as the university architect in early 1856": Richardson, *A Not Unsightly Building* at 53.

18. Page 56, para. 3 – "No competition was held for the job": Geoffrey Simmins, *Fred Cumberland: Building the Victorian Dream* (University of Toronto Press, 1997) at 94.

19. Page 56, para. 3 – "which were never built": Richardson, *A Not Unsightly Building* at 12.

20. Page 56, para. 3 – "as a university senator since 1853": He resigned when he got the commission: see Averill and Keith, "Daniel Wilson" at 147-8.

21. Page 56, para. 3 – "just south-east of the present Convocation Hall": Simmins, *Cumberland* at 95; Richardson, *A Not Unsightly Building* at 53.

22. Page 56, para. 3 – "which now serves as the offices of the Students' Administrative Council": Richardson, *A Not Unsightly Building* at 53.

23. Page 56, para. 4 – "Cumberland had come to Canada in 1847 at age 27": Ibid. at 53-54.

24. Page 57, para. 1 – "then nearing completion": Ibid. at 53.

25. Page 57, para. 1 – "and the Seventh Post Office on Toronto Street": Ibid. at 55.

26. Page 57, para. 1 – "now the International Student Centre": Richardson, *A Not Unsightly Building* at 14 and 120; Simmins, *Cumberland* at 200 and 279.

27. Page 57, para. 1 – "the glory of Toronto": Simmins, *Cumberland* at 92.

28. Page 57, para. 1 – "existed upon the American continent": Ibid.

29. Page 57, para. 2 – "would be but a mushroom at that distance": Langton, "University of Toronto" at 142.

30. Page 57, para. 3 – "one of the ugliest buildings I ever saw": Ibid. Note that in the original, "shewing" is used instead of "showing."

31. Page 58, para. 1 – "on his return His Excellency approved": Ibid.

32. Page 58, para. 2 – "you Canadians have a prejudice against trees": Ibid. at 143.

33. Page 58, para. 2 – "half so pretty": Ibid. at 144.

34. Page 58, para. 2 – "The tree was toppled in a storm the following year": "Eric Arthur Talks About University College," *University of Toronto Graduate* (June, 1970) at 104.

35. Page 58, para. 3 – "nearly 400 feet long": Richardson, *A Not Unsightly Building* at 72. This includes the round chemistry building: see ibid., fn 3 at 158.

36. Page 58, para. 3 – "that then could then be seen from the city and the lake": Ibid. at 72.

37. Page 58, para. 3 – "the most photographed bit of architecture in Toronto": "Eric Arthur Talks About University College" at 103.

38. Page 58, para. 3 – "borrowed from an abbot's kitchen in western England": Richardson, *A Not Unsightly Building* at 65 and 111.

39. Page 58, para. 3 – "its ruggedness was appropriate to Canada": Simmins, *Cumberland* at 103.

40. Page 58, para. 3 – "the 'Canadian style'": Langton, "University of Toronto" at 142.

41. Page 58, para. 3 – "influenced by John Ruskin": "Eric Arthur Talks About University College" at 39. The Exhibition on Ruskin at the Tate Gallery (seen by the author in March 2000), which includes Ruskin's design for a window of the Oxford Museum, dated 1855, illustrates Ruskin's influence on University College.

42. Page 58, para. 3 – "breadth and solidity": Richardson, *A Not Unsightly Building* at 61.

43. Page 58, para. 3 – "the importance of craftsmanship": Simmins, *Cumberland* at 104.

44. Page 60, para. 1 – "for reasons of economy": Richardson, *A Not Unsightly Building* at 73; Simmins, *Cumberland* at 113. There was a financial crisis in Toronto in 1887: see Richardson, *A Not Unsightly Building,* fn 5 at 158.

45. Page 60, para. 1 – "It served as the architects' office for the project": Richardson, *A Not Unsightly Building* at 73.

46. Page 60, para. 1 – "the present Junior Common Room was the dining hall": Richardson, *A Not Unsightly Building* at 108.

47. Page 60, para. 1 – "to slide the cow down from the top": Ibid.; W.S. Wallace, "The Case of the Bell-Ringing Cow," *University of Toronto Monthly,* (May, 1945) at 200. The cow incident became an enduring part of the University's lore. In 1937, T. A. Reed mentioned "that almost every graduate since has claimed to have had a part in the prank": See Toronto *Daily Star,* October 30, 1937.

48. Page 60, para. 2 – "unless there was 'conscientious objection'": Richardson, *A Not Unsightly Building* at 103 and 105.

49. Page 60, para. 2 – "when it opened": Ibid. at 93.

50. Page 60, para. 2– "in the west wing of the second floor": Ibid. at 93 and 95.

51. Page 62, para. 1– "where Ramsden Park now stands": Ibid. at 73.

52. Page 62, para. 1 – "from German-speaking cantons in Switzerland": Ibid. at 74; Simmins, *Cumberland* at 104.

53. Page 62, para. 1 – "survived the 1890 fire": Alice Hamilton and Douglas Richardson, "Joseph McCausland," *DCB,* v.13 at 612; Richardson, *A Not Unsightly Building* at 99.

54. Page 62, para. 1 – "a major marble supply company": Sheldon J. Godfrey, "Newman Leopold Steiner," *DCB,* v. 13 at 986. Although known as Toronto's first Jewish alderman, he left the faith in about the year 1880.

55. Page 62, para. 1 – "shows that the tree is a maple": Richardson, *A Not Unsightly Building* at 88 and 160.

56. Page 62, para. 1 – "They left the beaver, however": Office of the Secretary to the Board of Governors, UTA/A73-0015/042 – Original Warrants, 1917; Ian L. Campbell, *The Identifying Symbols of Canadian Institutions* (Renison College and Canadian Heraldry Associates, 1990), pt. 1 at 164-5; Alan Beddoe, *Beddoe's Canadian Heraldry* (Belleville: Mika Publishing, 1981) at 100.

57. Page 62, para. 2 – "pubs in University College have been named after them": Reznikoff's Pub, a fixture in University College student life in the 1980s, ran into trouble in the early 1990s and is no longer held: see *Gargoyle,* January 28, 1993 and January 13, 1994. It was largely replaced by Diablo's Latenight, which is still held. Diablo's Coffee Bar, after which the Latenight series was named, was re-opened after the JCR was renovated in 1989 and still operates.

58. Page 62, para. 2 – "Reznikoff's ghost then departed from the college": Richardson, *A Not Unsightly Building* at 146. Richardson's account is adapted from W.J. Loudon's, *Studies of Student Life,* v. 5.

59. Page 62, para. 3 – "north-east of the college": Richardson, *A Not Unsightly Building* at 119-120.

60. Page 62, para. 3 – "by residents of Yorkville upstream": Ibid. at 119.

61. Page 62, para. 3 – "proposes to re-create part of the stream": *University of Toronto Bulletin,* January 11, 1999.

62. Page 62, para. 4 – "the capstone for the 120-foot tower": *The Great Good Place: Exploring University College* (Toronto: University College, 1984) at 1.

63. Page 62, para. 4 – "was set in place by Governor General Head": Richardson, *A Not Unsightly Building* at 56.

64. Page 63, para. 1 – "and afterwards a banquet in the library": Ibid. at 13.

65. Page 63, para. 1 – "the children of the most affluent and the most influential": Wallace, *A History of the University of Toronto* at 76-77.

CHAPTER 7 – 1860 – SAVING THE UNIVERSITY

1. Page 64, para. 1 – "many prizes and scholarships": The tuition in 1856 was £2 10s. for the academic year for a full-time student: see *Return to An Address from the Legislative Assembly to His Excellency the Governor General* (June 18, 1856) at 39. At the same time, the University was paying labourers between $0.75 and $1.00 a day. A year's tuition was thus equal to approximately two weeks' wages of an unskilled labourer or cleaning woman. In 1857, there were available 29 scholarships of £30, ten medal prizes, and 6 book prizes. A student could not hold more than one scholarship: see *The Calendar of University College, Toronto* (Toronto, Henry Rowsell, 1857) at 46-9.

2. Page 64, para. 1 – "the number had increased to more than 100": W.S. Wallace, *A History of the University of Toronto* (University of Toronto Press, 1927) at 77.

3. Page 64, para. 1 – "for the cows which supplied milk": Douglas Richardson, *A Not Unsightly Building: University College and Its History* (Toronto: Mosaic Press, 1990) at 14.

4. Page 64, para. 1 – "professors spent the afternoon taking walks": Ibid.; William James Loudon, *Sir William Mulock : A Short Biography* (Toronto: Macmillan, 1932) at 40.

5. Page 64, para. 1 – "which was reserved for recreation and walking": Loudon, *Sir William Mulock* at 39.

6. Page 64, para. 1 – "a cricket club – was formed": *The University of Toronto Literary and Scientific Society Annual* (Toronto: Henry Rowsell, 1869) at 88 notes that [English] football was played, but says specifically that cricket was not played. J.O. Miller and F.B. Hodgins, ed., *Year Book of the University of Toronto 1886-87* (Toronto: Rowsell and Hutchison, 1887) at 99 declares that the Toronto University Cricket Club "was founded in the year 1869," but no reliable source for its creation has been located.

7. Page 64, para. 2 – "removing its privileged position": Ibid. at 78; A.B. McKillop, *Matters of Mind: The University in Ontario 1791-1951* (University of Toronto Press, 1994) at 29-32; Harold Averill and Gerald Keith, "Daniel Wilson and the University of Toronto" in Elizabeth Hulse, ed., *Thinking With Both Hands* (University of Toronto Press, 1999) at 150.

8. Page 64, para. 2 – "[that is, in Britain]": "Sir Daniel Wilson's Journal," in UTA/Langton Family Papers/B65-0014/004 at 28 (c. 1865).

9. Page 65, para. 1 – "seriously affected the denominational colleges": C.B. Sissons, *A History of Victoria University* (University of Toronto Press, 1952) at 111; Wallace, *A History of the University of Toronto* at 78.

10. Page 65, para. 1 – "Victoria College was going deeply into debt": McKillop, *Matters of Mind* at 28.

11. Page 65, para. 1 – "justly entitled": Sissons, *Victoria* at 107; J.G. Hodgins, *Documentary History of Higher Education in Upper Canada*, v. 14 at 205-206.

12. Page 65, para. 2 – "a petition sent to the government in late 1859": The document was actually a "Memorial prepared by Order and in Behalf of the Conference of the Wesleyan Methodist Church in Canada": see Hodgins, *Documentary History*, v.14 at 225.

13. Page 66, para. 1 – "remained until 1884": G.S. French, "Samuel Sobieski Nelles," *DCB*, v. 11 at 640.

14. Page 66, para. 1 – "in what he called 'the present raid'": Sissons, *Victoria* at 107.

15. Page 66, para. 1 – "the Catholic institutions were mainly spectators": Ibid.

16. Page 66, para. 1 – "gave Victoria its active support": Sissons, *Victoria* at 111-113; Hilda Neatby, *"and not to yield": Queen's University, 1841-1917* (Kingston: McGill-Queen's University Press, 1978) at 104 et. seq.

17. Page 66, para. 2 – "will want to know who that stranger is": Hodgins, *Documentary History*, v.14 at 213.

18. Page 66, para. 2 – "that there shall be no 'surplus'": Ibid. at 209.

19. Page 66, para. 2 – "Wesleyan, Congregational, Baptist, Roman Catholic, etc.": Ibid. at 229.

20. Page 66, para. 2 – "the Toronto College monopoly": Sissons, *Victoria* at 108.

21. Page 66, para. 3 – "what it is in the best Colleges of the United States": Hodgins, *Documentary History*, v.14 at 226.

22. Page 66, para. 3 – "the study of classics and mathematics": Ibid. at 240.

23. Page 66, para. 3 – "and yet be a B.A. with honours": Ibid. at 241.

24. Page 66, para. 4 – "towards permitting greater specialization": Ibid., v. 15 at 182-189.

25. Page 67, para. 1 – "and similar practical courses": Ibid. at 117-118.

26. Page 67, para. 1 – "he did not think even law or medicine belonged in a university": See Chapter 5 (1853).

27. Page 67, para. 1– "from three to four years": Hodgins, *Documentary History,* v. 15 at 28 (Petition to the Legislative Assembly of the Chancellor, Vice-Chancellor and the Senate of the University of Toronto, March 16); Robert Falconer, "The Tradition of Liberal Education in Canada," *Canadian Historical Review* (1927) at 112.

28. Page 67, para. 1– "the so-called 'pass students'": Hodgins, *Documentary History*, v.14 at 241; "Speech of Dr. McCaul at the Recent Convocation of University College, Toronto," in *Journal of Education* (December, 1857) at 180.

29. Page 67, para. 1– "professors spent too much of their time with the honours students": Hodgins, *Documentary History*, v. 15 at 125.

30. Page 67, para. 1– "the term 'honour' referred to the student and not the course": C.B. Sissons, "Memorandum on the History of the Honour, General and Pass Courses," UTA/B89-0003/02 at 1; Hodgins, *Documentary History*, v.11 at 138. For a discussion of the honour course system at the University of Toronto, see Patricia Jasen, "Educating an Elite: A History of the Honour Course System at the University of Toronto" *Ontario History*, Volume 81, December 1989 at 269.

31. Page 68, para. 1 – "some other superior grammar school": Hodgins, *Documentary History*, v.15 at 179; Falconer, "Liberal Education" at 113.

32. Page 68, para. 2 – "who was sympathetic to the denominational colleges": J.K. Johnson and P.B. Waite, "Sir John Alexander MacDonald," *DCB*, v.12 at 593.

33. Page 68, para. 2 – "who was not": J.M.S. Careless, *Brown of the Globe* (Toronto: Macmillan Company of Canada Ltd., 1963), v.2 at 23.

34. Page 68, para. 2 – "having been a schoolmate of his in Edinburgh": Elizabeth Hulse, "'A Long and Happy Life': Daniel Wilson with Friends and Family" in Hulse, ed., *Thinking with Both Hands* at 270; Careless, *Brown*, v. 2 at 24.

35. Page 68, para. 2 – "Witnesses appeared for Victoria, Queen's, and Trinity": Sissons, *Victoria* at 111.

36. Page 68, para. 2 – "was not required": C.B. Sissons, *Egerton Ryerson: His Life and Letters* (Toronto: Clark Irwin and Co., 1947), v.2 at 418.

37. Page 68, para. 2 – "now at Trinity": Averill and Keith, "Sir Daniel Wilson" at 150; H.H. Langton, *Sir Daniel Wilson* at 78.

38. Page 68, para. 2 – "for the post of vice-chancellor in 1856": John Langton, "The University of Toronto in 1856," *Canadian Historical Review*, v.5 no.2 (1924) at 132.

39. Page 68, para. 2 – "stick to me like bricks": W. A. Langton, ed., *Early Days in Upper Canada: From the Backwoods of Upper Canada and the Audit Office of the Province of Canada* (Toronto: Macmillan Company of Canada Ltd., 1926) at 284. It is also possible that some of the more puritanical of the professors, such as the strait-laced Wilson, may have been alienated by reports of looseness of conduct on McCaul's part: see Squair Memoirs (5 November, 1921). Langton (which Langton is not clear) read a letter from John Langton, regarding the investigation into McCaul's "immoral conduct." John A. Macdonald was reported to have said, "Not Guilty, but don't do it again." John Langton also mentions that McCaul had a reputation for hypocrisy and was mistrusted by his staff. See Loudon, *Sir William Mulock* at 38: "that the old doctor was not as strict in his habits or his customs as some of the other professors."

40. Page 68, para. 3 – "commonly taught in university education": Hodgins, *Documentary History*, v.15 at 148

41. Page 68, para. 3 – "in which he has not had the slightest experience": Ibid. at 208.

42. Page 68, para. 3 – "they justly claim in a liberal education": Ibid. at 209.

43. Page 69, para. 1 – "the practical duties of life": Ibid. at 211.

44. Page 69, para. 2 – "at the Scottish universities": Ibid. at 259.

45. Page 69, para. 2 – "Is he a graduate himself?": Ibid. at 268.

46. Page 69, para. 2 – "the affairs of the educational institutions of our country?": Ibid.

47. Page 69, para. 2 – "the most unscrupulous and jesuitically untruthful intriguer I ever had to do with": Averill and Keith, "Daniel Wilson" at 146.

48. Page 69, para. 3 – "the chair of the committee, Malcolm Cameron": Margaret Coleman, "Malcolm Cameron," *DCB*, v.10 at 128.

49. Page 70, para. 1 – "'an old friend' of Victoria College": Sissons, *Ryerson* at 427.

50. Page 70, para. 1 – "no doubt with help from Ryerson": Hodgins, *Documentary History*, v.15 at 306.

51. Page 70, para. 1 – "never brought in a final report": Ibid.

52. Page 70, para. 1 – "was not acted upon": Sissons, *Ryerson* at 425-426.

53. Page 70, para. 1 – "with the help of Ryerson": Sissons, *Ryerson* at 428-436; Sissons, *Victoria* at 113; Hodgins, *Documentary History*, v.16 at 300-304.

54. Page 70, para. 1 – "without weakening their efficiency": Hodgins, *Documentary History*, v. 16 at 310 (report of the Attorney-General [John A. Macdonald] to the Governor-General); Sissons, *Ryerson* at 429-30; Sissons, *Victoria* at 114.

55. Page 70, para. 1 – "an early graduate of King's College": George Maclean Rose, *A Cyclopaedia of Canadian Biography* (Toronto: Rose Publishing Co., 1888), v.2 at 174.

56. Page 70, para. 1 – "was in the camp of the opposition": Indeed, when Patton was re-elected as vice-chancellor in 1862, Adam Crooks, a loyal senator, seconded the motion: see Hodgins, *Documentary History*, v.17 at 141. Sissons, *Victoria* at 113, insists that "Queen's and Victoria had no part in a conspiracy to influence the elections of 1860"; Wallace, *A History of the University of Toronto* at 83, however, says they did.

57. Page 70, para. 2 – "the best mode of affiliation": Sissons, *Ryerson* at 434; Sissons, *Victoria* at 120.

58. Page 70, para. 2 – "including faculties of law and medicine": Hodgins, *Documentary History*, v. 17 at 76-77 (Reply of the Senate of the University of Toronto to the Questions on the Affiliation of Colleges to the University); Sissons, *Victoria* at 120.

59. Page 70, para. 2 – "should be limited to $28,000 a year": Hodgins, *Documentary History*, v.17 at 73; Sissons, *Victoria* at 121.

60. Page 70, para. 2 – "and maintain their libraries": Hodgins, *Documentary History*, v.17 at 74.

61. Page 70, para. 2 – "was to become King's College": Hodgins, *Documentary History*, v.17 at 72; Sissons, *Victoria* at 121.

62. Page 70, para. 2 – "were to be excluded from the senate": Hodgins, *Documentary History*, v.17 at 72; Sissons, *Victoria* at 121.

63. Page 71, para. 1 – "including Edward Blake": Sissons, *Victoria* at 122.

64. Page 71, para. 1 – "public support of denominational colleges": Bruce W. Hodgins, "John Sandfield Macdonald," *DCB*, v.10 at 467; Sissons, *Victoria* at 132.

65. Page 71, para. 1 – "had been appointed by the government": Sissons, *Victoria* at 109; Wallace, *A History of the University of Toronto* at 77 and 85.

66. Page 71, para. 1 – "in any future decisions": Sissons, *Victoria* at 122.

67. Page 71, para. 1 – "favourable to the denominational colleges appointed": Hodgins, *Documentary History*, v.18 at 12-15; Wallace, *A History of the University of Toronto* at 85-86.

68. Page 71, para. 1 – "be maintained intact": Hodgins, *Documentary History*, v.17 at 308.

69. Page 71, para. 1 – "will receive a fatal blow": Ibid., v.18 at 6-7.

70. Page 71, para. 2 – "filled Toronto's St. Lawrence Hall": The *Globe*, March 6, 1863; Hodgins, *Documentary History*, v.17 at 133 (meeting of March 5, 1863); Sissons *Victoria* at 121-2; Joseph Schull, *Edward Blake: The Man of the Other Way 1833-1881* (Toronto: Macmillan of Canada, 1975) at 23.

71. Page 71, para. 2 – "of which we were so proud": The *Globe*, March 6, 1863.

72. Page 71, para. 2 – "would introduce into the senate": Hodgins, *Documentary History*, v.17 at 308.

73. Page 71, para. 2 – "professorships of law and medicine be restored": Ibid., v.17 at 133 (meeting of March 5, 1863).

74. Page 71, para. 2 – "the *Globe* reporter did not know": The *Globe*, March 6, 1863.

75. Page 71, para. 2 – "and three groans for the Commissioners": Ibid.

76. Page 71, para. 3 – "who had died suddenly": Hodgins, *Documentary History*, v.17 at 307-312.

77. Page 72, para. 1 – "were passed with healthy majorities": Ibid. at 313-314.

78. Page 72, para. 1 – "at least in many things": Ibid., v.18 at 10.

79. Page 72, para. 2 – "with their tails between their legs": "Daniel Wilson Journal" at 28.

80. Page 72, para. 2 – "how narrowly their university escaped extinction": Averill and Keith, "Daniel Wilson" at 152, quoting Daniel Wilson, "The University of Toronto and University College," in J.O. Miller and F.B. Hodgins, ed., *The Year Book of the University of Toronto 1886-1887* (Toronto: Rowsell and Hutchinson, 1887) at 26-27.

81. Page 72, para. 2 – "and Crooks became the vice chancellor": Hodgins, *Documentary History* v.18 at 152 (Senate meeting of December 22, 1864); Wallace, *A History of the University of Toronto* at 87; Averill and Keith, "Daniel Wilson" at 151-152.

82. Page 72, para. 2 – "without affecting the University of Toronto's endowment": Neatby, *"and not to yield": Queen's University, 1841-1917* at 106.

83. Page 73, para. 1 – "abolished grants to the denominational colleges": Sissons, *Victoria* at 132-137; Neatby, *"and not to yield": Queen's University, 1841-1917* at 114-115.

84. Page 73, para. 1 – "to challenge and meet the enemy in open combat": Sissons, *Victoria* at 133.

85. Page 73, para. 1 – "at least at present": Ibid. at 137.

86. Page 73, para. 2 – "primarily from the towns and villages of Ontario": W.S. Wallace, "Background" in Claude T. Bissell, ed., *University College: A Portrait* (University of Toronto Press, 1953) at 7.

87. Page 73, para. 2 – "and later, a lawyer": Hilary Dawson, "Alfred M. Lafferty, M.A. 1839-1912: An Early Black Graduate of the University of Toronto," *Ontario Black History News* (1998), v. 20, n. 37 at 5-6.

88. Page 73, para. 2 – "Louis Riel's provisional government at Red River": W.D. Smith, "James Ross," *DCB*, v. 10 at 629-631; Lewis H. Thomas, "Louis Riel," *DCB*, v.11 at 738; Wallace, *A History of the University of Toronto* at 90.

89. Page 73, para. 3 – "under the shadow of the American Civil War": See Robin W. Winks, *Canada and the United States: The Civil War Years* (Baltimore: Johns Hopkins Press, 1960).

90. Page 73, para. 3 – "from a British ship on the Atlantic Ocean": This event, in 1861, was known as the Trent Affair: see Bruce W. Hodgins, "John Sandfield Macdonald," in J.M.S. Careless, ed., *The Pre-Confederation Premiers: Ontario Government Leaders 1841-1867* (University of Toronto Press, 1980) at 265; Bruce W. Hodgins, *John Sandfield Macdonald 1812-1872* (University of Toronto Press, 1971) at 52.

91. Page 73, para. 3 – "the University Rifle Corps": See Wallace, *History of the University of Toronto* at 90; Loudon, *Sir William Mulock* at 51-3; *Resolution of the Senate of the University of Toronto, Recording the Great Services Rendered to the University by the Chancellor, The Right Honourable Sir William Mulock, P.C., K.C.M.G.* at 7. The Resolution gives William Mulock credit for suggesting the creation of the company. Loudon says that Mulock made the suggestion to McCaul, who called the organizing meeting. The unit was officially known as K. Company of the Queen's Own Rifles.

92. Page 73, para. 3 – "and the ubiquitous Adam Crooks an ensign": Wallace, *A History of the University of Toronto* at 90.

93. Page 73, para. 3 – "and William Tempest, were killed": Ibid.; James Loudon and William Mulock were with the company but did not take part in the battle: see W.J. Loudon and W.F. MacLean, eds., *University of Toronto FASTI From 1850 to 1887* (Toronto: Williamson and Company, 1887) at 94.

94. Page 73, para. 3 – "in the East Hall of University College": Wallace, *History* at 91.

95. Page 74, para. 2 – "Crooks became one of his ministers": Ibid. at 94.

96. Page 74, para. 2 – "Mowat, a strong supporter of the University, became premier": Paul Romney, "Sir Oliver Mowat," *DCB*, v. 13 at 729.

97. Page 74, para. 2 – "being captured by hostile persons": *An Act Respecting the University of Toronto*, 36 Vic. (1873) c.29; Averill and Keith, "Daniel Wilson" at 153.2

98. Page 74, para. 2 – "by graduates of the University": *An Act Respecting the University of Toronto* ss. 2, 5, and 23. Senators would be elected for five-year terms. The Chancellor was elected for a three-year term.

99. Page 74, para. 2 – "nine persons for three-year periods": *An Act Respecting the University of Toronto*, s. 2. There were also seven named ex-officio members, two of which were from the University College Council. This brought the total composition of the Senate to thirty-one members, plus "all former Chancellors and Vice-Chancellors" of the University: see s. 3. Only thirteen members of the new Senate could in theory have no connection to the University at all.

100. Page 74, para. 2 – "unless they affiliated": Averill and Keith, "Daniel Wilson" at 153.

CHAPTER 8 – 1871 – SCIENCE AND TECHNOLOGY

1. Page 75, para. 1 – "died suddenly": J. Donald Wilson, "William Hincks," *DCB*, v. 10 at 349; E. Horne Craigie, *A History of the Department of Zoology of the University of Toronto up to 1962* (Toronto: Department of Zoology, 1966) at 10.

2. Page 75, para. 1 – "was forced to retire": T.R. Millman, "James Beaven," *DCB*, v. 10 at 39 .

3. Page 75, para. 2 – "the professor of philosophy at Knox College": R.D. Gidney, "George Paxton Young," *DCB*, v.11 at 942; John G. Slater, "Philosophy at Toronto" (unpublished manuscript, 1998) at 70.

4. Page 75, para. 2 – "logical proof of the existence of God": Slater, "Philosophy" at 63-64.

5. Page 75, para. 2 – "the supernatural aspects of Christianity": D.C. Masters, *Henry John Cody: An Outstanding Life* (Toronto: Dundurn Press, 1995) at 16.

6. Page 75, para. 2 – "truly great teacher": Slater, "Philosophy" at 82.

7. Page 75, para. 2 – "his friend from their Edinburgh days": Marinell Ash, "The Early Years" in Elizabeth Hulse, ed., *Thinking with Both Hands: Sir Daniel Wilson in the Old World and the New* (University of Toronto Press, 1999) at 13.

8. Page 75, para. 2 – "most popular of all their College studies": Slater, "Philosophy" at 70.

9. Page 75, para. 3 – "the laws of thought": Ibid. at 68; see Susan Zeller, "'Merchants of Light': The Culture of Science in Daniel Wilson's Ontario 1853-1892" in Hulse, ed., *Thinking with Both Hands* at 133, on parallelograms of forces.

10. Page 75, para. 3 – "the professorship of mathematics at Victoria College": C.B. Sissons, *A History of Victoria University* (University of Toronto Press, 1952) at 140; Slater, "Philosophy" at 70.

11. Page 76, para. 1 – "the *Canadian Journal*": Zeller, "'Merchants of Light'" at 119; Trevor H. Levere, "The Most Select and the Most Democratic: A Century of Science in the Royal Society of Canada" (unpublished paper, 1998) at 9; "Sir Daniel Wilson's Journal," in UTA/Langton Family Papers/B65-0014/004 at 44 (January 26, 1879); James Loudon, "Memoirs of James Loudon" UTA/B72-0031/016(11) at 41.

12. Page 76, para. 2 – "a chair at Durham University": Craigie, *Department of Zoology* at 10. Nicholson moved to the University of Aberdeen in 1882, where he was a seminal figure in the development of modern paleontology. Some of the fossils he collected in Canada as part of his private collection now form part of Aberdeen's paleontological museum: see Nigel Trewin, "History of Geology at Aberdeen," http://info.abdn.ac.uk/-gmi265/history.html.

13. Page 76, para. 2 – "a wilderness of stuffed birds": Craigie, *Department of Zoology* at 11.

14. Page 76, para. 2 – "some twenty-six articles": Ibid.

15. Page 77, para. 1 – "until his retirement in 1912": "Robert Ramsay Wright," Henry James Morgan, ed., *The Canadian Men and Women of Our Time* (Toronto: William Briggs, 1912) at 1189; Craigie, *Department of Zoology* at 13.

16. Page 77, para. 1 – "using both hands": Craigie, *Department of Zoology* at 14.

17. Page 77, para. 1 – "'definitely settled' by Darwin": Zeller, "'Merchants of Light'" at 128.

18. Page 77, para. 2 – "in zoology than botany": Dorothy F. Forward, *The History of Botany at the University of Toronto* (Toronto, 1977) at 5.

19. Page 77, para. 2 – "until the First World War": Craigie, *Department of Zoology* at 15.

20. Page 77, para. 2 – "abolished in 1853": See Chapter 4 (1850), where James Beaven was elected the dean of arts.

21. Page 77, para. 2 – "in 1901 and 1902, respectively": Craigie, *Department of Zoology* at 14.

22. Page 77, para. 2 – "the history of Canadian education": Ibid. at 13-14.

23. Page 78, para. 1 – "a consulting actuary for Confederation Life": Loudon, "Memoirs" at 32.

24. Page 78, para. 2 – "and a graduate of the University": W.S. Wallace, *A History of the University of Toronto* (University of Toronto Press, 1927) at 100.

25. Page 78, para. 2 – "and died during exams": T.R. Loudon, "Introduction" in Loudon, "Memoirs" at 1.

26. Page 78, para. 2 – "and the dean of residence": Ibid. at 1-2.

27. Page 78, para. 3 – "'decided against' him": Loudon, "Memoirs" at 32; Harold Averill and Gerald Keith, "Sir Daniel Wilson and the University of Toronto," in Hulse, ed., *Thinking with Both Hands* at 154.

28. Page 78, para. 3 – "presumably for Loudon": Averill and Keith, "Sir Daniel Wilson and the University of Toronto" at 154.

29. Page 78, para. 4 – "'mathematical tutor in University College'": Daniel Wilson to James Loudon, July 27, 1875, Ireton Papers, UTA/B92-0030/009(04). While Averill and Keith, in "Sir Daniel Wilson" at 154, describe the letter as "gracious," it gives Loudon more praise for his conduct as Dean of Men than for his scholarship.

30. Page 78, para. 4 – "such as Edward Blake": Averill and Keith, "Sir Daniel Wilson" at 155; Ben Forster and Jonathan Swainger, "Edward Blake," *DCB*, v. 14 at 74. Goldwin Smith was, at the time, promoting Edward Blake as a future national leader as the head of the "Canada First" movement, a loose group of literary and intellectual figures who wanted to emphasize Canadian nationalism rather than Canada's connection with Britain.

31. Page 78, para. 4 – "to Premier Oliver Mowat": Averill and Keith, "Sir Daniel Wilson" at 155.

32. Page 78, para. 4 – "but kept the closing date very short": Ibid.

33. Page 79, para. 1 – "it happened to do both": Loudon, "Memoirs" at 32-34.

34. Page 79, para. 2 – "knowledge for its own sake": Zeller, "'Merchants of Light'" at 128.

35. Page 79, para. 2 – "the first in Canada for undergraduate students": Elizabeth J. Allin, *Physics at the University of Toronto* (Department of Physics, University of Toronto, 1981) at 3.

36. Page 79, para. 2 – "into his laboratory in the roundhouse": W.A.E McBryde, "History of the Chemistry Department" (unpublished manuscript, 1998), chap. 2 at 14.

37. Page 79, para. 2 – "from those offered in traditional textbooks": Yves Gingras, *Physics and the Rise of Scientific Research in Canada* (Montreal: McGill-Queen's University Press, 1991) at 19-20.

38. Page 79, para. 2 – "a major researcher and a splendid teacher": Craigie, *A History of the Department of Zoology at the University of Toronto* at 13-14.

39. Page 79, para. 2 – “and even single atoms”: Zeller, “‘Merchants of Light’” at 127, citing his lecture to the Br. Ass. For the Adv. of Science in 1874.

40. Page 79, para. 3 – “usually referred to as A. & M’s”: J.G. Hodgins, *Documentary History of Education in the Province of Ontario,* v.23 at 4.

41. Page 79, para. 3 – “how best to provide technical education”: Ibid. at 1; one of the authors was Hodgins, who did the documentary history of education in Ontario, and the other was a medical doctor from London Ontario, who headed a chemical company that manufactured acid: C.R. Young, *Early Engineering Education at Toronto 1851-1919* (University of Toronto Press, 1958) at 25; Loudon “Memoirs” at 19-22.

42. Page 79, para. 3 – “the recent established Massachusetts Institute of Technology”: Young, *Engineering* at 7. M.I.T. was founded in 1865.

43. Page 79, para. 3 – “New York’s Rensselaer Polytechnic”: Ibid. Rensselaer Polytechnic was the first such institution.

44. Page 79, para. 3 – “control of the government itself”: Hodgins, *Documentary History,* v.23 at 10-11; see also Richard White, *The Skule Story: The University of Toronto Faculty of Applied Science and Engineering 1873-2000* (University of Toronto Press, 2000) at 7-10.

45. Page 80, para. 1 – “the site of the present Ryerson Polytechnical University”: Ibid., v.23 at 8; Loudon “Memoirs” at 19; Young, *Engineering* at 28.

46. Page 80, para. 1 – “the north-east corner of Church and Adelaide streets”: Young, *Engineering* at 27; Loudon, “Memoirs” at 22; Geoffrey Simmins, *Fred Cumberland: Building the Victorian Dream* (University of Toronto Press, 1997) at 168-9.

47. Page 80, para. 1 – “taught their business?”: The *Globe,* February 11, 1871 (debates of the Legislature of Ontario); Loudon, “Memoirs” at 19-20; Young, *Engineering* at 28.

48. Page 80, para. 1 – “would benefit from such a school”: The *Globe,* February 11, 1871, reported his remarks as follows: “Hon J.B. MACDONALD said it was proposed to erect the college on the grounds of the Normal School. Institutions of this kind had been very successful in the United States and would be so here, especially schools of minearology; for ignorance of minearology had cost many of the inhabitants of this country dear. He would ask was it not time that the drivers of our locomotives, who were entrusted with so many lives, should be thoroughly taught their business. This would be done in this college, where amongst other things there would be lectures on the machinery of engines.”

49. Page 80, para. 2 – “a school of mines for the University”: Young, *Engineering* at 20.

50. Page 80, para. 2 – “under his own auspices”: Loudon, “Memoirs” at 20; see also Young, *Engineering* at 21, 28, and 32-34.

51. Page 80, para. 2 – “had already been purchased”: Young, *Engineering* at 35.

52. Page 80, para. 2 – “in the spring of 1872”: Loudon, “Memoirs” at 22-23; White, *The Skule Story* at 10.

53. Page 80, para. 2 – “lectured in chemistry”: Hodgins, *Documentary History,* v.24 at 232. Loudon did not join the staff until the second year: White, *The Skule Story* at 14.

54. Page 80, para. 2 – “after Hincks died”: McBryde, “Chemistry,” chap. 3 at 3-5; Young, *Engineering* at 38-39.

55. Page 81, para. 1 – “mining, engineering, mechanics and manufacturing”: *An Act to Establish a School of Practical Science* (1873), preamble; White, *The Skule Story* at 12.

56. Page 81, para. 1 – "a diploma after three years": *Act to Establish School of Practical Science*, ss. 1 and 8; White, *The Skule Story* at 12.

57. Page 81, para. 1 – "for artisans and others": *Act to Establish School of Practical Science*, s. 8.

58. Page 81, para. 1 – "available to University College": White, *The Skule Story* at 15-16.

59. Page 82, para. 1 – "the affiliation of SPS with the University": *Act to Establish School of Practical Science*, s. 10; White, *The Skule Story* at 12.

60. Page 82, para. 1 – "for work in the physical sciences": White, *The Skule Story* at 16-17; Hodgins, *Documentary History*, v. 27 at 87-8 (Professor James Loudon to the Honourable S.C.V. Wood, provincial secretary, December 17, 1875 – written at the request of Crooks).

61. Page 82, para. 1 – "well received by the government": Young, *Engineering* at 52.

62. Page 82, para. 1 – "an influential engineer": Loudon, "Memoirs" at 36.

63. Page 82, para. 1 – "now minister of education": Robert M. Stamp, "Adam Crooks," *DCB*, v. 11 at 222.

64. Page 82, para. 1 – "decided to sell the Mechanics' Institute": The Building was demolished in 1949: Young, *Engineering* at 40.

65. Page 82, para. 1 – "on the grounds of the University": Young, *Engineering* at 42; Loudon, "Memoirs" at 37; Averill and Keith, "Daniel Wilson" at 156; UTA/ B72-0013/001(01), James Loudon to Edward Blake, December 27, 1875; Thomas Moss to Edward Blake, March 21 and December 29, 1876; UTA/A70-0024/056(03), Adam Crooks to Thomas Moss, June 17, 1878; White, *The Skule Story* at 16-17.

66. Page 82, para. 1 – "and Vice-chancellor Moss": Averill and Keith, "Daniel Wilson" at 156.

67. Page 82, para. 1 – "the evening working-men's classes": Loudon, "Memoirs" at 37.

68. Page 82, para. 1 – "The three-storey red-brick building": Young, *Engineering* at 59.

69. Page 82, para. 1 – "the little red Schoolhouse": McBryde, "Chemistry," chap. 2 at 18.

70. Page 82, para. 1 – "the architect of Trinity College": Young, *Engineering* at 59.

71. Page 82, para. 2 – "his experience as an Engineer": Loudon, "Memoirs" at 37A; Young, *Engineering* at 63 and 65; Averill and Keith, "Daniel Wilson" at 156. Wilson would have chosen one of McGill Principal Dawson's sons: Loudon at 37; Averill and Keith at 156; Young at 62.

72. Page 82, para. 2 – "and a dagger in the other": W.J. Loudon, *Studies of Student Life* (University of Toronto Press, 1928), v.5 at 95-96.

73. Page 82, para. 3 – "the professional kind": Young, *Engineering* at 64.

74. Page 82, para. 3 – "running through both terms": Young, *Engineering* at 80; "Annual Report of the School of Practical Science, Toronto, for the Year 1882-3," *Sessional Papers of the Ontario Legislature*, v.16 (1884) no. 28 at 3.

75. Page 82, para. 3 – "the theory of the steam engine to the next": Catherine Moriarty, *John Galbraith, 1846-1914; Engineer and Educator – A Portrait* (Toronto: Faculty of Applied Sciences and Engineering, University of Toronto, 1989) at 24.

76. Page 83, para. 1 – "had converted": Young, *Engineering* at 81; Charles Levi, "Eugene Stern: The First Jewish Staff Member at the University?" unpublished memorandum (1999). Stern was listed as an "Israelite" in the 1871 Canadian Census, (Toronto 047 B 2 54 19). This information has been independently confirmed by Sheldon J. Godfrey: see Godfrey to Friedland, February 3, 1999, enclosing census report and S.J. Birnbaum, "The History of the Jews in Toronto," *Canadian Jewish News*, v.16 (January 24, 1913) at 8.

77. Page 83, para. 2 – "the first chair of the board": Loudon, "Memoirs" at 37A; Young, *Engineering* at 67.

78. Page 83, para. 2 – "followed by Daniel Wilson": Averill and Keith, "Daniel Wilson" at 161. Wilson had added ethnology to the curriculum: Young, *Engineering* at 75.

79. Page 83, para. 2 – "Ramsay Wright was the secretary": Ramsay Wright to Minister of Education, January 26, 1880, *Sessional Papers*, v.12 (1880), no. 13 at 3.

80. Page 83, para. 2 – "and other rooms he could get at University College": Loudon, "Memoirs" at 38; Young, *Engineering* at 60.

81. Page 83, para. 2 – "facilities for University College professors": In the last few years of the 1870s there was a shortage of funds: see Averill and Keith, "Daniel Wilson" at 157.

82. Page 83, para. 2 – "and no engineering labs": Young, *Engineering* at 60 and 68.

83. Page 83, para. 2 – "a series of public lectures in 1881-82": Ibid. at 75.

84. Page 83, para. 2 – "in the Daily Business of Life": "Daniel Wilson Journal" at 55 (May 27, 1881).

85. Page 83, para. 2 – "and introducing every other one": Averill and Keith, "Daniel Wilson" at 162.

86. Page 84, para. 1 – "after the first lecture": Young, *Engineering* at 76.

87. Page 84, para. 2 – "to encourage industrial development in Canada": A.B. McKillop, *Contours of Canadian Thought* (University of Toronto Press, 1987) at 80-81.

88. Page 84, para. 2 – "there were more than 30 students": *Annual Report of School of Practical Science for the Year 1882-1883.*

89. Page 86, para. 2 – "and in 1884 more than 40": Young, *Engineering* at 81.

90. Page 84, para. 2 – "three years of approved engineering work": Ibid.

91. Page 84, para. 2 – "students from the private medical schools": McBryde, "History of the Chemistry Department," chap. 4 at 8.

92. Page 84, para. 2 – "increasingly inadequate": Young, *Engineering* at 82.

93. Page 86, para. 2 – "not mechanical or electrical engineering": Ibid. at 84.

94. Page 84, para. 2 – "lit at night by arc lamps": Fred Kee, "Electric Power in Canada" in *Electricity: The Magic Medium* (Thornhill: The Institute of Electrical and Electronics Engineers Inc., 1985) at 48. Kee says that arc lighting had been "invented" as early as 1812.

95. Page 84, para. 2 – "was clearly required": *Annual Report of the School for Practical Science, Toronto, for the Year 1882-3* (Sessional Papers), no.29, vol.16A, 1884 at 3.

96. Page 86, para. 3 – "for which Pike was being paid": McBryde, "History of the Chemistry Department," chap. 4 at 8-10; Young, *Engineering* at 78-82; "Wilson Journal" at 55 (May 27, 1881); White, *The Skule Story* at 24-27.

97. Page 84, para. 3 – "the reason for the conflict is not known": Young, *Engineering* at 79.

98. Page 84, para. 3 – "made up only of SPS members": White, *The Skule Story* at 36-37.

CHAPTER 9 – 1880 – THE ADMISSION OF WOMEN

1. Page 85, para. 1 – "as finally disposed of": *Varsity*, October 7, 1880. The predecessor of the *Varsity* was the *White and Blue*: see Claude Bissell, "Opinion," in *University College: A Portrait* (University of Toronto Press, 1953) at 85.

2. Page 85, para. 1 – "run by both graduates and undergraduates": Bissell, "Opinion" at 85.

3. Page 85, para. 1 – "a reporter for the *Globe* and other papers": Harold Averill and Gerald Keith, "Daniel Wilson and the University of Toronto" in Elizabeth Hulse, ed., *Thinking with Both Hands: Sir Daniel Wilson in the Old World and the New* (University of Toronto Press, 1999) at 167-168.

4. Page 85, para. 2 – "Never in my day Madam!": Gina Feldberg, "Emily Howard Jennings (Stowe)," *DCB*, v.13 at 508. Emily Stowe practiced without a license until 1880, at which point she could then practice in the open. Some sources support the claim that Dr. James Miranda Barry, inspector of hospitals in Canada in 1857, was actually a woman disguised as a man, but this is not universally accepted: see Jacalyn Duffin, *History of Medicine: A Scandalously Short Introduction* (University of Toronto Press, 1999) at 265; Charles G. Roland, "James Barry," *DCB*, v.9 at 34.

5. Page 86, para. 1 – "the 72-year-old McCaul announced his retirement": "Sir Daniel Wilson's Journal" in UTA/ Langton Family Papers/B65-0014/004 at 45 (July 7, 1879); Averill and Keith, "Daniel Wilson and the University of Toronto" at 157.

6. Page 86, para. 1 – "Things have been drifting of late": "Wilson Journal" at 46 (July 7, 1879).

7. Page 86, para. 1 – "since June of 1876": Averill and Keith, "Daniel Wilson and the University of Toronto" at 157.

8. Page 86, para. 1 – "an obstruction in every way": "Wilson Journal" at 47 (October 28, 1879).

9. Page 86, para. 1 – "the 39-year-old chief justice of Ontario, Thomas Moss": J.G. Snell, "Thomas Moss," *DCB*, v. 11 at 621. He had been registrar of UC from 1861 to 1873. He died in 1881 at the age of 42.

10. Page 86, para. 1 – "could also serve as president of University College": Wilson Journal" at 46 (July 7, 1879).

11. Page 86, para. 1 – "with a fitting increase of salary": Ibid. at 48 (November 12, 1879).

12. Page 86, para. 1 – "offered the presidency of University College to Wilson": Ibid. at 46 and 50 (October 1, 1879 and May 20, 1880).

13. Page 87, para. 1 – "in like fashion": Ibid. at 50 (May 30, 1880).

14. Page 87, para. 2 – "you will allow me to retire": Ibid. at 52 (January 1, 1881).

15. Page 87, para. 2 – "who later would be the principal of University College": "Maurice Hutton," in Henry James Morgan, ed., *The Canadian Men and Women of the Time*, 2nd ed. (Toronto: William Briggs, 1912) at 564.

16. Page 87, para. 2 – "there's life in the old dog yet": "Wilson Journal" at 51 and 53 (October, 1880 and January 1, 1881).

17. Page 87, para. 3 – "one needed a university degree in order to teach high school": R.D. Gidney and W.P.J. Millar, *Professional Gentlemen: The Professions in Nineteenth-Century Ontario* (University of Toronto Press, 1994) at 235-236. Women had been teaching at the elementary level as early as the 1820s: see Alison Prentice et al., *Canadian Women: A History* (Toronto: Harcourt Brace Jovanovich, 1988) at 80-82 and 93-95.

18. Page 87, para. 3 – "even acceptable assistants in them": Averill and Keith, "Daniel Wilson and the University of Toronto" at 168; *Varsity* of December 11, 1880. An Act of 1871 allowed them to attend the new High Schools and Collegiate Institutes: see A.B. McKillop, *Matters of Mind: The University in Ontario 1791-1951* (University of Toronto Press, 1994) at 138. From 1885 on, the specialist teacher qualifications normally required an honours BA.

19. Page 87, para. 3 – "Parliament to be appealed to, etc. etc.": "Wilson Journal" at 58 (February 3, 1882).

20. Page 87, para. 3 – "by the physician Emily Stowe": Paula J.S. LaPierre, "The First Generation: The Experience of Women University Students in Central Canada" (Ph.D. Thesis: University of Toronto, 1993) at 103 and 120; Heather Murray, "Daniel Wilson as Litterateur: English Professor, Critic, and Poet" in Elizabeth Hulse, ed., *Thinking With Both Hands* at 218.

21. Page 87, para. 4 – "the Canadian Women's Suffrage Association": Gina Feldberg, "Emily Howard Jennings (Stowe)" at 509.

22. Page 87, para. 4 – "by numbers instead of names": University of Toronto Senate Minutes, March 8, 1877.

23. Page 87, para. 4 – "wrote the exams in Toronto": See *Varsity* of November 13, 1880, in which William Houston wrote: "I hope to see the local examinations thrown open, before long, to both sexes."

24. Page 87, para. 4 – "those proposed to male candidates in the same subject": Senate Minutes, May 28, 1877.

25. Page 88, para. 1 – "his chemistry lectures given at S.P.S.": *Varsity*, November 13, 1880.

26. Page 88, para. 1 – "and listen to his anthropology lectures": M.E. Spence, "Once There were no Women at Varsity," *University of Toronto Monthly*, v.33 at 123.

27. Page 88, para. 1 – "only 1, Henrietta Charles, from St. Catharines, ever graduated": John Squair, "Admission of Women to the University of Toronto and University College" (pamphlet, 1924, in University of Toronto Pamphlet collections and also found in B84-0003/002) at 2-3.

28. Page 88, para. 1 – "for their private education": Ibid. at 6; Senate of July 26, 1880; also Senate of March 4, 1881.

29. Page 88, para. 1 – "Their requests to Wilson were turned down": Anne Rochon Ford, *A Path not Strewn with Roses: One Hundred Years of Women at the University of Toronto 1884-1984* (University of Toronto Press, 1985) at 7.

30. Page 88, para. 2 – "and a wrong to the individual and to society": *Varsity*, March 3, 1882.

31. Page 88, para. 2 – "The motion was rejected": Averill and Keith, "Daniel Wilson and the University of Toronto" at 169.

32. Page 88, para. 2 – "I say very decidedly No!": Wilson Journal" at 72 (September 26, 1883).

33. Page 88, para. 3 – "over an eight-year period commencing in the 1860s": Wilson Journal" at 31 (December 10, 1873); Averill and Keith, "Daniel Wilson and the University of Toronto" at 167.

34. Page 88, para. 3 – "and at Harvard and Columbia": Ford, *A Path not Strewn with Roses* at 4-5. At Oxford and Cambridge, however, women could not get degrees until the 20th century – at Oxford in 1920 and at Cambridge not until 1948: see Ford at 4.

35. Page 88, para. 3 – "were co-educational": Ford, *A Path not Strewn with Roses* at 4-5.

36. Page 88, para. 3 – "Mount Allison in New Brunswick in 1872": Ibid. at 5.

37. Page 88, para. 3 – "but she did not graduate": Ibid. at 25-26.

38. Page 88, para. 3 – "from the Victoria medical school in 1883": Ibid. at 27; C.B. Sissons, *A History of Victoria University* (University of Toronto Press, 1952) at 197.

39. Page 88, para. 3 – "her BSc degree from Victoria in 1884": Sissons, *Victoria,* at 197.

40. Page 89, para. 1 – "*A Path not Strewn with Roses*": Ford, *A Path not Strewn with Roses* at iv.

41. Page 89, para. 2 – "on the McGill campus": Ibid. at 17-18.

42. Page 89, para. 2 – "the power of steady passive resistance": "Wilson Journal" at 72 (September 26, 1883).

43. Page 89, para. 3 – "and high intellectual development of women": John Squair, "Admission of Women" at 8, citing Daniel Wilson to Ella Gardiner, September 25, 1883.

44. Page 89, para. 3 – "physical differences that distinguish the sexes": Averill and Keith, "Daniel Wilson and the University of Toronto" at 169. Some "authorities" held that the "physiology of women made serious study difficult, particularly during menstruation": see A. B. McKillop, *Matters of Mind* at 126.

45. Page 89, para. 3 – "at the excitable age of 18 to 22": Ford, *A Path not Strewn with Roses* at 4 (letter to Ross quoting Charles W. Eliot of Harvard.)

46. Page 89, para. 3 – "'or danger incurred,' he wrote": Averill and Keith, "Daniel Wilson and the University of Toronto" at 170.

47. Page 89, para. 3 – "what I fear is that your reception will be *too* cordial": Ford, *A Path not Strewn with Roses* at 9; M.E. Spence, "Eliza May Balmer," *University of Toronto Monthly,* v.33 at 147.

48. Page 89, para. 3 – "a source of mischievous jest to others": Murray, "Daniel Wilson as Litterateur: English Professor, Critic, and Poet" at 218-19.

49. Page 89, para. 3 – "Shakespeare's *Measure for Measure* or *Othello*": Ibid. at 219.

50. Page 89, para. 4 – "for the admission of women to University College": Ross' letter of August 20, 1884, cited in Nancy Ramsay Thompson, "The Controversy over the Admission of Women to University College, University of Toronto" (M.A. Thesis: University of Toronto, 1974) at 126; see also Squair, "Admission of Women" at 19, which is slightly different.

51. Page 89, para. 4 – "a prize-winning 1863 graduate of Toronto": "His Honour Col. The Hon John Morrison Gibson," in Morgan, ed., *The Canadian Men and Women of the Time* at 443.

52. Page 89, para. 4 – "in my opinion you are just the man": Ford, *A Path not Strewn with Roses* at 12; William Houston to J.M. Gibson, January 12, 1884 (copied from the letter books of William Houston and forwarded by Heather Murray).

53. Page 89, para. 4 – "allowing women to keep their scholarship money": Senate of July 21 and July 26, 1880; Thompson, "The Controversy over the Admission of Women" at 52.

54. Page 89, para. 4 – "a future minister of education": "Hon. Richard Harcourt" in Morgan, ed., *The Canadian Men and Women of the Time* at 499.

55. Page 90, para. 1 – "for women as University College does for men": *Varsity,* April 5, 1884.

56. Page 90, para. 1 – "but ready to enforce them": Ford, *A Path not Strewn with Roses* at 13; Houston to Wilson, June 11, 1884 (Houston letter books as forwarded by Heather Murray).

57. Page 90, para. 2 – "is rarely a spur to intellectual activity": *Varsity*, March 15, 1884.

58. Page 90, para. 2 – "as we probably should": Ibid.

59. Page 90, para. 2 – "to the simple University of Toronto crest": Claude Bissell, "Opinion" at 92-93.

60. Page 90, para. 3 – "for women students": John Squair, "Admission of Women" at 12-18.

61. Page 90, para. 3 – "an old school teacher and school inspector": "Wilson Journal" at 74-5 (November 23, 1883).

62. Page 90, para. 4 – "the amount – $20 – which you sent me": E. Gardiner, "A Reminiscence," *Sesame*, v.1 no.1 (1897) at 22.

63. Page 90, para. 4 – "and a delicately moulded face": Spence, "Balmer" at 148.

64. Page 90, para. 4 – "if he would permit her to attend his lectures": Ibid.

65. Page 90, para. 4 – "just as he did the other students": John G. Slater, "Philosophy at Toronto" (Unpublished manuscript, 1998) at 80.

66. Page 91, para. 1 – "the onus of ordering her out": Ibid., citing Andrew Stevenson in the *University of Toronto Monthly* of 1938.

67. Page 91, para. 2 – "as may be necessary in that behalf": Squair, "Admission of Women" at 24-5.

68. Page 91, para. 2 – "to 'show backbone'": "Wilson Journal" at 84 (October 1, 1884).

69. Page 91, para. 2 – "the judgment of experience": Ibid. at 78 (March 28, 1884).

70. Page 91, para. 3 – "a waiting room for the women students": E. Gardiner, "A Reminiscence" at 22.

71. Page 91, para. 3 – "when she retired at age 67": Ford, *A Path not Strewn with Roses* at 14; Gardiner, "Reminiscence" at 22; McKillop, *Matters of Mind* at 132; Squair, "Admission of Women" at 25-26.

72. Page 91, para. 3 – "Ella Gardiner": E. Gardiner, "A Reminiscence" at 22.

73. Page 92, para. 1 – "though the documents do not make it clear": It is apparent that the author was one of the three students, from the details of her narrative.

74. Page 92, para. 1 – "eight other women would join them over the course of the year": E. Gardiner, "A Reminiscence" at 22.

75. Page 92, para. 1 – "or even consult the library catalogues": Ibid. at 23.

76. Page 92, para. 2 – "a member of the 'committee' of a club": *Year Book of the University of Toronto, 1886-1887* (Toronto: Rowsell & Hutchinson) at 79, UTA/P78-0163.

77. Page 92, para. 2 – "and to encourage public speaking": Charles Levi, "Where the Famous People Were?: The Origins, Activities and Future Careers of Student Leaders at University College, Toronto 1854-1973" (Ph.D. Thesis: York University, 1998) at 235-236; Ford, *A Path not Strewn with Roses* at 19.

78. Page 92, para. 2 – "or recreation ground for women": Levi, "Where the Famous People Were?" at 237-238, 243, and 246.

79. Page 92, para. 3 – "almost eighty years later, in 1959": Helen Gurney, *A Century to Remember: Women's Sports at the University of Toronto* (Toronto: U of T Women's T-Holders' Association, 1993) at 35.

80. Page 93, para. 1 – "founded in 1895": Ibid. at 1-2.

81. Page 93, para. 1 – "recreational ice-skating rinks from 1896": Ibid. at 1; Harold Averill comments to Friedland, January 29, 2001.

82. Page 93, para. 1 – "over the northern end of the University": Gurney, *A Century to Remember* at 4.

83. Page 93, para. 1 – "a member of both the golf and the tennis clubs as an undergraduate in the 1890s": Ibid. at 2.

84. Page 94, para. 1 – "became principal of Albert College in Belleville": Ford, *A Path not Strewn with Roses* at 15; UTA/Graduate Records/"Gardiner, Ella"/A73-0026/113(26).

85. Page 94, para. 1 – "to complete their education with private tutors": Ford, *A Path not Strewn with Roses* at 14, UTA/Graduate Records/"Brown, Catherine Edith"/A73-0026/039(96).

86. Page 94, para. 1 – "and later taught at Harbord Collegiate": UTA/Graduate Records/"Balmer, Eliza May"/A73-0026/018a(17).

87. Page 94, para. 1 – "became the head of English and history at Parkdale Collegiate": UTA/Graduate Records/ "Spence, Nellie"/A73-0026/437(14).

88. Page 94, para. 1 – "having interrupted her studies to teach in Ottawa": Paula LaPierre, "The First Generation" at 120.

89. Page 94, para. 1 – "the path chosen by many of the early women graduates": Levi, "Where the Famous People Were?" at 275.

90. Page 94, para. 1 – "at University College were women": Ibid. at 292, adapted from *President's Report, 1912/13* at 38-39.

91. Page 94, para. 1 – "over each of the next two decades": McKillop, *Matters of Mind* at 141.

92. Page 94, para. 2 – "boarding houses on Bloor Street and in the Annex": Ford, *A Path not Strewn with Roses* at 21.

93. Page 94, para. 2 – "but it was never built": Levi, "Where the Famous People Were?" at 243.

94. Page 94, para. 2 – "on the site of the present Sidney Smith Hall, in 1919": Ford, *A Path not Strewn with Roses* at 21; Averill's comments to Friedland, January 29, 2001.

95. Page 94, para. 2 – "but that never happened": Ford, *A Path not Strewn* at 31-33.

96. Page 95, para. 1 – "as a women's residence for Victoria": Ibid. at 27-28; see also Jean O'Grady, *Margaret Addison: A Biography* (Montreal: McGill-Queen's University Press, 2001) at 83-90.

97. Page 95, para. 2 – "and applied chemistry, in 1912": Richard White, *The Skule Story: The University of Toronto Faculty of Applied Science and Engineering 1873-2000* (University of Toronto Press, 2000) at 73.

98. Page 95, para. 2 – "admitted to engineering by 1923": E-mail from Ruby Heap to Charles Levi, December 11,

2000, containing excerpt from upcoming work on "The Professional Education of Women Engineers in Quebec and Ontario 1920-1990."

99. Page 95, para. 2 – "(then part of engineering) in 1920": Ford, *A Path not Strewn with Roses* at 48. Many have identified Hill as the first woman to graduate from architecture: see for example *The Beaver* (December, 2000) at 30. However, the case of Mary Anna Kentner, who was reported in the press to have entered Architecture in 1916, has not been settled decisively either way: see UTA/Graduate Records/"Kentner, Mary Anna"/A7309926/ 197(13).

100. Page 95, para. 2 – "an important aeronautical engineer": Ford, *A Path not Strewn with Roses* at 49.

101. Page 95, para. 2 – "one of the first two women to graduate from Trinity College": Ibid. at 31.

CHAPTER 10 – 1883 – FEDERATION

1. Page 99, para. 1 – "between the denominational colleges and the University": Harold Averill and Gerald Keith, "Sir Daniel Wilson and the University of Toronto" in Elizabeth Hulse, ed., *Thinking with Both Hands* (University of Toronto Press, 1999) at 173.

2. Page 99, para. 1 – "that is controlled by the State": W.J. Loudon, *Sir William Mulock: A Short Biography* (Toronto: Macmillan Co. of Canada Ltd., 1932) at 229-230.

3. Page 99, para. 1 – "before Mulock's speech": Mulock "without previous consultation with anybody publicly raised the question": see James Loudon, "Memoirs of James Loudon," UTA/B72-0031/016(011) at 53.

4. Page 99, para. 1 – "to dream of a legislative grant": "Sir Daniel Wilson's Journal" in UTA/Langton Family Papers/ B65-0014/004 at 73-74 (October 17, 1883).

5. Page 99, para. 1 – "our chances of sharing in private munificence": Ibid. at 75 (November 29, 1883).

6. Page 99, para. 1 – "special financial treatment for the University of Toronto": C.B. Sissons, *A History of Victoria University* (University of Toronto Press, 1952) at 162.

7. Page 100, para. 1 – "after the death of Chief Justice Thomas Moss": J. G. Snell, "Thomas Moss," *DCB,* v. 11 at 621; "Hon. Sir Charles Moss," in Henry James Morgan, *The Canadian Men and Women of the Time* (Toronto: William Briggs, 1912) at 830; Loudon, "Memoirs" at 46-7. Wilson had been elected pro-Vice Chancellor when Moss tendered his resignation on November 1, 1880, but the contest for the vice-chancellorship only really opened with Moss' death: see Averill and Keith, "Sir Daniel Wilson" at 160-1.

8. Page 100, para. 1 – "he had campaigned strongly for the position": As a wealthy businessman and lawyer, Mulock had even tried to eliminate competition by successfully having the senate remove the $400 yearly payment for the position. Payment was reinstated after his election: see Loudon, "Memoirs" at 46-48.

9. Page 100, para. 1 – "11 votes to 4": Sissons, *Victoria* at 161. Three other votes were cast for F. W. Taylor: see James Loudon, "Memoirs" at 47.

10. Page 100, para. 1 – "devoid of the instincts of a gentleman": "Wilson Journal" at 75 (January 28, 1884).

11. Page 100, para. 2 – "by order in council in 1878": "Copy of an Order-In-Council approved by his Honor, the Lieut. Governors the 16th Day of May, A.D. 1878", UTA/A70-0024/reel 2.

12. Page 100, para. 2 – "as leader of the opposition": W. S. Wallace, *A History of the University of Toronto* (University of Toronto Press, 1927) at 134.

13. Page 100, para. 2 – "his career as a Liberal politician": Averill and Keith, "Sir Daniel Wilson" at 161 and 172.

14. Page 100, para. 2 – "a separate college for women should be built": Loudon, *Sir William Mulock* at 224. Mulock in his 1883 address talked about how a university education would help prepare women to be breadwinners, as well as wives and mothers, and saw it "as much their right as that of their brothers" to have a State education. He seemed to be most concerned about coping with the huge numbers of new students.

15. Page 100, para. 2 – "the largest religious denomination in the province": Marguerite Van Die, *An Evangelical Mind: Nathanael Burwash and the Methodist Tradition in Canada, 1839-1918* (Montreal: McGill-Queen's University Press, 1989) at 120. Almost a quarter of the population were Methodists: see J.M.S. Careless, "Beginning a New Life in Toronto" (undated and unpublished speech) at 2.

16. Page 100, para. 2 – "and were supporters of Victoria, did": "The Methodist vote was crucial to the vice-chancellor's success at the polls": see Averill and Keith, "Sir Daniel Wilson" at 172.

17. Page 100, para. 3 – "the various other great educational institutions of the province": Loudon, *Sir William Mulock* at 300; Sissons, *Victoria* at 159.

18. Page 101, para. 1 – "for an enlarged university": Sissons, *Victoria* at 163; Loudon, *Sir William Mulock* at 302; Sissons identified the friend as the Hon. John McDonald.

19. Page 101, para. 1 – "met with Mulock": Loudon, *Sir William Mulock* at 302.

20. Page 101, para. 1 – "the Reverend George Grant": D.B. Mack, "George Monro Grant," *DCB*, v. 13 at 403-408.

21. Page 101, para. 1 – "the Reverend Charles Body": For Body, see T. A. Reed, ed., *A History of the University of Trinity College, Toronto 1852-1952* (University of Toronto Press, 1952) at 87 and 97-98.

22. Page 101, para. 2 – "a good science program": A.B. McKillop, *Matters of Mind: The University in Ontario 1791-1951* (University of Toronto Press, 1994) at 46; Wallace, *A History of the University of Toronto* at 126.

23. Page 101, para. 2 – "A university": Technically, Victoria was a college until it merged with Albert College in Belleville to form Victoria University in 1884: see Neil Semple, "Federation and the New 'Old Vic'" (undated and unpublished speech notes) at 1.

24. Page 101, para. 2 – "Every sect cannot have a genuine university": G.S. French, "Prelude to Federation" (undated and unpublished speech) at 4; McKillop, *Matters of Mind* at 46.

25. Page 101, para. 2 – "with the Prince of Wales medal in 1859": Marguerite Van Die, "Nathanael Burwash," *DCB*, v. 14 at 161.

26. Page 102, para. 1 – "for the 'low church' Anglicans": French, "Prelude to Federation" at 3 and 5.

27. Page 102, para. 1 – "don't sell us for their own party purposes": "Wilson Journal" at 76 (February 22, 1884).

28. Page 102, para. 1 – "including the theological colleges": Nathanael Burwash, "The Development of the University, 1853-1887" in *The University of Toronto and Its Colleges, 1827-1906* (Toronto: University Librarian, 1906) at 44.

29. Page 102, para. 1 – "and not a little sectarian bigotry": "Wilson Journal" at 83 (July 24, 1884). Wilson claimed later, in a diary entry of April 16, 1887, that he was "kept entirely in the dark." However, he knew in general what was going on, even though he had not seen a key document prepared by the denominational colleges until it was shown to him by the principal of Wycliffe in November, 1884: see "Wilson Journal" at 118 (April 16, 1887). Wilson was no doubt preoccupied by the issue of the admission of women.

30. Page 102, para. 1 – "the various governing bodies of the universities and colleges": "Wilson Journal" at 90 (December 22, 1884); Sissons, *Victoria* at 165-7.

31. Page 102, para. 1 – "to lay their hands on the University endowment": "Wilson Journal" at 88 (December 5, 1884).

32. Page 102, para. 1 – "why not now?": Ibid. (December 12, 1884).

33. Page 102, para. 2 – "a scheme proposed by Burwash": Van Die, *An Evangelical Mind* at 123; French, "Prelude to Federation" at 7. For a discussion of Burwash's career, see Van Die's book.

34. Page 102, para. 2 – "responsible for the scientific subjects": Sissons, *Victoria* at 166; Burwash, "The Development of the University" at 48-51.

35. Page 102, para. 2 – "under the British North America Act of 1867": Wallace, *A History of the University of Toronto* at 115 and 130.

36. Page 102, para. 2 – "the English basis for a broad liberal culture": Cited in Van Die, *An Evangelical Mind* at 118.

37. Page 102, para. 2 – "so the subject-matter division was chosen": Sissons, *Victoria* at 166.

38. Page 102, para. 3 – "and all the denominational colleges": Ibid.

39. Page 103, para. 1 – "hiring college staff in those fields": Ibid.; Burwash, "The Development of the University" at 51; Wallace, *A History of the University of Toronto* at 131.

40. Page 103, para. 1 – "medieval and modern history went to the University": Sissons, *Victoria* at 166.

41. Page 103, para. 1 – "given to the University at Wilson's insistence": Ibid.; Wallace, *A History of the University of Toronto* at 131.

42. Page 103, para. 1 – "which he described as a 'Methodist grab'": "Wilson Journal" at 103 (April 5, 1886).

43. Page 103, para. 2 – "possibly in the downtown Upper Canada College site": "Wilson Journal" at 100 (April 2, 1886); Loudon, "Memoirs" at 56-57.

44. Page 103, para. 2 – "the old parliament buildings on Front Street": Averill and Keith, "Sir Daniel Wilson" at 173.

45. Page 103, para. 2 – "a figment of Wilson's imagination": Wallace, *A History of the University of Toronto* at 127. Burwash denied it in the *University of Toronto Monthly*, March, 1916.

46. Page 103, para. 2 – "other suitable accommodation for U.C.": Nelles to Mulock, November 29, 1884; Nelles to Ross, November 29, 1884, UTA/B92-0030/009(14); Sissons, *Victoria* at 178-79.

47. Page 103, para. 2 – "also dropped it": James Loudon, "Memoirs" at 56-57.

48. Page 103, para. 2 – "and for some of the university professors": Ibid. at 57.

49. Page 103, para. 3 – "accepted the proposal without amendment": Sissons, *Victoria* at 166-167.

50. Page 103, para. 3 – "as did the University College council": "Wilson Journal" at 90 (January 9, 1885).

51. Page 103, para. 3 – "Queen's, however, rejected it": Hilda Neatby, *Queen's University: vol. 1, 1841-1917* (Kingston: McGill-Queen's University Press, 1978) at 162.

52. Page 103, para. 3 – "any compensation for the college's moving to Toronto": Sissons, *Victoria* at 167; Wallace, *A History of the University of Toronto* at 124.

53. Page 103, para. 3 – "a major, $70,000 arts building": Neatby, *"and not to Yield"* at 158. It would have cost Queen's a quarter of a million dollars to move: see Neatby, *Queen's University* at 162; Sissons, *Victoria* at 167; Wallace, *A History of the University of Toronto* at 123-24.

54. Page 103, para. 3 – "and move to Toronto": Speech by Principal of 1885, as quoted in McKillop, *Matters of Mind* at 50.

55. Page 104, para. 1 – "to serve the needs of eastern Ontario": Neatby, *Queen's University* at 162.

56. Page 104, para. 1 – "'There is nothing in it for Queen's,' he remarked": Ibid.

57. Page 104, para. 2 – "a fine new Gothic chapel": Reed, *Trinity* at 89.

58. Page 104, para. 2 – "until its present building was constructed in 1925": Wallace, *A History of the University of Toronto* at 239.

59. Page 104, para. 3 – "happy to continue their association with the University": Sissons, *Victoria* at 167.

60. Page 104, para. 3 – "to continue focusing on ecclesiastical training": Wallace, *A History of the University of Toronto* at 119, 244, and 247.

61. Page 104, para. 3 – "a significant proportion of University College students": Ibid. at 245.

62. Page 104, para. 3 – "while studying for divinity degrees at Knox": J.G. Hodgins, *Documentary History of Education in Ontario*, v. 26 at 192 (Historical Sketch at the Laying of the Corner Stone of the New Building for Knox College, May, 1874); Brian J. Fraser, *Church, College, and Clergy: A History of Theological Education at Knox College, Toronto, 1844-1944* (Montreal: McGill-Queen's University Press, 1995) at 54; Wallace, *A History of the University of Toronto* at 244.

63. Page 105, para. 1 – "what would later be called King's College Circle": Wallace, *A History of the University of Toronto* at 245. King's College Circle does not appear on University maps until 1969.

64. Page 105, para. 1 – "heresies allegedly promoted by Trinity": French, "Prelude to Federation" at 3.

65. Page 105, para. 1 – "on university land near College Street": Wallace, *A History of the University of Toronto* at 246.

66. Page 105, para. 1 – "moved to its present location on Hoskin Avenue": Ibid. at 247.

67. Page 105, para. 2 – "an independent arts and theological college": "But the form of affiliation favoured by the TBC ultimately proved unacceptable at the University of Toronto. The alternative, virtual integration with that institution, was equally unacceptable" to the TBC: see Charles M. Johnston, *McMaster University, Volume 1: The Toronto Years* (University of Toronto Press, 1976) at 41-42. Averill and Keith identify the Toronto Baptist College as affiliating along with Wycliffe and Knox in 1885: see Averill and Keith, "Sir Daniel Wilson" at 174.

68. Page 105, para. 2 – "an annual contribution of $14,500 a year": Johnston, *McMaster University, volume 1* at 32.

69. Page 105, para. 2 – "participated in the federation discussions": Wallace, *A History of the University of Toronto* at 121; "Wilson Journal" at 83 (July 24, 1884).

70. Page 105, para. 2 – "in Galileo's time": "Wilson Journal" at 83 (July 18, 1884).

71. Page 105, para. 2 – "the more pronounced their dogmatism": Ibid. at 112 (March 7, 1887). Wilson himself was profoundly alienated by Russell Wallace's lectures. See Johnston, *McMaster University, volume 1* at 50 for other concerns.

72. Page 105, para. 3 – "with a Baptist arts college in Woodstock": Johnston, *McMaster University, volume 1* at 46.

73. Page 105, para. 3 – "to the new Baptist institution, McMaster University": Ibid. at 47.

74. Page 105, para. 3 – "close to $1 million came to the institution": Ibid. at 49.

75. Page 106, para. 1 – "with the Lordship of Christ as the controlling principle": Johnston, *McMaster University,*

volume 1 at 52. McMaster University decided to remain in Toronto, rather than to locate in Woodstock: see Johnston, *McMaster University, volume 1* at 57.

76. Page 106, para. 1 – "with its plans to relocate there": Johnston, *McMaster University, volume 1* at 127.

77. Page 106, para. 1 – "to be raised from time to time": Ibid. at 159 and 213.

78. Page 106, para. 1 – "physically moved to Hamilton, Ontario": Ibid. at xii and 213.

79. Page 106, para. 2 – "the sensitive subjects of history and philosophy": Lawrence Shook, *Catholic Post-Secondary Education in English-Speaking Canada: A History* (University of Toronto Press, 1971) at 141-143; see also Shook, "St. Michael's College and University Federation" (unpublished manuscript, 1958) for this and the next paragraph; Sissons, *Victoria* at 161. Note also that at about the same time Western wanted to affiliate, but it never worked out: "Wilson Journal" at 56 (October 1, 1881); Averill and Keith, "Sir Daniel Wilson" at 172.

80. Page 107, para. 1 – "calculated to utterly destroy free will": Archbishop Lynch to Father Vincent, October 6, 1884, cited in Shook, *Catholic Post-Secondary Education* at 145.

81. Page 107, para. 1 – "at any non-Catholic institution": Ibid.

82. Page 107, para. 2 – "he would become the superior of the college": Ibid. at 141 and 146.

83. Page 107, para. 2 – "closer relations with the denominational colleges": Ibid. at 141.

84. Page 107, para. 2 – "the 'best attainable' at the time": Ibid. at 142, quoting Alfred Baker in *University of Toronto Monthly* of 1911.

85. Page 107, para. 2 – "with the coming to Toronto of Etienne Gilson": Laurence K. Shook, *Etienne Gilson* (PIMS, 1984).

86. Page 107, para. 2 – "and Jacques Maritain": Donald Gallagher and Idella Gallagher, "Introduction," in *A Maritain Reader* (New York: Doubleday, 1966).

87. Page 107, para. 2 – "later called the Pontifical Institute": McKillop, *Matters of Mind* at 462.

88. Page 107, para. 2 – "primarily a theological college": Wallace, *A History of the University of Toronto* at 136.

89. Page 108, para. 1 – "between 1881 and 1910": Shook, *Catholic Post-Secondary Education* at 143-144.

90. Page 108, para. 2 – "finally fail of going into effect": Sissons, *Victoria* at 174.

91. Page 108, para. 2 – "was to meet in September 1886 in Toronto": Ibid. at 179.

92. Page 108, para. 2 – "to bring the scheme into practical operation": Wallace, *A History of the University of Toronto* at 124; Burwash, "The Development of the University" at 54-55.

93. Page 108, para. 2 – "turned against the scheme": Sissons, *Victoria* at 177.

94. Page 108, para. 2 – "such dignitaries as Sir John A. Macdonald, Mowat, Ross, and Blake": Ibid. at 180.

95. Page 108, para. 2 – "voted against federation": Ibid. at 181; Van Die, *An Evangelical Mind* at 118-119. Nelles was disappointed that Victoria was the only denominational institution which remained interested in federation, and Burwash supported him. After the Conference approved federation, Burwash returned to his original support for it.

96. Page 108, para. 3 – "the support of both parties later that month": Sissons, *Victoria* at 183; "Wilson Journal" at 119 (April 23, 1887).

97. Page 108, para. 3 – "until after Victoria indicated its support": Sissons, *Victoria* at 184.

98. Page 108, para. 3 – "which produced a new University of Toronto Act": *An Act Respecting the Federation of the University of Toronto and University College with other Universities and Colleges*, R.S.O 1887, c. 230.

99. Page 108, para. 3 – "would become the president of the new university council": *1887 Act*, ss. 9, 10, and 56; Averill and Keith, "Sir Daniel Wilson" at 176.

100. Page 108, para. 3 – "not just the president of University College": Assistant Secretary to Minister of Education, June 18, 1890, enclosing "draft for revision and approval" appointed Daniel Wilson "President of the University of Toronto," citing *1887 Act* at section 5(2), PAO/RG 2-29-1; see also Carl Berger, "Sir Daniel Wilson," *DCB*, v. 12 at 1112. Berger, who does not go into the 1887 Act in detail, describes "Wilson's life as President of University College and later of the University of Toronto."

101. Page 108, para. 4 – "the unanimous consent of the senate": *1887 Act*, ss. 5, 87, and 89.

102. Page 109, para. 1 – "that Victoria had sought": Sissons, *Victoria* at 168.

103. Page 109, para. 1 – "but Wilson had strongly opposed": "Wilson Journal" at 95 and 116 (July 3, 1885 and April 5, 1887).

104. Page 109, para. 1 – "again confer their own degrees": *1887 Act*, s. 6.

105. Page 109, para. 1 – "government control of the University": Sissons, *Victoria* at 182.

106. Page 109, para. 1 – "at the pleasure of the government": *1887 Act*, s. 5(2).

107. Page 109, para. 1 – "had to consent to every act of the senate": *1887 Act*, ss. 40-1.

108. Page 109, para. 2 – "as president of the council": *1887 Act*, s. 56; Victoria had insisted that members of the college councils be excluded from the University Council: "Wilson Journal" at 114-115 (March 26, 1887).

109. Page 109, para. 2 – "failing to discover my aim": "Wilson Journal" at 114 (March 23, 1887).

110. Page 109, para. 2 – "and servants of the University": *1887 Act*, ss. 56-58; Sissons, *Victoria* at 183.

111. Page 109, para. 2 – "and develop the University with its Council and Faculty": "Wilson Journal" at 122 (June 15, 1887).

112. Page 109, para. 3 – "a few months after the legislation had been enacted": G.S. French, "Samuel Sobieski Nelles," *DCB*, v. 11 at 641; Sissons, *Victoria* at 185.

113. Page 109, para. 3 – "as the new principal": Van Die, "Nathanael Burwash," *DCB*, v. 14 at 162; Sissons, *Victoria* at 187.

114. Page 109, para. 3 – "a token rent of a dollar a year": Sissons, *Victoria* at 184.

115. Page 109, para. 3 – "the former was chosen": Ibid. The original grant of land under a perpetual lease only extended as far north as Czar Street (present-day Charles Street). Victoria acquired parcels of land between Czar and Bloor under term leases. Finally, in 1949, these parcels were incorporated into the permanent leasehold: see *Vic News Letter* II:2 (November, 1949) at 4. See also Chapter 29 (1950).

116. Page 109, para. 3 – "on the now fashionable Bloor Street": The property was appraised in case Victoria later left the University and had to pay for the land: see Sissons, *Victoria* at 184.

117. Page 110, para. 1 – "the architect W.G. Storm": Ibid. at 187.

118. Page 110, para. 2 – "The Victoria senate rejected the board's decision": Ibid.

119. Page 110, para. 2 – "$25,000 plus yearly grants if it stayed": Ibid. at 184 and 188.

120. Page 110, para. 2 – "it was illegal for Victoria to move": Sissons, *Victoria* at 188.

121. Page 110, para. 2 – "for which Toronto has become notorious": "Should Victoria University Join the Proposed Federation of Colleges?" undated pamphlet, VUA/History File at 9. There were many pamphlets for and against: see Wallace, *A History of the University of Toronto* at 125.

122. Page 110, para. 2 – "more than double that in Cobourg": "Should Victoria Join" at 15.

123. Page 110, para. 2 – "had died of diphtheria in one week in 1889": Van Die, *An Evangelical Mind* at 127.

124. Page 110, para. 3 – "as an independent institution in Cobourg": Sissons, *Victoria* at 188.

125. Page 110, para. 3 – "the family's distillery business": Leo Johnson, "William Gooderham," *DCB*, v.11 at 360-361; Sissons, *Victoria* at 189.

126. Page 110, para. 3 – "was not made a condition of the bequest": Sissons, *Victoria* at 189.

127. Page 110, para. 3 – "who died in 1896": Ibid. at 217.

128. Page 110, para. 3 – "settled during the summer of 1890": Ibid. at 188-189. The University was required to pay back any donations that had been made in trust on the condition that it stay. B.M. Britton to Board of Victoria College, 5 May, 1891 puts judgment at $18,185.03, costs to the plaintiffs at $295.03: see Victoria University Archives – Federation.

129. Page 110, para. 3 – "165 to 83 in favour": Sissons, *Victoria* at 190.

130. Page 110, para. 3 – "reversed its earlier vote against the move": Ibid.

131. Page 110, para. 4 – "was proclaimed in force": Ibid.

132. Page 111, para. 1 – "and statesmanlike measure": Wallace, *A History of the University of Toronto* at 133.

133. Page 111, para. 1 – "from the whole area of the social sciences": Northrop Frye, "Preface," in *From Cobourg to Toronto: Victoria University in Retrospect* (Toronto: Chartres Books, 1989) at 8.

134. Page 111, para. 2 – "in its chapel": Sissons, *Victoria* at 208.

135. Page 111, para. 2 – "to erect a single structure": Ibid. at 205; Neil Semple, "Federation and the New 'Old Vic'" at 3.

136. Page 111, para. 2 – "where the main building now stands": Careless, "Beginning a New Life in Toronto" (undated and unpublished speech) at 2.

137. Page 111, para. 2 – "who had died suddenly that summer": Shirley G. Morriss, "William George Storm," *DCB*, v. 12 at 991; Semple, "Federation and the New 'Old Vic'" at 4.

138. Page 111, para. 2 – "and a cast-iron skeleton and staircases": Morriss, "William George Storm" at 993; Semple, "Federation and the New 'Old Vic'" at 4; Eric Arthur, *Toronto: No Mean City* (University of Toronto Press, 1986) caption to 5.63; Andrew Ballantyne, "America's rough-hewn Romano," *TLS*, July 10, 1998 at 18 shows that Trinity Church, Boston, completed in 1877, clearly resembles the Victoria building.

139. Page 112, para. 1 – "The churchlike": Van Die, *An Evangelical Mind* at 130.

140. Page 112, para. 1 – "with its red sandstone and grey limestone": Semple, "Federation and the New 'Old Vic'" at 4.

141. Page 112, para. 1 – "which had been completed earlier that year": Careless, "Beginning a New Life in Toronto" at 2.

142. Page 112, para. 1 – "to endow a new chair": Sissons, *Victoria* at 208.

143. Page 112, para. 1 – "the women's residence built in 1903": Van Die, "Nathanael Burwash" at 163.

144. Page 112, para. 1 – "completed in 1913": Ibid.; Careless, "Beginning a New Life in Toronto" (undated and unpublished speech) at 7.

145. Page 112, para. 1 – "without a Bible on the platform": Sissons, *Victoria* at 208.

CHAPTER 11 – 1887 – MORE NEW PROFESSORS

1. Page 113, para. 1 – "as anticipated": W.S. Wallace, *A History of the University of Toronto* (University of Toronto Press, 1927) at 140.

2. Page 113, para. 1 – "and in 1904, more than 400": Ibid. at 144.

3. Page 113, para. 1 – "the colour of the government's money": Ibid.

4. Page 113, para. 1 – "the city's default of its lease of Queen's Park": "Sir Daniel Wilson's Journal," in UTA/Langton Family Papers/B65-0014/004 at 140 (September 14, 1888); Harold Averill and Gerald Keith, "Sir Daniel Wilson at the University of Toronto," in Elizabeth Hulse, ed., *Thinking with Both Hands* (University of Toronto Press, 1999) at 163; Heather Murray, *Working in English: History, Institution, Resources* (University of Toronto Press, 1996) at 23.

5. Page 113, para. 2 – "going to England for a classicist": "Wilson Journal" at 52 (October 16, 1880).

6. Page 113, para. 2 – "Toronto for Torontonians": *Varsity* of March 30, 1889. The *Varsity* explicitly attacked this "whine" as a "pathetic appeal ... not at all likely to rouse great public indignation"; John G. Slater, "Philosophy at Toronto" (unpublished manuscript, 1998) at 88; Tory Hoff, "The Controversial Appointment of James Mark Baldwin to the University of Toronto in 1889" (M.A. Thesis: Carleton University, 1980) at 61 and 66.

7. Page 114, para. 1 – "the number of 'home products' was only 44 per cent": *University of Toronto Monthly*, v. 12 at 4; Slater, "Philosophy at Toronto" at 100.

8. Page 114, para. 2 – "and do the work myself": Wilson Journal" at 60 (May 27, 1882); Averill and Keith, "Sir Daniel Wilson" at 164.

9. Page 114, para. 2 – "who was subsequently hired by Cornell": Schurman was to be hired to teach history, and Wilson would then take over English Literature: see "Wilson Journal" at 208 (May 18, 1892).

10. Page 114, para. 2 – "as his assistant": Murray, *Working in English* at 39; "David Reid Keys" in Henry James Morgan, ed., *The Canadian Men and Women of Our Time* (Toronto: William Briggs, 1912) at 610. Keys became an associate professor in 1902 and identified himself strongly with Canadian nationalism. Averill and Keith, "Sir Daniel Wilson" at 164-165, refer to him as an "intellectual lightweight who gained the respect of neither the president nor his colleagues." In 1892 Wilson noted in his diary: "I see by this morning's papers that Dr. Schurman succeeds President White in Cornell University. Just ten years ago.....I was full of hope to secure him for the History Chair – I taking the English Literature. But I was thwarted. We lost the chance of an exceptionally able man, and got instead D.R. Keys!" (Wilson's exclamation mark): "Wilson Journal" at 208 (May 18, 1892). Wilson's opinion was not shared by all. At Keys' death he was called a "noted Canadian historian and philologist": see "David Reid Keys," *University of Toronto Monthly*, v. 40 (October, 1939) at 11.

11. Page 115, para. 1 – "taken over by a number of lecturers": Wallace, *A History of the University of Toronto* at 142.

12. Page 115, para. 1 – "William Henry Fraser": William Henry Fraser received a B.A. in 1880 and was full professor from 1901 until his death in 1916.

13. Page 115, para. 1 – "and not in literature": Maddalena Kuitunen and Julius Molinaro, *A History of Italian Studies at the University of Toronto 1840-1990* (Toronto: Department of Italian Studies, 1991) at 15.

14. Page 115, para. 1 – "had a similar career": John Squair received his B.A. in 1883 and retired as full Professor and Head of the Department of French in 1916: C.D. Rouillard, *French Studies at the University of Toronto 1853-1993* (Toronto: Department of French, 1994) at 5 and 41.

15. Page 115, para. 1 – "for generations of students": Rouillard, *French Studies* at 41.

16. Page 115, para. 2 – "was not a research mathematician": G. de B. Robinson, *The Mathematics Department in the University of Toronto* (Toronto: Department of Mathematics, 1979) at 16.

17. Page 115, para. 2 – "there was not even a competition for the position": PAO/RG-2-29-1-248/Daniel Wilson to George Ross, July 9, 1887.

18. Page 115, para. 2 – "*Good Will Hunting*": "Good Will Hunting" was distributed in Canada by Alliance Films and had a Canadian release date of January 9, 1998: see *The Internet Movie Database*, http://us.imdb.com.

19. Page 115, para. 2 – "now situated at the University of Toronto": www.fields.utoronto.ca/about.htm.

20. Page 115, para. 2 – "*Theory of the Algebraic Functions of a Complex Variable*": J. C. Fields, *Theory of the Algebraic Functions of a Complex Variable* (Berlin: Mayer & Muller, 1906).

21. Page 115, para. 2 – "membership in the Royal Society of London": *University of Toronto Monthly*, v. 33 at 56; *University of Toronto Monthly*, v. 7 at 178.

22. Page 115, para. 3 – "a chair in political science": Averill and Keith, "Sir Daniel Wilson" at 164.

23. Page 116, para. 1 – "the social and economic problems of industrial society": A.B. McKillop, *Matters of Mind: The University in Ontario 1791-1951* (University of Toronto Press, 1994) at 193.

24. Page 116, para. 1 – "the introduction of party politics": Daniel Wilson to Edward Blake, October 27, 1882, cited in Charles M. Johnston, *McMaster University Vol. 1: The Toronto Years* (University of Toronto Press, 1976) at 51 and 257.

25. Page 116, para. 1 – "the elements that go to the making of a gentleman": "Wilson Journal" at 96 (November 7, 1885); see also the John Squair Memoirs, UTA/A83-0036/043 (November 22 or 23): "Houston's career always strikes me as very pathetic." Houston in turn referred to Wilson as "my unseen enemy" and in a letter to Mulock charged that Wilson "has misrepresented me to the Government ... [and] has sought to bring me into personal contempt by writing anonymously against me in the press": see Houston to Mulock, April 15, 1884, and Houston to Ross, September 24, 1888, William Houston letterbooks (forwarded by Heather Murray).

26. Page 116, para. 1 – "and served as its president": Averill and Keith, "Sir Daniel Wilson" at 184; McKillop, *Matters of Mind* at 195.

27. Page 116, para. 1 – "all without success": Averill and Keith, "Sir Daniel Wilson" at 184; see for example PAO/RG-2-29-1/Guthrie to Ross, June 15, 1888 and William Houston to George Ross May 20, 1892: "Nothing but the hope of getting first the Political Economy chair and more recently the English chair, with some prospect of a chance for the history chair would have kept me so long". Houston earlier had claimed "I care little for the title if only I am allowed an opportunity of putting into practice the system of teaching which I advocate", see Houston to Ross, June, 1888, Houston letter books.

28. Page 116, para. 2 – "had specifically mentioned such a chair": *An Act Respecting the Federation of the University of Toronto and University College with other Universities and Colleges*, 1887, s. 5.

29. Page 116, para. 2 – "in the London *Athenaeum* in early 1888": Wilson Journal" at 128 (February 11, 1888).

30. Page 117, para. 1 – "including Houston": The application file appears to have been lost. It is known, however, that Charles G.D. Roberts applied, as well as Houston. Roberts withdrew his application in order to apply for a position at Queen's: see Murray, *Working in English* at 24.

31. Page 117, para. 1 – "be appointed": Wilson to Ross, May 31, 1887. See also Tory Hoff, "The Controversial Appointment" at 60; *University of Toronto Monthly*, 1903 at 60; "Testimonials of James W. Bell M.A. (Toronto) Ph.D. (Leipzig) Late Professor of Political Economy and History in the University of Colorado" (1888), James W. Bell Collection, University of Colorado Archives. Bell died in Boulder, Colorado in 1889 at the age of 34: see *The Boulder Sentinel*, January 10,1890 (copy from James W. Bell Collection, University of Colorado Archives).

32. Page 117, para. 1 – "'inclined to prefer Mr. Ashley' of Oxford": "Wilson Journal" at 131 (April 19, 1888).

33. Page 117, para. 1 – "to argue a case before the Privy Council": *The St. Catharine's Milling and Lumber Company* v. *The Queen* settled the boundary dispute between Ontario and Manitoba: see A. Margaret Evans, *Sir Oliver Mowat* (University of Toronto Press, 1992) at 179-180.

34. Page 117, para. 1 – "in June, Mowat announced Ashley's appointment": "Wilson Journal" at 137 (June 30, 1888).

35. Page 117, para. 1 – "I hope for excellent results in all ways": Ibid.

36. Page 117, para. 1 – "passing Canadians over": *World*, July 7, 1888.

37. Page 117, para. 2 – "The 28-year-old William Ashley": Sara Z. Burke, *Seeking the Highest Good: Social Service and Gender at the University of Toronto 1888-1937* (University of Toronto Press, 1996) at 17.

38. Page 117, para. 2 – "who would become even more distinguished": McKillop, *Matters of Mind* at 195.

39. Page 117, para. 2 – "*Introduction to English Economic History and Theory*": Burke, *Seeking the Highest Good* at 20.

40. Page 117, para. 2 – "*Toronto University Studies in Political Science*": Ibid. at 19-23; McKillop, *Matters of Mind* at 195.

41. Page 117, para. 2 – "by the bankers of Toronto": Burke, *Seeking the Highest Good* at 20.

42. Page 117, para. 2 – "for a chair in economic history": "Wilson Journal" at 210 (June 26, 1892); Burke, *Seeking the Highest Good* at 23-24. In 1901 Ashley left Harvard to take the Chair of Commerce at the University of Birmingham, where he fostered the development of its commercial programme. He was heavily involved in local affairs and was ultimately knighted for his work during World War I: see C.A. Ashley, "Sir William Ashley and the Rise of Schools of Commerce," *The Commerce Journal Annual Review* (March 1938) at 40-50.

43. Page 117, para. 2 – "His influence on developments at Toronto continued, however": McKillop, *Matters of Mind* at 198.

44. Page 117, para. 2 – "the program Ashley had developed": Burke, *Seeking the Highest Good* at 26.

45. Page 117, para. 2 – "for its model": Burke, *Seeking the Highest Good* at 26-7; Ian M. Drummond, *Political Economy at the University of Toronto: A History of the Department 1888-1982* (Toronto: Governing Council of the University of Toronto, 1983) at 39; C.A. Ashley, "Sir William Ashley" at 46. At Birmingham, Ashley insisted that students take two courses in the Faculty of Arts and Sciences, and study modern languages, as well as taking commerce courses.

46. Page 117, para. 3 – "James Mavor was appointed professor of political economy": Burke, *Seeking the Highest Good* at 24.

47. Page 117, para. 3 – "the only regular full-time instructor in the department": Drummond, *Political Economy* at 31; Alan F. Bowker, "Truly Useful Men: Maurice Hutton, George Wrong, James Mavor, and the University of Toronto 1880-1927" (Ph.D. Thesis: University of Toronto, 1975) at 317.

48. Page 117, para. 3 – "connected with Glasgow University": Bowker, "Truly Useful Men" at 118.

49. Page 117, para. 3 – "to seek his own replacement": Ibid. at 123.

50. Page 117, para. 3 – "a really first rate Economist": Cited in Burke, *Seeking the Highest Good* at 24. Mavor had attended Glasgow University but because of illness never received a degree. The University of Toronto, however, awarded him a Ph.D. in 1912 because of his scholarship: see "James Mavor," *Proceedings and Transactions of the Royal Society of Canada*, 3rd Series, v. 20, 1926 at xiv-xv.

51. Page 117, para. 3 – "to obtain a Canadian-born scholar": McKillop, *Matters of Mind* at 198. Houston was again a candidate: see Blake Papers, William Houston to Edward Blake, July 1, 1892, UTA/B-72/0013/01(13); "Political Science"/"List of Applications for the Chair of Political Science in University of Toronto," PAO/RG2-29-1.

52. Page 118, para. 1 – "his genius for friendship, his magnetism, and his wit": "James Mavor" at xiii and xv.

53. Page 118, para. 2 – "about slum life in Glasgow": Burke, *Seeking the Highest Good* at 25.

54. Page 118, para. 2 – "and formed the Socialist League": Bowker, "Truly Useful Men" at 116.

55. Page 118, para. 2 – "a major crusader against the public ownership of utilities": Ibid. at 127 and 140.

56. Page 118, para. 2 – "the anarchist Peter Kropotkin": Ibid. at 117.

57. Page 118, para. 2 – "on a visit to Toronto": James Mavor, *My Windows on the Street of the World* (London & Toronto: J. M. Dent & Sons, 1923), v. 1 at 371, v. 2 at 92-3. Kropotkin's visit took place in 1897 when the British Association for the Advancement of Science held its annual meeting in Toronto.

58. Page 118, para. 2 – "a physical resemblance between the two": Ibid., v. 1, frontispiece (portrait of Professor James Mavor by Horatio Walker); v. 2, facing 92 (portrait of Prince Peter Kropotkin by A. Dickson Patterson).

59. Page 118, para. 2 – "half a million words": Bowker, "Truly Useful Men" at 138.

60. Page 118, para. 2 – "a report for the Ontario government on workers' compensation": "James Mavor" at xv. He did a study on wheat production in western Canada for the British government in 1905, which caused the great Cambridge economist Alfred Marshall to say that, "Mavor knew more about [wheat production] that anyone else in the world": see Bowker, "Truly Useful Men" at 134.

61. Page 119, para. 1 – "a library of 30,000 volumes": Bowker, "Truly Useful Men" at 148.

62. Page 119, para. 1 – "of what is now the Art Gallery of Ontario": Ibid. at 145; see also E. Lisa Panayotidis, "James Mavor: Cultural Ambassador and Aesthetic Educator to Toronto's Elite," *Journal of Pre-Raphaelite Studies*, 1997-1998, v. 6-7.

63. Page 119, para. 1 – "cloistral aloofness and academic pedantry": "James Mavor" at xiii.

64. Page 119, para. 2 – "his role in supporting the student strike of 1895": Mavor, in part, helped provoke the strike by agreeing to, and then refusing, to allow two controversial speakers to address the Political Science Club: see Chapter 15 (1895).

65. Page 119, para. 2 – "a disgrace to the University": Bowker, "Truly Useful Men" at 125.

66. Page 119, para. 2 – "resented by the nationalists": Ibid. at 124.

67. Page 119, para. 2 – "to dismiss Professor Mavor": Ibid. at 126.

68. Page 119, para. 2 – "annual Canadian drama awards": www.culturenet.ca/tta/doras.htm.

69. Page 119, para. 3 – "and a disciplinary direction": Murray, *Working in English* at 17.

70. Page 119, para. 3 – "to literary studies": Ibid. As his student and successor as head, A.S.P. Woodhouse, stated in a memorial tribute, "He had to rescue the teaching of literature from the dead hand of linguistic analysis, to free it from the mere cramming of irrelevant information and unattached literary history, and to show how the subject could be presented as a thing of ideas, of beauty and of power": *University of Toronto Quarterly* (October 1944) at 9.

71. Page 119, para. 3 – "according to Woodhouse": *University of Toronto Quarterly* (October 1944) at 8-9.

72. Page 119, para. 3 – "and more sensitively": Claude Bissell, *Halfway up Parnassus: A Personal Account of the University of Toronto 1932-1971* (University of Toronto Press, 1974) at 5.

73. Page 120, para. 1 – "William Houston applied for the chair": Murray, *Working in English* at 29.

74. Page 120, para. 1 – "our foremost littérateur": Murray, *Working in English* at 33, citing *Varsity* of November 17, 1888.

75. Page 120, para. 1 – "would later become Manchester University": "Wilson Journal" at 145 (January 21, 1889); Murray, *Working in English* at 24 and 37.

76. Page 120, para. 1 – "or to persons personally contacted": "Wilson Journal" at 145 (January 21, 1889); Hoff, "The Controversial Appointment" at 60.

77. Page 120, para. 1 – "three men are thought necessary": Murray, *Working in English* at 28.

78. Page 120, para. 1 – "especially for Keys": "Wilson Journal" at 146 (January 30, 1889); see Averill and Keith, "Sir Daniel Wilson" at 184.

79. Page 120, para. 1 – "would succeed Wilson as president": "Wilson Journal" at 142 and 149 (November 12, 1886 and March 12, 1889). As Wilson points out in the 1889 entry, he considered Schurman equally qualified to hold the chair in English.

80. Page 120, para. 1 – "Schurman became president of Cornell a few years later": Morris Bishop has summed up Schurman's contribution to Cornell in the following terms: "His success was the success of Cornell ... In his time, Cornell became one of the great universities of America, indeed, of the world": see Morris Bishop, *A History of Cornell* (Ithaca: Cornell University Press, 1962) at 442. Schurman, after the end of his Presidency of Cornell in 1920, went on to a distinguished diplomatic career, culminating in the Ambassadorship to Germany from 1925-1930: see www.rzuser.uni-heidelberg.de/~g30/Engischurman.html.

81. Page 120, para. 2 – "the *American Journal of Philology*": *University of Toronto Quarterly*, October 1944 at 3; Murray, *Working in English* at 18.

82. Page 120, para. 2 – "before making his choice": Murray, *Working in English* at 26-27.

83. Page 120, para. 2 – "in the *Dominion Illustrated* magazine": Ibid. at 26.

84. Page 121, para. 1 – "what they were doing": *World* of February 14, 1889, as quoted in Hoff, "The Controversial Appointment" at 63.

85. Page 121, para. 1 – "so I believe we have got the best man available": "Wilson Journal" at 146 (January 30, 1889).

86. Page 121, para. 1 – "chosen the best man available": *Varsity*, February 2, 1889.

87. Page 121, para. 2 – "He was to have dined with me to-day": "Wilson Journal" at 148 (February 22, 1889).

88. Page 121, para. 2 – "There were twenty-two applications": Hoff, "The Controversial Appointment" at 69.

89. Page 121, para. 2 – "became even more active than in the previous appointments": "Wilson Journal" at 168 (September 26, 1889).

90. Page 122, para. 1 – "with the gold medal in both philosophy and classics": Hoff, "The Controversial Appointment" at 72.

91. Page 122, para. 2 – "having spent a year at Johns Hopkins": Ibid. at 72-73.

92. Page 122, para. 2 – "He had not yet published": Hoff, "The Controversial Appointment" at 94; Slater, "Philosophy at Toronto" at 93.

93. Page 122, para. 2 – "to be perpetuated through Hume": Slater, "Philosophy at Toronto" at 90.

94. Page 122, para. 2 – "Hume applied for the position": Ibid.

95. Page 122, para. 2 – "sent a letter supporting him for the position": Hoff, "The Controversial Appointment" at 74.

96. Page 123, para. 1 – "in which I have taught at Harvard": PAO/RG-2-29-2/James to Ross, September 17, 1889; see Hoff, "The Controversial Appointment" at 89; Slater, "Philosophy at Toronto" at 90.

97. Page 123, para. 1 – "if he were making the selection": Slater, "Philosophy at Toronto" at 90-91.

98. Page 123, para. 2 – "[that is, the nationalists] can go": "Wilson Journal" at 168 (September 26, 1889).

99. Page 123, para. 2 – "W.M. Wundt's famous laboratory in Leipzig": Wundt's lab had been established in 1879: see Mary J. Wright and C. Roger Myers, *History of Academic Psychology in Canada* (Toronto: C.J. Hogrefe, 1982) at 70.

100. Page 123, para. 2 – "He completed his doctorate at Princeton": Hoff, "The Controversial Appointment" at 79; Slater, "Philosophy at Toronto" at 91.

101. Page 123, para. 2 – "Baldwin's recommendations were excellent": Ibid.

102. Page 123, para. 2 – "at a small Presbyterian college in Illinois": Slater, "Philosophy at Toronto" at 91. The college was Lake Forest University.

103. Page 123, para. 2 – "his friend at Princeton, James McCurdy": Hoff, "The Controversial Appointment" at 80; "James Frederick McCurdy" in Morgan, ed., *The Canadian Men and Women of Our Time* at 759. McCurdy received his doctorate from Princeton in 1878. Baldwin and he were thus not contemporaries at Princeton.

104. Page 123, para. 2 – "who was teaching Oriental languages at Toronto": *University of Toronto Monthly*, October, 1935 at 12. McCurdy and Hirschfelder were at that point in dispute over who was to be head of the department: see PAO/RG-2-22-1-248/Wilson to Ross, May 31, 1887; see also UTA/B92-0030/009(16), Baker to James Loudon, November 16, 1886: "they differed even in the pronunciation of the Hebrew letters."

105. Page 123, para. 2 – "and had published four significant articles": Slater, "Philosophy at Toronto" at 91; Hoff, "The Controversial Appointment" at 94 and 100; James Mark Baldwin, *Handbook of Psychology* (New York: H. Holt, 1889), v. 1; *Handbook of Psychology* (New York: H. Holt, 1891), v. 2.

106. Page 123, para. 2 – "belonged to the department of philosophy": Hoff, "The Controversial Appointment" at 214; Slater, "Philosophy at Toronto" at 135.

107. Page 123, para. 3 – "the two leading candidates for the position": Ibid. at vii.

108. Page 123, para. 3 – "a weakened echo of Dr. Young's teaching": Slater, "Philosophy at Toronto" at 91.

109. Page 123, para. 3 – "asked to reply to their points on behalf of Hume": Hoff, "The Controversial Appointment" at 81 and 103; Slater, "Philosophy at Toronto" at 95.

110. Page 123, para. 3 – "who strongly supported Hume": "Wilson Journal" at 168 (September 27, 1889).

111. Page 123, para. 3 – "approached Mowat in favour of Hume": Hoff, "The Controversial Appointment" at 122; Slater, "Philosophy at Toronto" at 95.

112. Page 123, para. 3 – "to teach us this very subject": *The World*, cited in Hoff, "The Controversial Appointment" at 124.

113. Page 124, para. 1 – "further study in Germany": Hoff, "The Controversial Appointment" at 170 and 194; Slater, "Philosophy at Toronto" at 97.

114. Page 124, para. 1 – "on a miserable makeshift arrangement": "Wilson Journal" at 172 (October 19, 1889).

115. Page 124, para. 1 – "if his future career confirms his promise thus far": Ibid.; Hoff, "The Controversial Appointment" at 143.

116. Page 124, para. 1 – "or at least till I have shuffled off the mortal coil of presidency or of life": "Wilson Journal" at 173 (October 21, 1889); Hoff, "The Controversial Appointment" at 149.

117. Page 124, para. 1 – "the first American to be appointed to the Toronto faculty": Hoff, "The Controversial Appointment" at 144.

118. Page 124, para. 1 – "came to Toronto the next month": "Wilson Journal" at 175 (October 26, 1889).

119. Page 124, para. 1 – "He was a superb teacher and attracted large classes": Slater, "Philosophy at Toronto" at 94 and 102-3; Hoff, "The Controversial Appointment" at 161.

120. Page 124, para. 2 – "the first psychology lab in the British Empire": Hoff, "The Controversial Appointment" at 165 and 172.

121. Page 124, para. 2 – "authority customarily considered even more sacred": Slater, "Philosophy at Toronto" at 99. Baldwin's inaugural lecture was affected by an attack of influenza but, in Wilson's opinion, "in spite of a brief attack of faintness did well": see "Wilson Journal" at 177 (January 13, 1890).

122. Page 124, para. 2 – "including Wilson": Hoff, "The Controversial Appointment" at 136-137.

123. Page 124, para. 2 – "thought it should": See generally on this, Hoff, "The Controversial Appointment" at 31-34.

124. Page 124, para. 2 – "experiments he conducted with his young daughters": Hoff, "The Controversial Appointment" at 177, 181, and 185; Slater, "Philosophy at Toronto" at 111.

125. Page 124, para. 2 – "*Mental Development in the Child and the Race*": Hoff, "The Controversial Appointment" at 177 and 187; James Mark Baldwin, *Mental Development in the Child and in the Race* (New York: Macmillan, 1906) 3rd ed. A reprint was issued in 1968.

126. Page 124, para. 3 – "for a demonstrator for his lab": "Wilson Journal" at 203 (March 25, 1892); Hoff, "The Controversial Appointment" at 191-3.

127. Page 124, para. 3 – "demonstrating in the lab": Hoff, "The Controversial Appointment" at 194, fn11 and 205.

128. Page 124, para. 3 – "insisted that the person be a Toronto graduate": "Wilson Journal" at 203 (March 25, 1892).

129. Page 124, para. 3 – "it would be worse than the fire": Ibid. at 210 (June 26, 1892).

130. Page 124, para. 4 – "who undertakes to negotiate the whole matter with [Mowat]": Ibid. (June 29, 1892).

131. Page 125, para. 1 – "and died on August 5": Ibid. at 211.

132. Page 125, para. 2 – "one of the finest and best-known psychologists in North America": Hoff, "The Controversial Appointment" at 168, 205, and 215.

133. Page 125, para. 2 – "continued for many decades": Slater, "Philosophy at Toronto" at 111.

134. Page 125, para. 2 – "a Leipzig-trained psychologist": Hoff, "The Controversial Appointment" at 202; Slater, "Philosophy at Toronto" at 103.

135. Page 125, para. 2 – "who became an important experimental psychologist": Hoff, "The Controversial Appointment" at 208-9; Wright and Myers, *History of Academic Psychology in Canada* at 75-76.

136. Page 125, para. 2 – "took up Baldwin's interest in child psychology": Hoff, "The Controversial Appointment" at 210-13; Slater, "Philosophy at Toronto" at 111; Wright and Myers, *History of Academic Psychology in Canada* at 75.

137. Page 125, para. 3 – "a position of authority for the next 37 years": Slater, "Philosophy at Toronto" at 96.

138. Page 125, para. 3 – "he was just competent as a teacher": Ibid. at 131 and 134. There is some uncertainty about Hume's doctoral thesis. He was awarded the Ph.D. *summa cum laude* by Albert Ludwig University in Freiburg after only half a year's residence. Slater has suggested that the authorities there took into account his graduate work at Johns Hopkins and Harvard. The 40-page dissertation, *Political Economy and Ethics*, may indeed have been written after Hume received his doctoral degree: see Slater, "Philosophy at Toronto" at 127-128.

139. Page 125, para. 3 – "His retirement was not noted in the *University of Toronto Monthly*": Hume was given a year's leave of absence in June, 1926, after which he was to retire. He was born September 12, 1860. He was given leave of absence at the age of 65 and retired at 66: see ibid. at 138.

CHAPTER 12 – 1887 – MEDICINE

1. Page 126, para. 1 – "the establishment of a 'teaching faculty' of medicine at the University": *An Act respecting the Federation of the University of Toronto and University College with other Universities and Colleges*, Stat. Ont. 1887, c.20, s.5(1).

2. Page 126, para. 1 – "one of the best medical schools on the continent": "The laboratories are in point of construction and equipment among the best on the continent. Increasing attention has recently been devoted to the cultivation of research. There are both general and department libraries, an excellent museum, and all necessary teaching accessories": Abraham Flexner, *Medical Education in the United States and Canada: A Report to the Carnegie Foundation for the Advancement of Teaching* (New York: Arno Press Reprint, 1972) at 323. See also ibid. at 325, where McGill and Toronto are given an overall rating, on the continental scale, of "excellent." The original report was printed in 1910.

3. Page 126, para. 2 – "had to obtain them through a university": R.D. Gidney and W.P.J. Millar, *Professional Gentlemen: The Professions in Nineteenth-Century Ontario* (University of Toronto Press, 1994) at 357-358.

4. Page 126, para. 2 – "kept raising its standards": A.A. Primrose, "The Faculty of Medicine," in *The University of Toronto and Its Colleges 1827-1906* (Toronto: The University Library, 1906) at 176.

5. Page 126, para. 2 – "and fewer students took a Toronto degree": W.S. Wallace, *A History of the University of Toronto* (University of Toronto Press, 1927) at 210-211.

6. Page 126, para. 2 – "only ten degrees were granted in medicine by the University of Toronto": Sandra Frances McRae, "The 'Scientific Spirit' in Medicine at the University of Toronto 1888-1910" (Ph.D. Thesis, University of Toronto, 1987) at 85; R. D. Gidney and W. P. J. Millar, "The Reorientation of Medical Education in Late Nineteenth-Century Ontario: The Proprietary Medical Schools and the Founding of the Faculty of Medicine at the University of Toronto," *Journal of the History of Medicine*, v.49 (1994) at 67-68. In contrast, Trinity awarded 65 degrees and Victoria 20: see ibid.

7. Page 126, para. 3 – "had more than 500 students": A.B. McKillop, *Matters of Mind: The University in Ontario 1791-1951* (University of Toronto Press, 1994) at 77.

8. Page 126, para. 3 – "transferred to the Toronto School of Medicine": McRae, "The 'Scientific Spirit'" at 73; see also Chapter 4 (1850).

9. Page 127, para. 1 – "Trinity Mews condominiums at 40 Spruce Street": *Trinity Convocation Bulletin*, v.10, no.5 (1975) at 6; www.toronto.com.

10. Page 127, para. 1 – "at the urging of Emily Stowe": Anne Rochon Ford, *'A Path Not Strewn With Roses': One Hundred Years of Women at the University of Toronto 1884-1984* (Toronto: University of Toronto Press, 1985) at 37; Gina Feldberg, "Emily Howard Jennings (Stowe)," *DCB*, v. 13 at 509.

11. Page 127, para. 1 – "at 291 Sumach Street": Lykke De La Cour and Rose Sheinin, "The Ontario Medical College for Women 1883 to 1906: Lessons from Gender-separatism in Medical Education," in Marianne Ainley, ed., *Despite the Odds: Essays in Canadian Women and Science* (Montreal: Vehicule Press, 1990) at 113.

12. Page 127, para. 1 – "to the new University of Toronto medical school until 1906": Ibid. at 117; Ford, *'A Path Not Strewn With Roses'* at 38.

13. Page 127, para. 2 – "would become its instructors": David R. Keane, "William Thomas Aikins," *DCB*, v. 12 at 11; Gidney and Millar, *Professional Gentlemen* at 89.

14. Page 127, para. 2 – "founding the *Canadian Journal of Medical Science*": Gidney and Millar, *Professional Gentlemen* at 89.

15. Page 128, para. 1 – "and not the president of the University": Harold Averill and Gerald Keith, "Sir Daniel Wilson and the University of Toronto" in Elizabeth Hulse, ed., *Thinking with Both Hands* (University of Toronto Press, 1999) at 176. Wilson was not appointed President of the University Council until June 18, 1890. The portions of the Act allowing faculties of medicine and law came into effect on proclamation. There was a two year delay in the internal reorganization of the University and University College. During that time, Wilson was only the President of University College: see Chapter 10 (1883).

16. Page 128, para. 2 – "that was increasingly required in medicine": Gidney and Millar, "The Reorientation of Medical Education" at 53, 57, and 61-62; Primrose, "The Faculty of Medicine" at 176.

17. Page 128, para. 2 – "to medicine as a 'science'": Gidney and Millar, *Professional Gentlemen* at 362-368.

18. Page 128, para. 2 – "stopped granting money to the denominational colleges": Gidney and Millar, "The Reorientation of Medical Education" at 56 and 62.

19. Page 128, para. 2 – "such as Michigan and McGill": McRae, "The 'Scientific Spirit'" at 94.

20. Page 128, para. 2 – "after two years to study at McGill": "Sir William Osler", in Henry James Morgan, ed., *The Canadian Men and Women of the Time* (Toronto: William Briggs, 1912) at 875; T.A. Reed, *A History of the University of Trinity College* (University of Toronto Press, 1952) at 73.

21. Page 129, para. 1 – "the increasingly scientific University of Toronto medical exams": McRae, "The 'Scientific Spirit'" at 88 and 91.

22. Page 129, para. 1 – "to grant non-theological degrees": Gidney and Millar, "The Reorientation of Medical Education" at 69.

23. Page 129, para. 1 – "a faculty of medicine at the University of Toronto": Ibid.

24. Page 129, para. 2 – "but declined": George W. Spragge, "The Trinity Medical College," *Ontario History*, v. 58 (1966) at 87; *Return to an Order passed by the Legislative Assembly on the 24th day of April, 1893 giving the report of the Committee of the Senate of the University of Toronto appointed to inquire into the erection of the Biological Building...* (Ontario Department of Education, 1894) [Hereinafter 1894 *Return*] at 45.

25. Page 129, para. 2 – "technically separate from Trinity College": The school had become independent so that its students could take U of T degrees if they wished. The University of Toronto had prohibited the granting of degrees to students who "formed part of any other University empowered to grant degrees in medicine": see Spragge, "The Trinity Medical College" at 84. In 1877, the Toronto School of Medicine secured Government approval for a regulation that prohibited the affiliation with the University of Toronto of any medical school also affiliated with another institution entitled to grant medical degrees. This was done, it is alleged, to prevent Trinity students from competing for the state-funded medals and prizes awarded for performance in the University of Toronto's medical examinations. In response, the Trinity medical school secured the passage of a provincial act setting it up as an institution separate from Trinity College. The separation, however, was purely a formality: see ibid. at 84-7.

26. Page 129, para. 2 – "in re-establishing the Trinity medical school in 1871": Spragge, "The Trinity Medical College" at 82.

27. Page 129, para. 2 – "Ramsay Wright's 'frogology'": Gidney and Millar, "Reorientation" at 71, citing *Canadian Practitioner*, v. 12 (1887) at 101; McRae, "The 'Scientific Spirit'" at 159. The term may have been coined to refer to A. B. Macallum's work on amphibians.

28. Page 129, para. 2 – "as was Aikins": Keane, "William Thomas Aikins" at 12.

29. Page 129, para. 2 – "and why add more?": 1894 *Return* at 8.

30. Page 129, para. 3 – "the Toronto School of Medicine's building": *The University of Toronto, 1827-1906* (The University Library, 1906) at 211.

31. Page 129, para. 3 – "both the Toronto School of Medicine and the University of Toronto": 1894 *Return* at 14-16.

32. Page 129, para. 3 – "professors of chemistry and applied chemistry respectively": 1894 *Return* at 16.

33. Page 129, para. 3 – "lest he should offend Trinity College": "Sir Daniel Wilson's Journal," UTA/B65-0014/004 at 125 (October 10, 1887).

34. Page 129, para. 3 – "Aikins was elected dean by the teaching staff": 1894 *Return* at 13; Primrose, "The Faculty of Medicine" at 176; Charles Godfrey, *Aikins of the U of T Medical Faculty* (Madoc, Ontario: Codam Publishers, 1998) at 275-276.

35. Page 129, para. 4 – "an excellent reputation as a surgeon": Keane, "William Thomas Aikins" at 12; Godfrey, *Aikins* at 129-130.

36. Page 129, para. 4 – "a new technique for amputation above the knee": Charles W. Harris, "William Thomas Aikins," *Canadian Journal of Surgery*, v.5 (1962) at 135.

37. Page 129, para. 4 – "a charming disquisition on amputation at the thigh": "Wilson Journal" at 191 (May 7, 1891).

38. Page 129, para. 4 – "Lister's methods of preventing infections during surgery": Harris, "William Thomas Aikins" at 135; Godfrey, *Aikins* at 225-228.

39. Page 130, para. 1 – "to park his scalpel in his teeth to free his hands while operating": *Faculty of Medicine Tablet*, v. 3, no.2 (1987) at 12.

40. Page 130, para. 1 – "and I did": William E. Gallie, "First Annual Medical Alumni Oration", *Medical Graduate*, v.3 (1956-57) at 6-7.

41. Page 130, para. 1 – "trained George Peters": Peters married Sir William Meredith's daughter and was a Lt.-Colonel of the Governor-General's Guards. He also invented the Peters "self-registering target" and was an active member of the Hunt Club. He was a member of the staff of the Ontario Veterinary College: UTA/Graduate Records/"Peters, George Armstrong," A73-0026/362(34).

42. Page 130, para. 1 – "the best surgeon I ever knew": Gallie, "First Annual Medical Alumni Oration" at 7.

43. Page 130, para. 1 – "a prominent surgeon at the Hospital for Sick Children": "Frederic Newton Gisborne Starr", in Morgan, ed., *Canadian Men and Women of the Time* at 1055. Frederic Newton Gisborne Starr received his M.B. in 1889.

44. Page 130, para. 1 – "was to take place every five years": 1894 *Return* at 14 and 58; Primrose, "The Faculty of Medicine" at 176.

45. Page 130, para. 1 – "a number of professors were dropped": Primrose, "The Faculty of Medicine" at 176-177; McRae, "The 'Scientific Spirit'" at 175-178.

46. Page 130, para. 1 – "including Dean Aikins' brother": "Wilson Journal" at 207 (May 14, 1892).

47. Page 130, para. 1 – "professors of anatomy and pathology were appointed": James Loudon, "Memoirs of James Loudon," UTA/B72-0031/16(11) at 90; McRae, "The 'Scientific Spirit'" at 175-8. The faculty was, however,

unhappy with the concept of five-year reviews and future reviews were cancelled: see Primrose, "The Faculty of Medicine" at 177. The science professors were very good. Gallie later wrote that Macallum and Wright were "outstanding": see Gallie, "First Annual Medical Alumni Oration" at 7.

48. Page 130, para. 2 – "on the site of the present medical school": Wallace, *A History of the University of Toronto* at 144.

49. Page 130, para. 2 – "as well as the diffusion of learning": Wright in the *Globe* of October 4, 1887, as cited in Gidney and Millar, *Professional Gentlemen* at 363.

50. Page 131, para. 1 – "which were about to be constructed": "Wilson Journal" at 129 (March 21, 1888).

51. Page 131, para. 1 – "and two from Johns Hopkins": Ibid. at 176 (December 21, 1889).

52. Page 131, para. 1 – "between Johns Hopkins and Toronto": McRae, "The 'Scientific Spirit'" at 187.

53. Page 131, para. 2 – "after his favourite poet": See Donald Jones, "Medical School is his monument but it does not bear his name," in UTA/A83-0036/042.

54. Page 131, para. 2 – "he received his medical degree from Toronto": Macallum received an M.B. degree: see University of Toronto Commencement Program, June 7, 1889; "Archibald Byron Macallum," *Proceedings of the Royal Society of Canada*, 3rd Series, v. 28 (1934) at xix. *Obituary Notices of the Royal Society*, no. 3, December, 1934 gave the date as 1890.

55. Page 131, para. 2 – "and the following year, a professor": "Copy of an Order in Council approved by His Honor the Lieutenant Governor the 22nd day of October A.D. 1891" states "inasmuch as there is not Professor of Physiology exclusively in said [Medical] Faculty that A.B. McCallum [sic] B.A. M.B. (Tor) Ph.D. (Johns Hopkins) at present Lecturer, be appointed Professor of Physiology": 1894 *Return* at 40. This was an unpaid position. The following year, he was made an "associate professor" in the Faculty of Arts, to discourage him from leaving the University. This was at the suggestion of Edward Blake: UTA/B72/0013/1-Correspondence, June, 1892, Edward Blake to George Ross, June 13, 1892. Both *Proceedings of the Royal Society of Canada* and *Obituary Notices of the Royal Society* give the date of his professorship as 1890.

56. Page 131, para. 2 – "their evolutionary origins in the ocean": "Archibald Byron Macallum" at xx.

57. Page 132, para. 1 – "to be elected a fellow of the Royal Society of London": *Obituary Notices of the Royal Society*, no. 3, December, 1934 at 289. McCallum was elected in 1906. J.C. Fields was not elected until 1913: see www.math.toronto.edu/fields.html.

58. Page 132, para. 1 – "who just previously had moved to Johns Hopkins": Charles G. Roland, "William Osler," *DCB*, v.14 at 801 says Osler "took up the post in May 1889". Michael Bliss says that he was appointed September, 1888: see Michael Bliss, *William Osler: A Life in Medicine* (University of Toronto Press, 1999) at 172.

59. Page 132, para. 1 – "discussed recent scientific work on malaria": William Osler, "The Etiology of Malaria," in *Formal Opening of the New Building of the Biological Department December 19, 1889* (Toronto: J.E. Bryant Company Ltd., 1890) at 13.

60. Page 132, para. 2 – "plans were being made to enlarge it": 1894 *Return* at 27.

61. Page 132, para. 2 – "no indication of the use that would be made of those rooms": Loudon, "Memoirs of James Loudon" at 88.

62. Page 132, para. 2 – "wanted dissection at the University": W.J. Loudon, *Sir William Mulock: A Short Biography* (Toronto: Macmillan, 1932) at 85-86.

63. Page 132, para. 2 – "had combined the two activities": 1894 *Return* at 101.

64. Page 132, para. 3 – "was contrary to government policy": Wallace, *A History of the University of Toronto* at 150; Loudon, "Memoirs of James Loudon" at 85 et seq.

65. Page 132, para. 3 – "rent the space from the University": Loudon, "Memoirs of James Loudon" at 85-87; McRae, "The 'Scientific Spirit'" at 177-78.

66. Page 132, para. 3 – "our Machiavellian Doctor": "Wilson Journal" at 190 (April 11, 1891).

67. Page 132, para. 3 – "this 'underhand proceeding'": "Wilson Journal" at 201 (February 20, 1892); Loudon, "Memoirs of James Loudon" at 88.

68. Page 132, para. 3 – "so I said nothing about it": "Wilson Journal" at 202 (March 1, 1892).

69. Page 132, para. 3 – "the danger of infection from such use": Loudon, *Sir William Mulock* at 86-87; 1894 *Return* at 82 and 88-89.

70. Page 132, para. 4 – "would cause problems": 1894 *Return* at 82.

71. Page 132, para. 4 – "a few miles away": William Edward Gallie, "The University of Toronto Medical School; Fifty Year's Growth" 3(2) *Medical Graduate* (1956-7) at 7.

72. Page 133, para. 1 – "was open only to children": Primrose, "The Faculty of Medicine" at 179.

73. Page 133, para. 1 – "(not Sir John A.)": Michael Bliss, "John McDonald," *DCB*, v. 12 at 551-552.

74. Page 133, para. 1 – "another $60,000 in his will": "Wilson Journal" at 205 (May 7, 1892).

75. Page 133, para. 1 – "that he fund such an institution": 1894 *Return* at 74 and 76. It was at one time to be called the "Amy Macdonald Hospital."

76. Page 133, para. 1 – "then called the University Park": 1894 *Return* at 74.

77. Page 133, para. 1 – "facing McCaul Street": Loudon, "Memoirs of James Loudon" at 93; 1894 *Return* at 77.

78. Page 133, para. 1 – "was about to open such a hospital": Bliss, "William Osler" at 332.

79. Page 133, para. 2 – "where Wycliffe College now stands": "Wilson Journal" at 206 (May 7, 1892); 1894 *Return* at 79.

80. Page 133, para. 2 – "for several lots on College Street were arranged": "Wilson Journal" at 206; 1894 *Return* at 76.

81. Page 133, para. 2 – "some were very agitated": 1894 *Return* at 75.

82. Page 133, para. 2 – "should be restored to the University": Loudon, "Memoirs of James Loudon" at 92; 1894 *Return* at 49 and 73.

83. Page 133, para. 2 – "no money for a hospital": "Wilson Journal" at 206 (May 7, 1892).

84. Page 133, para. 2 – "our restored medical faculty": Ibid.

85. Page 133, para. 2 – "on the south side of College Street until 1913": C. K. Clarke, *A History of the Toronto General Hospital* (Toronto: W. Briggs, 1913).

86. Page 133, para. 3 – “in the university senate in the spring of 1892”: Loudon, S*ir William Mulock* at 87; “Wilson Journal” at 207-209 (May 14, 1892 to June 4, 1892); Loudon, “Memoirs of James Loudon” at 92.

87. Page 133, para. 3 – “or the senate”: Loudon, “Memoirs of James Loudon” at 92-93 and 97.

88. Page 133, para. 3 – “The amendment was carried 29 to 6”: 1894 *Return* at 85; Loudon, *Sir William Mulock* at 88-89.

89. Page 133, para. 3 – “Loudon was one of the six dissenters”: Wallace, *A History of the University of Toronto* at 151.

90. Page 133, para. 3 – “small claim on me for my courtesy”: “Wilson Journal” at 208-209 (June 4, 1892); Averill and Keith, “Sir Daniel Wilson” at 188.

91. Page 133, para. 3 – “to hear evidence on the matter”: 1894 *Return* at 86-87.

92. Page 134, para. 1 – “Loudon was appointed president”: Loudon, “Memoirs of James Loudon” at 100.

93. Page 134, para. 1 – “for his immediate appointment”: Loudon, “Memoirs of James Loudon” at 100-101; Wallace, *A History of the University of Toronto* at 148; see also Blake to Ross, July 27, 1892, UTA/B72-0013/001.

94. Page 134, para. 1 – “whom he usually described in his diary as ‘the Mole’”: “Wilson Journal” at 169 (September 27, 1889).

95. Page 134, para. 1 – “is the prize”: “Wilson Journal” at 209 (June 4, 1892); Averill and Keith, “Sir Daniel Wilson” at 187.

96. Page 134, para. 2 – “and the Park Hospital”: Loudon, “Memoirs Of James Loudon” at 103-05; McRae, “The ‘Scientific Spirit’” at 179-183.

97. Page 134, para. 2 – “Justice (later the chief justice) Glenholme Falconbridge”: 1894 *Return* at 49.

98. Page 134, para. 2 – “impugning the integrity of Mulock”: Wallace, *A History of the University of Toronto* at 151.

99. Page 134, para. 2 – “such as Ramsay Wright”: 1894 *Return* at 97 et seq.

100. Page 134, para. 2 – “the rest of the nine-person committee”: 1894 *Return* at 123.

101. Page 134, para. 2 – “a word not found in his vocabulary”: Wallace, *A History of the University of Toronto* at 149.

102. Page 134, para. 2 – “disinterested and honourable”: 1894 *Return* at 89.

103. Page 134, para. 3 – “a white-brick Renaissance-style building”: V.E. Henderson, “The Architecture of the University,” *University of Toronto Monthly*, v.23 at 331.

104. Page 134, para. 3 – “on the site of the present medical building”: Loudon, “Memoirs of James Loudon” Section C at 10.

105. Page 134, para. 3 – “as the use of the building changed”: James Loudon, “Buildings and Equipment” in *The University of Toronto and Its Colleges* at 211.

106. Page 134, para. 3 – “had to cling to the lectern for support”: J.H. Cameron and J.T. Fotheringham, “The Inauguration of New Medical Laboratories,” *University of Toronto Monthly*, v. 4 at 11-12 and 19.

107. Page 135, para. 1 – “the cause of scientific medical education in Ontario”: Ibid. at 23.

108. Page 135, para. 1 – "every nook and corner of the globe": McRae, "The 'Scientific Spirit'" at 301.

109. Page 135, para. 1 – "I need scarcely mention in this audience": Ibid.

110. Page 135, para. 1 – "after him was unsuccessful": Robin S. Harris to [unidentified], 24 May, 1983, UTA/A83-0036/042. Harris identified the proposal as emanating from Dean Lowy: Donald Jones, "Historical Toronto," UTA/A83-0036/032.

111. Page 136, para. 1 – "when he accepted the position of provost": T. A. Reed, *Trinity* at 116-117; Wallace, *A History of the University of Toronto* at 136. The discussions had started a year earlier: see letter from James Loudon to [W. F.?] Maclean, November 14, 1899, UTA/B77-0031/004(29).

112. Page 136, para. 1 – "to stand aloof from one another": T.C.S. Macklem, "The Future of the University," *University of Toronto Monthly*, v.1 at 36.

113. Page 136, para. 1 – "a committee to discuss amalgamation": Primrose, "The Faculty of Medicine" at 177.

114. Page 136, para. 1 – "remained uninterested": Spragge, "The Trinity Medical College" at 91.

115. Page 136, para. 2 – "to erect their own new medical building": Spragge, "The Trinity Medical College" at 93.

116. Page 136, para. 2 – "leaving the Trinity medical school isolated": Ibid. at 94.

117. Page 136, para. 2 – "the Niagara Falls of Amalgamation": Ibid. at 95.

118. Page 136, para. 3 – "to quote Macklem": T.C.S. Macklem, "Federation Days," *Trinity University Review*, January 1927 at 18.

119. Page 136, para. 3 – "at the end of July 1903": Reed, *Trinity* at 127.

120. Page 136, para. 3 – "was amended to this end": Ibid. at 126; *An Act Respecting the University of Toronto and University College* (1901), s. 23. As well, the position "President of the University Council" was renamed "President of the University of Toronto." The president of the University would no longer be president of University College. Classicist Maurice Hutton became the principal of University College: see *Act Respecting the University of Toronto and University College*, ss. 38-40; Reed, *Trinity* at 124-125; "Maurice Hutton," in Morgan, ed., *Canadian Men and Women* at 564.

121. Page 136, para. 3 – "but eventually was dismissed": Ibid. at 128-129; Macklem, "Federation" at 19; *University of Trinity College* v. *Macklem* (1903) 2 O.W.R. 804 (High Court).

122. Page 136, para. 3 – "as a federated college on October 1, 1904": T. A. Reed, *Trinity* at 128; Spragge, "The Trinity Medical College" at 95.

123. Page 138, para. 1 – "The women's medical school": Now called the Ontario Medical College for Women: see De la Cour and Sheinin, "The Ontario Medical College for Women" at 116.

124. Page 138, para. 1 – "Dr. Augusta Stowe-Gullen would be the dean": De la Cour and Sheinin, "The Ontario Medical College for Women" at 117.

125. Page 138, para. 1 – "following the report of the 1906 Royal Commission": McRae, "The 'Scientific Spirit'" at 81-82.

126. Page 138, para. 1 – "The women's medical school thereupon was then closed": De la Cour and Sheinin, "The Ontario Medical College for Women" at 117.

CHAPTER 13 – 1889 – LAW, DENTISTRY, AND OTHER PROFESSIONS

1. Page 139, para. 1 – "the re-establishment of a 'teaching faculty' of law in 1889": October, 1888 Senate Statute 201; J. McGregor Young, "The Faculty of Law", in *The University of Toronto and Its Colleges 1827-1906* (Toronto: The University Librarian, 1906) at 159; C. Ian Kyer and Jerome E. Bickenbach, *The Fiercest Debate: Cecil A. Wright, the Benchers and Legal Education in Ontario 1923-1957* (Toronto: The Osgoode Society, 1987) at 28 and 35.

2. Page 139, para. 1 – "as the 1887 Act had contemplated": *An Act Respecting the Federation of the University of Toronto and University College with other Universities and Colleges*, Stat. Ont., 1887, s.5(1).

3. Page 139, para. 1 – "had been closed in 1853": See Chapter 4 (1850).

4. Page 139, para. 1 – "very few students took the optional LLB degree": See Chapter 4 (1850). Young, "The Faculty of Law" at 158, says that between 1865 and 1880 only 39 LL.B.s were given. These included the great criminal lawyer, B.B. Osler, and the leader of the Ontario Conservatives, William Meredith.

5. Page 139, para. 2 – "three-year postgraduate programs": For this, see Robert Stevens, *Law School: Legal Education in America from the 1850s to the 1980s*, as cited in R.D. Gidney and W.P.J. Millar, *Professional Gentlemen: The Professions in Nineteenth-Century Ontario* (University of Toronto Press, 1994) at 490, fn59; Christopher Moore, *The Law Society of Upper Canada and Ontario's Lawyers 1797-1997* (University of Toronto Press, 1997) at 164. Both Columbia and Michigan had enrolments of over 600 law students: see G. Blaine Baker, "Legal Education in Upper Canada 1785-1889: The Law Society as Educator" in David H. Flaherty, *Essays in the History of Canadian Law* (Toronto: The Osgoode Society, 1983) at 110.

6. Page 139, para. 2 – "recently had established a similar one": For Dalhousie, see P.B. Waite, *The Lives of Dalhousie University*, volume 1 (Montreal: McGill-Queen's University Press, 1994) at 137-140; John Willis, *A History of Dalhousie Law School* (University of Toronto Press, 1979).

7. Page 139, para. 2 – "simply offered voluntary lectures": Christopher Moore, *The Law Society of Upper Canada* at 166-167.

8. Page 139, para. 2 – "to consider the matter": *Varsity*, February 6, 1886.

9. Page 140, para. 1 – "a Teaching Faculty in law in the University": Law Society, *Minutes of Convocation*, v. 1 at 213.

10. Page 140, para. 1 – "the work of a political scientist": Mulock to Ross, April 7, 1888, PAO/RG-2-29-1.

11. Page 140, para. 2 – "jointly by the Law Society and the University": Law Society, *Minutes of Convocation* at 233; *Canada Law Journal*, March 16, 1888 at 130-31; Christopher Moore, *The Law Society of Upper Canada* at 168; Kyer and Bickenbach, *The Fiercest Debate* at 29; Curtis Cole, "A Hand to Shake the Tree of Knowledge: Legal Education in Ontario 1871-1889," *Interchange* (Autumn, 1986) at 22.

12. Page 140, para. 2 – "coupled with practical lectures": Ibid.

13. Page 140, para. 2 – "to four years": Cole, "A Hand to Take Shake the Tree" at 23. Students could still choose the non-university five year route: see Gidney and Millar, *Professional Gentlemen* at 369.

14. Page 140, para. 2 – "it would take five years under articles": Baker, "Legal Education in Upper Canada" at 85.

15. Page 140, para. 3 – "and the county law associations": Law Society, *Minutes of Convocation* at 238-239; *Canada Law Journal* of August 1, 1888 at 393 et seq.; Baker, "Legal Education in Upper Canada" at 108.

16. Page 140, para. 3 – "jealousy of Toronto University": *Canada Law Journal* of March 16, 1888 at 132; Gidney and Millar, *Professional Gentlemen* at 369.

17. Page 140, para. 3 – "the present course of seven years?": Law Society, *Minutes of Convocation* at 235.

18. Page 140, para. 3 – "the effect of the scheme on its arts program": They were also worried about the effect on their B.C.L. degree: ibid. at 236.

19. Page 140, para. 3 – "the articling period would be shortened": Moore, *The Law Society of Upper Canada* at 167.

20. Page 140, para. 3 – "Students were a form of cheap labour": Kyer and Bickenbach, *The Fiercest Debate* at 31.

21. Page 140, para. 3 – "the introduction of shorthand and the typewriter": Gidney and Millar, *Professional Gentlemen* at 374-375.

22. Page 140, para. 3 – "whether run by the University or the Law Society": Ibid. at 370; Moore, *The Law Society of Upper Canada* at 167. The newspapers were filled with letters to the editor: see Gidney and Millar, *Professional Gentlemen* at 370 and 490-491.

23. Page 141, para. 1 – "or service of students": Law Society, *Minutes of Convocation* at 263; Kyer and Bickenbach, *The Fiercest Debate* at 30.

24. Page 141, para. 1 – "the Law Society approved the committee's report": Ibid.

25. Page 141, para. 1 – "was officially established": Cole, "A Hand to Take Shake the Tree" at 23.

26. Page 141, para. 1 – "general professional autonomy": Curtis Cole, "A Learned and Honorable Body: The Professionalization of the Ontario Bar, 1867-1929" (Ph.D. thesis, University of Western Ontario, 1987) as cited in Moore, *The Law Society of Upper Canada* at 169.

27. Page 141, para. 1 – "about half had degrees": Gidney and Millar, *Professional Gentlemen* at p 488, note 6, citing *the Canada Law Journal* of February 1, 1889; Moore, *The Law Society of Upper Canada* at 171; Kyer and Bickenbach, *The Fiercest Debate* at 34.

28. Page 141, para. 1 – "an extra two years articling": Moore, *The Law Society of Upper Canada* at 169.

29. Page 141, para. 1 – "it is not expedient at present": Law Society, *Minutes of Convocation* at 266.

30. Page 141, para. 2 – "two part-time professors": J. McGregor Young, "The Faculty of Law" at 163; Kyer and Bickenbach, *The Fiercest Debate* at 35.

31. Page 141, para. 2 – "directly addressed to himself": "Sir Daniel Wilson's Journal," UTA/B65-0014/004 at 183 (April 25, 1890). William Lyon Mackenzie King was not enamoured with Proudfoot, who he claimed had set a "very unfair paper" in 1895: see Mackenzie King Diaries, May 8, 1895.

32. Page 141, para. 2 – "Proudfoot remained a professor until 1900": G. Blaine Baker, "William Proudfoot," *DCB*, v.13 at 849.

33. Page 141, para. 2 – "eventually he resigned his professorship": Robert C. Vipond, "David Mills," *DCB*, v. 13 at 709-710; R.C.B. Risk, "Constitutional Scholarship in the Late Nineteenth Century: Making Federalism Work" (1996), 46 *University of Toronto Law Journal* 427 at 431.

34. Page 141, para. 3 – "and more than thirty substantial articles": R.C.B. Risk, "Augustus Henry Frazer Lefroy," *DCB*, v.14 at 638. See also R.C.B. Risk, "A.H.F. Lefroy: Common Law Thought in Late Nineteenth-Century Canada: On Burying One's Grandfather," *University of Toronto Law Journal*, v.41 (1991).

35. Page 142, para. 1 – "to concentrate on the practice of law": UTA/Graduate Records/"Young, James McGregor"/ A73-0026/531(70).

36. Page 142, para. 1 – "and B.B. Osler": Young, "The Faculty of Law" at 163.

37. Page 142, para. 1 – "was abandoned after a few years": Ibid. at 165; Kyer and Bickenbach, *The Fiercest Debate* at 35.

38. Page 142, para. 2 – "only a handful of LLB students each year": In 1902, the University conferred 6 LL.B.s; in 1905, 13 were granted. In 1929, just before the onset of the Great Depression, only 3 were awarded: see President's Report, 1901/02; *President's Report, 1904/05*; *President's Report, 1928/29.*

39. Page 142, para. 2 – "the graduates included Chief Justice Lyman Duff": David Ricardo Williams, *Duff: A Life in the Law* (Vancouver: University of British Columbia Press, 1984) at 20.

40. Page 142, para. 2 – "Prime Minister Mackenzie King": R. MacGregor Dawson, *William Lyon Mackenzie King: A Political Biography 1874-1923* (University of Toronto Press, 1958) at 51.

41. Page 142, para. 2 – "the first woman barrister in the British Empire": Anne Rochon Ford, *"A Path Not Strewn With Roses": One Hundred Years of Women at the University of Toronto 1884-1984* (University of Toronto Press, 1985) at 41; Constance Backhouse, *Petticoats and Prejudice: Women and Law in Nineteenth-Century Canada* (Toronto: Women's Press, 1991) at 313.

42. Page 142, para. 2 – "individual law courses as part of their BA": Young, "The Faculty of Law" at 167. In the academic year of 1905-6, for example, law courses were included in the programme leading to a general B.A., and in the Honours programmes for History and Political Science: see *The Calendar of the University of Toronto for the year 1904-1905* (Toronto: The University Press) at 115-30.

43. Page 142, para. 2 – "an LLM was introduced": Young, "The Faculty of Law" at 166.

44. Page 143, para. 1 – "the hundreds at Osgoode Hall Law School": Moore, *The Law Society of Upper Canada* at 170.

45. Page 143, para. 1 – "to avoid duplication of work": *Report of the Royal Commission on the University of Toronto* (Toronto: L.K. Cameron, Printer to the King's Most Excellent Majesty, 1906) at xxxv.

46. Page 143, para. 1 – "once again the Law Society was not interested": Kyer and Bickenbach, *The Fiercest Debate* at 36.

47. Page 143, para. 1 – "practical on-the-job training": Gidney and Millar, *Professional Gentlemen* at 369.

48. Page 143, para. 1 – "its monopoly on professional legal education in the province": See Chapter 4 (1850); Baker, "Legal Education in Upper Canada" at 109. See also A.B. McKillop, *Matters of Mind: The University in Ontario 1791-1951* (University of Toronto Press, 1994) at 74.

49. Page 143, para. 2 – "independent of the universities": Gidney and Millar, *Professional Gentlemen* at 372.

50. Page 143, para. 2 – "eager to improve their status and prestige": Ibid. at 360.

51. Page 143, para. 2 – "on all major roads entering Toronto": D.W. Gullett, *A History of Dentistry in Canada* (University of Toronto Press, 1971) at 75.

52. Page 143, para. 2 – "more of a learned profession": Ibid. at 74.

53. Page 143, para. 2 – "to make Latin an entrance requirement": Gidney and Millar, *Professional Gentlemen* at 359.

54. Page 143, para. 3 – "it affiliated with the University": Gullet, *A History of Dentistry* at 73.

55. Page 143, para. 3 – "from two to three years in 1890": *The Ontario Dental Association: A Profile: The First One Hundred Years* (Ontario Dental Association, 1967) at 19.

56. Page 143, para. 3 – "the first such awarded in Canada": Gullet, *A History of Dentistry* at 73.

57. Page 143, para. 3 – "also started awarding degrees in dentistry": Ibid. at 82-83.

58. Page 143, para. 3 – "are no more entitled to the doctorate than barbers": Gidney and Millar, *Professional Gentlemen* at 360, citing *Ontario Medical Journal* of February, 1893.

59. Page 143, para. 4 – "east of University Avenue": Gullet, *A History of Dentistry* at 137.

60. Page 143, para. 4 – "had become dean of the college in 1893": Anne Carlyle Dale, "James Branston Willmott," *DCB*, v. 14 at 1068; Gullet, *A History of Dentistry* at 74.

61. Page 143, para. 4 – "Early in the Christian era it had its foundation": *Daily Mail and Empire*, October 2, 1896.

62. Page 144, para. 1 – "increased from three to four years": Gullet, *A History of Dentistry* at 137.

63. Page 144, para. 1 – "to a site closer to the University": Ibid.

64. Page 144, para. 1 – "now occupied by the faculty of architecture": Gullet, *A History of Dentistry* at 138; *The Ontario Dental Association: A Profile* at 24.

65. Page 144, para. 1 – "over the College Street entrance": As of October 29, 1999. The words "Royal College of Dental Surgeons" only remain as marks on the stone from which the letters were removed.

66. Page 144, para. 1 – "with accommodation for 350": "Formal Opening of the New Dental College, Toronto," *Dominion Dental Journal*, v.22 (1910) at 38; *The Ontario Dental Association: A Profile* at 24.

67. Page 144, para. 1 – "just under half a million dollars": Gullet, *A History of Dentistry* at 137 and 168.

68. Page 144, para. 1 – "a master of science in dentistry": Ibid. at 183.

69. Page 145, para. 1 – "seven years after dentistry's first course": Gullet, *A History of Dentistry* at 59.

70. Page 145, para. 1 – "22 bachelor of pharmacy degrees were awarded in 1895": Ernst W. Steib, "A Century of Formal Pharmaceutical Education in Ontario," *Canadian Pharmaceutical Journal*, v. 116 (1983) at 105.

71. Page 145, para. 1 – "only in the late 1940s": Ibid. at 106.

72. Page 145, para. 1 – "It did not physically move to the campus until 1963": Ibid. at 106 and 154; *Varsity News* (October 1963) at 12.

73. Page 145, para. 1 – "three-storey building on Gerrard Street East in 1887": Steib, "A Century of Formal Pharmaceutical Education in Ontario" at 105.

74. Page 145, para. 1 – "a larger building next door in 1941": *Ontario College of Pharmacy Calendar for 1949-1950* at 13.

75. Page 145, para. 1 – "was licensed in 1893": *The Ontario Dental Association: A Profile* at 19.

76. Page 145, para. 1 – "even before Confederation": Ernst W. Steib et al., "Women in Ontario Pharmacy 1867-1927," *Pharmacy in History*, v. 28 (1986) at 125.

77. Page 145, para. 1 – "the charms of the domestic hearth": Cited in Gidney and Millar, *Professional Gentlemen* at 327.

78. Page 145, para. 2 – "became a University of Toronto diploma": Alexander M. Ross, *The College on the Hill: A History of the Ontario Agricultural College 1874-1974* (Toronto: Copp Clark Publishing, 1974) at 35-36.

79. Page 145, para. 2 – "purchased near Guelph": Ibid. at 12; A. Margaret Evans, *Sir Oliver Mowat* (University of Toronto Press, 1992) at 84 and 213.

80. Page 145, para. 2 – "a Toronto bachelor of science of agriculture degree (BSA)": Alexander M. Ross and Terry Crowley, *The College on the Hill: A New History of the Ontario Agricultural College 1874-1999* (Toronto: Dundurn Press, 1999) at 48.

81. Page 145, para. 2 – "our practical minded farmers would like it": *Globe*, as cited in Alexander M. Ross, *The College on the Hill* at 36.

82. Page 145, para. 3 – "the responsibility of the Ontario government": Evans, *Sir Oliver Mowat* at 213.

83. Page 147, para. 1 – "when the college became the University of Guelph": Ross and Crowley, *The College on the Hill* at 164.

84. Page 147, para. 1 – "best all-round equipped institution of its kind in the world": C.C. James, "The Ontario Agricultural College," *University of Toronto Monthly*, v.3 at 302.

85. Page 147, para. 1 – "increased the length of the course to four years": Ibid. at 301. C.C. James was at the time he wrote the article the Professor of Chemistry at the College. Alexander M. Ross has argued, however, that it was only after 1905, when the curriculum was changed and technical innovations were introduced, that the College had any real impact on Ontario farming: see Ross, *College on the Hill* at 73. Ross also points out that that until 1903 the administrators sent the University misleading reports about the College: see ibid. at 36-37.

86. Page 147, para. 1 – "and more than 700 students": James, "The Ontario Agricultural College" at 301.

87. Page 147, para. 1 – "many of them from outside Ontario": Ross, *College on the Hill* at 37.

88. Page 147, para. 1 – "professors in American agricultural colleges": James, "The Ontario Agricultural College" at 302.

89. Page 147, para. 1 – "a domestic science school for women": Ross and Crowley, *The College on the Hill* at 52 and 54; James, "The Ontario Agricultural College" at 303.

90. Page 148, para. 1 – "and relocated to Guelph in 1922": See generally F. Eugene Gattinger, *A Century of Challenge: A History of the Ontario Veterinary College* (University of Toronto Press, 1962); A.M. Evans, "Smith, Andrew," *DCB*, v.11 at 961-963.

CHAPTER 14 – 1890 – THE FIRE AND NEW CONSTRUCTION

1. Page 149, para. 1 – "was destroyed by fire": W.S. Wallace, *A History of the University of Toronto* (University of Toronto Press, 1927) at 145-147; Douglas Richardson, *A Not Unsightly Building: University College and Its History* (Toronto: Mosaic Press, 1990) at 19-20 and 117 et seq.; Robert H. Blackburn, *Evolution of the Heart: A History of the University of Toronto Library up to 1981* (University of Toronto Press, 1989) at 58 et seq.; James Loudon, "Memoirs of James Loudon," UTA/A72-0031/16(11) at 72-81.

2. Page 149, para. 1 – "a ruin tottering to the ground": Joseph Schull, *Edward Blake: Leader and Exile* (Toronto: Macmillan of Canada, 1976) at 179-180.

3. Page 149, para. 1 – "swept away in a single night": Sir Daniel Wilson's Journal," UTA/Langton Family Papers/ B65-0014/004(02) at 178 (February 15, 1890).

4. Page 149, para. 2 – "that Friday evening, at 8 o'clock": James Loudon, "Memoirs" at 72.

5. Page 149, para. 2 – "around 3,000 people": Douglas Richardson, *A Not Unsightly Building* at 19.

6. Page 149, para. 2 – "and 'promenading' to two bands": In the late Victorian era, 'promenades' were held, rather than dances, the latter still being regarded as too risqué for young people: see Charles Levi, "Where the Famous People Were? The Origins, Activities and Future Careers of Student Leaders at University College, Toronto, 1854-1973" (Ph.D. thesis, York University, Canada, 1998) at 63, n3; Richardson, *A Not Unsightly Building* at 18.

7. Page 149, para. 2 – "to illuminate the rooms and the exhibits": Ibid. at 125.

8. Page 149, para. 2 – "for lighting in University College": Ibid., at 165, n35, indicates that there was not even very much gas lighting in the building.

9. Page 149, para. 2 – "While they were climbing the staircase": Ibid., at 165, n36, suggests that it was between the first and second floors.

10. Page 149, para. 2 – "at the south-east end of the building": Ibid. at 19; Blackburn, *Evolution of the Heart* at 58.

11. Page 150, para. 1 – "to send water to the upper storeys": Richardson, *A Not Unsightly Building* at 126 and 165, n38.

12. Page 150, para. 1 – "by 11 o'clock it was largely out": Ibid. at 19 and 126.

13. Page 150, para. 1 – "there were no casualties": Blackburn, *Evolution of the Heart* at 59.

14. Page 150, para. 2 – "the great bell had plunged to the ground and shattered": Wallace, *A History of the University of Toronto* at 145.

15. Page 150, para. 2 – "The massive oak doors to the college were destroyed": Richardson, *A Not Unsightly Building* at 127.

16. Page 150, para. 2 – "were burned": Blackburn, *Evolution of the Heart* at 59.

17. Page 150, para. 2 – "Audubon's *Birds of America*": Richardson, *A Not Unsightly Building* at 165, n52.

18. Page 150, para. 2 – "now worth about $10 million": Richard Landon e-mail to Friedland, February 8, 2001. A

copy of *Birds of America* was auctioned for £5.5 million in March 2000: see *Daily Mail*, March 13, 2000. There is, of course, no way to know whether the University Library's copy would have survived in a similar condition and fetched a similar price.

19. Page 150, para. 2 – "Professor Chapman's mineral specimens were lost": Ibid. at 126.

20. Page 150, para. 2 – "Wilson also lost all his lecture notes": "Wilson Journal" at 179 (February 15, 1890).

21. Page 151, para. 1 – "was not visibly damaged": Richardson, *A Not Unsightly Building* at 126-127.

22. Page 151, para. 2 – "'Varsity in Ruins,' headlined the *Globe*": Ibid. at 19; *Globe*, February 15, 1890.

23. Page 151, para. 2 – "50,000 persons turned up to view the damage": Richardson, *A Not Unsightly Building* at 126.

24. Page 151, para. 2 – "met on Saturday to assess the situation": Board of Trustees Minutes, February 15, 1890, UTA/A70-0024/reel 6.

25. Page 151, para. 2 – "board member and engineer Casimir Gzowski": Board of Trustees Minutes, February 15, 1890; Richardson, *A Not Unsightly Building* at 126-127. For David Dick, see Richardson, *A Not Unsightly Building* at 122; also Eric Arthur, *Toronto: No Mean City* (3rd Edition, University of Toronto Press, 1986) at 151. For Sir Casimir Gzowski, see H.V. Nelles, "Sir Casimir Stanislaus Gzowski," *DCB*, v.12 at 389-396.

26. Page 151, para. 2 – "admit of roofing in and restoring": "Wilson Journal" at 179 (February 21, 1890).

27. Page 152, para. 1 – "at about $260,000": Ibid.

28. Page 152, para. 1 – "only $90,000 of insurance on the building": Board of Trustees, February 17, 1890, UTA/A70-0024 (Memorial to the Honourable the Minister of Education); Richardson, *A Not Unsightly Building* at 129.

29. Page 152, para. 1 – "and the provincial treasurer": "Wilson Journal" at 179 (February 21, 1890).

30. Page 152, para. 1 – "the insurance money it would receive": Board of Trustees, February 17, 1890.

31. Page 152, para. 1 – "turned down a request for help": Richardson, *A Not Unsightly Building* at 130. But it did remit duty on gifts of books from outside Canada: see Blackburn, *Evolution of the Heart* at 62.

32. Page 152, para. 1 – "as did the city of Toronto": Richardson, *A Not Unsightly Building* at 129; Board of Trustees, March 3, 1890.

33. Page 152, para. 1 – "promised $10,000": Board of Trustees, July 24, 1890; Blackburn, *Evolution of the Heart* at 90.

34. Page 152, para. 2 – "Almost no classes were cancelled": Wallace, *A History of the University of Toronto* at 145. Bessie Scott in her diary noted on February 21, 1890 that Van der Smissen cancelled his German class: see Blackburn, *Evolution of the Heart* at 59.

35. Page 152, para. 2 – "with the minister of education": "Wilson Journal" at 179 (February 21, 1890).

36. Page 153, para. 1 – "devoted much of his time to university affairs": Robert Craig Brown, *Canadian National Policy 1883-1900: A Study in Canadian-American Relations* (Princeton: Princeton University Press, 1964) at 245-246. Blake had given up the leadership of the Liberal Party in Ottawa in 1890 and for the first time in ten years was able to devote significant time and energy to the University. This was to be his last hurrah in terms of active interest: see Averill and Keith, "Sir Daniel Wilson" at 192-193.

37. Page 153, para. 1 – "St Andrew's Presbyterian Church on King Street": Richardson, *A Not Unsightly Building* at 122 and 125; Shirley G. Morriss, "William George Storm," *DCB,* v.12 at 993.

38. Page 153, para. 1 – "was not looked on with favour": Richardson, *A Not Unsightly Building* at 130.

39. Page 153, para. 2 – "a reading and retiring room for women students": Ibid. at 134.

40. Page 153, para. 2 – "but that did not come about": Paula J.S. LaPierre, "The First Generation: The Experience of Women University Students in Central Canada" (Ph.D. Thesis, University of Toronto, 1993) at 106-107.

41. Page 153, para. 2 – "four rooms for his psychology labs": Tory Hoff, "The Controversial Appointment of James Mark Baldwin to the University of Toronto in 1889" (M.A. Thesis, Carleton University, 1980) at 171.

42. Page 153, para. 2 – "the newel post on the east staircase": Richardson, *A Not Unsightly Building* at 138. Some have called it a Gryphon, Griffin, or Gargoyle: see ibid. at 140.

43. Page 153, para. 2 – "and was not replaced": "Wilson Journal" at 201 (February 14, 1892).

44. Page 153, para. 2 – "New water mains were placed on the campus": Minutes of the Board of Trustees, October 15 and 30, 1891, UTA/A70-0024/reel 6; Richardson, *A Not Unsightly Building* at 165, n39.

45. Page 153, para. 2 – "the abominable engine-house and chimney stalk": "Wilson Journal" at 201 (February 14, 1892).

46. Page 153, para. 3 – "only $50,000 insurance money available": Board of Trustees, February 17, 1890 (Memorial to the Honorable the Minister of Education); Blackburn, *Evolution of the Heart* at 59.

47. Page 153, para. 3 – "potential donors throughout the world": Blackburn, *Evolution of the Heart* at 61.

48. Page 154, para. 1 – "a set of his work in eleven volumes": Ibid. at 63 and 65.

49. Page 154, para. 1 – "Queen Victoria donated a book on royal residences": William Henry Pyne, *History of the Royal Residences of Windsor Castle, St. James Palace, Carlton House and Kensington Palace* (London: Dry, 1819). The Queen donated four other books: see communication from Dr. Richard Landon, Director, Thomas Fisher Library, University of Toronto, 14 February, 2000.

50. Page 154, para. 1 – "from 3,000 duplicates": Blackburn, *Evolution of the Heart* at 61and 64-65.

51. Page 154, para. 2 – "richer as well as larger": Ibid. at 66.

52. Page 154, para. 2 – "had recently trebled in size": Richardson, *A Not Unsightly Building* at 121; Blackburn, *Evolution of the Heart* at 67-68.

53. Page 154, para. 2 – "there were 55,000 items on the shelves": Blackburn, *Evolution of the Heart* at 93.

54. Page 154, para. 2 – "after the parliamentary library in Ottawa": Professor W.H. Van der Smissen estimated that before the fire, the library had contained 33,000 volumes, making it, in his estimation, the second largest library in the country, after the parliamentary library: see Blackburn, *Evolution of the Heart* at 59. In 1865, when the parliamentary library arrived in Ottawa, it was already estimated at 60,000 volumes. No major losses affected the parliamentary library during the rest of the century: see Marjory Ayleene Bolick, "An Observation Study of the Library of Parliament, Ottawa, Canada" (M.L. thesis, University of Washington, 1957) at 17-18. McGill University's library contained 19,000 volumes in 1881. The massive expansion supported by William Macdonald was just about to begin: see Robert Bruce Frost, McGill University: For the Advancement of Learning (Montreal: McGill-Queen's University Press, 1980), v. 1 at 247, v. 2 at 14.

55. Page 154, para. 2 – "and Yale's four times, as large": Richardson, *A Not Unsightly Building* at 166, n68. The comparison was made in the Legislature on February 21, 1890. It was based on the relative sizes of universities' libraries prior to the fire; it can be assumed that Harvard and Yale continued to add to their collections while Toronto recovered from its loss. In 1893 the Harvard University library contained 437,747 volumes: see "Report of the President and Treasurer of Harvard College, 1893-4," communicated by Brian A. Sullivan, Reference Archivist, Harvard University Archives, Pusey Library.

56. Page 154, para. 3 – "until after the Second World War": Blackburn, *Evolution of the Heart* at 88-89.

57. Page 154, para. 3 – "to make it as fireproof as possible": Ibid. at 86.

58. Page 154, para. 3 – "allowed light to penetrate from floor to floor": Ibid. at 91-92.

59. Page 154, para. 4 – "designed to contain 120,000 volumes": Ibid.

60. Page 154, para. 4 – "200 students at large oak desks": Richardson, *A Not Unsightly Building* at 131; Blackburn, *Evolution of the Heart* at 91.

61. Page 154, para. 4 – "half for men and half for women": Blackburn, *Evolution of the Heart* at 91.

62. Page 154, para. 4 – "could be open in the evenings": Ibid. at 91 and 93.

63. Page 154, para. 4 – "and 7 to 10:30 in the evening": Ibid.

64. Page 154, para. 4 – "in one of his early books": Ibid. at 89-91; see Daniel Wilson's, *Prehistoric Annals of Scotland,* vol. 2 (London, England: Macmillan and Co., 1863).

65. Page 154, para. 4 – "6 feet lower than originally planned": Blackburn, *Evolution of the Heart* at 89.

66. Page 154, para. 4 – "in full operation in January 1893": Ibid. at 93.

67. Page 154, para. 5 – "into the ravine had been completed": Ibid. at 122-123.

68. Page 155, para. 1 – "was also growing": J.M.S. Careless, "Beginning a New Life in Toronto" (Unpublished and undated manuscript) at 7. By 1906 it had nearly 20,000 volumes.

69. Page 155, para. 1 – "the so-called collegiate Gothic style": C.B. Sissons, *A History of Victoria University* (University of Toronto Press, 1952) at 240.

70. Page 155, para. 2 – "had been destroyed in the fire": Blackburn, *Evolution of the Heart* at 68.

71. Page 155, para. 2 – "for what is needed": *Varsity,* February 2, 1889.

72. Page 155, para. 2 – "in his King's College days": Blackburn, *Evolution of the Heart* at 69 and 71.

73. Page 156, para. 1 – "and HCan for Canadian history": Ibid.

74. Page 156, para. 1 – "after Claude Bissell became president": Ibid. at 184 et seq. The remains of the old-classification system have continued to mystify graduate students to this day: personal knowledge of Charles Levi.

75. Page 156, para. 2 – "taken down in 1912 to build Hart House": T.A. Reed, *The Blue and White: A Record of Fifty Years of Athletic Endeavour at the University of Toronto* (University of Toronto Press, 1944) at 12 and 15.

76. Page 156, para. 2 – "close to what became Varsity Stadium several years later": Ibid. at 20.

77. Page 156, para. 2 – "to build the new Biology Building": Ibid. at 3-7.

78. Page 156, para. 3 – "the wearing of rubber-soled shoes on the gymnasium floor": Ibid. at 8-9, 11-12 and 15.

79. Page 156, para. 3 – "used the basement of their college for athletics": A.E.M. Parkes, "The Development of Women's Athletics at the University of Toronto" (1961), quoted in Helen Gurney, *A Century to Remember 1893-1993: Women's Sports at the University of Toronto* (University of Toronto Women's T-Holders' Association, 1993) at 2-3.

80. Page 156, para. 3 – "until Convocation Hall was erected in 1906": James Loudon, "Buildings and Equipment" in *The University of Toronto and Its Colleges 1827-1906* (University Librarian, 1906) at 215; H.H. Langton, *Sir John Cunningham McLennan: A Memoir* (University of Toronto Press, 1939) at 24.

81. Page 156, para. 4 – "the present Wallberg building": Loudon, "Buildings and Equipment" at 212. It was torn down in 1963: see W.A.E . McBryde, "History of the Chemistry Department" (Unpublished manuscript, 1999), chapter 4 at 16.

82. Page 156, para. 4 – "and was used for arts and medical students": McBryde, "History of the Chemistry Department," chapter 4 at 16 and 18; Loudon, "Buildings and Equipment" at 212-213.

83. Page 157, para. 1 – "or interest in experimental research": McBryde, "History of the Chemistry Department," chapter 4 at 21.

84. Page 157, para. 1 – "related to his PhD thesis": Ibid.

85. Page 157, para. 1 – "for a subdivision": Ibid. at 22.

86. Page 157, para. 1 – "a fellow of Merton College": Ibid.

87. Page 157, para. 1 – "some of his laboratory demonstrations": Ibid., chapter 4, n.50.

88. Page 157, para. 2 – "and one at Heidelberg": Ibid. at 14 and n.33.

89. Page 157, para. 2 – "the others at Michigan, California, and Stanford": Ibid. at n.33.

90. Page 157, para. 2 – "and returned to England": McBryde, "History of the Chemistry Department," chapter 5 at 6 and 11.

91. Page 157, para. 2 – "future Nobel laureate, Frederick Soddy": Ibid. at 6. Soddy went to McGill and worked with Rutherford, out of which came the hypothesis of spontaneous disintegration of atoms by which the phenomena of radioactivity could be explained: ibid. at 7.

92. Page 157, para. 2 – "He appears to have been a poor choice": Ibid. at 7-8 and 10.

93. Page 157, para. 2 – "appears to be rather trivial": Ibid. at 8.

94. Page 157, para. 2 – "His later publications were also unimpressive": Ibid. at 23.

95. Page 157, para. 2 – "the sub-department of physical chemistry": Ibid. at 11-12.

96. Page 157, para. 2 – "and the board of governors to resign": Ibid. at 26 and 30; *University of Toronto Report of the Board of Governors for the Year Ending 30th June, 1920* at 121; *University of Toronto Report of the Board of Governors for the Year Ending 30th June, 1921* at 131.

97. Page 157, para. 2 – "Lash Miller then became the head of the department": McBryde, "History," chapter 5 at 30.

CHAPTER 15 – 1895 – THE STRIKE

1. Page 158, para. 1 – "largest mass meeting in the history of the University": *Varsity*, February 20, 1895. This issue of the *Varsity*, for reasons unknown, is not included in the microfilmed reels of the periodical. A photocopy of it can be found in the Dale Family Papers, B75-0013/001 and in the Hellems papers at the University of Colorado Archives.

2. Page 158, para. 1 – "half a block south of College Street": Arthur M. Chisholm, "When I Went to College," *University of Toronto Monthly* (November, 1926) at 66. Wardell's Hall was later known as Broadway Hall: see Hector Charlesworth, *More Candid Chronicles* (Toronto: Macmillan Co. of Canada, 1928) at 78.

3. Page 158, para. 1 – "often used for religious and political meetings": Charlesworth, *More Candid Chronicles* at 78.

4. Page 158, para. 1 – "Gentlemen Will Please Not Spit on the Floor": Ibid.

5. Page 158, para. 1 – "including a hundred women": Sara Z. Burke, "New Women and Old Romans: Co-education at the University of Toronto 1884-1895," *Canadian Historical Review* (June, 1999) at 237.

6. Page 158, para. 1 – "professor of Latin, William Dale": Burke, "New Women and Old Romans" at 239; "Partial Memoirs of the Rev. D.B. Macdonald" (1953), UTA/B83-1295 at 3.

7. Page 158, para. 1 – "publicly announced earlier in the day": Mackenzie King Diary, February 15, 1895.

8. Page 158, para. 1 – "called 'Billy' by his classmates": See Arthur M. Chisholm letters, Fisher Rare Book Library; "Macdonald memoir" at 3. King was also occasionally called "Rex": see R. MacGregor Dawson, *William Lyon Mackenzie King: A Political Biography 1874-1923* (University of Toronto Press, 1959) at 30.

9. Page 158, para. 1 – "I scarcely ate any lunch": King Diary, February 15, 1895.

10. Page 158, para. 2 – "rather solemn, moon faced": H.S. Ferns and B. Ostry, *The Age of Mackenzie King: The Rise of the Leader* (London: William Heinemann Ltd, 1955) at 19.

11. Page 158, para. 2 – "the difficulties existing in the University": *Varsity*, February 20, 1895.

12. Page 158, para. 2 – "the age-old cult of tyranny": Charlesworth, *More Candid Chronicles* at 78.

13. Page 158, para. 2 – "as one of the leaders of the 1837 rebellion": Ferns and Ostry, *The Age of Mackenzie King* at 21.

14. Page 158, para. 2 – "seconded by Tom Greenwood": Charlesworth, *More Candid Chronicles* at 78.

15. Page 160, para. 1 – "the aftermath of the Irish uprising": "Major Thomas Hamar Greenwood", Henry James Morgan ed., *The Canadian Men and Women of the Time* (Toronto: William Briggs 1912) at 473; UTA/Graduate Records/"Viscount Thomas Hamar Greenwood"/A73-0026/128(34); *Monthly*, October 1938 at 11.

16. Page 160, para. 1 – "editor of the *Varsity*": Charlesworth, *More Candid Chronicles* at 78.

17. Page 160, para. 1 – "The secretary of the meeting was Bruce Macdonald": "Macdonald memoir" at 3; *Monthly*, October 1938 at 10.

18. Page 160, para. 1 – "The motion passed with five dissenting votes": *Varsity*, February 20, 1895.

19. Page 160, para. 1 – "was passed unanimously": Ibid.

20. Page 160, para. 2 – "The strike was confined to University College": B.K. Sandwell, "Student '97," in Claude T. Bissell, ed., *University College: A Portrait 1853-1953* (University of Toronto Press, 1953) at 117.

21. Page 160, para. 2 – "counselled abstention": C.B. Sissons, *A History of Victoria University* (University of Toronto Press, 1952) at 215.

22. Page 160, para. 2 – "They took his advice": Ibid.; *Globe,* February 18, 1895.

23. Page 160, para. 2 – "The boycott of classes was successful": King Diary, February 18, 1895.

24. Page 160, para. 2 – "then a member of parliament in England": Ben Forster and Jonathan Swainger, "Edward Blake," *DCB*, v.14 at 82.

25. Page 160, para. 2 – "was certainly ridiculous": Wrong to Blake, February 20, 1895, UTA/B72-0013/002(03).

26. Page 160, para. 3 – "large number of future politicians at University College": W.S. Wallace, *A History of the University of Toronto* (University of Toronto Press, 1927) at 154 refers to "budding politicians."

27. Page 160, para. 3 – "was in the class of '96": *Monthly,* October 1938 at 10.

28. Page 160, para. 3 – "may carry me into political life": King Diary, February 5, 1895. It was said after attending a Liberal meeting at Massey Hall.

29. Page 160, para. 3 – "in the years leading up to the strike": Burke, "New Women and Old Romans" at 234.

30. Page 160, para. 4 – "of the freshmen (the class of '96)": James Loudon, "Hazing and Hustling Affairs" (1895), UTA/B72-0031/003(49) at 3; Burke, "New Women and Old Romans" at 234; see Keith Walden, "Hazes, Hustles, Scraps, and Stunts: Initiations at the University of Toronto 1880-1925" in Paul Axelrod and John G. Reid, eds., *Youth, University and Canadian Society: Essays in the Social History of Higher Education* (Montreal: McGill-Queen's University Press, 1989).

31. Page 160, para. 4 – "by turning a fire hose on the students": Loudon, "Hazing" at 3.

32. Page 160, para. 4 – "actually manned the hose": Burke, "New Women and Old Romans" at 234.

33. Page 160, para. 4 – "hazing would lead to expulsion": Loudon, "Hazing" at 4. This memo has attached to it the minutes of the University Council of October 26, 1892, where it is stated "in future those taking part in them will be suspended."

34. Page 160, para. 4 – "another future politician, Arthur Chisholm": UTA/Graduate Records/"Arthur Murray Chisholm"/A73-0026/057(57).

35. Page 161, para. 1 – "we had neglected to cut the hose": Chisholm, "When I Went" at 66.

36. Page 161, para. 1 – "And in our final year came the blow-off": Ibid.

37. Page 161, para. 1 – "pranks that were part of student life": Charlesworth, *More Candid Chronicles* at 57; A.B. McKillop, *Matters of Mind: The University in Ontario 1791-1951* (University of Toronto Press, 1994) at 231; "Sir Daniel Wilson's Journal," UTA/Langton Family Papers/B65-0014 at 199 (November 2, 1891). For Hallowe'en disturbances in general, see Keith Walden, "Respectable Hooligans: Male Toronto College Students Celebrate Hallowe'en, 1884-1910," *Canadian Historical Review,* v. 68 (1987).

38. Page 161, para. 1 – "tore down an old shed beside the college": "Shed Affair" memorandum, UTA/B72-0031/001(27) at 3-4; King diary of October 31, and Nov. 2 and 3, 1893.

39. Page 161, para. 1 – "until the fine was paid": Loudon, *The Memoirs of James Loudon,* UTA/B72-0031/016(11) at

111; "Shed memo" at 4. The following year, King was involved in violence at a convocation at Massey Hall, for which he had to apologize to the College Council: see Loudon, "Hazing" at 5.

40. Page 161, para. 2 – "Wrong applied for the position": Wrong to Ross, August 10, 1892, PAO/RG2-29-2.

41. Page 161, para. 2 – "from Wycliffe College in 1883": Alan F. Bowker, "Truly Useful Men: Maurice Hutton, George Wrong, James Mavor and the University of Toronto 1880-1927" (Ph.D. Thesis, University of Toronto, 1975) at 75.

42. Page 161, para. 2 – "had become an Anglican priest in 1886": Ibid. at 78.

43. Page 161, para. 2 – "had taught church history at Wycliffe since 1883": Ibid. at 82-83.

44. Page 162, para. 1 – "to seek a lecturer at $800 a year": Robert Bothwell, *Laying the Foundation: A Century of History at the University of Toronto* (Toronto: Department of History, 1991) at 23.

45. Page 162, para. 1 – "who was at Oxford over the summer": Bowker, "Truly Useful Men" at 82.

46. Page 162, para. 1 – "a professor was being sought": Bothwell, *Laying the Foundation* at 24; Wrong to Ross, August 31, 1892, PAO/RG2-29-2.

47. Page 162, para. 1 – "his salary at Wycliffe was $1,800": *Varsity*, November 14, 1894.

48. Page 162, para. 1 – "he could apply for the professorship the following year": Wrong to Ross, September 5, 1892, PAO/RG2-29-2.

49. Page 162, para. 1 – "who were paid only $800": Loudon, "Memoirs," at 109.

50. Page 162, para. 1 – "who was seven years older than Wrong": UTA/Graduate Records/"William Dale"/A73-0026/077(29). James Reaney, *The Dismissal: Or Twisted Beards and Tangled Whiskers* (Erin, Ontario: Press Porcépic, 1978) at 58 says that he was born in 1853; other bios say 1850.

51. Page 162, para. 1 – "was still a lecturer at $800 a year": Dale became an Associate Professor on November 3, 1892 at a salary of $1,800 a year: see "Copy of an Order in Council Approved… the 3rd Day of November, 1892," A70-0024/reel 3; see also "Wilson Journal" at 204-205 (April 25, 1892).

52. Page 162, para. 1 – "had received his MA in 1873": UTA/Graduate Records/"Dale"; Reaney, *The Dismissal* at 58.

53. Page 162, para. 1 – "as principal of a high school in Quebec": *Toronto Star*, February 15, 1895.

54. Page 162, para. 2 – "Mr. Wrong is a son-in-law of the Hon. Edward Blake": Sheraton to Ross, August 18, 1892, PAO/RG2-29-2.

55. Page 162, para. 2 – "doing so would inevitably lead to an attack on Blake": Guthrie to Harcourt, September 27, 1892, PAO/RG2-29-1 (Houston file).

56. Page 162, para. 3 – "as an Irish member of the British parliament": Forster and Swainger, "Edward Blake" at 82. The election was finished by July 13, 1892: see Joseph Schull, *Edward Blake: Leader and Exile 1881-1912* (Toronto: Macmillan of Canada, 1976) at 191.

57. Page 162, para. 3 – "in all probability gone": Blake to Ross, July 27, 1892, UTA/B72-0013/001.

58. Page 162, para. 3 – "and he died several weeks later": "Wilson Journal" at 211.

59. Page 162, para. 3 – "do good work for the University": Blake to Ross, July 27, 1892. Blake himself, the Globe informed its readers, had earlier been offered the position but turned it down to enter Imperial politics: *Globe*,

August 19, 1892. Loudon's name had also been put forward by W.F. MacLean, the editor of the Toronto *World*. *Globe*, August 19, 1892.

60. Page 163, para. 1 – "he intends to apply for the Chair": *Globe*, August 19, 1892. In 1892, Wrong published *The Crusade of MCCCLXXXIII* (London: James Parker and Co., 1892). He wrote in the preface at vi, "The contents of this book were at first intended to form part of a larger work on the history of England in the latter part of the fourteenth century. Circumstances have made necessary the immediate publication of this portion of it."

61. Page 163, para. 1 – "was certainly not necessary": William D. Meikle, "And Gladly Teach: G.M. Wrong and the Department of History at the University of Toronto" (Ph.D. Thesis: Michigan State University, 1977) at 41-42. Ross would not have been surprised at Blake's letter. He wrote a similar letter himself to Loudon on August 30, 1893 using a pretext to tell Loudon that Ross's son was an applicant for a fellowship in political science: see Ross to Loudon, August 30, 1893, B72-0031/013(05).

62. Page 163, para. 2 – "William Houston applied unsuccessfully": See "Testimonials in Support of the Application of William Houston M.A. for the Position of Teacher of Constitutional History in the University of Toronto," PAO/RG2-29-2; also Houston to Blake, July 29, 1892, UTA/B72-0013/001(12).

63. Page 163, para. 2 – "to Columbia University on a fellowship": UTA/Graduate Records/"Charles A. Stuart"/A73-0026/452(76).

64. Page 163, para. 2 – "to return to lecture on his behalf": Wilson, however, noted ruefully of Stuart that "he evades the fulfilment of what I counted on," but this may have been in reference to the fact Stuart completed his lectures ahead of schedule: see "Wilson Journal" at 204 (April 14, 1892).

65. Page 163, para. 2 – "around the beginning of September 1892": Alex Stuart to Blake, August 25, 1892, UTA/B72-0013/001(12).

66. Page 163, para. 2 – "his health was apparently not good": G. W. Ross to Edward Blake, July 22, 1892, UTA/B72-0013/001(12).

67. Page 163, para. 2 – "the acting minister of education, William Harcourt": Internal memo from George Ross, August 29, 1892, PAO/RG2-29-2 (Stuart File).

68. Page 163, para. 2 – "during his illness": Ibid.

69. Page 163, para. 3 – "to discuss a number of appointments": "Report of the Commissioners on the Discipline in the University of Toronto" (1895), in UTA/B75-0013(002) at 7.

70. Page 163, para. 3 – "still not having been decided": Ibid.

71. Page 163, para. 3 – "as Mr. Wrong is my son-in-law": Ibid.

72. Page 163, para. 3 – "During his 35-year career at the University": Chester Martin, "George MacKinnon Wrong," *Transactions of the Royal Society of Canada*, 3rd Series, 1949 at 147.

73. Page 163, para. 3 – "in promoting the study of Canadian history": Ibid. at 147-148; "George MacKinnon Wrong" citation for Toronto LL.D., UTA/A83-0036/043. See also D.C. Masters, *Henry John Cody: An Outstanding Life* (Toronto: Dundurn Press, 1995) at 57: "He was the real founder of the school of Canadian history that became such an important part of the Toronto contribution to historiography."

74. Page 163, para. 3 – "the creator of the Champlain Society": Bothwell, *Laying the Foundation* at 35. In 1897, Wrong established the *Review of Historical Publications relating to Canada*, the precursor to the *Canadian Historical Review* With B. E. Walker, he helped found the Champlain Society in 1905: see UTA/A83-0036/043.

75. Page 163, para. 3 – "the doyen of Ontario's historians": McKillop, *Matters of Mind* at 473.

76. Page 163, para. 3 – "writes historian Robert Bothwell": Ibid. Lower wrote he was a "good if not a great scholar": see A.R.M. Lower, *My First Seventy Five Years* (Toronto: Macmillan of Canada, 1967) at 49.

77. Page 163, para. 3 – "because he turned to the law": Graduate Records, "Stuart."

78. Page 163, para. 3 – "until his death in 1924": Ibid.

79. Page 163, para. 4 – "Two years later, in September 1894": "Copy of an Order in Council approved… the 28th day of September 1894," UTA/A70-0024/reel 3; Meikle, "And Gladly Teach" at 41.

80. Page 164, para. 1 – "history at $2,500 a year": "Copy of an Order in Council."

81. Page 164, para. 1 – "in which other candidates could apply": See Ross to Loudon, July 12, 1894, and Loudon to Ross, July 12, 1894, B72-0031/13(07); Wrong to Loudon, July 24 and August 4, 1894, B72-0013/011(08); Loudon to Ross, August 11, 1894, B72-0013/013(04). As of August 11, the decision to fill the chair was still referred to by Loudon as a "new one." Wrong's printed application is dated September 17, 1894, see "Application and Testimonials of George M. Wrong, B.A., for the Post of Professor of History in the University of Toronto." We have been unable to find records of a competition and the many historians that have delved into the matter have not turned up anything. Perhaps they were borrowed by the Royal Commission and never returned.

82. Page 164, para. 1 – "Soon after the appointment": Blake addressed Convocation in October, 1894: see *Varsity*, October 11, 1894.

83. Page 164, para. 1 – "the paper asked": *Varsity*, October 17, 1894.

84. Page 164, para. 1 – "a weekly run by undergraduates": Claude T. Bissell, "Opinion," in *University College: A Portrait 1853-1953* (University of Toronto Press, 1953) at 102.

85. Page 164, para. 1 – "let the fact be known": *Varsity*, November 7, 1894; Charlesworth, *More Candid Chronicles* at 71; John G. Slater, "Philosophy at Toronto" (Unpublished Manuscript, 1999) at 129.

86. Page 164, para. 2 – "the outstanding man of our year": Chisholm, "When I Went" at 66.

87. Page 164, para. 2 – "We are having quite a time re Wrong apptmt. etc.": King Diary, November 12, 1894.

88. Page 164, para. 2 – "Wrong had done so and lowered the mark": Robert H. Blackburn, "Mackenzie King, William Mulock, James Mavor, and the University of Toronto Student Strike of 1895," *Canadian Historical Review*, December, 1988 at 492. Blackburn recounted that the University Librarian, W. Stewart Wallace, told him the anecdote many times.

89. Page 164, para. 2 – "which killed his chances for a renewal of his scholarship": King Diary, Oct. 1, 1894; Blackburn, "Mackenzie King" at 492.

90. Page 164, para. 3 – "in the University College students' residence": Burke, "New Women and Old Romans" at 236.

91. Page 164, para. 3 – "became head of mathematics": UTA/Graduate Records/"Alfred T. DeLury"/A73-0026/83(23).

92. Page 164, para. 3 – "when Dale was fired": Wallace, *A History of the University of Toronto* at 153. The following year he went to Chicago where he received his Ph.D. He then taught at the University of Colorado, where he was the dean of arts and science for 30 years: see UTA/Graduate Records/"Frederick Hellems"/A73-0026/146(04).

93. Page 164, para. 3 – "was also acting behind the scenes": Blackburn, "Mackenzie King" at 490.

94. Page 164, para. 3 – "following the fire of 1890": Harold Averill and Gerald Keith, "Sir Daniel Wilson and the University of Toronto," in Elizabeth Hulse, ed., *Thinking with Both Hands* (University of Toronto Press: 1999) at 187; Blackburn, "Mackenzie King" at 497.

95. Page 164, para. 3 – "with respect to the medical faculty": See Chapter 12 (1887).

96. Page 164, para. 3 – "Mulock wanted to be the chancellor": Ross to Blake, May 6, 1895, UTA/B72-0013/002(03); see also Walker to Blake, April 12, 1895, Fisher Rare Book Library, Edmund Walker papers, Box 18, file 33.

97. Page 164, para. 3 – "a position he would obtain many years later": Mulock became Chancellor in 1924: see W.S. Wallace, "Sir William," *University of Toronto Monthly*, v.37 at 5.

98. Page 164, para. 3 – "during the course of the controversy": Blackburn, "Mackenzie King" at 493.

99. Page 165, para. 1 – "with Mulock": Ibid. at 494.

100. Page 165, para. 1 – "to quote Loudon's memoirs": Loudon, "Memoirs" at 113.

101. Page 165, para. 2 – "involving two workers' advocates": The two were Alfred Jury and Phillips Thompson: see "University of Toronto Political Science Club 1894-1895," UTA/B73-0007/001.

102. Page 165, para. 2 – "one of them being an agnostic": Charlesworth, *More Candid Chronicles* at 72-73; *Varsity*, January 16, 1895; Bothwell, *Laying the Foundation* at 29.

103. Page 165, para. 2 – "arranged to have the meeting take place off campus": The meeting took place at Forum Hall: see *Varsity*, January 26, 1895.

104. Page 165, para. 2 – "strong student backing at a mass meeting": *Varsity*, January 26, 1895.

105. Page 165, para. 2 – "before applying for an assembly room": *Varsity*, January 16, 1895.

106. Page 165, para. 2 – "some manifestly honest principle": Ibid.

107. Page 165, para. 2 – "religious 'sceptics'": Ibid.

108. Page 165, para. 2 – "The *Varsity*'s current editor, Joseph Montgomery": Reaney, *The Dismissal* at 60.

109. Page 165, para. 2 – "was ordered by the council to apologize": King Diary, January 19, 1895.

110. Page 166, para. 1 – "but the editorial board would not hear of it": King Diary, January 22, 1895.

111. Page 166, para. 1 – "freedom of the press and freedom of assembly": *Varsity*, January 16, 1895.

112. Page 166, para. 1 – "suspended him from attending lectures": *Varsity*, February 1, 1895; *Toronto Daily Mail*, January 23, 1895.

113. Page 166, para. 1 – "for which we have been contending": *Varsity*, February 1, 1895. That Friday a mass meeting was held denouncing the actions of the Council: see *Mail*, February 2, 1895.

114. Page 166, para. 2 – "a remarkable letter to the editor from Dale": *Globe*, February 9, 1895. In part, this was motivated by a letter from Walker dated February 2, 1895 and one from Wrong dated February 2, 1895, both published in the *Globe* of February 4, 1895.

115. Page 166, para. 2 – "without Dale's name": Charlesworth, *More Candid Chronicles* at 75.

116. Page 166, para. 2 – "It appeared on the front page of the paper": *Globe*, February 9, 1895.

117. Page 166, para. 2 – "It is the letter of a madman": Wrong to Blake, February 13, 1895, B72-0013/002(003).

118. Page 166, para. 2 – "the results to learning will be most disastrous": *Globe*, February 9, 1895.

119. Page 166, para. 3 – "and pitching in Wrong's apptmt.": King Diary, February 9, 1895.

120. Page 166, para. 3 – "and demanded that something be done": Loudon to Ross, February 12, 1895, UTA/B72-0031/013(08); Pike to Loudon, February 9, 1895, B72-0031/11(09); see also letter from Macallum to Loudon, Feb. 11 1895, B72-0031/011(09).

121. Page 166, para. 3 – "they had decided to dismiss Professor Dale": Loudon, "Memoirs" at 113.

122. Page 166, para. 3 – "This I agreed to furnish": Ibid.

123. Page 166, para. 3 – "Loudon produced the letter on Wednesday": James Loudon to Ross, February 12, 1895.

124. Page 166, para. 3 – "his dismissal was announced officially": Ross to Loudon, February 15, 1895, UTA/B72-0031/013(08).

125. Page 167, para. 1 – "to appoint a commission": King Diary, February 20, 1895.

126. Page 167, para. 1 – "negotiated with the administration": Burke, "New Women and Old Romans" at 237.

127. Page 167, para. 1 – "which the government accepted": Ross to Loudon, February 27, 1895, UTA/B72-0031/013(08).

128. Page 167, para. 2 – "the first that had been held since the fire in 1890": King Diary, February 22, 1895.

129. Page 167, para. 2 – "was part of the program": Charles M. Levi, "Where the Famous People Were?: The Origins, Activities and Future Careers of Student Leaders at University College, Toronto 1854-1973" (Ph.D. Thesis, York University, 1998) at 63.

130. Page 167, para. 2 – "but the students preferred dancing": *Toronto Star*, February 23, 1895.

131. Page 167, para. 2 – "Dancing was not officially permitted at the college until the following year": The 1896 Conversazione programme was the first to list dancing: see *University Literary & Scientific Society – Conversazione, 14 February, 1896*, UTA/B72-1034-11.

132. Page 167, para. 2 – "dancing was not allowed until 1926": Northrop Frye, "Preface," *From Cobourg to Toronto: Victoria University in Retrospect* (Toronto: Chartres Books, 1989) at 7.

133. Page 167, para. 2 – "at intervals until nearly three o'clock": *Toronto Star*, of Feb. 23, 1895; see also King Diary of February 22, 1895.

134. Page 167, para. 2 – "suitable to boys in lower grades": Charlesworth, *More Candid Chronicles* at 64.

135. Page 168, para. 1 – "a former member of the university senate": Taylor received his M.A. from the University in 1856. He received a Jubilee Knighthood in 1897: see UTA/Grad Records/"Sir Thomas Wardlaw Taylor"/ A73-0026-463 (28). He served on the university senate from 1873 to 1883: see *University of Toronto – Class and Prizes*

Lists, 1873 (Toronto: Henry Rowsell, 1873); see also Richard A. Willie, "Sir Thomas Wardlaw Taylor," *DCB*, v. 14, at 990-2.

136. Page 168, para. 1 – "as its chair": Wallace, *A History of the University of Toronto* at 153; "Report of the Commissioners" at 1; Ferns and Ostry, *The Age of Mackenzie King* at 26.

137. Page 168, para. 1 – "Hearings were held from April 8 to 23": Wallace, *A History of the University of Toronto* at 153.

138. Page 168, para. 1 – "at certain points during these troubles": "Report of the Commissioners" at 12.

139. Page 168, para. 1 – "beyond the line of fair comment": Ibid. at 4.

140. Page 168, para. 1 – "and addresses within the University": Ibid. at 9.

141. Page 168, para. 1 – "that Blake had used his influence in Wrong's appointment": Ibid. at 7.

142. Page 168, para. 1 – "could have been pursued towards him": Ibid. at 6.

143. Page 168, para. 1 – "a distinct triumph for the University authorities": Wallace, *A History of the University of Toronto* at 154.

144. Page 168, para. 1 – "rather a whitewashing affair": King Diary, April 22, 1895; Burke, "New Women and Old Romans" at 239.

145. Page 168, para. 2 – "had directed their attack against him": Charlesworth, *More Candid Chronicles* at 83.

146. Page 168, para. 2 – "lying in wait to entrap him": "Report of the Commissioners" at 5.

147. Page 168, para. 2 – "their lawyer, W.R. Riddell": Loudon, "Memoirs" at 115.

148. Page 168, para. 2 – "enough to destroy my future usefulness": Ibid. at 114.

149. Page 168, para. 2 – "or by his opponents in the Senate": Walker to Blake, April 12, 1895.

150. Page 168, para. 3 – "King turned down a fellowship to Chicago": Graduate Records, "Hellems"; R. MacGregor Dawson, *William Lyon Mackenzie King: A Political Biography 1874-1923* (University of Toronto Press, 1959) at 49.

151. Page 168, para. 3 – "which he never received": Ferns and Ostry, *The Age of Mackenzie King* at 28; Mulock to Loudon, June 21, 1897, UTA/B72-0031/005(26).

152. Page 168, para. 3 – "obtaining his LLB from Toronto": Dawson, *King* at 50-51.

153. Page 168, para. 3 – "subsequently to Harvard to study with Ashley": Dawson, *King* at 53-71.

154. Page 168, para. 3 – "brought him in as his deputy": Blackburn, "Mackenzie King" at 501, n44; Charlesworth, *More Candid Chronicles* at 91.

155. Page 168, para. 3 – "but then turned to law and politics": Charlesworth, *More Candid Chronicles* at 88-90; Graduate Records/"Greenwood"; Reaney, *The Dismissal* at 58.

156. Page 168, para. 3 – "while maintaining his interest in politics": Graduate Records/"Chisholm."

157. Page 169, para. 1 – "It really makes a man doubt a lot of things": Arthur M. Chisholm to Clark, March 20, 1925, Chisholm Papers, Fisher Rare Book Library.

158. Page 169, para. 1 – "became a corporate lawyer": Reaney, *The Dismissal* at 60.

159. Page 169, para. 2 – "but was not allowed to do so": The university senate declined to allow Tucker to write exams while he was still under suspension, and his suspension was not lifted in time for exams: see Senate Minutes, April 11 and May 10, 1895, UTA/A68-0012/reel 2. Mulock recommended that Tucker be able to write: see Brebner to Mulock, March 18, 1895, UTA/B72-0031/007(35).

160. Page 169, para. 2 – "the following year at Stanford University": Arthur Stringer, "A Prefatory Memoir" in James A. Tucker, *Poems* (Toronto: William Briggs, 1904) at xv.

161. Page 169, para. 2 – "probably financed by Mulock": Blackburn, "Mackenzie King" at 493.

162. Page 169, para. 2 – "but was refused": See Tucker to Loudon, June 24, 1899, and Loudon to Tucker, undated, UTA/B72-0031/007(34).

163. Page 169, para. 2 – "assistant editor of *Saturday Night* magazine": Charlesworth, *More Candid Chronicles* at 87.

164. Page 169, para. 2 – "died at the age of 31 in 1903": Reaney, *The Dismissal* at 62.

165. Page 169, para. 2 – "a volume of his poetry after his death": Tucker, *Poems.*

166. Page 169, para. 2 – "just when he was beginning to find himself": Arthur M. Chisholm to Clark, March 20, 1925.

167. Page 169, para. 2 – "Tucker should have one from Toronto": *Saturday Night,* September 10, 1938, as clipped in Graduate Records, "Greenwood".

168. Page 169, para. 2 – "He took up farming": UTA/Graduate Records/"Dale."

169. Page 169, para. 2 – "became the mayor of St. Marys": Ibid.

170. Page 169, para. 2 – "sessional lecturing at McMaster and Queen's universities": Ibid.

171. Page 169, para. 2 – "a member of the University of Toronto senate": Slater, "Philosophy" at 107. Further information may yet emerge on the controversy and the characters involved. Dale and Tucker's papers have still not been made public by their families: see Ferns and Ostry, *The Age of Mackenzie King* at 27, note 1 with respect to Tucker. Harold Averill says that the Dale papers are to be deposited in the U of T Archives sometime in the future.

172. Page 169, para. 3 – "for their role in the strike": See generally, Burke, "New Women and Old Romans." Two women from the class of '95 had been members of the board of the *Varsity.* Miss Fraser was a member of the Business Board and Miss E. Durand was a member of the Editorial Board. Fraser went on to become head of the Romance Languages Department of Randolph Macon Women's College in Lynchburg, Virginia: see UTA/Graduate Records/"Margaret Emma Nicholas Fraser"/A73-0026/108(97). Durand, like Tucker, died young – in 1900 at age 30 – and, like Tucker, her poetry was published posthumously: see UTA/Graduate Records/"Evelyn Durand"/A73-0026/090(77).

173. Page 169, para. 3 – "unladylike behaviour": Burke, "New Women and Old Romans" at 238, citing the *Star*; see also the *Mail and Empire,* cited by Burke, "New Women and Old Romans" at 238, calling it 'unwomanly'.

174. Page 169, para. 3 – "even than the young men": *Mail and Empire,* February 20, 1895, as cited in Burke, "New Women and Old Romans" at 238.

175. Page 169, para. 3 – "from what we used to have ten years ago": Blake to Mowat, February 28, 1895, UTA/B72-

0031/11(09). He did not become a senator until the late 1890s, according to John D. Blackwell, "Samuel Hume Blake," *DCB,* v.14 at 87.

176. Page 169, para. 3 – "there may be scandals arising from co-education": Blake to Mowat, February 28, 1895.

177. Page 169, para. 3 – "a sense of ease in their surroundings": Burke, "New Women and Old Romans" at 233.

178. Page 169, para. 3 – "are much more easy to entertain": "Wilson Journal" at 186 (December 13, 1890).

179. Page 169, para. 3 – "unless they were related": Burke, "New Women and Old Romans" at 240; UC Council minutes, September 12, 1895.

180. Page 170, para. 1 – "whose directions as to conduct are to be observed": Ibid.

181. Page 170, para. 1 – "after 6 o'clock in the evening": Burke, "New Women and Old Romans" at 240.

182. Page 170, para. 2 – "There had been earlier attempts to close it": See "Wilson Journal" at 120-121 and 181 (June 14, 1887 and March 16, 1890).

183. Page 170, para. 2 – "for much of the student agitation": *The Calendar of the University of Toronto for the Year 1893-4* (Toronto: Rowsell & Hutchinson, 1893) at 68.

184. Page 170, para. 2 – "lived in the residence": Burke, "New Women and Old Romans" at 236.

185. Page 170, para. 2 – "ran student life in the college": *Varsity,* November 25, 1897; see also Wallace, *A History of the University of Toronto* at 107.

186. Page 171, para. 1 – "and the space was needed for other purposes": *Varsity,* October 25, 1899; Minutes of University College Council June 10 and 16, 1899; "Annual Report of the Council of University College 1898-99," UTA/A69-0016.

187. Page 171, para. 1 – "Fraternities were starting to emerge": *Varsity,* October 17, 1894. This article was written by King: see King Diary, October 10, 13, 17, 1894.

188. Page 171, para. 1 – "and could house students": *Varsity,* October 25, 1899.

189. Page 171, para. 1 – "the first fraternity residence for students in 1893": *Catalogue of the Alpha Delta Phi 1832-1956* (New York: Executive Council of the Alpha Delta Phi Fraternity, 1956) at 247; see also Falconbridge to Loudon, February 11, 1903, UTA/B72-0031/002(44).

190. Page 171, para. 1 – "Zeta Psi in 1879": Wallace, *A History of the University of Toronto* at 109; C.A. Moss, "Zeta Psi at Toronto," *University of Toronto Monthly,* v. 1 at 174; *The Story of Zeta Psi* (New York: Zeta Psi Fraternity, 1932) at 474 et seq.

191. Page 171, para. 1 – "two of Edward Blake's sons were members": *Zeta Psi Semi-Centennial Biographical Catalogue* (Published for the Fraternity in the City of New York, 1899) at 762.

192. Page 171, para. 1 – "and Kappa Alpha": For Kappa Alpha, see *Kappa Alpha Record 1825-1940* (Clinton, Mass.: The Colonial Press, 1941) at 353 et seq.

193. Page 171, para. 1 – "Mackenzie King's fraternity": See King Diary, October 30, 1893, "the afternoon, evening were taken up with the KAPPA ALPHA Society. I was initiated today"; and also November 20, 21, and 22, 1893.

194. Page 171, para. 1 – "in 1892": *Kappa Alpha Record* at 353.

195. Page 171, para. 1 – "encouraged fraternities during the late 1890s and early 1900s": Minutes of University College Council, June 5, 1899.

196. Page 171, para. 1 – "now occupied by Massey College": See map of "Group Plan of University of Toronto Buildings," UTA/A65-0001/16.

197. Page 171, para. 1 – "at favourable interest rates": *Varsity*, December 3, 1901, and January 13, 1904.

198. Page 171, para. 1 – "sold the residence furniture to the fraternity": Minutes of University College Council, October 26, 1899.

199. Page 171, para. 1 – "would dissociate itself from fraternities and sororities": Claude Bissell, *Halfway up Parnassus: A Personal Account of the University of Toronto 1932-1971* (University of Toronto Press, 1974) at 101-2; *Varsity*, February 3, 1960; Caput minutes, October 24, 1959 UTA/A68-0012/reel 23; Board of Governors minutes, January 28, 1960, UTA/A70-0012/reel 19.

200. Page 171, para. 2 – "to find the courage to challenge authority": Personal knowledge of Charles Levi, who found the reference while working on his history of the University College Literary and Athletic Society, but has temporarily misplaced it.

201. Page 171, para. 2 – "nothing has been altered": *Varsity*, October 9, 1895.

202. Page 171, para. 2 – "having power to act for the undergraduates as a whole": *Acta Victoriana*, March, 1895 at 179; Levi, "Where the Famous People Were?" at 128.

203. Page 171, para. 2 – "would be renamed the Students' Administrative Council": The organization was known as the Undergraduate Union in 1900 and was renamed the Student's Parliament in 1905: see Levi, "Where the Famous People Were?" at 129-132.

204. Page 171, para. 3 – "are still unanswered": Michiel Horn, *Academic Freedom in Canada: A History* (University of Toronto Press, 1999) at 24.

205. Page 171, para. 3 – "an exercise of one's academic freedom?": Ibid. at 23.

206. Page 172, para. 1 – "in the hands of an independent body": *Globe*, February 9, 1895.

207. Page 172, para. 1 – "living in splendour at the Grange in Toronto": Ramsay Cook, "Goldwin Smith," *DCB*, v.13 at 970-971.

208. Page 172, para. 1 – "responsible for overseeing its affairs": "Report of the Commissioners on the Discipline in the University of Toronto" at 27.

209. Page 172, para. 1 – "which would make just such a recommendation": *Report of the Royal Commission on the University of Toronto* (Toronto: L. K. Cameron, 1906) at xx-xxi.

CHAPTER 16 – 1897 – GRADUATE STUDIES

1. Page 175, para. 1 – "the introduction of the PhD degree in 1897": Senate minutes of April 30 and May 14, 1897, UTA/A68-0012, reel 3; Peter N. Ross, "The Origins and Development of the Ph.D. Degree at the University of Toronto 1871-1932" (Ed.D. Thesis: University of Toronto, 1972) at 194; Peter N. Ross, "The Establishment of the Ph.D. at Toronto: A Case of American Influence," *History of Education Quarterly* (Fall, 1973) at 372 says that the regulations were proposed on March 12, 1897 and adopted May 14, 1897.

2. Page 175, para. 1 – "fifteen years earlier": James Loudon, "The Memoirs of James Loudon," B72-0031/016(11) at 52. Loudon does not discuss the 1897 Ph.D. in the memoirs.

3. Page 175, para. 1 – "no regulations implementing it had been established": Ross, "The Establishment of the Ph.D." at 364.

4. Page 175, para. 1 – "the feasibility of offering the degree": Ibid. at 372.

5. Page 175, para. 1 – "had never been revoked": Ross, "The Origins and Development of the Ph.D." at 193.

6. Page 175, para. 1 – "again on Macallum's motion": Ross, "The Establishment of the Ph.D." at 372.

7. Page 175, para. 1 – "due to Professor A.B. Macallum": *Annual Report of the President of the University of Toronto for the year ending June 30th, 1902* at 4.

8. Page 175, para. 2 – "the lesser qualification, the MB": The M.D. was an uncommon degree. Most degrees in Medicine at the time were M.B. degrees. From 1854 to 1906, the University granted 1,485 M.B. degrees and only 175 M.D. degrees: see *The University of Toronto and its Colleges, 1827-1906* (Toronto: The University Library, 1906) at Appendix F.

9. Page 175, para. 2 – "a research degree requiring a thesis": The university's power to grant doctorates had been confirmed by legislation in 1873, which allowed the university to award doctorates in "any Department of knowledge whatsoever, except theology.": see *An Act Respecting the University of Toronto (1873)*, section 41. This declaratory section of the act may have been inspired by the controversy between 1860 and 1868 in England over the legal power of the University of London to grant the degree of D.Litt. see: Renate Simpson, *How the Ph.D. Came to Britain: A Century of Struggle for Postgraduate Education*, (Sturminster Newton, England: Direct Design Ltd, 1983) at 48-9.

10. Page 175, para. 2 – "by either thesis or examination": Ross, "The Origins and Development of the Ph.D." at 87. The D. Paed. that Loudon had steered through the Senate in 1894 was based only on examination: see ibid. at 164-5.

11. Page 175, para. 3 – "the first convocation of King's College": King's College, Toronto, *Faculty of Arts* (Toronto: H. & W. Rowsell, 1845) at pt. IV (Degrees) UTA/B88/002/001(20); *The University of Toronto and its Colleges, 1827-1906* at Appendix F. A Convocation held in 1844 awarded degrees *ad eundem*, but no M.A.s.

12. Page 175, para. 3 – "But the degree was not highly regarded": Ross, "The Origins and Development of the Ph.D." at 92; A.B. Macallum, "The Foundation of the Board of Graduate Studies," *University of Toronto Monthly*, v.16 (February, 1916) at 220; R. Ramsay Wright and W.J. Alexander, "The Arts Faculty" in *The University of Toronto and its Colleges 1827-1906* (Toronto: University Librarian, 1906) at 92 says there was only a "perfunctory treatment" of M.A. theses.

13. Page 176, para. 1 – "nor was residence at the University required": In 1871, the M.A. degree requirements were "Candidates … must be of the standing of one year from admission to the Degree of B.A., and must have

composed an approved Thesis upon some subject in one of the Departments in the Faculty of Arts": see *Revised Statutes of the University of Toronto, 1871* (Toronto: Henry Rowsell, 1872) at 2 (Faculty of Arts).

14. Page 176, para. 1 – "or to other aids": John G. Slater, "Philosophy at Toronto" (Unpublished manuscript, 1999) at 162.

15. Page 176, para. 1 – "any original research worthy of mention": *Varsity*, March 7, 1900; Macallum, "The Foundation of the Board of Graduate Studies" at 220.

16. Page 176, para. 1 – "no references to authorities": Mavor's comment written on cover page of W.L.M. King, "The International Typographical Union" (M.A. Thesis, University of Toronto, 1897) in UTA/T79-0075.(83).

17. Page 176, para. 1 – "The requirements were tightened in 1903": Ross, "The Origins and Development of the Ph.D." at 119 and 216; Macallum, "The Foundation of the Board of Graduate Studies" at 220.

18. Page 176, para. 1 – "a year's residence would be required for the degree": W.S. Wallace, *A History of the University of Toronto* (University of Toronto Press, 1927) at 223.

19. Page 176, para. 2 – "four of them at Leipzig": See Chapter 14 (1890). See also Ross, "The Origins and Development of the Ph.D." at 171-72.

20. Page 177, para. 1 – "post-graduate work at the University of Berlin": UTA/Graduate Records/"William John Alexander"/A73-0026/004(23).

21. Page 177, para. 1 – "from Freiburg University": Ross, "The Origins and Development of the Ph.D." at 171.

22. Page 177, para. 2 – "at least far from being friendly to her": Simpson, *How the Ph.D. Came to Britain* at 81.

23. Page 177, para. 2 – "received their doctorates from Johns Hopkins": See Elsie M. Pomeroy, *William Saunders and His Five Sons: The Story of the Marquis Wheat Family* (Toronto: The Ryerson Press, 1956).

24. Page 177, para. 2 – "at Hamilton College in New York": See Elsie M. Pomeroy, *William Saunders* at 156.

25. Page 177, para. 2 – "the chair of physics at Harvard": See Elsie M. Pomeroy, *William Saunders* at 173.

26. Page 177, para. 2 – "the developer of Marquis wheat": Elsie M. Pomeroy, *William Saunders* at 141. A populist ranking of Canadians important in the twentieth century placed Charles Saunders first: see H. Graham Rawlinson and J. L. Granatstein, *The Canadian 100: the 100 most influential Canadians of the twentieth century* (Toronto: Little, Brown and Company, 1997) at 15-18.

27. Page 177, para. 3 – "McGill did not introduce the PhD degree until 1906": Stanley Brice Frost, *McGill University, v. 2 1895-1971* (Montreal: McGill-Queen's University Press, 1980) at 80-82.

28. Page 177, para. 3 – "before the turn of the century": Ross, "The Origins and Development of the Ph.D." at 15; Robin Harris, *A History of Higher Education in Canada 1663-1960* (University of Toronto Press, 1976) at 187, states that Mount Allison and New Brunswick also had Ph.D.s by 1890.

29. Page 177, para. 3 – "could not receive a PhD in England": Simpson, *How the Ph.D. Came to Britain* at 135.

30. Page 177, para. 3 – "work of a very high standard": James G. Greenlee, *Sir Robert Falconer: A Biography* (University of Toronto Press, 1988) at 187; Simpson, *How the Ph.D. Came to Britain* at 74.

31. Page 177, para. 3 – "towards the end of the First World War": Simpson, *How the Ph.D. Came to Britain* at 135; Negley Harte, *The University of London 1836-1986* (London: The Athlone Press, 1986) at 200; Greenlee, *Sir Robert Falconer* at 239.

32. Page 177, para. 3 – "gone to Germany for graduate work": Simpson, *How the Ph.D. Came to Britain* at 121.

33. Page 177, para. 3 – "from the United States": Ibid. at 145.

34. Page 177, para. 3 – "very few scholarships were available": Harris, *History of Higher Education* at 188 describes the Gilchrist Scholarships at the University of London. See also Simpson, *How the Ph.D. Came to Britain* at 72 and Yves Gingras, *Physics and the Rise of Scientific Research in Canada* (Montreal: McGill-Queen's University Press, 1991) at 41-45 for the 1851 Exhibition scholarship; Simpson, *How the Ph.D. Came to Britain* at 73 et seq. for the Rhodes.

35. Page 177, para. 4 – "by Yale since 1860": Ross, "The Establishment of the Ph.D." at 360.

36. Page 178, para. 1 – "since the 1870s": Ibid.

37. Page 178, para. 1 – "in academic life in the United States": Ross, "The Establishment of the Ph.D." at 358.

38. Page 178, para. 1 – "from its founding until 1900": Ross, "The Origins and Development of the Ph.D." at 149.

39. Page 178, para. 1 – "with Toronto graduates receiving 19 of them": Ibid. at 181.

40. Page 178, para. 1 – "only 40 PhDs from 1897 until 1921": *University of Toronto Register of Graduates 1920* (University of Toronto Press, 1921) at 156.

41. Page 178, para. 1 – "financial assistance from that university": Ross has calculated that 21 of the 31 University of Toronto graduates enrolled at Johns Hopkins during this period received funding from that university: see Ross, "The Origins and Development of the Ph.D." at 181.

42. Page 178, para. 1 – "were Toronto graduates": Ross, "The Origins and Development of the Ph.D." at 181.

43. Page 178, para. 1 – "I should much like to see their Alma Mater": Ibid. at 130-131.

44. Page 178, para. 1 – "Pelham Edgar in French and, later, English": C.B. Sissons, *A History of Victoria University* (University of Toronto Press, 1952) at 220.

45. Page 178, para. 1 – "the reputation of J.J. Sylvester": Ross, "The Origins and Development of the Ph.D." at 182 says that Sylvester attracted students. However, Sylvester was appointed to Oxford in December, 1883, and gave up "complete control of the Mathematical studies of the University" to "the person who may succeed to my positions there": see Karen Hunger Parshall, *James Joseph Sylvester: Life and Work in Letters* (Oxford: Clarendon Press, 1998) at 235. Thus, Sylvester did not supervise Fields, who arrived in 1884, but the records at Johns Hopkins do not indicate who Fields' supervisor actually was.

46. Page 178, para. 1 – "a position at King's College in 1843": See Chapter 2 (1842).

47. Page 178, para. 2 – "(founded in 1892)": Ross, "The Establishment of the Ph.D." at 361.

48. Page 178, para. 2 – "which was restricted to graduate students": Ross, "The Origins and Development of the Ph.D." at 175.

49. Page 178, para. 2 – "though far fewer obtained their PhDs there": Ibid. at 181.

50. Page 178, para. 2 – "39 Toronto graduates had gone to Chicago": Ibid.

51. Page 178, para. 2 – "Mackenzie King": R. MacGregor Dawson, *William Lyon Mackenzie King: A Political Biography 1874-1923* (University of Toronto Press, 1958) at 51.

52. Page 178, para. 2 – "and F.B.R. Hellems": UTA/Graduate Records/"Frederick Hellems"/A73-0026/146(004).

53. Page 178, para. 2 – "building is named after him": Ibid.; Ross, "The Origins and Development of the Ph.D." at 13. See, for example, http://bus.colorado.edu/campus.html, a map of the campus which prominently notes Hellems Hall.

54. Page 178, para. 2 – "forty-six American universities awarded the PhD degree": Ross, "The Origins and Development of the Ph.D." at 149.

55. Page 178, para. 2 – "to establish the doctorate at Toronto": See James Loudon, "The Universities in Relation to Research," *Proceedings of the Royal Society of Canada*, 1902 at LVIII and LIX.

56. Page 179, para. 1 – "or Chicago take snuff": *Varsity*, October 14, 1897.

57. Page 179, para. 1 – "had research doctorates": *University of Toronto and its Colleges*, Appendices at 223.

58. Page 179, para. 1 – "the faculty of applied science and engineering": *University of Toronto and its Colleges*, Appendices at 226-7.

59. Page 179, para. 1 – "not a supporter of post-graduate degrees": Ross, "The Origins and Development of the Ph.D." at 207.

60. Page 179, para. 1 – "which no single university fully supplies": Ross, "The Origins and Development of the Ph.D." at 131.

61. Page 179, para. 2 – "after two years of residence": *Calendar of University and University College, 1897-98* at 196; Ross, "The Establishment of the Ph.D." at 372.

62. Page 179, para. 2 – "spent at another university": Ross, "The Origins and Development of the Ph.D." at 200.

63. Page 179, para. 2 – "a three-year residency until 1910": Slater, "Philosophy at Toronto" at 165.

64. Page 179, para. 2 – "restricted to University of Toronto graduates until 1905": Macallum, "The Foundation of the Board of Graduate Studies" at 220.

65. Page 179, para. 2 – "an original investigation conducted by himself": *Calendar*, 1897-98 at 196; Ross, "The Origins and Development of the Ph.D." at 196.

66. Page 179, para. 2 – "and political science": Ross, "The Origins and Development of the Ph.D." at 194. The *University of Toronto Calendars* from 1897 to 1913 give a slightly different story. The departments offering major fields remained fixed at seven from 1897 to 1904-5: Biology, Chemistry, Physics, Geology, Philosophy, Oriental Languages and Political Science. Four departments offered minor courses: Modern Languages, Latin and Greek, History and Mathematics. From 1904-5 to 1909-10, Mathematics moved from the minor to the major category. From 1909 until the end of the period examined, no departments were "minor." Instead, 11 programmes were offered: Biology, Physiology and Biochemistry, Geology and Mineralogy, Chemistry, Physics, Mathematics, Philosophy, Political Science, Oriental Languages and Romance Languages.

67. Page 179, para. 2 – "until after Fields came in 1902": *University of Toronto Calendar*, 1902-03 at 135; Peter N. Ross, "The Origins and Development of the Ph.D." at 209.

68. Page 179, para. 2 – "as it was commonly called": Peter N. Ross, "The Origins and Development of the Ph.D." at 206.

69. Page 179, para. 2 – "because James McCurdy of University College": He had come to Toronto in 1885 after

spending 11 years at Princeton, where he had received his doctorate in 1878: see "The Founder of Oriental Studies in the University of Toronto," *University of Toronto Monthly* (October, 1935). Between 1894 and 1896, he produced three editions of his massive, three-volume work, *History, Prophecy and the Monuments: or Israel and the Nations* (New York: Macmillan, 1894). The third edition appeared in 1896. In 1911, its three volumes were reprinted as one. Three of his Ph.D. students went on to senior positions at the University. Richard Davidson became the principal of Emmanuel College (from 1932 until 1944): see UTA/Graduate Records/"Richard Davidson"/A73-0026/079. Thomas Eakin became the principal of Knox College (from 1926 until 1944): see UTA/Graduate Records/"Thomas Eakin"/A73-0026/091(79); see also Chapter 19 (1907). William Taylor became the principal of University College (from 1944 to 1951): see A.S.P. Woodhouse, "William Robert Taylor," *Proceedings of the Royal Society of Canada* (1951) at 116.

70. Page 179, para. 2 – "up to the end of the First World War": Charles Levi, "Thirty-Nine PhDs" (unpublished research note, University of Toronto History Project).

71. Page 179, para. 3 – "had to read more than 1,500 essays": Ross, "The Origins and Development of the Ph.D." at 210.

72. Page 179, para. 3 – "in a Johns Hopkins-style degree": Robert Bothwell, *Laying the Foundation: A Century of History at the University of Toronto* (Toronto: Department of History, 1991) at 65.

73. Page 179, para. 3 – "aims at the understanding of a subject": Ibid. at 66.

74. Page 179, para. 3 – "were not awarded until 1925": Ibid. at 67.

75. Page 180, para. 1 – "most American universities that offered the degree": Slater, "Philosophy at Toronto" at 165.

76. Page 180, para. 1 – "an ad hoc committee appointed by the senate": Ross, "The Origins and Development of the Ph.D." at 195. The Board's membership was drawn from the Council of the University, the Council of University College and the Senate of Victoria University. It had limited powers. Macallum secured its replacement by the Board of Post-Graduate Studies in 1903. This Board had "wider powers": see ibid. at 205-206.

77. Page 180, para. 1 – "a board of graduate studies was established": Macallum, "The Foundation of the Board of Graduate Studies" at 221; Slater, "Philosophy at Toronto" at 107; Ross, "The Origins and Development of the Ph.D." at 223.

78. Page 180, para. 1 – "chaired the senate committee and, later, the board": Ross, "The Origins and Development of the Ph.D." at 206.

79. Page 180, para. 1 – "though advocated by the senate over the years": Ross, "The Origins and Development of the Ph.D." at 211 states that the Senate had recommended a separate faculty to the 1906 Royal Commission .

80. Page 180, para. 1 – "not established in the University until 1922": Wallace, *A History of the University of Toronto* at 223.

81. Page 180, para. 2 – "a total of 35 PhDs were awarded by the University": *Register of Graduates 1920.*

82. Page 180, para. 2 – "his massive work on Russian economic history": Judy Mills and Irene Dombra, eds., *University of Toronto Doctoral Theses, 1897-1967* (University of Toronto Press, 1968) at 615; James Mavor, *An Economic History of Russia* (London: J.M. Dent and Sons Ltd., 1914). The degree was awarded before the publication of the work. The regulations of the programme were explicitly waived for Mavor and for Van der Smissen: see Ross, "The Origins and Development of the Ph.D." at 289-90.

83. Page 180, para. 2 – "also based on published work": W.H. Van der Smissen, *Shorter Poems of Goethe and Schiller, in Chronological Order* (New York: D. Appleton, 1912).

84. Page 180, para. 3 – "his thesis on nerve cells in 1899": Ross, "The Origins and Development of the Ph.D." at 198. Another of Macallum's doctoral students was George Nasmith, who for forty years was the deputy health officer for Toronto and an expert on water supplies. During the First World War, he went overseas and developed the first mobile water filtration units and, after the chlorine gas attack near Ypres in 1915, devised the first gas mask: see UTA/Graduate Records/"George Gallie Nasmith"/A73-0026/345. Another doctoral student was J.B. Collip, who was intimately involved in the discovery of insulin. Collip went on to a distinguished career at Alberta and later McGill and still later Western, where he was the dean of medicine: see UTA/Graduate Records/"James B. Collip"/A73-0026/65. A further student – though not a doctoral student – of Macallum's, Maude Menten, should be mentioned. She was a 1904 graduate in natural science from the University and then studied medicine at the women's medical college. When it closed, she transferred to the University's medical school. While there, she was a demonstrator in the physiology department and worked closely with Macallum, publishing a paper with him on nerve cells in 1906 in the *Proceedings of the Royal Society of Canada.* Her later work led to her co-authorship of the first monograph of the Rockefeller Institute in New York, and her work on enzymes in Berlin led to the important discovery with Leonor Michaelis of the "Michaelis-Menten Equation." She subsequently received her Ph.D. from the University of Chicago and spent most of her career as a professor of pathology at the University of Pittsburgh, where her scholarly output continued, chiefly on cancer research: see UTA/Current People/ "Maud Leonora Menten."

85. Page 180, para. 3 – "for other publications with other libraries": Ross, "The Origins and Development of the Ph.D." at 197-8.

86. Page 180, para. 3 – "was not good enough": F. H. Scott, "On the Structure, Micro-Chemistry and Development of Nerve Cells, with Special Reference to Their Nuclein Compounds," *Transactions of the Canadian Institute*, v. 6, pts. 1 and 2 (December, 1999) at 405.

87. Page 180, para. 3 – "reprint the text of his thesis in that series": F. H. Scott, "On the Structure, Micro-Chemistry and Development of Nerve Cells, with Special Reference to Their Nuclein Compounds," *University of Toronto Studies, Physiological Series* no. 1 (1900).

88. Page 180, para. 3 – "had been accepted for publication": Ross, "The Origins and Development of the Ph.D." at 199-200.

89. Page 180, para. 3 – "fifteen years after his death": F.C. MacIntosh, "Canada's First Ph.D. in Physiology," *Physiology Canada*, v.10 (1985) at 94 calls the two concepts "chemical transmission and axonal transport" and says that they "have since been recognized as among the most basic in neurosciences." The description in the text was George Connell's translation of the terms.

90. Page 180, para. 3 – "into a first-class institution": Maurice B. Visscher, "Dr. Scott – An Appreciation," *The Journal-Lancet* (Minneapolis), v.71 (November, 1951) at 509, as forwarded by the University of Minnesota Archives.

91. Page 180, para. 4 – "awarded to John McLennan in physics": *University of Toronto and its Colleges,* Appendices at 256.

92. Page 182, para. 1 – "the acknowledged leader of Science in Canada": A.S. Eve, "Sir John Cunningham McLennan 1867-1935," *Obituary Notices of Fellows of the Royal Society 1932-1935* (London: Harrison and Sons, 1936) at 577.

93. Page 182, para. 1 – "in the physics division": H. H. Langton, *Sir John Cunningham McLennan: A Memoir* (University of Toronto Press, 1939) at 11.

94. Page 182, para. 1 – "immediately appointed an assistant demonstrator": Ibid. at 12.

95. Page 182, para. 1 – "with sir J.J. Thomson in the Cavendish Laboratory": Ibid. at 15-17.

96. Page 182, para. 1 – "the great Wilhelm Ostwald of Leipzig": Eve, "Sir John Cunningham McLennan 1867-1935" at 578.

97. Page 182, para. 1 – "the basis for the awarding of a doctorate by Toronto": *University of Toronto and its Colleges,* Appendices at 256.

98. Page 182, para. 1 – "Loudon supported the granting of the doctorate": James Loudon was McLennan's friend and supporter throughout his career at Toronto: see Langton, *Sir John Cunningham McLennan* at 12.

99. Page 182, para. 1 – "for supervising McLennan's work": Neither did W.J. Loudon, James Loudon's nephew, supervise McLennan's work.

100. Page 182, para. 1 – "up to the Second World War": Levi, "Thirty-Nine PhDs"; Charles Levi, "Doctoral Theses by Discipline 1915-1939 as taken from *Doctoral Theses 1897-1967*" (Memorandum, June 30, 1999).

101. Page 182, para. 1 – "head of physics at the University of Toronto": After receiving his B.A. in 1904 he worked with McLennan and then received one of the few scholarships available for study in England, the 1851 Exhibition scholarship, made possible by a surplus of money left over from the 1851 Royal Exhibition. Like McLennan he studied and worked with Thomson, but unlike McLennan he in the end received a Cambridge B.A. He returned to the University of Toronto and under McLennan's supervision received his Ph.D. in 1910. Burton supervised two students, James Hilliar and Albert Prebus, who actually built the microscope: see UTA/Graduate Records/"Eli Franklin Burton"/A73-0026/046(78).

102. Page 182, para. 2 – "to William Parks in 1900": *University of Toronto and its Colleges,* Appendices at 256.

103. Page 182, para. 2 – "the head of geology, Arthur Coleman": Ross, "The Origins and Development of the Ph.D." at 8-9; UTA/Graduate Records/"Arthur Philemon Coleman"/A73-0026/64(81-2).

104. Page 182, para. 2 – "during the First World War": Ross, The Origins and Development of the Ph.D." at 306-7.

105. Page 182, para. 2 – "at the School of Practical Science": J.B. Tyrrell, "Arthur Philemon Coleman," *Transactions of the Royal Society of Canada,* Series 3, v. 33 (1939) at 125-6.

106. Page 182, para. 2 – "being evidences of glaciation": W.W. Watts, "Arthur Philemon Coleman," *Obituary Notices of Fellows of the Royal Society 1939-1941,* volume 3 (London: Morrison and Gibb Ltd., 1942) at 117.

107. Page 182, para. 2 – "when Coleman retired in 1922": E.S. Moore, "Memorial of William Arthur Parks," *Proceedings of the Geological Society of America for 1936* at 230.

108. Page 182, para. 2 – "at the Royal Ontario Museum from 1915 to 1936": Ibid.

109. Page 182, para. 2 – "dinosaur specimens at the museum": Ibid. at 229.

110. Page 182, para. 3 – "who had received his PhD in Germany": See Chapter 14 (1890).

111. Page 182, para. 3 – "one teaching at Wisconsin": This was John R. Roebuck: see electronic mail message from Cathy Jacob, University of Wisconsin Archives to Charles Levi, March 17, 1999.

112. Page 182, para. 3 – "one teaching at Utah": "University of Utah Historical Records: Walter D. Bonner" (forwarded by University of Utah Archives).

113. Page 184, para. 1 – "in Schenectady, New York": UTA/Graduate Records/"Saul Dushman"/A73-0026/090. William Lang, also in chemistry, supervised the fourth doctorate the University awarded. Francis Allan, Lang's student, became the professor of organic chemistry at the University and in 1934 the dean of arts: see UTA/ Graduate Records/"Francis Allan"/A73-0026/004.

114. Page 184, para. 1 – "at the Dominion Observatory in Ottawa": C.S. Beals, "Ralph Emerson DeLury," *Proceedings of the Royal Society of Canada* (1957).

115. Page 184, para. 1 – "and headed its school of engineering research": Ross, "The Origins and Development of the Ph.D." at 284. Boswell received his doctorate in 1907. He was appointed a Demonstrator in Chemistry for the academic year 1906-7: see *The Calendar of the University of Toronto for the year 1906-7* at 22. Maitland C. Boswell outlined the creation of the School of Engineering Research in the first issue of School of Engineering Research, *Bulletin* (1919).

116. Page 184, para. 1 – "was named after Lash Miller": The building is now named the John and Edna Davenport Chemical Research Building, which incorporates the Lash Miller Chemical Research Laboratories: see *University of Toronto Bulletin*, December 18, 2000.

117. Page 184, para. 2 – "in the *Journal of Physical Chemistry*": *University of Toronto and its Colleges*, Appendices at 256.

118. Page 184, para. 2 – "under August Kirschmann": Ibid.; Tory Hoff, "The Controversial Appointment of James Mark Baldwin to the University of Toronto in 1889" (M.A. Thesis, Carleton University 1980) at 209. After a year in Paris and another year at Cambridge, Baker became the vice-principal of the women's college at Mount Allison University and in 1913 accepted a chair in psychology at the Maryland college for women, later becoming its principal: see *Allisonia*, v. 11, no.2 (February 1914), from documents forwarded by Mount Allison Department of Philosophy to John Slater, 1997. Kirschmann supervised three other Ph.D.s in psychology before returning to Germany in 1909: see Hoff, "The Controversial Appointment of James Mark Baldwin" at 206. Hume, the head of the department, supervised only one student, who, after a period as a missionary in China, became a professor at Wycliffe College. This was William E. Taylor: see UTA/Graduate Records/"William Edington Taylor"/A73-0026/463(37). After Kirschmann left, no Ph.D.s were awarded in psychology until 1927: see Slater, "Philosophy at Toronto" at 117.

119. Page 184, para. 2 – "positions for women chemists were not easy to find": Ruby Heap, "From the Science of Housekeeping to the Science of Nutrition: Pioneers in Canadian Nutrition and Dietetics at the University of Toronto's Faculty of Household Science, 1900-1950" (Unpublished paper, presented June 7, 1997 at the CHA conference, Memorial University of Newfoundland, 8) at 14.

120. Page 184, para. 2 – "like many women chemists at the time": Ibid.

121. Page 184, para. 2 – "She joined the School of Household Science": Kerrie J. Kennedy, "Womanly Work: The Introduction of Household Science at the University of Toronto" (M.A. Thesis, University of Toronto, 1995) at 33.

122. Page 184, para. 2 – "started by Lillian Massey Treble": David Roberts, "Lillian Frances Massey (Treble)," *DCB*, v.14 at 746.

123. Page 184, para. 2 – "from Lillian Massey's cooking classes": Heap, "From the Science of Housekeeping" at 5-6.

124. Page 184, para. 2 – "a school training teachers of household science": Kennedy, "Womanly Work" at 40; Heap, "From the Science of Housekeeping" at 6.

125. Page 184, para. 2 – "were first offered by the University in 1902": Heap, "From the Science of Housekeeping" at 6.

126. Page 184, para. 3 – "the household science degree to the senate": Kennedy, "Womanly Work" at 43; Heap, "From the Science of Housekeeping" at 6.

127. Page 184, para. 3 – "a true woman's life in our university": Kennedy, "Womanly Work" at 43.

128. Page 184, para. 3 – "should remain in the home": Although many women were at the time entering the workforce, it was precisely this phenomenon that generated discussion of the nature of a "true" woman and how society could both protect the individual and promote the ideal: see Carolyn Strange, *Toronto's girl problem: the perils and pleasures of the city, 1880-1930* (University of Toronto Press, 1995).

129. Page 184, para. 3 – "of such a course in the University": Heap, "From the Science of Housekeeping" at 7.

130. Page 184, para. 3 – "from physical chemistry to physiological chemistry": Ibid. at 15.

131. Page 184, para. 3 – "Macallum's department of physiology": Ibid. at 15.

132. Page 184, para. 3 – "above the rank of demonstrator": Ibid.; *The University of Toronto and its Colleges,* Appendices at 221-222 lists two other women on staff in 1906 – Miss L.B. Johnson, an assistant demonstrator in physics, and Miss M.L. Menten, class assistant in physiology – neither of which are, of course, professorial appointments.

133. Page 184, para. 4 – "and the principal, Annie Laird": Kennedy, "Womanly Work" at 52; Heap, "From the Science of Housekeeping" at 3 et seq.; *The University of Toronto and its Colleges,* Appendices at 229.

134. Page 185, para. 1 – "under the direction of able men": Clara Benson, "Household Science," *University of Toronto Monthly,* v. 7 at 63; see Kennedy, "Womanly Work" at 67.

135. Page 185, para. 1 – "half a million dollars from Lillian Massey Treble": Kennedy, "Womanly Work" at 46.

136. Page 185, para. 1 – "a listing in *American Men of Science*!": Ibid. at 17.

137. Page 185, para. 1 – "28 of them in the sciences": Anne Rochon Ford, *'A Path Not Strewn With Roses': One Hundred Years of Women at the University of Toronto 1884-1984* (University of Toronto Press, 1985) at 46.

CHAPTER 17 – 1901 – THE TURN OF THE CENTURY AND THE RISE OF THE ALUMNI ASSOCIATION

1. Page 186, para. 1 – "a new era in the history of the University": *Varsity*, December 18, 1900. The new century began in 1901, not 1900.

2. Page 186, para. 1 – "were rung": The *Toronto World*, December 31, 1900, said that most churches would have services.

3. Page 186, para. 1 – "the recently opened Toronto City Hall": The City Hall was completed in 1899: see Eric Arthur, *Toronto: No Mean City*, 3rd edition (University of Toronto Press, 1986) at 190-191.

4. Page 186, para. 1 – "twenty more for the new century": *Globe*, January 1, 1901.

5. Page 186, para. 2 – "brighter days in store": *Varsity*, January 15, 1901.

6. Page 186, para. 2 – "large annual deficits": James Loudon, "The University and State Aid," *University of Toronto Monthly*, v.1 (January, 1901) at 135; Edward E. Stewart, "The Role of the Provincial Government in the Development of the Universities of Ontario 1791-1964" (D.Ed. Thesis, University of Toronto, 1970) at 265-270. See also F.A. Moure, "Outline of the Financial History of the University," *The University of Toronto and Its Colleges 1827-1906* (University Librarian, 1906) at 71 et seq.

7. Page 186, para. 2 – "the deficit amounted to over $30,000": Richard Harcourt's speech on the second reading of his 1901 bill, cited in Ontario Public Records and Archives Department, "Newspaper Hansard" at 131.

8. Page 186, para. 2 – "on average, under $125,000 a year": Loudon, "State Aid" at 136.

9. Page 186, para. 2 – "only $7,000 of that amount": Ibid. at 138; John Squair, "Alumni Associations in the University of Toronto" (University of Toronto Press, 1922) at 19; W.S. Wallace, *A History of the University of Toronto* (University of Toronto Press, 1927) at 158-59.

10. Page 186, para. 2 – "the University of California more than $300,000": Loudon, "State Aid" at 138. Harcourt gave other figures for state contributions, such as $318,000 for Pennsylvania, $255,000 for Ohio, and $235,000 for New York: see "Newspaper Hansard" at 131.

11. Page 186, para. 2 – "was needed by the University of Toronto": Loudon, "State Aid" at 137.

12. Page 187, para. 1 – "the designs of the denominational colleges": Wallace, *History of the University of Toronto* at 158.

13. Page 187, para. 1 – "they could turn things around again": Both Chancellor Edward Blake and Vice-chancellor William Mulock had been involved with the struggle: see Chapter 7 (1860). Both resigned in 1900. Mulock resigned the Vice-chancellorship a few days before Blake's letter of resignation arrived in Toronto: see James Loudon, "Memoirs," UTA/B72-0031/16(11) at 127.

14. Page 187, para. 1 – "the brunt of the battle": *Varsity*, January 15, 1901.

15. Page 187, para. 1 – "and collectively on public opinion": Loudon, "State Aid" at 139.

16. Page 187, para. 2 – "the greatest constructive feat of his administration": Wallace, *History of the University of Toronto* at 157.

17. Page 187, para. 2 – "confidant of William Ross's Liberal government": John D. Blackwell, "Samuel Hume Blake," *DCB*, v. 14 at 85-88.

18. Page 188, para. 1 – "a man like Seth Low [of Columbia]": Gerald Kurland, *Seth Low: The Reformer in an Urban and Industrial Age* (New York: Twayne Publishers, 1971) at 61.

19. Page 188, para. 1 – "or Principal Grant [of Queen's]": Loudon, "Memoirs" at 128. Blake expressed similar views in a speech to the Political Science Association in the fall of 1900 when he said: "We want a man! ... We want a strong personality – one full of life and vigor – a man of deep sympathy ..." This was clearly not Loudon: see *Varsity*, December 4, 1900; see also James Tucker, "Mr. S.H. Blake and the University," *Saturday Night*, December 1, 1900.

20. Page 188, para. 1 – "immediately wrote to Chancellor Edward Blake in England": Loudon, "Memoirs" at 125.

21. Page 188, para. 1 – "which has characterized this affair": Ibid. at 127.

22. Page 188, para. 1 – "acted on *immediately*": Ibid. at 128 (emphasis in original). The letter of resignation was dated February 2, 1900.

23. Page 188, para. 1 – "and form an Alumni Association": Ibid. at 129.

24. Page 188, para. 2 – "wanted a wider association of graduates": Otto J. Klotz, "Toronto University Club of Ottawa," *University of Toronto Monthly*, v. 1 at 5.

25. Page 188, para. 2 – "of such an organization": *Varsity*, March 21, 1900.

26. Page 188, para. 2 – "not a substitute for an organized alumni association": Squair, "Alumni Association" at 6-7; Wallace, *History of the University of Toronto* at 158.

27. Page 188, para. 2 – "the driving force behind the organization": "Sir Daniel Wilson's Journal," Langton Family Papers, UTA/B65-0014/004(02) at 204-205 (April 25, 1892).

28. Page 188, para. 2 – "led to the student strike of 1895": Squair, "Alumni Association" at 8-9; Wallace, *History of the University of Toronto* at 158.

29. Page 188, para. 2 – "to promote a residence for women, without success": *Sesame*, January 1899 at 26. The alumnae association was founded in 1898. Before that, there was a Women's Residence Association made up of alumnae and faculty wives: see Sara Burke, "Research Memo: Alumnae and Faculty Wives"; Loudon, "Memoirs" at 115 et seq.

30. Page 188, para. 2 – "the University of Michigan Alumni Association": *Varsity*, March 21, 1900; Otto Klotz in the *Globe*, April 18, 1900.

31. Page 188, para. 2 – "after spending a year at Toronto": UTA/Graduate Records/"Otto Julius Klotz"/A73-0026/207(69).

32. Page 188, para. 3 – "calling for a university-wide body": Squair, "Alumni Association" at 9.

33. Page 188, para. 3 – "was meeting in Toronto": *Globe*, April 17, 1900.

34. Page 188, para. 3 – "in the chemistry lecture hall": W.H. Fraser, "The Alumni Association," *University of Toronto Monthly*, v. 1 at 2.

35. Page 188, para. 3 – "and Otto Klotz": *Daily Mail and Empire*, April 18, 1900.

36. Page 189, para. 1 – "of importance to Victoria, a Methodist": Wallace, *History of the University of Toronto* at 159.

37. Page 189, para. 1 – "to block Toronto's medical ambitions": H.H. Langton, *Sir John Cunningham McLennan: A Memoir* (University of Toronto Press, 1939) at 23. The *Globe*, April 18, 1900, referred to the "recent attack on the medical faculty."

38. Page 189, para. 1 – "contagious enthusiasm": Langton, *Sir John Cunningham McLennan* at 23.

39. Page 189, para. 1 – "succeeded A.B. Macallum as president in 1913": H.H. Langton became secretary-treasurer in 1908. In 1910, McLennan returned as acting secretary-treasurer, to be succeeded in 1911 by H. A. McTaggart, who was replaced in 1912 by J. Patterson. Similarly, the Presidency changed. Reeve left in 1907, replaced by I. H. Cameron, who was replaced in 1908 by Barlow Cumberland, who was replaced by J.M. Gibson in 1909. A.B. Macallum became President in 1912: see *University of Toronto Monthly*, vols. 6-14; R.A. Reeve, "Professor McLennan and the Alumni Association," *University of Toronto Monthly*, v. 15 at 183-184.

40. Page 189, para. 1 – "the head of English at Harbord Collegiate": UTA/Graduate Records/"Gertrude Lawler"/ A73-0026/221(42).

41. Page 189, para. 1 – "a former chancellor of Victoria, Samuel Nelles": *Acta Victoriana*, May 1897 at 404 and April 1899 at 517; *University of Toronto Register of Graduates, 1920* (University of Toronto Press, 1921) at 117.

42. Page 189, para. 2 – "It also included undergraduates": Fraser, "The Alumni Association" at 3.

43. Page 189, para. 2 – "on the basis of local branches": Ibid.

44. Page 189, para. 2 – "there were 17 branches": Squair, "Alumni Association" at 10; Wallace, *History of the University of Toronto* at 159.

45. Page 189, para. 2 – "twelve of the organizational meetings": Loudon, "Memoirs," Section B at 2.

46. Page 189, para. 2 – "the number of Toronto graduates in the west": "Toronto University and the West" in *The Educational Monthly of Canada*, v. 25 (1903) at 423.

47. Page 189, para. 2 – "they met with thirty-five": Ibid.

48. Page 189, para. 2 – "rather than go to the United States": Peter N. Ross, "The Origins and Development of the Ph.D. Degree at the University of Toronto 1871-1932" (D.Ed. Thesis, University of Toronto, 1972) at 218-219, citing McLennan's Scrapbook #1; "Toronto University and the West" at 424.

49. Page 189, para. 2 – "23 of them in Ontario": Squair, "Alumni Association" at 27.

50. Page 189, para. 3 – "the night before graduation, June 1900": Ibid. at 13.

51. Page 189, para. 3 – "The new chancellor, Chief Justice William Meredith": "The Hon. Sir William Ralph Meredith" in Henry James Morgan, ed., *The Canadian Men and Women of The Time* (Toronto: William Briggs, 1912) at 797-8.

52. Page 189, para. 3 – "would receive his PhD the following day": Squair, "Alumni Association" at 14.

53. Page 189, para. 3 – "on Lake Ontario in the evening": Ibid. at 13.

54. Page 189, para. 3 – "in the examination hall of the School of Practical Science": Other convocations had taken place in such odd venues as a circus tent and a music hall: see Langton, *Sir John Cunningham McLennan* at 24.

55. Page 189, para. 3 – "by the ubiquitous McLennan": Squair, "Alumni Association" at 14.

56. Page 190, para. 1 – "as the professor of surgery": UTA/Graduate Records/"Irving Heward Cameron"/A73-0026/048(84).

57. Page 190, para. 1 – "all articles had to be signed": I.H. Cameron, "Salutory," *University of Toronto Monthly*, v.1 at 1; Loudon, "Memoirs," section B at 1.

58. Page 190, para. 1 – "a paid editor was hired": Harold Averill, "The University of Toronto Monthly and its Successors" (Unpublished manuscript, 1981) at 1.

59. Page 190, para. 1 – "incorporated into the new *Varsity Graduate*": Ibid. at 2.

60. Page 190, para. 2 – "the state university": Loudon, "State Aid" at 135.

61. Page 190, para. 2 – "school of mining and engineering": Loudon, "Memoirs," Section B at 7-8; C.R. Young, *Early Engineering Education at Toronto 1851-1919* (University of Toronto Press, 1958) at 100; A.B. McKillop, *Matters of Mind: The University in Ontario 1791-1951* (University of Toronto Press, 1994) at 172; H.V. Nelles, *The Politics of Development: Forests, Mines, and Hydro-Electric Power in Ontario 1849-1941* (Toronto: Macmillan of Canada, 1974) at 140-41; Edward E. Stewart, "The Role of the Provincial Government" at 260; Hilda Neatby, *Queen's University: volume 1, 1841-1917* (Kingston: McGill Queen's University Press, 1978) at 218. As Neatby acknowledges, the story of the arrangement is complex. It would appear that Principal Grant used his college's multiple connections to the Premier, Sir Oliver Mowat, to their best advantage.

62. Page 190, para. 2 – "and put it at a side entrance": Loudon, "Memoirs," Section B at 8.

63. Page 190, para. 2 – "dissociated itself from University College": W.H. Ellis, "The Faculty of Applied Science," *University of Toronto* (1906) at 182; McKillop, *Matters of Mind* at 171.

64. Page 190, para. 2 – "rather than by University College professors": Young, *Early Engineering Education* at 88.

65. Page 190, para. 2 – "the government more than doubled the space": James Loudon, "Buildings and Equipment" in *The University of Toronto and Its Colleges* at 213.

66. Page 190, para. 2 – "a large addition to the east": Young, *Early Engineering Education* at 90.

67. Page 190, para. 2 – "now faced Queen's Park": Loudon, "Buildings" at 213.

68. Page 190, para. 2 – "as it had until then": Young, *Early Engineering Education*, sketch facing 56.

69. Page 190, para. 2 – "the existing three-year diploma course": *Calendar of the School of Practical Science* (Toronto: Warwick & Sons, 1891) at 37; *Calendar of the School of Practical Science* (Toronto: Warwick & Sons, 1893) at 46-7; Young, *Early Engineering Education* at 90-92; Richard White, *The Skule Story: The University of Toronto Faculty of Applied Science and Engineering 1873-2000* (University of Toronto Press, 2000) at 43-44; Ellis, "The Faculty of Applied Science" at 183.

70. Page 190, para. 3 – "there were only 70 regular engineering students": Young, *Early Engineering Education* at 87.

71. Page 190, para. 3 – "there were 200 students": Ibid. at 108.

72. Page 190, para. 3 – "by 1905 there would be more than 500": Ibid. at 123.

73. Page 190, para. 3 – "were attending university": For careers of engineers, see Philip A. Lapp, "The Nation Builders" in Robin S. Harris and Ian Montagnes, eds., *Cold Iron and Lady Godiva: Engineering Education at Toronto 1920-1972* (University of Toronto Press, 1972) at 109 et seq. See also *University of Toronto Calendar Faculty of Applied Science and Engineering, 1912-1913* at 106-133.

74. Page 191, para. 1 – "later the head of the department of architecture": Young, *Early Engineering Education* at 91.

75. Page 191, para. 1 – "in the new engineering laboratory": Ibid.

76. Page 191, para. 1 – "when Victoria moved to Toronto": J.B. Tyrrell, "Arthur Philemon Coleman," *Proceedings of the Royal Society of Canada*, 3rd Series, v. 33 (1939) at 125; Young, *Early Engineering Education* at 93.

77. Page 191, para. 1 – "while continuing his association with engineering": Tyrrell, "Arthur Philemon Coleman" at 126.

78. Page 191, para. 1 – "of mechanical and electrical engineering": *Calendar of the School of Practical Science* (Toronto: Warwick & Sons, 1891) at 5. The department remained combined until the academic year of 1909-10. Even then, the relationship of the two departments remained so close that their programmes were identical for the first two years: see *The Calendar of the University of Toronto Faculty of Applied Science and Engineering, 1909-10* (Toronto: The University Press, 1909) at 27.

79. Page 191, para. 2 – "to the government for its funding": *Report of the Royal Commission on the University of Toronto* (Toronto: L.K. Cameron, 1906) at xxx.

80. Page 191, para. 2 – "the faculty of applied science of the University": Young, *Early Engineering Education* at 110 and 116; Ellis, "The Faculty of Applied Science" at 183.

81. Page 191, para. 2 – "at a dinner given in his honour": John Galbraith, "The Function of the School of Applied Science in the Education of the Engineer," *University of Toronto Monthly*, v.1 at 150.

82. Page 191, para. 2 – "the ancient faculties of Arts, Medicine and Law": Galbraith, "The Function of the School of Applied Science in the Education of the Engineer" at 157.

83. Page 191, para. 2 – "into the University until 1906": *Calendar of the Ontario School of Practical* Science (Toronto: 1905-6) at 18; *Statute of the Senate of the University of Toronto, 14 December, 1900*. "No liability shall be incurred by the University of Toronto for the support or maintenance of the faculty hereby established"; *An Act Respecting the University of Toronto and University College (1906)*, Appendix L, s. 6.

84. Page 191, para. 3 – "sometimes referred to as the 'New Ontario'": H.V. Nelles, *The Politics of Development* at 108. For development of the north, see also Michael Bliss, *Northern Enterprise: Five Centuries of Canadian Business* (Toronto: McClelland and Stewart, 1987) at 314 et seq.; Robert Craig Brown and Ramsay Cook, *Canada 1896-1921: A Nation Transformed* (Toronto: McClelland and Stewart, 1974) at 87 et seq.; McKillop, *Matters of Mind* at 171.

85. Page 191, para. 3 – "a provincial equivalent to the opening of the west": Nelles, *The Politics of Development* at 109.

86. Page 191, para. 3 – "make such development remunerative": Ibid. at 61, citing *Globe*, April 3, 1900.

87. Page 191, para. 3 – "the new Chicago of the North": Ibid. at 55, citing F.A. Wightman, *Our Canadian Heritage* (Toronto, 1905).

88. Page 192, para. 1 – "for support for science and engineering": Loudon, "Memoirs," Section B at 6.

89. Page 192, para. 1 – "300 graduates from eighteen Ontario counties": Ibid. at 13.

90. Page 192, para. 1 – "to press the claims of the University": Langton, *Sir John Cunningham McLennan* at 23.

91. Page 192, para. 1 – "like the historical red flag": Loudon, "Memoirs," Section B at 11.

92. Page 192, para. 1 – "but Loudon did take part": Ibid. at 12.

93. Page 192, para. 1 – "efficient scientific teaching at the University": Langton, *Sir John Cunningham McLennan* at 23.

94. Page 192, para. 1 – "qualified Canadians to head their departments": Ibid. at 14.

95. Page 192, para. 1 – "that has ever gathered at the Parliament Buildings": Cited in Loudon, "Memoirs," Section B at 13.

96. Page 192, para. 2 – "outlining why funds were required": "Petition of the Undergraduates of the Ontario School of Practical Science presented to the Lieut. Governor-in-Council, March 6, 1901," UTA/A74-0008/008(05); see also Young, *Early Engineering Education* at 110.

97. Page 192, para. 2 – "that face the legislative buildings so threateningly": Squair, "Alumni Association" at 16; *University of Toronto Monthly*, v. 31 at 400. The Engineering Society apparently had no part in the petition. Founded in 1885, at that time the Society was a voluntary organization which concentrated on scholarly endeavours, such as the publication of papers presented at meetings of the society: see Barry G. Levine, *A Century of Skill and Vigour* (Toronto: T.H. Best Printing, 1985) at 3-4.

98. Page 193, para. 1 – "sunk by General Wolfe in 1758": *University of Toronto Monthly*, v. 31 at 400.

99. Page 193, para. 1 – "that of other engineering colleges": "Petition" at 1-3.

100. Page 193, para. 1 – "cannot be over-emphasized": Ibid. at 3.

101. Page 193, para. 1 – "of her mineral and forest wealth": Ibid.

102. Page 193, para. 1 – "paid close attention to scientific study": Ibid. at 4.

103. Page 193, para. 1 – "he could make no promises": Loudon, "Memoirs," Section B at 11.

104. Page 193, para. 2 – "he wrote to a cabinet colleague in 1901": Ross to "Cabinet Colleague," 1901, as cited in Charles W. Humphries, "James P. Whitney and the University of Toronto," in Edith G. Firth, ed., *Profiles of a Province: Studies in the History of Ontario* (Toronto: Ontario Historical Society, 1967) at 119. This article does not have references, but in Charles W. Humphries, *"Honest Enough to be Bold": The Life and Times of Sir James Pliny Whitney* (University of Toronto Press, 1985) at 235, n.28 is a reference to a letter from Ross to W. Harty which is probably the right one.

105. Page 193, para. 2 – "as to the effect upon the country": Humphries, "James P. Whitney" at 119.

106. Page 193, para. 3 – "like the coffin of Mohammed": Ibid.

107. Page 193, para. 3 – "from the provincial succession duties": Ibid. Note that Samuel Blake had suggested this in the fall of 1900, as reported in the *Varsity*, November 27, 1900. See also Squair, "Alumni Association" at 19.

108. Page 193, para. 3 – "our young men will go elsewhere for higher education": Humphries, "James P. Whitney" at 119.

109. Page 193, para. 3 – "under Chancellor Meredith's influence": Ibid. at 120.

110. Page 193, para. 3 – "for the support of the Alumni of Toronto": Ibid.

111. Page 193, para. 3 – "as leader of the Conservatives in Ontario": Humphries, *"Honest Enough to Be Bold"* at 62.

112. Page 193, para. 4 – "a bill was introduced by the government": As we saw in an earlier section, to pave the way for Trinity's federation with U of T the *1901 Act* also created a separate principal for University College. See also *1901 Act*, ss. 38-41.

113. Page 193, para. 4 – "responding to the University's requests": *Globe*, March 22, 1901, cited in "Newspaper Hansard" at 122; Edward E. Stewart, "The Role of the Provincial Government" at 268-273.

114. Page 194, para. 1 – "with the exception of biology": *An Act Respecting the University of Toronto and University College (1901)*, 1 Edw. VII, cap. 41, s. 16; Harcourt's speech reported on March 22, 1901 in the "Newspaper Hansard" at 122.

115. Page 194, para. 1 – "an additional $25,000 a year to the University": "Newspaper Hansard" at 132.

116. Page 194, para. 1 – "a cost of about $200,000": Ibid.

117. Page 194, para. 1 – "and for the extension of SPS": *1901 Act*, s. 17.

118. Page 194, para. 2 – "called the Chemistry and Mining Building": Young, *Early Engineering Education* at 112.

119. Page 194, para. 2 – "which was opened in 1904": Ibid. at 122.

120. Page 194, para. 2 – "more than doubled the space available to engineering": Loudon, "Buildings" at 213. Loudon gives the floor space of the "Skulehouse" as 55,299 square feet and that of the new building at 75,000 square feet.

121. Page 194, para. 2 – "directly north of the new main building": Ellis, "The Faculty of Applied Science" at 183.

122. Page 194, para. 2 – "Haultain became a professor of mining in 1910": G. R. Mickle was promoted from Lecturer in Mining to become the first Professor of Mining in 1906: see *Calendar of the Ontario School of Practical Science* (Toronto 1906-7 Session) at 14. Haultain's appointment appears in the calendar for 1909-10: see *The Calendar of the University of Toronto Faculty of Applied Science and Engineering, 1909-1910* (Toronto: The University Press) at 8.

123. Page 194, para. 2 – "'Iron Ring' ceremony": Levine, *A Century of Skill and Vigour* at 6; White, *The Skule Story* at 67.

124. Page 194, para. 2 – "the former Wycliffe College building be torn down": The old college was opened on October 24, 1882 but had proven inadequate by 1891. A new college was built on its present site on Hoskin Avenue. The old college at College and McCaul streets was torn down for the new science building: see *The Jubilee Volume of Wycliffe College* (Toronto: Wycliffe College, 1927) at 39, 55-6.

125. Page 194, para. 2 – "one of its many locations over the years": John Squair, "How the University Press has Developed," *University of Toronto Monthly*, v.21 at 118.

126. Page 194, para. 3 – "had not gone far enough": "Newspaper Hansard" at 132.

127. Page 194, para. 3 – "for the biology department as well": Ibid. at 162.

128. Page 194, para. 3 – "through succession duties": Ibid. at 133 and 188.

129. Page 194, para. 3 – "was clearly a result of its influence": Wallace, *History of the University of Toronto* at 160.

130. Page 194, para. 3 – "of the former University College residence": Squair, "Alumni Association" at 15. The term "Faculty Union" was in use at the time to identify a social organization rather than a negotiating group.

131. Page 194, para. 4 – "and in the Boer War": Ibid. at 21.

132. Page 194, para. 4 – "agreed to contribute another $50,000": R.A. Reeve, "The Convocation Hall," *University of Toronto Monthly*, v.5 at 58; Loudon, "Memoirs," Section B at 5.

133. Page 194, para. 4 – "The sum was raised": Wallace, *History of the University of Toronto* at 160.

134. Page 194, para. 4 – "Goldwin Smith of the Grange gave the final $5,000": Loudon, "Memoirs," Section D at 17.

135. Page 194, para. 4 – "was laid in June 1904": Squair, "Alumni Association" at 23.

136. Page 194, para. 4 – "designed by Darling and Pearson": Reeve, "The Convocation Hall" at 59.

137. Page 194, para. 4 – "for the businessman Joseph Flavelle in Queen's Park": Michael Bliss, *A Canadian Millionaire: The Life and Business Times of Sir Joseph Flavelle, Bart., 1858-1939* (Toronto: Macmillan of Canada, 1978) at 97.

138. Page 194, para. 4 – "modelled on the Sorbonne theatre in Paris": Reeve, "The Convocation Hall" at 60.

139. Page 196, para. 1 – "2,000 people": Ibid. at 59.

140. Page 196, para. 1 – "before the hall could be used": Squair, "Alumni Association" at 23.

141. Page 196, para. 2 – "in what had been the residence": Langton, *Sir John Cunningham McLennan* at 25.

142. Page 196, para. 2 – "The space was clearly inadequate": Ibid.

143. Page 196, para. 2 – "with over 30,000 for chemistry": Loudon, "Memoirs," Section C at 13. Section C of the Loudon Memoirs is oddly paginated and the reader is duly warned.

144. Page 196, para. 2 – "was engaged in his path-breaking research": Yves Gingras, *Physics and the Rise of Scientific Research in Canada* (Montreal: McGill-Queen's University Press, 1991) at 29; Stanley Brice Frost, *McGill University* (Montreal: McGill-Queen's University Press), v. 1 (1980) at 273 and v.2 (1984) at 37-39.

145. Page 196, para. 2 – "prepared a design": Loudon, "Memoirs," Section C at 13.

146. Page 196, para. 2 – "with Galbraith's approval": Loudon, "Memoirs," Section C at 18-19; Catherine Moriarty, *John Galbraith 1846-1914: Engineer and Educator* (Faculty of Applied Science and Engineering, University of Toronto, 1989) at 64.

147. Page 196, para. 2 – "SPS thereupon hired its own physics lecturer": Loudon, "Memoirs," Section C. The person in question was named Anderson.

148. Page 196, para. 2 – "much to the annoyance of Loudon": Ibid. The pagination of the Loudon memoirs at this point is truly difficult to decipher.

149. Page 196, para. 3 – "sought an interview with the premier": Ibid. at 14.

150. Page 196, para. 3 – "and invite the premier to meet the deputation there": Ibid.

151. Page 196, para. 3 – "at Queen's Park on March 23, 1904": Ibid. at 15; Wallace, *History of the University of Toronto* at 160; *Globe*, March 24, 1904.

152. Page 196, para. 3 – "with 1,400 signatures": Loudon, "Memoirs," Section C at 15.

153. Page 196, para. 3 – "to the University and its alumni": Langton, *Sir John Cunningham McLennan* at 26.

154. Page 196, para. 3 – "at a cost of $180,000": Ibid. at 27.

155. Page 196, para. 3 – "came as a veritable surprise": *University of Toronto Monthly,* vol. 5 (December, 1904) at 60.

156. Page 196, para. 4 – "that the grant would help their chances": In the aftermath of a large provincial convention, Liberal associations started to name candidates at the end of November: see *Globe,* November 26, 1904. The announcement of the funding of the physics building was made on November 28: see *Globe,* November 29, 1904.

157. Page 196, para. 4 – "with 69 seats to the Liberals' 29": Humphries, *"Honest Enough to be Bold"* at 94.

CHAPTER 18 – 1905 – WHITNEY AND THE ROYAL COMMISSION

1. Page 197, para. 1 – "that removed the existing university deficit": The deficit was almost $50,000 in 1905: "Speech Delivered by the Hon. J.P. Whitney, Premier and Attorney General of Ontario on Introducing the Act respecting the University of Toronto on Wednesday, May 17th, 1905" (Toronto: L.K. Cameron, 1905) at 6; Charles Humphries, "James P. Whitney and the University of Toronto," in Edith G. Firth, ed., *Profiles of a Province: Studies in the History of Ontario* (Toronto: Ontario Historical Society, 1967) at 119.

2. Page 197, para. 1 – "and generously provided for future funding": *An Act Respecting the University of Toronto (1905)*; Humphries, "Whitney" at 120; W.S. Wallace, *A History of the University of Toronto* (University of Toronto Press, 1927) at 166-7.

3. Page 197, para. 1 – "and also to those in control of the University": "Speech Delivered" at 7.

4. Page 197, para. 1 – "a sound, stable, and permanent footing": Ibid. at 13.

5. Page 197, para. 1 – "suspended between heaven and earth": Humphries, "Whitney" at 119.

6. Page 197, para. 2 – "and the physics building": *1905 Act*, ss. 6 and 8.

7. Page 197, para. 2 – "than originally anticipated": "Speech Delivered" at 14.

8. Page 197, para. 2 – "the operating expenditures for the year": *1905 Act*, s. 2.

9. Page 197, para. 2 – "in future years": "Speech Delivered" at 18.

10. Page 197, para. 2 – "grants to the University approached half a million dollars": "Speech Delivered" at 16; Wallace, *History of the University of Toronto* at 167; Humphries, "Whitney" at 120; James Loudon, "Memoirs of James Loudon," UTA/B72-0031/16(11), Section G at 1.

11. Page 197, para. 2 – "to borrow money for future construction": *1905 Act*, preamble and s. 2; "Speech Delivered" at 16.

12. Page 197, para. 2 – "ought to bear its fair share of the burden": "Speech Delivered" at 16.

13. Page 198, para. 1 – "a museum for the School of Practical Science": *1905 Act*, preamble and s. 5; "Speech Delivered" at 14-15.

14. Page 198, para. 1 – "the hospital near the Don River": *1905 Act*, preamble and s. 5; "Speech Delivered" at 15.

15. Page 198, para. 1 – "administration of the affairs of the University": "Speech Delivered" at 21.

16. Page 198, para. 1 – "10 years past by the former government": Humphries, "Whitney" at 120; Charles Humphries, *'Honest Enough to be Bold': The Life and Times of Sir James Pliny Whitney* (University of Toronto Press, 1985) at 109.

17. Page 199, para. 1 – "open to students of all faculties": T.H.B. Symons, "Devonshire House," *Varsity Graduate* (January, 1957).

18. Page 199, para. 1 – "and the John W. Graham library for Trinity": www.facilities.utoronto.ca/PMDC/projects/munktrin.html

19. Page 199, para. 1 – "to compensate those whose property would be affected": *An Act Respecting the University of Toronto and University College (1906)*, s. 143.

20. Page 200, para. 1 – "and opened in 1907": Symons, "Devonshire" at 18.

21. Page 200, para. 1 – "and not, as many believe, the premier": See "Memorandum re: E.C. Whitney Bequest," Bursar's Office, June 24, 1952, UTA/A86-0038/24, with extracts from Whitney will of February 19, 1920.

22. Page 200, para. 1 – "for the construction of government buildings": Alyson King, "Centres of 'home-like influence': Residences for women at the University of Toronto," *Material History Review*, v.49 (Spring, 1999) at 45.

23. Page 200, para. 2 – "not that of his minister of education": Humphries, "Whitney" at 121.

24. Page 200, para. 2 – "He wanted Goldwin Smith to chair it": Michael Bliss, *A Canadian Millionaire: The Life and Business Times of Sir Joseph Flavelle, Bart. 1858-1939* (Toronto: Macmillan of Canada, 1978) at 164.

25. Page 200, para. 2 – "Smith was a highly respected intellectual": James G. Greenlee, *Sir Robert Falconer: A Biography* (University of Toronto Press, 1988) at 110.

26. Page 200, para. 2 – "the commission of inquiry set up after the 1895 strike": See Chapter 15 (1895); Wallace, *History of the University of Toronto* at 165.

27. Page 200, para. 2 – "but agreed to be a member": Bliss, *Canadian Millionaire* at 164; *Telegram* of October 3, 1905, as cited in "Bliss Research Notes."

28. Page 200, para. 2 – "former Toronto mayor William Boulton": Ramsay Cook, "Goldwin Smith," *DCB*, v. 13 at 968-970.

29. Page 200, para. 2 – "Smith's elegant residence, the Grange": See Commissioners to Smith, April 4, 1906, Goldwin Smith Papers, Cornell University.

30. Page 200, para. 3 – "He moved to Toronto in 1887": Bliss, *Canadian Millionaire* at 1, 9 and 27.

31. Page 200, para. 3 – "in meat packing, merchandising, and finance": See generally, Bliss, *Canadian Millionaire.*

32. Page 200, para. 3 – "rivalled the Grange in grandeur": Michael Bliss and William Dendy, "Holwood," *Canadian Collector* (November/December, 1975) at 21.

33. Page 200, para. 3 – "meetings of the commission were held at the Grange": For liquor and Holwood, see Bliss, *Canadian Millionaire* at 501.

34. Page 201, para. 1 – "which had responsibility for its finances": Bliss, *Canadian Millionaire,* at 141-145.

35. Page 201, para. 1 – "of the University for more than thirty years": Ibid. at 180.

36. Page 201, para. 1 – "Reverend Bruce Macdonald later stated": D.B. MacDonald, "Partial Memoirs of the Rev. D. Bruce MacDonald pertaining to the University of Toronto" (1953), UTA/B83-1295 at 35.

37. Page 201, para. 1 – "a mind of marvellous clarity": H.J. Cody, "A Chapter in the Organization of Higher Education in Canada 1905-6," *Transactions of the Royal Society of Canada*, Section II, 1946 at 92, copy in UTA/A83-0036/020.

38. Page 201, para. 1 – "Flavelle's daily paper, the *News*": Greenlee, *Sir Robert Falconer* at 110.

39. Page 201, para. 1 – "One of his employees at the paper, A.H.U. Colquhoun": Ibid.; UTA/Graduate Records/ "Arthur Hugh Urquhart Colquhoun"/A73-0026/065(86).

40. Page 201, para. 1 – "and a member of the commission": Humphries, "Whitney" at 121.

41. Page 201, para. 1 – "for a businessman to chair the commission": Flavelle to Smith, April 7, 1906, Goldwin Smith Papers.

42. Page 201, para. 2 – "the 58-year-old Byron Edmund Walker": B.E. Walker was known as "Byron" until 1910, when he styled himself "Sir Edmund Walker": see comments from Wentworth Walker, December, 1999. Hereafter he will be referred to as "Edmund Walker."

43. Page 201, para. 2 – "in spite of his being both a Liberal": Although Walker was more or less non-partisan, when offered a post in the Conservative cabinet in 1910, he replied, "I still like to think I am a Liberal": see G.P. de T. Glazebrook, *Sir Edmund Walker* (Oxford: Oxford University Press, 1933) at 1 and 109. By 1911 he had left the Liberal party over the issue of reciprocity: ibid. at 110-111.

44. Page 201, para. 2 – "and an agnostic": Bliss, *Canadian Millionaire* at 87.

45. Page 201, para. 2 – "would become chancellor of the University": "The New Chancellor," *University of Toronto Monthly*, v. 24 at 57.

46. Page 201, para. 2 – "had left school in Hamilton at age 12": Glazebrook, *Sir Edmund Walker* at 3.

47. Page 201, para. 2 – "to enter his uncle's *bureau de change* business": UTA/Graduate Records/"Byron Edmund Walker"/A73-0026/490(97).

48. Page 201, para. 2 – "including the Metropolitan Museum of Art": Glazebrook, *Sir Edmund Walker* at 12 and 23.

49. Page 201, para. 2 – "in 1907 he became its president": Ibid. at 83.

50. Page 201, para. 2 – "on the east side of St. George": 99 St. George. See Donald Jones, "Banker's Imagination was Fired to Help in Building Our Museum," in UTA/A83-0036/043.

51. Page 201, para. 2 – "now the site of the business school": 97 St. George is immediately to the south of the Business School.

52. Page 201, para. 2 – "apart from the government itself": Glazebrook, *Sir Edmund Walker* at 40.

53. Page 201, para. 2 – "a member of the University's board of trustees and senate": Ibid. at 41.

54. Page 201, para. 3 – "one of the founders of the Royal Ontario Museum": Lovat Dickson, *The Museum Makers: The Story of the Royal Ontario Museum* (Toronto: The Royal Ontario Museum, 1986) at 27; Glazebrook, *Sir Edmund Walker* at 92-93.

55. Page 201, para. 3 – "and the Champlain Society": Glazebrook, *Sir Edmund Walker* at 70-71, 78, and 90-91. The Gallery was originally known as the Art Museum of Toronto. It became the Art Gallery of Toronto in 1919: see David Kimmell, "Toronto Gets a Gallery: The Origins and Development of the City's Permanent Public Art Museum," *Ontario History*, v. 84, no. 3 (September 1992) at 202-206.

56. Page 201, para. 3 – "one of the promoters of a reference library for the city": Ibid. at 72 and 78-79. Although established by Royal charter in 1851, it was not until 1914 that the Canadian Institute was allowed to use the prefix, "Royal": see http://psych.utoronto.ca/~rci/History.html.

57. Page 201, para. 3 – "but expert geologist and palaeontologist": Greenlee, *Sir Robert Falconer* at 110.

58. Page 201, para. 3 – "a member of the Royal Society of Canada": *Proceedings and Transactions of the Royal Society of Canada*, 3rd Series, v. 5 (1912) at IV.

59. Page 202, para. 1 – "he would have preferred to be an academic": Greenlee, *Sir Robert Falconer* at 110.

60. Page 202, para. 2 – "as leader of the Conservatives": Humphries, "Whitney" at 118; Greenlee, *Sir Robert Falconer* at 110.

61. Page 202, para. 2 – "chief justice of the Common Pleas Division of Ontario in 1894": "The Hon. Sir William Ralph Meredith," in Henry James Morgan, ed., *The Canadian Men and Women of the Time* (Toronto: William Briggs, 1912) at 798.

62. Page 202, para. 2 – "in the drafting of the subsequent legislation": Humphries, *Honest* at 128.

63. Page 202, para. 2 – "on Bloor Street, east of Yonge": D.C. Masters, *Henry John Cody: An Outstanding Life* (Toronto: Dundurn Press, 1995) at 13 and 95.

64. Page 202, para. 2 – "the famous University College class of 1895": "Macdonald memoirs" at 3.

65. Page 202, para. 2 – "and the head of St Andrew's boys' school": UTA/Graduate Records/"Donald Bruce Macdonald"/A73-0026/260(38).

66. Page 202, para. 2 – "Cody having graduated from Wycliffe College": In 1893: Masters, *Cody* at 32.

67. Page 202, para. 2 – "and Macdonald from Knox": In 1897: Graduate Records/"Macdonald."

68. Page 202, para. 2 – "and then president of the University": Masters, *Cody* at 87, 177, and 292.

69. Page 202, para. 2 – "when Cody became president": Graduate Records/"Macdonald."

70. Page 202, para. 3 – "and report on the issues": Humphries, "Whitney" at 121-122.

71. Page 202, para. 3 – "took place two days later": *Report of the Royal Commission on the University of Toronto* (Toronto: L.K. Cameron, 1906) at 196.

72. Page 202, para. 3 – "for the next thirteen years": UTA/Graduate Records/"Robert Allan Pyne"/A73-0026/370(73).

73. Page 202, para. 3 – "was present and was in control": Humphries, "Whitney" at 121.

74. Page 202, para. 4 – "The commission met seventy-seven times": *Commission* at 196.

75. Page 202, para. 4 – "in Goldwin Smith's elegant dining room": Patricia H. Gaffney, ed., *Goldwin Smith Papers at Cornell University* (Ithaca, New York: John M. Olin Library, 1971) at 9.

76. Page 202, para. 4 – "between afternoon and evening meetings": "Macdonald memoirs" at 6.

77. Page 202, para. 4 – "including Harvard, Yale, and Princeton": Bliss, *Canadian Millionaire* at 165.

78. Page 202, para. 4 – "on proposals for the University's reform": The sole mention of it in the Commission's report is at xviii.

79. Page 203, para. 1 – "were his 'present views'": Flavelle to Whitney, January 19, 1906, "Bliss Papers."

80. Page 203, para. 1 – "the tentative views of the commission": Ibid.

81. Page 203, para. 1 – "to outline their conclusions": Commission Minutes, March 1, 1906, "Bliss Papers."

82. Page 203, para. 1 – "seated on the floor of the chamber": *Globe*, May 3, 1906 in "Bliss Papers"; "Macdonald memoirs" at 6.

83. Page 203, para. 1 – "published by the *World* in early March": *World*, March 12, 1906.

84. Page 203, para. 1 – "Charges of theft were brought": Bliss, *Canadian Millionaire* at 166; *Globe*, March 20, 1906.

85. Page 203, para. 2 – "permanently valuable document": *Globe*, April 7, 1906.

86. Page 203, para. 2 – "but for the Dominion": *World*, April 7, 1906.

87. Page 203, para. 2 – "with two exceptions": Flavelle to Smith, May 10, 1906, Goldwin Smith Papers, Cornell University.

88. Page 204, para. 1 – "20 members from the commission's 15": See Draft Act, s. 24 in *Commission* at 10 and *1906 Act*, s. 24.

89. Page 204, para. 1 – "be given to the University": *Globe*, May 3, 1906 in "Bliss Papers."

90. Page 204, para. 2 – "exists either in Great Britain or in North America": *Commission* at xviii-xix.

91. Page 204, para. 2 – "and financial control now vested in the State": Ibid. at xxi.

92. Page 204, para. 2 – "not intentionally inject poison into the Bill": *Globe*, May 3, 1906 in "Bliss Papers."

93. Page 204, para. 2 – "received royal assent on May 14, 1906": *1906 Act*. An amendment regarding veto power was defeated: see *Globe*, May 11, 1906 in "Bliss Papers."

94. Page 204, para. 3 – "and removable at the pleasure of the government": *Commission* at xxiii.

95. Page 204, para. 3 – "Only the president would be a member": *1906 Act*, sections 24 and 34.

96. Page 204, para. 3 – "in some the alumni would elect members to the board": *Commission* at 52-54. The University of Toronto Alumni Association wanted to elect three members, and the Toronto Branch four: see *Commission* at 156-160.

97. Page 204, para. 3 – "in the governance of the University": J.G. Hodgins, *Documentary History of Education in Ontario* (Toronto: Warwick Bros. & Rutter, 1895), v.17 at 313-314.

98. Page 204, para. 4 – "were members of the senate": *1906 Act*, s. 47.

99. Page 204, para. 4 – "as their representative": Ibid., s. 48.

100. Page 205, para. 1 – "with the president of the University as its chair": Ibid., ss. 73,76-78, and 88.

101. Page 205, para. 2 – "relieved of all teaching duties": *Commission* at xx and xxvi.

102. Page 205, para. 2 – "we have had divided authority": *Commission* at xviii.

103. Page 205, para. 2 – "eliminated entirely the position of vice-chancellor": Ibid. at xxvii.

104. Page 205, para. 2 – "on the recommendation of the president": *1906 Act*, s. 39.

105. Page 205, para. 2 – "to be made up of the deans and principals": C.B. Sissons, *A History of Victoria University* (University of Toronto Press, 1952) at 227-228.

106. Page 205, para. 2 – "through a body called the Caput": *1906 Act*, s. 85.

107. Page 205, para. 2 – "founded in the west and elsewhere": Michiel Horn, *Academic Freedom in Canada: A History* (University of Toronto Press, 1999) at 38 and 362-363.

108. Page 205, para. 3 – "what today we would call a multiversity": Clark Kerr, *The Uses of the University* (New York: Harper & Row, 1966).

109. Page 205, para. 3 – "would no longer be funded directly by the government": *Commission* at xxxi; Wallace, *History of the University of Toronto* at 170.

110. Page 205, para. 3 – "would also be the responsibility of the University": *Commission* at xxxi-xxxiii.

111. Page 205, para. 3 – "for medical education would no longer apply": Ibid.; Wallace, *History of the University of Toronto* at 171.

112. Page 205, para. 3 – "the acceptance of women into the faculty of medicine": *Commission* at xxxiv and 142 et seq.

113. Page 205, para. 3 – "to give up its monopoly on legal education": Ibid. at xxxiv-xxxv and 198-199; C. Ian Kyer and Jerome E. Bickenbach, *The Fiercest Debate: Cecil A. Wright, the Benchers, and Legal Education in Ontario, 1923-1957* (Toronto: The Osgoode Society, 1987) at 36.

114. Page 205, para. 4 – "Technical education was supported by the commission": *Commission* at xix; A.B. McKillop, *Matters of Mind: The University in Ontario 1791-1951* (University of Toronto Press, 1994) at 167-168.

115. Page 206, para. 1 – "of our Province and of the Dominion": *Commission* at 165-168.

116. Page 206, para. 1 – "of the Manufacturers' Association brief": McKillop, *Matters of Mind* at 167.

117. Page 206, para. 1 – "which only a modern university can supply": *Commission* at xix.

118. Page 206, para. 1 – "'mutually satisfactory and beneficial' relationship": Ibid. at xliv.

119. Page 206, para. 1 – "in close proximity to the University": Ibid. at xlvii.

120. Page 206, para. 1 – "an equal place with culture in the University": Ibid. at lix-lx.

121. Page 206, para. 1 – "in its way untrammelled by the union": Ibid. at lx.

122. Page 206, para. 2 – "and the federated bodies": Ibid. at xxiv. But they added astronomy, psychology, and education to the list of University subjects: see draft bill, s. 127 at 34.

123. Page 206, para. 2 – "such as philosophy and modern history": Flavelle to Whitney, January 19, 1906, "Bliss Papers."

124. Page 206, para. 2 – "that come from membership in a great University": *Commission* at xlvii-xlviii.

125. Page 206, para. 3 – "with Toronto's faculty of medicine": Ibid. at lviii. See also Flavelle to Whitney, February 8, 1906, "Bliss Papers"; Chapter 12 (1887).

126. Page 206, para. 3 – "and how a new building would be financed": See Flavelle to Osler, March 10, 1906 and Flavelle to Whitney, March 10, 1906, "Bliss Papers."

127. Page 206, para. 3 – "Trinity's demand for space was excessive": Ibid.

128. Page 206, para. 3 – "the value would increase in the near future": *Commission* at lviii.

129. Page 207, para. 1 – "by the new board of governors": Ibid. at lix.

130. Page 207, para. 1 – "he had failed in leadership at a critical time": Flavelle to Whitney, April 1, 1906, "Bliss Papers."

131. Page 207, para. 1 – "when the new university board was established": "Report form Trinity College Committee on Removal to Queen's Park, to be read at the adjourned meeting with the Committee of the Board of Governors of the University of Toronto, on 9th January, 1907," Trinity College Archives, 986-0008/004(10).

132. Page 207, para. 1 – "but nothing came of it": Flavelle to Smith, April 10, 1906, Goldwin Smith Papers, Cornell University.

133. Page 207, para. 1 – "separate duplicate lectures at Trinity was continued": *Commission* at lvii-lix.

134. Page 207, para. 2 – "in the vicinity of Queen's Park": *Commission* at lii.

135. Page 207, para. 2 – "a superintendent of buildings and grounds be appointed": Ibid. at liii.

136. Page 207, para. 2 – "on account of the growth of the city": Ibid. at 124.

137. Page 207, para. 2 – "had just been published": This book was originally published as *Tomorrow: A Peaceful Path to Real Reform* in 1898 and was republished as *Garden Cities of Tomorrow* in 1902: see F.J. Osborn, "Preface," in Ebeneezer Howard, *Garden Cities of Tomorrow* (Cambridge, Massachusetts: The M.I.T. Press, 1965) at 9.

138. Page 207, para. 2 – "away from the pollution of factories": Howard, *Garden Cities* at 52-55.

139. Page 207, para. 3 – "from Bloor Street down to the Biology Building": *Commission* at xxxvii.

140. Page 207, para. 3 – "had been brought underground in the 1880s": See *Varsity*, October 20, 1883.

141. Page 207, para. 3 – "for a botanical garden": *Commission* at xxxvi-xxxvii.

142. Page 207, para. 3 – "Such a garden, in fact, was developed": See John P.M. Court, "Out of the Woodwork: The Wood Family's Benefactions to Victoria College," *Canadian Methodist Historical Society Papers*, v. 11 (1997).

143. Page 207, para. 4 – "said little about graduate work": *Commission* at xxxviii-xxxix.

144. Page 208, para. 1 – "whereas Toronto had fewer than 10": Ibid. at 181-182.

145. Page 208, para. 1 – "than to develop basic knowledge": See Ibid. at xxxix regarding engineering.

146. Page 208, para. 1 – "for only another three years": Ibid.

147. Page 208, para. 1 – "and a major addition was completed by 1910": Robert H. Blackburn, *Evolution of the Heart: A History of the University of Toronto Library up to 1981* (University of Toronto Library, 1989) at 91-93 and 123.

148. Page 208, para. 1 – "is a properly equipped Museum": *Commission* at xl-xli.

149. Page 208, para. 1 – "extending the buildings in the distant future": Ibid.

150. Page 208, para. 2 – "were by their governments": Ibid. at liii-liv.

151. Page 208, para. 2 – "should be linked to succession duties": Ibid. at lv-lvi.

152. Page 208, para. 2 – "to the growth of the University requirements": Ibid. at lv.

153. Page 208, para. 2 – "the substantial sum of about $400,000 a year": Ibid. at lv.

154. Page 208, para. 2 – "violently against this form of taxation": "Macdonald memoirs" at 7; "Goldwin Smith," *University of Toronto Monthly*, v. 12 at 214-215.

155. Page 208, para. 2 – "which may be subject to change in the future": Goldwin Smith, *Reminiscences* (New York: The Macmillan Company, 1910) at 464. The incident in the 1890s when there was opposition to giving him an honorary degree because of his pro-American views – during which he was called a 'traitor' – may also have played a role: see Cook, "Smith" at 971. He got one in 1902.

156. Page 208, para. 2 – "a certain percentage of the revenues from succession duties": Gaffney, *Goldwin Smith Papers at Cornell University* at 11; Morris Bishop, *A History of Cornell* (Ithaca, New York: Cornell University Press, 1962) at 356.

157. Page 208, para. 2 – "without spelling out what that percentage would be": *Commission* at lv.

158. Page 208, para. 3 – "(averaging the previous three years)": Ibid. at lvi; Wallace, *History of the University of Toronto* at 182.

159. Page 208, para. 3 – "it be added to the endowment": Section 141 of the proposed act in *Commission* at 37.

160. Page 208, para. 3 – "the amount the University could receive": See Flavelle to Smith, May 10, 1906.

161. Page 208, para. 3 – "his wealthy wife had died the year before": *1906 Act*, s. 140.

162. Page 209, para. 1 – "about $700,000": B.E. Walker, "Succession Duties and University Finance," *University of Toronto Monthly*, v.22 at 11; Greenlee, *Sir Robert Falconer* at 167-168.

163. Page 209, para. 2 – "in the history of higher education in Ontario": McKillop, *Matters of Mind* at 166.

164. Page 209, para. 2 – "the greatest friend the institution has ever had": Humphries, *Honest* at 128.

165. Page 209, para. 3 – "had only one session with him": Loudon, "Memoirs," Section G, at 6. Wallace notes his run-in with Flavelle and Walker over the Victoria residence affair in *History of the University of Toronto* at 156-157. See also for this Loudon, "Memoirs" at 116 and 126; Greenlee, *Sir Robert Falconer* at 109. Discussion of the 1851 scholarship can be found in Loudon, "Memoirs," Section F at 15-16; Wallace, *History of the University of Toronto* at 155; *Report of the Commissioners Appointed to Inquire into and Report upon the matters referred to in a resolution of the Senate of the University of Toronto passed on the 20th day of January, 1905* (Toronto: L.K. Cameron, 1905); John Squair, "Alumni Organization at the University of Toronto," *University of Toronto Monthly*, v.22 at 107.

166. Page 209, para. 3 – "are wanting in president Loudon": Letter of March 3, 1906, cited in Bliss, *Canadian Millionaire* at 522 and Greenlee, *Sir Robert Falconer* at 112.

167. Page 209, para. 3 – "a pension equivalent to his full salary": Wallace, *History of the University of Toronto* at 162.

168. Page 209, para. 3 – "after the new board was in place": Bliss, *Canadian Millionaire* at 168.

169. Page 209, para. 3 – "Loudon, then 65, agreed": Letter of March 14, 1906, referred to in Loudon, "Memoirs," Section G at 12.

170. Page 209, para. 3 – "and moreover was having heart problems": Loudon, "Memoirs," Section G at 8-9.

171. Page 209, para. 3 – "and he could retire with some dignity": Ibid. at 10.

172. Page 209, para. 4 – "had become deputy minister of education": Wallace, *History of the University of Toronto* at 172.

173. Page 209, para. 4 – "and the editor of the *Globe*, J.A. Macdonald": Wallace, *History of the University of Toronto* at 172; Humphries, *Honest* at 128.

174. Page 209, para. 4 – "The chair of the previous board of trustees, John Hoskin": Wallace, *History of the University of Toronto* at 172.

175. Page 209, para. 4 – "the law firm of Osler, Hoskin and Harcourt": Curtis Cole, *Osler, Hoskin, and Harcourt: Portrait of a Partnership* (Toronto: McGraw-Hill Ryerson Ltd., 1995) at 30-31.

176. Page 209, para. 4 – "and after whom Hoskin Avenue is named": Eric Arthur, *Toronto: No Mean City*, 3rd edition (University of Toronto Press, 1986) at 282.

177. Page 209, para. 5 – "until a new president was appointed": Loudon, "Memoirs," Section G at 13. See also Resignation Correspondence, UTA/B72-0031/006(30).

178. Page 209, para. 5 – "the registrar of the University, James Brebner": UTA/Graduate Records/"James Brebner"/ A73-0026/036(47). See also Loudon, "Memoirs," Section G at 5. Loudon withdrew from chairing most senate committees because of conflict with Brebner: see Resignation Correspondence at 2-3.

179. Page 210, para. 1 – "or given a leave of absence": Loudon, "Memoirs," Section G at 14.

180. Page 210, para. 1 – "The board was not prepared to change Brebner's status": Ibid. at 19.

181. Page 210, para. 1 – "and accepted Loudon's resignation": James Grant Greenlee, "James Loudon," *DCB*, v.14 at 666; Resignation Correspondence at 4.

182. Page 210, para. 1 – "was appointed acting president": Wallace, *History of the University of Toronto* at 162.

183. Page 210, para. 1 – "learning the rudiments of golf": Loudon to Wrong, August 29, 1906, Wrong Papers, Fisher Rare Book Room.

184. Page 210, para. 1 – "He continued to live in his house on St George Street": 83 St. George: Loudon, "Memoirs," Section G at 14.

185. Page 210, para. 1 – "continually blamed others for the problems he had faced": Bliss, *Canadian Millionaire* at 141; Greenlee, *Sir Robert Falconer* at 108 and 355.

CHAPTER 19 – 1907 – ROBERT FALCONER CHOSEN

1. Page 211, para. 1 – "fourth president of the University of Toronto": "University Appointments," *University of Toronto Monthly*, v.7 at 163.

2. Page 211, para. 2 – "then a professor at Oxford, to become president": Including Chancellor Meredith and Samuel Blake: see Charles Humphries, *'Honest Enough to be Bold': The Life and Times of Sir James Pliny Whitney* (University of Toronto Press, 1985) at 129.

3. Page 211, para. 2 – "if he would be interested": Michael Bliss, *Sir William Osler* (University of Toronto Press, 1999) at 338.

4. Page 211, para. 2 – "and I am 15 years too old": Osler to Macallum, June 12, 1906, cited in Bliss, *Sir William Osler* at 338.

5. Page 211, para. 3 – "must of necessity have lost its keenness": Flavelle to Smith, May 8, 1906, in Research Notes of Michael Bliss.

6. Page 212, para. 1 – "rather than the scientific side": Michael Bliss, *A Canadian Millionaire* (Toronto: Macmillan of Canada, 1978) at 177.

7. Page 212, para. 1 – "to appoint him than go afield": Hutton to Walker, July 5, 1906, "Bliss Papers."

8. Page 212, para. 1 – "the view of the new Board of Governors": Walker to Van Hise, August 8, 1906, "Bliss Papers"; James G. Greenlee, *Sir Robert Falconer: A Biography* (University of Toronto Press, 1988) at 113.

9. Page 212, para. 1 – "and could scarcely be a new start": Smith to Walker, March 19, 1907, Fisher Rare Book Library, Manuscript Collection 1, Walker (Sir Edmund) papers, box 7, file 24.

10. Page 212, para. 2 – "an opportunity to look him over": Smith to Walker, August 15, 1906, James Greenlee President Search Committee note cards, card 33.

11. Page 212, para. 2 – "to take a place in another university": Schurman to Smith, October 18, 1906, "Greenlee Cards," card 42; Greenlee, *Sir Robert Falconer* at 114.

12. Page 212, para. 3 – "Houston recommended Chancellor William Meredith": Flavelle to Houston, May 9, 1906, "Bliss Papers."

13. Page 212, para. 3 – "George Wrong wanted Edmund Walker": Greenlee, *Sir Robert Falconer* at 112; Wrong to Walker, May 15, 1907, Fisher Rare Book Library, Manuscript Collection 1, Walker (Sir Edmund) papers, box 7, file 24; Wrong to Flavelle, May 4, 1906, "Bliss Papers."

14. Page 212, para. 3 – "his former roommate at University College, Canon Cody": D.C. Masters, *Henry John Cody: An Outstanding Life* (Toronto: Dundurn, 1995) at 76. Cody had been nominated by J.D. Swanson: see Greenlee, *Sir Robert Falconer* at 112.

15. Page 212, para. 3 – "which he did": Peter Oliver, *G. Howard Ferguson: Ontario Tory* (University of Toronto Press, 1977) at 12; Humphries, *Honest* at 247-248.

16. Page 212, para. 3 – "against the Roman Catholic Church": D.B. Macdonald, "Partial Memoirs of D. Bruce Macdonald," UTA/B83-1295 at 9.

17. Page 212, para. 4 – "there were at least ninety on their list": Greenlee, *Sir Robert Falconer* at 114.

18. Page 212, para. 4 – "(the Canadian secretary of the Rhodes Trust)": George Parkin: see Greenlee, *Sir Robert Falconer* at114.

19. Page 212, para. 4 – "a non-Canadian teaching at the University of Michigan": Mark Wenley was born in Scotland in 1861, educated at Glasgow and Edinburgh, and came to the University of Michigan in 1896, where he was professor and department head of philosophy until his death in 1929: *Who was Who in America, Vol. 1, 1897-1942* (Chicago: A.N. Maquis, 1943) at 1322; King to White of the Board, Sept 6, 1906, "Greenlee Cards," card 40.

20. Page 213, para. 1 – "Osler said he would think about it": Macdonald, "Memoirs" at 8.

21. Page 213, para. 1 – "neither by training nor disposition am I adapted to it": Osler to Hoskin, December 31, 1906, "Greenlee Cards," card 46; Greenlee, *Sir Robert Falconer* at 114.

22. Page 213, para. 2 – "in danger of losing our power of choice": Greenlee, *Sir Robert Falconer* at 114; Smith to Walker, January 10, 1907, Walker Papers, box 7, file 22.

23. Page 213, para. 2 – "full board of governors met on February 7, 1907": UTA/A73-0015/041(05), Office of the Secretary of the Board of Governors.

24. Page 213, para. 2 – "a report on the candidates": UTA/A73-0015/041/(06).

25. Page 213, para. 2 – "had met on earlier occasions": Greenlee, *Sir Robert Falconer* at 115; J.A. Macdonald to Walker, January 23, 1907, UTA/A73-0015/51(14).

26. Page 213, para. 2 – "and had just seen in Halifax": Greenlee, *Sir Robert Falconer* at 102. Both Falconer and Macdonald were interested in church union (between Presbyterians and Methodists).

27. Page 214, para. 1 – "Falconer, then just under 40": Falconer was born February 10, 1867 and would have been 39 years, 362 days old when the Board first considered his name: see Greenlee, *Sir Robert Falconer* at 5.

28. Page 214, para. 1 – "Flavelle's paper, the *News*": Greenlee, *Sir Robert Falconer* at 95.

29. Page 214, para. 1 – "the chair of New Testament literature by Knox College": Ibid. at 103.

30. Page 214, para. 1 – "received his divinity degree in 1892": Ibid. at 11, 19, 29, and 46.

31. Page 214, para. 1 – "several summers studying in Germany": Ibid. at 40-41.

32. Page 214, para. 1 – "the great biblical dictionaries then being prepared": Ibid. at 50, 65, and 67.

33. Page 214, para. 1 – "based on his scholarship": Ibid. at 67.

34. Page 214, para. 1 – "unanimously endorsed as principal of Pine Hill": Ibid. at 76.

35. Page 214, para. 2 – "contained only four names": UTA/A73-0015/041(06), Office of the Secretary of the Board of Governors.

36. Page 214, para. 2 – "dean of the teachers' college of the University of Missouri": "Greenlee Cards", card 5; Greenlee, *Sir Robert Falconer* at 114.

37. Page 214, para. 2 – "a British educational reformer at Manchester": Greenlee, *Sir Robert Falconer* at 114; Sir Michael Ernest Sadler (1861-1943) was educated in classics at Trinity College, Oxford. From 1895 to 1903 he

directed the governmental department of Education's office of special enquiries and reports. He then became professor of education at Manchester until 1911. See below for source.

38. Page 214, para. 2 – "became vice-chancellor of Leeds University": L.G. Wickham Legg and E.T. Williams, ed., *Dictionary of National Biography: 1941-1950* (Oxford University Press, 1959) at 753-4. Sadler went on to become master of University College, Oxford.

39. Page 214, para. 2 – "a good chance Sadler would accept": "Greenlee Cards," card 53.

40. Page 214, para. 2 – "the news that Sadler was the board's choice": J.A. Macdonald to Walker, Feb 23, 1907, "Greenlee Cards," card 52.

41. Page 214, para. 2 – "the appointment of a non-Canadian": Goldwin Smith to Walker, March 9, 1907, "Greenlee Cards," card 54. The note reads "disclosure in the *Globe* may do harm by stimulating opposition" – so Smith is speculating. There was no sign of any opposition in the *World* or the *Globe* in early March, 1907.

42. Page 214, para. 2 – "in the person of Dr Loudon": Smith to Walker, March 8, 1907, "Bliss Papers."

43. Page 214, para. 2 – "Sadler, however, turned down the offer": Sadler to Walker, March 15, 1907, "Greenlee Cards," card 56. The offer was renewed, but again turned down: see Sadler to Walker, April 16, 1907, "Greenlee Cards," card 57.

44. Page 214, para. 3 – "continually growing in intellectual development": G.H. Murray to Walker, April 6, 1907, "Greenlee Cards," card 68.

45. Page 214, para. 3 – "will go on growing": D. Macgillivary to Walker, April 6, 1907, "Greenlee Cards," card 62.

46. Page 214, para. 4 – "meet with the board on Monday": J.A. Macdonald to Walker, April 6, 1907, "Greenlee Cards," card 71.

47. Page 214, para. 4 – "still catch the ship leaving from Boston on Tuesday": Greenlee, *Sir Robert Falconer* at 117; "Greenlee Cards," card 60.

48. Page 214, para. 4 – "and at other times during the day": "Greenlee Cards," card 71.

49. Page 215, para. 1 – "unanimous approval of the board": Greenlee, *Sir Robert Falconer* at 117; F.C.A Jeanneret, "The Early Contribution of Sir Robert Falconer to Higher Education," UTA/B83-1230 at 11.

50. Page 215, para. 1 – "a distinct handicap": Humphries, *Honest* at 248, n17.

51. Page 215, para. 1 – "he would prove acceptable to the denominational colleges": Flavelle to Mackenzie Bowell, April 26, 1907, "Bliss Papers."

52. Page 215, para. 1 – "from St Francis Xavier, a Catholic college": "Falconer, Sir Robert," *Canadian Who's Who, 1936-1937* at 351.

53. Page 215, para. 1 – "subject to the agreement of the Pine Hill board": Greenlee, *Sir Robert Falconer* at 117.

54. Page 215, para. 2 – "(he later changed his view)": Ibid. at 118 and 121.

55. Page 215, para. 2 – "a rather serious leap in the dark": Ibid. at 118.

56. Page 215, para. 2 – "Falconer could become 'a great president'": Ibid.; "Greenlee Cards," card 85.

57. Page 215, para. 2 – "His inaugural address would be in September": Greenlee, *Sir Robert Falconer* at 121-122.

58. Page 215, para. 3 – "dignity and acceptability": W.S. Wallace, *A History of the University of Toronto* (University of Toronto Press, 1927) at 173.

59. Page 215, para. 3 – "during his tenure that the faculty of household science": James Loudon received approval (by Order-in-Council) from the Government to establish the faculty in 1905, but on the advice of the University solicitors this decision was left to the new Board of Governors, which approved their statute establishing Household Science on August 2, 1906: see minutes of the Board of Trustees, November 18, 1905 and February 24, 1906 and the minutes of the Board of Governors, August 2, 1906, UTA/A70-0024/reel 9.

60. Page 215, para. 3 – "and the faculty of education": See Chapter 20 (1908).

61. Page 215, para. 3 – "and engineering within the University": It came into being on June 15, 1906: see *An Act Respecting the University of Toronto and University College (1906)*, s. 6. See also C.R. Young, *Early Engineering Education at Toronto 1851-1919* (University of Toronto Press, 1958) at 129.

62. Page 215, para. 3 – "the establishment of all three of these faculties": See *Report of the Royal Commission on the University of Toronto* (Toronto: L.K. Cameron, 1906) at xxx-xxxi for School of Practical Science, xxxvi-xxxvii for Household Science, and li for Education (called Pedagogy).

63. Page 215, para. 4 – "also recommended a school of forestry": *Commission* at xxxv-xxxvi.

64. Page 215, para. 4 – "for its establishment for several years": Loudon to Harcourt, Oct. 29, 1902, quoted in James Loudon, "Memoirs of James Loudon," UTA/B72-0031/16(11), Section D at 3-4.

65. Page 215, para. 4 – "to establish such a school in Kingston": James Loudon, "Forestry and the University Question," *University of Toronto Monthly*, v.3 at 178; J.W.B Sisam, *Forestry Education at Toronto* (University of Toronto Press, 1961) at 9-12.

66. Page 215, para. 4 – "there was no money to hire a professor": Loudon, "Memoirs," Section D at 6 and 16; Sisam at 12.

67. Page 215, para. 4 – "with a staff of three": Sisam, *Forestry* at 19-20. Enrolment was, however, low – there were only 8 students in its first year – and the faculty was housed along with botany in a reconstructed home on the east side of Queen's Park Crescent: see Wallace, *History of the University of Toronto* at 221; Dorothy F. Forward, *The History of Botany at the University of Toronto* (Toronto: Botany Department, 1977) at 9, 13, and 15.

68. Page 215, para. 4 – "was appointed dean": "Dr. Fernow, Toronto's First Dean of Forestry," *University of Toronto Monthly*, v.23 at 300. One botanist, C.D. Howe (not the future cabinet minister), became the dean of forestry after Fernow and another, J.H. White, became "a pillar" of the forestry faculty: see Forward, *Botany* at 13.

69. Page 216, para. 1 – "the first such school in North America": The forestry school at Cornell was closed down in 1903 because the State withdrew funding when objections were made to using for forestry purposes the large block of land that Cornell had been given in the Adirondacks: see Waterman T. Hewett, *Cornell University: A History* (New York, The University Publishing Society, 1905), v.2 at 377-378.

70. Page 216, para. 1 – "the creator of modern forestry in the United States": "Dr. Fernow" at 300.

71. Page 216, para. 1 – "51 students enrolled in a four-year program": Sisam, *Forestry* at 26.

72. Page 216, para. 1 – "on the east side of St George Street": C.D. Howe, "The New Forestry Building," *University of Toronto Monthly*, v. 26 at 14.

73. Page 216, para. 1 – "to accommodate the new engineering building": Ian Montagnes, "They're Still Pushing Forestry Around," *Varsity Graduate* (May/June, 1982) at 17.

74. Page 216, para. 2 – "simply as a theological college": *Commission*, draft bill, s. 7(4) at 5; Lawrence Shook, *Catholic Post-Secondary Education for English-speaking Canada – A History* (University of Toronto Press, 1971) at 151: "Never once in the report itself, is St. Michael's mentioned as a prospective arts college in the new university."

75. Page 216, para. 2 – "which for the most part it was": Wallace, *History of the University of Toronto* at 136.

76. Page 216, para. 2 – "received degrees from the University of Toronto": Shook, *Catholic Post-Secondary* at 143, actually says "about 9."

77. Page 216, para. 2 – "such as Goldwin Smith": Ramsay Cook, "Smith, Goldwin," *DCB*, v. 13 at 972: "mistrusted Roman Catholicism everywhere."

78. Page 216, para. 2 – "and William Meredith": Humphries, *Honest* at 18-19.

79. Page 216, para. 2 – "their first objective was to produce priests": Shook, *Catholic Post-Secondary* at 150.

80. Page 216, para. 2 – "eligible for admission to the University": Ibid. at 149-50; Robert J. Scollard, *Dictionary of Basilian Biography* (Toronto: Basilian Press, published to the World Wide Web 1997 at www.basilian.org) at 1; Edmund J. McCorkell, *Father Henry Carr* (Toronto: Basilian Teacher, 1964) at 303.

81. Page 216, para. 2 – "modelled on European classical lines": McCorkell, *Father Henry Carr* at 303.

82. Page 216, para. 2 – "from entering the University of Toronto": Irene Poelzer, "Fr. Henry Carr and the Federated Model for Catholic Higher Education in Canada," *The Basilian Way of Life and Higher Education* (Saskatoon: St. Thomas More College, 1995) at 62; Shook, *Catholic Post-Secondary* at 150.

83. Page 216, para. 3 – "to the satisfaction of the Board": Shook, *Catholic Post-Secondary* at 152.

84. Page 216, para. 3 – "is not quite clear": Ibid.

85. Page 216, para. 3 – "It appears likely that Father Carr helped engineer it": Ibid.

86. Page 216, para. 3 – "who had open-minded views on Catholicism": Humphries, *Honest* at 7.

87. Page 217, para. 1 – "he received his degree in 1903": Scollard, *Dictionary of Basilian Biography.*

88. Page 217, para. 1 – "was one of Hutton's favourite honour classics students": Edmund J. McCorkell, *Henry Carr – Revolutionary* (Toronto: Griffin House, 1971) at 19.

89. Page 217, para. 1 – "while taking their college subjects at St Michael's": Shook, *Catholic Post-Secondary* at 152-53; McCorkell, *Henry Carr – Revolutionary* at 19; Henry Carr, "The very reverend J.R. Teefy C.S.B. L.L.D.," *Canadian Catholic Historical Association Report*, v.7 (1939/40), UTA/A83-0036/028 at 94.

90. Page 217, para. 1 – "with University College degrees": Shook, *Catholic Post-Secondary* at 150 and 153; McCorkell, *Henry Carr – Revolutionary* at 19; Carr, "Teefy" at 94.

91. Page 217, para. 1 – "was approved by the board as an arts college": Board of Governors Minutes, December 8, 1910, UTA/A70-0024 reel 9; Shook, *Catholic Post-Secondary* at 153.

92. Page 217, para. 1 – "was in 1911": Shook, *Catholic Post-Secondary* at 150 and 153.

93. Page 217, para. 1 – "of the three other arts colleges": McCorkell, *Henry Carr – Revolutionary* at 19.

94. Page 217, para. 1 – "University of Toronto degrees through St. Michael's": Carr, "Teefy" at 94.

95. Page 217, para. 1 – "taught the college subjects": *Moments: St. Michael's College – 125 years, University of Toronto – 150 years: An Exhibition of Historic Photographs* (Toronto: University of St. Michael's College Archives, 1978) at 18.

96. Page 217, para. 1 – "only when Carr Hall opened in 1954": Ibid.

97. Page 217, para. 1 – "of St Mary Street until 1959": Shook, *Catholic Post-Secondary* at 191.

98. Page 218, para. 1 – "had ambitious plans for the college": Scollard, *Dictionary of Basilian Biography*, Alexander Reford, "St. Michael's College at the University of Toronto, 1958-1978: The Frustrations of Federation," *CCHA, Historical Studies* 61 (1995) at 171-194. Carr was both president of the college and superior of the order at St. Michael's.

99. Page 218, para. 1 – "the greatest Catholic education centre in the world": Carr to Falconer, May 10, 1916, UTA/ A67-0007/038a.

100. Page 218, para. 2 – "Falconer's inauguration": At the time it was called an inauguration, today the common term is installation.

101. Page 218, para. 2 – "particularly warm applause when he received his": "Inauguration of President Falconer and Opening of the Physics Building," *University of Toronto Monthly*, v. 8 at 1-4.

102. Page 218, para. 2 – "in recognition of her nursing work during the war": *President's Report, 1919/20* at 11; UTA/ Graduate Records/"Edith Catherine Rayside"/A73-0026/373(71); James Coyne to Falconer, July 9, 1919, UTA/ A67-0007/62; Falconer to Rayside, October 14 and November 1, 1919, UTA/A67-0007/60a; Jean Bannerman, *Leading Ladies Canada* (Belleville: Mika Publishing Company, 1977) at 97, says the Master of Household Science Degree was "slightly incongruous." Edith Rayside was the great aunt of David Rayside: see Chapter 36 (1967). In 1923, Dr. Helen McMurchy became the first woman to receive an honorary M.D. in recognition of her achievements in the field of child welfare. It was not until 1925 that Caroline Macdonald received the first honorary LL.D. awarded to a woman by the University of Toronto. Macdonald, a 1901 graduate of University College, had been a YMCA missionary in Japan where she had worked in prisons and established a settlement house in Tokyo. For these services, she was decorated by the Japanese Emperor in 1924: UTA/Graduate Records/"Annie Caroline Macdonald"/A73-0026/259(90).

103. Page 219, para. 1 – "having been totally reconditioned in 1979-80": "Convocation Hall, University of Toronto," document prepared by Hart House Theatre, undated.

104. Page 219, para. 2 – "is a great university": Robert Falconer, "Inaugural Address of President Falconer," *University of Toronto Monthly*, v.8 at 6.

105. Page 219, para. 2 – "the central position of arts in a university": Ibid. at 7.

106. Page 219, para. 2 – "under the same academical roof": *Commission* at lx.

107. Page 219, para. 2 – "is not a technical school": Falconer, "Inaugural Address" at 8.

108. Page 219, para. 2 – "for the extension of the boundaries of knowledge": Ibid.

109. Page 219, para. 3 – "professors' salaries should be raised": Ibid. at 13-14.

110. Page 219, para. 3 – "would appeal to the ordinary citizen": Ibid. at 9.

111. Page 219, para. 3 – "The press gave its approval": Greenlee, *Sir Robert Falconer* at 124.

112. Page 219, para. 3 – "it is the University": Ibid. at 125.

113. Page 219, para. 4 – "or some combination of the three?": Ibid. at 136.

114. Page 219, para. 4 – "Falconer embraced all three concepts": Ibid. at 142-143.

115. Page 219, para. 4 – "but organically integrated university": Ibid. at 142.

116. Page 221, para. 1 – "are so manifest": Falconer, "Inaugural Address" at 10.

117. Page 221, para. 2 – "with Falconer as its president": Sara Z. Burke, *Seeking the Highest Good: Social Service and Gender at the University of Toronto 1888-1937* (University of Toronto Press, 1996) at 54 and 59. See also H.C.F. Wasteneys, "A History of the University Settlement of Toronto 1910-1958" (Ph.D. Social Work, U of T, 1975).

118. Page 221, para. 2 – "an Oxford-linked house in the east end of London": Burke, *Seeking the Highest Ground* at 8 et seq.

119. Page 221, para. 2 – "which was connected with the University of Chicago": Ibid. at 43.

120. Page 221, para. 2 – "conditions in the poorer areas of the city": Ibid. at 42-47.

121. Page 221, para. 2 – "they were permitted to participate": Ibid. at 59 and 72.

122. Page 221, para. 3 – "which would also address the YMCA's needs": Ibid. at 58.

123. Page 221, para. 3 – "conducted by university athletes": Ibid. at 41.

124. Page 221, para. 3 – "and elevate the other": Ibid. at 59.

125. Page 221, para. 3 – "maintain the University of Toronto connection": *Working Together: celebrating 85 years of community service.* (Toronto, 1985) .

126. Page 222, para. 1 – "you may possess": Burke, *Seeking the Highest Good* at 52-53.

127. Page 222, para. 1 – "I should be wise in keeping out of pulpits": Greenlee, *Sir Robert Falconer* at 119

128. Page 222, para. 1 – "their extension and correspondence schemes": Greenlee, *Sir Robert Falconer* at 154; Falconer to Earl Grey, April 27, 1910, UTA/A67-007/09.

129. Page 222, para. 1 – "he would put these ideas into practice": For example, enrolment for pass teachers' courses went from just under 100 in 1920 to just under 500 in 1930: J.A. Blyth, "A Foundling at Varsity: A History of the Division of University Extension, University of Toronto" (Privately published, 1976) at 204. The department of University Extension was established on July 1, 1920 under the direction of W.J. Dunlop.

130. Page 222, para. 2 – "had urged Falconer to take this step": Greenlee, *Sir Robert Falconer* at 189-190.

131. Page 222, para. 2 – "the first large missionary group left for China": Source misplaced.

132. Page 223, para. 1 – "or one of its affiliated medical colleges": Source misplaced.

133. Page 223, para. 1 – "were opening their doors to Chinese students": Greenlee, *Sir Robert Falconer* at 189-190.

134. Page 223, para. 1 – "the head tax continued to apply to them until 1917": Ibid. at 190-192.

135. Page 223, para. 2 – "the funds raised were inadequate": Ibid. at 192-195.

136. Page 223, para. 2 – "until after the First World War": Ibid. at 239-240.

CHAPTER 20 – 1908 – FALCONER'S EARLY YEARS

1. Page 224, para. 1 – "a new era in the history of a great University": *Globe*, September 27, 1907.

2. Page 224, para. 1 – "on how the building would be used": "Opening of the Physics Building", *University of Toronto Monthly*, v.8 at 4.

3. Page 224, para. 1 – "excelled by none on this continent": Ibid.

4. Page 224, para. 1 – "did not have an adequate observatory": C.A. Chant, *Astronomy in the University of Toronto: The David Dunlap Observatory* (University of Toronto Press, 1954) at 3.

5. Page 224, para. 2 – "was inadequate from many points of view": I.R. Dalton and G.D. Garland, "The Old Observatory's Noble History", *The Cannon*, October 31, 1980 at 5.

6. Page 224, para. 2 – "made observation of the heavens difficult": Chant, *Astronomy* at 12. The six-inch telescope had been built in 1881 in order to watch the transit of Venus across the sun, which would help determine the earth's distance from the sun: ibid. at 3.

7. Page 224, para. 2 – "made accurate magnetic reading difficult": The exception was Sundays, when the street cars were not operating. In 1897, however, the city allowed street cars to operate on Sundays and, as a result, that aspect of the observatory's work moved outside Toronto: see Dalton and Garland, "The Old Observatory" at 5.

8. Page 224, para. 2 – "now King's College Road": *Report of the Royal Commission on the University of Toronto* (Toronto: L.K. Cameron, 1906) at xli.

9. Page 225, para. 1 – "a new and larger meteorological building": Dalton and Garland, "The Old Observatory" at 5.

10. Page 225, para. 1 – "was relocated east of University College": Ibid.

11. Page 225, para. 1 – "used by engineering students for earth measurements": Ibid.; *University of Toronto Calendar*, 1908-1909 at 76-77.

12. Page 225, para. 2 – "Kingston Road in the east end of the city": James Loudon, "Memoirs of James Loudon", UTA/B72-0031/16, Section I at 9.

13. Page 225, para. 2 – "with his various small telescopes": Chant, *Astronomy* at 10.

14. Page 226, para. 1 – "in the history of astronomy at Toronto": Don Fernie to author, undated letter.

15. Page 226, para. 1 – "he obtained a PhD from Harvard": Helen S. Hogg, "Clarence Augustus Chant", *Proceedings of the Royal Society of Canada*, 3rd Series, v. 51 (1957) at 69.

16. Page 226, para. 1 – "he would remain its head until 1935": Elizabeth J. Allin, *Physics at the University of Toronto, 1843-1980* (Toronto: Department of Physics, 1981) at 9; Richard A. Jarrell, *The Cold Light of Dawn: A History of Canadian Astronomy* (University of Toronto Press, 1988) at 129; Hogg, "Chant" at 69-70.

17. Page 226, para. 1 – "continued as its editor for the next fifty years": Hogg, "Chant" at 70.

18. Page 226, para. 1 – "simply the history of the Department of Astronomy, University of Toronto": Jarrell, *Cold Light* at 127.

19. Page 226, para. 2 – "just north of the bridge": Chant, *Astronomy* at 10 et seq.

20. Page 226, para. 2 – "farther south, had objected": Ibid. at 11.

21. Page 226, para. 2 – "financing the construction of an observatory": Ibid. at 18-19 and 22.

22. Page 226, para. 2 – "the comet missed the earth by 10 million miles": Ibid. at 22-23.

23. Page 226, para. 2 – "a wealthy amateur astronomer, David Dunlap": Ibid. at 23-24.

24. Page 226, para. 2 – "the second largest in the world": Ibid. at 39-40, 53, 62; Hogg, "Chant" at 70. The largest was the 100-inch telescope placed in 1917 at Mount Wilson Observatory in California, which retained that title until a 200-inch telescope was installed at Mount Palomar in 1947. See www.mtwilson.edu/History/ca188/cal0288.html.

25. Page 226, para. 3 – "a delegation of ministers from various denominations": These were Albert Carman, general superintendent of the Methodist Church; William McLaren of the Presbyterian Knox College; Elmore Harris, the pastor of Walmer Road Baptist Church; and N.W. Hoyles, a lay member of the Board of Wycliffe and a prominent lawyer: see James G. Greenlee, *Sir Robert Falconer: A Biography* (University of Toronto Press, 1988) at 128.

26. Page 226, para. 3 – "in its Oriental studies department": Greenlee, *Sir Robert Falconer* at 127 et seq.

27. Page 227, para. 1 – "and lectured on the English Bible at University College": Ibid. at 128-129.

28. Page 227, para. 1 – "satisfied with things as they were being taught": "Proceedings of Committee", February 23, 1909, UTA/A83-0036/006 at 37-38.

29. Page 227, para. 2 – "took up the cause of the delegation": Greenlee, *Sir Robert Falconer* at 129.

30. Page 227, para. 2 – "raising the same issues as the earlier delegation": Blake to Hoskin, December 22, 1908, UTA/A83-0036/026; Blake to Macdonald, March 16, 1909, Fisher Rare Book Library, Manuscript Collection 1, Walker (Sir Edmund) papers.

31. Page 227, para. 2 – "any nation has given to man": Blake to Hoskin at 6.

32. Page 227, para. 2 – "are mere myths and allegories": Ibid. at 7.

33. Page 228, para. 1 – "in the classes of this department": Ibid. at 5.

34. Page 228, para. 1 – "as the defence of the Bible": Blake to Macdonald, March 16, 1909 at 6.

35. Page 228, para. 1 – "a reign of lawlessness and anarchy": Ibid. at 11.

36. Page 228, para. 1 – "Scopes 'monkey' trial of 1925 in the United States": *Tennessee vs. John Thomas Scopes* was a 1925 trial over the "Butler Law" of Tennessee, which prohibited the teaching of 'evolutionary theory' in any state supported school, college, or university. Scopes was fined $100, and the ACLU appealed to the Tennessee Supreme Court, which did not overturn the verdict and declared the Butler Law constitutional. It was not repealed until 1968: see Paul K. Conklin, *When All the Gods Trembled: Darwin, Scopes, and American Intellectuals* (Lanham, Maryland: Rowman and Littlefield, 1998); Ray Ginger, *Six Days or Forever: Tennessee v. John Thomas Scopes* (London: Oxford University Press, 1974); Edward J. Larson, *Summer for the Gods: The Scopes Trial and America's Continuing Debate Over Science and Religion* (New York: Basic Books, 1997).

37. Page 228, para. 2 – "to investigate the allegations": February 11, 1909 – see Greenlee, *Sir Robert Falconer* at 130.

38. Page 228, para. 2 – "avoid touching them": "Proceedings of Committee" at 9.

39. Page 228, para. 2 – "for the purpose of getting at the truth": Ibid.

40. Page 228, para. 2 – "probably fifty per cent of the work": Ibid. at 11.

41. Page 228, para. 2 – "the greatest code of Ethics known to the world": *Report of the Special Committee to the Board of Governors University of Toronto Adopted 20th December, 1909* (University of Toronto Press, 1909) at 5-6. Teefy dissented in part, according to the minutes of the board of December 20, 1909, but it is not clear on what point.

42. Page 228, para. 3 – "a victory of sorts for academic freedom": Michiel Horn, *Academic Freedom in Canada: A History* (University of Toronto Press, 1999) at 36.

43. Page 228, para. 3 – "the domain of Theology contrary to the statute": *Report* at 6.

44. Page 228, para. 3 – "stayed out of the controversy": Greenlee, *Sir Robert Falconer* at 134.

45. Page 229, para. 1 – "knocked our hats off": Ibid. at 133.

46. Page 229, para. 2 – "contain not history but tradition": Blake to Macdonald at 4.

47. Page 229, para. 2 – "and the chairman of the board of Victoria": Michael Bliss, *A Canadian Millionaire* (Toronto: Macmillan of Canada, 1978) at 200-202; Greenlee, *Sir Robert Falconer* at 130-31; Horn, *Academic Freedom* at 35-37; Margaret Prang, *N.W. Rowell: Ontario Nationalist* (University of Toronto Press, 1975) at 70-79.

48. Page 229, para. 2 – "and the board held firm": C.B. Sissons, *A History of Victoria University* (University of Toronto Press, 1952) at 237. Conference also upheld Jackson: see ibid. at 239.

49. Page 229, para. 2 – "a relatively liberal view of religion": Greenlee, Sir *Robert Falconer* at 129-130; Marguerite Van Die, *An Evangelical Mind: Nathanael Burwash and the Methodist Tradition in Canada 1839-1918* (Montreal: McGill-Queen's University Press, 1989) at 104 and 112.

50. Page 229, para. 2 – "The Truth Shall Make You Free": Van Die, *An Evangelical Mind* at 128.

51. Page 229, para. 3 – "a separate college for women in the University": Senate Minutes, November 8, 1907.

52. Page 229, para. 3 – "argued for such a college in the early 1880s": See Chapter 10 (1883).

53. Page 229, para. 3 – "more than 1,000 students at University College alone": George M. Wrong, "Report of the Committee Appointed to Enquire in Regard to a Possible College for Women", March 10, 1909, UTA/A67-0007/026; *President's Report 1908/09* at 9.

54. Page 229, para. 3 – "would obviously reduce the numbers": George Wrong, "A College for Women", *University of Toronto Monthly*, v. 10 at 5.

55. Page 229, para. 3 – "had almost 5,000 women students": Ibid.

56. Page 229, para. 4 – "and at Harvard and McGill": Paula J.S. LaPierre, "The First Generation: The Experience of Women University Students in Central Canada" (Ph.D. Thesis, University of Toronto, 1993) at 107. Women's colleges were first established at Cambridge's Newnham College in 1871, Oxford's Lady Margaret Hall in 1879, and at Harvard in 1879 (Harvard Annex, subsequently renamed Radcliffe in 1894): see Elizabeth Seymour Eschbach, *The Higher Education of Women in England and America, 1865-1920* (New York: Garland, 1993) at 72-75 and 109.

57. Page 229, para. 4 – "were dominated by men": Wrong, "Report."

58. Page 229, para. 4 – "in its chosen sphere of labor": Ibid.

59. Page 230, para. 1 – "is to fit her for this sphere": Undated letter drafted, as cited in LaPierre, "The First Generation" at 109; UTA/B83-1288, Wrong Papers; see also Wrong, "College" at 7.

60. Page 230, para. 1 – "related specifically to 'good housekeeping'": Memo from Wrong, as cited in LaPierre, "The First Generation" at 108; Wrong Papers, "Memorandum for the Consideration of the Committee on the College for Women": see also Kerrie Johan Kennedy, "Womanly Work: The Introduction of Household Science at the University of Toronto" (M.A. Thesis, Graduate Department of Education, University of Toronto, 1995) at 55.

61. Page 230, para. 1 – "women's special needs": Wrong, "College" at 7.

62. Page 230, para. 1 – "in its first few years of operation": The Faculty did, however, have a fair number of "non-degree seeking occasional students, and educational students who were seeking specialist status in household science": see Kennedy, "Womanly Work" at 56-57.

63. Page 230, para. 2 – "had been established in 1901": See Dorothy N.R. Jackson, *A Brief History of Three Schools* (Toronto: T. Eaton Co. Ltd., 1953); Heather Murray, *Working in English: History, Institution, Resources* (University of Toronto Press, 1996); and Heather Murray, "Making the Modern: Twenty Five Years of the Margaret Eaton School of Literature and Expression", *Essays in Theatre*, v. 10 (November, 1991); David R. Keys, "The Margaret Eaton School of Literature and Expression", *University of Toronto Monthly* (March, 1907) at 124; John Byl, "The Margaret Eaton School, 1901-1942: Women's Education in Elocution, Drama, and Physical Education" (Ph.D. Thesis, State University of New York at Buffalo, 1992); John Byl, "Margaret Eaton School 1901-1942 Finder's Guide".

64. Page 230, para. 2 – "and other faculty members": Murray, *English* at 46 and 63n7; Murray, "Modern" at 42-43.

65. Page 230, para. 2 – "the year after he arrived": Murray, "Modern" at 58.

66. Page 230, para. 2 – "at its Annesley Hall residence": Murray, "Modern" at 42.

67. Page 230, para. 2 – "a prototype for a women's college": Murray, *English* at 49.

68. Page 230, para. 2 – "the Frenchman François Delsarte": Ibid. at 63. The proponent of modern dance, Isadora Duncan, came out of the movement: ibid. at 52.

69. Page 230, para. 2 – "and vocal expression": Ibid. at 51, quoting the founder of the school, Emma Scott Raff.

70. Page 230, para. 2 – "professional and practical education for women": Ibid. at 49, citing *Calendar* of 1908-09. James Mavor's daughter, Dora Mavor, studied drama there after several unsuccessful attempts in an arts program at the University. She taught at the school for a period of time and later, as Dora Mavor Moore, became influential in developing the theatre in Canada. See David Gardner, "Dora Mavor Moore", *Theatre History in Canada*, v.1 (Spring 1980) at 5; Paula Sperdakos, "Dora Mavor Moore: Before the New Play Society", *Theatre History in Canada*, v. 10 (Spring 1989) at 43 and 47; Jackson at 35; Murray, *English* at 57.

71. Page 230, para. 3 – "to construct a building for the school": Murray, "Modern" at 44.

72. Page 230, para. 3 – "just south of Bloor Street": Jackson, *Three Schools* at 8-9; Murray, *English* at 47.

73. Page 230, para. 3 – "when the street was widened": Murray, "Modern" at 44; Murray, *English* at 61.

74. Page 230, para. 3 – "established the previous year": Jackson, *Three Schools* at 29; Murray, *English* at 47-48, 54, and 61.

75. Page 230, para. 4 – "the establishment of a separate college": Wrong, "Report"; "Report of the Committee Appointed to Enquire in Regard to a Possible College for Women", *University of Toronto Monthly,* v.9 at 286.

76. Page 230, para. 4 – "28 votes to 8": "Report of the Committee" at 286; UTA/A68-0012, roll 5 (Senate Minutes, April 16, 1909).

77. Page 230, para. 4 – "having earlier expressed cautious approval": The Women's Club expected that the proposed college would "be placed on an equality with the men's colleges in the University": see "Committee of the University Women's Club appointed to confer with the Committee of the Senate of the University of Toronto on the proposed College for Women", UTA/A67-0007/026. See also M. Jennifer Brown, *"A Disposition to Bear the Ills... ": Rejection of a Separate College by University of Toronto Women* (Toronto: The Women in Canadian History Project, 1977) at 13; Anne Rochon Ford, *A path not strewn with roses: One Hundred Years of Women at the University of Toronto, 1884-1984* (University of Toronto Press, 1985) at 43; and Alyson E. King, "The Experience of the Second Generation of Women Students at Ontario Universities" (Ph.D. Thesis, University of Toronto, 1999) at 130-132.

78. Page 230, para. 4 – "was now strongly opposed to the idea": "Report of the Committee Appointed to Consider the Report of the Senate in Regard to a Possible College for Women", UTA/A67-0007/026.

79. Page 230, para. 4 – "also rejected the report": Brown, *"A Disposition to Bear the Ills"* at 1.

80. Page 231, para. 2 – "'coeducation which exists' at the University": "Reply of the Alumnae", *University of Toronto Monthly,* v. 9 at 289 and 291.

81. Page 231, para. 2 – "at certain American universities": Ibid. at 290, regarding the curtailment of Harvard library and laboratory privileges of Radcliffe students. See also Elizabeth Seymour Eschbach, *The Higher Education of Women in England and America, 1865-1920* (New York: Garland, 1993) at 77; Eugenia Kaledin, *The Education of Mrs. Henry Adams* (Philadelphia: Temple University Press, 1981) at 45-50.

82. Page 231, para. 2 – "there were high school jobs in that field": Mabel Cartwright, "A College for Women", *University of Toronto Monthly,* v.10 at 2.

83. Page 231, para. 2 – "but not classics or mathematics": Ibid.

84. Page 231, para. 2 – "to mistrust 'special courses' for women": Ibid. at 4; "Reply of the Alumnae" at 290.

85. Page 231, para. 2 – "that was the end of it": Minutes of United Alumnae Committee", May 22, 1909, UTA/B65-0030/01(01); University Women's Club report of May 18, 1910.

86. Page 231, para. 2 – "was now effectively dead": "Minutes of United Alumnae Committee", December 3, 1909. The issue did however linger for another year: see Burke to Friedland, May 28, 1999.

87. Page 231, para. 2 – "the arts program for the 1909-10 academic year": Kennedy, "Womanly Work" at 57.

88. Page 232, para. 1 – "access to the president's office": "Minutes of United Alumnae Committee", October 28, 1909.

89. Page 232, para. 1 – "the rejection of Wrong's report by the alumnae": "Minutes of University College Alumnae Association", May 1909, UTA/A69-0011/014. She gave the opening speech and seconded the motion disassociating the alumnae from the report.

90. Page 232, para. 1 – "that she herself obviously enjoyed": UTA/Graduate Records/ "Patterson, Annie"/A73-0026/358(15).

91. Page 232, para. 2 – "prepared on these and other subjects": See for example, "Report of Committee on Dean of Women", UTA/A67-0007/026.

92. Page 232, para. 2 – "in teaching as well as in learning?": Cartwright, "College" at 3.

93. Page 233, para. 1 – "entirely controlled and directed by men": Saint Hilda's *Chronicle*, Lent, 1908 at 3, as cited in Brown, *"A Disposition to Bear the Ills"* at 9.

94. Page 233, para. 1 – "the faculty of education that excluded women?": UTA/A67-0007/010 (Helen Macmurchy).

95. Page 233, para. 2 – "by each of the alumnae associations": Circular letter from United Alumnae Committee, June 30, 1910, UTA/B65-0030/001(05).

96. Page 233, para. 2 – "was elected by the medical alumni": See Chapter 12 (1887).

97. Page 233, para. 2 – "she was awarded an honorary LLD by the University": UTA/Graduate Records/"Gertrude Lawler"/A73-0026/221(92).

98. Page 233, para. 2 – "head of English at Havergal College": Murray, *English* at 49 and 61; UTA/Graduate Records/ "Charlotte Ross"/A73-0026/386(97).

99. Page 233, para. 3 – "to over 4,000 by 1910": Greenlee, *Sir Robert Falconer* at 165; Robert Falconer, "Development in the University of Toronto", *University of Toronto Monthly*, v. 13 at 213.

100. Page 233, para. 3 – "and Dalhousie fewer than 500": In 1914, McGill had approximately 2,500 students: see Stanley Brice Frost, *McGill University: For The Advancement of Learning* (Montreal: McGill-Queen's University Press, 1980), v.2 at 89. In 1909-10, Queen's had 1,517 students: see Hilda Neatby, *Queen's University: : vol. 1, 1841-1917* (Kingston: McGill-Queen's University Press, 1978) at 334n48. In 1910-1911, Dalhousie had 412 students: see P.B. Waite, *The Lives of Dalhousie University* (Montreal: McGill-Queen's University Press, 1994), v.1 at 294. By contrast, Harvard had 5,265 students in 1908-09: see Samuel Eliot Morison, *The Development of Harvard University since the Inauguration of President Eliot, 1869-1929* (Cambridge: Harvard University Press, 1930) at xc. Yale had 3,306 students in 1907-08: see *Report of the President of Yale University with the Deans and Directors of its Several Departments for the Academic Year 1907-1908* at 14.

101. Page 233, para. 3 – "to an average mark of 60 per cent": See Falconer, "Development" at 213: "the requirement of matriculation rose in 1909 from 33% to 40% on each paper; in 1911 to 40% with an average of 50% on all the papers; and in 1912 to 40% with an average of 60%". See also Greenlee, *Sir Robert Falconer* at 169.

102. Page 233, para. 3 – "whereupon enrolment levelled off": Greenlee, *Sir Robert Falconer* at 170.

103. Page 233, para. 3 – "for entrance to the University of Toronto": Greenlee, *Sir Robert Falconer* at 170 et seq.; Falconer, "Development" at 213.

104. Page 233, para. 3 – "and an honours degree four": Greenlee, *Sir Robert Falconer* at 170.

105. Page 233, para. 3 – "to devote more time to graduate work": Ibid. at 173.

106. Page 233, para. 3 – "for all applicants to the University of Toronto until 1931": See Robin S. Harris, *Quiet Evolution: A Study of the Educational System of Ontario* (University of Toronto Press, 1967) at 51.

107. Page 234, para. 1 – "experiencing a $40,000 deficit": Greenlee, *Sir Robert Falconer* at 164; Falconer, "Development" at 219.

108. Page 234, para. 1 – "succession duty income was limited to $500,000": Ibid.

109. Page 234, para. 2 – "to build a national university": Greenlee, *Sir Robert Falconer* at 156-7.

110. Page 234, para. 3 – "to recruit the most desirable candidates": Ibid. at 182.

111. Page 234, para. 3 – "begins at a low scale and advances very slowly": Falconer, "Development" at 219.

112. Page 234, para. 3 – "who had reached the age of 70": Horn, *Academic Freedom* at 289. The University was authorized by the government in 1891 to start a retirement fund for each staff member. It was compulsory for those appointed after that date. Staff members would contribute according to their salaries. The higher the salary, the more a person would contribute. The university would provide 6% interest on that sum, which was a generous interest rate at the time: see e-mail from H.V. Nelles to Friedland, February 14, 2001, citing E.P. Neufeld, *The Canadian Financial System* at 562-563. This sum could not be touched while the person was employed by the University. When the person retired, the sum would be payable to him. If he died in office, it would be payable to his estate. This scheme would still have been in existence when the Carnegie scheme came into operation: see "Copy of an Order in Council approved by His Honor the Lieutenant Governors the 20th day of November A.D. 1891", with attached regulations dated November 19, 1891 (documents forwarded by John Slater). The Carnegie scheme provided for yearly payments and not a lump sum, as the 1891 scheme did. The board of governors adopted a resolution requesting admission on June 11, 1908: see Order-in-council approved by Premier Whitney and the Ontario legislature on March 5 and 8, 1909, respectively. The University admitted to the allowance system by the Carnegie foundation on June 4, 1909: see Carnegie Foundation for the Advancement of Teaching, *Fourth Annual Report of the President and of the Treasurer* (New York, 1909) at 34. McGill and Dalhousie were admitted in 1906.

113. Page 234, para. 3 – "the requirement that half the board be ministers": Sissons, *Victoria* at 267.

114. Page 234, para. 4 – "appointments for approval by the board": *An Act Respecting the University of Toronto and University College (1906)*, Section 88.

115. Page 234, para. 4 – "or abroad to interview candidates": Greenlee, *Sir Robert Falconer* at 180.

116. Page 234, para. 4 – "who had completed their studies in Britain": Ibid.

117. Page 234, para. 4 – "keen on persons who had studied in Britain": Ibid.

118. Page 234, para. 4 – "four possible candidates from Britain": Mavor to Falconer, July 20, 1911, UTA/A67-0007/021.

119. Page 234, para. 4 – "a new prospect, L. Bernstein Naymier": That is how Namier described himself at the time: see letter from Namier, dated June 14, 1911, UTA/A67-0007/021.

120. Page 235, para. 1 – "later known as Louis Namier?": For Namier, see Julia Namier, *Lewis Namier: A Biography* (London: Oxford University Press, 1971); see also Linda Colley, *Lewis Namier* (London: Weidenfeld and Nicolson, 1989).

121. Page 235, para. 1 – "we have had in economics and history for some years": Smith to Falconer, July 5, 1911, UTA/A67-0007/021.

122. Page 235, para. 1 – "worried about Namier's spoken English": Cannon to Lloyd, June 14, 1911, UTA/A67-0007/021.

123. Page 235, para. 1 – "from Poland some five years earlier": Namier, *Lewis Namier* at xv.

124. Page 235, para. 1 – "the safer choice": Lloyd to Mavor, July 12, 1911, UTA/A67-0007/021.

125. Page 235, para. 1 – "indistinct articulation strongly developed": Mavor to Falconer, July 20, 1911.

126. Page 235, para. 1 – "who accepted the position": Lloyd to Falconer, August 4, 1911, UTA/A67-0007/021.

127. Page 235, para. 2 – "decided to remain there for family reasons": Bell to Wrong, July 15, 1911, UTA/A67-0007/021.

128. Page 235, para. 2 – "colourless or second-rate successor": Bell to Wrong, July 26, 1911, UTA/A67-0007/021.

129. Page 235, para. 2 – "for which Falconer had asked": Falconer to Walker, September 8, 1911, Ibid.

130. Page 235, para. 2 – "who by his broken accent constantly proclaims it": Flavelle to Falconer, September 10, 1911, Flavelle Papers, Box 38, Queen's University Archives. Although Michael Bliss came across a couple of anti-Semitic remarks by Flavelle in his study of Flavelle, they were made at a time when he was closely associated with Goldwin Smith, whose anti-Jewish views are well known: see Ramsay Cook, "Goldwin Smith", *DCB,* v. 13 at 972. There is no evidence that Falconer ever expressed any anti-Semitic views and in one letter in the Namier file he wrote that "the fact of his being a Jew has no influence one way or another with us": see Falconer to Hull, September 14, 1911, UTA/A67-0007/021.

131. Page 235, para. 2 – "The other candidate, Hodder Williams, was appointed": *President's Report, 1911/12* at 8.

132. Page 235, para. 2 – "appointed a lecturer in the law faculty in 1930": See Chapter 26 (1931).

CHAPTER 21 – 1909 – EDUCATION, MEDICINE, AND THE MUSEUM

1. Page 236, para. 1 – "the greatest economic boom in its history": Robert Bothwell, Ian Drummond and John English, *Canada, 1900-1945* (University of Toronto Press, 1987) at 55. The chapter is entitled "The Great Boom of 1900-1913".

2. Page 236, para. 1 – "with the help of provincial capital grants": See Chapter 18 (1905).

3. Page 236, para. 2 – "in developing mines": Robert Falconer, "The Needs of the University of Toronto", *University of Toronto Monthly*, v.9 at 139.

4. Page 236, para. 2 – "Many of these leaders would come out of engineering": Philip A. Lapp, "The Nation Builders" in Robin S. Harris and Ian Montagnes, ed., *Cold Iron and Lady Godiva: Engineering Education at Toronto 1920-1972* (University of Toronto Press, 1974.)

5. Page 236, para. 2 – "to be used for steam, gas, and hydraulic work": Falconer, "Needs" at 141; Robert W. Angus, "The New Laboratories of the University of Toronto, for Steam, Gas, and Hydraulic Work", *Applied Science*, (February, 1910) at 7-8; C.R. Young, *Early Engineering Education at Toronto 1851-1919* (University of Toronto Press, 1958) at 132. It was designed to be hidden. The architects – once again Darling and Pearson – realized that it would be difficult to make a building that contained steam engines and other heavy equipment look attractive, so it was planned eventually to attach a more attractive building to the west side of it: see Angus, "The New Laboratories" at 8-9.

6. Page 236, para. 2 – "from a three to a four-year program": Falconer, "Needs" at 141; Young, *Early Engineering Education* at 132, links both the construction of the building and the introduction of the four-year course to the 1909-10 academic year. The three-year diploma was eliminated: see Richard White, *The Skule Story: The University of Toronto Faculty of Applied Science and Engineering 1873-2000* (University of Toronto Press, 2000) at 68.

7. Page 236, para. 2 – "brought out from time to time": White, *Skule Story* at 74-77.

8. Page 237, para. 1 – "the corner of Bloor Street and Spadina Avenue in 1910": H.T.J. Coleman, "The University Schools", *University of Toronto Monthly*, v.10 at 396-397.

9. Page 237, para. 1 – "had been established in late 1906": J. George Hodgins, *The Establishment of Schools and Colleges in Ontario 1792-1910*, v. 3 (Toronto: King's Printer, 1910) at 272.

10. Page 237, para. 1 – "on the recommendation of the royal commission": *Report of the Royal Commission on the University of Toronto* (Toronto: L.K. Cameron, 1906) at li; W.S. Wallace, *A History of the University of Toronto* (University of Toronto Press, 1927) at 219.

11. Page 237, para. 1 – "to supplement each other": *Commission* at li.

12. Page 237, para. 1 – "still the northern end of the city": *Commission* at li; "Report of the Committee re Faculty of Education, University of Toronto, October 16, 1906", UTA/A83-0036/007 at 2.

13. Page 237, para. 1 – "conduct educational experiments": "Report of the Committee" at 5.

14. Page 237, para. 1 – "the superintendent of education, John Seath": Ian Dowbiggin, "Seath, John", *DCB*, v.14 at 918.

15. Page 237, para. 1 – "Normal School in Hamilton to the University of Toronto": *Commission* at 141. He became

the superintendent in May, 1906 and so at the time of his submission he was actually inspector of high schools. Loudon had also been urging that this be done: see James Loudon, "Memoirs of James Loudon", UTA/B72-0031/16(11), Section G at 6.

16. Page 237, para. 1 – "a shortage of high school teachers in the province": "Report of the Committee" at 1-2.

17. Page 237, para. 1 – "to the new faculty of education in October 1907": Hodgins, *Establishment of Schools and Colleges* at 272.

18. Page 237, para. 1 – "were used for practice teaching": Coleman, "Schools" at 396; Wallace, *History of the University of Toronto* at 219; Hutton to "Dear Sir", May 2, 1907, UTA/A83-0036/007. Robin Harris identifies the "Sir" as "W. Wilkinson, Sec'y S B", but it is not clear who this is.

19. Page 238, para. 1 – "and a large model school of more than 1,000 students": Recommendations of the Special Committee on the Organization of the Faculty of Education, "Historical Sketch" (undated), UTA/A83-0036/007; Jack Batten, *UTS: 75 Years of Excellence* (Toronto: University of Toronto Schools, 1985) at 2.

20. Page 238, para. 1 – "both boys and girls": In separate wings: see "Historical Sketch".

21. Page 238, para. 1 – "University of Toronto Schools (UTS)": At first it was simply referred to as the University Schools: see Coleman, "Schools" at 396; H.J. Coleman, "The Faculty of Education", *University of Toronto Monthly*, v.11 at 29; Batten, *UTS* at 4.

22. Page 238, para. 1 – "and the higher grades of a primary school": "Report of a Special Committee on the Organization of the Faculty of Education", May 6, 1910, UTA/A83-0036/007.

23. Page 238, para. 1 – "what is to be the leading Secondary School": Undated minutes of the United Alumnae Committee, UTA/B65-0030/001(03).

24. Page 238, para. 1 – "because there are no girls there to teach": McMurchy to Falconer, June 29, 1910, UTA/A67-0007/010.

25. Page 238, para. 1 – "to include women": Falconer to McMurchy, May 13, 1910, UTA/A67-0007/010.

26. Page 238, para. 1 – "almost seventy years later": Jill Rutherford, "Co-Education Debated", *UTS Alumni Association Newsletter* (March, 1999) at 15.

27. Page 238, para. 2 – "who was strongly favoured by the government": Seath to Hutton, November 14, 1906, UTA/A83-0036/007 at 8.

28. Page 238, para. 2 – "having received a BA in the early 1890s": "William Pakenham", in Henry James Morgan, ed., *Canadian Men and Women of the Time* (Toronto: William Briggs, 1912) at 879.

29. Page 238, para. 2 – "to take examinations for education degrees": See Chapter 16 (1897).

30. Page 238, para. 2 – "would remain dean until 1934": "William Pakenham"; Seath to Hutton at 8; UTA/Graduate Records/"Pakenham, William"/A73-0026/354(88).

31. Page 238, para. 2 – "would serve until 1922": Coleman, "Faculty" at 30; Wallace, *History of the University of Toronto* at 220; Batten, *UTS* at 6-7.

32. Page 238, para. 3 – "both the University of Toronto and Queen's University": "Extract from Report to the Minister of Education From the Superintendent", UTA/A83-0036/007. According to Falconer to Pyne, May 15, 1917, UTA/A83-0036/007, this report was completed in the spring of 1917.

33. Page 238, para. 3 – "was not attracting enough students": "Extract" at 1.

34. Page 238, para. 3 – "and it had inadequate facilities": Ibid. at 2-5.

35. Page 238, para. 3 – "no gymnasium connected with the model school": Ibid. at 2.

36. Page 238, para. 3 – "in which practice teaching was done": Ibid. at 8.

37. Page 239, para. 1 – "and in factories during the war": Falconer to Pyne, May 15, 1917, refers to "national service".

38. Page 239, para. 1 – "threatened to withdraw financial support": Pyne to Board of Governors, July 23, 1917, UTA/A83-0036/007.

39. Page 239, para. 2 – "to establish the government's own school": This was the *School Law Amendment Act.* The minister of education was now Canon Cody, who, as a member of the Royal Commission of 1906, had recommended that the University establish a faculty of education: see D.C. Masters, *Henry John Cody: An Outstanding Life* (Toronto: Dundurn Press, 1995) at 60 and 116.

40. Page 239, para. 2 – "be more efficient than the university?": "The Argument for the Retention of the Faculty of Education in the University of Toronto", President's Office, April 30, 1920, UTA/A83-0036/007 at 4-5.

41. Page 239, para. 2 – "for the Carnegie pension scheme": Ibid. at 6-7.

42. Page 239, para. 2 – "to the authority of the senate": "Memorandum of Agreement" between the Board of Governors and the Minister of Education, June 30, 1920, UTA/A75-0021/07, clauses 1 and 6; Robin Harris, "Faculty of Education/Ontario College of Education", UTA/A83-0036/008.

43. Page 239, para. 2 – "and its students transferred to Toronto": Falconer to Taylor, October 29, 1920, UTA/A83-0026/007; A.B. McKillop, *Matters of Mind: The University in Ontario 1791-1951* (University of Toronto Press, 1994) at 651n80.

44. Page 239, para. 3 – "allowing them to teach primary school": UTA/A83-0036/001 "Professional Education."

45. Page 239, para. 3 – "before being admitted": Wallace, *History of the University of Toronto* at 220.

46. Page 239, para. 3 – "was added to the Toronto staff": Harris, "Faculty of Education".

47. Page 239, para. 3 – "would require the approval of government": "Memorandum of Agreement", clauses 4 and 5.

48. Page 239, para. 3 – "It became the faculty of education in 1972": See UTA/Corporate Authority Binder.

49. Page 239, para. 4 – "was declared open": Michael Bliss, *A Canadian Millionaire: The Life and Business Times of Sir Joseph Flavelle, Bart. 1858-1939* (Toronto: Macmillan of Canada, 1978) at 207. See generally, J.T.H. Connor, *Doing Good: The Life of Toronto's General Hospital in the Nineteenth and Twentieth Centuries* (University of Toronto Press, 2000).

50. Page 239, para. 4 – "one of the best in the world": Bliss, *Millionaire* at 207.

51. Page 239, para. 4 – "the hospital's board of trustees": Ibid. at 145; W.G. Cosbie, *The Toronto General Hospital 1819-1965: A Chronicle* (Toronto: Macmillan of Canada, 1975) at 141-149; J.W. Flavelle, "The Toronto General Hospital" speech to the Canadian Club, April 4, 1910.

52. Page 239, para. 4 – "near the Don River": See Chapter 12 (1887).

53. Page 239, para. 4 – "closer to the University": Bliss, *Millionaire* at 145.

54. Page 240, para. 1 – "an out-patient building for the hospital": Ibid. at 145.

55. Page 240, para. 1 – "as part of a new complex": Ibid.; Cosbie, *Toronto General* at 142.

56. Page 240, para. 1 – "donate $200,000 to purchase a site for it": *An Act Respecting the University of Toronto (1905),* sections 5 and 11.

57. Page 240, para. 2 – "at a cost of $3,450,000": Bliss, *Millionaire* at 207.

58. Page 240, para. 2 – "double its grant to $600,000": Ibid at 205; *An Act respecting the Toronto General Hospital (1991),* schedule 1.

59. Page 240, para. 2 – "to contribute major sums": Bliss, *Millionaire* at 160 and 205.

60. Page 240, para. 2 – "His eventual donation was more than $350,000": Ibid. at 205.

61. Page 241, para. 1 – "were purchased or expropriated": Ibid. at 206. See the powers given to the hospital in *An Act Respecting the Toronto General Hospital (1906),* particularly section 12.

62. Page 241, para. 1 – "on the corner of College and Huron streets": See Chapter 13 (1889). The hospital conveyed land to the University on the north side of College Street: see Robert B. Kerr and Douglas Waugh, *Duncan Graham: Medical Reformer and Educator* (Toronto: Dundurn Press, 1989) at 29.

63. Page 241, para. 1 – "extend from University Avenue to Elizabeth Street": See Chapter 12 (1887).

64. Page 241, para. 1 – "Darling and Pearson were chosen as the architects": Bliss, *Millionaire* at 204.

65. Page 241, para. 1 – "make it look cold and uninviting": Cosbie, *Toronto General* at 144-5; Bliss, *Millionaire* at 206.

66. Page 241, para. 1 – "and the Shields emergency building": Bliss, *Millionaire* at 207.

67. Page 241, para. 1 – "after two philanthropic sisters": Ibid. at 160.

68. Page 241, para. 1 – "and an obstetrics building were also erected": Ibid. at 207; Cosbie, *Toronto General* at 143.

69. Page 241, para. 2 – "south-west of the main hospital building": Bliss, *Millionaire* at 207; *TGH Act*, 1911, schedule 1, clauses 5 and 6; Cosbie at 146.

70. Page 241, para. 2 – "the distinguished pathologist J.J. Mackenzie": A.B. Macallum, "John Joseph Mackenzie", *Proceedings of the Royal Society of Canada*, 3rd series, v. 17 (1923) at vi.

71. Page 241, para. 2 – "appointed to the chair of pathology": Ibid. at iv and vi.

72. Page 242, para. 1 – "profound factors in the problems of disease": Ibid. at vi.

73. Page 242, para. 1 – "T.G. Brodie, a British physiologist": "Thomas Gregor Brodie", *Proceedings of the Royal Society of Canada* (1917) at ix-xi.

74. Page 242, para. 1 – "and pathology of the kidney": Macallum, "Mackenzie" at vi.

75. Page 242, para. 1 – "professor of chemical pathology in 1909": Rudolph Peters, "John Beresford Leathes" *in Biographical Memoirs of Fellows of the Royal Society*, v. 4 (London: The Royal Society, 1958).

76. Page 242, para. 1 – "Leathes returned to England in 1914": UTA/Graduate Records/"Leathes, J.B"/A73-0026/225(14).

77. Page 242, para. 2 – "during this period": Jones was appointed an assistant psychiatrist on July 7, 1909: see notes on Minutes of the Board of Toronto General Hospital, "Bliss Papers".

78. Page 242, para. 2 – "highly recommended by William Osler": Clarke to Hanna, October 23, 1908, reprinted in Cyril Greenland, *Charles Kirk Clarke: A Pioneer of Canadian Psychiatry* (Toronto: Clarke Institute, 1966) at 18-19. Jones had been charged with indecently assaulting two young "mentally defective" girls in England before he came to Canada. He was acquitted, but Philip Kuhn has made a convincing case that he might have been guilty: see Philip Kuhn, "'Romancing with a Wealth of Detail': Narratives of Dr. Ernest Jones's 1906 arrest for indecent assault" (Unpublished paper, November 23, 2000). It is not known whether Osler knew the circumstances of the case, but it is likely that he did because of the extensive publicity given the case in England. Whether C.K. Clarke knew is less certain. In his autobiography, Jones states that the English trial constituted "the most disagreeable experience in [his] life: see Kuhn at 2. See also R.A. Paskauskas, "Ernest Jones: A Critical Study of his Scientific Development" (Ph.D. Thesis, University of Toronto,1986).

79. Page 242, para. 2 – "the professor of psychiatry and dean of medicine": R.A. Paskauskas, ed., *The Complete Correspondence of Sigmund Freud and Ernest Jones 1908-1939* (Cambridge, Massachusetts: The Belknap Press, 1993) at 72 and 88. For Clarke, see Greenland, *Charles Kirk Clarke.*

80. Page 242, para. 2 – "like everything else in dead seriousness": Paskauskas, *Complete Correspondence* at 11.

81. Page 242, para. 3 – "inoculated with psychoanalytic doctrines": Ibid. at 73.

82. Page 242, para. 3 – "the stress I lay on sexual matters": Ibid. at 60.

83. Page 242, para. 3 – "had to be guarded by detectives": Ibid. at 87-88.

84. Page 242, para. 3 – "if they did not return to England": Ibid. at 96.

85. Page 243, para. 1 – "as head of a special unit in neurology at TGH": Ibid. at 114-116.

86. Page 243, para. 1 – "he stayed in Canada only two more years": Ibid. at 116n2.

87. Page 243, para. 2 – "which had been meeting for a year": Flavelle to Meredith, May 9, 1908, UTA/A67-0007/001. See also Bliss notes on the minutes of the hospital board of November 7, 1906.

88. Page 243, para. 2 – "This was the Johns Hopkins model": James G. Greenlee, *Sir Robert Falconer: A Biography* (University of Toronto Press, 1988) at 127. The official term used at the time for these departments was "services".

89. Page 243, para. 2 – "assisted by two other associate professors": Letter of W.T. White to the *Evening Telegram*, May 14, 1906, cited in "The General Hospital and the University of Toronto" at 9.

90. Page 243, para. 2 – "passed by in favour of younger men": Ibid.; Flavelle to Falconer, April 4, 1908, UTA/A83-0036/010 at 6.

91. Page 243, para. 2 – "well publicized in the press": See the articles in the *Evening Telegram* collected in the pamphlet, "The General Hospital and the University of Toronto".

92. Page 243, para. 2 – "by the former president, Loudon": Greenlee, *Sir Robert Falconer* at 127. The professors preferred the English system where doctors were given individual autonomy: see Bliss, *Millionaire* at 204 and 525n53; "Meeting of Toronto General Hospital Board On Staff Re-Organization With the Permanent Members

of the Medical Faculty of the University of Toronto", October 10, 1907 at 67 (Document forwarded by J.T.P. Connor of the Toronto General Hospital History Project.)

93. Page 243, para. 2 – "would make the appointments": Loudon to Whitney, July 8, 1908, UTA/A83-0036/010.

94. Page 244, para. 1 – "was their responsibility": See, e.g., White to Flavelle of April 3, 1908, UTA/A83-0036/010 at 3 and 4; Flavelle to Falconer, April 4, 1908 at 6.

95. Page 244, para. 1 – "ultimate responsibility for patient care was theirs": Moreover, the city of Toronto and some of the subscribers had given substantial amounts of money and did not want the hospital to be completely controlled by academics: see White letter to *Telegram* at 10; Flavelle to Meredith, May 13, 1908, UTA/A67-0007/001.

96. Page 244, para. 2 – "'mischievous and troublesome' professors": Flavelle to Meredith, May 13, 1908 at 3.

97. Page 244, para. 2 – "we should work this out ourselves": Falconer to Flavelle, May 16, 1908, UTA/A67-0001/001 at 2.

98. Page 244, para. 2 – "three for medicine and four for surgery": *TGH Act (1911)*, by-law, clause 6; Greenlee, *Sir Robert Falconer* at 127.

99. Page 244, para. 2 – "was enshrined in legislation in 1911": *TGH Act (1911).*

100. Page 244, para. 2 – "a single head for each department": Bliss, *Millionaire* at 525n53. See insulin section, where this will be discussed. On March 12, 1919, the board centralized the services in medicine and surgery to one service each: see notes on Toronto General Hospital board minutes in "Bliss Notes" at 10.

101. Page 244, para. 2 – "hospital trustees and the university governors": Greenlee, *Sir Robert Falconer* at 127; notes on Toronto General Hospital Board minutes, May 5, 1909, "Bliss Papers"; *TGH Act (1911)*, schedule 1, clauses 9 and 15.

102. Page 244, para. 2 – "age limits, however, were maintained": *TGH Act*, 1911, by-law, clause 9.

103. Page 244, para. 2 – "all positions were open to women": Ibid. by-law, clause 4.

104. Page 244, para. 2 – "the heads of the WCH departments": Flavelle to Lady Eaton, January 24, 1917, "Bliss Papers".

105. Page 244, para. 2 – "the first wing of the present hospital was opened": Geraldine Maloney, "The Women's College Hospital as a Teaching Institution", UTA/A83-0036/012 at 6; Edward Shorter, *A Century of Radiology in Toronto* (Toronto: Wall and Emerson, 1995) at 98.

106. Page 244, para. 3 – "was formally opened": "Addresses given at the Opening of the Royal Ontario Museum, March 19, 1914", *University of Toronto Monthly*, v. 15 at 73.

107. Page 244, para. 3 – "with its entrance on Bloor Street": Lovat Dickson, *The Museum Makers: The Story of the Royal Ontario Museum* (Toronto: Royal Ontario Museum, 1986) at 38.

108. Page 244, para. 3 – "had about it the air of a temple": Ibid.

109. Page 244, para. 3 – "by two columns of UTS military cadets": *Mail and Empire*, March 20, 1914; "Minutes of Seventh Meeting, Committee of Directors Royal Ontario Museum, March 13, 1914", UTA/A67-0007/032.

110. Page 245, para. 1 – "and other New York museums": Dickson, *The Museum Makers* at 10 and 12.

111. Page 245, para. 1 – "along with related library material": Madeleine A. Fritz, "The Royal Ontario Museum of

Palaeontology", UTA/P78-0626 at 3-4; Walker to Hoskin, July 14, 1904, UTA/B72-0031/001(59); "Mr. B.E. Walker's Gift to the University", *University of Toronto Monthly*, v. 5 at 21.

112. Page 245, para. 1 – "be built as early as possible": *Report of the Royal Commission* at xl-xli.

113. Page 245, para. 2 – "Victoria had brought its museum from Cobourg": C.B. Sissons, *A History of Victoria University* (University of Toronto Press, 1952) at 147.

114. Page 245, para. 2 – "large contributors in the future": *Commission* at xl.

115. Page 246, para. 1 – "had been saved from the fire": See Chapter 14 (1890).

116. Page 246, para. 1 – "and kept growing": J.R. Dymond, "The Royal Ontario Museum of Zoology", UTA/A83-0036/019 at 7.

117. Page 246, para. 1 – "by her late husband": Ibid. at 10.

118. Page 246, para. 1 – "a fine series of birds of paradise": Ibid. at 9.

119. Page 246, para. 1 – "had been destroyed in the fire": See Chapter 14 (1890); "150 Years of Geology at the University of Toronto" (Toronto: Department of Geology, 1998) at 11.

120. Page 246, para. 1 – "in the tower of University College": T.L Walker, "The Royal Ontario Museum: Mineralogy", *University of Toronto Monthly*, v. 14 at 157.

121. Page 246, para. 1 – "in the new Mining Building": Fritz, "ROM" at 3; E.S. Moore, "The Royal Ontario Museum of Geology", UTA/A83-0036/019 at 3.

122. Page 246, para. 1 – "the building to house the collections": Moore, "Geology" at 3.

123. Page 246, para. 1 – "to be part of a larger museum": Fritz, "ROM" at 3.

124. Page 246, para. 1 – "readily accessible to the public": *Commission* at xl.

125. Page 246, para. 1 – "help the economic development of the province": G.P. de T. Glazebrook, *Sir Edmund Walker* (Oxford: Oxford University Press, 1933) at 93-94. Walker declared it open "for the public generally": see speech by Walker at opening.

126. Page 246, para. 1 – "artefacts fashioned in earlier times": T.F. McIlwraith, "Charles Trick Currelly", *Proceedings of the Royal Society of Canada*, 3rd series, v. 51 (1957) at 75.

127. Page 246, para. 2 – "an important role in creating the museum": See Dickson, *The Museum Makers* at 12 et seq.; Charles Trick Currelly, *I Brought the Ages Home* (Toronto: The Ryerson Press, 1956).

128. Page 246, para. 2 – "became interested in political science": Currelly, *I Brought* at 14 and 30-32.

129. Page 246, para. 2 – "for a thesis on anarchism": Ibid. at 32; Dickson, *The Museum Makers* at 15.

130. Page 246, para. 2 – "and invited Currelly to join him": Currelly, *I Brought* at 36.

131. Page 246, para. 2 – "during his student days": Ibid. at 13-14.

132. Page 246, para. 2 – "advised him to seize the opportunity": Ibid. at 36.

133. Page 246, para. 2 – "a cultural missionary": Northrop Frye, "Editor's Introduction", in Currelly, *I Brought* at vii.

134. Page 246, para. 3 – "were Currelly's close friends": Currelly, *I Brought* at 37 and 129; Dickson, *The Museum Makers* at 13 and 14.

135. Page 246, para. 3 – "and would shed light on Christianity": Currelly, *I Brought* at 38. Burwash thought Currelly might also do some "teaching in Biblical archeology". Therefore Currelly's expertise was sought, and not just the artefacts he had collected.

136. Page 246, para. 3 – "Walker's own personal collection": Dickson, *The Museum Makers* at 13.

137. Page 247, para. 1 – "utterly out of the question": Currelly, *I Brought* at 128-29; Dickson, *The Museum Makers* at 19.

138. Page 247, para. 1 – "before the University's board of trustees": Currelly, *I Brought* at 129-30.

139. Page 247, para. 1 – "the great Fitzwilliam Museum in Cambridge": Ridgeway to Mavor, November 28, 1907, UTA/A67-0007/001.

140. Page 247, para. 1 – "and $1,500 for purchases": Hutton to Currelly, July 19, 1906, UTA/A67-0007/001. He had originally been offered $500 salary and $500 towards his collecting: see "Memorandum of an informal interview between President Burwash, Professor MacCurdy and Mr. Walker", January 29, 1906, UTA/B72-0031/005(28).

141. Page 247, para. 1 – "sums that increased over the years": For this, see Currelly, *I Brought* passim.

142. Page 247, para. 2 – "went to see Premier Whitney": Glazebrook, *Sir Edmund Walker* at 93-94.

143. Page 247, para. 2 – "wanted $50,000 with which to start construction": Currelly, *I Brought* at 183; "Report of the Property Committee regarding Museum", May 23, 1907 in Minutes of the Board of Governors, UTA/A70-0024, roll 9.

144. Page 247, para. 2 – "plans for an H-shaped building": In the press release at the opening the ROM said that it would "eventually form a quadrangle": see "Opening of the Royal Ontario Museum by His Royal Highness the Duke of Connaught", UTA/A67-0007/032 at 2.

145. Page 247, para. 2 – "and the other beside Taddle Creek": Dickson, *The Museum Makers* at 34-35. Pearson to Walker, March 5, 1914 says that they had started plans in the early part of 1907.

146. Page 247, para. 2 – "Construction would begin with the latter": Pearson to Walker, March 5, 1914. Whitney, however, was concerned about what the legislature would say. At that point, financier and board of governors member, E.B. Osler, said that if the legislature turned it down, he, Osler, would give the money: see Currelly, *I Brought* at 183.

147. Page 247, para. 2 – "Currelly was sending back": Currelly, *I Brought* at 193; Pearson to Walker, March 5, 1914.

148. Page 247, para. 2 – "by the University and the government": *An Act to Provide for the Establishment of a Provincial Museum (1912)*, sections 7 and 15-16; Dickson, *The Museum Makers* at 27; "Memorandum on the History of Museum-University Relations (1962)", UTA/A83-0036/019 at 3; Walker, "Mineralogy" at 157. The ROM was governed jointly but not equally. Of the 10 members, 6 were ex-officio or appointed by the government, 4 were ex-officio or appointed by the University.

149. Page 247, para. 2 – "Walker was elected chairman of the board of trustees": "Opening of the Royal Ontario Museum" at 3.

150. Page 247, para. 2 – "a significant supporter of the museum": Dickson, *The Museum Makers* at 40.

151. Page 247, para. 2 – "was appointed a trustee in 1921": Dickson, *The Museum Makers* at 30. Sigmund Samuel's first contribution to the Museum was in 1915: see Ian Montagnes, "A Philanthropist Tells Why he is One", *Varsity Graduate* (Christmas 1960) at 72; UTA/Graduate Records/"Sigmund Samuel"/A73-0026/396(53).

152. Page 247, para. 2 – "of such a major public institution in Toronto": Stephen Speisman has suggested this honour might properly be awarded to Lewis Samuel, Sigmund's father, who served as President of the Mechanics Institute in Toronto in the 1870s: Charles Levi conversation with Stephen Speisman, December 1, 2000.

153. Page 247, para. 3 – "each reporting to the board of trustees of the museum": Currelly, *I Brought* at 209; Walker, "Mineralogy" at 158.

154. Page 247, para. 3 – "had university appointments": Currelly, *I Brought* at 183.

155. Page 247, para. 3 – "had suffered in the past": Ibid.

156. Page 247, para. 3 – "the museum was part of the University": "Museum and University Serve One Another", *University of Toronto Monthly*, v. 23 at 72.

157. Page 247, para. 3 – "later changed to archaeology": McIlwraith, "Charles Trick Currelly" at 75. Originally he was called the professor of the history of industrial art: Currelly, *I Brought* at 210.

158. Page 247, para. 3 – "to house its extensive holdings": Currelly, *I Brought* at 197; Dickson, *The Museum Makers* at 36.

159. Page 248, para. 1 – "the museum's major Chinese collection": Currelly, *I Brought* at 181-182.

160. Page 248, para. 1 – "the museum's West Asian collection": Dickson, *The Museum Makers* at 30.

161. Page 248, para. 1 – "important Paul Kane paintings of Indian life": "Opening of the Royal Ontario Museum" at 3; *Star*, March 28, 1914. In addition to Kane's paintings, the collection also included works by John Gatlin and Edmund Morris.

162. Page 248, para. 2 – "relegated to the basement": Moore, "Geology" at 5-6; "150 Years" at 9-10; Currelly, *I Brought* at 197.

163. Page 248, para. 2 – "specialized in ores": W.A. Parks, "The Royal Ontario Museum: Geology", *University of Toronto Monthly*, v. 14 at 163.

164. Page 248, para. 2 – "nickel from Sudbury and silver from Cobalt": Ibid. at 164.

165. Page 248, para. 2 – "to the idea of 'continental drift'": Moore, "Geology" at 6; "150 Years" at 10.

166. Page 248, para. 2 – "later by the Toronto geophysicist Tuzo Wilson": G.D. Garland, "John Tuzo Wilson", *Biographical Memoirs of Fellows of the Royal Society*, v. 41 (1995) 524-552; "150 Years" at 17.

167. Page 248, para. 3 – "working on the Geological Survey of India": "150 Years" at 10.

168. Page 248, para. 3 – "Flavelle Medal for outstanding work in science": "The Late Professor T.L Walker", *University of Toronto Monthly* (October, 1942) at 14; A.L. Parsons, "Thomas Leonard Walker", *Proceedings of the Royal Society of Canada*, 3rd series, v. 37 (1943) at 93.

169. Page 248, para. 3 – "was carried over to the museum": "150 Years" at 5 and 10; Walker, "Mineralogy" at 157.

170. Page 248, para. 3 – "as the department of geological sciences": "150 Years" at 5.

171. Page 248, para. 4 – "director of the natural sciences division": Dymond, "The Royal Ontario Museum of Zoology" at 12 and 37; "Benjamin Arthur Bensley", *Proceedings of the Royal Society of Canada*, 3rd series, v. 28 (1934) at xxi.

172. Page 248, para. 4 – "and other marsupials": "Bensley" at 21; E. Horne Craigie, *A History of the Department of Zoology of the University of Toronto up to 1962*, (Toronto: Department of Zoology, 1966) at 29.

173. Page 248, para. 4 – "at Go Home Bay in Georgian Bay": Madawaska Club, *1898-1923 Go Home Bay* (Privately published, 1923).

174. Page 248, para. 4 – "on the fish of Georgian Bay": Craigie, *Zoology* at 28 and 40.

175. Page 248, para. 4 – "one of Canada's most eminent entomologists": Ibid. at 46 et seq.; Glenn B. Wiggins, "Edmund Murton Walker, 1877-1969", *Rotunda*, v.2, no. 2 (Spring, 1969) at 37; *Proceedings of the Royal Society of Canada*, 3rd series, v. 28 (1934) at iv.

176. Page 248, para. 4 – "also winning the Royal Society's Flavelle Medal": Wiggins, "Walker" at 38.

177. Page 250, para. 1 – "Coleman's colleague in geology": "150 Years" at 11; "William Arthur Parks", *Proceedings of the Royal Society of Canada*, 3rd series, v. 31 (1937) at xviii.

178. Page 250, para. 1 – "and his first PhD student, W.A. Parks": See Chapter 16 (1897). See also "Parks"; Madeline A. Fritz, "William Arthur Parks" (Toronto: Royal Ontario Museum, 1971).

179. Page 250, para. 1 – "a fellow of the Royal Society of London in 1934": "Parks" at xx; "150 Years" at 11.

180. Page 250, para. 1 – "and finally to vertebrate fossils": "Parks" at xix; "150 Years" at 11; Fritz, "Parks" at 8 et seq.

181. Page 250, para. 1 – "for his work on dinosaurs": See W.A. Parks, "Dinosaurs in the Royal Ontario Museum", *University of Toronto Quarterly* (1935).

182. Page 250, para. 1 – "and a professor of geology": "150 Years" at 14.

183. Page 250, para. 1 – "the second best collection of dinosaurs in the world": Fritz, "ROM" at 19. It appears that the best collection was at the American Museum of Natural History in New York: see Lyle Rexer and Rachel Klein, *American Museum of Natural History: 125 years of Expedition and Discovery* (New York: Harry N. Abrams, 1995) at 206.

184. Page 250, para. 1 – "elected a fellow of the Royal Society of Canada": "150 Years" at 14; "Madeleine Fritz", *Proceedings of the Royal Society of Canada*, 6th series, v. 4 (1993) at 53. Margaret Newton, a plant physiologist, was elected in the same year. Jean Bannerman, *Leading Ladies Canada* (Belleville: Mika Publishing Company, 1977), mentions Alice Wilson at 533 and Margaret Newton at 549-551 but does not include Fritz.

185. Page 250, para. 1 – "Alice Wilson in 1938": Barbara Meadowcroft, "Alice Wilson, 1881-1964: Explorer of the Earth Beneath her Feet", in Marianne Ainley, *Despite the Odds: Essays on Canadian Women and Science* (Montreal: Vehicule Press, 1990).

186. Page 250, para. 1 – "with the Geological Survey of Canada": G.W. Sinclair, "Alice Evelyn Wilson", *Proceedings of the Royal Society of Canada*, 4th series, v. 4 (1966).

187. Page 250, para. 2 – "who first collected whole skeletons": Fritz, "ROM" at 7-8.

188. Page 250, para. 2 – "helped expose the specimens": Ibid. at 8.

189. Page 250, para. 2 – "in the possession of a Canadian institution": Fritz, "ROM" at 9 says over 50 million; *University of Toronto Monthly*, vol. 23 at 72 says that it is three million years old.

190. Page 250, para. 2 – "It is still on display in the museum": Museum #764. See the picture of the dinosaur in Fritz, "Parks" at 10.

191. Page 250, para. 2 – "a hooded duck-billed dinosaur": Fritz, "ROM" at 9.

192. Page 250, para. 2 – "this species of dinosaur travelled on two legs": Museum #845; Dr. Kevin Seymour, assistant curator of Palaeobiology at the ROM, personal communication, May 31, 1999. Parks, "Dinosaurs" carries a picture of the dinosaur between pages 192 and 193.

193. Page 250, para. 2 – "sometimes scientists get things wrong": Kevin Seymour to author, May 31, 1999.

CHAPTER 22 – 1914 – THE GREAT WAR

1. Page 253, para. 1 – "even in Hamburg": James G. Greenlee, *Sir Robert Falconer: A Biography* (University of Toronto Press, 1988) at 198-99; *Globe*, September 8, 1914.

2. Page 253, para. 1 – "before heavy clouds gather": Robert Falconer, "Inaugural Address", *University of Toronto Monthly*, v. 8 at 14.

3. Page 253, para. 2 – "for our own sakes and for our children's": *University of Toronto Roll of Service 1914-1918* (University of Toronto Press, 1921) at xi.

4. Page 253, para. 2 – "and undergraduates had left for England": A.B. McKillop, *Matters of Mind: The University in Ontario 1791-1951* (University of Toronto Press, 1994) at 267.

5. Page 253, para. 2 – "and 70 faculty members were on active service": Greenlee, *Falconer* at 221 and Donald B. Smith, "Lost Youth", *University of Toronto Graduate* (Autumn, 1989) at 20, both citing *President's Report 1914/15* at 8.

6. Page 253, para. 2 – "who were about to leave for overseas": *Roll of Service* at xiv.

7. Page 254, para. 1 – "just after the war began": Ibid. at xxxvi et seq. See also James William Noel Leatch, "Military Involvement in Higher Education: A History of the University of Toronto Contingent, Canadian Officers' Training Corps" (Ph.D. Thesis, University of Toronto, 1995) at 94-96; Robert A. Spencer, "A Parade of Proud Memories", *Varsity Graduate* (April 1965).

8. Page 254, para. 1 – "of the University of Toronto's contingent": See Acting Adjutant General to Falconer, October 17, 1914, UTA/A83-0036/035.

9. Page 254, para. 1 – "for recruits for the COTC": Barbara M. Wilson, ed., *Ontario and the First World War 1914-1918: A Collection of Documents* (University of Toronto Press, 1977) at civ.

10. Page 254, para. 1 – "more than 500 students had enrolled in the corps": Ibid.

11. Page 254, para. 1 – "Professor W.R. Lang, the head of chemistry": Ibid.; McKillop, *Matters of Mind* at 267. *Roll of Service* at xxxviii also says there were this many students drilling a few days after term opened.

12. Page 254, para. 1 – "to permit their attendance": Greenlee, *Falconer* at 220, citing *President's Report 1914/15* at 9.

13. Page 254, para. 1 – "vacant farm land north of St. Clair Avenue": Ian Urquhart, "Memoirs" at 6: unpublished document sent to the author by Donald Urquhart, February, 1998.

14. Page 254, para. 1 – "the unfinished theatre as a rifle range": Smith, "Lost Youth" at 21; Urquhart, "Memoirs" at 10; Ian Montagnes, *Uncommon Fellowship: The Story of Hart House* (University of Toronto Press, 1969) at 17 and 29-30.

15. Page 254, para. 1 – "were used on the range": Montagnes, *Uncommon Fellowship* at 16-17; Montagnes, "The Founder and the Animator" in David Kilgour, ed., *A Strange Elation: Hart House, the First Eighty Years* (Toronto: Hart House, 1999) at 9.

16. Page 254, para. 2 – "I could scarcely do otherwise": Kent Duff to his mother, October 28, 1914, cited in Richard White, *The Skule Story: The University of Toronto Faculty of Applied Science and Engineering 1873-2000* (University of Toronto Press, 2000) at 89.

17. Page 254, para. 2 – "Leave this matter to the boys and their parents": Douglas to Falconer, December 9, 1915, UTA/A67-0007/038a.

18. Page 254, para. 2 – "joined a Victoria company": There were two companies: McKillop, *Matters of Mind* at 267, citing C.B. Sissons, *A History of Victoria University* (University of Toronto Press, 1952) at 271.

19. Page 254, para. 2 – "that was led by Vincent Massey": John English, *Shadow of Heaven: The Life of Lester Pearson, Volume One: 1897-1948* (Toronto: Lester & Orpen Dennys, 1989) at 26.

20. Page 254, para. 2 – "and dean of Burwash Hall": McKillop, *Matters of Mind* at 267.

21. Page 254, para. 2 – "pinned on me": Lester Pearson, *Mike: The Memoirs of the Right Honourable Lester B. Pearson*, vol. 1 (University of Toronto Press, 1972) at 17. On this page, Pearson also mentions his fumbled punt which allowed Medicine to beat Victoria for the intramural championship and the Mulock Cup. "It was a nightmare mistake which haunted me for ages."

22. Page 254, para. 2 – "and St. Michael's students": *Roll of Service* at xxxviii.

23. Page 254, para. 2 – "while training at Owen Sound": Ibid. at xvii.

24. Page 254, para. 2 – "would become principals of University College": "O.T.C. Officers", *University of Toronto Monthly*, v. 15 at 260.

25. Page 254, para. 3 – "female enrolment stayed about the same": *President's Report 1916/17* at 7; Wilson, *Ontario and the First World War* at cv.

26. Page 254, para. 3 – "the proportion of women increased considerably": W.P.J. Millar and R.D. Gidney, "'Medettes': Thriving or Just Surviving? Women Students in the Faculty of Medicine, University of Toronto, 1910-1951" in Elizabeth Smyth et al., eds., *Challenging Professions: Historical and Contemporary Perspectives on Women's Professional Work* (University of Toronto Press, 1999) at 215-216.

27. Page 254, para. 3 – "by the end of the 1916 academic year": Greenlee, *Falconer* at 221, citing *President's Report 1915/16* at 8.

28. Page 254, para. 3 – "there were more women than men": McKillop, *Matters of Mind* at 275.

29. Page 255, para. 1 – "but there were fewer than 200 in 1916—1917": Falconer, "The Khaki University", *University of Toronto Monthly*, v. 19 , 18-22 at 21. The *President's Reports* give an indication of where Falconer found these figures: *1913/14* at 5 says there were 627 students in engineering while *1916/17* puts it at 196 and *1917/18* at 5 puts the number at 168.

30. Page 255, para. 1 – "to 60 at its conclusion": McKillop, *Matters of Mind* at 277.

31. Page 255, para. 1 – "and in munitions factories": *Roll of Service* at xiv.

32. Page 255, para. 1 – "Falconer wrote about the 'quietness'": Falconer to Murray, December 24, 1915, as cited in Greenlee, *Falconer* at 222.

33. Page 255, para. 1 – "and 'loneliness'": Falconer to William Peterson, October 14, 1916, as cited in Greenlee, *Falconer* at 222.

34. Page 255, para. 1 – "interfaculty Mulock Cup competition, continued": *Roll of Service* at xvi; *President's Report 1915/16* at 7.

35. Page 255, para. 1 – "Afternoon dances were, however, permitted": *Varsity*, January 7, 1918.

36. Page 255, para. 2 – "for the British Royal Flying Corps": *Roll of Service* at xix; Elizabeth Milne, "The Royal Flying Corps at the University of Toronto 1917-1918", UTA/A83-0036/036.

37. Page 255, para. 2 – "and in front of Victoria College": *Roll of Service* at xix.

38. Page 255, para. 2 – "but as yet unopened Hart House": Montagnes, *Uncommon Fellowship* at 17 and 29-30; *President's Report 1917/18* at 8-9. Note they also took over the examination hall in the rear of Convocation Hall, the three men's residences, and the Dining Hall.

39. Page 255, para. 2 – "on the second floor of Wycliffe College": Michael Millgate, "William Faulkner, Cadet", *University of Toronto Quarterly*, vol. 35 (January 1966) at 117. See also D.J. MacMillan, "Fictional Facts and Factual Fiction: William Faulkner and World War I", *The Faulkner Journal*, Spring 1987 at 47; Frederick R. Karl, *William Faulkner: American Writer* (New York: Weidenfeld and Nicolson, 1989) at 112-116. See also Joel Williamson, *William Faulkner and Southern History* (New York: Oxford University Press, 1993) at 182. Faulkner greatly exaggerated his experience in Canada to his friends and family at home. In a series of letters home, he said he first flew in August and had four hours of solo flying by the end of November. This could not have been true, as no one in Faulkner's class had time to complete the course.

40. Page 255, para. 2 – "by members of the engineering faculty": Milne, "Royal Flying Corps" at 2.

41. Page 255, para. 2 – "After conscription was legislated in 1917": Greenlee, *Falconer* at 224 et seq.

42. Page 255, para. 2 – "they go around whistling now": *Globe*, March 14, 1918, as cited in McKillop, *Matters of Mind* at 290.

43. Page 255, para. 3 – "more than 600 persons – died": McKillop, *Matters of Mind* at 268. For precise numbers, see *Roll of Service* at 529.

44. Page 255, para. 3 – "The former president, James Loudon, lost a son": *Roll of Service* at 87.

45. Page 255, para. 3 – "so did Chancellor Meredith": Ibid. at 100-101; McKillop, *Matters of Mind* at 289.

46. Page 255, para. 3 – "and the former vice-chancellor Charles Moss": UTA/Graduate Records/"Charles A. Moss"/A73-0026/339(10). The vice-chancellor had already died in October of 1912.

47. Page 255, para. 3 – "and so did George Wrong": *Roll of Service* at 155; McKillop, *Matters of Mind* at 289.

48. Page 255, para. 3 – "W.H. Van der Smissen": UTA/Graduate Records/"W.H. Vander Smissen"/A73-0026/483(85).

49. Page 255, para. 3 – "later the dean of medicine": UTA/Graduate Records/"Harold Primose"/A73-0026/368(87); Nancy Joy, "Doctor Primrose: 'The Colonel'", excerpt from unpublished memoirs, 1998; UTA/Graduate Records/"Alexander Primrose"/A73-0026/368(86).

50. Page 256, para. 1 – "and 4 from the class of 1918": "Killed in Action or Died on Service June-October", *University of Toronto Monthly*, v.19 at 1-5.

51. Page 256, para. 1 – "starting with the Amiens offensive": Stephen Pope and Elizabeth Anne Wheal, *The Macmillan Dictionary of the First World War* (London: Macmillan Reference Books, 1995) at 23; J.F.B. Livesay, *Canada's Hundred Days* (Toronto: Thomas Allen, 1919) at 2 et seq.

52. Page 256, para. 1 – "the Armistice of November 11, 1918": Smith, "Lost Youth" at 19; Livesay, *Canada's Hundred Days* at 400.

53. Page 256, para. 1 – "had not been kept together as a fighting force": *Roll of Service* at xvi.

54. Page 256, para. 1 – "normally to the infantry": McKillop, *Matters of Mind* at 268, citing Ralph Hodder-Williams, *Princess Patricia's Canadian Light Infantry, 1914-1919,* 2nd ed. (Edmonton: PPCLI, 1968) at 83.

55. Page 256, para. 1 – "some of the fiercest battles in the war": McKillop, *Matters of Mind* at 268.

56. Page 258, para. 1 – "at the Somme in September 1918": R. Douglas Francis, *Frank H. Underhill: Intellectual Provocateur* (University of Toronto Press, 1986) at 38 and 45. This is not to be confused with the more famous Battle of the Somme in 1916.

57. Page 258, para. 1 – "from McMaster University in May 1916": Donald G. Creighton, *Harold Adams Innis: Portrait of a Scholar* (University of Toronto Press, 1986) at 31.

58. Page 258, para. 1 – "and that may have saved his life": E-mail to the author from Anne Innis Dagg, February 28, 2001.

59. Page 258, para. 1 – "as Alfred Marshall's *Principles of Economics*": Creighton, *Harold Adams Innis* at 33-37.

60. Page 258, para. 2 – "and so brought about their surrender": UTA/Graduate Records/"Thain MacDowell"/A73-0026/265(072).

61. Page 258, para. 3 – "in an army medical corps": Roderick Stewart, *Bethune* (Toronto: New Press, 1973) at 6.

62. Page 258, para. 3 – "He was wounded by shrapnel": Smith, "Lost Youth" at 20.

63. Page 258, para. 3 – "spent three months in a British military hospital": Wendell MacLeod and Hilary Russell, "Norman Bethune: A Biographical Outline" in David A.E. Shephard and Andree Levesque, eds., *Norman Bethune: His Times and His Legacy* (Ottawa: Canadian Public Health Association, 1982) at 2, 7. The second battle of Ypres was noted for the first use of poison gas, fired by the Germans on Canadian troops: see www.lib.byu.edu/~rdh/wwi/1915/chlorgas.html.

64. Page 258, para. 3 – "as a surgeon in the Royal Navy": MacLeod and Russell, "Norman Bethune" at 7; Smith, "Lost Youth" at 20.

65. Page 258, para. 3 – "of meningitis and double pneumonia": John F. Prescott, "John McCrae", *DCB,* v. 14 at 679-680.

66. Page 258, para. 4 – "a 1,000-bed base hospital": *Roll of Service* at xxx et seq.; "The University Hospital", *University of Toronto Monthly,* v. 15 at 411; J.J McKenzie, "The University of Toronto Hospital in the Eastern Mediterranean", *University of Toronto Monthly,* v. 17 at 68.

67. Page 258, para. 4 – "at the request of the Serbian government": There is a plaque to this effect put up in 1984 in the Medical Sciences Building: see "Plaque commemorates war service of U of T doctors, nurses", *University of Toronto Bulletin,* November 19, 1985 at 4.

68. Page 258, para. 4 – "in heavy trench warfare against the Germans": *Roll of Service* at xxxi.

69. Page 259, para. 1 – "woman doctor, Harriet Cockburn": See UTA/B65-0005.

70. Page 259, para. 1 – "many of whom were Toronto undergraduates": *Roll of Service* at xxx.

71. Page 259, para. 1 – "to the championship of the Macedonian front": English, *Shadow of Heaven* at 35 and 37.

72. Page 259, para. 2 – "became a scientific centre for the district": *Roll of Service* at xxx.

73. Page 259, para. 2 – "the professor of pathology": J.J. and K.C. Mackenzie, *Number 4 Canadian Hospital: The Letters of Professor J.J. Mackenzie from the Salonika Front* (Toronto: Macmillan Canada, 1933).

74. Page 259, para. 2 – "and Lady Eaton Professor of Medicine at the University": R.B. Kerr and D. Waugh, *Duncan Graham: Medical Reformer and Educator* (Toronto: Dundurn Press, 1989) at 22.

75. Page 259, para. 2 – "who would become the dean of medicine": Joy, "Doctor Primrose"; UTA/Graduate Records/ "Primrose, Alexander"/A73-0026/368(86).

76. Page 259, para. 2 – "later the professor of clinical surgery": Falconer to Minister of Militia, March 18, 1915, UTA/A83-0036/036.

77. Page 259, para. 2 – "would eventually grow to 2,000 beds": W.B. Hendry to Falconer, April 30, 1917, UTA/A83-0036/036.

78. Page 259, para. 2 – "by the University Women's Hospital Supply Association": *Roll of Service* at xxiii-xxxiv.

79. Page 260, para. 1 – "undergraduate women": Margaret Wrong, "War Work of University Women at Home", *The Varsity Magazine* (1918) at 133.

80. Page 260, para. 1 – "reconstituted in Basingstoke, England": *Roll of Service* at xxxii. Basingstoke was 75 kilometres south-west of London. The descendants of the Canadian medical team at Salonika have been meeting and collecting material on the hospital: see letter from Mary Louise Gaby, January 5, 2000, enclosing report of meeting held May 30, 1998.

81. Page 260, para. 2 – "loss of German culture, scholarship, and language": McKillop, *Matters of Mind* at 290.

82. Page 260, para. 2 – "for all specialist courses except chemistry": *President's Report 1917/18* at 9.

83. Page 260, para. 2 – "in which German works were read": John G. Slater, "Philosophy at Toronto" (Unpublished manuscript, 1999) at 136.

84. Page 260, para. 2 – "as it had in the years since the 1870s": McKillop, *Matters of Mind* at 291.

85. Page 260, para. 3 – "of professors with German roots": See Greenlee, *Falconer* at 201-14; Michiel Horn, *Academic Freedom in Canada: A History* (University of Toronto Press, 1999) at 41; McKillop, *Matters of Mind* at 259-62.

86. Page 260, para. 3 – "were forced to leave the University of Toronto": Greenlee, *Falconer* at 201-207. For a discussion of Trinity College, see Horn, *Academic Freedom* at 43-45.

87. Page 260, para. 3 – "and none had yet become a Canadian citizen": Greenlee, *Falconer* at 205.

88. Page 260, para. 3 – "was not made permanent": Ibid.

89. Page 260, para. 3 – "was drafted into the German army": Ibid. at 206.

90. Page 260, para. 3 – "neither had he taken out Canadian citizenship": Ibid. at 201.

91. Page 260, para. 4 – "for trading with the enemy": *Telegram*, November 25, 1914, as cited in McKillop, *Matters of Mind* at 260; Michael Bliss, *A Canadian Millionaire: The Life and Business Times of Sir Joseph Flavelle, Bart. 1858-1939* (Toronto: Macmillan of Canada, 1978) at 243.

92. Page 260, para. 4 – "then let us close the universities": Horn, *Academic Freedom* at 43. There were later sugges-

tions that the University should be closed in any case: see Leonard to Falconer, January 6, 1917, UTA/A67-0007/043; McKillop, *Matters of Mind* at 290.

93. Page 260, para. 4 – "they are injurious alien enemies": *Globe*, November 17, 1914; McKillop, *Matters of Mind* at 260.

94. Page 261, para. 1 – "wanted them to stay": Greenlee, *Falconer* at 208-210; Horn, *Academic Freedom* at 42.

95. Page 261, para. 1 – "after a two-day board meeting in November 1914": Horn, *Academic Freedom* at 42.

96. Page 261, para. 1 – "until the end of the academic year": Greenlee, *Falconer* at 210.

97. Page 261, para. 1 – "and spoke of resigning": Osler to Walker, November 18, 1914, as cited in Greenlee, *Falconer* at 208.

98. Page 261, para. 1 – "are being killed by Germans at the front": *Canadian Annual Review (1914)* at 267-68; McKillop, *Matters of Mind* at 261.

99. Page 261, para. 1 – "but without success": Greenlee, *Falconer* at 212; Horn, *Academic Freedom* at 43.

100. Page 261, para. 2 – "a teaching position in a small college": Greenlee, *Falconer* at 212.

101. Page 261, para. 2 – "at McMaster University on Bloor Street": Ibid. at 213.

102. Page 261, para. 2 – "was taken back from him": Falconer to Mueller, December 18, 1914, UTA/A67-0007/035.

103. Page 261, para. 2 – "but the board would not have him": See Mueller to Falconer, May 25, 1915 and Falconer to Mueller, June 14, 1915, UTA/A67-0007/035.

104. Page 261, para. 2 – "academic freedom was a losing cause": Horn, *Academic Freedom* at 61. There were others in the University with a German background. The dean of forestry, Bernhard Fernow, had been born in Germany and had fought in the Franco-Prussian war, but he was an American citizen: see UTA/Graduate Records/"Fernow, Bernard Edward"/A73-0026/101(53). There were rumours that he had not encouraged students to volunteer. It turned out, however, that he had been a strong supporter of the COTC and nothing was done: see Horn, *Academic Freedom* at 45-46. In any event, he was one year away from retirement. The psychologist, August Kirschmann, had returned to Germany a number of years before the war on sick leave. He was still being granted partial salary when war broke out, but this and his appointment were quickly cancelled. He remained in Germany after the war: see Chapter 16 (1897).

105. Page 261, para. 2 – "foremost Goethe scholars in the English-speaking world": *London Times*, December 2, 1986.

106. Page 261, para. 2 – "the faculty at Alberta, was hired": Ibid.

107. Page 261, para. 3 – "in comparison with Germany and the United States": See generally Mel Thistle, *The Inner Ring: The Early History of the National Research Council of Canada* (University of Toronto Press, 1966); Trevor Levere, *Research and Influence: A Century of Science in the Royal Society of Canada* (Ottawa: Royal Society of Canada, 1998) at 30-31; McKillop, *Matters of Mind* at 285 et seq.; Yves Gingras, *Physics and the Rise of Scientific Research in Canada*, Peter Keating, trans., (Montreal: McGill-Queen's University Press, 1991) at 53 et seq.

108. Page 261, para. 3 – "the faculties of applied science in Canada together": Thistle, *Inner Ring* at 29.

109. Page 261, para. 3 – "50 pure research men all told": Ibid.

110. Page 261, para. 3 – "had been less than $300,000": Thistle, *Inner Ring* at 5; McKillop, *Matters of Mind* at 286.

111. Page 262, para. 1 – "scientific research": Thistle, *Inner Ring* at 9.

112. Page 262, para. 1 – "was made its full-time chairman": Ibid. at 10.

113. Page 262, para. 1 – "President Falconer": Falconer to Flavelle, June 3, 1916, as cited in ibid. at 8-9.

114. Page 262, para. 1 – "the committee member John McLennan": Thistle, *Inner Ring* at 16.

115. Page 262, para. 1 – "favoured centralizing the laboratories in Ottawa": Ibid. at 30 et seq.

116. Page 262, para. 1 – "which individual universities would receive support": See ibid. at 42, showing the jealousies amongst the universities.

117. Page 262, para. 1 – "the creation of central laboratories in Ottawa": Ibid. at 47 and 68.

118. Page 262, para. 1 – "who had shown capacity for scientific research": Ibid. at 27.

119. Page 262, para. 2 – "engaged in organized industrial research": White, *Skule Story* at 93-94.

120. Page 262, para. 2 – "that the royal commission of 1906 had recommended": *Report of the Royal Commission on the University of Toronto* (Toronto: L.K. Cameron, 1906) at xxxix.

121. Page 262, para. 2 – "had advocated for many years": McKillop, *Matters of Mind* at 168 and 285 et seq.

122. Page 262, para. 2 – "Galbraith had died a month before the war began": Falconer to Mackenzie, September 8, 1914, UTA/A67-0007/035.

123. Page 262, para. 2 – "and organization of industrial research": W.H. Ellis, "The University and Industrial Research", *Applied Science*, v. 10, no. 5 (June, 1916) at 125.

124. Page 262, para. 2 – "the foundation of a School of Engineering Research": Ibid.

125. Page 262, para. 2 – "from a special provincial grant for research": Richard White writes, "although born in wartime, research undertaken with its funds in 1918 did not all have a direct connection with the war". Research included voltage regulation for high-tension transmission lines, plant growth enzymes, and a new type of reinforced concrete for the construction of large buildings. The School of Engineering Research was "the Faculty's first step into institutionalized research support for its academic staff": see White, *Skule Story* at 94-95; Maitland C. Boswell, "The School of Engineering Research", UTA/A83-0036/003; Philip C. Enros, "The University of Toronto and Industrial Research in the Early Twentieth Century", in Richard A. Jarrell and Arnold E. Ross, eds., *Critical Issues in the History of Canadian Science, Technology, and Medicine* (Thornhill: HSTC Publications, 1983).

126. Page 262, para. 3 – "mainly in relation to munitions": Falconer to Comptroller, Munitions Inventions Department, March 11, 1916, UTA/A83-0036/017.

127. Page 262, para. 3 – "tested the steel casings of shells": Ibid.; Wilson, *Ontario and the First World War* at cvi; *President's Report 1914/15* at 10.

128. Page 262, para. 3 – "and chemical engineers tested chemical explosives": Falconer to Comptroller, March 11, 1916, UTA/A83-0036/017.

129. Page 262, para. 3 – "and the shrapnel within them": Ibid.

130. Page 262, para. 3 – "to the chemistry of explosives": Ruby Heap, "From the Science of Housekeeping to the Science of Nutrition: Pioneers in Canadian Nutrition and Dietetics at the University of Toronto's Faculty of Household Science, 1900-1950" (Unpublished manuscript) at 16.

131. Page 262, para. 4 – "but only up to about 60 miles an hour": E-mail from Ben Etkin to Charles Levi, January 31, 2001; J.H. Parkin, "The Toronto Aerodynamic Laboratory", *University of Toronto Monthly*, v.24 at 25-26. The speed is better reckoned as 80 feet per second.

132. Page 263, para. 1 – "in the thermodynamics building": Parkin, "Aerodynamic Laboratory" at 25.

133. Page 263, para. 1 – "over a lake in New York state": Gordon N. Patterson, *Pathway to Excellence* (Toronto: Institute of Aerospace Studies, 1977) at 3.

134. Page 263, para. 1 – "in the 'Silver Dart' in Nova Scotia": Ibid.

135. Page 263, para. 1 – "Bell's research group in the Maritimes": "Course in Aeronautical Engineering Established", *University of Toronto Monthly*, v. 28 at 319.

136. Page 263, para. 1 – "in charge of aeronautical research in the University": Ibid.

137. Page 263, para. 1 – "just south of the thermodynamics building": Parkin, "Aerodynamic Laboratory" at 26.

138. Page 263, para. 1 – "more than double the speed of the old tunnel": Ibid. The new speed would be 200 feet per second: see e-mail from Etkin to Levi, January 31, 2001.

139. Page 263, para. 1 – "was introduced": "Course" at 319.

140. Page 263, para. 2 – "in aiding the war effort": H.H. Langton, *Sir John Cunningham McLennan: A Memoir* (University of Toronto Press, 1939) at 41 et seq.

141. Page 263, para. 2 – "from natural gas in Canada": Ibid. at 46; Barry Countryman, *Helium for Airships and Science: The Search in Canada 1916-1936* (Toronto: Barry Countryman, 1992) at 5-6.

142. Page 264, para. 1 – "asked to produce quantities of helium": Langton, *McLennan* at 46.

143. Page 264, para. 1 – "to produce the necessary quantities more quickly": Ibid. at 47 and 104-105.

144. Page 264, para. 1 – "could be used in military operations": Ibid. at 47.

145. Page 264, para. 1 – "expertise in low-temperature physics": Ibid. at 62 et seq.

146. Page 264, para. 2 – "for the British navy on anti-submarine devices": Ibid. at 43 et seq. He also did work on testing periscope sights: see McKillop, *Matters of Mind* at 284, citing "Research" (Unpaginated), Papers of University Historian, UTA/A83-0036/001.

147. Page 264, para. 2 – "research in England for the navy": Langton, *McLennan* at 45.

148. Page 264, para. 2 – "graduates to assist him": Ibid. at 48-49.

149. Page 264, para. 2 – "magnetic characteristics": Ibid. at 44, 50; communication with Craig Brown, June, 1999.

150. Page 264, para. 2 – "would make sea mines more stable": Langton, *McLennan* at 50; Arthur J. Marder, *From the Dreadnought to Scapa Flow: The Royal Navy in the Fisher Era 1904-1919*, v.4 (London: Oxford University Press, 1969) at 87-88. Marder is generally dismissive of the effect scientific discoveries had on the outcome of the naval war and instead stresses the eventual efficacy of the convoy system.

151. Page 264, para. 2 – "two subs and a launch": Langton, *McLennan* at 55. Craig Brown commented in January,

2001 on a draft of the manuscript: "This is, indeed, what he wrote, but there is no evidence to support this claim."

152. Page 264, para. 2 – "fully accepted by the Navy as standard devices": Langton, *McLennan* at 55.

153. Page 264, para. 2 – "director of research for the navy": Ibid. at 58-59.

154. Page 264, para. 2 – "was to be part of the arrangement": Ibid. at 59.

155. Page 264, para. 2 – "decided not to fund the laboratory": Ibid. at 60-61.

156. Page 264, para. 3 – "of wounds in the respiratory system": *President's Report 1915/16* at 10.

157. Page 264, para. 3 – "developed special techniques for blood transfusions": UTA/Graduate Records/"Lawrence Bruce Robertson"/A73-0026/382(11); Lawrence Bruce Robertson, "The Transfusion of Whole Blood", *British Medical Journal*, July 8, 1916; L. Bruce Robertson and C. Gordon Watson, "Further Observations on the Results of Blood Transfusion in War Surgery", *British Medical Journal*, November 24, 1917; Peter H. Pinkerton, "Canada's transfusion medicine pioneer: Lawrence Bruce Robertson", *Transfusion*, vol. 41 (February 2001) at 283.

158. Page 265, para. 1 – "blood with saline solutions": Robertson, "The Transfusion of Whole Blood" at 38.

159. Page 265, para. 1 – "in cases of severe hemorrhage": Dawson Williams, "The Transfusion of Whole Blood", *British Medical Journal*, November 24, 1917 at 695.

160. Page 265, para. 2 – "demonstrator in psychiatry at the University of Toronto": Donald T. Fraser, "John Gerald FitzGerald", *Proceedings of the Royal Society of Canada*, 3rd Series, v. 35 (1941) at 113.

161. Page 265, para. 2 – "to use Jones's words": Jones to FitzGerald, April 4, 1910, supplied by his grandson James FitzGerald.

162. Page 265, para. 2 – "at the Pasteur Institutes in Paris and Brussels": Fraser, "John Gerald FitzGerald" at 113.

163. Page 265, para. 2 – "as an associate professor of hygiene": Ibid.

164. Page 265, para. 2 – "the first full-time member of the department": Robert D. Defries, *The First Fifty Years* (University of Toronto Press, 1968) at 9.

165. Page 265, para. 2 – "the Pasteur anti-rabies vaccine": Paul A. Bator with Andrew James Rhodes, *Within Reach of Everyone: A History of the University of Toronto School of Hygiene and the Connaught Laboratories, Vol. 1, 1927-1955* (Ottawa: Canadian Public Health Association, 1990) at 18.

166. Page 265, para. 2 – "a much-needed diphtheria antitoxin": Ibid.

167. Page 265, para. 2 – "involved in a commercial venture": McKillop, *Matters of Mind* at 284; Donald Jones, "Turning an Idea into a World Reputation", *Toronto Star*, October 5, 1985 at M3.

168. Page 265, para. 2 – "and FitzGerald at his own expense": C.B. Farrar, "I Remember J. G. FitzGerald", *American Journal of Psychiatry*, v. 120, no. 1 (1963) at 50.

169. Page 266, para. 1 – "where the four horses": Defries, *First Fifty Years* at 5.

170. Page 266, para. 1 – "used in its production were kept": Bator, *Within Reach* at 18; Jones, "Turning an Idea" at M3.

171. Page 266, para. 1 – "as part of the department of hygiene": Bator, *Within Reach* at 18; Defries, *First Fifty Years* at 8; Jones, "Turning an Idea" at M3.

172. Page 266, para. 2 – "for the Canadian Expeditionary Forces": Falconer to Osler, February 8, 1915, UTA/A67-0007/035.

173. Page 266, para. 2 – "to get $5,000 from the federal government": Ibid; Falconer to Minister of Militia, February 23, 1915, UTA/A67-0007/035.

174. Page 266, para. 2 – "as well as to many civilians": Bator, *Within Reach* at 21.

175. Page 266, para. 2 – "who was chairman of the Red Cross": Defries, *First Fifty Years* at 20.

176. Page 266, para. 2 – "for the production of vaccines and antitoxins": It was actually 58 acres: see Bator, *Within Reach* at 21; Defries, *First Fifty Years* at 25.

177. Page 266, para. 2 – "the Duke of Connaught": Falconer to Henderson, September 18, 1917, UTA/A67-0007/47a.

178. Page 266, para. 2 – "with FitzGerald as its head": Fraser, "John Gerald FitzGerald" at 114.

179. Page 266, para. 2 – "named the FitzGerald Building": Jones, "Turning an Idea" at M3.

180. Page 266, para. 3 – "and the professor of hygiene, John Amyot": Bator, *Within Reach* at 8-9.

181. Page 266, para. 3 – "and controlling contagious diseases": Ibid. at 21-22. FitzGerald did not go overseas until 1918 although he had enlisted in the Royal Army Medical Corps in 1915.

182. Page 266, para. 3 – "more men dying from disease than from wounds": Ibid. at 21, citing "Dr. Amyot Outlines Health Work in War", UTA/Graduate Records/A73-0026/007(35).

183. Page 266, para. 4 – "from wounds or shock": *Roll of Service* at xx-xxi; see Edward A. Bott, "Re-Educational Work for Soldiers", *University of Toronto Monthly*, v. 17 at 269.

184. Page 267, para. 1 – "to supervise related work": *Roll of Service* at xxi.

185. Page 267, para. 2 – "were taught": Ibid. at xxi; Ruby Heap, "Training Women for a New 'Women's Profession': Physiotherapy Education at the University of Toronto, 1917-1940", *History of Education Quarterly*, v.35 (Summer 1995) at 140.

186. Page 267, para. 2 – "a distinguished professor of history at the University": Robert Bothwell, *Laying the Foundation: A Century of History at the University of Toronto* (Toronto: Department of History, 1991) at 81; e-mail from Lynn Bullock (Curator, PPCLI Regimental Museum) to Charles Levi, October 26, 2000.

187. Page 267, para. 2 – "for the next thirty years": Slater, "Philosophy at Toronto" at 124.

188. Page 267, para. 2 – "had been rejected by the philosophy department": Ibid. at 119-120.

189. Page 267, para. 2 – "who did not know Greek": Ibid. at 120.

190. Page 267, para. 3 – "for the Invalided Soldiers Commission": *Roll of Service* at xxiii.

191. Page 268, para. 1 – "in its head office on Spadina Avenue": Keens Building at 185 Spadina Ave: see Haultain to Falconer, June 14, 1919, UTA/A67-0007/052a.

192. Page 268, para. 1 – "as auto mechanics and applied electricity": *Roll of Service* at xxiii; *President's Report 1917/18* at 15-16.

193. Page 268, para. 1 – "more than 300 women as occupational therapists": *Roll of Service* at xxiii; Judith Friedland, "Occupational Therapy and Rehabilitation: An Awkward Alliance", *The American Journal of Occupational Therapy*, v. 52, no. 5 (May 1998) 373-380 at 376, putting the number at 350.

194. Page 268, para. 1 – "for occupational therapy on McCaul Street": *Roll of Service* at xxiii.

195. Page 268, para. 1 – "woodwork, book-binding, and basketry": Ibid.

196. Page 268, para. 1 – "I can't do it": Helen LeVesconte, Oral Interview Transcript, UTA/B76-0008 at 26.

197. Page 268, para. 1 – "to brood over his troubles": A. Primrose, "Ontario Society of Occupational Therapy", *University of Toronto Monthly*, v. 23 at 292.

198. Page 268, para. 1 – "was initiated at the University in 1926": W.J. Dunlop, "A Brief History of Occupational Therapy", *Canadian Journal of Occupational Therapy*, v. 1, no. 1 (1933) at 9.

199. Page 268, para. 1 – "Helen LeVesconte was a member of that first class": LeVesconte transcript at 45.

200. Page 268, para. 2 – "gave themselves up to common rejoicing": *Roll of Service* at xxvi. The losses, however, continued. A few days after the armistice, for example, a Victoria College student, William Hanna, who had enlisted in 1915 and been severely wounded at the battle of the Somme but then joined the Royal Flying Corps, died in an accidental plane crash while observing the Austrian retreat: see *Roll of Service* at 61. Many others died of influenza, which affected so many in the fall of 1918: see generally, Janice P. Dickin McGinnis, "The Impact of Epidemic Influenza: Canada, 1918-1919", *Papers Presented to the Canadian Historical Association Annual Meeting* (1977), 121-140; Eileen Pettigrew, *The Silent Enemy: Canada and the Deadly Flu of 1918* (Saskatoon: Western Producer Prairie Books, 1983). The University was closed between October 18 and November 5, 1918: see *President's Report 1918/1919* at 9.

CHAPTER 23 – 1919 – POST WAR

1. Page 269, para. 1 – "the foundation stone for a memorial tower was laid": "Armistice Day", *University of Toronto Monthly*, v. 20 at 53; "Corner Stone of the Memorial Tower is Laid", *University of Toronto Monthly*, v.20 at 87; Montagnes, *Uncommon Fellowship* at 38.

2. Page 269, para. 1 – "at the official opening of Hart House": Ian Montagnes, *Uncommon Fellowship: The Story of Hart House* (University of Toronto Press, 1969) at 27.

3. Page 269, para. 1 – "immediately after the end of the war": "The Memorial Committee's Report", *University of Toronto Monthly*, v. 19 at 131-132.

4. Page 269, para. 1 – "was to be constructed": James M. MacCallum, "Progress of the Memorial Committee", *University of Toronto Monthly*, v. 19 at 96.

5. Page 269, para. 1 – "on King's College Circle was selected": Ibid.

6. Page 269, para. 1 – "to keep the land for the expansion of the library": "Memorial Committee's Report" at 132.

7. Page 269, para. 1 – "to situate the building on its present site": Ibid.

8. Page 269, para. 2 – "as long as the University endures": "Corner Stone of the Memorial Tower is Laid" at 88.

9. Page 269, para. 2 – "to the simple, impressive service": Ibid.

10. Page 271, para. 1 – "not actually completed until 1924": *University of Toronto Bulletin*, November 11, 1996 at 1. See also Paul Gary Russell, "The Mutable Monument: The Architecture of Hart House" in David Kilgour, ed., *A Strange Elation: Hart House: The First Eighty Years* (Hart House, 1999).

11. Page 271, para. 1 – "of those who had not returned": Macallum, "Progress of the Memorial Committee" at 96.

12. Page 271, para. 1 – "that education was a provincial responsibility": James Greenlee, *Sir Robert Falconer: A Biography* (University of Toronto Press, 1988) at 248, citing J.A. Calder to Falconer, April 15, 1919, UTA/A67-0007/55.

13. Page 271, para. 1 – "Borden wrote to Falconer": Ibid. at 249, citing Borden to Falconer, July 16, 1919, UTA/A67-0007/57.

14. Page 271, para. 1 – "embarking upon business enterprises, etc.": Ibid.

15. Page 271, para. 1 – "were ex-soldiers": A.B. McKillop, *Matters of Mind: The University in Ontario 1791-1951* (University of Toronto Press, 1994) at 335.

16. Page 271, para. 1 – "and construction began": "Corner Stone of the Memorial Tower is Laid" at 87.

17. Page 271, para. 1 – "making a total today of 51 bells": Micah Raynor, "Towering Reminder", *University of Toronto Bulletin*, November 11, 1996; Karina Dahlin, "Making sure the carillon carries on", *Bulletin*, September 11, 1989; "Ring out sweet bells", *Bulletin*, November 21, 1975; "The bells – all 51 of them – ring out again", *Bulletin*, May 14, 1976.

18. Page 271, para. 2 – "unique in North America": Montagnes, *Uncommon Fellowship* at 5.

19. Page 271, para. 2 – "had planned to erect a new building": Ibid. at 9.

20. Page 271, para. 2 – "student centre in one building": Ibid. at 6. See also Ian Montagnes, "The Founder and the Animator" in *A Strange Elation.*

21. Page 271, para. 2 – "Vincent's grandfather, Hart Massey": Montagnes, *Uncommon Fellowship* at 10 and 13. The name Massey Foundation was in fact not adopted until 1919. Until then it was called the Hart Massey Estate. See e-mail from Karen Finaly of January 22, 2002.

22. Page 271, para. 2 – "was therefore added to the plans": D.B. Macdonald, "Partial Memoirs of D.B. Macdonald", UTA/B83-1295 at 16.

23. Page 271, para. 2 – "were completed before the war": Montagnes, *Uncommon Fellowship* at 16-17.

24. Page 271, para. 3 – "cost close to $2 million": Massey to Bickersteth, January 17, 1929, UTA/A75-0021/048.

25. Page 271, para. 3 – "and smooth Indiana limestone": Montagnes, *Uncommon Fellowship* at 22.

26. Page 272, para. 1 – "and residences at Victoria College": Ibid. at 16.

27. Page 272, para. 1 – "massive foundations were required for support": Ibid.

28. Page 272, para. 1 – "looked like a proscenium arch": Ibid. at 19; Nathaniel A. Benson, "Varsity's Little Theatre", *University of Toronto Alumni Bulletin* (February, 1952); Montagnes, "The Founder and the Animator" at 9; Vincent Massey, *What's Past is Prologue* (Toronto: Macmillan Company of Canada Ltd., 1963) at 55-56.

29. Page 272, para. 1 – "before construction started": *University of Toronto Monthly,* vol. 11 (July, 1911) at 414-415 et seq.

30. Page 272, para. 1 – "than on the east wall": Montagnes, *Uncommon Fellowship* at 26-27; Sirluck to Friedland, December 29, 2000; Ernest Sirluck, ed., *Complete Prose Works of John Milton 1643-1648* (New Haven: Yale University Press, 1959).

31. Page 273, para. 1 – "infused the life of this institution": Ibid. at 29.

32. Page 273, para. 1 – "It has continued to guide wardens": Margaret Hancock, introduction to Kilgour, ed., *A Strange Elation* at 2.

33. Page 273, para. 2 – "of true religion and high endeavour": Montagnes, *Uncommon Fellowship* at 29.

34. Page 273, para. 3 – "he meant 'men'": Ibid. at 18.

35. Page 273, para. 3 – "on equal terms with men until 1972": Anne Rochon Ford, *A Path not Strewn with Roses: One Hundred Years of Women at the University of Toronto 1884-1984* (University of Toronto Press, 1985) at 74; *Bulletin,* January 28, 1972 at 1.

36. Page 273, para. 3 – "in the conversation of the wise and the earnest": Hart House Five-Year Plan, 1997-2002 at 1.

37. Page 273, para. 3 – "and possibly only Protestantism": For example, Catholics are treated as outside the S.C.M., which took over the work of the YMCA in Hart House: see Ernest A. Dale, *Twenty-one years a-building : a short account of the Student Christian Movement of Canada, 1920-1941* (Toronto: Student Christian Movement of Canada, 1941) at 18; see also the document by Bickersteth dated March 4, 1957.

38. Page 273, para. 3 – "were not allowed official space for meetings": For example, at a meeting of the House Committee, the Jewish "Menorah Society" was refused permission to use a room: see Minutes of the Hart House Committee, October 8, 1919.

39. Page 273, para. 4 – "were open to women": Minutes of Music Committee, October 19, 1920.

40. Page 273, para. 4 – "provided no ladies are present": Minutes of House Committee, February 18, 1921.

41. Page 273, para. 4 – "by the lower south-east door": Minutes of House Committee, February 23, 1921.

42. Page 273, para. 4 – "pool for club contests": Minutes of House Committee, March 9, 1921.

43. Page 274, para. 1 – "to hold a dinner in the House": Ibid.

44. Page 274, para. 1 – "while it was in Hart House": Irene M. Spry, "Economic History and Economic Theory: Innis's Insights", in Charles R. Acland and William J. Buxton, eds., *Harold Innis in the New Century: Reflections and Refractions* (Montreal: McGill-Queen's University Press, 1999) at 107. One of the primary reasons the Faculty Club moved out of Hart House in 1960 was so that women could be members: see Montagnes, *Uncommon Fellowship* at 177.

45. Page 274, para. 1 – "to raise funds to acquire their own premises": Minutes of the House Committee, March 10, 1920.

46. Page 274, para. 1 – "for dining and meetings and other activities": The building was acquired in 1922 but not opened until January of 1923: see *Varsity*, October 2, 1922 and January 10, 1923; *University of Toronto Monthly*, v.23 at 105. An earlier, smaller house had been equipped as a Women's Union by Margaret Wrong, the daughter of George Wrong. Falconer quite rightly noted that "but one house cannot service even as a modest social headquarters for the 450 women students of the college alone, to say nothing of those of other faculties": see *President's Report 1919/1920* at 8. Falconer here ignored the existence of Queen's Hall, which functioned as a social centre for approximately 100 U.C. students: see Charles Levi, "Phyllis Grierson, Margaret Ross and the Queen's Hall Girls: Intergroup Conflict among University College Students 1910-1921" (Unpublished paper, CHEA Conference, 2000). Margaret Wrong had left the University in 1921 and never made use of the new building.

47. Page 274, para. 2 – "a student union for all women students": Joseph Flavelle donated Holwood house to the University to be used as a "club or meeting place" for women staff and students, but it was never used as such: see Michael Bliss, *A Canadian Millionaire: The Life and Business Times of Sir Joseph Flavelle, Bart. 1858-1939* (Toronto: Macmillan of Canada, 1978) at 508-509.

48. Page 275, para. 1 – "a similar recommendation of the musical club": Minutes of House Committee, December 16, 1919.

49. Page 275, para. 1 – "in some form or shape": Sproatt and Rolph to Massey, December 17, 1919, UTA/A73-0050/001/65.

50. Page 275, para. 2 – "first warden of Hart House, Walter Bowles": Montagnes, *Uncommon Fellowship* at 30; Montagnes, "The Founder and the Animator" at 13.

51. Page 275, para. 2 – "the CBC's newscast reader": Montagnes, *Uncommon Fellowship* at 36.

52. Page 275, para. 2 – "as a lay member of a church mission": Ibid. at 38-39.

53. Page 275, para. 2 – "as warden until 1947": Ibid. at vi; Montagnes, "The Founder and the Animator" in Kilgour, ed., *A Strange Elation* at 14-15.

54. Page 275, para. 2 – "and faculty members": Montagnes, *Uncommon Fellowship* at 31.

55. Page 275, para. 2 – "was the first chair of the art committee": Ibid. at 52.

56. Page 275, para. 2 – "were members of the music committee": See Montagnes, *Uncommon Fellowship* at 69 for MacMillan; and see Minutes of Board of Stewards meeting, January 8, 1920 for Willan.

57. Page 275, para. 2 – "of the debates committee": Montagnes, *Uncommon Fellowship* at 111.

58. Page 275, para. 3 – "the Hart House String Quartet established": Ibid. at 66-68 and 75. See generally Jim Bartley, Brian Pronger, and Rupert Schieder, "Music: No Ragtime in the House" in *A Strange Elation*. For the string quartet, see Kilgour, ed., *A Strange Elation* at 63.

59. Page 275, para. 3 – "until the end of the Second World War": Montagnes, *Uncommon Fellowship* at 76.

60. Page 275, para. 3 – "be excluded from the piano": Minutes of Meeting of Music Committee, December 3, 1919.

61. Page 275, para. 4 – "on the bare walls of the House": See Catherine D. Siddall, "Art: An Audience for the Future" in Kilgour, ed., *A Strange Elation*.

62. Page 275, para. 4 – "two or three paintings a year": Montagnes, *Uncommon Fellowship* at 41.

63. Page 275, para. 4 – "*Georgian Bay, November*": Ibid. at 53; Micah Raynor, "The Pupil's Palette", *University of Toronto Bulletin*, September 11, 2000.

64. Page 275, para. 4 – "Lawren Harris and J.E.H. MacDonald": Montagnes, *Uncommon Fellowship* at 53.

65. Page 275, para. 4 – "who died at Oxford after the war": Ibid. at 55; Siddall, "Art: An Audience for the Future" at 51.

66. Page 275, para. 4 – "were purchased with these funds": *Gifts and the Great Wrong Gift* (Toronto: Justina M. Barnicke Gallery, Hart House, 1998).

67. Page 275, para. 5 – "and of the wider community": See Richard Partington, "Theatre: A Matter of Direction" in Kilgour, ed., *A Strange Elation*.

68. Page 276, para. 1 – "and played by Healey Willan": Judith Knelman, "School for Directors", *The Graduate* (September/October 1984) at 12; Claude Bissell, *The Young Vincent Massey* (University of Toronto Press, 1981) at 68.

69. Page 276, para. 1 – "seventeen plays were produced": Montagnes, *Uncommon Fellowship* at 107.

70. Page 276, para. 2 – "The first Hart House debate was held in 1924": Ibid. at 109. See John Duffy, "Debates: Academy and Agora" in Kilgour, ed., *A Strange Elation*.

71. Page 276, para. 2 – "along with speeches from the floor": Montagnes, *Uncommon Fellowship* at 109-111.

72. Page 276, para. 2 – "and 88 opposed it": *Varsity*, December 5, 1924.

73. Page 276, para. 3 – "because of his role in the strike thirty years earlier": Montagnes, *Uncommon Fellowship* at 112-113.

74. Page 276, para. 3 – "greater independence for the Dominions": Ibid. at 113.

75. Page 276, para. 3 – "Three hundred more were turned away": Ibid. at 114.

76. Page 276, para. 3 – "which he had not even debated as yet at Ottawa": Letter home to England from Bickersteth of February 9, 1927, cited in Montagnes, *Uncommon Fellowship* at 115.

77. Page 276, para. 3 – "408 to 125 in favour of the prime minister": Minutes of the Debates Committee, February 4, 1927.

78. Page 277, para. 1 – "to occupy the building for five years": T.A. Reed, ed., *A History of the University of Trinity College Toronto 1852-1952* (University of Toronto Press, 1952) at 139-141.

79. Page 277, para. 1 – "stone of the present building was laid": *Trinity University Review*, v. 35, no. 8 (May-June, 1923) at 3.

80. Page 277, para. 1 – "from the old building on Queen Street was discovered": Ibid. at 10.

81. Page 277, para. 1 – "was used by the Archbishop of Algoma": Ibid. at 7.

82. Page 277, para. 1 – "usages of the Church of England in Canada": Ibid. at 3.

83. Page 278, para. 1 – "would agree to unite": Reed, *Trinity College* at 140. Reed does not name the donor, but clear evidence that it was E.C. Whitney can be found in Whitney to Macklem, January 26, 1910 and Macklem to Whitney, February 4, 1910, Trinity College Archives/986-0009/005(05).

84. Page 278, para. 1 – "another one, in 1921, also failed": Reed, *Trinity College* at 150; *Globe*, April 23, 1921.

85. Page 278, para. 2 – "part of the building facing Hoskin Avenue": Reed, *Trinity College* at 149.

86. Page 278, para. 2 – "over the previous twenty years": See Chapter 17 (1901) and Chapter 21 (1909).

87. Page 278, para. 2 – "to resemble the old college": *Varsity*, October 2, 1925.

88. Page 278, para. 2 – "Trinity moved to its new site": Reed, *Trinity College* at 151.

89. Page 278, para. 2 – "continued to wear gowns to lectures": *Telegram*, October 20, 1925; Reed, *Trinity College* at 158.

90. Page 278, para. 2 – "and to meals": "[G]owns are worn essentially to meals": see *Trinity This Year* (1989).

91. Page 278, para. 2 – "who could not then be divinity students": Reed, *Trinity College* at 150.

92. Page 278, para. 2 – "there were more than 300 students": Ibid. at 161.

93. Page 278, para. 2 – "were purchased for women's residences": *Telegram*, March 2, 1925. Walker had been knighted in 1910 and died in 1924: see G.P. de T. Glazebrook, *Sir Edmund Walker* (Oxford: Oxford University Press, 1933) at 106. Walker's home was used for a men's residence after World War II: George Connell comments on draft manuscript, January 2001.

94. Page 278, para. 2 – "St. Hilda's was not built until 1937": Reed, *Trinity College* at 171.

95. Page 278, para. 2 – "renamed Trinity House": Ibid. at 160.

96. Page 278, para. 2 – "was purchased for a men's residence": Ibid. at 149.

97. Page 278, para. 2 – "during the Second World War": Ibid. at 171.

98. Page 278, para. 2 – "to be used initially as the chapel": *Varsity*, October 2, 1925.

99. Page 278, para. 2 – "was completed in 1955": *Trinity University Review*, v. 58, no.2 (December, 1955); "Trinity College Chapel and Sir Giles Gilbert Scott", *Trinity Convocation Bulletin*, v.18, no.1 (Summer, 1980).

100. Page 278, para. 3 – "Enrolment was rising": "Adequate Support of the Provincial University", UTA/B72-0015/001 at 2.

101. Page 278, para. 3 – "and had doubled again by 1920": Greenlee, *Falconer* at 257, citing *President's Report 1917-1918* at 3 and *President's Report 1919/20* at 3.

102. Page 278, para. 3 – "and were becoming uncompetitive": Ibid. at 259; McKillop, *Matters of Mind* at 298 et seq.

103. Page 278, para. 3 – "about $8,000 Canadian": Alumni Association of the University of Toronto, "Some observations on the New outlook and the New financial needs of the University of Toronto", UTA/B72-0015/001 at 6.

104. Page 278, para. 3 – "I am doubtful about cooking my own dinner!": Greenlee, *Falconer* at 259, citing Wrong to A.L. Smith, September 30, 1919.

105. Page 279, para. 1 – "was approaching $1 million": Greenlee, *Falconer* at 258, citing Board of Governors Minutes, May 19, 1918; June 20, 1919; June 24, 1920.

106. Page 279, para. 1 – "the United Farmers of Ontario government in October 1919": "Ernest Charles Drury", in W.S. Wallace, ed., *The Macmillan Dictionary of Canadian Biography* (Toronto: Macmillan of Canada, 1978) at 225; Greenlee, *Falconer* at 258.

107. Page 279, para. 1 – "was considerably less secure": Greenlee, *Falconer* at 258.

108. Page 279, para. 1 – "Its mind is isolated": *Globe*, December 13, 1922 at 13.

109. Page 279, para. 1 – "several vacancies with its own supporters": Greenlee, *Falconer* at 264.

110. Page 279, para. 1 – "in the budget it inherited": Ibid. at 258.

111. Page 279, para. 1 – "a maximum increase of $500 per person": Greenlee, *Falconer* at 261.

112. Page 279, para. 2 – "on university finances would be appointed": Greenlee, *Falconer* at 261; Edward E. Stewart, "The Role of the Provincial Government in the Development of the Universities of Ontario 1791-1964" (D.Ed. Thesis, University of Toronto, 1970) at 345-353.

113. Page 279, para. 2 – "Canon Cody, its chair": D.C. Masters, *Henry John Cody: An Outstanding Life* (Toronto: Dundurn Press, 1995) at 119 and 125-127.

114. Page 279, para. 2 – "as was the businessman T.A. Russell": McKillop, *Matters of Mind* at 301.

115. Page 279, para. 2 – "given each year to the University of Toronto": Greenlee, *Falconer* at 262; McKillop, *Matters of Mind* at 304. See *Report of the Royal Commission on University Finances* (Toronto: Clarkson W. James, 1921) at 8 for a summary of the recommendations.

116. Page 279, para. 2 – "and the University of Western Ontario": McKillop, *Matters of Mind* at 304.

117. Page 279, para. 2 – "would receive from this source": See Chapter 21 (1909); see also Greenlee, *Falconer* at 168.

118. Page 279, para. 2 – "and was expected to rise in future years": O.D. Skelton to Cody, December 31, 1920, UTA/B72-0015/001 at 3-4.

119. Page 279, para. 2 – "the government ignored the recommendation": Greenlee, *Falconer* at 263.

120. Page 279, para. 2 – "and the crying needs of the Province": *Globe*, April 15, 1921, cited in Stewart, "Role of Provincial Government" at 351.

121. Page 279, para. 3 – "to the University for capital expenditures": Greenlee, *Falconer* at 262; McKillop, *Matters of Mind* at 305; *Report of the Royal Commission on University Finances* at 8.

122. Page 279, para. 3 – "$500,000 for a new anatomy building": Greenlee, *Falconer* at 263; Stewart, "Role of Provincial Government" at 352.

123. Page 279, para. 3 – "the building was completed in 1923": W.S. Wallace, *A History of the University of Toronto* (University of Toronto Press, 1927) at 188.

124. Page 280, para. 1 – "that has continued to this day": Charles Levi, "Where the Famous People Were?: The Origins, Activities, and Future Careers of Student Leaders at University College, Toronto, 1854-1973" (Ph.D. Thesis, York University, 1998) at 8 and 319.

125. Page 280, para. 1 – "and a women's gymnasium": *University Finances* at 11 and 24-25.

126. Page 280, para. 1 – "would not take place until the 1930s": See Chapter 26 (1909).

127. Page 280, para. 1 – "and the women's gymnasium, the late 1950s": Stewart, "Role of Provincial Government" at 351n36; Helen Gurney, *A Century to Remember, 1893-1993: Women's Sports at the University of Toronto* (University of Toronto Women's T-Holders' Association, 1993) at 33.

128. Page 280, para. 2 – "by a select committee of the legislature": Greenlee, *Falconer* at 269; Stewart, "Role of Provincial Government" at 355-357.

129. Page 281, para. 1 – "the leader of the opposition, Howard Ferguson": "Legislative Committee on University Affairs to Meet in October", *University of Toronto Monthly*, v. 23 at 3.

130. Page 281, para. 1 – "held between October 1922 and January 1923": "The Legislative Committee Reports", *Monthly*, v. 23 at 421.

131. Page 281, para. 1 – "Falconer attended every sitting": Greenlee, *Falconer* at 271.

132. Page 281, para. 2 – "their names for the head of medicine": Robert B. Kerr and Douglas Waugh, eds., *Duncan Graham: Medical Reformer and Educator* (Toronto: Dundurn Press, 1989) at 31; "The President's Opening Address", *University of Toronto Monthly* (1921) at 15; "Sir John and Lady Eaton's Gift to the University", *University of Toronto Monthly*, v.19 at 215.

133. Page 281, para. 2 – "for other purposes in the faculty of medicine": Kerr and Waugh, *Duncan Graham* at 49; *University Finances*, appendix 1 at 9; "The President's Opening Address".

134. Page 281, para. 2 – "though only 37 years old": Kerr and Waugh, *Duncan Graham* at 15 and 42-44.

135. Page 281, para. 2 – "first full-time professor of medicine in the British Empire": J.K.W. Ferguson, "Duncan Archibald Lamont Graham", *Proceedings of the Royal Society of Canada*, 4th Series, v.12 (1974) at 44.

136. Page 281, para. 2 – "at least we will attempt to secure this": Letter from Falconer to Goldie, November 6, 1918, cited in Kerr and Waugh, *Duncan Graham* at 42.

137. Page 281, para. 2 – "became the sole clinical head of medicine": Kerr and Waugh, *Duncan Graham* at 47; Duncan Graham, "The Department of Medicine, University of Toronto", *University of Toronto Monthly*, v.21 at 293-296.

138. Page 281, para. 2 – "and the Toronto General Hospital": Greenlee, *Falconer* at 266.

139. Page 281, para. 2 – "with Dr Alan Brown as its head": *President's Reports 1919/1920* at 9; Allison B. Kingsmill, *Dr. Alan Brown: Portrait of a Tyrant* (Markham, Ontario: Fitzhenry and Whiteside, 1995) at 54-57.

140. Page 281, para. 3 – "director general of army medical services": Kerr and Waugh, *Duncan Graham* at 48 and 52; Greenlee, *Falconer* at 268; Wallace, *History of the University of Toronto* at 198.

141. Page 281, para. 3 – "deputy minister of overseas forces": UTA/Graduate Records/"Thomas A. Gibson"/A73-0026/117(23). Gibson was closely involved with the Alumni Association, but did not represent the Association: see "Committee of Legislature on University Administration", *University of Toronto Monthly*, v. 23 at 106.

142. Page 281, para. 3 – "autocratic in the extreme": "Committee of Legislature", *University of Toronto Monthly*, v. 23 at 106.

143. Page 281, para. 3 – "the graduate body and the staff": Thomas Gibson, "The Purpose of My Suggestions", *University of Toronto Monthly* v. 23 at 107.

144. Page 282, para. 1 – "agreed with much of the criticism": *Report of the Special Committee Appointed by the Legislature to Inquire into the Organization and Administration of the University of Toronto* (Toronto: Clarkson W. James, 1923) at 8-9, 12, and 15-18.

145. Page 282, para. 1 – "illegal and unauthorized": "Legislative Committee Reports on the University's Administration", *University of Toronto Monthly*, v. 23 at 427; *Report* at 16.

146. Page 282, para. 1 – "It should have been approved by cabinet": Ibid.

147. Page 282, para. 1 – "and irregularly terminated": Ibid.

148. Page 282, para. 1 – "8 of its 24 members": Greenlee, *Falconer* at 271; *Report* at 15.

149. Page 282, para. 1 – "should require the approval of the senate": Greenlee, *Falconer* at 271; "Legislative Committee Reports", *Monthly*, v. 23 at 425; *Report* at 10.

150. Page 282, para. 2 – "in the selection of the holder of the chair": Kerr and Waugh, *Duncan Graham* at 32; also see the agreement between the Eatons and the University, "Deed of Gift", Clause 2, UTA/A67-0007/052a.

151. Page 282, para. 2 – "the reorganization of the department of medicine": Kerr and Waugh, *Duncan Graham* at 47 and 110-112; R.D. Gidney and W.P.J. Millar, "Quality and Quantity: The Problem of Admissions in Medicine at the University of Toronto", *Historical Studies in Education*, v. 9, no. 2 (Fall, 1997) at 174.

152. Page 282, para. 2 – "most of the clinical teaching staff in the hospitals": Kerr and Waugh, *Duncan Graham* at 50-51. For $200,000 required to be spent on clinical labs, see *Globe*, January 11, 1923 at 9.

153. Page 282, para. 2 – "such as new anatomy laboratories": *University Finances* at 11; see also Edwin R. Embree, Secretary of the Rockefeller Foundation to Falconer, November 19, 1920, UTA/A67-0007/062.

154. Page 282, para. 2 – "and better pathological laboratories": "Faculty of Medicine, University of Toronto, Memorandum from the Dean Presented to the University Commission, December 1920", UTA/A67-0007/69; Robin Harris, "Developments 1919-1932", UTA/A91-0020/001 at 11-12.

155. Page 282, para. 3 – "unless given unconditionally": *Report* at 17.

156. Page 282, para. 3 – "in the system of funding the University": Greenlee, *Falconer* at 271; "Legislative Committee Reports", *University of Toronto Monthly*, v.23 at 426.

157. Page 282, para. 3 – "to appeal to the government for additional support": "Legislative Committee Reports", *University of Toronto Monthly*, v. 23 at 426.

158. Page 282, para. 4 – "and wanted to encourage": Greenlee, *Falconer* at 271.

159. Page 282, para. 4 – "since its formal establishment as a department in 1920": Greenlee, *Falconer* at 252 et seq.; Wallace, *History* at 194; *University Finances* at 22-23.

160. Page 282, para. 4 – "never on a very systematic basis": Robin Harris, "Extension", UTA/A83-0036/001 at 1-7; Allen M. Tough, "The Development of Adult Education at the University of Toronto Before 1920" (M.A. Thesis, University of Toronto, 1962) at 32-41; J.A. Blyth, *A Foundling at Varsity: A History of the Division of University Extension University of Toronto* (Toronto: Privately Published, 1976) at 2-5.

161. Page 282, para. 4 – "a practical need to demonstrate its commitment": Greenlee, *Falconer* at 252-253.

162. Page 282, para. 4 – "There were not only correspondence": *Globe*, November 18, 1922 at 18.

163. Page 283, para. 1 – "for teachers": "Memorandum on University Extension, November 23, 1920", UTA/A67-0007/69 at 1.

164. Page 283, para. 1 – "and bank employees": Greenlee, *Falconer* at 253.

165. Page 283, para. 1 – "also lectures for working men and women": "Memorandum on University Extension" at 4.

166. Page 283, para. 1 – "established at Toronto in 1918": Greenlee, *Falconer* at 253; Joan Sangster, "The Toronto WEA 1919-50", UTA/A83-0036/016 at 4-8.

167. Page 283, para. 1 – "paid an even more welcome $400": Vincent Bladen, *Bladen on Bladen: Memoirs of a political economist* (Toronto: Scarborough College, 1978) at 32-33.

168. Page 283, para. 1 – "were given to farmers in rural settings": "Memorandum on University Extension" at 8.

169. Page 283, para. 1 – "anxious to serve all the people": Greenlee, *Falconer* at 256, citing Dunlop to Falconer, March 5, 1921, UTA/A67-0007/064.

170. Page 283, para. 1 – "enrolled in extension courses": Greenlee, *Falconer* at 256.

171. Page 283, para. 1 – "courses were offered in Windsor and Fort William": Ibid. at 257.

172. Page 283, para. 1 – "offered through the extension department": Harris, "Extension" at 11. Occupational Therapy was established in 1926: see W.J. Dunlop, "A Brief History of Occupational Therapy", *Canadian Journal of Occupational Therapy* (1933) at 9. Physical Therapy was introduced in 1929: see Ruby Heap, "Training Women for a New 'Women's Profession': Physiotherapy Education at the University of Toronto, 1917-1940", *History of Education Quarterly*, v.35 (Summer, 1995) at 135.

173. Page 283, para. 1 – "were involved in extension courses": Wallace, *History of the University of Toronto* at 194.

174. Page 284, para. 1 – "under Howard Ferguson was elected": Greenlee, *Falconer* at 272.

175. Page 284, para. 1 – "no intention of implementing the report": Greenlee, *Falconer* at 272; Walker to Leonard, September 10, 1923, cited in Greenlee Cards, card 231, UTA/A67-0007/35.

176. Page 284, para. 1 – "even though Ferguson had signed it": Greenlee, *Falconer* at 272.

177. Page 284, para. 1 – "when vacancies occurred": "University Act Amended", *University of Toronto Monthly*, v. 24 at 249-250; "The Amendment to the University Act", *University of Toronto Monthly*, v. 24 at 298-299.

CHAPTER 24 – 1922 – RESEARCH AND GRADUATE STUDIES

1. Page 285, para. 1 – "established Toronto's international reputation": *New York Times*, October 8, 1922; *The Times* (London), November 17, 1922.

2. Page 285, para. 1 – "becoming the leading university in Canada": James Greenlee, the author of a biography of Sir Robert Falconer, believes that the establishment of the School of Graduate Studies was the turning point: Greenlee to author, June, 1998.

3. Page 285, para. 2 – "at the Toronto General Hospital on January 23, 1922": Michael Bliss, *Banting: A Biography* (University of Toronto Press, 2nd paperback edition, 1992) at 80 and 82.

4. Page 285, para. 2 – "only be touched on here": See Bliss, *Banting*, Bliss, *The Discovery of Insulin* (University of Toronto Press, 1982); Bliss, "Rewriting Medical History: Charles Best and the Banting and Best Myth", *Journal of the History of Medicine*, v. 48 (July, 1993).

5. Page 285, para. 2 – "known for more than thirty years": Bliss, *Banting* at 52.

6. Page 285, para. 2 – "had tried to extract such a substance": Ibid. at 55.

7. Page 285, para. 2 – "even before its actual 'discovery'": "John James Rickard Macleod", *Proceedings of the Royal Society of Canada*, 3rd Series, v. 29 (1935) at x; M.L. Barr and R.J. Rossiter, "James Bertram Collip", *Biographical Memoirs of the Royal Society of Canada*, v.19 (1973) at 241.

8. Page 285, para. 3 – "a young doctor in London, Ontario": Bliss, *Banting* at 48.

9. Page 285, para. 3 – "from the pancreas of dogs": Ibid. at 53.

10. Page 285, para. 3 – "the head of physiology at the University of Toronto": Ibid. at 54.

11. Page 285, para. 3 – "had graduated in the class of 1917": Ibid. at 36. Banting graduated on December 9, 1916 but officially belonged to the class of 1917, which was accelerated because of the war. He reported for military duty on December 10th.

12. Page 286, para. 1 – "in Cleveland since 1903": Ibid at 54-55; "MacLeod" at ix.

13. Page 286, para. 1 – "quite willing to let Banting come": Bliss, *Banting* at 56.

14. Page 286, para. 1 – "he had to repeat his first year": Ibid. at 28.

15. Page 286, para. 1 – "only an average student in medical school": Ibid. at 32-33; Andrew Hunter, "Sir Frederick Grant Banting ", *Proceedings of the Royal Society of Canada*, 3rd Series, v.35 (1941) at 87 says "undistinguished".

16. Page 286, para. 1 – "could enter medical school at Toronto": R.D. Gidney and W.P.J. Millar, "Quality and Quantity: The Problem of Admissions in Medicine at the University of Toronto 1910-51", *Historical Studies in Education*, v.9, no. 2 (Fall, 1997) at 184-185; Bliss, *Banting* at 28-29. Banting failed German in his first university year (which meant he had to repeat the whole first year) and re-entered in 1911. His petition to enter medical school was accepted on condition that he make up the course he had failed. Once cleared to enter in 1912, he dropped out of 1911-12 term.

17. Page 286, para. 1 – "and received the Military Cross": Bliss, *Banting* at 37, 39, and 41.

18. Page 286, para. 1 – "disliked each other": Ibid. at 44 and 48.

19. Page 286, para. 2 – "Macleod's two summer research assistants": Ibid. at 58-59.

20. Page 286, para. 2 – "Charles Best won the toss": Ibid. at 59; Bliss, "Rewriting" at 253.

21. Page 286, para. 2 – "who became a general practitioner in Toronto": Bliss, "Rewriting" at 260n14. Noble rejoined the team in February 1922 and contributed to several key papers.

22. Page 286, para. 2 – "regretted for the rest of his life": Bliss, *Banting* at 65.

23. Page 286, para. 2 – "in physiology and biochemistry": Reginald E. Haist, "Charles Herbert Best", *Proceedings of the Royal Society of Canada*, 4th Series, v. 16 (1978) at 45.

24. Page 286, para. 3 – "under the supervision of A.B. Macallum": Barr and Rossiter, "Collip" at 236-237. Collip was about the same age as the 30-year-old Banting and was an extremely well-trained researcher. He had led his class in the then recently established physiology and biochemistry course.

25. Page 286, para. 3 – "for the year to work with Macleod": See Bliss, *Banting* at 63, 73, and 76.

26. Page 286, para. 3 – "he later modestly stated": Barr and Rossiter, "Collip" at 241.

27. Page 286, para. 3 – "purified the extract that was to be used": Bliss, *Banting* at 82; Collip to President Tory, January 25, 1922, Tory Papers, University of Alberta Archives (forwarded by Allison Li).

28. Page 286, para. 3 – "were 'spectacular'": Ibid.

29. Page 288, para. 1 – "greeted with a standing ovation": Ibid. at 61 and 86.

30. Page 288, para. 1 – "in alphabetical order": Ibid. at 86.

31. Page 288, para. 1 – "dissuaded from turning it down": Ibid. at 133-134.

32. Page 288, para. 1 – "the first Canadian to win a Nobel prize": Ibid. at 133.

33. Page 288, para. 1 – "as did Macleod with Collip": Ibid. at 134.

34. Page 288, para. 2 – "who should have received the prize": See Bliss, "Rewriting".

35. Page 289, para. 1 – "probably not have reached insulin": Bliss, *Banting* at 90; A.B. McKillop, *Matters of Mind: The University in Ontario 1791-1951* (University of Toronto Press, 1994) at 349.

36. Page 289, para. 1 – "and experience at their disposal": *President's Report 1921/22* at 13.

37. Page 289, para. 2 – "when he first received insulin in July 1922": Bliss, *Banting* at 98. Elizabeth, the 14-year-old daughter of Charles Evans Hughes, the American secretary of state, was close to death, weighing under 50 pounds, when she was brought to Toronto in the summer of 1922. After being treated with insulin, her blood sugar dropped to normal levels and her weight increased: see ibid. at 101-102.

38. Page 289, para. 2 – "celebrating the discovery of insulin": Ibid. at 6.

39. Page 289, para. 3 – "not a very good scientist": Ibid. at 9.

40. Page 290, para. 1 – "the Banting and Best Chair of Medical Research": Ibid. at 123 and 126.

41. Page 290, para. 1 – "a lifetime annuity of $7,500": Ibid. at 126.

42. Page 290, para. 1 – "establish the medical school in the 1880s": See Chapter 12 (1887).

43. Page 290, para. 1 – "appointed chief justice in Ontario": Bliss, *Banting* at 121.

44. Page 290, para. 1 – "newly established Banting Research Foundation": Ibid. at 153-154.

45. Page 290, para. 1 – "opposite the Toronto General Hospital": Ibid. at 182.

46. Page 290, para. 1 – "of the five-storey building": Ibid. at 183.

47. Page 290, para. 1 – "significant contributions to medical research": See ibid. at 187. Up to 1945, 242 BRF-supported scientific papers resulted: see Seymour Kanowitch, "The Banting Research Foundation," UTA/A83-0036/011.

48. Page 290, para. 1 – "to blacken the reputation of J.J.R. Macleod": Bliss, *Banting* at 158.

49. Page 290, para. 2 – "did not speak to each other": Ibid. at 159.

50. Page 290, para. 2 – "the University of Aberdeen": Ibid. at 179. "Macleod" at x says he accepted in 1927. Lloyd G. Stevenson, "John James Rickard Macleod" in *Dictionary of Scientific Biography*, v. 8 (New York: Charles Scribner's Sons, 1980) at 615, says he left in 1928.

51. Page 290, para. 2 – "excellent work in endocrinology": "Archibald Byron Macallum", *Proceedings of the Royal Society of Canada*, 3rd Series, v. 28 (1934) at XIX. Collip returned to the University of Alberta in 1922 and later assumed the Chair of Biochemistry at McGill in 1928 at the age of 35: see *RSC*, 4th series, vol. 4 (1966) at 74, 77. Bliss, *The Discovery of Insulin* at 237, says Collip went to McGill in 1928, having turned down a "staggering salary" from the Mayo Clinic the previous year.

52. Page 290, para. 2 – "to teach and conduct research at Toronto": Bliss, *Banting* at 160.

53. Page 290, para. 2 – "and open-heart surgery": Susan E. Belanger, "Continuing the Banting Legacy: The Banting Research Foundation 1925-1995, 70 Years of Medical Research in Canada" (Toronto: The Banting Research Foundation, 1995) at 4-6. See generally, Gordon Murray, *Medicine in the Making* (Toronto: The Ryerson Press, 1960).

54. Page 290, para. 2 – "and connected to the Banting Institute": Bliss, *Banting* at 310. The buildings are still called (separately) the Best Institute and the Banting Institute. The Banting and Best Department of Medical Research is located in the Best Institute, while the Banting Institute contains labs for medical microbiology, pathology, and clinical biochemistry and the office of the Banting Research Foundation. The two institutes were fittingly joined by a bridge in 1961 – the "Banting and Best Bridge": *Varsity Graduate* (April, 1961) at 60.

55. Page 290, para. 2 – "his importance in the discovery of insulin": See generally, Bliss, "Rewriting".

56. Page 290, para. 3 – "had not been good": Bliss, "Rewriting" at 255.

57. Page 291, para. 1 – "I'll never rest in my grave": Bliss, *Banting* at 5; Bliss, "Rewriting" at 255.

58. Page 291, para. 1 – "his good friend John FitzGerald died": Donald T. Fraser, "John Gerald FitzGerald", *Proceedings of the Royal Society of Canada*, 3rd Series, v. 35 (1941) at 113.

59. Page 291, para. 1 – "he bled to death": Conversation in 1998 and April, 2001 with his grandson, James FitzGerald, who is researching a book on his grandfather, to be entitled *An Irish Madness*, to be published by

Macfarlane, Walter & Ross in 2003; see also correspondence in the possession of James FitzGerald. See also two articles by James FitzGerald, "Dr. John Gerald FitzGerald: The Troubled Healer" in the Spring 2002 issue of the *U of T Magazine* and "Sins of the Fathers" in February 2002 *Toronto Life.*

60. Page 291, para. 2 – "*because* of the discovery of insulin": Bliss, "Build it and They will come: Why insulin was discovered in Toronto", address at the *Medicine in Toronto, 200 Years* symposium, October 16, 1993 at 2.

61. Page 291, para. 2 – "over the practice of medicine at Toronto": Bliss, *Banting* at 124; McKillop, *Matters of Mind* at 350-352. See also Chapter 20 (1908) and Chapter 23 (1919).

62. Page 291, para. 3 – "of the quality of the staff and facilities": Bliss, "Build it" at 4-5.

63. Page 291, para. 3 – "some of the finest research facilities in the world": Bliss, *Banting* at 32.

64. Page 291, para. 3 – "among the best on the continent": Sandra F. McRae, "The 'Scientific Spirit' in Medicine at the University of Toronto 1880-1910" (Ph.D. Thesis, University of Toronto, 1987) at 1-2 and 344; Abraham Flexner, *Medical Education in the United States and Canada: A Report to the Carnegie Foundation for the Advancement of Teaching* (Boston: The Merrymount Press, 1950 reprint) at 323. Flexner also noted that "the graduates of McGill and Toronto have passed through a scientific and clinical discipline of high quality": see ibid. at 15.

65. Page 291, para. 3 – "for research and animal quarters": Bliss, *Banting* at 152.

66. Page 291, para. 3 – "were ready to assist researchers": Ibid. at 83.

67. Page 291, para. 3 – "in the course of construction": Ibid. at 71.

68. Page 292, para. 1 – "discovered someplace else": Charles Hollenberg to author, June, 1998.

69. Page 292, para. 2 – "other departments of the University": McMurrich to Falconer, November 13, 1919, UTA/A67-0007/059, cited in James Greenlee, *Sir Robert Falconer: A Biography* (University of Toronto Press, 1988) at 251.

70. Page 292, para. 2 – "the creation of the board of graduate studies": See Chapter 16 (1897).

71. Page 292, para. 2 – "like an American Graduate School of first rank": A.B. Macallum to A.S. Mackenzie, November 28, 1918, quoted in Mel Thistle, *The Inner Ring: The Early History of the National Research Council of Canada* (University of Toronto Press, 1966) at 42; Peter N. Ross, "The Origins and Development of the Ph.D. Degree at the University of Toronto 1871-1932" (D.Ed. Degree, University of Toronto, 1972) at 294-295.

72. Page 292, para. 2 – "Germany grew rich and strong": *Report of the Royal Commission on University Finances* (Toronto: Clarkson W. James, 1921) at 16.

73. Page 292, para. 2 – "to the wealth of his native country": Ross, "Origins and Development" at 302.

74. Page 292, para. 2 – "later was appointed as its first dean": Robin Harris, "Graduate Studies at Toronto: The Role of the Dean", talk delivered March 12, 1986 at University College at 8.

75. Page 292, para. 3 – "as well as graduate studies": Ross, "Origins and Development" at 308; Harris, "The Role of the Dean" at 12.

76. Page 292, para. 3 – "had made a similar proposal": *Royal Commission* at 8; Ross, "Origins and Development" at 250; McKillop, *Matters of Mind* at 305.

77. Page 292, para. 3 – "became dean of the graduate school": Ross, "Origins and Development" at 324.

78. Page 292, para. 3 – "and graduate studies be joined": Ibid. at 326.

79. Page 292, para. 3 – "to control their research agenda": Ross, "Origins and Development" at 326; Robin Harris, "Graduate Studies", UTA/A83-0036/015 at 8.

80. Page 292, para. 3 – "could not lightly be sacrificed": Harris, "Graduate Studies" at 8.

81. Page 292, para. 3 – "Shortly after the rejection of his scheme": Harris, "The Role of the Dean" at 13.

82. Page 293, para. 1 – "retired to England at the age of 63": Ross, "Origins and Development" at 327; Harris, "The Role of the Dean" at 13.

83. Page 293, para. 1 – "until his death in 1944": Harris, "The Role of the Dean" at 16.

84. Page 293, para. 2 – "grew significantly": In 1920, there were 33 candidates registered for the Ph.D. degree; in 1922, there were 57; and in 1932, there were 131: see Ross, "Origins and Development" at 317.

85. Page 293, para. 2 – "and 131 registered for the degree": Ibid. at 240 and 317.

86. Page 293, para. 2 – "to bind Canada together": *President's Report 1919/20* at 10; Greenlee, *Falconer* at 250-51.

87. Page 293, para. 2 – "would be with the United States": Robert Falconer, "A Factor in Canadian Unity", *Globe*, January 21, 1922.

88. Page 293, para. 2 – "such as the Canadian Pacific Railway and Imperial Oil": Harris, "Graduate Studies" at 3.

89. Page 293, para. 2 – "primarily for non-Toronto students": McMurrich and Brett to Falconer, May 8, 1930, UTA/A67-0007/121; Harris, "Graduate Studies" at 3.

90. Page 293, para. 2 – "not eligible for National Research Council awards": Ross, "Origins and Development" at 331.

91. Page 293, para. 2 – "relatively poor research potential": Yves Gingras, *Physics and the Rise of Scientific Research in Canada*, Peter Keating, trans., (Montreal: McGill-Queen's University Press, 1991) at 59; Ross, "Origins and Development" at 330-31. Macallum had estimated at the time that in all of Canada there were "not many more than 50 pure research men all told", cited in Thistle, *Inner Ring* at 29.

92. Page 293, para. 2 – "who had held National Research Council awards": Ross, "Origins and Development" at 330.

93. Page 294, para. 1 – "with 9 each": Ross, "Origins and Development" at 331 and 331n1. Gingras, *Physics* at 59-60, says that from 1917 to 1938 Toronto got twice as many awards in physics as McGill did.

94. Page 294, para. 2 – "a nonentity in the life of the University": Executive Committee of the Graduate Student's Union to the Board of Graduate Studies, c. 1919, UTA/A83-0036/015.

95. Page 294, para. 2 – "with living accommodations": Ibid.; *Varsity*, December 13, 1918 and February 3, 1919. The idea of forming a Graduate Student Union was put forward in the fall of 1918, and a committee was established to draft a constitution, which was presented and approved at the first meeting of the G.S.U. on December 11, 1918.

96. Page 294, para. 2 – "for women graduate students": W.S. Wallace, *A History of the University of Toronto* (University of Toronto Press, 1927) at 224.

97. Page 294, para. 2 – "with the secretary of the school": Ross, "Origins and Development" at 245; Clarke G. Ashworth, "Post-Graduate Work at Toronto", *University of Toronto Monthly*, v. 24 at 297.

98. Page 294, para. 2 – "the policy, etc. of the School": Ross, "Origins and Development" at 323; McMurrich to Falconer, February 15, 1927, UTA/A67-0007/102.

99. Page 294, para. 2 – "would get adequate facilities": *Summer Varsity*, July 10, 1964; *President's Report 1964/65* at 103. The school had spent 1946-1961 at 44 Hoskin Avenue and 1961-1964 in the temporary building which stood next to SAC, but neither can be considered permanent facilities.

100. Page 294, para. 2 – "at the corner of Spadina Avenue and Harbord Street": University of Toronto Archives/Subject files/Buildings/"Graduate House".

101. Page 294, para. 3 – "by footnotes to an absurd extent": Robert Bothwell, *Laying the Foundation: A Century of History at the University of Toronto* (Toronto: Department of History, 1991) at 65.

102. Page 294, para. 3 – "was not awarded until 1925": Two Ph.D.'s were awarded in 1925, to W.B. Kerr and Walter Sage: see ibid. at 67.

103. Page 294, para. 3 – "and 4 in classics": Charles Levi, "Doctoral Theses by Discipline 1915-1939 as taken from *Doctoral Theses 1897-1967* (Memorandum, June 30, 1999). It should be noted here that *Doctoral Theses* (cited below) represents a 1967 understanding of the organization of disciplines that is often unrelated to how departments were organized in the period 1915-1939.

104. Page 294, para. 3 – "and Italian and Spanish 1 each": Ibid.

105. Page 294, para. 3 – "received her PhD in Italian in 1932": Judy Mills and Irene Dombra, eds., *University of Toronto Doctoral Theses, 1897-1967* (University of Toronto Press, 1968) at 86.

106. Page 294, para. 3 – "a major force in Italian studies at the University": Maddalena Kuitunen, *A History of Italian Studies at the University of Toronto 1840-1990* (Toronto: Department of Italian Studies, 1991) at 54.

107. Page 294, para. 3 – "from 1937 until 1950": UTA/Graduate Records/"Robert Kay Gordon"/A73-0026/122(27).

108. Page 294, para. 3 – "completed their doctorates in English in 1936": Mills and Dombra, *Doctoral Theses* at 36.

109. Page 294, para. 3 – "became the chair of the department in 1947": UTA/Current People/"J. Roy Daniells".

110. Page 295, para. 1 – "19 PhDs were awarded in psychology": Levi, "Doctoral Theses". Again, note that some of these were not granted by the Department of Psychology.

111. Page 295, para. 1 – "which had formed its own department in 1927": John G. Slater, "Philosophy at Toronto" (Unpublished manuscript) at 135.

112. Page 295, para. 1 – "was published in 1921": Harris, "The Role of the Dean" at 17.

113. Page 295, para. 1 – "the most learned man in the university": Harris, "The Role of the Dean" at 16, quoting Leslie Armour, *The Faces of Reason: An essay on philosophy and culture in English Canada 1850-1950* (Wilfrid Laurier Press, 1983) at 436.

114. Page 295, para. 1 – "Brett is said to have supervised 20 of them": Harris, "The Role of the Dean" at 17. See generally, John A. Irving, "The Achievement of George Sidney Brett", *University of Toronto Quarterly*, vol. 14, no. 4 (July, 1945) at 329.

115. Page 295, para. 2 – "renamed the Pontifical Institute in 1939": Martin Dimnik, ed., *Jubilee 1989: Pontifical Institute of Mediaeval Studies Foundation 1929 – Papal Charter 1939* (Toronto: Pontifical Institute of Mediaeval

Studies, 1989) at 5 and 11; Lawrence K. Shook, *Catholic Education in English-speaking Canada: A History* (University of Toronto Press, 1971).

116. Page 295, para. 2 – "through the graduate school": Ibid. at 10. Brett was a member of the Institute from the beginning and during his tenure as dean of the graduate school there were 24 Ph.D.s awarded through the Pontifical Institute: see Harris, "The Role of the Dean" at 18.

117. Page 295, para. 2 – "invariably had ambitious plans for the college": Alexander Reford, "St. Michael's College at the University of Toronto 1958-1978: The Frustrations of Federation", *CCHA Historical Studies*, v.61 (1995) at 175.

118. Page 295, para. 2 – "an anthropologist and Catholic writer": Ibid.; Dimnik, *Jubilee 1989* at 16.

119. Page 295, para. 2 – "then a professor of English literature": Dimnik, *Jubilee 1989* at 16.

120. Page 295, para. 2 – "Etienne Gilson and Jacques Maritain": Reford, "Frustrations of Federation" at 175.

121. Page 295, para. 2 – "to deliver some lectures": Doug Fetherling, "Pontifical Institute Loses Father Boyle", *Graduate* (November/December, 1984) at 13.

122. Page 295, para. 2 – "The institute will be there or it will be nowhere!": Etienne Gilson, "St. Michael's Establishes Institute of Mediaeval Studies", *University of Toronto Monthly*, v. 28 at 120.

123. Page 295, para. 2 – "in 1939 because of the war": Dimnik, *Jubilee 1989* at 39-40.

124. Page 295, para. 2 – "he spent a term at Toronto": Fetherling, "Pontifical Institute" at 13.

125. Page 295, para. 2 – "also a philosopher": Ibid.

126. Page 295, para. 2 – "in Belgium a few years earlier": J. Reginald O'Donnell, "Gerald Bernard Phelan", Royal Society of Canada obituary, reproduced in UTA/A83-0036/043 at 155.

127. Page 295, para. 2 – "work under Gilson, Phelan, and Maritain": Pegis' doctorate on *St. Thomas and the Problem of the Soul in the Thirteenth Century* was published in 1934: see J. Owens, "Anton Charles Pegis", *Proceedings of the Royal Society of Canada*, 4th Series, v. 16 (1978) at 103.

128. Page 295, para. 2 – "a constituent part of the University": Slater, "Philosophy at Toronto" at 322.

129. Page 297, para. 1 – "oversaw a major growth in graduate studies": Ian M. Drummond, *Political Economy at the University of Toronto: A History of the Department, 1888-1982* (Toronto: Faculty of Arts and Science, 1983) at 113 and 125.

130. Page 297, para. 1 – "doctorate on the Canadian Manufacturers' Association": Ibid. at 174.

131. Page 297, para. 1 – "supervised by Harold Innis and Alexander Brady": Marlene Shore, *The Science of Social Redemption: McGill, the Chicago School, and the Origins of Social Research in Canada* (University of Toronto Press, 1987) at 302n95; Harry H. Hiller, *Society and Change: S.D. Clark and the Development of Canadian Sociology* (University of Toronto Press, 1982) at 47.

132. Page 297, para. 1 – "when it was made a separate department in 1963": R. Helmes-Hayes, ed., *A Quarter-Century of Sociology at the University of Toronto 1963-1988* (Toronto: Canadian Scholars' Press, 1988) at 7; Hiller, *Society and Change* at 50. During his tenure as head, Clark helped stimulate a modest growth in graduate work in his department. From 1963 to 1969 (when Clark was head), six Ph.D. theses were produced in sociology at the University, while in Canada there were 15. As Hiller says at 22, "Sociology was one of the poorest in providing

native-trained faculty"; at 159, he adds, "Clark's own direct personal impact on the discipline in sociology in Canada is somewhat obscure".

133. Page 297, para. 1 – "such as Innis, Alexander Brady": Brady received his doctorate in history in 1926: see Mills and Dombra, *Doctoral Theses* at 71.

134. Page 297, para. 1 – "and all had doctorates": Professors with doctorates were still rare at the time. The department, writes Ian Drummond in *Political Economy* at 61, "was not very interested in the Ph.D., although when and if it could recruit the holder of a Ph.D. degree it was delighted to do so." Kennedy had hoped to succeed Urwick as Head of the Department of Political Economy: see Innis to Falconer, undated, UTA/A83-0036/041.

135. Page 297, para. 2 – "due to the demands of the undergraduate programs": Drummond, *Political Economy* at 4.

136. Page 297, para. 2 – "professor of social philosophy at the University of London": Sara Z. Burke, *Seeking the Highest Good: Social Service and Gender at the University of Toronto 1888-1937* (University of Toronto Press, 1996) at 116.

137. Page 297, para. 2 – "predecessor of the London School of Economics": McKillop, *Matters of Mind* at 506.

138. Page 297, para. 2 – "in McMaster Hall on Bloor Street": Ibid. at 506-507 and 511. McMaster moved to Hamilton between 1927 and 1930: see ibid. at 316.

139. Page 297, para. 3 – "such as W.A. Parks in geology": See Chapter 21 (1909).

140. Page 297, para. 3 – "and E.M. Walker in zoology": Ibid.

141. Page 297, para. 3 – "have the same advertising value": E. Horne Craigie, *A History of the Department of Zoology of the University of Toronto up to 1962* (Toronto: Department of Zoology, 1966) at 71.

142. Page 297, para. 3 – "received his PhD in 1937": Mills and Dombra, *Doctoral Theses* at 58.

143. Page 297, para. 3 – "later move to physiology in the faculty of medicine": "Curriculum Vitae – H.L. Atwood" (January, 1998).

144. Page 297, para. 3 – "had a significant number of graduate students": Charles Levi, "Memorandum on the Supervision of PhD Theses at the University of Toronto 1915-1939" (Memorandum, July 8, 1999) at 4-5.

145. Page 297, para. 3 – "and later was head of botany": UTA/Graduate Records/"Herbert S. Jackson"/A73-0026/172(20).

146. Page 298, para. 1 – "D.L. Bailey": Levi, "Memorandum on Supervision" at 4.

147. Page 298, para. 1 – "had attained their PhDs under his guidance": UTA/Graduate Records/"Dixon Lloyd Bailey"/A73-0026/15(16-17).

148. Page 298, para. 2 – "Best did": See Levi, "Doctoral Theses" and Levi, "Memorandum on Supervision".

149. Page 298, para. 2 – "little experimental research in the clinical departments": "Faculty of Medicine, University of Toronto – Memorandum from the Dean Presented to the University Commission, December, 1920", UTA/A67-0007/069 at 10.

150. Page 298, para. 2 – "because of the many standard texts produced": These include: J.J.R. Macleod, *Physiology and Biochemistry in Modern Medicine*, second edition 1919, seventh edition 1930; William Boyd, *Surgical Pathology*, published 1925 with three more texts in 1931, 1932, and 1937; John Charles Boileau Grant, *A Method of Anatomy*, second edition, 1940, sixth edition, 1958; Grant, *An Atlas of Anatomy*, first edition, 1943, seventh

edition, 1979; Grant, *A Dissector of Anatomy*, first edition, 1940, ninth edition, 1984; James Playfair McMurrich, *The Development of the Human Body*, first edition, 1902, seventh edition 1923; Charles H. Best, *Physiological Basis of Medical Practice*, first edition 1937, twelfth edition 1991.

151. Page 298, para. 2 – "were available in radiology and psychiatry": Harris, "The Role of the Dean" at 9.

152. Page 298, para. 2 – "had been introduced before the war": Ibid.

153. Page 298, para. 3 – "and 139 for MAs": *President's Report 1924/25* at 25.

154. Page 298, para. 3 – "for possible advancement in their profession": Between 1914 and 1922 there were 220 candidates for the D.Paed. degree: see Ross, "Origins and Development" at 304-305.

155. Page 298, para. 3 – "such as dentistry and forestry": Harris, "The Role of the Dean" at 9.

156. Page 298, para. 3 – "given each year to the School of Engineering Research": Richard White, *The Skule Story: The University of Toronto Faculty of Applied Science and Engineering 1873-2000* (University of Toronto Press, 2000) at 107 and 110.

157. Page 298, para. 3 – "was established in 1922": Harris, "Graduate Studies" at 4.

158. Page 298, para. 3 – "the year Eric Arthur arrived from England": White, *The Skule Story* at 112.

159. Page 298, para. 3 – "and analysis of historic architecture in Ontario": Ibid. at 135.

160. Page 298, para. 3 – "were in chemical engineering": Ibid. at 138. M.C. Boswell, the head of the division of engineering research and himself a productive researcher, was one of the few engineering professors with a doctorate, having received his from the department of chemistry in 1907: see Mills and Dombra, *Doctoral Theses* at 24. Most of the research in engineering was not, by most standards, scientific. "The research," historian Richard White has written, "usually took the form of trials, or tests, for which reporting was observational rather than analytical": see White, *The Skule Story* at 109. The total cited here includes Roland McLaughlin, the dean of engineering between 1954 and 1966, although extensive research has failed to turn up exactly where his degree should be classified. McLaughlin had an M.A.Sc., and it seems natural to assume that his Ph.D., awarded in 1926, would have been in engineering. That Faculty, however, did not offer the Ph.D. degree that early, a fact which Mills and Dombra failed to note when they compiled *Doctoral Theses*. There is also no evidence that McLaughlin was ever supervised by any member of the Department of Chemistry, even though the title of his thesis suggests it was on a chemical subject, and White has accepted that the Ph.D. was in chemistry.

161. Page 298, para. 4 – "by E.F. Burton": Levi, "Memorandum on Supervision" at 3.

162. Page 298, para. 4 – "research productivity in the department": McKillop, *Matters of Mind* at 344; Gingras, *Physics* at 31.

163. Page 298, para. 4 – "under Rutherford passed to Toronto": David Wilson, *Rutherford: Simple Genius* (London: Hodder and Stoughton, 1983) at 188; McKillop, *Matters of Mind* at 344.

164. Page 299, para. 1 – "women graduate students received doctorates": Mills and Dombra, *Doctoral Theses* at 109-110. The other two were Mattie Levi and Elizabeth Cohen. Mattie Levi is the great aunt of University of Toronto history project researcher Charles Levi. Vivian Pound, who also received a Ph.D. under McLennan's supervision, was a man: see Alison Prentice, "Vivian Pound was a Man? The Joys and Sorrows of Studying Gender in University Physics" (Paper delivered at Canadian History of Education Association conference, October, 2000).

165. Page 299, para. 1 – "this was regarded as evidence of lack of endeavour": Elizabeth J. Allin, *Physics at the University of Toronto 1843-1980* (University of Toronto Press, 1981) at 19-20.

166. Page 299, para. 1 – "and remained there until her retirement in 1970": Ibid. at 70.

167. Page 299, para. 2 – "the spectra of atoms and molecules": Ibid. at 14.

168. Page 299, para. 2 – "on which he started to work in 1910": Gingras, *Physics* at 31 and 71; Allin, *Physics* at 13-15.

169. Page 299, para. 2 – "who received his PhD in 1936": Mills and Dombra, *Doctoral Thesis* at 111; McLennan supervised Welsh's M.A. Welsh began his Ph.D. in Gottingen under James Franck, but returned to Toronto in 1933 where he resumed his studies. See Robin L. Armstrong, "Harry Lambert Welsh", Proceedings of the Royal Society of Canada, 4th series, v. 23 (1985).

170. Page 299, para. 2 – "supervise about 65 PhD students": UTA/Current People/"Harry L. Welsh".

171. Page 299, para. 2 – "who received his PhD in 1950": "Stoicheff, Boris Peter", *Canadian Who's Who 1998* at 1201.

172. Page 299, para. 2 – "in physics, electrical engineering, and chemistry": Boris Stoicheff to author, December 16, 1999. The Toronto faculty member is Peter Herman of electrical engineering.

173. Page 299, para. 3 – "facilitates the study of atoms and other particles": Stoicheff to author; Gingras, *Physics* at 71-72.

174. Page 299, para. 3 – "and similar lighter-than-air vehicles": See Chapter 22 (1914).

175. Page 299, para. 3 – "to create the desired low temperatures": The process is described in Gordon Shrum, *Gordon Shrum: An Autobiography* (Vancouver: University of British Columbia Press, 1986) at 41 and in "Further Triumph in Research for University of Toronto, *University of Toronto Monthly*, v.23 at 228-229.

176. Page 299, para. 3 – "produced by McLennan's team": Shrum, *Gordon Shrum* at 42; "Further Triumph" at 228.

177. Page 299, para. 4 – "the 'green line' of the Northern Lights": Shrum, *Gordon Shrum* at 43-46.

178. Page 299, para. 4 – "as others had thought": Ibid. at 43 and 46; Gingras, *Physics* at 72.

179. Page 299, para. 4 – "for the discovery": Gingras, *Physics* at 72.

180. Page 299, para. 4 – "there were 84 graduate students in physics": G.M. Volkoff, "Gordon Merritt Shrum", *Proceedings of the Royal Society of Canada*, 4th Series, v. 23 (1985) at 157-158.

181. Page 300, para. 1 – "Arthur Schawlow in 1981": *Toronto Star*, April 29, 1999.

182. Page 300, para. 1 – "Bertram Brockhouse in 1994": http://www.physics.mcmaster.ca/people/faculty/Brockhouse_BN.html.

183. Page 300, para. 1 – "and Walter Kohn in 1998": "Nobel Origins", *University of Toronto Magazine* (Winter, 1998) at 27.

184. Page 300, para. 2 – "not visible with ordinary microscopes": Allin, *Physics* at 28-29.

185. Page 300, para. 2 – "became the leader in spectroscopy": Ibid. at 27.

186. Page 300, para. 3 – "Lash Miller, the head of the department": Lang had become the professor of Military Studies in the University: see W.A.E. McBryde, "William Lash Miller" (Proof for American Chemical Society, 1989) at 167.

187. Page 300, para. 3 – "a graduate fellowship to one of his own students": W.A.E. McBryde, "William Lash Miller: Canada's Unique Chemist", *Journal of Canadian Studies*, v. 26, no. 3 (Fall, 1991) at 116.

188. Page 300, para. 3 – "and the best-known chemist in Canada": McBryde, "Miller" at 165.

189. Page 300, para. 3 – "who were invited to give addresses": Ibid. at 170.

190. Page 300, para. 4 – "they don't know atoms exist": Shrum, *Gordon Shrum* at 17.

191. Page 300, para. 4 – "Ostwald's laboratory in Leipzig": McBryde, "Miller" at 166.

192. Page 300, para. 4 – "who published in the 1870s and 80s": McBryde, "Unique" at 104.

193. Page 300, para. 4 – "Ostwald changed his view": Ibid. at 111.

194. Page 300, para. 4 – "F.B. Kenrick, did not": Miller continued to teach directly from Gibbs: see McBryde, "Miller" at 169.

195. Page 301, para. 1 – "passing reference to atomic theory": McBryde, "Unique" at 113-114.

196. Page 301, para. 1 – "on the speed or outcome of chemical reactions": Ibid. at 112.

197. Page 301, para. 1 – "and reproduction of micro-organisms": McBryde, "Miller" at 168.

198. Page 301, para. 1 – "inconsequential results that it yielded": Ibid.

199. Page 301, para. 1 – "did not affect most graduates": McBryde, "Unique" at 112.

200. Page 301, para. 1 – "the strong position it occupies today": Ibid. at 114. One exception to the pre-war somnolence of the Chemistry Department was the dynamic G.F. Marrian, biochemistry professor from 1933 to 1938. He made significant advances in understanding how hormones affect childbirth, and his work was mentioned in the 1939 Nobel chemistry citation. In 1939, Marrian returned to Scotland to become Professor of Chemistry at the University of Edinburgh. An obituary noted, "Marrian's arrival brought new life to the community of organic chemists and biochemists in Canada and especially Toronto": Gordon C. Butler, "Guy Frederic Marrian", *Proceedings of the Royal Society of Canada*, 4th series, v. 21 (1983).

201. Page 301, para. 2 – "celebrated the hundredth anniversary of its founding": W.J. Dunlop, "The Centenary Celebrations", *University of Toronto Monthly*, v. 28 at 64-67.

202. Page 301, para. 2 – "and optimism about its future": *Torontonensis* 1927 at 18. Falconer's message to the graduating class was optimistic about the future, but he saved his best words for the present: "The oak has driven its roots deeper into the soil of the country as it has been swayed by strong winds; to-day its branches spread wide, new departments and faculties have been shooting forth, and to its shade there come every year increasing numbers of students from the province, from Canada, and from other countries."

203. Page 301, para. 2 – "came from all over the civilized world": Falconer to Ferguson, September 20, 1928, cited in Ross, "Origins and Development" at 315.

CHAPTER 25 – 1926 – GOOD YEARS

1. Page 302, para. 1 – "treated the University well": James Greenlee, *Sir Robert Falconer: A Biography* (University of Toronto Press, 1988) at 284; D.C. Masters, *Henry John Cody: An Outstanding Life* (Toronto: Dundurn Press, 1995) at 145-146. Ferguson's regard for the University was not absolute, particularly when it came to academic freedom: see Peter Oliver, *G. Howard Ferguson: Ontario Tory* (University of Toronto Press, 1977) at 240-243 and 327-328.

2. Page 302, para. 1 – "Cody's good friend and college roommate, Ferguson": See Chapter 19 (1907).

3. Page 302, para. 1 – "appointed him to the position in 1923": Sidney Smith, "Henry John Cody", *Transactions of the Royal Society of Canada*, 3rd Series, v. 45 (1951) at 87.

4. Page 302, para. 1 – "after Sir Edmund Walker had stepped down": Walker had been elected chancellor: see "The New Chancellor", *University of Toronto Monthly*, v.24 at 57.

5. Page 302, para. 1 – "greater than that of any cabinet minister": *Telegram*, January 14, 1927.

6. Page 302, para. 1 – "while prices generally declined": A.B. McKillop, *Matters of Mind: The University in Ontario 1791-1951* (University of Toronto Press, 1994) at 319 and 628n53.

7. Page 302, para. 1 – "from a little over $1,500,000 to over $2,000,000": Ibid. at 320.

8. Page 302, para. 1 – "the night before the election": Oliver, *Ferguson* at 363; Masters, *Cody* at 166-169. Cody spoke on the Liquor Control Act, the burning issue of the time.

9. Page 302, para. 1 – "signalling the onset of a worldwide depression": October 29, 1929, "black Tuesday".

10. Page 302, para. 2 – "were gaining in stature": See Chapter 24 (1922).

11. Page 303, para. 1 – "W.J. Alexander in English in 1926": M.W. Wallace, "In Memoriam William John Alexander", UTA/A87-0002/02 at 4.

12. Page 303, para. 1 – "George Wrong in history in 1927": W.S. Wallace, "The Life and Work of George M. Wrong", *Canadian Historical Review*, v. 29 (September, 1948) at 236.

13. Page 303, para. 1 – "and Maurice Hutton in classics in 1928": Ward W. Briggs, Jr., ed., *Biographical Dictionary of North American Classicists* (Westport, Connecticut: Greenwood Press, 1994) at 302.

14. Page 303, para. 2 – "replaced him as head of English at University College": UTA/Graduate Records/"Malcolm Wallace"/A73-0026/492(83).

15. Page 303, para. 2 – "after serving five years at the University of Manitoba": F.E.L. Priestley, "A.S.P. Woodhouse", *Proceedings of the Royal Society of Canada*, 4th Series, v. 3 (1965) at 183.

16. Page 303, para. 2 – "head of the University College department in 1944": Ibid.

17. Page 304, para. 1 – "of such diverse and splendid power": Claude Bissell, *Halfway up Parnassus: A Personal Account of the University of Toronto 1932-1971* (University of Toronto Press, 1974) at 5.

18. Page 304, para. 1 – "became a professor of English at the University of Chicago": For E.K. Brown, see Laura Smyth Groening, *E.K. Brown: A Study in Conflict* (University of Toronto Press, 1993).

19. Page 304, para. 1 – "to become head of St Hilda's College": UTA/Current People/"Kirkwood, Mossie May".

20. Page 304, para. 1 – "who became head of English at Cornell": Davis later became president of Smith College: Bissell, *Parnassus* at 5 and 12; UTA/Graduate Records/"Herbert John Davis"/A73-0026/80(02).

21. Page 304, para. 2 – "which included the poet E.J. Pratt": David G. Pitt, *E.J. Pratt: The Truant Years 1882-1927* (University of Toronto Press, 1984) at 192-193.

22. Page 304, para. 2 – "in the spring of 1928": Kathleen Coburn, *In Pursuit of Coleridge* (Toronto: Clarke, Irwin and Company, 1993) at 17.

23. Page 304, para. 2 – "A turning point": Ibid.

24. Page 304, para. 2 – "Would I not switch to Wordsworth?": Ibid. at 19.

25. Page 304, para. 2 – "to supervise her post-graduate work": Ibid. at 18-19.

26. Page 304, para. 2 – "She later discovered": William McGuire, *Bollingen: An Adventure in Collecting the Past* (Princeton: Princeton University Press, 1982) at 228.

27. Page 304, para. 2 – "the research for which she is best known": J.R. De J. Jackson, "Kathleen Coburn", *Proceedings of the Royal Society of Canada*, 6th Series, v. 4 (1993) at 27.

28. Page 304, para. 2 – "of which Coburn was the general editor": E-mail from Heather Jackson to author, September 9, 1999; e-mails from Heather Jackson to author, January 30, 2001; Alida Minchella, "A Cause to Champion", *University of Toronto Bulletin*, February 5, 1996.

29. Page 304, para. 3 – "he 'was hooked'": McKillop, *Matters of Mind* at 468.

30. Page 304, para. 3 – "to Pelham Edgar": Ibid.

31. Page 304, para. 3 – "who died in 1991": See generally, Alvin A. Lee and Robert D. Denham, eds., *The Legacy of Northrop Frye* (University of Toronto Press, 1994).

32. Page 304, para. 3 – "predicted to number thirty-five volumes": Ronald Schoeffel to author, November 1999.

33. Page 304, para. 3 – "being deciphered by a team of scholars": E-mail from Ron Schoeffel to Charles Levi, May 3, 2000. Northrop Frye's late notebooks are being published by the University of Toronto Press, the first volumes appeared in July, 2000 and further ones in 2001.

34. Page 304, para. 4 – "and Hermann Boeschenstein in German": Alan Latta, "The Story of German at the University of Toronto" (Notes for Speech given November 7, 1991) at 5-6.

35. Page 305, para. 1 – "and Robert Finch in French": For Finch, see C.D. Rouillard and Colleagues, *French Studies at the University of Toronto 1853-1993* (Toronto: Department of French, 1994). C.D. Rouillard did not join the staff until 1937 but remained until 1972: ibid. at 95 and 292.

36. Page 305, para. 1 – "and Milton Buchanan in Italian and Spanish": Maddalena Kuitunen and Julius Milinaro, *A History of Italian Studies at the University of Toronto 1840-1990* (Toronto: Department of Italian Studies, 1991) at 22 and 24.

37. Page 305, para. 1 – "and F.V. Winnett": Fred V. Winnett and W. Stewart McCullough, "A Brief History of the Department of Near Eastern Studies (formerly Oriental Languages) in the University of Toronto to 1976-1977" (Unpublished manuscript, 1978), UTA/B2000-0009/001 at 18-20.

38. Page 305, para. 1 – "and, still later, the Yale classics departments": Briggs, *Biographical Dictionary* at 267.

39. Page 305, para. 1 – "theories of communication": Ibid. at 268.

40. Page 305, para. 1 – "who came in 1928 as Hutton's successor": Ibid. at 449.

41. Page 305, para. 1 – "was published in 1940": Ibid. at 104.

42. Page 305, para. 2 – "would remain as head at Toronto until 1953": Robert Bothwell, *Laying the Foundation: A Century of History at the University of Toronto* (Toronto: Department of History, 1991) at 84. G.M. Smith was the chair for a few years: ibid. at 79; McKillop, *Matters of Mind* at 476.

43. Page 305, para. 2 – "his interest was in Canadian history": As Martin told the *Varsity* in 1929, "we shall continue to emphasize Canadian History": see UTA/Graduate Records/"Chester Martin"/A73-0026/308(60).

44. Page 305, para. 2 – "in 1929": Bothwell, *Laying the Foundation* at 84; McKillop, *Matters of Mind* at 475.

45. Page 305, para. 2 – "including Donald Creighton": Donald Creighton was appointed a lecturer in the fall of 1927: see UTA/Graduate Records/"Donald Grant Creighton"/A73-0026/072(92a).

46. Page 305, para. 2 – "Frank Underhill": Underhill was appointed in 1927: see *President's Report 1927/28* at 3.

47. Page 305, para. 2 – "and Donald McDougall": Bothwell, *Laying the Foundation* at 81 and 83.

48. Page 305, para. 2 – "the acquisition of talent in foreign affairs": J.L Granatstein, *The Ottawa Men: The Civil Service Mandarins, 1935-1957* (University of Toronto Press, 1998) at 36 et seq.

49. Page 305, para. 2 – "both joined the Department of External Affairs": Bothwell, *Laying the Foundation* at 80 and at 82-83.

50. Page 305, para. 2 – "with scholars such as Creighton and Innis": Ibid. at 82.

51. Page 305, para. 3 – "who had a Chicago PhD": J.M.S. Careless, "George Williams Brown", *Proceedings of the Royal Society of Canada,* 4th Series, v.2 (1964) at 89.

52. Page 305, para. 3 – "the running of the *Canadian Historical Review* in 1930": Ibid.

53. Page 305, para. 3 – "become editor at the University of Toronto Press": Marsh Jeanneret, *God and Mammon: Universities as Publishers* (Toronto: Macmillan of Canada, 1989) at 37.

54. Page 306, para. 1 – "is the runner up": Bothwell, *Laying the Foundation* at 87.

55. Page 306, para. 1 – "reached 30 million copies": See Keith Wilson, *Charles William Gordon* (Winnipeg: Peguis Publishers, 1981) at 30. One of David Foot's books has recently sold more that 250,000 copies. Adel Sedra is likely to overtake Brown in sales, but many of these represent translations: see Chapter 35 (1966) and Chapter 42 (1997).

56. Page 306, para. 1 – "sold only 136 copies in its first year": McKillop, *Matters of Mind* at 664n86. The book was originally published by Yale University Press.

57. Page 306, para. 2 – "as a special lecturer on federal institutions": Ian Drummond, *Political Economy at the University of Toronto: A History of the Department, 1888-1982* (Toronto: Governing Council, 1983) at 42 and 170; R.C.B. Risk, "The Many Minds of W.P.M. Kennedy", *University of Toronto Law Journal,* v. 48 (1998) at 365.

58. Page 306, para. 2 – "the law side of the department": P.B. Waite, *Lord of Point Grey: Larry MacKenzie of U.B.C.* (Vancouver: University of British Columbia Press, 1987) at 58.

59. Page 306, para. 2 – "who had taught with Kennedy at St Michael's": Oral Interview of Revered Edmund Joseph McCorkell, June 19, 1974, UTA/B74-0050 at 76.

60. Page 306, para. 2 – "had married one of his history students": McCorkell Interview at 78. Risk, "Many Minds" at 354n4 says Kennedy's first wife died in the influenza epidemic of 1919, and he married again in 1921 – to a non-Catholic. He left the Catholic church at this time, and this is likely the reason he left St. Michael's: Risk, "Many Minds" at 365n50.

61. Page 306, para. 2 – "and had no legal training": Alexander Brady, "William Paul McClure Kennedy", *Proceedings of the Royal Society of Canada*, 4th Series, v. 11 (1964) at 109-110.

62. Page 306, para. 2 – "a new and fascinating theme": Brady, "Kennedy" at 109.

63. Page 306, para. 2 – "he had written ten books": Risk, "Many Minds" at 353 and 365.

64. Page 306, para. 2 – "a performer as much as a teacher": Jack Batten, *Robinette: The Dean of Canadian Lawyers* (Toronto: Macmillan of Canada, 1984) at 27.

65. Page 306, para. 3 – "MacKenzie, a Maritimer": MacKenzie hailed from Nova Scotia: see Waite, *Lord of Point Grey* at 1-11.

66. Page 306, para. 3 – "an accomplished international law scholar": Ibid. at 69 et seq.

67. Page 306, para. 3 – "introduced only after second year": Kennedy to Falconer, December 21, 1928, UTA/A82-0041/001.

68. Page 306, para. 3 – "and then after first year": Ibid.

69. Page 306, para. 3 – "under the wing of political economy in 1930": C.A. Wright, "Legal Education", *University of Toronto Alumni Bulletin*, (June 1952) at 15.

70. Page 306, para. 3 – "an independent School of Law in 1941": "School of Law has New Dean", *University of Toronto Monthly*, v. 44 at 172.

71. Page 307, para. 1 – "and many more": See C. Ian Kyer and Jerome E. Bickenbach, *The Fiercest Debate: Cecil A. Wright, the Benchers, and Legal Education in Ontario 1923-1957* (University of Toronto Press, 1987) at 58.

72. Page 307, para. 1 – "of all instruments in the service of mankind": Kennedy, "Law as a Social Science", *South African Law Journal*, v.3 (1934) at 100, quoted in Risk at 371-372.

73. Page 307, para. 1 – "was appointed a lecturer in 1930": Oral Interview with Jacob Finkelman, January 10, 1995 at 13.

74. Page 308, para. 1 – "this is no objection": Kennedy to Falconer, January 31, 1930, UTA/A67-0007/121.

75. Page 308, para. 1 – "among the least anti-Semitic types of his generation": Greenlee correspondence with the author, August, 1999.

76. Page 308, para. 1 – "the chairman of the board": Finkelman interview at 13.

77. Page 308, para. 1 – "and there would be no difficulty about that": Ibid. at 16.

78. Page 308, para. 1 – "first Jew appointed to a full-time position at the University": Ibid. at 15; see also Chapter 20 (1908).

79. Page 308, para. 2 – "captured virtually every honour they sought": E-mail from Bruce Kidd to author, December 9, 1999.

80. Page 308, para. 2 – "of energetic sport for women in the community": Ibid.

81. Page 308, para. 2 – "and the public service": Ibid.

82. Page 308, para. 3 – "from 1920 until1929": T.A. Reed, *The Blue and White: A Record of Fifty Years of Athletic Endeavour at the University of Toronto* (University of Toronto Press, 1944) at 201.

83. Page 308, para. 3 – "defeating Brandon, Manitoba": Ibid. at 200.

84. Page 309, para. 1 – "but lost to Port Arthur": *Torontonensis*, 1926 at 230.

85. Page 309, para. 1 – "and allowed only 13": Ibid. at 232.

86. Page 309, para. 1 – "winning the international intercollegiate title 6—1": Ibid.

87. Page 309, para. 2 – "would face Port Arthur for the Allan Cup": *Torontonensis*, 1927 at 138.

88. Page 309, para. 2 – "Joseph 'Stonewall'": *Globe*, February 20, 1928.

89. Page 309, para. 2 – "a member of the Canadian Senate": "Joseph Sullivan", at University of Toronto's Hall of Fame website, www.utoronto.ca/dar/physical.

90. Page 309, para. 2 – "and Toronto the second": *Torontonensis*, 1927 at 138; *Globe*, March 25-31, 1926.

91. Page 309, para. 2 – "until later that year": Ibid.

92. Page 309, para. 2 – "after three ten-minute overtime periods": *Globe*, March 30, 1926.

93. Page 309, para. 2 – "Port Arthur beat Sullivan and won the cup": *Globe*, March 31, 1926.

94. Page 309, para. 2 – "the greatest Championship series ever played in Canada": *Torontonensis*, 1927 at 139.

95. Page 309, para. 3 – "in the 1928 Olympics in St Moritz, Switzerland": Reed, *Blue and White* at 201-203; *Torontonensis*, 1927 at 140.

96. Page 309, para. 3 – "that ever wore the 'Blue and White'": Ibid. at 201.

97. Page 309, para. 3 – "the greatest hockey team ever seen in Europe": *Globe*, February 7, 1928.

98. Page 309, para. 3 – "and Great Britain, 14-0": Andrew Podnieks, *Canada's Olympic Hockey Teams: The Complete History 1920-1998* (Toronto: Doubleday Canada Limited, 1997) at 31.

99. Page 309, para. 3 – "received the nickname 'Stonewall'": *Globe*, February 20, 1928.

100. Page 309, para. 3 – "which has produced Dr. Banting?": *Globe*, March 23, 1928.

101. Page 311, para. 1 – "the women's intercollegiate basketball tournament": Helen Gurney, *A Century to Remember, 1893-1993, Women's Sports at the University of Toronto* (Toronto: University of Toronto Women's T-Holders Association, 1993) at 64 and 81.

102. Page 311, para. 1 – "winning 7 of the 10 championships": Ibid. at 159.

103. Page 311, para. 1 – "and Toronto won": Ibid. at 81 and 172.

104. Page 311, para. 1 – "but McGill dropped out": Ibid. at 82.

105. Page 311, para. 1 – "a scramble in front of the Queen's net": *Varsity*, February 17, 1925.

106. Page 311, para. 1 – "was also the University women's tennis champion": "Marion Hilliard", Hall of Fame website.

107. Page 311, para. 1 – "*A Woman Doctor Looks at Love and Life*": *Star*, October 24, 1964.

108. Page 311, para. 1 – "and allowed body checking": Brian McFarlane, *Proud Past, Bright Future: One Hundred Years of Canadian Women's Hockey* (Toronto: Stoddart Publishing, 1994) at 53; Joanna Avery and Julie Stevens, *Too Many Men on the Ice: Women's Hockey in North America* (Victoria, British Columbia: Polestar, 1997) at 66.

109. Page 311, para. 1 – "Thora McIlroy, the goalie": Gurney, *A Century to Remember* at 82.

110. Page 311, para. 1 – "no face masks and no indoor ice": McFarlane, *Proud Past, Bright Future* at 53-54, citing *Star* of 1985.

111. Page 311, para. 1 – "without suffering a loss": Gurney, *A Century to Remember* at 82; Webb, "She Shoots, She Scores", *University of Toronto Magazine* (Winter, 1997) at 16.

112. Page 311, para. 1 – "for the rest of the decade": Gurney, *A Century to Remember* at 172.

113. Page 311, para. 1 – "would not be resumed until after the war": Ibid. at 82 and 172.

114. Page 311, para. 2 – "in the 1924 Olympics in Paris": Patrick Okens, "Blues before Sunrise: rowing at the University of Toronto" (Unpublished M.A. Thesis, University of Toronto, 1999) at 49.

115. Page 311, para. 2 – "the son of the physicist W.J. Loudon": Ibid. at 28.

116. Page 311, para. 2 – "to the great Ned Hanlan in 1873": Thomas R. Loudon, "Autobiography", UTA/B76-0003/001(10) at 5.

117. Page 311, para. 2 – "coached by Hanlan": Bruce Kidd, "Edward (Ned) Hanlan", *DCB*, v. 13 at 440; Reed, *Blue and White* at 259.

118. Page 311, para. 2 – "he weighed only 135 pounds": Loudon, "Autobiography" at 10.

119. Page 311, para. 2 – "which he did for the next ten years": Okens, "Blues Before Sunrise" at 30.

120. Page 311, para. 2 – "made up mainly of returned veterans": One member of the crew had been gassed, another had won the Distinguished Flying Cross: see ibid. at 36.

121. Page 311, para. 2 – "had been wounded at Passchendaele": UTA/Graduate Records/"Thomas Richardson Loudon"/A73-0026/241(90).

122. Page 311, para. 2 – "adopt a scientific approach to rowing": Okens, "Blues Before Sunrise" at 36.

123. Page 312, para. 1 – "the swells of Lake Ontario more effectively": Ibid. at 31.

124. Page 312, para. 1 – "and a biology professor, Alan Coventry": Ibid. at 37n29. Coventry's Oxford oar is in the warden's office of Hart House. He was on the team for one year.

125. Page 312, para. 1 – "the four-year period from 1920 to 1923": Ibid. at 38-43; Reed, *Blue and White* at 259-261.

126. Page 312, para. 2 – "on the Seine outside Paris": Thomas R. Loudon, "Report on the Olympic Eight-Oared Races at Argenteuil, Paris, July 15, 16, and 17, 1924", in *Canada at the VIIIth Olympiad, France 1924*, copy in UTA/ B95-0024/001; Reed, *Blue and White* at 261.

127. Page 312, para. 2 – "they were unable to catch up": Okens, "Blues Before Sunrise" at 49.

128. Page 312, para. 2 – "better than we should have been": R.S. Hunter, *Rowing in Canada Since 1848* (Hamilton: Davis-Lisson Limited, 1933) at 116.

129. Page 312, para. 2 – "The Americans had brought their own water to Europe": A lack of sleep caused by the noise of Bastille Day celebrations a few days earlier was also blamed: see ibid. at 115-116.

130. Page 312, para. 3 – "starting in 1926": *Varsity*, October 18, 1926; *Globe*, October 18, 1926.

131. Page 312, para. 3 – "in an Oxford and Cambridge-style event": Hunter, *Rowing in Canada*, at 83.

132. Page 313, para. 1 – "and the second on the Toronto waterfront": Reed, *Blue and White* at 263; Okens, "Blues Before Sunrise" at 52.

133. Page 313, para. 1 – "and Toronto Blues football game": Ibid. at 53 to 57.

134. Page 313, para. 1 – "was disbanded in 1936": Reed, *Blue and White* at 263; Okens, "Blues Before Sunrise" at 57.

135. Page 313, para. 1 – "as an intercollegiate sport until the 1960s": Okens, "Blues Before Sunrise" at 70.

136. Page 313, para. 1 – "would not appear until the 1970s": Ibid. at 84.

137. Page 313, para. 1 – "winners Kay Worthington and Emma Robinson": Ibid. at 50n56; "Kay Worthington", Hall of Fame website.

138. Page 313, para. 2 – "from 1920 to 1926": "Warren Snyder", Hall of Fame website.

139. Page 313, para. 2 – "later became the solicitor of the University": "Hamilton 'Laddie' Cassels", Hall of Fame Website.

140. Page 313, para. 2 – "defeated the Argos 16-3 for the Grey Cup": Stephen Thiele, *Heroes of the Game: A History of the Grey Cup* (Norval, Ontario: Moulin Publishing Ltd., 1997) at 23; Reed, *Blue and White* at 110.

141. Page 313, para. 2 – "was the intercollegiate champion": Reed, *Blue and White* at 110-111.

142. Page 313, para. 2 – "Canadian male athlete of the half century": "Donald Carrick", Hall of Fame website.

143. Page 313, para. 2 – "refereed a record 16 Grey Cup games": "Hector Naismith 'Hec' Crighton", Hall of Fame website.

144. Page 313, para. 2 – "coached by Lester Pearson": *Torontonensis*, 1926 at 220.

145. Page 313, para. 2 – "long line-ups for season tickets": *Varsity*, October 8, 1926.

146. Page 313, para. 2 – "to seat 19,000 persons": Rick Kollins, "The History of Varsity Blues Football", updated in 1993 by Paul Carson (Unpublished and undated manuscript) at 2.

147. Page 313, para. 2 – "he would later design the new Varsity Arena": *Varsity*, March 17, 1998.

148. Page 313, para. 3 – "'noisy, jostling crowd' at Varsity Stadium": *Varsity*, November 29, 1926.

149. Page 313, para. 3 – "for the Grey Cup": *Star*, December 6, 1926; *Globe*, December 6, 1926. The Regina Roughriders, the western champions, had declined to participate in the Cup finals because of the lateness of the season: see Thiele, *Heroes of the Game* at 34.

150. Page 313, para. 3 – "cake of ice": *Globe*, December 6, 1926.

151. Page 313, para. 3 – "I couldn't move": Scott Young, *Hello Canada!: The Life and Times of Foster Hewitt* (Toronto: McClelland and Stewart, 1985) at 42.

152. Page 313, para. 3 – "much better but not more thrilling football": *Globe*, December 6, 1926; see also *Star*, December 6, 1926.

153. Page 314, para. 1 – "as many as 20,000 spectators": Kollins, "History of Varsity Blues" at 3.

154. Page 314, para. 1 – "the first touchdown pass in Canadian Grey Cup history": Ibid.; "Warren Stevens", Hall of Fame website; *Varsity*, February 17, 1948.

155. Page 314, para. 1 – "senior football, basketball, and hockey": Reed, *Blue and White* at 57; "Warren Stevens," Hall of Fame website; DeCourcy H. Raynor, "Stevens Coaches Senior Hockey", *University of Toronto Monthly*, v. 34 at 59.

156. Page 314, para. 1 – "the first such degree program in the Commonwealth": "Warren Stevens," Hall of Fame website.

157. Page 314, para. 1 – "until his retirement in 1970": Ibid.

158. Page 314, para. 2 – "in Convocation Hall for the first time": Ezra Schabas, *Sir Ernest MacMillan: The Importance of Being Canadian* (University of Toronto Press, 1994) at 68. While this is being written the author is listening to the Passion played by the Munich Bach Orchestra and Choir.

159. Page 314, para. 2 – "played the continuo parts on the organ": John Beckwith, *Music at Toronto: A Personal Account* (University of Toronto Press, 1995) at 14.

160. Page 314, para. 2 – "would be repeated annually for many years": Schabas, *Sir Ernest MacMillan* at 68.

161. Page 314, para. 2 – "A.S. Vogt, who also had held both positions, died": Ibid. at 73 and 77.

162. Page 314, para. 2 – "the largest in the British Empire": Earl Davey, "The Faculty of Music of the University of Toronto, 1918-1945", UTA/A83-0036/013.

163. Page 314, para. 2 – "one of several affiliated with the University": Davey, "The Faculty of Music" at 12, cites a senate resolution that mentions the affiliation of the Toronto Conservatory of Music, the Toronto College of Music, and the Hamilton Conservatory of Music.

164. Page 314, para. 2 – "in 1919": Schabas, *Sir Ernest MacMillan* at 74.

165. Page 314, para. 2 – "corner of College Street and University Avenue": Ibid.; Beckwith, *Music at Toronto* at 2. The Faculty of Music was established on March 7, 1918 and had its first council meeting on June 25, 1918.

166. Page 314, para. 3 – "as dean of the faculty until 1952": Schabas, *Sir Ernest MacMillan* at x.

167. Page 314, para. 3 – "when he was succeeded by Boyd Neel": In 1953: Schabas, *Sir Ernest MacMillan* at 292.

168. Page 314, para. 3 – "of the Toronto Mendelssohn Choir for fifteen": He was with the TSO from 1931-1956 and the Mendelssohn from 1942-1957: see Schabas, *Sir Ernest MacMillan* at x.

169. Page 314, para. 3 – "spend the next four years in a civilian internment camp": Ibid. at 13, 25-27, and 37 et seq.

170. Page 315, para. 1 – "based on a Swinburne poem": Ibid. at 41 and 45. He had also received a B.Mus. from Oxford by examination in 1911.

171. Page 315, para. 1 – "by the Mendelssohn Choir at Massey Hall in 1921": Ibid. at 47.

172. Page 315, para. 2 – "he conducted Mozart's *Requiem*": Ibid. at 79.

173. Page 315, para. 2 – "the following year at Hart House Theatre": Ibid. at 81.

174. Page 315, para. 2 – "would be a victim of the depression": Ibid. at 83.

175. Page 316, para. 1 – "Music is rare here": See Chapter 21 (1909).

176. Page 316, para. 2 – "like those depicted in some of F. Scott Fitzgerald's novels": Such as *This Side of Paradise*: see McKillop, *Matters of Mind* at 405 et seq.

177. Page 316, para. 2 – "from that of flappers and gin flasks": Ibid. at 407.

178. Page 316, para. 2 – "less drinking than shortly after the war": Ibid. at 418.

179. Page 316, para. 2 – "in revolt against a meaningless past": Ibid. at 420.

180. Page 316, para. 2 – "could be easily overstated": Paul Axelrod, *Making a Middle Class: Student Life in English Canada During the Thirties* (Montreal: McGill-Queen's University Press, 1990) at 16.

181. Page 317, para. 1 – "a Student Christian Movement meeting in Hart House": *Varsity*, February 4, 1929.

182. Page 317, para. 1 – "not wilfully blind to existing conditions": *Varsity*, January 22, 1929.

183. Page 317, para. 1 – "wanted the editor fired": *Varsity*, February 1, 1929. The minutes of the Board of Governors clearly show that the Board recommended that SAC "take immediate steps looking to a proper and adequate control of the situation": see Board of Governors Minutes, UTA/A70-0024/12, January 24, 1929. After that, verbal word came from a few Board members asking that the S.A.C. consider dismissal of Ryan: see UTA/A70-0012/03(03), SAC minutes, January 25, 1929.

184. Page 317, para. 1 – "eventually dismissed Ryan": *Varsity*, February 7, 1929. The whole incident goes well beyond "petting". Ryan had, in a series of editorials, offended and insulted Victoria College (October 11, 1928), Queen's Hall (November 16, 1928), Engineering (November 21, 1928), University College (December 6, 1928), and the entire professoriate (January 18, 1929), and had already been reprimanded twice by SAC. On February 6th, he overstepped his editorial boundaries and was finally dismissed. Since SAC was made up of representatives of the faculties and contained professorial representatives as well, Ryan could hardly have expected their support: see UTA/A70-0012/03(03), SAC minutes, February 6, 1929.

185. Page 317, para. 1 – "was prominent on the campus": *Varsity*, February 25, 1931.

186. Page 317, para. 1 – "He was suspended by SAC": SAC Minutes, February 27, 1931, UTA/A70-0012/03(03); see also Andrew Allan, *Andrew Allan: A Self-Portrait* (Toronto: Macmillan of Canada, 1974) at 54-59.

187. Page 317, para. 1 – "for the remainder of the year": Board of Governors Minutes, March 12, 1931, UTA/A70-0024/reel 12.

188. Page 317, para. 2 – "about an ideal world": Bissell at 16; McKillop, *Matters of Mind* at 453.

189. Page 317, para. 2 – "and provost of Trinity College George Ignatieff": See *Register of Rhodes Scholars 1903-1945* (London: Oxford University Press, 1950). Bissell twice applied unsuccessfully for a Rhodes, complaining in his diary that it went to "that stuffed shirt" Ignatieff: Bissell Diaries, UTA/B88-0091/001(03), November 11, 1936.

CHAPTER 26 – 1931 – DEPRESSING TIMES

1. Page 318, para. 1 – "from holding a public meeting": James G. Greenlee, *Sir Robert Falconer: A Biography* (University of Toronto Press, 1988) at 289; Michiel Horn, *Academic Freedom in Canada: A History* (University of Toronto Press, 1999) at 89; Michiel Horn, "'Free Speech within the Law': The Letter of the Sixty-Eight Toronto Professors, 1931," *Ontario History*, v. 72, no. 1 (March 1980); J.F. White, "Police Dictatorship", *Canadian Forum*, v. 11, no. 125 (February, 1931) at 167-168. A permit for the meeting was not required, but rather the police could exert pressure on hall and theatre owners to deny the owners a license if they used the premises for communist organizations. As Horn points out in his *Ontario History* article, the F.O.R lost their booking in January, 1931 at the Empire Theatre after a sergeant of detectives met with the owner of the theatre. No permit was required for the meeting.

2. Page 318, para. 1 – "a communist front": Greenlee, *Falconer* at 290; Horn, *Academic Freedom* at 89.

3. Page 318, para. 1 – "anyone of average intelligence": White, "Police Dictatorship" at 168.

4. Page 318, para. 1 – "and Malcolm Wallace": Horn, *Academic Freedom* at 89 and 97.

5. Page 318, para. 1 – "and intolerable": Greenlee, *Falconer* at 290-91.

6. Page 318, para. 1 – "signed by other professors": As reported in the *Varsity* of January 26, 1931.

7. Page 318, para. 2 – "section of our community": *Varsity*, January 22, 1931.

8. Page 318, para. 2 – "by a margin of 5 to 1": *Varsity* of January 23, 1931; A.B. McKillop, *Matters of Mind: The University in Ontario, 1791-1951* (University of Toronto Press, 1994) at 445.

9. Page 318, para. 2 – "in the previous chapter": See Chapter 25 (1926).

10. Page 320, para. 1 – "in public controversies": Greenlee, *Falconer* at 293-294.

11. Page 320, para. 1 – "on this or other political matters": Cited in Greenlee, *Falconer* at 294 and Horn, *Academic Freedom* at 90.

12. Page 320, para. 1 – "the views of the 68 professors": Greenlee, *Falconer* at 294; Horn, *Academic Freedom* at 90.

13. Page 320, para. 2 – "handling of imperial relations": Greenlee, *Falconer* at 298; Horn, *Academic Freedom* at 91.

14. Page 320, para. 2 – "endangers the autonomy of the University": Greenlee, *Falconer* at 298.

15. Page 320, para. 2 – "that autonomy is already lost": Ibid. at 298-299.

16. Page 320, para. 2 – "irritates onlookers": Ibid. at 299.

17. Page 320, para. 3 – "in Convocation Hall": Ibid. at 275 and 278.

18. Page 320, para. 3 – "burning political questions": Ibid. at 281-282.

19. Page 320, para. 3 – "ultra-socialistic teachings": Leonard to Walker, cited in Horn, *Academic Freedom* at 68.

20. Page 320, para. 3 – "*Labour in the Changing World* (1919)": Horn, *Academic Freedom* at 68; Greenlee, *Falconer* at 278.

21. Page 320, para. 3 – "mining engineer Colonel Reuben Wells Leonard": Greenlee, *Falconer* at 275; "Reuben Wells Leonard" in Henry James Morgan, ed., *The Canadian Men and Women of the Time* (Toronto: William Briggs, 1912) at 652. See generally Bruce Ziff, *Unforeseen Legacies: Reuben Wells Leonard and the Leonard Foundation Trust* (University of Toronto Press, 2000).

22. Page 320, para. 3 – "wanted MacIver fired": Horn, *Academic Freedom* at 68. Leonard never actually called for the firing of MacIver, but he did say the board should prevent "any teaching tending to upset [Western Capitalist] civilization", which is essentially the same thing.

23. Page 320, para. 3 – "Chair of Political Anarchy and Social Chaos": Greenlee, *Falconer* at 277-278.

24. Page 320, para. 3 – "a 'steadying influence' on labour": Ibid. at 276.

25. Page 320, para. 4 – "at the end of the following academic year": Ibid. at 326.

26. Page 320, para. 4 – "a severe heart disorder in June 1930": Ibid. at 292.

27. Page 321, para. 1 – "before retiring": Robin Harris, "Notes on Interview with A.B. Fennell, November 24, 1971", UTA/A83-0036/040.

28. Page 321, para. 1 – "to be his replacement": D.C. Masters, *Henry John Cody: An Outstanding Life* (University of Toronto Press, 1995) at 171; *Telegram* of April 29, 1931, cited in Robin Harris, "The Depression", UTA/A83-0036/001 at 3.

29. Page 321, para. 1 – "will have to watch our step": R. Douglas Francis, *Frank H. Underhill: Intellectual Provocateur* (University of Toronto Press, 1986) at 95; McKillop, *Matters of Mind* at 387.

30. Page 321, para. 2 – "the 'obvious choice'": Masters, *Cody* at 171.

31. Page 321, para. 2 – "the new premier, George Henry": "Henry, George Stewart", *Canadian Who's Who, 1938-1939* at 317.

32. Page 321, para. 2 – "in Buckingham Palace": Masters, *Cody* at 135.

33. Page 321, para. 2 – "the most sought-after speaker in Canada": Ibid. at 207.

34. Page 321, para. 2 – "with whom he came in contact": Ibid. at x.

35. Page 321, para. 3 – "was a parishioner": Ibid. at 183.

36. Page 321, para. 3 – "and many other influential professors": See Masters, *Cody* at 208 for Innis; see UTA/B98-0006 for Kennedy.

37. Page 321, para. 3 – "on the 1922 commission": See Chapter 18 (1905) and Chapter 23 (1919); Masters, *Cody* at 172.

38. Page 321, para. 3 – "the treatment of cancer by radium": Masters, *Cody* at 183.

39. Page 321, para. 3 – "had been disciplined": The new editors the following year certainly had good things to say about him: see *Varsity* editorial of October 13, 1931 – "Dr. Cody has paid the University a signal honour in accepting the appointment".

40. Page 321, para. 4 – "when he took office": Masters, *Cody* at 176.

41. Page 321, para. 4 – "which they did in 1934": John T. Saywell, *"Just Call me Mitch": The Life of Mitchell F. Hepburn* (University of Toronto Press, 1991) at 164-165.

42. Page 321, para. 4 – "regarded Cody with suspicion": Masters, *Cody* at 169.

43. Page 321, para. 4 – "in his earlier years": Sidney Smith, "Henry John Cody", *Proceedings of the Royal Society of Canada*, 3rd Series, v. 45 (1951) at 87.

44. Page 321, para. 4 – "for the presidency in 1906": See Chapter 19 (1907).

45. Page 321, para. 5 – "the ambassador to the United States": Massey was ambassador to the United States from 1926 to 1930: see Claude Bissell, *The Young Vincent Massey* (University of Toronto Press, 1981) at 114.

46. Page 321, para. 5 – "president of the University of Alberta": Frederick W. Gibson, *Queen's University, vol. II, 1917-1961* (Kingston: McGill-Queen's University Press, 1983) at 136-37.

47. Page 322, para. 1 – "but neither was interviewed": Robin S. Harris, "The Depression", UTA/A83-0036/001 at 2 says "no name except Cody's appears to have been considered", but Frederick Gibson says that Wallace "was seriously considered for the presidencies of Toronto and McGill": see Gibson, *Queen's University, vol. II* at 137.

48. Page 322, para. 1 – "appointed principal of Queen's University": Gibson, *Queen's University, vol. II* at 141.

49. Page 322, para. 1 – "and must evidently have it": Bissell, *Parnassus* at 193; Masters, *Cody* at 174.

50. Page 322, para. 2 – "who did not attend the meeting": Harris, "The Depression" at 4. The Board of Governors on October 8 discussed immediately appointing a new President. There was dissent; the motion, however, passed on division. Once that motion was passed, the Board voted without any recorded dissent to offer the position to Cody. The minority apparently wanted a proper selection committee to be set up, or such is inferred in the report of the small group sent to meet with Cody which reported back to the board of October 9th. Although Vincent Massey was a member of the Board and had been suggested for the Presidency, he did not attend either meeting of the Board, or any further meeting until January of 1932: see Board of Governors Minutes, UTA/A70-0024/reel 12; Masters, *Cody* at 174.

51. Page 322, para. 2 – "a matter for speculation": Masters, *Cody* at 175.

52. Page 323, para. 1 – "and not one of creation": D.B. MacDonald, "Partial Memoirs of the Rev. D. Bruce MacDonald pertaining to the University of Toronto" (1953), UTA/B83-1295 at 26.

53. Page 323, para. 2 – "thought about Cody's appointment": Harris was at that time still working on his history of the University of Toronto, which was never finished: see generally, UTA/A83-0036.

54. Page 323, para. 2 – "certainly not with satisfaction": Craigie to Harris, March 25, 1981, UTA/A83-0036/038.

55. Page 323, para. 2 – "and women visitors at 73 St. George": Birney to Harris, April 1, 1981, UTA/A83-0036/038.

56. Page 323, para. 2 – "particularly I think in the colleges": Havelock to Harris, Sept. 23, 1981, UTA/A83-0036/038. This accords with Grant's view that "Vincent is on the whole the most popular among the staff": see Grant to Lothian, May 4, 1931.

57. Page 323, para. 2 – "and obtain the necessary funding": Havelock to Harris, September 23, 1981, UTA/A83-0036/038.

58. Page 323, para. 3 – "by another $600,000": Edward E. Stewart, "The Role of the Provincial Government in the Development of the Universities of Ontario 1791-1964" (D.Ed. Thesis, University of Toronto, 1970) at 559-560. The following year the grant was for the most part restored.

59. Page 323, para. 3 – "to recover from the depression": Saywell, *Hepburn* at 144-145.

60. Page 323, para. 3 – "remained constant": Stewart, "The Role of the Provincial Government" at 559-560.

61. Page 324, para. 1 – "tuition fees had to rise": Cody to Chancellor E.W. Wallace of Victoria, April 16, 1935, UTA/A68-0006/018(02).

62. Page 324, para. 1 – "from $75 to $130 that year": Masters, *Cody* at 191; Harris, "The Depression" at 11 says fees went from $75 to $100 in 1932, and from $100 to $125 in 1935.

63. Page 324, para. 1 – "to drop out of university": Paul Axelrod, *Making a Middle Class: Student Life in English Canada during the Thirties* (Kingston: McGill-Queen's University Press, 1990) at 27.

64. Page 324, para. 1 – "as had administrative expenses": Masters, *Cody* at 191; Harris, "The Depression" at 10.

65. Page 324, para. 1 – "now had secretaries": Ibid. at 212.

66. Page 324, para. 1 – "with the registrar's office": Ibid.

67. Page 324, para. 1 – "throughout Cody's presidency": Harris, "The Depression" at 11.

68. Page 324, para. 1 – "such as the Students' Administrative Council": Ibid. at 12. For S.A.C. and its benevolent activities during the 1930s, see Charles Levi, "The S.A.C. Historical Project 1930-1950" (Toronto: Self-published, 1992) at 13-16.

69. Page 324, para. 1 – "from modest middle class ... families": Paul Axelrod, *Making a Middle Class* at 24.

70. Page 324, para. 1 – "by the Ontario Court of Appeal in 1990": *Canada Trust Co.* v. *Ontario Human Rights Commission* (1990), 69 D.L.R. (4th) 321 (Ont. C.A.); Ziff, *Unforeseen Legacies* at 53, 132 and 135.

71. Page 324, para. 1 – "who graduated in 1935": "Sydney Morris Hermant", *Canadian Who's Who, 1991* at 456.

72. Page 324, para. 1 – "maintain first class honours": Masters, *Cody* at 213.

73. Page 324, para. 1 – "the future dean of the graduate school": "Board appoints A.E. Safarian Dean of School of Graduate Studies", *University of Toronto Bulletin*, October 29, 1970.

74. Page 324, para. 1 – "would not have attended university": Edward Safarian to author, November 20, 1997.

75. Page 324, para. 1 – "the number of Jews at the University": Paul Bator, "Memorandum on the Cody Papers", UTA/A83-0036/001 at 10.

76. Page 324, para. 1 – "he added": Cody to General C.F. Winter, February 8, 1934, quoted in Bator, "Memorandum" at 9. Charles Francis Winter was born in 1863 and from the age of 18 served with the British Army in various colonial campaigns, including the Red River expedition of 1885. He joined the Canadian army in 1896 and served with the Royal Canadian Regiment during the Boer War: see "Major Charles Francis Winter" in Morgan, ed., *The Canadian Men and Women of the Time* at 1176. Winter had no connection with the University, and in his original letter to Cody expressed the hope that he would not be "considered a busybody in butting in on what may be considered none of my business": see Winter to Cody, February 7, 1934, UTA/A68-0006/12.

77. Page 324, para. 2 – "during the 1930s": McKillop, *Matters of Mind* at 425-427.

78. Page 324, para. 2 – "the highest it had ever been": Harris, "The Depression" at 1.

79. Page 324, para. 2 – "for all degree courses in 1931-32": Ibid. at 15; *President's Report, 1931/32* at 4; Axelrod, *Making a Middle Class* at 45.

80. Page 324, para. 2 – "such as commerce and finance": McKillop, *Matters of Mind* at 329, notes the increase from 60 in 1919-20 to 352 in 1931-32. Whereas C&F was booming up to 1932, the depression eventually stopped that growth and led to reverses. From its peak of 352 in 1932, enrolment was down to 207 by 1935: see the exam tables from the President's reports. Masters, *Cody* at 193, says that all the commerce grads for 1933 got jobs.

81. Page 324, para. 2 – "dropped after 1932": McKillop, *Matters of Mind* at 328-329. Enrolment in engineering dropped from 914 in 1932/1933 to around 800, see Richard White, *The Skule Story: The University of Toronto Faculty of Applied Science and Engineering 1873-2000* (University of Toronto Press, 2000) at 124.

82. Page 325, para. 1 – "with professional or business backgrounds": McKillop, *Matters of Mind* at 29.

83. Page 325, para. 1 – "such as the Student Christian Movement": Ibid. at 129.

84. Page 325, para. – "it made most students more cautious": Ibid. at 135. See also Chapter 29 (1950).

85. Page 325, para. 2 – "40 per cent of the total": McKillop, *Matters of Mind* at 427.

86. Page 325, para. 2 – "or dentistry": Ibid. at 428-430 and 437. In 1932, for instance, there were only five female engineering students out of a total of 914: see the *President's Report, 1932/33* at 109.

87. Page 325, para. 2 – "with her future husband in 1923": UTA/Graduate Records/"Mabel Gertrude Killins"/A73-0026/201(14).

88. Page 325, para. 2 – "and its instincts": McKillop, *Matters of Mind* at 429.

89. Page 325, para. 2 – "and physical therapy": Ibid. at 437.

90. Page 325, para. 2 – "the numbers in those fields doubled": Harris, "The Depression" at 14.

91. Page 325, para. 2 – "They also entered nursing": McKillop, *Matters of Mind* at 437.

92. Page 325, para. 2 – "in a new School of Nursing": "Financial Arrangements of the School of Nursing and its predecessor the Department of Public Health Nursing", April 23, 1946, UTA/A83-0036/013.

93. Page 325, para. 2 – "or physical therapy in this period": McKillop, *Matters of Mind* at 437.

94. Page 325, para. 2 – "the School of Social Work in 1941": UTA/A83-0036/014 "School of Social Work Fiftieth Anniversary Document"; Sara Z. Burke, *Seeking the Highest Good: Social Service and Gender at the University of Toronto 1888-1937* (University of Toronto Press, 1996) at 139.

95. Page 325, para. 2 – "the proportion of women declined to about 40 per cent": McKillop, *Matters of Mind* at 432.

96. Page 325, para. 3 – "with the support of the Rockefeller Foundation": "Financial Arrangements".

97. Page 325, para. 3 – "for nurses in the University": "The School of Nursing" (excerpt from the School of Nursing Calendar of 1956-57), UTA/A83-0036/013 at 1-3.

98. Page 325, para. 3 – "in the form of a building": Russell to Falconer, September 24, 1930, UTA/A83-0036/013.

99. Page 325, para. 3 – "reluctant to promise support": See Falconer to the Trustees of the Rockefeller Foundation, November 13, 1931, UTA/A83-0036/013.

100. Page 326, para. 1 – "nursing at the University": For Russell's title, see Russell to Falconer, October 24, 1931, UTA/A83-0036/013.

101. Page 326, para. 1 – "of help for nursing": Ibid.

102. Page 326, para. 1 – "was eventually provided": Robin Harris, "Nursing", UTA/A83-0036/013 at 3.

103. Page 326, para. 1 – "$17,500 from Rockefeller": "Financial Arrangements".

104. Page 326, para. 1 – "as a permanent endowment for the school": "Financial Arrangements"; Cody to W.A. Sawyer, June 15, 1938, UTA/A83-0036/013.

105. Page 326, para. 1 – "was established in 1942": "The School of Nursing" at 4.

106. Page 326, para. 2 – "by the royal commission of 1906": *Report of the Royal Commission on the University of Toronto* (Toronto: L.K. Cameron, 1906) at xxvii.

107. Page 326, para. 2 – "the offer was withdrawn": Forster to Falconer, July 16, 1927, UTA/A67-0007/107a; Forster to Falconer, May 12, 1932, UTA/A67-0007/131a; Falconer to Forster, May 13, 1932, ibid.

108. Page 326, para. 2 – "as its first professor of fine art": Dorothy Farr, "The Fine Art Department of the University of Toronto – A History", UTA/A83-0036/005.

109. Page 326, para. 2 – "added to the faculty in 1936": Farr, "The Fine Art Department" at 5.

110. Page 326, para. 2 – "with the help of Carnegie money": See Chapter 27 (1939).

111. Page 326, para. 2 – "the department of art and archeology": Farr, "The Fine Art Department" at 3-5.

112. Page 326, para. 3 – "under Bishop William C. White": For White, see Lewis C. Walmsley, *Bishop in Honan: Mission and Museum in the life of William C. White* (University of Toronto Press, 1974); Lovat Dickson, *The Museum Makers: The Story of the Royal Ontario Museum* (Toronto: Royal Ontario Museum, 1986) at 80-83.

113. Page 326, para. 3 – "who joined the faculty in 1934": George F.G. Stanley, "William Charles White", *Proceedings of the Royal Society of Canada*, 3rd Series, v.54 (1960) at 150.

114. Page 326, para. 3 – "the Royal Ontario Museum's Chinese collection": Walmsley, *Bishop in Honan* at 159.

115. Page 326, para. 3 – "for a number of years": Walmsley, *Bishop in Honan* at 167; Dickson, *The Museum Makers* at 81.

116. Page 326, para. 3 – "of the Chinese library collection": Sigmund Samuel to Currelly, December 24, 1937 (ROM Archives).

117. Page 326, para. 3 – "in China for the museum": Walmsley, *Bishop in Honan* at 153 says about 50,000 volumes; White to Cody April 5, 1933 (ROM Archives) says over 41,000. See also "Notes by Bishop White on Questions Relating to the Mu Chinese Library", April 10, 1956 (ROM Archives).

118. Page 326, para. 3 – "collector of artifacts in China, George Crofts": Dickson, *The Museum Makers* at 45.

119. Page 326, para. 3 – "obtained the 'Ming tomb'": Ibid. at 169. Patty Proctor of the ROM points out that "it was certainly bought as the tomb of a Ming general who died early in the Qing Dynasty, but there is some debate about the dating of various elements of the tomb. It has always been referred to as the 'Ming Tomb' but it is, strictly-speaking, a misnomer" (E-mail to author, September 13, 1999).

120. Page 327, para. 1 – "each of which weighs 17 tons": Ibid.

121. Page 327, para. 1 – "and the large bronze Buddha": Ibid. The plaque, however, says that it was given by David Dunlap in 1931 and doesn't say that it was purchased by Crofts.

122. Page 327, para. 1 – "at the west end of the Currelly Court": So the plaque says.

123. Page 327, para. 2 – "opened to Western influence": Stanley, "White" at 149-150; Dickson, *The Museum Makers* at 73-74 and 85.

124. Page 327, para. 2 – "many centuries earlier": Walmsley, *Bishop in Honan* at 137; Dickson, *The Museum Makers* at 74.

125. Page 327, para. 2 – "for the museum": Walmsley, *Bishop in Honan* at 140-141; Dickson, *The Museum Makers* at 76.

126. Page 328, para. 1 – "notably early bronzes": Walmsley, *Bishop in Honan* at 141.

127. Page 328, para. 1 – "even his interest in religion": Ibid.

128. Page 328, para. 1 – "the finest Chinese objects in the world": Ibid. at 150-151.

129. Page 328, para. 1 – "Bishop White Gallery": Walmsley, *Bishop in Honan* at 152; Dickson, *The Museum Makers* at 77 and 169.

130. Page 328, para. 1 – "in northern China": Walmsley, *Bishop in Honan* at 152-153; Gallery dedication document says 1238 or 1298, from Shansi province.

131. Page 328, para. 1 – "into sixty-three sections": E-mail from Patty Proctor to author, September 13, 1999.

132. Page 328, para. 1 – "which they hid": Walmsley, *Bishop in Honan* at 153; White, *Bulletin of the Royal Ontario Museum of Archaeology*, no. 12, July 1937 at 10.

133. Page 328, para. 1 – "restored to its original grandeur": Ibid.

134. Page 328, para. 1 – "by Sir Joseph Flavelle": "ROM Gallery Dedicated to Late Bishop White", June 19, 1969 (ROM Archives) says that it was the Flavelle Foundation.

135. Page 328, para. 1 – "put an end to their exportation": Dickson, *The Museum Makers* at 77-79.

136. Page 328, para. 1 – "while the sun shines": Ibid. at 77.

137. Page 328, para. 1 – "Bishop White left China in 1934": Walmsley, *Bishop in Honan* at 158.

138. Page 328, para. 2 – "with Canon Cody": Walmsley, *Bishop in Honan* at 159; Dickson, *The Museum Makers* at 80 et seq.

139. Page 328, para. 2 – "who had taught him at Wycliffe College": Dickson, *The Museum Makers* at 80.

140. Page 328, para. 2 – "with White as its director": Walmsley, *Bishop in Honan* at 159 and 167; Dickson, *The Museum Makers* at 83.

141. Page 328, para. 2 – "*Chinese Jews*": Walmsley, *Bishop in Honan* at 138 and 164.

142. Page 328, para. 2 – "presented a threat": Ibid. at 169.

143. Page 328, para. 2 – "remained at heart a medieval bishop": Ibid.

144. Page 328, para. 2 – "later renamed East Asian Studies": Ibid. at 182.

145. Page 328, para. 2 – "had joined the department": Walmsley, *Bishop in Honan* at 168; *President's Report, 1947/48* at 13.

146. Page 329, para. 1 – "triple the space available": Walmsley, *Bishop in Honan* at 160 says that the new addition was twice the size of the original building.

147. Page 329, para. 1 – "as a make-work project": Dickson, *The Museum Makers* at 66.

148. Page 329, para. 1 – "could be used": Walmsley, *Bishop in Honan* at 160; Dickson, *The Museum Makers* at 66-67.

149. Page 329, para. 1 – "was opened in 1933": Walmsley, *Bishop in Honan* at 160.

150. Page 329, para. 2 – "by museum officials": The figures on the poles are not properly "totems" but more akin to "crests": see e-mail from Ken Lister of the ROM to author, September 15, 1999.

151. Page 329, para. 2 – "Nisga'a Eagle Chief, Sagawen": Lister to author, September 15, 1999; Marius Barbeau, "Totem Poles for Our Provincial Museum" (undated memorandum), UTA/B79-0011/04(24) at 2.

152. Page 329, para. 2 – "is over 80 feet": Marius Barbeau, "The Mountain Totem Pole From the Nass River, northern British Columbia Collected by Marius Barbeau, 1928" (undated memorandum), UTA/B79-0011/04(24) at 1.

153. Page 329, para. 2 – "(24.5 metres)": From the plaque in front of the pole

154. Page 330, para. 1 – "of its kind in existence": Barbeau, "The Mountain Totem Pole" at 1; Barbeau, "Totem Poles" at 1; see also e-mail from Ken Lister to author, September 15, 1999, which states that "there are taller poles in existence now."

155. Page 330, para. 1 – "who worked with the National Museum": Marius Barbeau, F.R.S.C., was born in 1883 in Quebec, received a B.A. and LL.L. from Laval, and then won a Rhodes Scholarship. He attended Oxford but did not take a degree, returning in 1911 to become Ethnologist and Folklorist at the National Museum of Canada, a position he held for over fifty years: see "Barbeau, Marius", *Canadian Who's Who, 1958-60* at 53.

156. Page 330, para. 1 – "The red cedar totem pole": Barbeau, "Totem Poles" at 12.

157. Page 330, para. 1 – "by the expert craftsman Oyai": Barbeau, "The Mountain Totem Pole" at 1; Barbeau to McIlwraith, September 29, 1929, UTA/B79-0011/01.

158. Page 330, para. 1 – "about sixty years earlier": The museum plaque says it was carved in 1870.

159. Page 330, para. 1 – "for all time": Barbeau, "Totem Poles" at 9.

160. Page 330, para. 1 – "of a deceased relative of its owner": Ibid. at 14.

161. Page 330, para. 1 – "close to the Alaskan border": Ibid. at 1.

162. Page 330, para. 1 – "the keeper of ethnology": Dickson, *The Museum Makers* at 53.

163. Page 330, para. 1 – "their general lack of funds": McIlwraith to Barbeau, July 25, 1929 and August 30, 1929, UTA/B79-0011/01.

164. Page 330, para. 1 – "published in two volumes in 1948": S.D. Clark, "Thomas Forsyth McIlwraith", *Proceedings of the Royal Society of Canada*, 4th Series, v. 11 (1964) at 125.

165. Page 330, para. 2 – "of my grand-uncle": Barbeau, "Totem Poles" at 2-3.

166. Page 330, para. 2 – "from his nephews for $600": Ibid. at 4; "Totem Poles sent by Barbeau" (undated memorandum), UTA/B79-0011/04(24); see also Laurence Nowry, *Man of Mana: Marius Barbeau* (Toronto: New Canada Publications, 1995) at 234-236.

167. Page 330, para. 2 – "tumbled to the ground and decayed": Barbeau, "Totem Poles" at 4.

168. Page 330, para. 2 – "to transport it to Toronto": Barbeau to McIlwraith, November 15, 1929, UTA/B79-0011/01.

169. Page 330, para. 2 – "we will find some way": McIlwraith to Barbeau, September 23, 1929, UTA/B79-0011/01.

170. Page 330, para. 2 – "and the Currelly Gallery": Barbeau also acted as a middle-man for collectors of poles in Edinburgh, London, New York, and Paris, in order to "save as many as possible and in the interests of propagation". He did also, on occasion, insist on preservation of poles on their original sites, especially in the lower Skeena district: see Lowry, *Man of Mana* at 221-222 and 236.

171. Page 330, para. 3 – "the new department of geography": UTA/Graduate Records/"Griffith Taylor"/UTA/A73-0026/462(36); Marie Sanderson, *Griffith Taylor: Antarctic Scientist and Pioneer Geographer* (Ottawa: Carleton University Press, 1988) at 142; Nancy J. Christie, "'Pioneering in a Civilized World': Griffith Taylor and the Ecology of Geography", *Scientica Canadensis*, v. 17, nos. 1-2 at 142; Donald Kerr, "A Short History of the Department of Geography University of Toronto" (address delivered at the 50th anniversary of the Department, October, 1985) at 1.

172. Page 330, para. 3 – "kept up the campaign": Patrick W. Naughton, "The Development of the Department of Geography at the University of Toronto," UTA/A83-0036/005 (student paper, 1977) at 2, 7 and 9; Kerr, "A Short History" at 1.

173. Page 330, para. 3 – "the usual route in universities": Naughton at 1, citing Taylor.

174. Page 330, para. 3 – "could not be found": Sanderson, *Griffith Taylor* at 129.

175. Page 330, para. 3 – "teaching at the University of Chicago": Ibid. at x, 130, and 143.

176. Page 330, para. 3 – "had grown up in Australia": Arriving with his family from England in 1893 at age 12: Sanderson, *Griffith Taylor* at 4-5.

177. Page 330, para. 3 – "studied at Cambridge": Sanderson, *Griffith Taylor* at 22.

178. Page 330, para. 3 – "from the University of Sydney": Graduate Records, "Taylor".

179. Page 330, para. 3 – "until coming to Chicago": Sanderson, *Griffith Taylor* at x.

180. Page 331, para. 1 – "to the Antarctic in 1911-12": Scott had called him a "remarkable character": see Sanderson, *Griffith Taylor* at xi; Graduate Records, "Taylor".

181. Page 331, para. 1 – "wrote a book about his experiences": Sanderson, *Griffith Taylor* at x.

182. Page 331, para. 1 – "would strengthen Australia 'biologically'": Christie, "'Pioneering in a Civilized World'" at 129.

183. Page 331, para. 1 – "far less than the official estimates": Graduate Records, "Taylor".

184. Page 331, para. 2 – "matching his Chicago salary": Sanderson, *Griffith Taylor* at 139 et seq.; Masters, *Cody* at 197-98.

185. Page 331, para. 2 – "at the Ontario College of Education": Sanderson, *Griffith Taylor* at 142. The support was dropped the following year when an honours course in geography was instituted: Naughton, "The Development of the Department" at 15-16.

186. Page 331, para. 2 – "in the faculty of arts": Christie, "'Pioneering in a Civilized World'" at 142.

187. Page 331, para. 2 – "(about twice his yearly salary)": Sanderson, *Griffith Taylor* at 143. The house is no longer standing.

188. Page 331, para. 2 – "he wrote in 1936": Christie, "'Pioneering in a Civilized World'" at 142n53.

189. Page 331, para. 2 – "head of geography until 1951": Graduate Records, "Taylor".

190. Page 331, para. 2 – "200 articles over the course of his career": Sanderson, *Griffith Taylor* at x.

191. Page 331, para. 2 – "almost as controversial in Canada": Graduate Records, "Taylor".

192. Page 332, para. 1 – "how the environment influences history": Sanderson, *Griffith Taylor* at 149.

193. Page 332, para. 1 – "cultural geography": Ibid. at x.

194. Page 332, para. 1 – "a population exceeding 100 million persons": Christie, "'Pioneering in a Civilized World'" at 148.

195. Page 332, para. 1 – "as the political centre of the British Empire": Ibid. at 149.

196. Page 332, para. 1 – "enthusiastically republished the article": Ibid. at 148-149.

197. Page 332, para. 1 – "relatively small population growth": Graduate Records, "Taylor".

198. Page 332, para. 2 – "had left his estate to his sister": "The Wallberg Memorial Building", *University of Toronto Monthly*, v. 48 at 18; UTA/A85-0033/08 "Wallberg Fund, Historical". For biographical material on Emil Wallberg, see UTA/A74-0008/008(02). Wallberg left approximately $2,750,000 to his sister, who bequeathed $1,000,000 for the building. In 1946 the balance remaining in her estate went into a trust for engineering scholarships, fellowships, lectures and grants.

199. Page 332, para. 2 – "was a graduate of the University of Toronto": Harris, "The Depression" at 12.

200. Page 332, para. 2 – "where he practised as an engineer": Ibid.

201. Page 332, para. 2 – "including Canada Wire and Cable": "The Wallberg Memorial Building", *University of Toronto Monthly*, v. 48 at 18.

202. Page 332, para. 3 – "her late husband, David Dunlap": Peter M. Millman, "The David Dunlap Observatory Nears Completion", *University of Toronto Monthly*, v. 35 at 143; "David Dunlap Observatory is Opened", *University of Toronto Monthly*, v. 35 at 223; C.A. Chant, *Astronomy in the University of Toronto: The David Dunlap Observatory* (University of Toronto Press, 1954) at 32-34.

203. Page 332, para. 3 – "was a University of Toronto graduate": The Dunlaps both attended school in Pembroke.

Jessie Bell Dunlap apparently never went to University. David studied law in the 1880s, but was called to the Bar only in 1894: see Common Rolls and Barrister's Rolls of the Law Society of Upper Canada.

204. Page 332, para. 3 – "the head of astronomy": See Chapter 21 (1909).

205. Page 332, para. 3 – "and the very wealthy Dunlap": Chant, *Astronomy* at 33.

206. Page 332, para. 3 – "and mining promoter in Northern Ontario": *The David Dunlap Observatory: The First Fifty Years 1935-1985* (Toronto: University of Toronto, 1985) at 3.

207. Page 332, para. 3 – "died in 1924": *First Fifty Years* at 3.

208. Page 333, para. 1 – "to Mr. Dunlap": Chant, *Astronomy* at 33.

209. Page 333, para. 1 – "93 Highland Avenue": Ibid. at 39.

210. Page 333, para. 1 – "for presidents of the University": Claude Bissell, *Halfway up Parnassus: A Personal Account of the University of Toronto 1932-1971* (University of Toronto Press, 1974) at 37-38.

211. Page 333, para. 1 – "a number of years later": Chant, *Astronomy* at 34.

212. Page 333, para. 2 – "a large block of land on a gentle rise": Millman, "Observatory" at 143.

213. Page 333, para. 2 – "25 kilometres north of the campus": *First Fifty Years* at 3.

214. Page 333, para. 2 – "on a government map": Chant, *Astronomy* at 39.

215. Page 333, para. 2 – "to purchase the property": *First Fifty Years* at 3.

216. Page 333, para. 2 – "of his retirement from the University": Helen Sawyer Hogg, "Clarence Augustus Chant", *Proceedings of the Royal Society of Canada*, 3rd Series, v. 51 (1957) at 70.

217. Page 334, para. 1 – "was given an honorary degree": "David Dunlap Observatory is Opened" at 223.

218. Page 334, para. 1 – "(1.88-metre)": "The David Dunlap Observatory of the University of Toronto" (pamphlet, no publisher, October, 1993).

219. Page 334, para. 1 – "the Mount Wilson Observatory in California": Millman, "Observatory" at 143.

220. Page 334, para. 1 – "the largest in Canada": "David Dunlap Observatory".

221. Page 334, para. 1 – "contain smaller telescopes": Ibid.

222. Page 334, para. 1 – "at the Lick Observatory": Peter M. Millman, "Reynold Kenneth Young", *Proceedings of the Royal Society of Canada*, 4th Series, v. 16 (1978) at 121.

223. Page 334, para. 1 – "with her future husband": Judith Knelman, "Helen Hogg", *University of Toronto Graduate* (September/October, 1985) at 6.

224. Page 334, para. 1 – "for the next thirty years": Knelman, "Hogg" at 8.

225. Page 334, para. 1 – "a full professor in 1957": Ibid. at 9.

226. Page 334, para. 1 – "and officially retired in 1976": "A star in academic constellation, Dr Hogg retires", *Bulletin*, September 10, 1976.

227. Page 334, para. 1 – "opened in 1971": "David Dunlap Observatory". It is given as 0.6 meters.

228. Page 334, para. 1 – "the development of the surrounding area": "David Dunlap Observatory and the Problems Raised by Urbanization of the Surrounding Area" (Office of the Comptroller, November 19, 1953), UTA/A83-0036/020; "David Dunlap Observatory faces problems of light pollution", *Bulletin*, September 6, 1974.

229. Page 334, para. 1 – "the Helen Sawyer Hogg Telescope": *Globe and Mail*, January 21, 1998; Steven De Sousa, "Goodbye Chile, Hello Argentina!", *Bulletin*, February 3, 1998.

230. Page 334, para. 2 – "were mostly tranquil": Horn, *Academic Freedom* at 125.

231. Page 334, para. 3 – "have nothing to do with democracy": Ibid. at 118, citing the *Globe and Mail*, which cites Grube.

232. Page 334, para. 3 – "attacked Grube in the legislature": Ibid. at 119.

233. Page 335, para. 1 – "have no further interest for us": Ibid. at 119 and 121.

234. Page 335, para. 1 – "smacks of rank sedition": McKillop, *Matters of Mind* at 397.

235. Page 335, para. 1 – "trying to scuttle our ship of state": This was Colonel Fraser Hunter: see Horn, *Academic Freedom* at 119.

236. Page 335, para. 1 – "whether I came out of the business safely": Horn, *Academic Freedom* at 120.

237. Page 335, para. 2 – "had a low tolerance": Horn, *Academic Freedom* at 94.

238. Page 335, para. 2 – "had the highest regard": Masters, *Cody* at 185.

239. Page 335, para. 2 – "not with the British Empire": McKillop, *Matters of Mind* at 389.

240. Page 335, para. 2 – "gave no more extension lectures": Horn, *Academic Freedom* at 96-97.

241. Page 335, para. 2 – "will require his removal": Cody to MacDonald, November 24, 1933, UTA/A68-0006/010.

242. Page 335, para. 2 – "to the scrap heap": McKillop, *Matters of Mind* at 393.

243. Page 335, para. 2 – "the British propaganda about democracy": Horn, *Academic Freedom* at 97.

244. Page 335, para. 2 – "of expressing his ideas": Horn, *Academic Freedom* at 96; McKillop, *Matters of Mind* at 390.

245. Page 335, para. 2 – "no more public speeches for a year": Horn, *Academic Freedom* at 97; McKillop, *Matters of Mind* at 393.

246. Page 335, para. 2 – "anonymous pieces for the *Canadian Forum*": Horn, *Academic Freedom* at 97.

247. Page 335, para. 3 – "praising aspects of Mussolini's regime": Horn, *Academic Freedom* at 94; McKillop, *Matters of Mind* at 390.

248. Page 336, para. 1 – "to carry it out": Horn, *Academic Freedom* at 94; McKillop, *Matters of Mind* at 390.

249. Page 336, para. 1 – "the individual has duties toward it": McKillop, *Matters of Mind* at 392. He had expressed the same idea relating to the University in his first annual report, where he wrote that "while academic freedom is

rightly held to be essential to true university teaching, academic responsibility accompanies it, and is equally imperative": Horn, *Academic Freedom* at 94; see also Masters, *Cody* at 180.

250. Page 336, para. 1 – "the political activities of his professoriate": McKillop, *Matters of Mind* at 392.

251. Page 336, para. 1 – "from the Italian government": Masters, *Cody* at 231; see also Maddalena Kuitunen and Julius Molinaro, *A History of Italian Studies at the University of Toronto 1840-1990* (Toronto: Department of Italian Studies, 1991) at 34-41.

252. Page 336, para. 2 – "in the coming federal election": McKillop, *Matters of Mind* at 446.

253. Page 336, para. 2 – "told the *Globe and Mail* in 1935": *Globe and Mail,* October 4, 1935, as cited in Bator, "Memorandum on the Cody Papers" at 13; see also Horn, *Academic Freedom* at 125.

254. Page 336, para. 2 – "members of the staff of Victoria College": Bator, "Memorandum on the Cody Papers" at 12; see also Horn, *Academic Freedom* at 111.

255. Page 336, para. 2 – "the English Fabian Society": Horn, *Academic Freedom* at 93; McKillop, *Matters of Mind* at 388.

256. Page 336, para. 2 – "of the CCF party": Horn, *Academic Freedom* at 93.

257. Page 336, para. 2 – "between the League and the CCF": Ibid.

258. Page 336, para. 2 – "*Social Planning for Canada,* in 1935": McKillop, *Matters of Mind* at 395.

259. Page 336, para. 2 – "with which they were associated": Horn, *Academic Freedom* at 93-94; McKillop, *Matters of Mind* at 388.

260. Page 336, para. 3 – "for his 'Flanders fields' statement": Francis, *Underhill* at 113.

261. Page 337, para. 1 – "head of political economy in 1937": UTA/Graduate Records/"Harold Adams Innis"/A73-0026/167(94); McKillop, *Matters of Mind* at 398.

262. Page 337, para. 1 – "to support Underhill": Francis, *Underhill* at 113; Horn, *Academic Freedom* at 120.

263. Page 337, para. 1 – "in favour of Underhill and Grube": Horn, *Academic Freedom* at 121; McKillop, *Matters of Mind* at 398.

264. Page 337, para. 1 – "for those who lost their lives in Flanders": Horn, *Academic Freedom* at 121.

265. Page 337, para. 1 – "had been wounded in the war": See Chapter 22 (1914).

266. Page 337, para. 1 – "would expect a professor to behave": Horn, *Academic Freedom* at 121.

267. Page 337, para. 1 – "by members of the faculty": Horn, *Academic Freedom* at 122; Francis, *Underhill* at 112-13.

268. Page 337, para. 1 – "to a subsequent meeting of the board": Francis, *Underhill* at 113.

269. Page 337, para. 1 – "take no further action at present": Horn, *Academic Freedom* at 122.

270. Page 337, para. 1 – "Both lost their jobs": Horn, *Academic Freedom* at 127 and generally, chapter 6.

271. Page 337, para. 1 – "would once again be under threat of dismissal": Horn, *Academic Freedom* at 154; Francis, *Underhill* at 126-127.

CHAPTER 27 – 1939 – THE SECOND WORLD WAR

1. Page 338, para. 1 – "on September 10, 1939": J.L. Granatstein, *Canada's War: The Politics of the Mackenzie King Government, 1939-1945* (Toronto: Oxford University Press, 1975) at 11. Britain had declared war on September 3rd.

2. Page 338, para. 1 – "the storm has broken upon us": A.B. McKillop, *Matters of Mind: The University in Ontario 1791-1951* (University of Toronto Press, 1994) at 522.

3. Page 338, para. 1 – "from whom we sprang demands it": D.C. Masters, *Henry John Cody: An Outstanding Life* (Toronto, Dundurn Press, 1995) at 234.

4. Page 338, para. 1 – "to the cheers of the great assemblage": "The King and Queen Come to the University", *University of Toronto Monthly*, v. 39.

5. Page 338, para. 2 – "General A.G.L. McNaughton": Donald H. Avery, *The Science of War: Canadian Scientists and Allied Military Technology during the Second World War* (University of Toronto Press, 1998) at 276-277.

6. Page 338, para. 2 – "dentistry and agriculture": Cited in Avery, *Science of War* 43.

7. Page 339, para. 1 – "making satisfactory progress": McKillop, *Matters of Mind* at 523-524, citing the Department of War Services National Resources Mobilization Act.

8. Page 339, para. 1 – "(including 500 graduates)": McKillop, *Matters of Mind* at 523.

9. Page 339, para. 2 – "were cancelled": McKillop, *Matters of Mind* at 527.

10. Page 339, para. 2 – "exhibition games took place": "Sport News", *University of Toronto Monthly*, v.42 at 53.

11. Page 339, para. 2 – "with various RCAF teams": Ibid.

12. Page 339, para. 2 – "increased during this period": McKillop, *Matters of Mind* at 527; "Sport News" at 53.

13. Page 339, para. 2 – "reluctantly suspended its debates": McKillop, *Matters of Mind* at 527; Charles Levi, "The S.A.C. Historical Project 1930-1950" (self-published, 1992) at 67-72.

14. Page 339, para. 2 – "the number of dances was reduced": McKillop, *Matters of Mind* at 527; Levi, "S.A.C. Historical Project" at 61-63.

15. Page 339, para. 3 – "totalled 557": *University of Toronto Memorial Book Second World War 1939-1945* (Toronto: Soldiers' Tower Committee, 1994) at v.

16. Page 339, para. 3 – "who died in the First World War": 613 died in the First World War: see *University of Toronto Roll of Service 1914-1918* (University of Toronto Press, 1921) at 529.

17. Page 340, para. 1 – "in the first war": *President's Report, 1944/45* at 6.

18. Page 340, para. 1 – "had served in the RCAF": *Memorial Book* at v.

19. Page 340, para. 1 – "on November 29, 1939": "The University and the War", *University of Toronto Monthly*, v.40 at 63.

20. Page 340, para. 2 – "had won a Rhodes to Oxford in 1929": UTA/Graduate Records/"George Stevenson Cartwright"/A73-0026/53(55).

21. Page 340, para. 3 – "Dishforth Cemetery, Yorkshire, England": *Memorial Book* at 11.

22. Page 340, para. 4 – "was John Kenneth Macalister": Ibid. at 39.

23. Page 340, para. 4 – "in the summer of 1940": According to P.B. Waite, MacKenzie consulted with W.P.M. Kennedy about his U.N.B. offer sometime in late March or early April of 1940. The appointment was not made until July 30: see P.B. Waite, *Lord of Point Grey: Larry MacKenzie of U.B.C.* (Vancouver: University of British Columbia Press, 1987) at 90-92.

24. Page 341, para. 1 – "an interest in an appointment": Kennedy to Macalister, July 10, 1940, UTA/A82-0041/(004).

25. Page 341, para. 1 – "MANY THANKS – MACALISTER": Macalister to Kennedy, September 17, 1940, UTA/A82-0041/(004). See also correspondence with Larry MacKenzie in the MacKenzie Papers in the U.B.C. Archives, provided to the author by Philip Gerard, who is writing a biography of Bora Laskin. See, in particular, letters from Macalister to MacKenzie of Aug. 24, 1940, box 20, file 3, and June 29, 1942, box 29, file 5.

26. Page 341, para. 1 – "had joined the Canadian infantry": *Memorial Book* at 39.

27. Page 341, para. 1 – "future cabinet minister Jack Pickersgill": For Pickersgill, see George H. Ford, ed., *The Making of a Secret Agent: Letters of 1934-1943 Written by Frank Pickersgill and Edited with a Memoir* (Toronto: McClelland and Stewart, 1978).

28. Page 341, para. 1 – "to act as a secret agent": Douglas LePan, *Macalister, or Dying in the Dark: A fiction based on what is known of his life and fate* (Kingston, Ontario: Quarry Press, 1995) at 97-100.

29. Page 341, para. 1 – "on September 14, 1944": *Memorial Book* at 39 and 54; Ford, *Making of a Secret Agent* at 271 gives the date as September 11, 1944.

30. Page 341, para. 2 – "their own women's corps": Nancy Kiefer and Ruth Roach Pierson, "The War Effort and Women Students at the University of Toronto 1939-1945", in Paul Axelrod and John Reid, eds., *Youth, University, and Canadian Society: Essays in the Social History of Higher Education* (Montreal: McGill-Queen's University Press, 1989) at 173. The navy followed in 1942.

31. Page 341, para. 2 – "of the three services": Ibid. at 176.

32. Page 341, para. 2 – "had studied physical and occupational therapy": Ibid.

33. Page 341, para. 2 – "graduate Mary Susannah McLaren": Atkinson was killed in an aircraft accident near Calgary, Britton in an accident in Toronto, and McLaren in a vehicle accident in England: see *Memorial Book* at 2, 7, and 44.

34. Page 341, para. 2 – "and sewing": Kiefer and Pearson, "The War Effort and Women Students" at 164-5.

35. Page 341, para. 2 – "had been produced that year": University Women Report on Year's War Work", *University of Toronto Monthly*, v. 43 at 75.

36. Page 341, para. 2 – "is to preserve the home": Kiefer and Pierson, "The War Effort and Women Students" at 175. Some women, however, wanted to be more actively involved in the war effort. The idea had been rejected in a University College parliamentary debate in October 1939, one speaker stating that "women would have a serious disrupting effect on the morale of the army": see ibid. at 164; Alison Prentice et al., *Canadian Women: A History*, (Toronto: Harcourt Brace Jovanovich, 1988) at 301-303.

37. Page 341, para. 3 – "and drill every week": Kiefer and Pierson, "The War Effort and Women Students" at 167-168.

38. Page 341, para. 3 – "offered by the Ford Motor Company": Ibid. at 172.

39. Page 341, para. 3 – "to war work": Ibid. at 174-175.

40. Page 342, para. 1 – "were offered": Ibid. at 175-176.

41. Page 342, para. 1 – "and popular conceptions of femininity": Ibid. at 161 and 178; Elsie Gregory MacGill, a 1927 graduate in engineering at the University of Toronto, was one notable exception. She was in charge of all Canadian production of Hurricane and Helldiver fighter planes: see Chapter 9 (1880) and Prentice et al., *Canadian Women* at 300.

42. Page 342, para. 2 – "for most of the 1930s": Masters, *Cody* at 233; McKillop, *Matters of Mind* at 521.

43. Page 342, para. 2 – "but a world": Masters, *Cody* at 234.

44. Page 342, para. 2 – "No country would allow them refuge": Irving Abella and Harold Troper, *None is Too Many: Canada and the Jews of Europe 1933-1948* (Toronto: Lester Publishing, 1991) at 63-64.

45. Page 342, para. 2 – "head of the immigration service in Ottawa": Ibid. at 64.

46. Page 342, para. 2 – "a more open policy": James G. Greenlee, *Sir Robert Falconer: A Biography* (University of Toronto Press, 1988) at 336.

47. Page 342, para. 3 – "the worst record toward Jewish refugees": Irving Abella and Harold Troper, "Canada and the Refugee Intellectual", in Jarrell C. Jackman and Carla M. Borden, eds., *The Muses Flee Hitler: Cultural Transfer and Adaptation* (Washington, Smithsonian Institution Press, 1983) at 259.

48. Page 342, para. 3 – "and Jewish refugees in particular": Abella and Troper, *None* at 50. Those excluded included non-Jews such as the 250,000 Spanish exiles located primarily in France: see Avery, *Reluctant Host: Canada's Response to Immigrant Workers, 1896-1994* (Toronto: McClelland and Stewart, 1995) at 121-122. See also Paul Stortz, "Refugee Professors at the University of Toronto, 1935-1945" (Fall 2001), *Historical Studies in Education*, vol. 13 (forthcoming).

49. Page 342, para. 3 – "barely exceeded twenty": Michiel Horn, *Academic Freedom in Canada: A History* (University of Toronto Press, 1999) at 166. McGill "did next to nothing to help refugee faculty" says Horn, *Academic Freedom* at 138; see also Avery, *Reluctant Host* at 118-121.

50. Page 342, para. 3 – "who could fill the position concerned": Abella and Troper, "Canada" at 260-161; Avery, *Reluctant Host* at 121.

51. Page 343, para. 1 – "that would pay his salary for two years": Lawrence D. Stokes, "Canada and an Academic Refugee from Nazi Germany: The Case of Gerhard Herzberg", *Canadian Historical Review*, v.57 (1976) at 153-154 and 157-158.

52. Page 343, para. 1 – "a permanent position for the scholar": Carnegie Corporation to Cody, January 24, 1935, UTA/A68-0006/18(12).

53. Page 343, para. 1 – "at the University of Saskatchewan, however": Stokes, "Canada and an Academic Refugee" at 158-159. Avery, in *Reluctant Host* at 119 credits John Spinks, later the president of the University of Saskatchewan and the chairman of Ontario's Spinks Commission, for persuading the University to take him.

54. Page 343, para. 1 – "unusual qualifications": Stokes, "Canada and an Academic Refugee" at 163-164.

55. Page 343, para. 2 – "came with Carnegie money": See Chapter 26 (1931).

56. Page 343, para. 2 – "when his Carnegie money ran out": See Chapter 26 (1931). Rockefeller also would sometimes offer half salaries for a three year period if the institution would undertake to hire the person at the end of the period: see Tracy B. Kittredge to Professor Foltin, November 17, 1938, UTA/A68-0006/040. Regarding Foltin, Vincent Massey noted, "I may say that he is not of Jewish race": see Massey to Cody, December 20, 1938, UTA/A68-0006/040. For Massey's views on immigrants, see Abella and Troper, *None* at 48-50. It does not appear that Toronto ever used the Rockefeller route.

57. Page 344, para. 1 – "to Canada late in 1939": Mary Burbidge, "Lives Lived: Gretl Deutsch Helleiner", *Globe and Mail*, October 20, 1997.

58. Page 344, para. 1 – "political economy in 1940": Elizabeth Wallace, "Karl Helleiner", *Proceedings of the Royal Society of Canada*, 4th Series, v. 22 (1984) at 79.

59. Page 344, para. 1 – "in biochemistry at Dalhousie": "Helleiner, Gerald", *Canadian Who's Who, 1984* at 531. See e-mail by Gerry Helleiner to the author of April 10, 2001.

60. Page 344, para. 2 – "I'd ever have gone into it": Michael Bliss, *Banting: A Biography* (University of Toronto Press, 1984) at 100-101 and 252; see also Masters, *Cody* at 216, stating that Banting allowed his name to be used by the Canadian Committee to Aid Jewish Refugees.

61. Page 344, para. 2 – "to finance his research": Bliss, *Banting* at 236.

62. Page 344, para. 2 – "and the son of a Nobel laureate": Hermann Emil Fischer, his father, won the Nobel Prize for Chemistry in 1902 and died in 1919, predeceased by his wife and two of his three sons. See www.nobel.se/laureates/chemistry-1902-1-bio.html.

63. Page 344, para. 2 – "was appointed in 1937": Karl Paul Link, "Hermann O.L. Fischer: A Tribute on his 70th Birthday", *Archives of Biochemistry and Biophysics*, v.78 (December, 1958).

64. Page 344, para. 2 – "to support him for ten years": Masters, *Cody* at 216-17. Fischer brought with him his former student, Erich Baer, who joined the staff of the Banting and Best Institute. Baer won the 1962 Chemical Institute of Canada Medal and stayed at the University until his death: see UTA/Graduate Records/"Baer, Erich"/A73-0026/14(94).

65. Page 344, para. 2 – "a more open policy on refugees": H.J. Cody, "Canada and the Refugee Problem" (text of radio address), *University of Toronto Monthly*, v. 39 at 139-141; Masters, *Cody* at 216 and 218.

66. Page 344, para. 2 – "we are expecting Fischer to accomplish": Masters, *Cody* at 217.

67. Page 344, para. 2 – "at the University of California, Berkeley": Link, "Fischer".

68. Page 344, para. 2 – "helped bring a number of scientists to the University": Paul Bator with Andrew Rhodes, *Within Reach of Everyone: A History of the University of Toronto School of Hygiene and the Connaught Laboratories 1927-1955* (Toronto: Canadian Public Health Association, 1990) at 71.

69. Page 344, para. 2 – "the field of chemotherapeutics": "Refugee Sketches" (undated), UTA/A68-0006/48(09).

70. Page 344, para. 2 – "all their new chemotherapeutic products": Ibid.

71. Page 344, para. 3 – "who became head of mathematics in 1934": Gilbert De B. Robinson, "Samuel Beatty",

Proceedings of the Royal Society of Canada, 4th Series, v. 9 (1971) at 33; Gilbert De B. Robinson, *The Mathematics Department in the University of Toronto 1827-1978* (Toronto: Department of Mathematics, 1979) at 40.

72. Page 344, para. 3 – "the strength of the department": Robinson, *Mathematics* at 41.

73. Page 344, para. 3 – "at Princeton's Institute for Advanced Study": Ibid. at 40-41.

74. Page 344, para. 3 – "of our generation": Ibid. at 44.

75. Page 344, para. 3 – "were supervised by Brauer": Ibid. at 96-97.

76. Page 344, para. 3 – "the chair of applied mathematics": Ibid. at 41-42.

77. Page 345, para. 1 – "the popular *Evolution of Physics*": Ibid. at 42.

78. Page 345, para. 2 – "for his entire career": Ibid. at 66; Michael Smith, "Digression", *University of Toronto Magazine* (Spring, 1997) at 13; Geoff Hancock, "The Many Sides of Donald Coxeter", *Graduate* (September/October, 1979) at 10.

79. Page 345, para. 2 – "most distinguished mathematician": Hancock, "Many Sides" at 10.

80. Page 345, para. 2 – "just as Brauer did in algebra": Robinson, *Mathematics* at 66.

81. Page 345, para. 2 – "in other universities": For more on these individuals, see Ernst J. Kani and Robert A. Smith, eds., *The Collected Papers of Hans Arnold Heilbronn* (New York: John Wiley and Sons, 1988); Joseph W. Dauben, *Abraham Robinson: The Creation of Nonstandard Analysis: A Personal and Mathematical Odyssey* (Princeton: Princeton University Press, 1995); P.G. Rooney, "Peter Scherk", *Proceedings of the Royal Society of Canada*, 5th Series (1986).

82. Page 346, para. 1 – "it was eligible to compete": H.S.M. Coxeter, "Achievement in Maths", *Varsity Graduate*, (April 1986) at 17.

83. Page 346, para. 1 – "to Putnam candidates": Ibid.

84. Page 346, para. 1 – "(a future chair of the department)": Robinson, *Mathematics* at 94.

85. Page 346, para. 2 – "as enemy aliens": Masters, *Cody* at 273.

86. Page 346, para. 2 – "accidental immigrants": Paula Jean Draper, "Muses behind Barbed Wire: Canada and the Interned Refugees", in Jackman and Borden at 272.

87. Page 346, para. 2 – "sent to internment camps in Canada": Avery, *Science of War* at 205; Draper, "Muses" at 273 says "over twenty-two hundred".

88. Page 346, para. 2 – "stayed in Canada": Draper, "Muses" at 276.

89. Page 346, para. 2 – "more former internees": Levi, "S.A.C. Historical Project" at 77-78.

90. Page 346, para. 3 – "wanted to study at a university": Ibid.

91. Page 346, para. 3 – "the board of governors was opposed": Masters, *Cody* at 273-277.

92. Page 346, para. 3 – "against their exclusion": Masters, *Cody* at 276; Levi, "S.A.C. Historical Project" at 77-89.

93. Page 346, para. 3 – "the released internees could take military training": Masters, *Cody* at 276.

94. Page 346, para. 3 – "who had to take military training": See letter from Cody to MacKenzie January 21, 1943, UTA/A83-0036/002, outlining the history of the issue. Only nine of this group of interned students ended up at the University of Toronto in 1942-43, and of that group only 5 were Jewish, although all had fled Germany because, according to the Nazis, they had some "Jewish blood": see "A Statement Concerning the Admission of Certain Refugees to the University of Toronto in the Fall Term of 1942, by the President, Dr. H.J. Cody", UTA/ A83-0036/002 at 2.

95. Page 346, para. 3 – "Miss T. Nikaido": Bursar to Registrar, November 16, 1942, UTA/A83-0036/002.

96. Page 346, para. 3 – "like his father": Cody to Myers, January 21, 1943, UTA/A83-0036/002 at 3.

97. Page 346, para. 3 – "throughout North America": Eric Koch, *Deemed Suspect: A Wartime Blunder* (Toronto: Methuen, 1980) at 255-259.

98. Page 347, para. 1 – "Kohn said": "Nobel Origins", *University of Toronto Magazine* (probably published in 1998); see Beatty to Bruce Macdonald, October 7, 1942, UTA/A83-0026/0002, urging the University to accept the interned students.

99. Page 347, para. 1 – "and student of the Holocaust": Draper, "Muses" at 277.

100. Page 347, para. 1 – "ahead of the Gestapo": John G. Slater, "Philosophy at Toronto: A Documented History of the Philosophy Department of the University of Toronto" (unpublished draft, 1999) at 203.

101. Page 347, para. 1 – "a camp in Sherbrooke, Quebec": Ibid. at 203.

102. Page 347, para. 1 – "is good enough for us": Ibid.

103. Page 347, para. 1 – "a member of the philosophy department": Ibid. at 199 and 203. According to Slater, Fackenheim was brought in as a temporary replacement for Anderson. He did so well that he was hired.

104. Page 347, para. 1 – "theologian at St Michael's College": Draper, "Muses" at 277.

105. Page 348, para. 1 – "than getting out of the Camp": Blair to Wasteneys, April 1, 1942, in "Cody Statement" at 3.

106. Page 348, para. 1 – "the department of Spanish and Portuguese": "Portugal Honours Kurt Levy", *University of Toronto Bulletin*, November 19, 1984 at 9; "Honouring the past, investing in the future", *University of Toronto Campaign Spring Quarterly* (April, 1999) as cited at www.uoftcampaign.com/quartspring_honouring.htm.

107. Page 348, para. 1 – "before the war started six weeks later": "Honouring the past".

108. Page 348, para. 1 – "released from the camp": Ibid. There are others that could have been included, such as Henry Kreisel, who received his Ph.D. at Toronto and went on to become the head of the department of English at the University of Alberta.

109. Page 348, para. 2 – "the subject of great controversy": See Horn, *Academic Freedom at* 154-165; Masters, *Cody* at 249-268; R. Douglas Francis, *Frank H. Underhill: Intellectual Provocateur* (University of Toronto Press, 1986) at 114-126; McKillop, *Matters of Mind* at 541-543.

110. Page 348, para. 2 – "the Battle of Britain was about to be fought": Horn, *Academic Freedom* at 154; Masters, *Cody* at 257-258.

111. Page 348, para. 2 – "the Permanent Joint Board on Defence": Horn, *Academic Freedom* at 154.

112. Page 348, para. 2 – "all our eggs in the British basket": Underhill did not speak from a prepared text – the quotes

are Francis's version taken from his rough notes, newspaper reports and a reconstruction of what he said prepared ten days later: Francis, *Underhill* at 115.

113. Page 348, para. 2 – "in Britain's hour of greatest need": Masters, *Cody* at 259.

114. Page 348, para. 2 – "blooming in Flanders fields": See Chapter 26 (1931).

115. Page 348, para. 2 – "shrink with the British Empire": Brendan O'Brien to author, May 19, 1998.

116. Page 348, para. 3 – "to intern Underhill": Horn, *Academic Freedom* at 154. Arthur Meighen's complex relationship with the University of Toronto bears more scrutiny. In 1953, he was suggested as the successor to Vincent Massey for the Chancellorship of the University: see Charles Godfrey, "Biography of Herbert Bruce, Draft Chapter 14" at 15-18.

117. Page 348, para. 3 – "without the president's recommendation": Horn, *Academic Freedom* at 155.

118. Page 348, para. 3 – "would split the University": Ibid. at 156.

119. Page 349, para. 1 – "and I so recommend": Ibid. at 156 and 158.

120. Page 349, para. 1 – "agreed with the board's position": Ibid. at 159.

121. Page 349, para. 2 – "contributed by the University": Horn, *Academic Freedom* at 159; Masters, *Cody* at 265; Francis, *Underhill* at 121.

122. Page 349, para. 2 – "Underhill refused": Masters, *Cody* at 263.

123. Page 349, para. 2 – "not to dismiss Underhill": Horn, *Academic Freedom* at 160; Masters, *Cody* at 264; Francis, *Underhill* at 122.

124. Page 349, para. 2 – "of the First World War": See Chapter 22 (1914).

125. Page 349, para. 2 – "different from anyone who has not": Masters, *Cody* at 265.

126. Page 349, para. 2 – "history student Ken McNaught": Kenneth McNaught, *Conscience and History: A Memoir* (University of Toronto Press, 1999) at 27.

127. Page 349, para. 2 – "was sent to Cody": Horn, *Academic Freedom* at 161; Francis, *Underhill* at 123.

128. Page 349, para. 2 – "was also sent": Horn, *Academic Freedom* at 161.

129. Page 349, para. 3 – "at a meeting of the board in June 1941": Horn, *Academic Freedom* at 163; Masters, *Cody* at 267.

130. Page 349, para. 3 – "on relations with the United States": Horn, *Academic Freedom* at 161-162.

131. Page 349, para. 3 – "and add to our difficulties abroad": Ibid. at 161.

132. Page 349, para. 3 – "to a subsequent meeting": Horn, *Academic Freedom* at 163.

133. Page 349, para. 3 – "seriously contemplated his own resignation": Masters, *Cody* at 267.

134. Page 349, para. 3 – "did not recommend dismissal": Horn, *Academic Freedom* at 164.

135. Page 349, para. 3 – "without the president's concurrence": Horn, *Academic Freedom* at 164; Masters, *Cody* at 268.

136. Page 349, para. 3 – "for his pro-American sentiments": Horn, *Academic Freedom* at 156.

137. Page 349, para. 4 – "out of the public spotlight in the future": Ibid. at 164-165.

138. Page 350, para. 1 – "on political or public questions": Kennedy to Cody, September 21, 1940, UTA/A68-0006/046; Horn, *Academic Freedom* at 165; Irving Abella, "The Making of a Chief Justice: Bora Laskin, the Early Years", *Law Society Gazette*, v. 25 (1991) at 426.

139. Page 350, para. 2 – "with organized or unorganized Communism": Cited in Horn, *Academic Freedom* at 165.

140. Page 350, para. 2 – "was not yet an ally": Germany attacked the Soviet Union on June 22, 1941: see Horn, *Academic Freedom* at 149.

141. Page 350, para. 2 – "of possessing communist pamphlets": Horn, *Academic Freedom* at 148-49. According to the *Globe and Mail* of September 21, 1940 (their first report on the matter), Levine was arrested on Friday, September 20th. His house had been raided on the 18th. They picked up Levine officially two days later.

142. Page 350, para. 2 – "elected as president": Avery, *Science of War* at 221.

143. Page 350, para. 2 – "*Salute to the USSR*": Ezra Schabas, *Sir Ernest MacMillan: The Importance of Being Canadian* (University of Toronto Press, 1994) at 180.

144. Page 350, para. 3 – "as radar technicians": McKillop, *Matters of Mind* at 530-31.

145. Page 350, para. 3 – "of the first group of veterans": Ibid. at 524-25.

146. Page 350, para. 3 – "that in the faculty of arts decreased": Ibid. at 529.

147. Page 350, para. 3 – "at the final examinations": Ibid. at 535.

148. Page 350, para. 3 – "be curtailed or closed": McKillop, *Matters of Mind* at 677n29.

149. Page 350, para. 3 – "of the Humanities Research Council": Ibid. at 532-535. See also the unpublished papers given to the author by Francess Halpenny, May 2001, attached to her edited copy of Chapter 27 (1939) of this manuscript.

150. Page 352, para. 1 – "of limiting enrolment was devised": R.D. Gidney and W.P.J. Millar, "Quantity and Quality: The Problem of Admissions in Medicine at the University of Toronto 1910-1951", *Historical Studies in Education*, v. 9 (Fall/Autumn 1997) at 186.

151. Page 352, para. 1 – "only about 140 applications": Ibid. at 185.

152. Page 352, para. 1 – "more than 350 applications for 150 places": "Report of Committee on Admissions", 1943, UTA/A86-0027/23 at 221. In both 1942 and 1943 the number of Jews admitted was 32, that is, 21% of the class: "Report of the Committee on Admission of First Year Students", October 2, 1942, UTA/A86-0027/23 at 32 and "Report of the Committee", 1943 at 223. The percentage of Jewish applicants admitted in 1943 (64%) was, in fact, higher than that for non-Jews (55%): see "Report of the Committee", 1943 at 223. We have, unfortunately, not been able to find records showing what the high school marks were of the candidates and so cannot compare Jewish candidates with others. There is some indication that the Jewish candidates had higher marks because in 1944 the medical school admission committee referred to the fact that it "had to deal with a formidable array of Jewish applicants, many of whom had a very good matriculation score": see "Report of Committee on Admission to First Year Session 1944-1945", October 6, 1944, UTA/A86-0027/24 at 26. Another indication is that the committee finds it a 'serious problem' that only 6% of the Jews the previous year failed, whereas the overall failure rate in first year was 27%. Why would this be considered a serious problem, unless

there was some interest in limiting the number of Jews? The committee also noted in its 1944 report "the almost vitriolic criticism from parents and others on three points, namely: the large number of Jews, the large number of women, and the failure to admit the sons and daughters of medical men": see "Report of Committee on Admission to First Year Session 1944-1945" at 27. See also the presidential address by Jacalyn Duffin to the Canadian Society for the History of Medicine, May 2001 ("The Quota: 'An Equally Serious Problem' For Us All"). Nine months after leaving the U of T History project and long after this and the other footnotes on the subject were written, Charles Levi accidentally came across a memo from Robin Ross, the U of T registrar, to Claude Bissell, making it absolutely clear that discrimination existed in the medical faculty. Ross' memo is dated December 4, 1959: UTA A71-0011/33(07). See Levi's e-mails to me of December 18, 2001. It was too late to include a reference to the memo in the text of the history, but not too late to include it in this note. The memo states, in part: 'This office admits candidates to the Pre-medical Years of the Faculty of Medicine. It does so on the advice of a Selection Committee of the Council of the Faculty of Medicine. I am deeply disturbed by one aspect of the selection process. There is a definite limitation imposed by the Selection Committee on the number of Jewish students whom they are prepared to accept in the Pre-medical Years. There are, of course, solid practical reasons for this restriction and I am the first to sympathize with the Council in what is an awkward dilemma. Against that, however, is the very real danger that the University can be charged – and rightly so – with exercising the very kind of discrimination that we disavow publicly. As an example, during the session 1957-58 eleven well-qualified applicants were refused. These figures became nine in 1958-59 and fourteen in the session 1959-60. In each year, a fairly large number of candidates with lower academic standing were admitted. In most cases it was quite unrealistic to argue that the rejected candidates were refused on any other grounds than that they were Jewish. Whatever the practical difficulties may be, I think that this should stop. One way out of the dilemma would be to abolish the two Pre-medical years. Candidates for Medicine should be advised to take the General Science course and after that proceed to the First Medical Year. I have not discussed this in any detail with the Dean of Medicine as yet. I would like a chance of talking with yourself at your convenience." There is no record of Bissell's response in his papers or in his diary except an ambiguous entry in his diary on December 11, 1959 stating, "Long talk with Robin Ross about problems and Senate."

153. Page 352, para. 1 – "at the provincial university": Gidney and Millar, "Quantity" at 171 and 180.

154. Page 352, para. 1 – "the number of clinical places available": Ibid. at 176-177.

155. Page 352, para. 1 – "other medical schools in Canada": See, for example, Percy Barsky, "How 'Numerus Clausus' Was Ended In the Manitoba Medical School", *Jewish Historical Society of Canada Journal*, v. 1, no. 2 (Fall 1977) at 75.

156. Page 352, para. 1 – "limit enrolment at the University of Toronto": R.D. Gidney and W.P.J. Millar, "Medical Students at the University of Toronto 1910-1940: A Profile", *Canadian Bulletin of Medical History*, v.13 (1996) at 40.

157. Page 352, para. 1 – "was Jewish": Ibid. at 38-39.

158. Page 352, para. 2 – "were given special consideration": Gidney and Millar, "Quantity and Quality" at 186 and 188-189.

159. Page 352, para. 2 – "such as New York City": See Stephen Steinberg, "How Jewish Quotas Began" in *Commentary*, vol. 52, no. 23, September 1971. The article ends by stating that "whatever merit these arguments have, the concept of 'regional balance' unquestionably originated as a rationale for discrimination and may well continue as such today."

160. Page 352, para. 2 – "of the faculty of medicine": W.P.J. Millar, "'We wanted our children should have it better': Jewish Medical Students at the University of Toronto" (unpublished CHA paper, May 20, 2000) at 23.

161. Page 352, para. 2 – "the large number of jews": "Report of Committee on Admission to First Year Session 1944-1945" at 27. "Jew" is in lower case in the original. See also the statistical footnote in the above paragraph.

162. Page 352, para. 2 – "after the new policy was introduced": See also the statistical footnote in the paragraph above. Anecdotal evidence of discrimination is ample: see Harold Wiezel conversation with author, September 16, 2000; various conversations with other doctors including 1954 graduate Robert Ehrlich; Jan Steiner Oral Interview transcript, UTA/B87-0044 at 57-59; Edward Shorter, *A Century of Radiology in Toronto* (Toronto: Wall and Emerson, Inc., 1995) at 129; Gerald Tulchinsky, *Branching Out: The Transformation of the Canadian Jewish Community* (Toronto: Stoddart, 1998) at 275; Lesley Marrus Barsky, *From Generation to Generation: A History of Toronto's Mount Sinai Hospital* (McClelland & Stewart: Toronto, 1998) at 17. There remains no hard evidence that this was ever accepted policy. Statistical proof is also less than decisive. Jewish enrolment in Medicine from 1929 to 1942 ranged from 19% to 27%: see Gidney and Millar, "Medical Students" at 39; Fennell to Cody, November 12, 1929, UTA/A83-0036/002; UTA/A83-0036/002; Harris note, March 20, 1942, "Proportion of Jewish Students in Medicine"; Ryerson to Cody, October 27, 1939, UTA/A68-0006/042. Statistics for subsequent years are scarce – 14% in 1950 (see UTA/A65-0013/77, Evans to Smith, October 20, 1950) and 20% in 1953 (see UTA/A68-0007/097(07), B'nai B'rith Hillel Foundation, 1952-53 Annual Report). For two years, admissions statistics are available which add extra support. In 1949/50, 57.8% of all non-Jewish applications were accepted, but only 45.5% of all Jewish applications. In 1951/52 the ratios were 44.7% non-Jewish acceptance and 38.3% Jewish acceptance: see UTA/A86-0028/014. As Millar puts it, "it appears that the admissions committee limited the numbers of Jews as a routine procedure", but she adds, "Though after the second world war they [Jews] faced discrimination as a result of biased admissions policies, that may have been a short-term reversal, and one that apparently lessened over the next decade in response to demographic pressures as well as more liberalized attitudes": see Millar, "Jewish Medical Students" at 24 and 27. George Connell, who served on the admissions committee for Medicine beginning in 1958, declared, "I never heard any allusion to race and religion and could detect no bias on those grounds": see Connell marginal note of January, 2001 on author's draft.

163. Page 352, para. 2 – "but no longer did so": The letter explained, "Some years ago, in the Faculty of Medicine, there was a policy of discrimination against woman applicants in the form of a quota. For the last two admission seasons, however, there has been no such policy": see UTA/B83-0040/15, D.F. Forster to Mrs. Bird, chairman of the Royal Commission on the Status of Women in Canada, October 22, 1968, UTA/B83-0040/15; see also Jan Steiner Oral Interview transcript, UTA/B87-0044 at 59; see also the presidential address by Jacalyn Duffin to the Canadian Society for the History of Medicine, May 2001 ("The Quota: 'An Equally Serious Problem' For Us All") and her e-mails to Friedland, February 13, 2001.

164. Page 353, para. 1 – "posed a problem": Avery, *Science of War* at 84.

165. Page 353, para. 1 – "the work of teaching efficiently": Masters, *Cody* at 271.

166. Page 353, para. 1 – "by the autumn of 1942": McKillop, *Matters of Mind* at 529.

167. Page 353, para. 1 – "for the Royal Air Force": Masters, *Cody* at 271.

168. Page 353, para. 1 – "had been seconded to the military": Avery, *Science of War* at 84.

169. Page 353, para. 1 – "became assistant professors": Alison Prentice, "Three women in Physics" in Elizabeth Smyth, et al., *Challenging Professions: Historical and Contemporary Perspectives on Women's Professional Work* (University of Toronto Press, 1999) at 128.

170. Page 353, para. 1 – "became a full professor in 1963": "Staff Cards" University of Toronto Archives.

171. Page 353, para. 2 – "to the Department of Finance": McKillop, *Matters of Mind* at 529.

172. Page 353, para. 2 – "the first principal of Scarborough College": UTA/A83-0036/043 "Arthur Fitzwalter Wynne Plumptre".

173. Page 353, para. 2 – "to 600 engineers": Vincent Bladen, *Bladen on Bladen: Memoirs of a political economist* (Scarborough College in the University of Toronto, 1978) at 90.

174. Page 353, para. 3 – "A number of engineers": Richard White, *The Skule Story: The University of Toronto Faculty of Applied Science and Engineering 1873-2000* (University of Toronto Press, 2000) at 155.

175. Page 353, para. 3 – "to Research Enterprises Limited": Avery, *Science of War* at 84.

176. Page 353, para. 3 – "as chairman of the board of governors": *Varsity Graduate* (February, 1965) at 21.

177. Page 353, para. 3 – "used by the RCAF": C.R. Young to Cody, November 8, 1940, UTA/A68-0006/48(01).

178. Page 353, para. 3 – "on the theory of flight": "The University and the War", *University of Toronto Monthly*, v.40 at 91.

179. Page 353, para. 3 – "but this arrangement did not work out": White, *The Skule Story* at 154.

180. Page 353, para. 3 – "could work as instructors": Ibid.

181. Page 354, para. 1 – "the National Research Council at Ottawa": Avery, *Science of War* at ix and 15; C.P. Stacey, *Arms, Men and Governments: The War Policies of Canada 1939-1945* (Ottawa: The Queen's Printer, 1970) at 512; McKillop, *Matters of Mind* at 522.

182. Page 354, para. 1 – "during the First World War": See Chapter 22 (1914).

183. Page 354, para. 1 – "Its single, well-equipped laboratory": Avery, *Science of War* at 44.

184. Page 354, para. 1 – "which had been opened in 1932": Ibid. at 267.

185. Page 354, para. 1 – "had 300 professional staff by 1939": Ibid. at 44.

186. Page 354, para. 1 – "and a staff of about 3,000": Stacey, *Arms, Men and Governments* at 507; Wilfrid Eggleston, *National Research in Canada: The NRC 1916-1966* (Toronto: Clarke, Irwin & Company Limited, 1978) at 278. Eggleston's figure of 3,000 is for 1950.

187. Page 354, para. 1 – "work relating to chemistry": Avery, *Science of War* at 47.

188. Page 354, para. 1 – "employed over 1,000 scientists": Ibid. at 77.

189. Page 354, para. 1 – "to the Allied victory": Stacey, *Arms, Men and Governments* at 512; Avery, *Science of War* at 9.

190. Page 354, para. 2 – "some work on radar development": Avery, *Science of War* at 84. The work was highly secret and was concentrated in Ottawa: see ibid. at 86; George R. Lindsey, ed., *No Day Long Enough: Canadian Science in World War II* (Toronto: Canadian Institute of Strategic Studies, 1997) at 48.

191. Page 354, para. 2 – "for the Canadian and British navies": Avery, *Science of War* at 84. White, *The Skule Story* at 155, refers to the work of R.J. Montgomery of ceramic engineering who helped Research Enterprises manufacture optical glass for radar sets.

192. Page 354, para. 2 – "of the atomic bomb": Avery, *Science of War* at 176-177.

193. Page 354, para. 2 – "transferred from Cambridge": Ibid. at 181.

194. Page 354, para. 3 – "without a direct hit": Avery, *Science of War* at 98-99; Lindsey, *No Day Long Enough* at 110.

195. Page 354, para. 3 – "and the United States in 1940": Avery, *Science of War* at 66.

196. Page 354, para. 3 – "headed by the physicist Arnold Pitt": Stacey, *Arms, Men and Governments* at 513; Avery,

Science of War at 102-106 and 277. Dr. R.W. McKay and Mr. W.H. McPherson were senior members of the research group, according to Stacey, *Arms, Men and Governments* at 513.

197. Page 354, para. 3 – "joined the faculty in 1927": Elizabeth Allin, *Physics at the University of Toronto 1843-1980* (Toronto: Department of Physics, 1981) at 25.

198. Page 354, para. 3 – "proximity to an object": See generally, Avery, *Science of War* at 98-106.

199. Page 354, para. 3 – "a number of important innovations": Avery, *Science of War* at 277.

200. Page 354, para. 3 – "the launching of the shell": Ibid. at 100.

201. Page 354, para. 3 – "head of computer science at the University": Allin, *Physics* at 30.

202. Page 354, para. 3 – "the fuses on British guns": Avery, *Science of War* at 104. The others were Morris Rubinoff and Ted Pashler.

203. Page 355, para. 1 – "that powered the radio": Lindsey, *No Day Long Enough* at 110; Avery, *Science of War* at 104;Wilfrid Eggleston, *Scientists at War*, (Toronto: Oxford University Press, 1950) at 69.

204. Page 355, para. 2 – "in the development of the fuse": Avery, *Science of War* at 101.

205. Page 355, para. 2 – "could fall into enemy hands": Ibid. at 104-5.

206. Page 355, para. 2 – "that began in 1944": Ibid. at 105.

207. Page 355, para. 2 – "being destroyed in the air": Ibid.

208. Page 355, para. 2 – "would not have been available in time": Stacey, *Arms, Men and Governments* at 513. Avery, *Science of War* at 106, notes that towards the end of the war the fuses were used against German tanks and by Allied bombers.

209. Page 355, para. 3 – "involving shell propellants and explosives": Avery, *Science of War* at 274 and 279. Another chemist who made significant contributions to the war effort was Lloyd Pidgeon, who joined the staff of the University of Toronto in 1943, two years after he was appointed director in charge of research at Dominion Magnesium Ltd.: see *Globe and Mail*, December 18, 1999.

210. Page 355, para. 3 – "from the United States in 1936": Avery, *Science of War* at 279; UTA/Current People/"George F. Wright".

211. Page 355, para. 3 – "conducted at Canadian universities": Avery, *Science of War* at 113.

212. Page 355, para. 3 – "noted for his eccentricities": Ibid. Wright was "brash, temperamental, and dictatorial": see ibid. at 118.

213. Page 355, para. 3 – "drove his team ruthlessly": Ibid. at 110.

214. Page 355, para. 3 – "since the First World War": Ibid. at 109.

215. Page 355, para. 3 – "various methods of production": Ibid. at 109-112.

216. Page 355, para. 3 – "the official reported": Ibid. at 110.

217. Page 355, para. 3 – "for use by the American forces": Ibid. at 116.

218. Page 355, para. 3 – "by the Canadian and US navies": Ibid. at 117-119.

219. Page 355, para. 3 – "for his contributions": Ibid. at 317n146.

220. Page 355, para. 4 – "did work on burn dressings": Lindsey, *No Day Long Enough* at 139.

221. Page 355, para. 4 – "the new wonder drug penicillin": Bator and Rhodes, *Within Reach of Everyone* at 72 and 74.

222. Page 356, para. 1 – "for the production of the antibiotic": Ibid. at 72.

223. Page 356, para. 1 – "a whole-blood replacement for military use": Ibid. at 73-74 and 79-82; Lindsey, *No Day Long Enough* at 123.

224. Page 356, para. 1 – "in experimental animals": Bator and Rhodes, *Within Reach of Everyone* at 73.

225. Page 356, para. 1 – "dried human blood serum, or plasma": Lindsey, *No Day Long Enough* at 123.

226. Page 356, para. 1 – "of blood serum a week": Bator and Rhodes, *Within Reach of Everyone* at 73.

227. Page 356, para. 1 – "almost a million blood donations": Ibid. at 74.

228. Page 356, para. 2 – "who from 1941": Ibid. at 126.

229. Page 356, para. 2 – "and related biophysical matters": Charles H. Best, "Donald Young Solandt", *Proceedings of the Royal Society of Canada*, 3rd Series, v. 49 at 137.

230. Page 356, para. 2 – "from the University in 1935": UTA/Graduate Records/"Jeanne F. Manery"/A73-0026/303(53). It is possible Manery also obtained a doctorate at the University of London.

231. Page 356, para. 2 – "to the study of night vision": Best, "Donald Solandt" at 137.

232. Page 356, para. 2 – "at the age of 48": Ibid.

233. Page 356, para. 2 – "chancellor of the University": C.E. Law, "Omond McKillop Solandt", *Proceedings of the Royal Society of Canada*, 6th Series, v. 4 (1993) at 130.

234. Page 356, para. 3 – "Canada's efforts in aviation medicine": Bliss, *Banting* at 254-262; Lindsey, *No Day Long Enough* at 127-134; D.J. Goodspeed, *A History of the Defence Research Board of Canada* (Ottawa: Queen's Printer, 1958) at 224-225.

235. Page 356, para. 3 – "such as Edward Hall": Bliss, *Banting* at 267.

236. Page 356, para. 3 – "president of the University of Western Ontario": Ibid. at 309.

237. Page 356, para. 3 – "on aviation medicine before the war": Goodspeed, *Defence Research Board* at 224; Lindsey, *No Day Long Enough* at 7-8; Bliss, *Banting* at 250.

238. Page 356, para. 3 – "by a number of American scientists": Bliss, *Banting* at 280.

239. Page 356, para. 3 – "by high speeds and high altitudes": Goodspeed, *Defence Research Board* at 224.

240. Page 356, para. 3 – "by the effects of accentuated gravity": T.M. Gibson and M.H. Harrison, *Into Thin Air: A History of Aviation Medicine in the RAF* (London: Robert Hale, 1984) at 148; Lindsey, *No Day Long Enough* at 128.

241. Page 356, para. 4 – "north of Eglinton Avenue": Bliss, *Banting* at 277.

242. Page 356, para. 4 – "the effects of high altitudes": Ibid. at 281.

243. Page 356, para. 4 – "was the first in North America": Peter Allen, "The Remotest of Mistresses: The Story of Canada's Unsung Tactical Weapon: The Franks Flying Suit", *Canadian Aviation Historical Society Journal*, v. 21 (Winter 1983) at 112; Lindsey, *No Day Long Enough* at 17; Bliss, *Banting* at 277, says it was the first in the British Commonwealth.

244. Page 358, para. 1 – "at least eighty such chambers": Allen, "Remotest of Mistresses" at 111; Lindsey, *No Day Long Enough* at 131.

245. Page 358, para. 1 – "a temperature of –59°F": Bliss, *Banting* at 281.

246. Page 358, para. 1 – "he had tested on himself": Ibid. at 272.

247. Page 358, para. 1 – "the staff wisely said no": Ibid. at 281.

248. Page 358, para. 1 – "was an improved oxygen mask": Lindsey, *No Day Long Enough* at 17.

249. Page 358, para. 2 – "a cancer researcher in Banting's laboratory": Lindsey, *No Day Long Enough* at 116; Bliss, *Banting* at 187.

250. Page 358, para. 2 – "the world's first anti-gravity suit": Allen, "Remotest of Mistresses" at 114; Lindsey, *No Day Long Enough* at 8; Bliss, *Banting* at 309.

251. Page 358, para. 2 – "and stronger liquid-filled bottles": Gibson and Harrison, *Into Thin Air* at 149; Bliss, *Banting* at 255.

252. Page 358, para. 2 – "in water-filled condoms": Allen, "Remotest of Mistresses" at 114; Bliss, *Banting* at 255.

253. Page 358, para. 2 – "with the help of the department of electrical engineering": Lindsey, *No Day Long Enough* at 117.

254. Page 358, para. 2 – "the amphibious landing in North Africa": Lindsey, *No Day Long Enough* at 117. They weren't used by the RAF because by the time they were ready dog fights were no longer common: see Allen, "Remotest of Mistresses" at 120; see also Bliss, *Banting* at 290.

255. Page 358, para. 2 – "without the pilots blacking-out": Gibson and Harrison, *Into Thin Air* at 148.

256. Page 358, para. 2 – "of Franks' flying suit": Allen, "Remotest of Mistresses" at 120.

257. Page 358, para. 3 – "would use such weapons": Bliss, *Banting* at 232; Avery, *Science of War* at 153.

258. Page 358, para. 3 – "of destroying an enemy": Bliss, *Banting* at 232-233.

259. Page 358, para. 3 – "rats harbouring infected fleas": Ibid. at 233.

260. Page 358, para. 3 – "even a scratch would be deadly": Avery, *Science of War* at 153.

261. Page 358, para. 3 – "with the government's": Avery, *Science of War* at 157; John Bryden, *Deadly Allies: Canada's Secret War 1937-1947* (Toronto: McClelland and Stewart, 1989) at 43.

262. Page 358, para. 3 – "and President Cody's": Avery, *Science of War* at 325n11.

263. Page 358, para. 4 – "during the Second World War": Ibid. at 175.

264. Page 358, para. 4 – "to counter the enemy's use of these weapons": Ibid. at 153.

265. Page 359, para. 1 – "weapons in Ethiopia": Ibid. at 23.

266. Page 359, para. 1 – "against Chinese troops": Ibid. at 134.

267. Page 359, para. 1 – "their use by the enemy less likely": Ibid. at 163.

268. Page 359, para. 1 – "threatened such a response": Ibid. at 136.

269. Page 359, para. 1 – "in charged munitions": Lindsey, *No Day Long Enough* at 152.

270. Page 359, para. 2 – "the department of physiological hygiene": Bator and Rhodes, *Within Reach of Everyone* at 77.

271. Page 359, para. 2 – "in the department of chemistry": Masters, *Cody* at 236; Bryden, *Deadly Allies* at 62.

272. Page 359, para. 2 – "became superintendent of research": Goodspeed, *Defence Research Board* at 146-47.

273. Page 359, para. 2 – "at the 2,000-square mile": Avery, *Science of War* at 130 says 1,825.

274. Page 359, para. 2 – "where various weapons were tested": Ibid. at 124, 150, 163, and 164.

275. Page 359, para. 2 – "worked on biological warfare": Bryden, *Deadly Allies* at 43-50; Bliss, *Banting* at 282.

276. Page 359, para. 2 – "experimented with parrot fever": Bryden, *Deadly Allies* at 43-44.

277. Page 359, para. 2 – "and typhus": Goodspeed, *Defence Research Board* at 153.

278. Page 359, para. 2 – "The salmonella poisoning work": Bryden, *Deadly Allies* at 82.

279. Page 359, para. 2 – "specifically for use against humans": Ibid.

280. Page 359, para. 3 – "spearheaded the biological research": Avery, *Science of War* at 256.

281. Page 359, para. 3 – "not destroy them": Bryden, *Deadly Allies* at 83.

282. Page 359, para. 3 – "and Craigie's work on the typhus vaccine": Bator and Rhodes, *Within Reach of Everyone* at 74.

283. Page 359, para. 3 – "awarded a US Medal of Freedom": Ibid. at 96.

284. Page 359, para. 4 – "of similarity of equipment": Avery, *Science of War* at 21.

285. Page 360, para. 1 – "of advanced weapons and equipment": Ibid. at 95.

286. Page 360, para. 1 – "between science and government": Ibid. at 4.

CHAPTER 28 – 1944 – CHANGING THE GUARD

1. Page 363, para. 1 – "post-secondary education of veterans": See Chapter 23 (1919); Peter Neary, "Canadian Universities and Canadian Veterans of World War II", in Neary and Jack Granatstein, *The Veterans Charter and post-World War II Canada* (Montreal: McGill-Queen's University Press, 1998) at 110; A.B. McKillop, *Matters of Mind: The University in Ontario 1791-1951* (University of Toronto Press, 1994) at 547.

2. Page 363, para. 1 – "$150 a year for each veteran": Neary, "Canadian Veterans" at 110 and 118-119.

3. Page 363, para. 1 – "was about 7,000": E.A. Corbett, *Sidney Earle Smith* (University of Toronto Press, 1961) at 44.

4. Page 363, para. 1 – "at the beginning of the war": McKillop, *Matters of Mind* at 548.

5. Page 363, para. 1 – "it was over 17,000": Corbett, *Smith* at 44.

6. Page 363, para. 1 – "who went on to university": Neary, "Canadian Veterans" at 122 and 139.

7. Page 363, para. 2 – "Drew did not like Cody": D.C. Masters, *Henry John Cody: An Outstanding Life* (Toronto: Dundurn Press, 1995) at 287.

8. Page 363, para. 2 – "after he became premier": Ibid. at 291.

9. Page 363, para. 2 – "on the issue of 'enemy aliens'": Cody to Henry, March 1, 1943, NAC/George Alexander Drew Papers/MG32 C3, v. 32, file 297; Henry to Cody, March 10, 1943, ibid.

10. Page 364, para. 1 – "Cody turned 76 in 1944": Sidney Smith, "Henry John Cody", *Proceedings of the Royal Society of Canada*, 3rd Series, v. 45 (1951) at 87.

11. Page 364, para. 1 – "Cyril James": Cyril James was born in 1903 and was 36 when he was appointed principal of McGill in 1939. He would have been 41 in 1944: see Stanley Brice Frost, *The Man in the Ivory Tower: F. Cyril James of McGill* (Montreal: McGill-Queen's University Press, 1991) at 4 and 59.

12. Page 364, para. 1 – "His health was deteriorating": Masters, *Cody* at 226-228.

13. Page 364, para. 1 – "suffered from ulcers": Ibid. at 227.

14. Page 364, para. 1 – "head of the University Health Service": UTA/Graduate Records/"Richard William Ian Urquhart"/A73-0026/482(62).

15. Page 364, para. 1 – "just a little bit deaf": Extract from reminiscences of R.W.I. Urquhart, sent by Donald Urquhart February 25, 1998.

16. Page 364, para. 1 – "of what he had said": Ibid.

17. Page 364, para. 1 – "dean of medicine, W.E. Gallie": "Gallie, William Edward", *Canadian Who's Who 1949-1951* at 364.

18. Page 364, para. 1 – "an insulin reaction": Urquhart extract.

19. Page 364, para. 1 – "as he has been slipping badly": Bruce to Massey, May 9, 1944, UTA/B87-0082/371(02).

20. Page 364, para. 1 – "must contemplate resignation": D.B. Macdonald, "Partial Memoirs of the Rev. D.B. Macdonald pertaining to the University of Toronto", UTA/B83-1295 at 42.

21. Page 364, para. 2 – "to succeed Cody as president": Claude Bissell, *The Imperial Canadian: Vincent Massey in Office* (University of Toronto Press, 1986) at 178; Masters, *Cody* at 289. It may be that at this stage Drew also supported Massey as Cody's replacement. Drew visited Massey in England in December, 1943: see Bissell, *Massey* at 177; Masters, *Cody* at 289.

22. Page 364, para. 2 – "Massey made to Canada": Bissell, *Massey* at 178. Massey had wanted to succeed Falconer as President as well: see Chapter 22 (1931).

23. Page 364, para. 2 – "'ideal president,' they thought": Bruce to Massey, May 9, 1944.

24. Page 364, para. 2 – "and get back to him": Bissell, *Massey* at 178.

25. Page 364, para. 2 – "if it had been made": Massey to Bruce, June 24, 1944, UTA/B87-0082/371(02), simply says that there is "no point in dealing with the subject."

26. Page 364, para. 2 – "master of Balliol College in Oxford": Bissell, *Massey* at 171, 179, and 193-194.

27. Page 364, para. 3 – "prolong his presidency": Masters, *Cody* at 288.

28. Page 364, para. 3 – "was first revealed": Macdonald, "Memoirs" at 42.

29. Page 364, para. 3 – "only 7 out of 22 members attended": Board of Governors Minutes, March 9, 1944, UTA/A70-0024/reel 14.

30. Page 364, para. 3 – "on the day of the meeting": Macdonald, "Memoirs" at 42. Macdonald also had Sidney Smith in mind for the presidency.

31. Page 364, para. 3 – "was about to retire": Masters, *Cody* at 288.

32. Page 364, para. 3 – "for the previous ten years": Corbett, *Smith* at 35.

33. Page 365, para. 1 – "the 47-year-old Smith": Smith was born March 9, 1897: see "Smith, Sidney Earle", *Canadian Who's Who 1949-1951* at 934.

34. Page 365, para. 1 – "executive assistant to the president": Masters, *Cody* at 289.

35. Page 365, para. 1 – "later succeed to the office of President": Board of Governors Minutes, March 9, 1944.

36. Page 365, para. 2 – "growing work of this University": Cody to Smith, March 14, 1944, UTA/A68-0006/061(04).

37. Page 365, para. 2 – "the National Conference of Canadian Universities": Masters, *Cody* at 289; see Gwendoline Pilkington, "A History of the National Conference of Canadian Universities 1911-1961" (Ph.D. Thesis, University of Toronto, 1974).

38. Page 365, para. 2 – "president of the association in 1942": Pilkington, "National Conference" at 401-402.

39. Page 366, para. 1 – "rehabilitation of returning students": Cody to Smith, March 14, 1944.

40. Page 366, para. 2 – "were not pleased with Cody's actions": Bruce to Massey, May 9, 1944. George Drew was "upset and annoyed": see Henry Borden Oral Interview Transcript, B87-0044 at 16.

41. Page 366, para. 2 – "was deleted": Board of Governors Minutes, March 23, 1944.

42. Page 366, para. 2 – "for academic administration as Smith": Cody to Ferguson of April 14, 1944, Drew Papers, v.32, file 297. John English, Pearson's biographer, heard rumours about Pearson becoming president from Goldwin French: see conversation with John English, May 28, 2000.

43. Page 366, para. 3 – "a model administrator president": W.L. Morton, *One University* (Toronto: McClelland and Stewart, 1957) at 172.

44. Page 366, para. 3 – "would make a good president": Cody to Smith, May 4, 1944, UTA/A68-0006/61.

45. Page 366, para. 3 – "from 1925 to 1929": Corbett, *Smith* at 13.

46. Page 366, para. 3 – "dean of Dalhousie Law School": John Willis, *A History of Dalhousie Law School* (University of Toronto Press, 1979) at 101-102.

47. Page 366, para. 3 – "then president of the University of Manitoba": Corbett, *Smith* at 19.

48. Page 366, para. 3 – "the treasurer, Leslie Frost": "Frost, Hon. Leslie Miscampbell", *Canadian Who's Who 1949-1951* at 358; "Drew, Lieut-Col. George Alexander", *Canadian Who's Who 1949-1951* at 285. Drew and Frost had interrupted their studies at University College to enlist and went directly to Osgoode without obtaining a Toronto degree.

49. Page 366, para. 3 – "the attorney general, Leslie Blackwell": "Blackwell, Leslie Egerton", *Canadian Who's Who 1949-1951* at 89.

50. Page 366, para. 3 – "and development minister, Dana Porter": "Porter, Hon. Dana Harris", *Canadian Who's Who 1949-1951* at 814; Corbett, *Smith* at 28-29.

51. Page 366, para. 3 – "of Premier John Bracken of Manitoba": Corbett, *Smith* at 29-30; Mary Dale Muir, "Dr. Sidney E. Smith, University College Principal and Assistant to the President", *University of Toronto Monthly*, v. 44 at 256. Borden was responsible for assuring Drew that Smith was capable: see Borden Oral Interview at 16.

52. Page 366, para. 4 – "in due time": Board of Governors Minutes, April 27, 1944.

53. Page 366, para. 4 – "included a fine house": Macdonald to Smith, May 2, 1944, UTA/A83-0036/039. Cody, by contrast, was originally hired at a salary of $15,000, reduced to $12,602 in 1934 and to $12,300 plus $1,500 for expenses in 1945: see *Report of the Board of Governors for the Year Ended June 30, 1934* at 29 and *Report of the Board of Governors for the Year Ended June 30, 1945* at 34. The University valued Smith's house at $1,200, meaning the total package was only $600 less than Cody's final salary.

54. Page 367, para. 1 – "site of the present McLaughlin Planetarium": Claude Bissell, *Halfway up Parnassus: A Personal Account of the University of Toronto 1932-1971* (University of Toronto Press, 1974). At the time of writing, the Planetarium is being used as the Children's Own Museum.

55. Page 367, para. 1 – "being used as a women's residence": Cody to Smith, May 4, 1944. The building was originally purchased for Robert Falconer in 1921. See also UTA/A75-0027/002(56).

56. Page 367, para. 1 – "Falconer had lived there": Comments from Harold Averill to Friedland, February 18, 2001.

57. Page 367, para. 1 – "before the turn of the century": Masters, *Cody* at 309.

58. Page 367, para. 1 – "took effect as of July 1, 1944": Macdonald to Smith, May 2, 1944.

59. Page 367, para. 2 – "in the late summer of 1944": Corbett, *Smith* at 37.

60. Page 367, para. 2 – "to meet the new conditions": Masters, *Cody* at 291.

61. Page 367, para. 2 – "not what he had in mind": Ibid.

62. Page 367, para. 3 – "the 100-year-old chancellor": "The University Mourns the Loss of its Chancellor", *University of Toronto Monthly*, v. 45 at 9.

63. Page 367, para. 3 – "his great grandson, William J. Mulock": Ibid.

64. Page 367, para. 3 – "in a few paragraphs": See Masters, *Cody* at 287 et seq.; Bissell, *Massey* at 176-181.

65. Page 367, para. 3 – "to promote Massey as the next chancellor": Cody to Massey, May 17, 1944, UTA/B87-0082/371(02).

66. Page 367, para. 3 – "he wanted to die in office": Masters, *Cody* at 290.

67. Page 367, para. 3 – "withdrew it": Ibid.

68. Page 367, para. 4 – "for another four years": Ibid. at 292.

69. Page 367, para. 4 – "that might have favoured Massey": Ibid. at 293.

70. Page 368, para. 1 – "the only candidate": Bissell, *Massey* at 180.

71. Page 368, para. 1 – "in November 1944": Masters, *Cody* at 293.

72. Page 368, para. 1 – "the previous spring": Cody to Massey, May 17, 1944.

73. Page 368, para. 1 – "for a number of years": Bissell, *Massey* at 179.

74. Page 368, para. 2 – "according to his own wishes": Drew to Massey, October 18, 1944, UTA/B87-0082/371(02); Bissell, *Massey* at 180.

75. Page 369, para. 1 – "unsolicited advice": Masters, *Cody* at 302.

76. Page 369, para. 1 – "the method of selecting the chancellor": Masters, *Cody* at 299 et seq.; Bissell, *Massey* at 180-81.

77. Page 369, para. 1 – "and of the alumni": *University of Toronto Act, 1947*, ss. 62, 66, and 67; the key section was 62(1), which said, "There shall be a Chancellor of the University who shall be appointed by the Board and by the Senate on the nomination of the Committee of Nomination"; Bissell, *Massey* at 180-81.

78. Page 369, para. 1 – "from four to three years": *University of Toronto Act, 1947*, s. 63; Bissell, *Massey* at 181.

79. Page 369, para. 1 – "appeared to be to get rid of Cody": Masters, *Cody* at 301.

80. Page 369, para. 2 – "but the senate refused to accept it": Ibid. at 302.

81. Page 369, para. 2 – "of the Students' Administrative Council": Ibid. at 302 and 305.

82. Page 369, para. 2 – "of events on the campus": For the relationship between Cody and E.A. Macdonald, see Charles Levi, "The SAC Historical Project 1930-1950" (Toronto: Self-published, 1992) at 38-39.

83. Page 369, para. 2 – "Sydney Hermant was magnificent": Masters, *Cody* at 305.

84. Page 369, para. 2 – "gave an opposite opinion": Ibid. at 304-305.

85. Page 369, para. 2 – "installed as chancellor in November 1947": Ibid. at 303, 305, and 308. Herbert Bruce was suggested as Massey's successor in 1953, but he was reluctant to run against Arthur Meighen: see Charles Godfrey, "Biography of Herbert Bruce Draft Chapter 14" at 15-19.

86. Page 369, para. 2 – "Canon Cody did not attend": Masters, *Cody* at 308.

87. Page 369, para. 3 – "a member by the government": "Prominent Engineer Appointed to University's Board of Governors", *University of Toronto Monthly*, v. 45 at 46. Phillips was appointed on October 17, 1944, and attended his first meeting of the Board on October 26, 1944, at which Cody (but not Macdonald) was present: see Board of Governors Minutes, October 26, 1944, UTA/A70-0024/reel 15.

88. Page 369, para. 3 – "and the 52-year-old Phillips took over": "A New Chairman for the Board of Governors", *University of Toronto Monthly*, v. 45 at 120. Phillips was appointed chair on February 6, 1945, the same day that Henry Borden and O.D. Vaughan were appointed to the board. However, Phillips never gave his actual birthdate out, only his year – 1893. So he was either 51 or 52 when he was appointed: see Board of Governors Minutes, February 8, 1945.

89. Page 369, para. 3 – "a position he would hold until 1964": "Achievements Long Remembered", *Varsity Graduate*, (February, 1965) at 21.

90. Page 369, para. 3 – "conspicuous gallantry": Ibid. at 28.

91. Page 369, para. 3 – "when the war broke out": Ibid.

92. Page 369, para. 3 – "one of its youngest lieutenant-colonels": Ibid.

93. Page 369, para. 3 – "and radar sets": Ibid; see also previous chapter.

94. Page 370, para. 1 – "including Massey-Ferguson": Liz Lundell, *The Estates of Old Toronto* (Erin, Ontario: Boston Mills Press, 1997) at 163 and 169.

95. Page 370, para. 1 – "that carried him to the top": Bissell, *Parnassus* at 29.

96. Page 370, para. 1 – "and with his successor, Bissell": Ibid. at 30.

97. Page 370, para. 1 – "toughness, intelligence, and charm": Bissell, *Massey* at 189-190. Frances Ireland noted that no one was able to oppose anything Phillips ever wanted: see Frances Ireland oral interview transcript, B86-0052 at 4.

98. Page 370, para. 1 – "particularly history": Bissell, *Parnassus* at 29.

99. Page 370, para. 1 – "almost father-like toward me": UTA/B88-0091, Claude Bissell Diaries, December 26, 1964.

100. Page 370, para. 1 – "earlier in the century": Bissell, *Parnassus* at 29-30.

101. Page 371, para. 1 – "(later Edper Brascan)": "Borden, Henry", *Canadian Who's Who 1952-54* at 104.

102. Page 371, para. 1 – "he had been a Rhodes Scholar": "A New Chairman" at 120.

103. Page 371, para. 1 – "chairman of the Wartime Industries Control Board": Ibid.

104. Page 371, para. 1 – "when Phillips resigned in 1964": UTA/Current People/ "Borden, Henry".

105. Page 371, para. 1 – "was also appointed": "A New Chairman" at 120.

106. Page 371, para. 1 – "lawyers Beverley Matthews": Board of Governors cards, UTA/A83-0036/021.

107. Page 371, para. 1 – "and Arthur Kelly": "Recent Appointments to the Board of Governors", *University of Toronto Monthly*, v. 46 at 34.

108. Page 371, para. 1 – "general manager of the Metropolitan Opera": Ibid.

109. Page 371, para. 1 – "and the accountant Walter Gordon": Ibid.

110. Page 371, para. 1 – "and minister of finance in Pearson's government": "Gordon, Walter", *Canadian Who's Who 1984* at 458. For Gordon in general, see Walter Gordon, *Walter L. Gordon: A Political Memoir* (Toronto: McClelland and Stewart, 1977).

111. Page 371, para. 2 – "by Smith, Phillips, and Borden": Corbett, *Smith* at 45; Borden Oral Interview at 21-22.

112. Page 371, para. 2 – "a 1916 graduate of University College": "Miss Agnes MacGillvray '16 UC, New Secretary to President", *University of Toronto Monthly*, v.41 at 98.

113. Page 371, para. 2 – "over a period of forty years": Clara C. Benson, "Miss Annie Patterson Retires", *University of Toronto Monthly*, v.41 at 97.

114. Page 371, para. 2 – "before retiring in 1963": One of these was acting President Woodside: see UTA/Graduate Records/"Agnes MacGillvray"/A73-0026/269(81).

115. Page 371, para. 2 – "for the administration": Corbett, *Smith* at 45.

116. Page 371, para. 2 – "appeared in Simcoe Hall": See Smith to "Dear Colleague", June 4, 1946, with attached "Functional Chart – University of Toronto", UTA/A83-0036/021.

117. Page 371, para. 3 – "brought in a comptroller": Bissell, *Parnassus* at 30; McKillop, *Matters of Mind* at 550-51.

118. Page 371, para. 3 – "but rather to the board": "Functional Chart".

119. Page 371, para. 3 – "to take more direct responsibility": Bissell, *Parnassus* at 30.

120. Page 371, para. 3 – "between academic and financial matters": Ibid.

121. Page 371, para. 3 – "under the authority of the comptroller": "Functional Chart".

122. Page 371, para. 3 – "(later designated a vice president)": Bissell, *Parnassus* at 30.

123. Page 371, para. 3 – "at Research Enterprises Limited": "University Appointments", *University of Toronto Monthly*, v.46 at 98.

124. Page 372, para. 1 – "quote Claude Bissell": Bissell, *Parnassus* at 30.

125. Page 372, para. 1 – "when he became president": Ibid. at 19, 21 and 38.

126. Page 372, para. 1 – "and the system was changed": Bissell Diary, January 7, 1965.

127. Page 372, para. 2 – "in his welcoming address": *Varsity*, September 27, 1945; Neary, "Canadian Veterans" at 113, discusses the issue of segregation.

128. Page 372, para. 2 – "set up to assist veterans": *Varsity* of September 27, 1945; *President's Report, 1946/47* at 74-76; Frances Stewart and George Wodehouse, "University Health Service: University of Toronto", document compiled in 1976, UTA/A83-0036/034.

129. Page 372, para. 2 – "get jobs after graduation": *President's Report, 1947/48* at 78-79.

130. Page 372, para. 3 – "were a no-nonsense body": McKillop, *Matters of Mind* at 553. See Levi, "S.A.C. Historical Project" (self-published, 1992) at 111-120; conversation with Francess Halpenny and Joan Randall, April 2001.

131. Page 372, para. 3 – "during the previous three years": *Varsity*, September 26, 1946.

132. Page 372, para. 3 – "reported in 1948": Beatty to Evans, November 10, 1948, UTA/A83-0036/037.

133. Page 372, para. 3 – "in September 1947": *Varsity*, September 25, 1947.

134. Page 372, para. 3 – "without any additions": Phillips to Drew, March 12, 1948, Drew Papers, v. 177, file 23. The 1945 Toronto City Directory lists five establishments on this stretch of road which may have held cocktail licenses. Along with the King Cole Room at 178 Bloor St. West and Diana Sweets at 188, there was the Honey Dew at 204, the Chez Paree at 220, and the Meadonia Hotel at 257. The author will leave it to more knowledgeable alumni to say which two establishments had cocktail licenses, but he is sure it was not the Honey Dew.

135. Page 373, para. 1 – "to 27.5 per cent in 1950-51": There were 3,249 women enrolled in 1944-45 out of a population of 7,265: see *President's Report, 1944/45* at 132. By 1950-51, the number of women had increased to 3,611, but this was out of a larger population of 13,129: see *President's Report, 1950/51* at 195.

136. Page 373, para. 1 – "their primary sphere of activity – the home": Alison Prentice et al., *Canadian Women: A History* (Toronto: Harcourt-Brace Jovanovich, 1988) at 303.

137. Page 373, para. 1 – "and had more children": Ibid. at 311.

138. Page 373, para. 1 – "twenty years later": Ibid. at 312; McKillop, *Matters of Mind* at 556.

139. Page 373, para. 1 – "as they had before the war": McKillop, *Matters of Mind* at 556.

140. Page 373, para. 2 – "were given in Convocation Hall": *Varsity*, October 9, 1947.

141. Page 373, para. 2 – "the site of the present Massey College": McKillop, *Matters of Mind* at 552.

142. Page 373, para. 2 – "beside the old observatory": Marsh Jeanneret, *God and Mammon: Universities as Publishers* (Toronto: MacMillan of Canada, 1989) at 29.

143. Page 373, para. 2 – "chose engineering": Smith to Howe, June 25, 1945, Drew Papers, v. 177, file 23 at 5.

144. Page 373, para. 2 – "a continuing need for engineers": McKillop, *Matters of Mind* at 556.

145. Page 373, para. 2 – "the remainder of the 1940s": K.J. Rea, *The Prosperous Years: The Economic History of Ontario 1939-1975* (University of Toronto Press, 1985) at 4.

146. Page 373, para. 3 – "on the downtown campus": Jean-Louis Trudel, "Born in War: Canada's Postwar Engineers and Toronto's Ajax Division" (unpublished paper, 1998) at 8-9.

147. Page 373, para. 3 – "about 25 miles east of Toronto": Alan Heisey, "The Ajax Years", in Robin Harris and Ian Montagnes, eds., *Cold Iron and Lady Godiva: Engineering Education at Toronto 1920-1972* (University of Toronto Press, 1973) at 73.

148. Page 373, para. 3 – "had filled more than 40 million shells": "University Annex to Open at Ajax", *University of Toronto Monthly*, v. 46 at 3; F.C. Boyd, "Operation Ajax: From Shell Plant to University", *University of Toronto Monthly*, v. 47 at 147.

149. Page 373, para. 3 – "consisted of over 4,000 acres": See UTA/A74-0008/11. The University grounds at Ajax covered an area of 428 acres within the 4600-acre compound. See also LePan in UTA/A68-0006/63(01).

150. Page 373, para. 3 – "with more than 100 buildings": Heisey, "The Ajax Years" at 74.

151. Page 373, para. 3 – "and 600 wartime houses": Porter to Phillips, August 2, 1945, Drew Papers, v. 177, file 23.

152. Page 373, para. 3 – "for storing surplus planes": Drew memo of July 25, 1945.

153. Page 373, para. 3 – "other arrangements could not be made": Ibid.

154. Page 373, para. 4 – "well over 3,000 first and second year students": "Farewell to Ajax", *University of Toronto Graduate* (April, 1949) at 2.

155. Page 373, para. 4 – "studying engineering at Ajax": Corbett, *Smith* at 44-45; Richard White, *The Skule Story: The University of Toronto Faculty of Applied Science and Engineering 1873-2000* (University of Toronto Press, 2000) at 160, says that in 1946-47 there were 3,312 students at Ajax, the largest it would be. The enrolment in engineering was much higher because third and fourth year students took their classes on the Toronto campus: White, *The Skule Story* at 160-161.

156. Page 374, para. 1 – "Hart House Ajax": Boyd, "Operation Ajax" at 147.

157. Page 374, para. 1 – "than the one you have": Howe to Phillips, February 7, 1947, UTA/A67-0007/16(02).

158. Page 374, para. 1 – "'of the facilities' at Ajax": Young to Smith, January 25, 1947, UTA/A67-0007/16(02).

159. Page 374, para. 2 – "back on the main campus": "Farewell to Ajax" at 1 notes that the Ajax campus closed May, 1949.

160. Page 374, para. 2 – "fronting on King's College Road": "Million Dollar Extension to Mechanical Engineering Building", *University of Toronto Monthly*, v. 47 at 154.

161. Page 374, para. 2 – "was completed on College Street": "The Wallberg Memorial Building", *University of Toronto Monthly*, v. 48 at 18. It officially opened in 1950: see "His Excellency Opens the Wallberg", *Varsity Graduate* (March, 1950) at 13.

162. Page 374, para. 2 – "which cost four times the sum": UTA/A75-0027/002(14).

163. Page 374, para. 2 – "left by Miss Wallberg in the 1930s": "Wallberg Memorial" at 18.

164. Page 374, para. 2 – "and the department of chemistry": Ibid.

165. Page 374, para. 2 – "as jet propulsion and atomic energy": "Tupper, Kenneth Franklin", *Canadian Who's Who 1958-1960* at 1112. In 1941 Cody had tried to lure C.J. Mackenzie, the head of the NRC, to come to Toronto as dean, but Mackenzie had declined because of the importance of the work he was doing in Ottawa: see Richard White, *The Skule Story* at 152.

166. Page 375, para. 1 – "to other universities": Young to Ireton, May 12, 1947, excerpted in UTA/A83-0036/018. The University did not get its first research reactor until 1971, when R.E. Jervis was named director of the "Safe Low Power Kritical Experiment" (SLOWPOKE) reactor: see White, *The Skule Story* at 184.

167. Page 375, para. 1 – "by the millions of tons": Kenneth F. Tupper, *Engineering Yesterday, Today, and Tomorrow: Inaugural Address as Dean of the Faculty of Applied Science and Engineering* (University of Toronto Press, 1950). at 14-15.

168. Page 375, para. 1 – "exploded a hydrogen bomb": The United States detonated its first hydrogen bomb at Eniwetok Atoll on November 1, 1952: see www.pbs.org/wgbh/annex/bomb/peopleevents/pandeAMEX63.html.

169. Page 375, para. 2 – "just a short distance": Smith to Phillips, March 1, 1954, UTA/A83-0036/003.

170. Page 375, para. 2 – "to become its vice-president": UTA/Graduate Records/"Kenneth Tupper"/A75-0026/003(29).

171. Page 375, para. 2 – "in chemistry in 1926": Judy Mills and Irene Dombra, *University of Toronto Doctoral Theses, 1897-1967* (University of Toronto Press, 1968) at 46.

172. Page 375, para. 2 – "be appointed": Smith to Phillips, March 1, 1954.

173. Page 375, para. 2 – "has developed a graduate programme": Ibid.

174. Page 375, para. 2 – "in chemical engineering, approved": Ibid.

175. Page 375, para. 2 – "while serving as dean": P.B. Hughes, "The Faculty", in Harris and Montagnes, *Cold Iron and Lady Godiva* at 15. He gave up being head of chemical engineering in 1960.

176. Page 375, para. 2 – "more than he realizes": Smith to Phillips, March 1, 1954. C.R. Young reported in 1943 that only 0.6% of all engineering students were graduate students: see Young to the Council of the Faculty of Applied Science, September 28, 1943, UTA/A83-0036/003 at 17.

177. Page 375, para. 2 – "and later the president of the University": "Ham, James Milton", *Canadian Who's Who 1984*, at 499.

178. Page 375, para. 2 – "productive Pulp and Paper Centre": "Rapson, William Howard", *Canadian Who's Who 1984* at 985; George Cook, "Pulp and Paper Centre has good pedigree, high hopes", *University of Toronto Bulletin*, May 24, 1988.

179. Page 375, para. 2 – "a major tool in astronomical studies": "Yen: His VLBI is recognized internationally as a major instrument in astronomical studies", *University of Toronto Bulletin*, November 24, 1980. Yen, originally known as "Jui-Lin Yen", was hired as a research assistant in 1950 and appointed a lecturer in 1953: see UTA/Staff Cards/"Yen, J.L" and also Yen letter of appointment as Research Assistant, May 2, 1952, UTA/A68-0007/87(02).

180. Page 375, para. 3 – "in the late 1940s": For aerospace, see Gordon N. Patterson, *Pathway to Excellence: UTIAS – the first twenty-five years* (Toronto: Institute for Aerospace Studies, 1977); Ben Etkin, "Beginnings", *Canadian Aeronautics and Space Institute Journal*, vol. 45, no. 2, June 1999.

181. Page 375, para. 3 – "perception of the Soviet Union": Donald H. Avery, *The Science of War: Canadian Scientists and Allied Military Technology during the Second World War* (University of Toronto Press, 1998) at 228.

182. Page 375, para. 3 – "by the government during the war": Avery, *Science of War* at 228; Gordon W. Watson, "Defense Research Board: Policies, Concepts, and Organization" in C.E. Law et al., eds., *Perspectives in Science and Technology: The Legacy of Omond Solandt* (Kingston: Queen's Quarterly, 1994) at 64-65.

183. Page 375, para. 3 – "as many American universities": See Stuart Leslie, *The Cold War and American Science: The Military-Industrial-Academic Complex and MIT and Stanford* (New York: Columbia University Press, 1993) for a description of defence work in the US.

184. Page 376, para. 1 – "of American scientists and engineers": Leslie, *Cold War* at 9.

185. Page 376, para. 1 – "in which the weapons are devised": Hacking, 'Weapons Research and the Form of Scientific Knowledge' in *Can. J. of Phil.*, supplementary vol. 12, 1986 at 259; cited in Leslie, *Cold War* at 9.

186. Page 376, para. 1 – "on the frontiers of the subject": Corbett, *Smith* at 52; *President's Report, 1956/57* at 11.

187. Page 376, para. 2 – "then called the Institute for Aerophysics": Etkin, "Beginnings" at 69; Patterson, *Pathway to Excellence* at 132-3, stating that the name was changed in 1963.

188. Page 376, para. 2 – "the drive and determination of Gordon Patterson": Etkin, "Beginnings" at 69.

189. Page 376, para. 2 – "and head of aeronautical engineering": Patterson, *Pathway to Excellence* at 28, says he arrived in January 1947.

190. Page 376, para. 2 – "had left for the National Research Council": Ibid. at 2-4.

191. Page 376, para. 2 – "of the Spitfire and Hurricane aircraft": Ibid. at 4-5 and 14-16.

192. Page 376, para. 2 – "at Princeton": Ibid. at 14 and 16.

193. Page 376, para. 2 – "part of the department of civil engineering": Ibid. at 20 and 24-25; Etkin, "Beginnings" at 69.

194. Page 376, para. 3 – "in supporting Patterson's work": Patterson, *Pathway to Excellence* at 19 and 42.

195. Page 376, para. 3 – "the equipment required is so expensive": Solandt to Smith, March 16, 1948, UTA/A83-0036/016.

196. Page 378, para. 1 – "that other Canadian universities had": Smith to Solandt, September 3, 1948, UTA/A83-0036/016.

197. Page 378, para. 1 – "from other parts of the country": Patterson, *Pathway to Excellence* at 53-54.

198. Page 378, para. 1 – "the Institute for Aerophysics was created": Smith to Solandt, September 3, 1948; Young to Smith, May 7, 1948, UTA/A83-0036/016.

199. Page 378, para. 2 – "for the next three years": "Defense Research Board: Memoranda of Agreement Between the Defence Research Board and the University of Toronto with Respect to the Establishment and Operation of the Institute of Aerophysics", July, 1949, UTA/A83-0036/016 at 1 and 3.

200. Page 378, para. 2 – "on Dufferin Street until 1959": Patterson, *Pathway to Excellence* at 114.

201. Page 378, para. 2 – "were invited to attend": Ibid. at 61.

202. Page 378, para. 2 – "as a research associate": Ibid. at 60-61 and 66.

203. Page 378, para. 2 – "in aerospace studies at the University": Patterson, *Pathway to Excellence* at 148 says that by 1959 he was already "an internationally known authority on shock waves".

204. Page 378, para. 2 – "and Gerald Bull": Patterson, *Pathway to Excellence* at 60.

205. Page 378, para. 2 – "of a 'super gun' for Saddam Hussein": William Lowther, *Arms and the Man: Dr. Gerald Bull, Iraq, and the Supergun* (Novato, California: Presidio Press, 1991) at 264-273.

206. Page 378, para. 2 – "was pushed a second time": Patterson, *Pathway to Excellence* at 60-63.

207. Page 378, para. 3 – "of aeronautical engineering for teaching": "Defense Research Board Memoranda" at 1-2.

208. Page 378, para. 3 – "engineering science course": Ibid. Before that it was an option in mechanical engineering: Patterson, *Pathway to Excellence* at 3.

209. Page 378, para. 3 – "(then called engineering physics)": The name was changed in 1962: see "Dr Boris Stoicheff of Physics succeeds Dr. Etkin as head of the Division of Engineering Science", *University of Toronto Bulletin*, March 13, 1972 at 4.

210. Page 378, para. 3 – "for the engineering physics course": Patterson, *Pathway to Excellence* at 7.

211. Page 378, para. 3 – "in 1933 with 12 students": *President's Report, 1933/34* at 29.

212. Page 378, para. 3 – "with approximately 500 students": E-mail message from Zvonko Vranesic to author, November 3, 1999.

213. Page 378, para. 3 – "as a lecturer in 1942": "Bernard Etkin is appointed Dean of Applied Science and Engineering", *Bulletin*, January 19, 1973.

214. Page 379, para. 1 – "well known through his two books": Patterson, *Pathway to Excellence* at 149. The two books were *Dynamics of Atmospheric Flight*, published in 1972, and *Dynamics of Flight: Stability and Control*, first published in 1959 and in its third edition in 1996.

215. Page 379, para. 1 – "and the atmosphere was creative": B. Etkin, "Beginnings" at 70.

216. Page 379, para. 1 – "from Canadian and American sources": Patterson, *Pathway to Excellence* at 120; Etkin, "Beginnings" at 70.

217. Page 379, para. 1 – "security clearances": "Defense Research Board Memoranda" at 3.

218. Page 379, para. 1 – "and restrictions on publication": A.F.B. Stannard, Department of National Defense to Fennell, March 18, 1947, UTA/A68-0007/023.

219. Page 379, para. 2 – "and electrical engineer V.G. Smith": Michael R. Williams, "UTEC and Ferut: The University of Toronto's Computation Centre", *IEEE Annals of the History of Computing*, v. 16, no. 2 (1994) at 4.

220. Page 379, para. 2 – "to examine emerging computing equipment": The three were B.A. Griffiths, V.G. Smith and A.F.C. Stevenson: see C.C. Gotlieb, "Transcript of Presentation Given at Los Alamos" (Los Alamos: University of California Los Alamos Scientific Laboratory, 1976) at 1.

221. Page 379, para. 2 – "from the Defence Research Board": Williams, "UTEC and Ferut" at 5.

222. Page 379, para. 2 – "and later its director": Ibid. at 6.

223. Page 379, para. 2 – "The 27-year-old Gotlieb": Pamela Cornell, "Mister Computer", *University of Toronto Graduate* (March/April, 1982) at 15.

224. Page 379, para. 2 – "a mechanical relay-based computer": Williams, "UTEC and Ferut" at 7.

225. Page 379, para. 2 – "to begin work on one": Ibid. at 7; Calvin C. Gotlieb, "Early Canadian Developments in Computers and Electronics", in Law et al. at 107.

226. Page 379, para. 2 – "and electrical engineer Alfred Ratz": Martha Hendriks, "An Institutional History of the Department of Computer Science at the University of Toronto 1948-1971" (Unpublished paper, 1992) at 4. Ratz joined the Westinghouse company: see Henry S. Tropp, "Second Interview with Professor C.C. Gotlieb, July 29, 1971" at 4.

227. Page 379, para. 2 – "and chancellor of the University of Waterloo": "Kates, Joseph", *Canadian Who's Who 1995* at 609-610.

228. Page 379, para. 2 – "with a small pilot model": Williams, "UTEC and Ferut" at 8; Gotlieb, "Los Alamos" at 4.

229. Page 379, para. 2 – "based on the UTEC prototype": Gotlieb, "Early Canadian Developments" at 107.

230. Page 379, para. 3 – "became available": Williams, "UTEC and Ferut" at 10.

231. Page 380, para. 1 – "all contracts over £100,000": Ibid.; Gotlieb, "Los Alamos" at 6.

232. Page 380, para. 1 – "had built for Manchester University": Williams, "UTEC and Ferut" at 10.

233. Page 380, para. 1 – "into a big machine": Ibid.

234. Page 380, para. 1 – "and was not very reliable": Ibid.

235. Page 380, para. 1 – "purchased the Ferranti": Ibid. at 10; Gotlieb, "Early Canadian Developments" at 107.

236. Page 380, para. 1 – "work continued on UTEC": Williams, "UTEC and Ferut" at 10.

237. Page 380, para. 1 – "by Beatrice (Trixie) Worsley": Ibid. Worsley graduated from Trinity College in 1944, joined the navy, and was discharged in 1946. She received an MA from M.I.T. in 1947 and was doing research studies in mathematics at Cambridge in 1950: see UTA/A73-0026/526(64).

238. Page 380, para. 1 – "for a doctorate in physics": Gotlieb, "Los Alamos" at 2.

239. Page 381, para. 1 – "simply left to wither away": Williams, "UTEC and Ferut" at 10.

240. Page 381, para. 1 – "was beginning to show promise": Ibid.

241. Page 381, para. 2 – "computer in the world": J.N. Patterson Hume, "Development of Systems Software for the Ferut Computer at the University of Toronto, 1952 to 1955", *IEEE Annals of the History of Computing*, v.16, no. 2 (1994) at 13.

242. Page 381, para. 2 – "for the US Bureau of Census the previous year": Gotlieb, "Early Canadian Developments" at 109.

243. Page 381, para. 2 – "of the old physics building": The Burton Wing of the McLennan Laboratory was constructed in 1947-48 and officially opened on April 7, 1949: see UTA/A75-0027/002(15).

244. Page 381, para. 2 – "with the computer science pioneer Alan Turing": For Turing, see Andrew Hodges, *Alan Turing: The Enigma* (New York: Simon and Schuster, 1983) at 438.

245. Page 381, para. 2 – "they had just purchased": Gotlieb, "Los Alamos" at 7.

246. Page 381, para. 2 – "the complicated Ferut machine code": Hume, "Systems Software" at 13.

247. Page 381, para. 2 – "for complex atoms": Ibid. at 13 and 19.

248. Page 381, para. 2 – "a computer conference held in Toronto": Tropp, "Interview with Professor C.C. Gotlieb", June 29, 1971 at 8.

249. Page 381, para. 2 – "on water levels": Williams, "UTEC and Ferut" at 11; Hume at 14; Gotlieb, "Early Canadian Developments" at 108.

250. Page 381, para. 3 – "and easier maintenance": Williams, "UTEC and Ferut" at 11; Hume at 19; Gotlieb at 110.

251. Page 381, para. 3 – "than the previous machines": "Fastest research 'brain' inaugurated at Varsity", *Varsity News* (December, 1962) at 2.

252. Page 381, para. 3 – "the only large-scale computer in Canada": Gotlieb, "Early Canadian Developments" in Solandt at 109 and 111; Tropp, "Interview" at 21.

253. Page 381, para. 3 – "was established": Tropp, "Second Interview" at 7-8.

254. Page 381, para. 3 – "the first in Canada": *University of Toronto Department of Computer Science* (brochure, 1997) at 2. Gotlieb supervised the first Ph.D. awarded in computer science in Canada: see Pamela Cornell, "Mister Computer" *Computer Science*, March/April 1982 at 15.

255. Page 381, para. 3 – "the top ten research departments in North America": *University of Toronto Department of Computer Science* at 1.

CHAPTER 29 – 1950 – 'EASY STREET'

1. Page 382, para. 1 – "relatively little unemployment": K.J. Rea, *The Prosperous Years: The Economic History of Ontario 1939-1975* (University of Toronto Press, 1985) at 4.

2. Page 382, para. 1 – "if they were men": Author's discussion with a number of female graduates from the 1950s.

3. Page 382, para. 1 – "would continue": Paul Axelrod, *Scholars and Dollars: Politics, Economics and Universities of Ontario 1945-1980* (University of Toronto Press, 1980) at 22.

4. Page 382, para. 1 – "of the post-war veterans": See Chapter 28 (1944).

5. Page 382, para. 1 – "This was the apolitical": Seymour Kanowitch, "From Social Committee to Student Union: A History of the Students' Administrative Council 1955-56 to 1966-67", UTA/A83-0036/031. Donald Forster and Claude Bissell, both discussing the 1950s after living through the 1960s, considered students of the 1950s apolitical. Forster called them "passive" in a 1982 interview: see Donald Forster Oral Interview, UTA/B86-0043, tape 1 at 105. Bissell, writing in 1974, notes than he gave a speech in 1958 commenting on the "apathy of the preceding years", and also that the students he supervised in residence were "in the fifties, a non-political group, not greatly concerned about collective rights, and shirking from responsibilities": see Claude Bissell, *Halfway up Parnassus: A Personal Account of the University of Toronto 1932-1971* (University of Toronto Press, 1974) at 123.

6. Page 382, para. 1 – "silent generation": The term "Silent Generation" became current in the United States in the 1950s: see "The Younger Generation", *Time*, November 5, 1951 and "The So-Called Silent Generation" by Thornton Wilder, *Yale Alumni Magazine*, January 1953. It is still used today: see, "The Silent Generation Seeks Its Due", *New York Times*, May 7, 2000.

7. Page 382, para. 1 – "worried about their future": Author's personal observations during the 1950s. Not everyone will agree with this assessment. Ramsay Cook, for example, experienced a more politically active group of students at United College in Winnipeg and after he came to Toronto to do his Ph.D. in the latter half of the 1950s: see Ramsay Cook to Friedland, February 14, 2001. Ian Montagnes, who was active on the U of T campus in the early 1950s, rightly points out that many individual students were active during the period: see e-mail from Montagnes to Friedland, January 11, 2001.

8. Page 382, para. 2 – "the university yearbook *Torontonensis*": Kanowitch, "Social Committee" at 3-4.

9. Page 382, para. 2 – "including Wendy Michener": UTA/Graduate Records/"Michener, Wendy Roland"/A73-0026/320(85). Michener was most notorious for her editorial, "a woman's eye view" – see *Varsity*, February 1, 1956 – when she declared, "There are some days when a woman can't think. If she could she would probably write a real, man-type editorial. But ever since the days of the apple this insidious thing has crept up on the female gender once a month". She was immediately censured by SAC, one member stating "the editors of the *Varsity* had done themselves and womanhood a great injustice": see minutes of the SAC Publications Committee February 6, 1956, UTA/A70-0012. Michener attempted to clarify in an editorial on February 6, 1956, where she actually used the word "menstruation", but SAC confirmed the censure: see *Varsity*, February 9, 1956 and SAC Minutes February 8, 1956. Michener went on to become a prominent Canadian film critic before her death in 1969 at the age of 33.

10. Page 382, para. 2 – "and Peter Gzowski": Peter Gzowski was editor of the *Varsity* in 1956/57: see SAC Minutes February 22, 1956, UTA/A70-0012.

11. Page 382, para. 2 – "for remedial English instruction": *President's Report, 1950/51* at 3. The section on remedial English had been written by Claude Bissell: see Montagnes to Harris, December 3, 1976, UTA/A83-0036/032. See also Montagnes' comments to the author of January 10, 2001.

12. Page 384, para. 1 – "and a passion for the subject": *Varsity* of March 5, 1952.

13. Page 384, para. 1 – "in shockingly bad taste": *Varsity*, March 18, 1952. The Engineering Society passed a motion that it was "an intentionally irresponsible act": *Varsity*, March 18, 1952. Sidney Smith's assistant, Frances Ireland, recalls that the article "was killingly funny, but Dr. Smith was frightfully upset": see Frances Ireland Oral Interview, UTA/B86-0052 tape #2 at 480.

14. Page 384, para. 2 – "in wider issues until the late 50s": Notably, the SAC resolved to protest the firing of six Toronto Symphony Orchestra members. At the height of the McCarthy era, the 'Symphony Six' had been dismissed because they had been refused entry into the U.S. and thus could not tour with the orchestra: see UTA/A70-0012, SAC minutes, October 22, 1952 and November 26, 1952.

15. Page 384, para. 2 – "into a sorority": Kanowitch, "Social Committee" at 10-11: see Chapter 15 (1895). SAC had also dealt with the issue of discrimination on campus from 1946 to 1950, after an incident in which a West Indian student was barred from entering a bridge contest at Hart House by its American organizers: see Charles Levi, "The S.A.C. Historical Project 1930-1950" (Toronto: self-published, 1992) at 120-140.

16. Page 384, para. 2 – "intensified in the 1960s": See generally Kanowitch, "Social Committee".

17. Page 384, para. 3 – "enlivened by drinking": *Varsity*, October 27, 1954; comments from Harold Averill to Friedland, February 18, 2001.

18. Page 384, para. 3 – "to the property of the TTC": *Varsity*, October 1, 1951.

19. Page 384, para. 3 – "in all my years at the University": *Varsity*, November 1, 1951.

20. Page 384, para. 3 – "of the bus were broken": *Varsity*, October 5, 1953.

21. Page 384, para. 3 – "take quite a bit of time": "Yestersday's Protester, Today's Chancellor", *University of Toronto Bulletin*, December 8, 1997; conversation with Jackman, January 2000.

22. Page 384, para. 4 – "and the arrival of three fire trucks": *Varsity*, October 15, 1956.

23. Page 384, para. 4 – "did something": *Varsity*, October 10, 1957.

24. Page 385, para. 1 – "five Queen's students were injured": *Varsity*, October 31, 1955.

25. Page 385, para. 1 – "and silverware stolen": *Varsity*, November 6, 1957.

26. Page 385, para. 1 – "Professor W.J. McAndrew, was injured": *Varsity*, September 24, 1954; "Report of the Investigating Committee of the Engineering Society Re: Freshman Demonstrations September 23, 1954", UTA/A68-0007125(06).

27. Page 385, para. 1 – "as the entire incident itself": *Varsity*, September 27, 1954.

28. Page 385, para. 1 – "was fined $4,000": *Varsity*, October 20, 1954.

29. Page 385, para. 1 – "after Hurricane Hazel": *Varsity*, November 1, 1954.

30. Page 385, para. 1 – "debris in High Park": *Varsity*, October 4, 1957.

31. Page 386, para. 1 – "coached by Bob Masterson": *Torontonensis*, 1951 at 220.

32. Page 386, para. 1 – "at each game in 1950": Rick Kollins and Paul Carson, "The History of Varsity Blues Football" (unpublished paper, Department of Athletics and Recreation, 1993) at 3.

33. Page 386, para. 1 – "to form a U-shaped stadium": Ian Speers, "Varsity Stadium" (unpublished memorandum, 1997) at 1.

34. Page 386, para. 1 – "when 26,764 persons": Kollins and Carson, "Varsity Blues" at 3. Although larger crowds have attended Vanier Cup games at Skydome in recent years, this record still stands for a regular season game: e-mail from Paul Carson to the University of Toronto History Project, January 26, 2000.

35. Page 386, para. 1 – "Western beat Varsity 41 to 6": *Varsity*, October 22, 1950.

36. Page 386, para. 1 – "was Fraser Mustard": *Torontonensis*, 1951 at 220.

37. Page 386, para. 1 – "'Moose' Mustard according to *Torontonensis*": *Torontonensis*, 1950 at 410.

38. Page 386, para. 1 – "head of the Canadian Institute for Advanced Research": "Mustard, James Fraser", *Canadian Who's Who 1995* at 871.

39. Page 386, para. 1 – "on the championship team in 1948": *Torontonensis*, 1949 at 425.

40. Page 386, para. 1 – "'most worthy' player on the team": Johnny Copp trophy – *Torontonensis*, 1950 at 410; "John Fraser 'Moose' Mustard", U of T Hall of Fame bio, www.utoronto.ca/physical.

41. Page 386, para. 1 – "from behind the bench": *Torontonensis*, 1951 at 219-220.

42. Page 386, para. 2 – "as captain": *Torontonensis*, 1952 at 99; "John R. Evans", University of Toronto Sports Hall of Fame website.

43. Page 386, para. 2 – "who later played professionally for Hamilton": "Steve Oneschuk", Hall of Fame website.

44. Page 386, para. 2 – "who played for Calgary and Montreal": UTA/Graduate Records/"Bewley, William James"/ A73-0026/28(73). Bewley turned professional with Calgary in 1953 and played for Montreal from 1954-1961, when he took the coach's job at McGill University while working as assistant to the general manager of the Aqua Mining Corporation.

45. Page 386, para. 2 – "the current chief justice of Ontario": *Torontonensis*, 1952 at 101. McMurtry's future political colleague, Bill Davis, the premier of Ontario from 1971 to 1985, had met McMurtry when they both played for the intermediate team: see Claire Hoy, *Bill Davis* (Toronto: Methuen, 1985) at 19.

46. Page 386, para. 2 – "with the help of John Sopinka": *Torontonensis*, 1955 at 119.

47. Page 386, para. 2 – "and again in 1958": *Torontonensis*, 1959 at 207.

48. Page 386, para. 3 – "a major sport in the 1920s": See Chapter 25 (1926).

49. Page 386, para. 3 – "until the 1960s": Patrick Okens, "Blues Before Sunrise: Rowing at the University of Toronto" (M.A. Thesis, University of Toronto, 1999) at 70-71.

50. Page 386, para. 3 – "no 'Tommy' Loudon to promote it": Ibid.

51. Page 386, para. 3 – "and he promoted basketball at the University": UTA/Graduate Records/"Stevens, Warren"/ A73-0026/445(88); T.A. Reed, *The Blue and White: A Record of Fifty Years of Athletic Endeavour at the University of Toronto* (University of Toronto Press, 1944) at 57 and 220-221.

52. Page 388, para. 1 – "men's interfaculty teams in all sports": "Report of the Advisory Planning Committee to the Board of Governors, September 12, 1957", UTA/A83-0036/026 at 56.

53. Page 388, para. 1 – "its first title in eighteen years": *Torontonensis*, 1958 at 214.

54. Page 388, para. 1 – "was a member of that team": Ibid.

55. Page 388, para. 1 – "a number of intercollegiate records": *Torontonensis*, 1955 at 118.

56. Page 388, para. 1 – "and track and field": See Olympic Honour Roll on the wall inside the north entrance of the Athletic Centre.

57. Page 388, para. 1 – "winning the Biggs trophy in 1960": "W.A. 'Pete' Potter", Hall of Fame website.

58. Page 388, para. 1 – "of the basketball team in 1956-57": *Torontonensis*, 1957, at 205.

59. Page 388, para. 2 – "won the intercollegiate championship in 1950-51": *Torontonensis*, 1951 at 216.

60. Page 388, para. 2 – "in the years 1954 to 1959": *Torontonensis*, 1959 at 196.

61. Page 388, para. 2 – "for four of those years:" *Torontonensis*, 1955 at 137; "David 'Red' Stephen", Hall of Fame bio forwarded from DAR, 1999.

62. Page 388, para. 2 – "the well-known Varsity Grads": *Torontonensis*, 1955 at 137.

63. Page 388, para. 2 – "against in the 1928 Olympics": See Chapter 25 (1926).

64. Page 388, para. 2 – "but was not selected": *Torontonensis*, 1955 at 137; Andrew Podnieks, *Canada's Olympic Teams: The Complete History 1920-1998* (Toronto: Doubleday Canada Ltd., 1997) at 79.

65. Page 388, para. 2 – "including 5 Canadian titles in a row": "Tom Watt", Hall of Fame website.

66. Page 388, para. 3 – "from 1950 to 1954": Helen Gurney, *A Century to Remember 1893-1993 Women's Sports at the University of Toronto* (Toronto: University of Toronto Women's T-Holders' Association, 1993) at 159.

67. Page 388, para. 3 – "and Mary Macdonald": "Sallie Wallace Teasdale", Hall of Fame website; "Mary Macdonald", ibid.

68. Page 388, para. 3 – "for three of those years": She later became an anesthesiologist at Toronto General Hospital, see "Teasdale", Hall of Fame website.

69. Page 388, para. 3 – "intercollegiate archery and volleyball": She later taught high school, see "Macdonald", Hall of Fame website.

70. Page 389, para. 1 – "badminton and softball": "Mary Foster", Hall of Fame website.

71. Page 389, para. 1 – "women's hockey was discontinued": Gurney, *A Century to Remember* at 82 and 172. The two other teams in the league, Queen's and McGill, withdrew from competition.

72. Page 389, para. 1 – "and won three league titles": "Foster", Hall of Fame website.

73. Page 389, para. 2 – "would soon be constructed": D.C. Masters, *Henry John Cody: An Outstanding Life* (Toronto: Dundurn Press, 1995) at 211.

74. Page 389, para. 2 – "south of the Royal Ontario Museum": Gurney, *A Century to Remember* at 28.

75. Page 389, para. 2 – "women's residence and social centre": John P.M. Court, "Out of the Woodwork: The Wood

Family's Benefactions to Victoria University", in Neil Semple, ed., *Canadian Methodist Historical Society Papers*, v. 11 (1997) at 36-39.

76. Page 389, para. 2 – "that had been leased to Victoria": Ibid. at 42-43; "Victoria Buys and Sells Properties", *Vic Newsletter* (November, 1949) at 4.

77. Page 390, para. 1 – "Margaret Addison Hall": Court, "Out of the Woodwork" at 43.

78. Page 390, para. 1 – "for $240,000": "Victoria Buys and Sells" at 4; Court, "Out of the Woodwork" at 43.

79. Page 390, para. 1 – "each year in rent to Victoria University": Court, "Out of the Woodwork" at 43.

80. Page 390, para. 2 – "announced by Sidney Smith in 1952": Gurney, *A Century to Remember* at 28.

81. Page 390, para. 2 – "'but not nude,' she added": *Varsity*, November 18, 1952.

82. Page 390, para. 2 – "entered the picture": Court, "Out of the Woodwork" at 43-44.

83. Page 390, para. 2 – "leader of the federal Conservative Party": "Frost, Hon. Leslie Miscampbell", *Canadian Who's Who, 1952-1954* at 378.

84. Page 390, para. 2 – "from the north to the legislative buildings": Court, "Out of the Woodwork" at 44; Gurney, *A Century to Remember* at 30; Zerada Slack, "A Brief on the Need and History of the Women's Athletic Building", November 7, 1956, in PAO/Pauline Emily McGibbon papers/F4161-4-1 Box 11 at 8.

85. Page 390, para. 2 – "comparable to the museum": Gurney, *A Century to Remember* at 31.

86. Page 390, para. 2 – "offered instead for the gymnasium": Ibid. at 30; Slack, "A Brief on the Need" at 8.

87. Page 390, para. 2 – "opened for women's athletics": Gurney, *A Century to Remember* at 33.

88. Page 390, para. 2 – "for both men and women": Ian Montagnes, *An Uncommon Fellowship: The Story of Hart House* (University of Toronto Press, 1969) at 163-164; Phillips to Smith, February 3, 1952, UTA/A68-0007/067.

89. Page 390, para. 2 – "is the most unrealistic": Phillips had "a strong fear that in the end it would be a charge against the University", see Phillips to Bissell, December 12, 1951, UTA/A68-0007/146(22).

90. Page 390, para. 3 – "the intense crowding in the years after the war": "Hart House Overcrowding Created Serious Problems", *University of Toronto Monthly*, v. 47 at 221; Montagnes, *An Uncommon Fellowship* at 152.

91. Page 390, para. 3 – "returned to England a few years after the war": Montagnes, *An Uncommon Fellowship* at 158.

92. Page 390, para. 3 – "was chosen as warden": Ibid. at 162.

93. Page 391, para. 1 – "during that difficult period": William Christian, *George Grant: A Biography* (University of Toronto Press, 1993) at 126-7.

94. Page 391, para. 2 – "the 1957 Senator John F. Kennedy debate": Montagnes, *An Uncommon Fellowship* at 183-184; *Varsity*, November 14, 1957.

95. Page 391, para. 2 – "'five o'clock' concerts": "Annual Report of the Music Committee 1952-1953".

96. Page 391, para. 2 – "sing in the 1952-53 season": Ibid.

97. Page 391, para. 2 – "but only on Wednesday afternoons": *President's Report, 1952/53* at 94.

98. Page 391, para. 3 – "that the pictures be taken down": *Varsity*, January 7, 1955.

99. Page 391, para. 3 – "is still firmly entrenched in Ontario": Ibid.

100. Page 391, para. 3 – "special Sunday evening concerts": *Varsity*, October 12, 21, and 25 1955; Boyd Neel, *My Orchestras and Other Adventures* (University of Toronto Press, 1985) at 161.

101. Page 391, para. 3 – "sporting events could charge admission on Sunday": *Varsity*, October 12, 1955.

102. Page 391, para. 3 – "but you can't play Beethoven": Ibid.

103. Page 391, para. 3 – "The concerts took place": *Varsity*, October 21, 1955.

104. Page 391, para. 4 – "after Ignatieff died suddenly": Montagnes, *An Uncommon Fellowship* at 168. Claude Bissell noted that he thought the death was mysterious: see Claude Bissell Diaries, March 29, 1952, UTA/B88-0091.

105. Page 391, para. 4 – "in the south wall of the building": McCulley to Smith, June 23, 1954, UTA/A68-0007/115(06).

106. Page 392, para. 1 – "then it was reserved for men": Varsity, October 1, 1954; Montagnes, *An Uncommon Fellowship* at 172.

107. Page 392, para. 1 – "purchased in 1949": Montagnes, *An Uncommon Fellowship* at 165.

108. Page 392, para. 1 – "commissioner of penitentiaries": Ibid. at 170.

109. Page 392, para. 1 – "a male preserve": Minutes of the House Committee of Hart House, January 10, 1957, UTA/A83-0036/032.

110. Page 392, para. 1 – "So did Vincent Massey": Inference from Bissell diary of August 13, 1968.

111. Page 392, para. 1 – "then the governor general of Canada": Vincent Massey was governor general from 1952 to 1959: see Claude Bissell, *The Imperial Canadian: Vincent Massey in Office* (University of Toronto Press, 1986) at ix.

112. Page 393, para. 1 – "Hart House to women": Bissell Diary, August 13, 1968.

113. Page 393, para. 1 – "on the same terms as male students": "Hart House Membership open to women students", *University of Toronto Bulletin*, January 28, 1972. The inaugural meeting of the committee was on February 10, 1969: Bissell diary of February 10, 1969. The solicitor to the University, Donald Guthrie, states, "On November 1, 1972, an order was made in the Supreme Court of Ontario approving a Deed of Arrangement between the University and the Massey Foundation, the effect of which was to admit women into full participation in the activities of the House": see Donald Guthrie comments to author, January, 2001.

114. Page 393, para. 2 – "separately from Hart House": Montagnes, *An Uncommon Fellowship* at 157; "Hart House Theatre Re-Opens", *University of Toronto Monthly*, v. 47 at 8.

115. Page 393, para. 2 – "used only sporadically since 1937": "Theatre Re-Opens" at 8.

116. Page 393, para. 2 – "to run the program for students": Montagnes, *An Uncommon Fellowship* at 157; "Theatre Re-Opens" at 8; *Forum*, April 6, 1948, says that he was "of Canadian parentage".

117. Page 393, para. 2 – "by amateur and semi-professional actors": Judith Knelman, "School for Directors", *University of Toronto Graduate* (September/October 1984) at 12.

118. Page 393, para. 2 – "of emotion and execution": *Globe and Mail*, January 28, 1947. The critic was J.A. McNeil.

119. Page 393, para. 2 – "theatre manager Jimmy Hozack": Knelman, "School for Directors" at 13.

120. Page 393, para. 2 – "and Eric House": "In memoriam: Robert Gill", *Bulletin*, October 18, 1974.

121. Page 394, para. 1 – "student productions": Jack Gray, "Robert Gill and Hart House Theatre", UTA/B95-0053.

122. Page 394, para. 1 – "Dostoyevsky's *Crime and Punishment*": "The Play Season at Hart House", *Varsity Graduate* (December, 1949) at 3.

123. Page 394, para. 1 – "outnumbering men three to one": "The Play Season" at 4.

124. Page 394, para. 1 – "and Donald Sutherland": Knelman, "School for Directors" at 12; "In Memoriam: Robert Gill"; Montagnes, *An Uncommon Fellowship* at 158.

125. Page 394, para. 1 – "in the development of Canadian theatre": "In Memoriam: Robert Gill".

126. Page 394, para. 1 – "in the Koffler Student Centre": Jane Stirling, "Hart House theatre ages gracefully", *Bulletin*, January 23, 1989. In the summer of 2000 a plan briefly circulated to close the theatre: see *Hart Beat* (June 2000) at 5; "Hope for Hart House Theatre", University of Toronto News and Events, September 11, 2000; *National Post*, June 5 and November 27, 2000.

127. Page 394, para. 2 – "almost exclusively from Europe": Ninette Kelly and Michael Trebilcock, *The Making of the Mosaic: A History of Canadian Immigration Policy* (University of Toronto Press, 1998) at 313, state that 165,000 refugees were admitted between 1947 and 1962.

128. Page 394, para. 2 – "on colour, race, and creed": Ibid. at 332 et seq.

129. Page 394, para. 2 – "from Canada's immigration laws": Ibid. at 351.

130. Page 394, para. 3 – "students at the University": "Friendly Relations with Overseas Students – Toronto Community Committee Report of Office Activities October 1951 – February 1952", in UTA/A83-0036/032.

131. Page 394, para. 3 – "to more than 2,000 today": The 1951/52 report gave the total number of overseas students at 450. As of 1997/98 it was 2,010: see "International Student Enrolment 1997-98", forwarded from the I.S.C.

132. Page 394, para. 3 – "began to be charged higher fees": Ibid.

133. Page 395, para. 1 – "closer contact with Canadian students": Kay Riddell, *The International Student Centre – How it all Began*, (Toronto, 1985) at 9.

134. Page 395, para. 1 – "Along with World University Service of Canada": World University Service of Canada (WUSC) developed out of the Canadian committees of the International Student Service (ISS). ISS changed its named to WUS in 1950, and the Canadians followed suit in 1952. ISS activity on campus can be traced back as early as 1932: see Charles Levi, "Decided Action Has Been Taken: Student Government, Student Activism, and University Administration at the University of Toronto and McGill University 1930-1950" (M.A. Thesis, York University, revised version September 8, 1994) at 45-48; "WUSC Chronology", www.wusc.ca/who/chronolo.html. Smith was National President of WUSC Canada in 1956/57: see for example Principal of George Williams College to Smith, December 6, 1956, UTA/A71-0011/008(13).

135. Page 395, para. 1 – "and later the principal of Havergal College": Riddell, *The International Student Centre* at 10; UTA/Current People/"Steele, Catherine".

136. Page 395, para. 1 – "the sudden death of her husband": UTA/Current People/"Riddell, Robert G."

137. Page 395, para. 1 – "at the corner of Bloor Street and Avenue Road": Riddell, *The International Student Centre* at 11.

138. Page 395, para. 1 – "became the first volunteer typist": Ibid.

139. Page 396, para. 1 – "after Catherine Steele's tenure": Riddell, *The International Student Centre* at 14-15 and 60-61.

140. Page 396, para. 1 – "were working for the organization": Ibid. at 17; Mary Ham to author, February 8, 2000.

141. Page 396, para. 2 – "had nine temporary homes": Ibid. at 3.

142. Page 396, para. 2 – "renamed the International Student Centre": Riddell, *The International Student Centre* at 41-42; "The ISC – Making the shock a little less severe", *Bulletin*, November 19, 1976.

143. Page 396, para. 2 – "Cumberland's magnificent home was saved": The building was formerly named Baldwin House after Robert Baldwin. Although he had once owned the land, Baldwin never lived on the property: see Lucy Booth Martyn, *Toronto: 100 Years of Grandeur* (Toronto: Pagurian Press, 1978) at 155 and 160-161.

144. Page 396, para. 2 – "by the Rotary clubs of Toronto": Ibid. at 161.

145. Page 396, para. 3 – "a student in engineering physics": Bosko Loncarevic to author, February 8, 2000; see also UTA/Current People/"Loncarevic, Bosko".

146. Page 396, para. 3 – "Are you going to be friendly?": Riddell, *The International Student Centre* at 13.

147. Page 396, para. 3 – "the intercollegiate water-polo title in 1953-54": Marijan Stipetic to Patrick Okens, January 28, 2000; *Torontonensis,* 1953 at 142; *Torontonensis,* 1954 at 150.

148. Page 396, para. 3 – "the school of mines of Sopron University": NCCU Report of 1957, excerpted in UTA/A73-0036/035 at 74-75; Smith to Farquharson, February 4, 1957, ibid.

149. Page 396, para. 3 – "the most advanced engineering school in Hungary": Cox to Smith, December 27, 1956, UTA/A83-0036/035.

150. Page 396, para. 3 – "involved in the uprising itself": Ibid.

151. Page 396, para. 3 – "provided financial assistance": NCCU Report at 75.

152. Page 396, para. 4 – "that developed on American campuses": See Ellen W. Schrecker, *No Ivory Tower: McCarthyism and the Universities* (New York: Oxford University Press, 1986) at 291-292.

153. Page 397, para. 1 – "permanent university employment in the United States": Chandler Davis, "The Purge", reprinted from *A Century of Mathematics in America* (Providence: American Mathematical Society, 1988) at 421, 423, and 427.

154. Page 397, para. 1 – "I am quite fed up": Cited in Schrecker, *No Ivory Tower* at 304.

155. Page 397, para. 2 – "witches to be hunted": Michiel Horn, *Academic Freedom in Canada: A History* (University of Toronto Press, 1999) at 218.

156. Page 397, para. 2 – "Smith shared Cody's concern": See Chapter27 (1939). All appointments had to have Cody's approval. It will be recalled that Dean Kennedy reported to Cody that he made Bora Laskin "declare unequivo-

cally" in front of witnesses that he had "no connection – public or private, expressly or implicitly – with organized or unorganized Communism".

157. Page 397, para. 2 – "medieval and Renaissance objects": Montagnes, *An Uncommon Fellowship* at 156. They were transferred to the Royal Ontario Museum in 1960 – ibid.

158. Page 397, para. 2 – "in the event of war": Smith to Ignatieff, November 9, 1951, UTA/A68-0007/94(05).

159. Page 397, para. 3 – "to establishing cells within universities": Smith to Newton, September 5, 1947, UTA/A68-0007/30(01).

160. Page 397, para. 3 – "or beyond the University": Ibid. The author has chosen not to speculate publicly as to the identity of suspected communists.

161. Page 397, para. 3 – "an imitation of Soviet methods": Massey to Boland, May 10, 1948, UTA/B87-0082/405(05).

162. Page 397, para. 3 – "can muster only 37 members": Smith to Kirkonnell of Feb 1, 1949, UTA/A83-0036/037. The *Varsity* noted in 1949 that there were less than 50 members of the Labour-Progressive Party club on campus: see *Varsity*, January 27, 1949. The L.P.P. was the label under which communists were allowed to organize in Canada in the late 1940s. They were reasonably active on campus in the late 1940s, when speakers friendly to communism could often be heard on campus, albeit with some difficulty. Dean Hewlett Johnson of Canterbury, called the "Red Dean" because of his belief that Stalin could be negotiated with, was invited to speak on campus in November, 1948. After the use of Convocation Hall and Hart House was denied, space was found at Trinity College for the speech: see Levi, "Decided Action" at 74-78. Tim Buck, leader of the L.P.P., also spoke at Hart House in 1947: see Balfour to Smith, November 6, 1947, UTA/A68-0007/30(01).

163. Page 397, para. 3 – "communist activities on the campus that year": *Varsity*, February 1, 1957. For a full analysis of RCMP activities on Canadian campuses, including the University of Toronto, see Steve Hewitt, *Spying 101: The RCMP's Secret Activities at Canadian Universities* (University of Toronto Press, forthcoming).

164. Page 398, para. 1 – "As mentioned in an earlier chapter": See Chapter 27 (1939). See also Hewitt, *Spying 101*, chapter 4.

165. Page 398, para. 1 – "with whom I had the pleasure to work": Einstein to Guggenheim foundation, November 16, 1947, cited in John Stachel, "Einstein and Infeld, Seen Through Their Correspondence" (unpublished paper, undated) at 33.

166. Page 398, para. 1 – "a Nobel Prize for Chemistry in 1998": Bruce Rolston, "Former MA Student Wins Nobel Prize for Chemistry", *Bulletin*, October 26, 1998.

167. Page 398, para. 1 – "as a post-doctoral student after the war": Ursula Franklin to author, 1998.

168. Page 398, para. 1 – "splendid work for the University": Horn, *Academic Freedom* at 204.

169. Page 399, para. 1 – "and Smith was sympathetic": Ibid.

170. Page 399, para. 1 – "and physics at the University of Toronto": Horn, *Academic Freedom* at 205.

171. Page 399, para. 2 – "to the Soviet masters of Poland": Ibid. at 206.

172. Page 399, para. 2 – "he was a communist": Sidney Smith, "Memorandum on Meeting with Dean Beatty and Professor Infeld on Thursday, April 13 [1950] in my office", UTA/A83-0036/030; Horn, *Academic Freedom* at 206.

173. Page 399, para. 2 – "I am left of Louis XIVth": Infeld to Einstein, November 6, 1949, cited in Stachel, "Einstein and Infeld" at 37.

174. Page 399, para. 2 – "the Canadian Soviet Friendship Society in 1941": Horn, *Academic Freedom* at 203.

175. Page 399, para. 2 – "after the Gouzenko revelations": Leopold Infeld, *Why I Left Canada: Reflections on Science and Politics*, Lewis Pyenson, ed., Helen Infeld, trans. (Montreal: McGill-Queen's University Press, 1978) at 29.

176. Page 399, para. 2 – "during his leave": Horn, *Academic Freedom* at 206.

177. Page 399, para. 2 – "though preferring that he not go": Ibid. at 206-7.

178. Page 399, para. 2 – "suddenly appeared": Ibid. at 207.

179. Page 399, para. 2 – "A.F.C. Stevenson": Arthur Stevenson went to Alexandria University in 1950 and then to Wayne State from 1953 to 1965. He died while hiking on the Niagara Escarpment in April, 1968, at the age of 68, three months after Infeld died: see Dimond to Prichard, June 15, 1994, forwarded from Office of the President; UTA/Graduate Records/"Stevenson, Arthur Frances Chesterfield"/A73-0026/445(97).

180. Page 399, para. 2 – "particularly for graduate teaching": Horn, *Academic Freedom* at 207; Beatty to Smith, May 29, 1950, UTA/A83-0036/030.

181. Page 399, para. 2 – "Infeld resigned": Horn, *Academic Freedom* at 208; Infeld, *Why I Left* at 55.

182. Page 399, para. 2 – "We are well rid of him": Horn, *Academic Freedom* at 208; Smith to Phillips, September 22, 1950 UTA/A83-0036/030.

183. Page 399, para. 3 – "head of the Institute of Theoretical Physics in Warsaw": G. De B. Robinson, "Leopold Infeld", *Proceedings of the Royal Society of Canada*, 4th Series, v. 6 (1968) at 124.

184. Page 399, para. 3 – "from his two children": Horn, *Academic Freedom* at 210.

185. Page 399, para. 3 – "Infeld died in 1968": Robinson, "Infeld" at 124.

186. Page 399, para. 3 – "subsequently restored, however": Eric Infeld to Prichard, July 5, 1994, forwarded from the Office of the President.

187. Page 399, para. 3 – "She took up his father's cause": Leonard Stern, "Cold War Pawn", in *Ottawa Citizen's Weekly*, July 19, 1998 at C3.

188. Page 400, para. 1 – "was under unfair public attack": Dimond to Prichard, June 15, 1994, forwarded from the Office of the President.

189. Page 400, para. 2 – "Professor Emeritus of the University of Toronto": Prichard to Eric Infeld, June 22, 1994, forwarded from the Office of the President.

190. Page 400, para. 2 – "Now this is no longer the case": Infeld to Prichard, July 5, 1994.

CHAPTER 30 – 1955 – PLANNING FOR GROWTH

1. Page 401, para. 1 – "approximately 67,000 within ten years": E.F. Sheffield, "Canadian University and College Enrolment Projected to 1965", in J.F. Leddy, ed., *Proceedings of the National Conference of Canadian Universities 1955* at 39; A.B. McKillop, *Matters of Mind: The University in Ontario 1791-1951* (University of Toronto Press, 1994) at 565.

2. Page 401, para. 1 – "coincided with Sheffield's": Paul Axelrod, *Scholars and Dollars: Politics, Economics, and the Universities of Ontario 1945-1980* (University of Toronto Press, 1982) at 85.

3. Page 401, para. 1 – "to publicize Sheffield's findings": Claude Bissell, *Halfway up Parnassus: A Personal Account of the University of Toronto 1932-1971* (University of Toronto Press, 1974) at 31 and 45.

4. Page 401, para. 2 – "would soon hit the universities": Sidney Smith, "Pressure of Numbers on Universities", *Saturday Night*, January 30, 1954 at 7-8.

5. Page 401, para. 2 – "that would continue into the future": Ibid. at 7; "Report of the Plateau Committee to the Senate, June 5, 1956", UTA/A75-0019/12 at 1; Smith to "Colleague", December 16, 1955, UTA/A68-0007/131(08). Smith did not use the word "plateau" in the *Saturday Night* article, but he did use it in June, 1955 immediately after Sheffield delivered his report to the NCCU: see *Proceedings* at 47.

6. Page 401, para. 2 – "what the University of Toronto should do": "Plateau" at 2.

7. Page 401, para. 2 – "its own statistical predictions": "Plateau" at 3. The projections were prepared by Professor B.A. Griffith of the department of mathematics, who resigned from the University in 1958 to become the Executive Vice-President of K.C.S. Limited: see "Griffith, Byron", *Canadian Who's Who 1958-1960* at 453.

8. Page 401, para. 2 – "a higher university participation rate": Smith, "Pressure" at 7.

9. Page 403, para. 1 – "rapidly rising": "Plateau" at 3. The figures are actually for York County.

10. Page 403, para. 1 – "somewhere between 21,000 and 25,000": Ibid.

11. Page 403, para. 1 – "to do some concrete planning": Smith to Phillips, February 9, 1956, UTA/A68-0007/134(10) at 2.

12. Page 403, para. 2 – "'to increase beyond' that": "Plateau" at 5.

13. Page 403, para. 2 – "to accommodate 500 students": Ibid. at 1.

14. Page 403, para. 2 – "become independent institutions": Ibid.

15. Page 403, para. 2 – "and harder to retain staff": Ibid. at 1 and 6.

16. Page 403, para. 2 – "about an overall planning process": Ibid. at 1.

17. Page 403, para. 3 – "by the board of governors in 1948": "Extract from Report 249 of the Property Committee dated April 14, 1948", in UTA/A83-0036/025.

18. Page 403, para. 3 – "about the University's planning process": Arthur to LePan, November 25, 1947, UTA/A83-0036/035.

19. Page 403, para. 3 – "James Murray and Anthony Adamson": Board of Governors Minutes, April 22, 1948, UTA/A70-0024/reel 16.

20. Page 403, para. 3 – "as the temporary building": Arthur to LePan, November 25, 1947.

21. Page 404, para. 1 – "taken down fifty years later": *University of Toronto Bulletin*, September 14, 1998.

22. Page 404, para. 1 – "Where can we put it?": Arthur to LePan, November 25, 1947.

23. Page 404, para. 2 – "The planning committee's report of 1949": Eric Arthur, "Report of the Committee Approved by the Board of Governors on April 22nd, 1948 on the Siting of Buildings and the Physical Growth of the University", June 1, 1949, UTA/A75-0019/012(01); "Extract from Minutes of Property Committee Report No. 254, June 21, 1949", in UTA/A83-0036/025.

24. Page 404, para. 2 – "in the area to the north": James Murray, "A Report on Problems of Building Expansion in the University of Toronto", 1947, in UTA/A83-0036/025 at 6.

25. Page 404, para. 2 – "and west as far as Spadina": Ibid. at 6-7.

26. Page 404, para. 2 – "or underpasses could solve this": Ibid. at 7-8.

27. Page 404, para. 2 – "from which vehicular traffic is excluded": Arthur, "Report" at 1; at 2 the report states that there should be "expansion to the South for playing fields and university staff housing".

28. Page 404, para. 3 – "O.D. Vaughan": UTA/Current People/"O.D. Vaughan".

29. Page 404, para. 3 – "made the decision to go west": Smith to Phillips, March 8, 1956, UTA/A68-0007/134(10) at 2.

30. Page 405, para. 1 – "money for expropriation": Ibid.

31. Page 405, para. 1 – "expropriated the property": Stone to Phillips, May 15, 1956 UTA/A68-0007/134(10) at 3.

32. Page 405, para. 1 – "as it then had the power to do": *The University of Toronto Act*, 1947, s. 32(e); press release from the University of Toronto, December 11, 1956, UTA/A71-0011/15(19); see also Henry Borden Oral Interview, UTA/B87-0044 at 38.

33. Page 405, para. 1 – "on the west side of St George": Stone to Phillips, May 15, 1956.

34. Page 405, para. 1 – "employees of the superintendent's office": Stone to Phillips, July 27, 1956, UTA/A71-00011/006(02) at 6.

35. Page 405, para. 1 – "for university purposes": Phillips to Dana Porter, December 7, 1956, UTA/A71-0011/006(02); see also Gordon Stephenson, "Notes on University Expansion", February 3, 1956, UTA/A68-0007/130(08).

36. Page 405, para. 2 – "more directly under the control of the board": "Report of the Planning Committee, University of Toronto, May 24, 1956", UTA/A83-0036/026 at 2.

37. Page 405, para. 2 – "a new city hall for Toronto": Geoffrey Simmins, *Ontario Association of Architects: A Centennial History 1889-1989* (Toronto: Ontario Association of Architects, 1989) at 142.

38. Page 405, para. 2 – "and inhuman piles of stone": *Varsity*, November 22, 1955; Simmins, *Ontario Association of Architects* at 143.

39. Page 405, para. 2 – "a dehumanized pile of stone": "Notes Taken from 'Lets Find Out' with Allan Anderson, heard over CJBC on Sunday, November 27th 1955", UTA/A68-0007/130(08) at 6 and 8 – emphasis in the original.

40. Page 405, para. 2 – "added the architecture student Peter Richardson": Ibid. at 8.

41. Page 405, para. 2 – "by the Massey Commission": The Massey Report declared, "all important buildings should be designed in open competition. Such a procedure would help to avoid the mediocrity which so easily besets government architecture": see *Report of the Royal Commission on National Development in the Arts, Letters, and Sciences 1949-1951* (Ottawa: Edmond Cloutier, 1951) at 220.

42. Page 405, para. 2 – "Viljo Revell's design was selected": Simmins, *Ontario Association of Architects* at 144-145.

43. Page 405, para. 3 – "was behind all this": R.S. Morris to Smith, December 1, 1955, UTA/A68-0007/130(08).

44. Page 405, para. 3 – "for the Massey Commission to that effect": Arthur to Smith, December 12, 1955, UTA/A68-0007/130(08).

45. Page 405, para. 3 – "for the city hall competition": Ibid.

46. Page 408, para. 1 – "the scuttling of the original design": Ibid.; Madill to Smith, December 21, 1955, UTA/A68-0007/130(08).

47. Page 408, para. 1 – "and were finalists in the competition": Muriel Emmanuel, ed., *Contemporary Architects*, third edition, (New York: St. James Press, 1993) at 33 and 262; Jennifer Taylor and John Andrews, *John Andrews: Architecture as a performing art* (Toronto: Oxford University Press, 1982) at 21-22.

48. Page 408, para. 1 – "such as Jack Diamond": Emmanuel, *Contemporary Architects* at 244.

49. Page 408, para. 1 – "who would design Massey College": Simmins, *Ontario Association of Architects* at 137.

50. Page 408, para. 2 – "when H.H. Madill retired in 1957": "Name New Head of Architecture", *Varsity News*, December, 1958 at 2.

51. Page 408, para. 2 – "to consider any name except mine": Eric Ross Arthur Oral History Interview, October 2, 1973 transcript, UTA/B74-0025 at 54.

52. Page 408, para. 2 – "not at present connected with the school": Mathers to Spragg, February 12, 1957, UTA/A71-0011/12(06).

53. Page 408, para. 2 – "that everyone believed he deserved": Peter Richardson to author, July 16, 1998.

54. Page 408, para. 2 – "Howarth from the University of Manchester": Woodside to staff in Architecture, December 19, 1957, UTA/A71-0011/12(06); "Name New Head"; Smith to Howarth, April 17, 1957, UTA/A71-0011/12(06).

55. Page 408, para. 3 – "a colleague he respected": Arthur Oral History Interview transcript at 32.

56. Page 408, para. 3 – "the new town of Stevenage after the war": "Stephenson, Gordon", *Canadian Who's Who, 1958-1960* at 1057. He became the head of civic design at the University of Liverpool and was appointed to the chair of planning at MIT, but after resigning from Liverpool could not get security clearance to enter the United States. He came to the University of Toronto after spending several years in Perth, Australia, where he eventually returned: see Arthur transcript at 33-34; Lloyd Rodwin, "Review of: *On A Human Scale: A Life in Urban Design: Gordon Stephenson*", originally published in the *Journal of the American Planning Association* (Autumn, 1995), cited at www.west.com.au/stephenson/rodwin/review.html.

57. Page 408, para. 3 – "in Arthur's architectural firm": W.A. Osbourne, "Report of the Advisory Planning Committee to the Board of Governors University of Toronto, September 12, 1957", UTA/A83-0036/026 at 3; Howard Chapman, "c.v." at 1; Howard Chapman to author, November 9, 1999.

58. Page 408, para. 3 – "extension of the Royal Ontario Museum": Howard Chapman, *Alfred Chapman: The man and his work* (Toronto: The Architectural Conservancy of Ontario, 1978) at 4 and 22.

59. Page 408, para. 3 – "before the First World War": Ibid. at 4.

60. Page 408, para. 3 – "into the Koffler Centre in the 1980s": Howard Chapman, "c.v." at 4.

61. Page 408, para. 4 – "for almost a year": It was appointed in October, 1956 and reported September 12, 1957: see Osbourne, "Report" at 1.

62. Page 409, para. 1 – "company in Galt, Ontario": "Osbourne, William Andrew", *Canadian Who's Who, 1952-1954.* J.S. Duncan was to be the chair, but Phillips didn't want him: see Phillips to Smith, September 27, 1956, excerpted in A83-0036/026. The next year, Duncan was fired as President of Massey-Harris and replaced by Phillips, at the instigation of E.P. Taylor: see Peter C. Newman, *The Canadian Establishment*, v. 1 (Toronto: McClelland and Stewart, 1975) at 34. Duncan says that Phillips and Taylor had disliked him since 1946, when he thwarted plans to sell a large chunk of Massey-Harris to U.S. investors: see James S. Duncan, *Not a One-Way Street* (Toronto: Clarke, Irwin and Company, 1971) at 147-151. See also Bissell, *Halfway Up Parnassus* at 97.

63. Page 409, para. 1 – "the dean of engineering": Osbourne, "Report" at cover.

64. Page 409, para. 1 – "and felt like a campus": "The Unfolding Plan", *Varsity Graduate* (November, 1957) at 142-146.

65. Page 409, para. 2 – "vehicles from the area": Osbourne, "Report" at 3, 45, and 65; see map.

66. Page 409, para. 2 – "from the main city streets": Ibid. at 65.

67. Page 409, para. 2 – "to lots on Spadina Avenue": Ibid. at 66.

68. Page 409, para. 2 – "the then contemplated Spadina Expressway": The expressway was then under consideration by city planners: see Eric Arthur to Smith, February 13, 1956, UTA/A83-0036/026; *Globe and Mail*, December 1, 1955.

69. Page 409, para. 2 – "on or close to St George Street": Osbourne, "Report", map and at 65.

70. Page 409, para. 2 – "rather than spread around the campus": Ibid. at 6, 11, 30, and 32.

71. Page 409, para. 2 – "several generations hence": Ibid. at 8.

72. Page 409, para. 3 – "would complete the quadrangle": Ibid. at 19.

73. Page 409, para. 3 – "on the west side of St George Street": Ibid. at 30 and 64-65.

74. Page 409, para. 3 – "should be constructed close by": Ibid. at 33.

75. Page 409, para. 3 – "on the east side of St George": Ibid. at 29 and 34.

76. Page 409, para. 3 – "should be constructed": Ibid. at 38-39.

77. Page 410, para. 1 – "the expropriated former Primrose Club": Ibid. at 46 and 53.

78. Page 410, para. 1 – "a new home on the west campus": Ibid. at 38.

79. Page 410, para. 1 – "to its new facility on Elm Street": Ibid. at 37.

80. Page 410, para. 1 – "and pharmacy got its own building": Ibid. at 36-37.

81. Page 410, para. 1 – "would not be necessary": Medicine "if pushed to the limit" could take another 100 students: see ibid. at 19-20.

82. Page 410, para. 1 – "some centre other than Toronto": Ibid. at 19.

83. Page 410, para. 2 – "would be about $10 million": Phillips to Porter, December 7, 1956.

84. Page 410, para. 2 – "for the projects already in progress": Osbourne, "Report" at 77.

85. Page 410, para. 2 – "It's good to dream": Conversation with Chapman on November 9, 1999.

86. Page 410, para. 2 – "not the $50 million, range": Smith to Etchen, December 5, 1955, UTA/A83-0036/026.

87. Page 410, para. 3 – "had recently been established": Axelrod, *Scholars and Dollars* at 80 and 83.

88. Page 410, para. 3 – "was founded in 1957": McKillop, *Matters of Mind* at 566.

89. Page 410, para. 3 – "to what I call 'quadrangles'": Phillips to Smith, July 30, 1957, UTA/A74-0011/24(12).

90. Page 411, para. 2 – "as minister of external affairs" : *Varsity*, September 25, 1957; E.A. Corbett, *Sidney Earle Smith* (University of Toronto Press, 1961) at 54-55.

91. Page 411, para. 2 – "of external affairs the next day": Corbett, *Smith* at 54-55 and 58.

92. Page 411, para. 2 – "would be good for all concerned": Ibid. at 54.

93. Page 412, para. 1 – "the most severe testing period in its history": Smith to Phillips, February 9, 1956. Bissell noted around the same time that Smith was "depressed by [the] prospect ahead" for the University, Bissell Diary, February 10, 1956.

94. Page 412, para. 1 – "who had been dean of arts": "Dr. Smith Joins Cabinet: Acting President Named", *Varsity News* (September, 1957) at 1.

95. Page 412, para. 2 – "as a 'great' university president": Caesar Wright speech in Senate, November 8, 1957, UTA/A83-0036/039 at 1.

96. Page 412, para. 2 – "was also Eric Phillips' view": Corbett, *Smith* at 46.

97. Page 412, para. 2 – "Others saw him differently": Some saw him as a good-natured Rotarian: McKillop, *Matters of Mind* at 550.

98. Page 412, para. 2 – "he'd find his spiritual home": Arthur Oral History Interview transcript at 55.

99. Page 412, para. 2 – "but actually deeply introspective": Corbett, *Smith* at 38.

100. Page 412, para. 2 – "complicated simplicity": Ibid. at 39. Smith was an administrator, not a scholar and always worried about his acceptance by scholars: ibid.

101. Page 412, para. 2 – "with a flexible point of view": Claude Bissell, "He Remained an Academic to the End", *Varsity Graduate* (December, 1961) at 27.

102. Page 412, para. 2 – "for harmony and strength": Bissell, *Parnassus* at 25.

103. Page 412, para. 2 – "as minister of external affairs": Bissell, *Parnassus* at 26-27; Corbett, *Smith* at 58.

104. Page 412, para. 2 – "almost servile before the business man": UTA/B88-091, Claude Bissell Diary, December 7, 1957 at 135.

105. Page 413, para. 1 – "resolution of the issue of legal education": Wright speech at 6.

106. Page 413, para. 2 – "as the standards within the University": Edgar McInnis, "Report of the Committee to Investigate the Pass and General Courses", UTA/A83-0036/004; Corbett, *Smith* at 49. There were earlier courses called the "general course" such as one introduced in the 1930s, but very few students entered the four year general course. In 1948, only 13 students entered the course: McInnis, "Report" at 2.

107. Page 413, para. 2 – "of the general course in 1951-52": "University of Toronto General Course in the Faculty of Arts", in UTA/A68-0007/74(06) at 6.

108. Page 413, para. 2 – "the so-called pass arts course": McInnis, "Report" at 9.

109. Page 413, para. 2 – "established in 1931": Ibid. at 3. At the time it was "called fifth form" or "senior matriculation".

110. Page 413, para. 2 – "the greater the failure rate": Ibid. at 46.

111. Page 413, para. 2 – "than those in the honours courses": Ibid. at 1.

112. Page 413, para. 3 – "at least third-class standing": Ibid. at 10.

113. Page 414, para. 1 – "in other subjects": Ibid. at 36-37.

114. Page 414, para. 1 – "stigma of inferiority": Ibid. at 4.

115. Page 414, para. 1 – "as higher entrance standards": Ibid. at 1.

116. Page 414, para. 2 – "replacement in the history department": Robert Bothwell, *Laying the Foundation: A Century of History at the University of Toronto* (Toronto: Department of History, 1991) at 83.

117. Page 414, para. 2 – "a generous expense allowance": "Conference with Chester Martin, 12:30 p.m., Saturday, September 22, 1951"; "Conference with Professor McInnis, Monday, October 29, 1951"; McInnis to Smith, January 29, 1952; Smith to McInnis, February 29, 1952, all in UTA/A68-0007/86(01).

118. Page 414, para. 2 – "had increased significantly": William H. Nelson, *The Search for Faculty Power: The University of Toronto Faculty Association 1942-1992* (Toronto: Canadian Scholars Press, 1993) at 10; K.J. Rea, *The Prosperous Years: The Economic History of Ontario* (University of Toronto Press, 1985) at 4.

119. Page 414, para. 2 – "it had fallen to about half": Nelson, *Faculty Power* at 10; Finding Aid to Interview of Professor J. Conacher, UTA/B86-0041.

120. Page 414, para. 3 – "and F.C.A. Jeanneret": In fact, the Committee was not actually formed until the fall of 1940, but the initial idea stemmed from the 1939 meeting: see Robin Harris, "The Development of the University of Toronto Faculty Association", UTA/A83-0036/001 at 1-2.

121. Page 414, para. 3 – "will be seriously affected": Harris, "Faculty Association" at 15.

122. Page 414, para. 3 – "by only 12 per cent": Nelson, *Faculty Power* at 10-11.

123. Page 414, para. 3 – "from $5,500 to $7,200": Ibid. at 11-12.

124. Page 414, para. 3 – "a little over 1 per cent a year": Rea, *Prosperous Years* at 4.

125. Page 415, para. 1 – "in 1954": Nelson, *Faculty Power* at 12.

126. Page 415, para. 1 – "brought in by the University in 1955": Corbett, *Smith* at 48-49; T.A. Goudge, "Address given at the staff meeting in honour of Sidney Smith, January 11, 1958" at 5. "At the same time" the official retirement age was raised" from 65 to 68: ibid.

127. Page 415, para. 1 – "for the next twenty years": Nelson, *Faculty Power* at 11.

128. Page 415, para. 1 – "for full professors by 50 per cent": Ibid. at 12.

129. Page 415, para. 1 – "worth more than the American": The *Globe* of November 3, 1959 said that the Canadian dollar was worth $1.05 U.S.

130. Page 415, para. 1 – "the highest salaries in the United States": Wright speech at 6.

131. Page 415, para. 1 – "on the North American continent": Goudge, "Address" at 3-4; Corbett, *Smith* at 48.

132. Page 415, para. 1 – "which has been made available to Canadians": Goudge, "Address" at 4, quoting Smith's remarks in 1956; see to the same effect, Nelson, *Faculty Power* at 12-13.

133. Page 415, para. 1 – "for his desk at his new job": Goudge, "Address" at 16.

134. Page 415, para. 2 – "of strengthening the school": Robin Harris, "Graduate Studies in Toronto: The Role of the Dean", speech delivered on March 12, 1986 at University College, at 20-23.

135. Page 415, para. 2 – "plus McGill in Canada": Ibid. at 21.

136. Page 415, para. 2 – "by the senate and the board": Senate Minutes, May 9, 1947, UTA/A68-0012/reel 10; Board of Governors Minutes, May 29, 1947, UTA/A70-0024/reel 15.

137. Page 415, para. 2 – "George Brett had died in 1944": Harris, "Graduate Studies" at 16.

138. Page 415, para. 2 – "to select a new dean": Ibid. at 19; "Two Staff Appointments", *University of Toronto Monthly*, v.45 at 146.

139. Page 415, para. 3 – "as the head of each division": "Report of the President's Committee on Graduate Studies", 1947, UTA/A83-0036/016 at 8.

140. Page 416, para. 1 – "was chair of the scientific division": "Graduate School Appointment", *University of Toronto Monthly*, v.48 at 40.

141. Page 416, para. 1 – "to chair all PhD orals": "Graduate Studies" at 6.

142. Page 416, para. 1 – "its graduate faculty members": Ibid. at 11.

143. Page 416, para. 1 – "also head of the graduate department": A.R. Gordon, "Report of the President's Committee on Statute 1844", February 2, 1956, UTA/A83-0036/016 at 3.

144. Page 416, para. 2 – "and more funding of graduate studies": "Graduate Studies" at 14-17.

145. Page 416, para. 2 – "on the name-plate above the door": Ibid. at 17.

146. Page 416, para. 2 – "as complete strangers from other universities": Ibid.

147. Page 416, para. 3 – "at the University of Manitoba": Laura Groening, *E.K. Brown: A Study in Conflict* (University of Toronto Press, 1993) at 138-141; Smith to Brown, April 2, 1947, UTA/A68-0007/19(04).

148. Page 416, para. 3 – "in the possibilities of the graduate school": Innis to Smith, May 1, 1947, transcribed in UTA/A83-0036/041.

149. Page 416, para. 3 – "resigning from the University": Innis to Smith, May 12, 1947, transcribed in UTA/A83-0036/041.

150. Page 416, para. 3 – "he had taken such action": McKillop, *Matters of Mind* at 517-8.

151. Page 416, para. 3 – "would be served by my resignation": Innis to Smith, May 12, 1947.

152. Page 417, para. 1 – "need you beyond words": Smith to Innis, May 14, 1947, UTA/B72-0003/005(11).

153. Page 417, para. 1 – "on very generous terms": Smith's notes of May 19, 1947, UTA/A68-0007/017(07); see also Smith to Board of Governors, June 26, 1947, UTA/A68-0007/019(03). Innis was paid a salary of $8,000.

154. Page 417, para. 1 – "was that of Harold Innis": Smith to Brown, June 17, 1947, UTA/A68-0007/019(04).

155. Page 417, para. 1 – "Innis became dean of the graduate school": "Graduate School Appointment".

156. Page 417, para. 2 – "Canada's senior academic statesman": Donald Creighton, *Harold Adams Innis: Portrait of a Scholar* (University of Toronto Press, 1957) at 120.

157. Page 418, para. 1 – "president of the Royal Society of Canada": A.R.M. Lower, "Harold Adams Innis", *Proceedings of the Royal Society of Canada*, 3rd Series, v. 47 (1953) at 89; Creighton, *Innis* at 124.

158. Page 418, para. 1 – "he had turned to during the war": Creighton, *Innis* at 120 and 123-124.

159. Page 418, para. 1 – "more unmistakably the mark of greatness": Bissell, *Parnassus* at 23.

160. Page 418, para. 2 – "for greater possibilities of delusion": Harold A. Innis, *The Bias of Communication* (University of Toronto Press: 1951) at 82; see also Robert Babe, *Canadian Communication Thought* (University of Toronto Press, forthcoming), chapter 3; Harris, "Graduate Studies" at 23. Other books by Innis from this period are *Empire and Communications* (1950) and *Changing Concepts of Time* (1952).

161. Page 418, para. 2 – "he showed us how to understand cultures": Marshall McLuhan, "Harold Innis", in *Explorations*, no. 25 (June, 1969), in *University of Toronto Graduate* (June, 1969) at 94-95.

162. Page 418, para. 3 – "mainly for the sciences": Undated draft letter from Smith, early 1951, UTA/A83-0036/016 at 1; Innis to Smith, November 7, 1950 with attached "Preliminary Memorandum for President Smith", UTA/A83-0036/016 at 2.

163. Page 418, para. 3 – "in the graduate school held fellowships": Undated draft letter.

164. Page 418, para. 3 – "students from the Toronto area": Harold Innis, speech of March 25, 1952, UTA/A83-0036/041 at 4-5.

165. Page 418, para. 3 – "a streetcar university": The subway was not opened until 1954: see "Official Opening Dates", www.city.toronto.on.ca/ttc/history.htm.

166. Page 418, para. 3 – "and almost half were from Toronto": Innis to Smith, November 7, 1950, with attached preliminary memo at 1. Innis argues that the University should show greater flexibility in dealing with out-of-province graduate students: see Innis speech at 7.

167. Page 418, para. 3 – "had been even higher": David Ross Keane, "Rediscovering Ontario University Students in the Mid-Nineteenth Century" (Ph.D. Thesis, University of Toronto, 1981), table 9.2, as cited in Charles Levi, "'Where the Famous People Were?': The Origins, Activities and Future Careers of Student Leaders at University College, Toronto 1854-197" (Ph.D. Thesis, York University, 1998) at 80; *President's Report 1913/1914* at 53; D.C. Masters, *Henry John Cody: An Outstanding Life* (Toronto: Dundurn Press, 1995) at 10.

168. Page 418, para. 4 – "about the role of the colleges": See Innis to Smith, received September 20, 1951, UTA/A83-0036/041 at 2; Innis to Smith, received October 10, 1951, UTA/A83-0036/041,where he refers to "the fatal divisiveness of the humanities".

169. Page 418, para. 4 – "and the professional courses": Moffat Woodside, "Report of the Special Committee on the Humanities", February 1, 1954, UTA/A83-0036/019 at 8.

170. Page 419, para. 1 – "social sciences": Masters, *Cody* at 288.

171. Page 419, para. 1 – "and asked Innis to head it": Woodside, "Report of the Special Committee" at 1.

172. Page 419, para. 2 – "when Innis became ill": Woodside, "Report" at 1.

173. Page 419, para. 2 – "and in May he underwent surgery": Creighton, *Innis* at 144-145.

174. Page 419, para. 2 – "the graduate school secretary": Ibid. at 145; Jack Sword to author, November 17, 1999. Innis had worked with Sword on the Royal Commission on Adult Education in Manitoba. Sword had come to Toronto to do graduate work in philosophy and was asked to join the graduate school shortly afterwards. He eventually completed his master's degree on a part-time basis in 1950.

175. Page 419, para. 2 – "at the age of 58": Lower, "Innis" at 89. Innis died three days after his 58th birthday; compare *American Economic Review*, v. 43 at 1.

176. Page 419, para. 2 – "published a rough draft of his intended speech": The speech was entitled "The Decline in the Efficiency of Instruments Essential to Equilibrium": see *American Economic Review*, v. 43 at 16.

177. Page 419, para. 2 – "the reissue of some of his books": UTA/Current People/"Mary Quayle Innis".

178. Page 419, para. 2 – "the path laid out by Innis": D.J. LeRoy, "Andrew Robertson Gordon", *Proceedings of the Royal Society of Canada*, 4th Series, v. 6 at 104.

179. Page 419, para. 2 – "that its members could not reach agreement": Woodside, "Report" at 10 and 35.

180. Page 419, para. 2 – "for another twenty years": See Chapter 32 (1960).

CHAPTER 31 – 1958 – FINANCING EXPANSION

1. Page 420, para. 1 – "let his name stand for the presidency": Claude Bissell, *Halfway up Parnassus: A Personal Account of the University of Toronto 1932-1971* (University of Toronto Press, 1974) at 36.

2. Page 420, para. 1 – "acting president, Moffat Woodside": F.C.A. Jeanneret referred to Woodside as the "runner-up": see Jeanneret to Bissell, February 4, 1958, UTA/A83-0036/043. Borden thought Woodside was "the obvious person": see Borden Oral Interview, UTA/B87-0044 at 47. Woodside also had been asked to apply for the job and expected it: see Murray Ross, *The Way Must be Tried: Memoirs of a University Man* (Toronto: Stoddart, 1992) at 62-63.

3. Page 420, para. 1 – "the president of the National Research Council": Stone to Vaughan, November 7, 1957, UTA/A88-0029/001; Frances Ireland Oral Interview Tape Summary, UTA/B86-0052 at 7.

4. Page 420, para. 1 – "and the discussion will end": Bissell, *Parnassus* at 36.

5. Page 420, para. 1 – "a decision by Colonel Phillips as chairman": Henry Borden Oral Interview at 48.

6. Page 420, para. 1 – "in that vast mind of yours?": Bissell, *Parnassus* at 36.

7. Page 420, para. 1 – "as his diary shows": Bissell Diary, October 20, 1957 at 134 contains the significant "But still..."

8. Page 420, para. 1 – "he would accept": Ibid. at 134.

9. Page 420, para. 1 – "by the board on December 12, 1957": Board of Governors Minutes, December 12, 1957, UTA/A70-0024/reel 18.

10. Page 420, para. 1 – "until the end of the academic year, however": Bissell, *Parnassus* at 38.

11. Page 420, para. 1 – "easily become a great university": Ibid. at 36.

12. Page 421, para. 1 – "had been acquired the previous year": Ibid. at 37-38. Bissell had lunched there the previous year: see Bissell Diary, October 12, 1956.

13. Page 421, para. 1 – "north of Toronto was named": Chapter 26 (1931).

14. Page 421, para. 1 – "and sell building lots on 220 feet": Smith to Phillips, December 20, 1955, UTA/A68-0007/134(10).

15. Page 421, para. 1 – "was kept intact": See *University of Toronto Bulletin*, June 12, 1989.

16. Page 421, para. 2 – "as the eighth president of the University": "The President Installed", *Varsity News* (November, 1958) at 1; Bissell, *Parnassus* at 50; UTA/B88-0091, Claude Bissell Diaries, November 9, 1958.

17. Page 421, para. 2 – "by Dean R.R. McLaughlin of engineering": "President Installed"; Bissell Diary, November, 1958.

18. Page 421, para. 2 – "one would occur during his speech": Bissell Diary, November, 1958.

19. Page 422, para. 1 – "tradition of vigorous individualism": Bissell, *Parnassus* at 51.

20. Page 422, para. 1 – "Old Toronto mother ever dear...": The *Blue and White* was written in the 1907/08 academic

year, words by Claris E. Silcox '08 and music by Clayton E. Bush '07: see James E. Jones, ed., *The University of Toronto Song Book* (Toronto: W.R. Draper, 1918) at 31.

21. Page 422, para. 1 – "reproduced in this chapter": Bissell, *Parnassus* at 52.

22. Page 422, para. 2 – "was a fund-raising campaign": Ibid.

23. Page 422, para. 2 – "a $5 million campaign in 1944": "University of Toronto Expansion Fund", UTA/A83-0036/024.

24. Page 422, para. 2 – "discouraging corporate donations": D.C. Masters, *Henry John Cody: An Outstanding Life* (Toronto: Dundurn Press, 1995) at 281-283.

25. Page 422, para. 2 – "to do the same": Cody to Ilsley, February 7, 1944, UTA/A83-0036/024.

26. Page 422, para. 2 – "the campaign was a failure": Ilsley to Cody, February 25, 1944, UTA/A83-0036/024, stated that a corporation could give an amount equal to the average that it had donated in the two years before the "excess profit" legislation. Corporations would probably not have given generous amounts in the early years of the war. Masters, *Cody* at 284, says the fundraising effort amounted to a little over $3 million including "promises and prospects".

27. Page 422, para. 2 – "and was abandoned discreetly": "$13,000,000 for Varsity", *Varsity Graduate* (April, 1948) at 1; Bissell, *Parnassus* at 53. According to one breakdown, only 34 individuals gave $1,000 or more and only 29 corporations gave $10,000 or more: see Rowney to Smith, November 23, 1956, UTA/A86-0002/005.

28. Page 422, para. 2 – "had encouraged him to write": Morley Callaghan, *The Varsity Story* (Toronto: Macmillan, 1948); see minutes of the Varsity Appeal Executive Committee, September 9, 1947, UTA/A83-0036/025; Gregory Clark, "The Varsity Story", *Varsity Graduate* (December, 1948) at 19.

29. Page 422, para. 3 – "and the possibility of another failure": In 1957 he confessed he had "many misgivings" about a new campaign: see Phillips to Frost, August 30, 1957, UTA/A71-0011/15(12).

30. Page 422, para. 3 – "had urged him to launch one": Smith had been interested in such a campaign for some time: see Smith to Phillips, February 9 and February 21, 1956, UTA/A68-0007/134(10).

31. Page 422, para. 3 – "to be left entirely to the state": Bissell to Phillips, January 10, 1958, UTA/A71-0011/15(12).

32. Page 422, para. 3 – "a successful campaign for $8 million": Bissell talk to the Senate, December 12, 1958, UTA/A86-0002/005 at 1-3.

33. Page 422, para. 4 – "campaign for $12.6 million": Bissell Diary, October 9, 1958; "$12,600,000 in Gifts Asked", *Varsity News* (June, 1959).

34. Page 422, para. 4 – "was a government responsibility": Brakeley to Smith, January 21, 1957, UTA/A86-0002/005.

35. Page 422, para. 4 – "to head the campaign": Bissell to Phillips, April 3, 1958, UTA/A71-0011/15(12); Phillips to Bissell, April 9, 1958, UTA/A71-0011/15(12).

36. Page 423, para. 1 – "to serve as co-chairs": "$12,600,000 in Gifts Asked". Phillips had tried to get Duncan to serve as chairman, but he refused: see Phillips to Frost, August 27, 1957, UTA/A71-0011/15(12).

37. Page 423, para. 1 – "being key members of the university board": University governors Eric Phillips, Henry Borden and James Duncan had connections to Argus when it was formed in September, 1945. Norman Urquhart, J.S.D. Tory and M.W. McCutcheon had an Argus affiliation when they were later appointed to the

board of governors: see orders-in-council from 1941 to 1958, UTA/A85-0024/011; *Canadian Who's Who*, vols. 5 and 6; and Richard Rohmer, *E.P. Taylor: The biography of Edward Plunket Taylor* (Toronto: McClelland & Stewart) at 86-7 and 170. Three of the four comptrollers during Phillips' tenure as chairman of the University – Arnold Gaine, A.C. Rankin, and F.R. Stone – had worked for Phillips previously: see Rohmer, *E.P. Taylor* at 166; Chapter 28 (1944); UTA/Graduate Records/"Rankin, Alexander Gormaly"/A73-0026/372(59); and UTA/Graduate Records/"Stone, Frank R."/A73-0026/450(75). Phillips surrounded himself with people he knew and trusted, both from inside and outside Argus. Referring to Phillips in *Parnassus* at 30, Bissell observes that "the university was to him, so to speak, a special slightly eccentric operation in the expanding empire over which he presided".

38. Page 423, para. 1 – "from Victoria College in maths and physics": Bissell, *Parnassus* at 53.

39. Page 423, para. 1 – "predecessor, Sir Edmund Walker": See Chapter 18 (1905).

40. Page 423, para. 1 – "had not gone to university": Bissell, *Parnassus* at 53.

41. Page 423, para. 2 – "which were to share in the proceeds": Ibid. at 52-53.

42. Page 423, para. 2 – "at the King Edward Hotel": Bissell Diary, October 28, 1959.

43. Page 423, para. 2 – "ever recorded in North America": "The National Fund: How the Victory was Won", *Varsity Graduate* (February, 1961) at 4.

44. Page 423, para. 2 – "establish Toronto as *The Canadian University*": Bissell diary, July 22, 1959 – Bissell's underlining.

45. Page 423, para. 2 – "Be Lured Home from U.S.": *Globe and Mail*, November 3, 1959.

46. Page 423, para. 2 – "over $15 million had been raised": "The National Fund" at 3.

47. Page 423, para. 3 – "engineering's Galbraith Building": "The Galbraith Building", *Varsity Graduate* (December, 1967) at 43.

48. Page 423, para. 3 – "with its Burton Tower": "The National Fund Harvest", *Varsity Graduate* (December, 1967) at 41.

49. Page 423, para. 3 – "of a heart attack the previous year": Bissell Diary, November 24, 1959; W.A. Mackintosh, "Sidney Earle Smith", *Proceedings of the Royal Society of Canada*, 3rd Series, v. 53 (1959) at 129.

50. Page 423, para. 3 – "was laid in October 1960": Bissell Diary, Oct 14, 1960; "In Memory of Sidney Smith", *Varsity Graduate* (1960) at 58.

51. Page 423, para. 3 – "from which the individual came": Bissell to Mackintosh, September 19, 1961, UTA/A71-0011/52(02).

52. Page 423, para. 3 – "their comfortable quarters in Flavelle House": Robert Bothwell, *Laying the Foundation: A Century of History at University of Toronto* (Department of History, University of Toronto: 1991) at 143-4.

53. Page 423, para. 3 – "for a building with so much glass": Hastie to Stone, November 19, 1964, UTA/B77-0001/16.

54. Page 425, para. 1 – "that her work was rejected": Bissell Diary, February 2 and 12, 1962.

55. Page 425, para. 2 – "quadrangle was completed": "Campaign Dollars Convert Blueprints into Buildings", *Varsity Graduate* (February, 1961) at 16. The quadrangle was completed in 1964: see Douglas Richardson, *A Not Unsightly Building: University College and its History* (Toronto: Mosaic Press, 1990) at 146.

56. Page 425, para. 2 – "its first dean of women, Margaret Addison": "Victoria turns a corner", *Varsity Graduate* (November, 1959) at 28. See generally, Jean O'Grady, *Margaret Addison: A Biography* (Montreal: McGill-Queen's University Press, 2001). Victoria also completed the new E.J. Pratt Library in 1961 and the New Academic Building (later named Northrop Frye Hall) in 1967: see Patricia McHugh, *Toronto Architecture: A City Guide* (Toronto: Mercury Books, 1985) at 8.

57. Page 425, para. 2 – "on St Joseph Street": "Loretto College Blends Yesterday and Today", *Varsity Graduate* (November, 1959) at 32; "Campaign Dollars" at 17. The John M. Kelly Library was opened in 1969 on land the College purchased from the Sisters Adorers of the Precious Blood in 1967: see J. Bernard Black, *Familiar Landmarks: Four Walks Through the Historic Campus of the University of St. Michael's College* (Toronto: University of St. Michael's College Archives, 1984) at 9.

58. Page 425, para. 2 – "on Devonshire Place": D.R.G. Owen, unpublished history of Trinity College 1952-1974, May, 1974, Trinity College Archives, 986-0012/020(07) at 7 and 15-17; "Campaign Dollars" at 17. Gerald Larkin, President of the Salada Tea Company of Canada, whose generosity to Trinity had already subsidized the new chapel and the Senior Common Room, donated $790,000 of the total $2.8 million needed for Trinity's complete building program from 1958 to 1963, almost as much as the National Fund's $895,000 contribution. His death in April, 1961 led to the decision to name the Academic Building after him.

59. Page 425, para. 3 – "in Ontario competing for funds": A list of all the new universities can be found in A.B. McKillop, *Matters of Mind: The University in Ontario 1791-1951* (University of Toronto Press, 1994) at 566.

60. Page 425, para. 3 – "that soon would be needed": Phillips to Frost, May 20, 1960, UTA/A88-0029/001 at 1 and 3.

61. Page 425, para. 3 – "was required in the mid-sixties": Bissell reported that annual net increases in staff between 1957-58 and 1962-63 varied from 26 to 54. In 1963-4 the net increase was 60, although 120 new staff were hired that year. In 1964-65 and 1965-66 new hires were "just over 100" each year, and in 1966-67 the figure was 160. Bissell, however, found these figures inadequate, noting that, "To achieve our goal we must advance this number well beyond 200": see *President's Reports*, 1963/64 at 14, 1964-65 at 8-9, and 1965-66 at 15.

62. Page 425, para. 3 – "the idea of three-year plans": Phillips to Frost, May 20, 1960 at 1.

63. Page 425, para. 3 – "should be each year": Paul Axelrod, *Scholars and Dollars: Politics, Economics, and the Universities of Ontario 1945-1980* (University of Toronto Press, 1982) at 89-90.

64. Page 425, para. 3 – "the former cosy arrangement with the premier": Ibid. at 90. He was also unhappy with the fact that Chancellor Beatty was appointed to the committee without his approval: ibid. at 90-91.

65. Page 426, para. 1 – "back to the universities themselves": Axelrod, *Scholars and Dollars* at 93.

66. Page 426, para. 1 – "and a system of community colleges": Ibid. at 94.

67. Page 426, para. 1 – "and an increasing number of staff": Ibid. at 95.

68. Page 426, para. 2 – "for the funding of Ontario universities": Ibid. at 98.

69. Page 426, para. 2 – "and headed by Toronto's Vincent Bladen": Vincent Bladen, *Bladen on Bladen* (Toronto: Scarborough College, 1978) at 159; Ernest Sirluck, *First Generation: An Autobiography* (University of Toronto Press, 1996) at 264.

70. Page 426, para. 2 – "with the CUA and the NCCU": Axelrod, *Scholars and Dollars* at 98.

71. Page 426, para. 2 – "a PhD student would be worth six units": Ibid.; Sirluck, *First Generation* at 266. The weighting was, in theory, designed to be neutral: see comments by Dan Lang to Friedland, February 2, 2001.

72. Page 426, para. 2 – "the ability to raise student fees was restricted": Charles Hanly, *Who Pays? University Financing in Ontario* (Toronto: James Lewis & Samuel, 1970) at 121.

73. Page 426, para. 2 – "the indirect costs of research": Comments from Dan Lang to Friedland, February 2, 2001.

74. Page 426, para. 2 – "the royal commission of 1906, fifty years earlier": Axelrod, *Scholars and Dollars* at 98; comments from Dan Lang to Friedland, February 2, 2001.

75. Page 427, para. 1 – "recommended in 1951": *Report of the Royal Commission on National Development in the Arts, Letters, and Sciences 1949-1951* (Ottawa: Edmond Cloutier, 1951) at 355.

76. Page 427, para. 1 – "of an outlet for his energies": Claude Bissell, *The Imperial Canadian: Vincent Massey in Office* (University of Toronto Press, 1986) at 193-194.

77. Page 427, para. 1 – "federal aid to the universities": Paul Litt, *The Muses, the Masses, and the Massey Commission* (University of Toronto Press, 1992) at 157. See generally, Karen Finlay, *The Forces of Culture: Vincent Massey and Canadian Sovereignty* (University of Toronto Press, forthcoming), chapter 6.

78. Page 427, para. 1 – "as the veterans left the universities": McKillop, *Matters of Mind* at 564.

79. Page 427, para. 1 – "to continue federal support": David A.A. Stager, "Federal Government Grants to Canadian Universities", *Canadian Historical Review*, v. 54, no. 3 (September, 1973) at 291-292; P.B.Waite, *Lord of Point Grey: Larry MacKenzie of U.B.C.* (Vancouver: University of British Columbia Press, 1987) at 149.

80. Page 427, para. 2 – "honorary degree from the University of Toronto": McKillop, *Matters of Mind* at 564. McKillop gives the date as October, 1949.

81. Page 428, para. 1 – "in the interest of the whole nation": Bissell, *Imperial* at 230; Stager, "Federal Government" at 292.

82. Page 428, para. 1 – "to that difficult problem": Bissell, *Imperial* at 230; Stager, "Federal Government" at 292; McKillop, *Matters of Mind* at 564; Waite, *Lord of Point Grey* at 154; *Toronto Star*, October 28, 1950; *Globe and Mail*, October 28, 1950.

83. Page 428, para. 1 – "overwhelmed by American influences": *Royal Commission* at 13-18 and 352. Massey wrote MacKenzie in September, 1951 saying that Massey and Neatby had arrived at the conclusion that "we can and should recommend Federal Aid to Universities": see Litt, *Muses* at 162.

84. Page 428, para. 1 – "their future usefulness": *Royal Commission* at 140-41 and 143.

85. Page 428, para. 1 – "had begun almost immediately": Draft Order-in-Council, 1951, UTA/A68-0007/95(01); Stager, "Federal Government" at 294; *Varsity*, September 27, 1951.

86. Page 428, para. 1 – "of our institutions of higher learning": *Varsity*, September 27, 1951.

87. Page 428, para. 1 – "government in 1951": Phillips to Frost of July 22, 1952, UTA/A68-0007/105(07). Deciding how to allocate part of it to the federated colleges was a continuing source of controversy: see Charles Levi, "Federal Aid or Federated Aid? 1951-1953", September 9, 1998.

88. Page 428, para. 1 – "shape the development of the University of Toronto": See Chapter 1 (1826), Chapter 2 (1842), Chapter 12 (1887), and Chapter 16 (1897).

89. Page 428, para. 2 – "on the Financing of Higher Education": Bladen, *Bladen* at 159; Sirluck, *First Generation* at 264. In January 1965 the US government announced a massive federal program for aid to education: see Bissell Diary, January 13, 1965.

90. Page 428, para. 2 – "to increase by $1 each year": Stager, "Federal Government" at 296.

91. Page 428, para. 2 – "to some $100 million in 1966-67": Ibid. at 297.

92. Page 428, para. 2 – "in the development of higher education": Ibid.

93. Page 428, para. 2 – "equal to half their cost": Ibid.

94. Page 428, para. 2 – "the level of its involvement": Glen Jones, "Governments, Governance, and Canadian Universities", in J. Smart, ed., *Higher Education: Handbook of Theory and Research,* v.11 (San Francisco: Jossey-Bass, 1996) at 352.

95. Page 428, para. 2 – "by the provinces on education": Axelrod, *Scholars and Dollars* at 181.

96. Page 428, para. 2 – "or anything else if a province wished": Sirluck, *First Generation* at 265.

97. Page 428, para. 3 – "in those areas": *Royal Commission* at 358-359.

98. Page 429, para. 1 – "and Sir James Dunn": Litt, *Muses* at 242.

99. Page 429, para. 1 – "administered by the Canada Council": Litt, *Muses* at 242; Bissell, *Imperial* at 232.

100. Page 429, para. 2 – "and obviously into the university": Bissell, *Parnassus* at 95.

101. Page 429, para. 2 – "of College Street and University Avenue": Boyd Neel, *My Orchestras and Other Adventures: The Memoirs of Boyd Neel* (University of Toronto Press, 1985) at 154.

102. Page 429, para. 2 – "from the conservatory": Ibid.

103. Page 429, para. 2 – "not noticeably tender to the arts": Ibid. at 158; Bissell, *Parnassus* at 97.

104. Page 429, para. 2 – "would not have assisted Neel's case": Neel, *My Orchestras* at 155.

105. Page 429, para. 2 – "to achieve his objective": Ibid. at 170.

106. Page 429, para. 2 – "on Bloor Street for the conservatory": Bissell, *Parnassus* at 96-97; John Beckwith, *Music at Toronto: A Personal Account* (University of Toronto Press, 1995) at 26-27.

107. Page 429, para. 3 – "as refugees before the war": Ezra Schabas, "Celebrating 50", *University of Toronto Bulletin,* January 6, 1997 at 6; *NUVO* (date unknown) at 124.

108. Page 431, para. 1 – "Teresa Stratas": Martin Hunter, "The Will to Sing: A Celebration of U of T's Opera School Stars", *University of Toronto Graduate* (Winter, 1988) at 9; Carl Morey, "Marshall Was Very Much a Canadian Singer", *Bulletin,* March 3, 199; see generally Ezra Schabas and Carl Morey, *Opera Viva: The Canadian Opera Company: The first fifty years* (Toronto: Dundurn Press, 2000).

109. Page 431, para. 1 – "a teacher at the school": Harry Rasky, *Stratas: An Affectionate Tribute* (Toronto: Oxford University Press, 1988) at 26-27.

110. Page 431, para. 1 – "at Eaton Auditorium": *NUVO* (date unknown) at 126.

111. Page 431, para. 1 – "and it was yes!": Neel, *My Orchestras* at 172.

112. Page 431, para. 2 – "It's a good question": Beckwith, *Music at Toronto* at 33-34.

113. Page 431, para. 2 – "a 'crazy set-up'": Neel, *My Orchestras* at 151.

114. Page 431, para. 2 – "gave academic degrees": The faculty has four divisions – composition, musicology, music education, and performance: John Beckwith to author, January 28, 1998; Lesa Donskov and Donald Graves, "A History of the Royal Conservatory of Music and the Faculty of Music, University of Toronto 1866-1982" (unpublished and undated manuscript), UTA/A83-0036/13 at 34.

115. Page 431, para. 2 – "learned only the piano": Neel, *My Orchestras* at 154.

116. Page 431, para. 2 – "who studied under Alberto Guerrero": Robert Craft, "Genius in Galoshes", *TLS*, November 28, 1997.

117. Page 431, para. 2 – "over a period of two decades": Beckwith, *Music at Toronto* at 45-47.

118. Page 431, para. 2 – "and the land on which it sits": Gay Abbate, "U of T releases RCM deed", *Bulletin*, February 12, 1990; "Separate Conservatory Neighbour Still", *University of Toronto Magazine* (Spring, 1990) at 31.

119. Page 431, para. 3 – "did not take place until that month": Bissell, *Parnassus* at 98. The cornerstone of the new music building was laid in 1961: see "Fanfare on Philosopher's Walk", *Varsity Graduate* (May, 1961) at 33.

120. Page 431, para. 3 – "conducted by Ettore Mazzoleni": "The Toast to the Faculty", *Varsity Graduate* (May, 1964) at 95. The fanfares were by MacMillan and Keith Bissell, Claude Bissell's brother: Schabas, *Sir Ernest MacMillan: The Importance of Being Canadian* (University of Toronto Press, 1996) at 45 and 294; Bissell, *Parnassus* at 98.

121. Page 431, para. 3 – "and John Weinzweig": See Beckwith, *Music at Toronto* at 30. The CBC Symphony, conducted by MacMillan and Neel, was slated to perform works by faculty members on March 7th: see the *Varsity*, March 2, 1964.

122. Page 432, para. 1 – "as many members of the Order of Canada": Beckwith, *Music at Toronto* at 57.

123. Page 432, para. 2 – "named after MacMillan": Bissell Diary, January 25, 1962; "March is Music Month at Varsity", *Varsity News* (February, 1964) at 5.

124. Page 432, para. 2 – "who had died in 1959": Bissell Diary, April 24, 1959 and August 31, 1960.

125. Page 432, para. 2 – "became general manager of the Metropolitan Opera": "Johnson, Edward", *Canadian Who's Who 1952-1954* at 541.

126. Page 432, para. 2 – "to be the former premier, George Drew": Beckwith, *Music at Toronto* at 28.

127. Page 432, para. 2 – "after the music man?": Ibid.

128. Page 432, para. 2 – "some gesture of the sort *was* deserved": Beckwith, *Music at Toronto* at 30. Ezra Schabas has rhetorically asked, "Shouldn't the *entire* building have been named after MacMillan, if it was going to be named after anybody?": see Schabas, *Sir Ernest MacMillan* at 292.

129. Page 432, para. 3 – "for the School of Business": "Campaign Dollars" at 16; "Report Number 350 of the Property Committee", March 11, 1969, UTA/A70-0025/24.

130. Page 432, para. 3 – "the first of its several moves": "Finding Aid, Interview of Professor O.W. Main by P.A. Bator", UTA/B88-0060.

131. Page 432, para. 3 – "had recently purchased": E-mail from Harold Averill to author, November 18, 1999; *President's Report, 1969/70* at 45; Bissell Diary, February 24, 1969; "Seminars, tours, and dinner to mark Business School opening", *Bulletin*, November 12, 1970.

132. Page 432, para. 4 – "within the graduate school": John Sawyer, "The Rotman School: A Historical Perspective 1901-1998", (draft article, June 30, 1998).

133. Page 432, para. 4 – "chaired by Harold Innis": Bladen, *Bladen* at 108-109.

134. Page 432, para. 4 – "during this period": See Chapter 30 (1955), outlining Innis' chairing of the committee on graduate studies and another committee on the humanities.

135. Page 432, para. 4 – "envisaged in graduate business": Bladen to Smith, May 13, 1949, UTA/A83-0036/009.

136. Page 432, para. 4 – "after Innis died": Bladen, *Bladen* at 110. Lionel Robbins of the London School of Economics had turned down the job: see correspondence between Louis Rasminsky and Robbins, January 23, 1953 and February 5, 1953, Lionel Robbins papers (made available by professor of economics Susan Howson, who is writing a biography of Robbins).

137. Page 432, para. 4 – "wasteful duplication": Bladen, *Bladen* at 110.

138. Page 433, para. 1 – "apparently was satisfied": Ibid.

139. Page 433, para. 2 – "in attracting full-time master's students": Ibid. at 109.

140. Page 433, para. 2 – "working at night": Transcript of Oral Interview with Vincent Bladen, UTA/B74-0038 at 140.

141. Page 433, para. 2 – "began to curtail the night work": Ibid. at 143.

142. Page 433, para. 2 – "begun under Innis": "Selected Excerpts from Warren Main Oral History Interview August 10, 1998". John C. Sawatsky was the other: see "The Annual Report of the Director of the Institute of Industrial Relations, 1950".

143. Page 433, para. 2 – "and that soon": Bladen to Bissell, May 26, 1958, UTA/A83-0036/009.

144. Page 433, para. 3 – "from the University of Saskatchewan in 1953": *Globe and Mail*, March 24, 1960.

145. Page 433, para. 3 – "was changed to the School of Business": Ibid.

146. Page 433, para. 3 – "to a master of business administration": Sawyer, "The Rotman School" at 24 gives this date as 1960.

147. Page 433, para. 3 – "under the aggressive [James] Gillies": Bissell Diary, October 18, 1966.

148. Page 433, para. 3 – "teaching at the University of California": "Gillies, James", *Canadian Who's Who, 1991* at 376.

149. Page 433, para. 3 – "impressed by him": Bissell Diary, December 2, 1959.

150. Page 433, para. 3 – "to the other members of the faculty": "Finding Aid: Dr Bator Interview with Professor O.W. Main"; Bissell Diary, December 23, 1959.

151. Page 433, para. 3 – "in the position": James Gillies and Colin Dickenson, "From the Faculty of Administrative Studies to the Schulich School of Business: The Origin and Evolution of Professional Education for Managers at

York University" (draft chapter, undated) at 132. We have found no correspondence in the Archives about Gillies with the exception of a program for his visit to the University of Toronto, November 30-December 2, 1959, UTA/A71-0011/31(07).

152. Page 433, para. 4 – "we could assert superiority": Bissell Diary, October 18, 1966; Bissell, *Parnassus* at 107.

153. Page 433, para. 4 – "was introduced in 1969": "Finding Aid: Dr. Bator Interview".

154. Page 433, para. 4 – "and by the students": Ibid.

155. Page 434, para. 1 – "that essential tool of research, the computer": "Put emphasis on research in Business", *Varsity News* (December, 1966) at 14; "In the School of Business they learn to play the game", *Varsity Graduate* (April, 1961) at 66.

156. Page 434, para. 1 – "of outstanding universities": "Development of Business School 'should have a high priority' the Board of Governors decides", *Bulletin*, November 4, 1971.

157. Page 434, para. 1 – "was purchased quickly": "Finding Aid: Dr. Bator Interview".

158. Page 434, para. 1 – "to build a leading school": "Development of Business School".

159. Page 434, para. 1 – "should receive a high priority": "Statement Issued by the Board of Governors, October 28, 1971", UTA/A96-0001/001.

160. Page 435, para. 1 – "as its first dean": "John B. Crispo", *Canadian Who's Who, 1991* at 223; "School of Business will become Faculty of Management Studies with John Crispo as first Dean", *Bulletin*, February 25, 1972. In 1982, political economy was split into the two departments of political science and economics and the commerce and finance program was transferred to the faculty of management – to be run jointly by them and the faculty of Arts and Science: see "Department of Political Economy split, commerce and finance merger with managerial studies", *University of Toronto Bulletin*, July 21, 1982; *The Faculty of Arts and Science St. George Campus 2000-2001 Calendar* at 24-25.

161. Page 435, para. 1 – "in financial derivatives": E-mail from Ed Safarian to Friedland, January 31, 2001; conversation with Paul Halpern, February 14, 2001.

162. Page 435, para. 1 – "with an MCom. in 1960": "Rotman Donates $3 Million", *University of Toronto Bulletin*, December 14, 1992

163. Page 435, para. 1 – "to hire and keep its faculty": John Sawyer, "From Commerce to Management: The Evolution of Business Education at the University of Toronto", in Barbara Austin, ed., *Capitalizing Knowledge: Essays on the History of Business Education in Canada* (University of Toronto Press, 2000), Chapter 4 at 162.

164. Page 435, para. 2 – "into the former Texaco building in 1970": E-mail from Harold Averill to author, November 18, 1999.

165. Page 435, para. 2 – "and also became a faculty in 1972": UTA/Corporate Name Authority/U-98.

166. Page 435, para. 2 – "before that the department of social service": *Teach us to Care and Not to Care: Fiftieth Anniversary 1914-1964 School of Social Work University of Toronto* (Toronto: U of T School of Social Work and Ontario Department of Public Welfare, 1964) at 13; Sara Z. Burke, *Seeking the Highest Good: Social Service and Gender at the University of Toronto 1888-1937* (University of Toronto Press, 1996) at 123.

167. Page 435, para. 2 – "to accept the position": John R. Graham, "A History of the University of Toronto School of Social Work" (University of Toronto Ph.D. Thesis, 1996) at 132-133. In 1929 he was appointed an assistant

professor in the department of social service, which that same year became the department of social science: see Burke, *Seeking the Highest Good* at 123.

168. Page 435, para. 2 – "in social welfare policy": Graham, "A History" at 124-125.

169. Page 436, para. 1 – "and planning in this field": Cassidy to King, December 10, 1943, UTA/A83-0036/14.

170. Page 436, para. 2 – "draft the CCF's Regina Manifesto": Graham, "A History" at 133, but Graham notes that he had adopted a more "centrist" position by 1945.

171. Page 436, para. 2 – "for which they stand": Allan Irving, "Social Science Research in the University: An Examination of the Views of Harry Cassidy and Harold Innis", *The Canadian Journal of Higher Education*, v. 10 (1980) at 100.

172. Page 436, para. 2 – "and undertaking research projects": Ibid. at 101.

173. Page 436, para. 2 – "and an associate professor": *Teach us to Care* at 39; Graham, "A History" at 161 and 163.

174. Page 436, para. 2 – "in an ever-changing department": Graham, "A History" at 163.

175. Page 436, para. 2 – "she will be pleased": Innis to Cody, April 11, 1944, UTA/A83-0036/14.

176. Page 436, para. 2 – "as chairman of the school's governing body": Graham, "A History" at 141; Burke, *Seeking the Highest Good* at 132.

177. Page 436, para. 3 – "an ambitious, dynamic, aggressive director": Graham, "A History" at 131.

178. Page 436, para. 3 – "I feel like ducking under my desk": *Teach us to Care* at 31.

179. Page 436, para. 3 – "bachelor of social work degree": "New Social Work Degrees Established at the University of Toronto", *University of Toronto Monthly* (May, 1947) at 204.

180. Page 436, para. 3 – "with a major research component": B.S.W. graduates could obtain the M.S.W. with one further year of study: see Graham, "A History" at 130 and 157-158; "New Social Work Degrees"; Burke, *Seeking the Highest Good* at 134.

181. Page 436, para. 3 – "first doctoral program in social work": Graham, "A History" at 130.

182. Page 436, para. 3 – "and stressed research": Ibid. at 140.

183. Page 436, para. 3 – "it would ever go through": Ibid. at 124.

184. Page 436, para. 3 – "more than doubled": Ibid. at 129.

185. Page 436, para. 3 – "the Canadian Mortgage and Housing Corporation": At that time known as the Central Mortgage and Housing Corporation.

186. Page 436, para. 3 – "of political economy at the University": Graham, "A History" at 158-159.

187. Page 437, para. 1 – "York University": Ibid. at 219. Malcolm Taylor would become principal of the University of Alberta (Calgary) and president of the University of Victoria: see "Taylor, Malcolm Gordon", *Canadian Who's Who, 1994* at 1120. John Morgan, another faculty member, would become the dean of the school of social work at the University of Pennsylvania.

188. Page 437, para. 1 – "the name he favoured": Graham, "A History" at 169.

189. Page 437, para. 1 – "he had sought for the school": Irving, "Social Science Research" at 106.

190. Page 437, para. 1 – "He died of cancer in 1951": Graham, "A History" at 170.

191. Page 437, para. 1 – "Chick, I am sure, will be a fine director": Harry Cassidy, "Memo to Chick", October 25, 1951, UTA/A83-0036/015.

192. Page 437, para. 2 – "for the next eighteen years": Graham, "A History" at 189.

193. Page 437, para. 2 – "increasing tension and division": Ibid. at 172-173.

194. Page 437, para. 2 – "the case work and group work teachers": Ibid. at 180-181.

195. Page 437, para. 2 – "in the service side": Ibid. at 173.

196. Page 437, para. 2 – "a balance between the two groups": Ibid. at 184, 190, and 196; see also J.R. Graham, "Charles Eric Hendry (1903-1979): The pre-war formational origins of a leader of post-World War II Canadian social work education", *Canadian Social Work Review*, vol. 11 (1994) at 150-67.

197. Page 437, para. 2 – "higher-paid men with doctorates": Ibid. at 184-185. This was a long-standing tension: see J.R. Graham and A. Al-Krenawi, "Contested terrain: Two competing views of social work at the University of Toronto, 1914-1945", *Canadian Social Work Review* (forthcoming).

198. Page 437, para. 2 – "always seemed to fall short of its potential": Ibid. at 210.

199. Page 437, para. 3 – "The BSW degree was dropped in 1965": Bissell Diary, January 21, 1965.

200. Page 437, para. 3 – "the thesis requirement for the MSW in 1967": Graham, "A History" at 284-285.

201. Page 437, para. 3 – "had reached 35 by 1972": Ibid. at 221 and 295.

202. Page 437, para. 3 – "were particularly productive scholars": Ibid. at 217.

203. Page 437, para. 3 – "Ben Schlesinger's *One-Parent Family*": *"Over and Out": Final Report of the Harry M. Cassidy Memorial Research Fund* (March, 1969); Graham, "A History" at 217. Some faculty members helped found new schools of social work, such as Betty Govan, who started the school in Baghdad and then returned to U of T: see Graham, "A History" at 218.

204. Page 437, para. 3 – "and John Gandy as a lecturer": Ibid. at 267 and 308-309.

205. Page 437, para. 3 – "a tenure stream appointment at the University": Howard McCurdy, who joined Assumption University in Windsor in 1959, was the first Black appointed to a Canadian University: see Michiel Horn, "Academic Freedom in Canada: A History" (unpublished draft manuscript, March, 1998) at 444.

206. Page 437, para. 3 – "but both were one-year appointments": Horn, "Academic Freedom" at 444. See McFarlane's curriculum vitae, forwarded by Bruce McFarlane, from Carleton University. For Hill, see staff card in University of Toronto Archives.

207. Page 438, para. 1 – "when the school became a faculty": Graham, "A History" at 294.

208. Page 438, para. 1 – "his doctorate in the United States": Allan Irving, "Outline of Topics for Interview with Dr. Albert Rose", July, 1978, UTA/B78-0011.

209. Page 438, para. 1 – "and accomplished scholar": Allan Irving, "One Just Man – Albert Rose, 1917-1996" (speech delivered December 3, 1996) at 1.

210. Page 438, para. 1 – "from 35 in 1972 to only 22": Graham, "A History" at 295.

211. Page 438, para. 1 – "the fortunes of the school would turn": Ibid. at 295-296.

212. Page 438, para. 2 – "from the University's fundraising activity": "Faculty of Law", *University of Toronto Graduate* (December, 1967) at 62.

213. Page 438, para. 2 – "in the fall of 1962": "Law Comes to the Home Campus", *Varsity Graduate,* March 1963 at 71; Bissell Diary, June 15, 1962 and November 22, 1962.

214. Page 438, para. 2 – "by the financier E.R. Wood": John P.M. Court, "Out of the Woodwork: The Wood Family's Benefactions to Victoria College", *Canadian Methodist Historical Society Papers,* v. 2 (1997) at 17.

215. Page 438, para. 2 – "as you realize, is no small matter": Bissell to Phillips, June 1, 1959, UTA/A71-0011/24(12); see also Bissell to Phillips, September 21, 1959, UTA/A71-0011/33(03). See also Bissell to Phillips, May 5, 1959, UTA/A71-0011/24(12): "I am afraid that Dean Wright is not sympathetic to the idea of going into the Arts Building, and is beginning to think of the possibility of taking over Flavelle House, with his library being housed in Falconer Hall".

216. Page 438, para. 2 – "moot court building were constructed": "Faculty of Law".

217. Page 438, para. 3 – "a professional law school": C. Ian Kyer and Jerome E. Bickenbach, *The Fiercest Debate: Cecil A. Wright, the Benchers, and Legal Education in Ontario 1923-1957* (Toronto: The Osgoode Society, 1987) at 167-168.

218. Page 438, para. 3 – "also had a professional law school": E.A. Corbett, *Sidney Earle Smith* (University of Toronto Press, 1961) at 13; "Report of the Manitoba Law School 1935-1936", in *The University of Manitoba Annual Reports 1935-1936* (Winnipeg, May 1936) at 124-126.

219. Page 438, para. 3 – "of the North American continent": Kyer and Bickenbach, *Fiercest Debate* at 188-189, where the memo is attributed to the Spring of 1947, perhaps May 1. A copy of the memo is found in UTA/A86-0019/001 and attributed to a non-existent box in the Smith papers. The original correspondence in the Smith papers has not surfaced. Smith used similar language in a draft which he sent to Arthur Kelly June 25, 1946: see Smith to Kelly, June 28, 1946, reproduced also in UTA/A86-0019, also referenced to the Smith papers, and also currently beyond locating. In that draft the phrase is "the outstanding Law School in Canada and one of the leading Law Schools of the North American continent".

220. Page 439, para. 1 – "and then into a separate division": C.A. Wright, "Legal Education in Ontario", *Alumni Bulletin* (June, 1952) at 15-16.

221. Page 439, para. 1 – "was given a doctorate at the age of 22": Kyer and Bickenbach, *Fiercest Debate* at 37, 51, and 97.

222. Page 439, para. 1 – "felt the time was not right": Ibid. at 168.

223. Page 439, para. 2 – "on the Osgoode program": Ibid. at 201-204; Christopher Moore, *The Law Society of Upper Canada and Ontario's Lawyers 1797-1997* (University of Toronto Press, 1997) at 251-252.

224. Page 439, para. 2 – "a large measure of publicity": Kyer and Bickenbach, *Fiercest Debate* at 210-211.

225. Page 439, para. 2 – "They just accept it": Undated clipping from unidentified newspaper assumed to be *Globe and Mail* and assumed to be in February, 1949, UTA/A83-0019/001.

226. Page 439, para. 2 – "and three of his colleagues resigned": Kyer and Bickenbach, *Fiercest Debate* at 210.

227. Page 439, para. 2 – "to join the University of Toronto faculty": Ibid. at 221. The fourth person, Stanley Edwards, joined the Toronto law firm of Fraser and Beatty: see *Canadian Legal Directory*, 1951 at 192.

228. Page 439, para. 2 – "from the University to Osgoode in 1945": This was in part to make more dramatic a possible later move to the University by both Wright and Laskin: see Kyer and Bickenbach, *Fiercest Debate* at 164-166. The key meeting to convince Kennedy of the wisdom of the plan was held at Kennedy's cottage at Beaver Lake just west of Algonquin Park: ibid. at 166. This cottage is now owned by the author.

229. Page 439, para. 2 – "had been engineered by Smith and Wright": Ibid. at 215. Laskin later claimed that he had no idea that he would be hired by the University, but it is reasonably clear that Smith had such an understanding with Wright. "It was conceived and implemented by Smith and Wright, who were close friends": Bissell, *Parnassus* at 99. Smith, however, told the Law Society that it wasn't until February 28th "that I approached these men and instituted negotiations": see Smith to Mason, March 10, 1949, UTA/A86-0019/001.

230. Page 439, para. 2 – "on our staff Wright, Laskin and Willis": Smith to LeMesurier, February 1, 1949, UTA/A68-0007/16(02). This was in response to LeMesurier's protest to Mason regarding the situation which led to Wright's resignation, on the 20th of January, 1949. C.S. LeMesurier was the dean of law at McGill: see Kyer and Bickenbach, *Fiercest Debate* at 209.

231. Page 439, para. 3 – "Wolfgang Friedmann were added": Kyer and Bickenbach, *Fiercest Debate* at 236-237.

232. Page 439, para. 3 – "LLB program was instituted": Ibid. at 223.

233. Page 440, para. 1 – "almost equals in number its students": Bruce to Frost, Feb 13, 1952, UTA/A86-0019/001. There were only 12 students in first year in 1953: see Kyer and Bickenbach, *Fiercest Debate* at 325n11. The Law Society required graduates from the Toronto program to spend a full year articling and a final year both articling and taking classes.

234. Page 440, para. 1 – "is to all intents and purposes dead": Willis to Wright, November 29, 1951, UTA/A68-0007/89(10).

235. Page 440, para. 2 – "the board of governor's legal education committee": Borden to Carson, January 31, 1952, UTA/A83-0036/008.

236. Page 441, para. 1 – "Caesar's hatred of Osgoode": Phillips to Smith, March 7, 1952, UTA/A68-0007/114(07).

237. Page 441, para. 1 – "no positive response from the Law Society": Wright to Smith, February 28, 1952, UTA/A86-0019/001; see also Bruce Dunlop, "How Did We Make Out?" *Nexus*, v. 5 (1995) at 10.

238. Page 441, para. 1 – "the equivalent of slave labour": *Varsity*, February 28, 1952.

239. Page 441, para. 1 – "before Call to the Bar": C.F.H. Carson, "The Law School Controversy", February 9, 1953, UTA/A86-0019/001 at 4.

240. Page 441, para. 2 – "the Law Society changed its tune": Kyer and Bickenbach, *Fiercest Debate* at 248-253; see John Arnup, "The 1957 Breakthrough" (1982) 18 *Law Society Gazette* at 180-203.

241. Page 441, para. 2 – "to attend law school in Ontario": "Memorandum on discussion at a meeting of members of a Special Committee of Convocation and heads of Universities or their representatives", April 30, 1955, UTA/A86-0019/001; Kyer and Bickenbach, *Fiercest Debate* at 249.

242. Page 441, para. 2 – "from the existing 900 students": Kyer and Bickenbach, *Fiercest Debate* at 251-252.

243. Page 441, para. 2 – "all the potential students": Moore, *Law Society* at 257-258 and 262.

244. Page 441, para. 2 – "in the negotiations": Kyer and Bickenbach, *Fiercest Debate* at 257.

245. Page 441, para. 2 – "Park Jamieson and John Arnup": Ibid. at 259; Moore, *Law Society* at 258.

246. Page 441, para. 2 – "would help at this stage": Mackintosh to Smith, December 6, 1956, UTA/A86-0019/001; Kyer and Bickenbach, *Fiercest Debate* at 258.

247. Page 441, para. 2 – "incredulous but ecstatic": Arnup, "The 1957 Breakthrough" at 198.

248. Page 441, para. 2 – "who would therefore save a year": Kyer and Bickenbach, *Fiercest Debate* at 262-263; Moore, *Law Society* at 261.

249. Page 441, para. 2 – "rose to about 400": Kyer and Bickenbach, *Fiercest Debate* at 266. Numbers actually declined before the move back to the campus: see Bissell to Phillips, September 21, 1959, UTA/A71-0011/33(03).

250. Page 442, para. 1 – "for eighteen years": Donald W. Clarke and Claude T. Bissell, "Reginald Evans Haist", *Transactions of the Royal Society of Canada*, 5th Series, v. 3 (1988) at 153-55.

251. Page 442, para. 1 – "and a return as professor": Bissell Diary, January 30, 1967.

252. Page 442, para. 1 – "the architect of legal education in Ontario": Kyer and Bickenbach, *Fiercest Debate* at 270.

253. Page 442, para. 2 – "Wright's successor as dean": "Friedland, Martin Lawrence", *Canadian Who's Who 1991* at 349.

254. Page 442, para. 2 – "leading schools of the North American continent": See *Maclean's*, October 6, 1997, at 30-38; "Law School Ranked Tops", *University of Toronto Bulletin*, October 14, 1997.

CHAPTER 32 – 1960 – NEW COLLEGES

1. Page 443, para. 1 – "affiliated with the University of Toronto": Claude Bissell, *Halfway up Parnassus: A Personal Account of the University of Toronto 1932-1971* (University of Toronto Press, 1974) at 67.

2. Page 443, para. 1 – "its first class of about 75 students": Murray Ross, *The Way Must be Tried: Memoirs of a University Man* (Toronto: Stoddart, 1992) at 24-25; Bissell, *Parnassus* at 68; UTA/B88-0091, Claude Bissell Diaries, September 12, 1960.

3. Page 443, para. 1 – "by the president of the University of Toronto": Agreement between the Governors of the University of Toronto and York University, Final Draft, November 8, 1960, UTA/A71-0011/46(11) at 1-4. The committee was chaired by Caesar Wright and Murray Ross was a member: see Ross, *Way* at 7.

4. Page 443, para. 1 – "when it returned to the downtown campus": Ross, *Way* at 15.

5. Page 443, para. 2 – "in a number of earlier reports": See Chapter 30 (1955).

6. Page 443, para. 2 – "with the aircraft company A.V. Roe": Ross, *Way* at 7; Paul Axelrod, *Scholars and Dollars: Politics, Economics, and the Universities of Ontario 1945-1980* (University of Toronto Press, 1982) at 63. Bissell had talked to Curtis about a second university when Bissell was president of Carleton: Bissell, *Parnassus* at 67.

7. Page 443, para. 2 – "what direction the new university would take": Bissell, *Parnassus* at 67 et seq.; Bissell Diary, passim.

8. Page 443, para. 2 – "would manage its own financial affairs": Bissell to Phillips, November 7, 1958, UTA/A71-0011/24(12).

9. Page 443, para. 3 – "as well as an arts and science college": Ross, *Way* at 6-7.

10. Page 444, para. 1 – "the creation of York University": Bissell, *Parnassus* at 67; "Agreement" at 1.

11. Page 444, para. 1 – "as York's first president": Bissell Diary, June 16 and 17, 1959; Bissell, *Parnassus* at 67.

12. Page 444, para. 1 – "with a fellow Cape Bretoner": Bissell, *Parnassus* at 26.

13. Page 444, para. 1 – "the members of York's organizing group": Axelrod, *Scholars and Dollars* at 65.

14. Page 444, para. 2 – "such as the mining executive Robert Winters": Ross, *Way* at 9; Axelrod, *Scholars and Dollars* at 65-67.

15. Page 444, para. 2 – "to finance the new university": Bissell, *Parnassus* at 68; Ross, *Way* at 6.

16. Page 445, para. 1 – "Phillips said": Ross, *Way* at 16.

17. Page 445, para. 1 – "persuaded Winters to take the job": Ibid. at 16-17; Bissell, *Parnassus* at 68.

18. Page 445, para. 1 – "became chancellor of the new university": Ross, *Way* at 16.

19. Page 445, para. 1 – "the Canadian Institute for International Affairs": Ibid. at 22. See also Chapter 30 (1955).

20. Page 445, para. 1 – "the geographer George Tatham": Ross, *Way* at 22 and 79.

21. Page 445, para. 1 – "and the historian John Saywell": Ibid. at 27 and 82. Sociologist John Seeley was also hired during this period: see ibid. at 22.

22. Page 445, para. 2 – "the site of Glendon Hall's 86 acres": Murray Ross, "The 4th Year of the White Rose at York", *Varsity Graduate* (December, 1963) at 82.

23. Page 445, para. 2 – "say by 1970": Bissell to Phillips, March 8, 1961, UTA/A71-0011/44(08).

24. Page 445, para. 2 – "a new and larger campus": Bissell to Phillips, February 27, 1961 and March 8, 1961, UTA/A71-0011/44(08); Phillips to Frost, April 8, 1961, UTA/A88-0029/001.

25. Page 445, para. 2 – "to the use of the property": Bissell to Phillips, February 27, 1961.

26. Page 445, para. 2 – "to be used for academic purposes": Glendon was sold for one dollar: see Ross, *Way* at 15.

27. Page 445, para. 2 – "in the north-west section of Metropolitan Toronto": Bissell, *Parnassus* at 68; Ross, *Way* at 88-89.

28. Page 445, para. 2 – "there would be 15,000 students by 1980": Ross, "White Rose" at 84. York actually had an enrolment of 24,293 students in 1980, but only 10,823 were full time: see Ministry of Colleges and Universities, *Statistical Summary 1980-81* at 12. John Deutsch's report of 1962 had said that "York University's projected enrollment is unrealistically low": see Ross, *Way* at 49.

29. Page 445, para. 3 – "a kind of junior branch": Ross, *Way* at 67.

30. Page 445, para. 3 – "nervous about our advances": Bissell, *Parnassus* at 69.

31. Page 445, para. 3 – "and competitive with, the University of Toronto": Ross, *Way* at 68.

32. Page 445, para. 3 – "completely independent of the University of Toronto": Ross to Bissell, December 29, 1964, UTA/A75-0021/24.

33. Page 446, para. 1 – "could not meet the expected demand": See "Expansion at Victoria", "Trinity Plans", and "St. Michael's Changes", *Varsity Graduate* (June, 1959) at 69-71.

34. Page 446, para. 1 – "west campus along Spadina Avenue": See Chapter 20 (1955); Bissell, *Parnassus* at 58; Linda Nye Poulos, "An Examination of the Multi-Faculty Concept at the University of Toronto and Innis College 1956-1980" (unpublished report, May, 1980) at 10-11.

35. Page 446, para. 1 – "for faceless dormitories": Bissell, *Parnassus* at 59.

36. Page 446, para. 1 – "destroy the college as a community": Ibid. at 60; Bissell to Phillips, May 5, 1959, UTA/A71-0011/24(12).

37. Page 446, para. 1 – "be limited to about 2,000 students": Bissell, *Parnassus* at 60.

38. Page 446, para. 1 – "be built on the campus": Ibid. at 59-60.

39. Page 446, para. 2 – "appropriately called New College": "Staff, Students Join Workmen in New College", *Varsity News*, (December, 1964) at 12. The name originally selected had been "New King's College," but the board of governors thought that King's College in Nova Scotia would be "irritated" with such a name, in spite of the fact that King's College had also been the name of the first college at the University of Toronto. So they dropped the word King's and it became simply "New College": see Brook to Bissell, April 2, 1962, UTA/A71-001/61(12); Bissell to Wetmore, March 29, 1962, UTA/A71-001/61(12). Bissell noted that King's felt it "had a proprietary right to the name." D.G. Ivey notes that New College is "an appropriate name ... because the creation of the

College marked a new and major step in the evolution of the college system at the University of Toronto": see D.G. Ivey, "New College 1962-1974" at 1.

40. Page 446, para. 2 – "and Huron streets on the west campus": Bissell Diary, October 21, 1964. Some of the administrative staff moved in to the unfinished building almost immediately: see "Staff, Students Join Workmen in New College", *Varsity News*, (December, 1964) at 12.

41. Page 447, para. 1 – "serpentine design": "Ceremony of Laying the Corner Stone of New College", UTA/A75-0021/004. The building was designed by architects Rounthwaite and Fairfield, and the second building by Fairfield and Dubois: see Ivey, "New College" at 3 and 8.

42. Page 447, para. 1 – "with nearly 600 in residence": "New College", *University of Toronto Graduate* (December, 1967) at 55.

43. Page 447, para. 1 – "it admitted the first students in 1962": Ibid. at 56.

44. Page 447, para. 1 – "officially opened the building": Borden had taken over the chair from Phillips in March of 1964. Phillips stayed on the Board as Honorary Chairman until his death in December, 1964: see "Achievements Long Remembered", *Varsity Graduate*, February, 1965 at 21 and 29.

45. Page 447, para. 2 – "as the first principal": Bissell Diary, December 4, 1961. The diary entry of November 15, 1962 says the first council meeting was on that date.

46. Page 447, para. 2 – "took part in the official opening": Bissell Diary, January 20 and March 14, 1963; D.J. Le Roy, "Frank Ellsworth Waring Wetmore", *Proceedings of the Royal Society of Canada*, 4th Series, vol. 1 (1967) at 119-120.

47. Page 447, para. 2 – "from the professional faculties": "Staff, Students" at 13; "New College", *University of Toronto Graduate* (December, 1967) at 56.

48. Page 447, para. 2 – "to be planned, Innis College": Bissell to Borden, March 14, 1967, UTA/A75-0021/591; Ivey, "New College" at 3; Poulos, "Multi-Faculty Concept" at 27-29.

49. Page 447, para. 2 – "came from science backgrounds": Andrew Baines, who succeeded Ivey, was a professor in the department of clinical biochemistry of the Faculty of Medicine at the time of his appointment in 1974: see "A.D. Baines to succeed Dr. Ivey as Principal of New College", *University of Toronto Bulletin*, May 24, 1974. See also *Varsity*, November 11, 1974 and Faculty of Medicine calendar for 1973-74, UTA/P78-0854. W.S. Wilson, a former assistant dean in the Faculty of Engineering, was appointed the first registrar of the college: see Ivey, "New College" at 4.

50. Page 447, para. 3 – "did not take place until the fall of 1973": "Barbecue and Street dance follow sod turning at Innis College site", *University of Toronto Bulletin*, September 21, 1973.

51. Page 447, para. 3 – "into being on July 1, 1964": "Staff, Students" at 12.

52. Page 447, para. 3 – "for Innis rather than Falconer": Bissell to Borden of January 31, 1964, UTA/A71-0011/76; Bissell Diary, January 23, 1964.

53. Page 447, para. 3 – "beside the old observatory": "Staff, Students" at 12.

54. Page 447, para. 3 – "in the fall of 1964": *President's Report, 1964/65* at 52-53.

55. Page 447, para. 3 – "but neither New nor Innis wanted that": Ivey, "New College" at 7.

56. Page 447, para. 3 – "twice as much as the first phase": Bissell Diary, October 20, 1965 and December 15, 1966.

57. Page 447, para. 3 – "a New College residence for women": Bissell Diary, October 8, 1969. The building is called Wetmore Hall.

58. Page 447, para. 3 – "a large new complex for Innis": Bissell Diary, December 7, 1965 and June 23, 1966.

59. Page 447, para. 3 – "a $12 million structure for 1,500 students": Robin Harris, "The Making of a College", *University of Toronto Graduate* (December, 1967) at 105.

60. Page 447, para. 3 – "between the towers": Peter Russell memo on Innis College (July, 1998) at 8; Harris, "Making of a College" at 105.

61. Page 447, para. 4 – "on capital contributions to universities": Bissell Diary, July 8, 1968; Russell memo on Innis at 2.

62. Page 447, para. 4 – "plans be reduced": Bissell Diary, February 17, 1967.

63. Page 447, para. 4 – "has been forgotten": Harris to Bissell, January 31, 1966, UTA/A75-0021/28.

64. Page 447, para. 4 – "emergency meeting of the Innis council": Russell to Innis College Council, July 8, 1968, UTA/A77-0019/003.

65. Page 448, para. 1 – "the most critical moment in the College's history": Ibid.

66. Page 448, para. 1 – "had adequate support from the University": "Motion passed by the Innis College Council at an Emergency Meeting on Thursday, July 11, 1968", UTA/A77-0019/003; Russell memo on Innis at 3.

67. Page 448, para. 1 – "the top of the University's list of capital priorities": Harris to Bissell, May 7, 1970, UTA/A77-0019/24; Ernest Sirluck, *First Generation: An Autobiography* (University of Toronto Press, 1996) at 287.

68. Page 448, para. 1 – "becoming more difficult to obtain": Bissell informed Harris that "housing funds from Central Mortgage and Housing Corporation are now being channeled through the Department of University Affairs, and the allocation of these funds to the various universities in the province will be on the basis of a list of priorities established by the Committee on University Affairs": Bissell to Harris, April 30, 1970, UTA/A77-0019/24; Bissell Diary, May 20, 1969 and July 8, 1969.

69. Page 448, para. 1 – "now to be designed by Diamond and Myers": "Barbecue"; Russell memo on Innis at 5-6.

70. Page 448, para. 1 – "was severely reduced": Bissell Diary, July 8, 1969.

71. Page 448, para. 1 – "and would be limited to 750 students": Bissell saw two possible options, one a building at St George and Sussex and a second using both 63 and 65 St. George Street: see Bissell to Rankin, June 25, 1970, UTA/A77-0019/24.

72. Page 448, para. 2 – "5 of the 25-member Innis council were students": Harris, "Making of a College" at 110.

73. Page 449, para. 1 – "such as modern art and film": Aba Bayefsky, noted Canadian artist, was a member of the college council: see "Bayefsky, Aba", *Canadian Who's Who, 1961-63* at 62; Russell memo on Innis at 6 and 8.

74. Page 449, para. 1 – "would have been pleased": See Bissell, *Parnassus* at 63.

75. Page 449, para. 1 – "from Robin Harris as principal in 1970": Bissell Diary, January 8, 1971. Harris continued as a professor of higher education and became the University Historian, commissioned to write the history of the University, a task he never completed. Bissell's diary shows that he also had thoughts about writing the university's history. The entry of November 11, 1969 records a meeting with Harris, stating that he told Harris "about [his]

plans for writing the History of the U of T and suggested a joint appointment as historians." It is not known why the idea was abandoned, but the collaboration could have produced a fine book, covering more than Bissell's personal account of his time at the University: see Harris to Bissell, July 9, 1970, UTA/A77-0019/43; Bissell to Harris, October 27, 1970, ibid.; "Resignation of Dr. Robin Harris as principal of Innis College", *Bulletin*, October 29, 1970; see Manuscript Material, Documents and Research Notes Compiled by Robin S. Harris, UTA/A83-0036; Bissell Diary, November 11, 1969.

76. Page 449, para. 1 – "its strong commitment to film": Russell memo on Innis at 8.

77. Page 449, para. 1 – "on the east side of St George Street in 1994": The residence was officially opened on November 5, 1994 – Harold Innis' 100th birthday: see *Bulletin*, November 21, 1994.

78. Page 449, para. 1 – "and Frank Cunningham": "Innis: A community of 'thoughtful pragmatists'", *Bulletin*, November 5, 1984.

79. Page 449, para. 2 – "as had the Plateau Committee's Report in 1956": See Chapter 30 (1955).

80. Page 449, para. 2 – "be established by the University of Toronto": "'Post Secondary Education in Ontario 1962-1970' Report of the Presidents of the Universities, Revised January 1963, Excerpts" (Hare Binder, Office of the Principal, Scarborough College).

81. Page 449, para. 2 – "with the encouragement of the government": The detailed history of the proposal is set out in Borden to Stewart, April 1, 1968, UTA/A73-0025/105(03).

82. Page 449, para. 2 – "east of the main campus": D.C. Williams, "The Development of Scarborough & Erindale Colleges and their relationship to the Queen's Park campus", December 6, 1963, UTA/A72-0026/001 at 1. Additional land north of Ellesmere Road was later expropriated, leading to concerns by the provincial government: see Frost to Borden, May 18, 1965, UTA/A73-0025/105(02); Bissell Diary, April 8, 1965.

83. Page 449, para. 2 – "20 miles west of the campus": Williams, "Development" at 1. Bissell and Stone had consulted Bill Davis about the purchase: see Bissell Diary, March 11, 1963. Bissell, *Parnassus* at 65, says 20 miles for each; however figures vary: see "Off-Campus Colleges Give University a 30-mile span", *Varsity News*, (October, 1963) at 8-9. "Scarborough, Erindale, say the 70s belong to them", *University of Toronto Graduate* (March, 1969) at 21, says each is 21 miles from St. George.

84. Page 449, para. 2 – "St George campus": "A Provisional Plan for Two Off-Campus Colleges in the University of Toronto" (Off-Campus College Committee, 1963), UTA/A72-0026/001 at 5; *President's Report, 1964/65* at 56.

85. Page 449, para. 2 – "the director of extension at the University": Bissell to Williams, October 29, 1962 (Hare Binder).

86. Page 449, para. 2 – "that Scarborough be built first": "Provisional Plan" at 4; Williams, "Development" at 2 .

87. Page 449, para. 2 – "wanted quick action": Bissell Diary, June 30, 1963.

88. Page 449, para. 2 – "would gradually achieve greater autonomy": Williams, "Development" at 2.

89. Page 449, para. 3 – "for planning of the two suburban colleges": Bissell Diary, April 25, 1963.

90. Page 451, para. 1 – "planner Michael Hugo-Brunt": John L. Ball, *The First Twenty-Five Years* (Toronto: Scarborough College, 1989) at 3; "A College is People", *Varsity Graduate* (December, 1966) at 32. Tom Howarth, the head of architecture was annoyed that he wasn't consulted first: Bissell Diary, September 6, 1963.

91. Page 451, para. 1 – "were delighted with the design": Bissell, *Parnassus* at 55; Bissell Diary, September 9, 1963.

92. Page 451, para. 1 – "and U of T graduate William Davis": Borden to Stewart, April 1, 1968 at 7.

93. Page 451, para. 1 – "had been planned for human beings": Bissell Diary, May 25, 1965.

94. Page 451, para. 1 – "and space into a single experience": Oscar Newman, "The New Campus", *The Architectural Forum* (May, 1966) at 54; see also Ball, *The First Twenty-Five Years* at 6.

95. Page 451, para. 1 – "conspicuous waste": Bissell Diary, January 17, 1966.

96. Page 451, para. 2 – "for one of the new colleges": Donald MacGregor, "Arthur Fitzwalter Wynne Plumptre", *Canadian Journal of Economics* (November, 1978) at 714 and 717.

97. Page 452, para. 1 – "first was towards Erindale": Bissell Diary, December 1, 1964.

98. Page 452, para. 1 – "principal of Scarborough College": Bissell Diary, March 4, 1965.

99. Page 452, para. 1 – "exclusively undergraduate institution": Williams to Bissell, February 14, 1966, UTA/A75-0021/29.

100. Page 452, para. 1 – "accept such a change": Woodside to Bissell, March 1, 1966, UTA/A75-0021/29.

101. Page 452, para. 1 – "University of Toronto at Scarborough": "New Name for Scarborough", *Bulletin*, September 30, 1996.

102. Page 452, para. 1 – "University of Toronto at Mississauga": Report Number 304 of the Executive Committee, Governing Council, UTA. Council officially approved the name change on April 21, 1998.

103. Page 452, para. 1 – "village just south of the college": Careless to Bissell, June 10, 1963, UTA/A72-0026/001.

104. Page 452, para. 1 – "once inhabited the area": C.E.A. Robinson to Bissell, May 17, 1963, UTA/A72-0026/001.

105. Page 452, para. 1 – "for retired veterans of the British army": Guy Collingwood Clarkson, "The History of the Grounds Comprising the New West Campus of the University of Toronto at Erindale" (1963), University of Toronto at Mississauga Archives.

106. Page 452, para. 2 – "into the design of the college": Ball, *The First Twenty-Five Years* at 9; Wynne Plumptre, "Scarborough's Noble Experiment", *University of Toronto Graduate* (May, 1972) at 12.

107. Page 452, para. 2 – "was original in North America": Quoted in Plumptre, "Noble Experiment" at 12.

108. Page 452, para. 2 – "in his own teaching": Ball, *The First Twenty-Five Years* at 9. See also Beckel to Sword, May 27, 1968, UTA/A75-0021/92; Plumptre, "Noble Experiment" at 12.

109. Page 452, para. 2 – "using videotaped lectures": Ball, *The First Twenty-Five Years* at 9.

110. Page 452, para. 2 – "incorporated into the building": Bissell estimated the television cost at close to a million dollars: see Bissell to Hermant, June 9, 1966, UTA/A75-0021/29.

111. Page 452, para. 2 – "enough staff members to teach the courses": Williams to Bissell, June 4, 1964, UTA/A72-0026/001; Williams to Bissell, November 25, 1964, UTA/A75-0021/004; "Teachers in Short Supply? Students Make Up For Lack In TV-Equipped Classrooms", *Varsity News* (March, 1966) at 11; Plumptre, "Noble Experiment" at 13.

112. Page 452, para. 3 – "lack of interaction with the lecturers": Plumptre, "Noble Experiment" at 15.

113. Page 452, para. 3 – "standardized instruction": Ibid. at 14.

114. Page 452, para. 3 – "did not save money": "Report of the Presidential Advisory Committee on the Status and Future of Scarborough College" (1970-71) at 7.

115. Page 452, para. 3 – "5,000 students planned for": Williams, "Development" at 3; Plumptre, "Noble Experiment" at 14.

116. Page 452, para. 3 – "there were fewer than 2,000 in 1970": Plumptre reported that there were 1,832 students as of December 1, 1969: see *President's Report, 1969/70*, part 2 at 74; "Status and Future" at 13.

117. Page 452, para. 3 – "ultimately turned over to other uses": Plumptre to Bissell, May 5, 1970, UTA/A77-0019/25 at 3; Plumptre, "Noble Experiment" at 57.

118. Page 453, para. 1 – "and other rooms at Scarborough": Principal Paul Thompson to author, June, 1998.

119. Page 453, para. 2 – "experienced another problem": Ball, *The First Twenty-Five Years* at 17. As Scarborough College Council expressed it, "Without a vigorous life of its own, there is a clear and present danger that Scarborough College will quickly degenerate into an embarrassing burden for the University, a suburban Siberia for dull faculty and inferior students": see "Submission to the Commission on University Government from Scarborough College as Approved by the College Council, April 28, 1969" (Hare binder).

120. Page 454, para. 1 – "be the undergraduate teaching function": Plumptre to Bissell, May 5, 1970 at 3. Plumptre also sent an official letter requesting a review: see Plumptre to Bissell, May 28, 1970 (Hare Binder).

121. Page 454, para. 2 – "the University of Toronto Faculty Association": "Scarborough College is suggested as a third major university", *Bulletin*, December 2, 1970.

122. Page 454, para. 2 – "receiving and rewarding loyalty": Colman to Bissell, May 4, 1970, UTA/A77-0019/25.

123. Page 454, para. 3 – "geographer Kenneth Hare": "Status and Future" at iv says the full membership was 30, although originally it was higher – see "Presidential committee will review Scarborough College status and future", *Bulletin*, September 24, 1970.

124. Page 454, para. 3 – "Birkbeck College in the University of London": "Hare, Frederick Kenneth", *Canadian Who's Who, 1999* at 533.

125. Page 454, para. 3 – "make recommendations for its future": Bissell to members of the Presidential Advisory Committee on the Status and Future of Scarborough College, August 28, 1970 (Hare Binder).

126. Page 454, para. 3 – "recent history of the University": Bissell Diary, January 7, 1971. The final report refers to the "often heated" debates: see "Status and Future" at 18.

127. Page 454, para. 3 – "University of Southern Ontario": "2 professors want Scarborough 'University of Southern Ontario'", *Bulletin*, April 27, 1971; "Status and Future" at 54-58.

128. Page 454, para. 3 – "many would leave the college": R.C. Roeder, "Statement to the Presidential Advisory Committee on the Status and Future of Scarborough College" (Hare Binder).

129. Page 454, para. 4 – "greater autonomy for the college": "Status and Future" at 19 and 38-39; "Keep U of T connection but with more autonomy", *Bulletin*, April 27, 1971.

130. Page 454, para. 4 – "but a prospective course of action": "Status and Future" at 19.

131. Page 455, para. 1 – "the Hare compromise": Bissell Diary, April 28, 1971.

132. Page 455, para. 1 – "and for the satellites": Bissell Diary, April 29, 1971. Bissell had told the Scarborough College Council of May 27, 1970 that "it was to be hoped that Scarborough College would think in terms of improvement of its position within a liberalized federal structure rather than in terms of a dissolution of the federal relationship": see minutes of the meeting of May 27, 1970 (Hare Binder).

133. Page 455, para. 1 – "implementing the Hare report": In 1972 academic appointment procedures were passed implementing the Hare report: see J.H. Sword, "University of Toronto Scarborough College Academic Appointments Procedure" (1972) (Hare Binder).

134. Page 455, para. 1 – "president of the University of Manitoba": "D. Ralph Campbell Manitoba President", *Bulletin*, March 5, 1976.

135. Page 455, para. 1 – "first woman principal of a college": Chemist Bert Allen succeeded Ralph Campbell but within a few months became ill, and Joan Foley became the acting principal. Allen died in December 1976, and Foley was later confirmed as the principal: see e-mail from Joan Foley to Friedland, February 4, 2001; "First woman principal", *Bulletin*, February 6, 1978. The appointment was retroactive to July 1, 1976: see "Senior administrative appointments announced", ibid., March 18, 1977. Alexandra Johnston was principal of Victoria College from 1981 to 1991: see "Johnston, Alexandra Ferguson", *Canadian Who's Who, 1994* at 573.

136. Page 455, para. 2 – "had expected did not come about": Comments from Dan Lang to Friedland, February 2, 2001.

137. Page 455, para. 2 – "as a distinctive feature of Scarborough": E-mails from Joan Foley to Friedland, February 4 and 18, 2001.

138. Page 455, para. 3 – "to follow the same path": "Status and Future" at 47. Oddly, he signed the report: see the mix-up described at 47.

139. Page 455, para. 3 – "outweigh the disadvantages": Ibid. at 47-48.

140. Page 455, para. 3 – "the Faculty of Arts and Science of the University of Toronto": Wilson to Bissell, January 13, 1971, UTA/A77-0019/43.

141. Page 455, para. 3 – "the principal from 1976 to 1986": "Next Erindale Principal Named", *Bulletin*, December 19, 1975; John R. Percy, ed., *Erindale College: The First Twenty-Five Years* (December, 1992) at 46.

142. Page 455, para. 3 – "any significant discussion of the issue": Fox to Friedland, March 23, 1998 at 2.

143. Page 455, para. 4 – "that of their colleagues at Scarborough": Fox to Friedland at 3.

144. Page 455, para. 4 – "for the future of the college": E-mail from Joan Foley to Friedland, February 18, 2001.

145. Page 456, para. 1 – "an imaginative plan for Erindale": "Interim Report re: Erindale Campus Master Plan" (1966). Bissell went to Andrew's office to view the plans for "a freer version of Scarborough": see Bissell Diary, August 24, 1965; see also the diary entry of December 12, 1966.

146. Page 456, para. 1 – "but various delays": Williams to Bissell, April 11, 1966, UTA/A75-0021/28; Williams confidential memo to Bissell of April 11, 1966, UTA/A75-0021/60.

147. Page 456, para. 1 – "against the expropriation of additional properties": "Statement by Dr. Claude Bissell, President, University of Toronto, Re: Erindale College Site", June 10, 1965, UTA/A75-0021/004; "Statement on Erindale College Site by Dr. Claude Bissell, President, the University of Toronto", June 28, 1965, A75-0021/28; Bissell to Borden, June 30, 1965, UTA/A75-0021/30; Bissell to Borden, July 5, 1965, UTA/A75-0021/28; Robarts to Bissell, July 8, 1965, UTA/A75-0021/28.

148. Page 456, para. 1 – "and financial concerns": Bissell Diary, December 12, 1966.

149. Page 456, para. 1 – "put off its implementation": Tuzo Wilson later referred to the "unsuitability of architects original plans – too complicated": see "Interview with Dr. J. Tuzo Wilson, Monday, August 15, 1983" at 2.

150. Page 456, para. 2 – "the first class that entered in 1967": "Progress Report from Erindale College", no. 2 (1967); "Official opening of Erindale a beginning and a fruition", *Bulletin*, October 19, 1973; "Scarborough, Erindale say that 70s belong to them", *University of Toronto Graduate* (March, 1969) at 21. The building was a functional two-story structure built by Olympia and York: see D. Carlton Williams, "Erindale College opens in autumn", *Varsity News* (May, 1967) at 4.

151. Page 456, para. 2 – "once the campus was developed": Erindale away to good start", *Varsity News* (November, 1968) at 14; "Official opening".

152. Page 456, para. 2 – "at the University of Toronto in the 1990s": Fox to Friedland at 5. She is currently working at Mount Sinai Hospital.

153. Page 456, para. 2 – "was all about the people": Percy, *Erindale College* at 3.

154. Page 457, para. 1 – "designed by Raymond Moriyama": In association with A.D. Margison and Associates: see "70s belong to them" at 21 and 25.

155. Page 457, para. 1 – "was not officially opened until 1973": "Official opening". The north building, a five-minute pleasant walk in good weather from the south building, continues to be used for academic purposes, but apparently creating in the staff located there – mainly persons in the humanities – some of the same feelings of neglect that are at times felt by both Scarborough and Erindale: see Paul Fox to author, March 1998. E.A. Robinson maintained that there were "no visible signs of separation at Erindale unlike Scarborough": see "University of Toronto Oral History Project Interview with Professor E.A. Robinson, Erindale College", summary, UTA/B86-0081 at 1.

156. Page 457, para. 2 – "president of the Royal Society of Canada in 1972": Karina Dahlin, "John Tuzo Wilson", *University of Toronto Magazine* (Summer, 1993) at 9; George D. Garland, "John Tuzo Wilson", *Proceedings of the Royal Society of Canada*, 6th Series, v. 4 (1993) at 133-135.

157. Page 457, para. 2 – "as principal of Erindale": "Progress Report from Erindale College", no. 2, 1967.

158. Page 457, para. 2 – "came of his proposal at the time": Bissell Diary, March 11, 1964.

159. Page 457, para. 2 – "as president of the University of Western Ontario": Percy, *Erindale College* at 51.

160. Page 457, para. 2 – "a product of the University": "Interview with Dr. J. Tuzo Wilson".

161. Page 457, para. 3 – "was being constructed nearby": Williams to Bissell, June 10, 1963, UTA/A72-0026/001; "70s belong to them" at 25.

162. Page 457, para. 3 – "content to spend time on the campus": Fox to Friedland at 3-4.

163. Page 457, para. 3 – "was less so in the physical sciences": E-mail from Joan Foley to Friedland, February 18, 2001.

164. Page 457, para. 4 – "by analysing moon rocks at Erindale": "Thousands line up to see Erindale's Moon (or portion thereof)', *University of Toronto Graduate* (December, 1969) at 66; Percy, *Erindale College* at 24-25 and 48.

165. Page 457, para. 4 – "3,000 people lined up to see the samples": "Thousands line up" at 65.

166. Page 457, para. 4 – "Mitchell Winnick of chemistry": Percy, *Erindale College* at 15.

167. Page 457, para. 5 – "one of Principal Paul Fox's goals": Karina Dahlin, "Erindale", *University of Toronto Magazine* (Spring, 1989) at 17; Fox to Friedland at 2. Some university departments also took a strong interest in the new college. The then chair of political economy, Stephen Dupré, symbolically taught a course at Erindale. The department of history, however, according to Desmond Morton, who taught his first course in Canadian history at Erindale and later would become its principal, took a more imperialistic view of the new campus. "The chair, A.P. Thornton," wrote Morton, "was a renowned historian of the British Empire and Commonwealth, and perhaps he saw his Erindale colleagues as a tiny dominion, remote, self-governing but, in all things, dutiful": see Percy, *Erindale College* at 28 and 34.

168. Page 457, para. 5 – "to almost every public event": Fox to Friedland at 2.

169. Page 458, para. 1 – "apartments": "Interview with Dr. J. Tuzo Wilson".

170. Page 458, para. 1 – "nine years after the first students arrived": "Report of the Presidential Advisory Committee on Erindale College" (June, 1965), UTA/A75-0021/004.

171. Page 458, para. 2 – "Martin Moscovits, chair of chemistry": Ibid.

172. Page 458, para. 2 – "Betty Roots, chair of zoology": Fox to Friedland at 8.

173. Page 458, para. 2 – "in neurochemistry at Erindale": Ibid. at 9.

174. Page 458, para. 2 – "the first Canadian woman in space": Ibid. at 7. The second Toronto graduate in space would be Julie Payette, who received her MASc in electrical engineering in 1990: see Rivi Frankle, "A Very Special Lecture Invitation", December, 1999; *University of Toronto News and Events*, January 7, 2000.

175. Page 459, para. 1 – "in 2001 the president of Victoria University": For Gooch, see *University of Toronto Bulletin*, February 12, 2001.

176. Page 459, para. 2 – "some 4,000 full-time students": Scarborough had about 3,500 full-time students: see Jane Stirling, "Scarborough", *University of Toronto Magazine* (Spring, 1989) at 16. Erindale had 3,872 full-time students: see Dahlin, "Erindale", ibid. at 17.

CHAPTER 33 – 1962 – GRADUATE STUDIES: FROM MASSEY COLLEGE TO THE ROBARTS LIBRARY

1. Page 463, para. 1 – "cornerstone of Massey College was laid": "A Royal Day at Massey College", *Varsity Graduate* (December, 1962) at 61.

2. Page 463, para. 2 – "in May 1962": Ibid.

3. Page 463, para. 2 – "of special promise": Massey to Phillips, December 14, 1959, UTA/A71-0011/76.

4. Page 463, para. 2 – "nature of the institution": UTA/B88-0091/001(05), Claude Bissell Diaries, December 27, 1959 at 150; Claude Bissell, *Halfway up Parnassus: A Personal Account of the University of Toronto 1932-1971* (University of Toronto Press, 1974) at 61, referring to "selective"; Bissell to Phillips, December 18, 1959, UTA/A71-0011/33(03).

5. Page 463, para. 2 – "Irene Clarke": "Clarke, Irene Fortune Irwin", *Canadian Who's Who 1983* at 209; Bissell Diary, December 27, 1959 at 150. Clarke was the first woman on the Board of Governors.

6. Page 463, para. 2 – "restricted to men": Bissell, *Parnassus* at 62.

7. Page 463, para. 2 – "accepted quickly": The gift was accepted at the board meeting of December 17, 1959: see Bissell Diary, December 27, 1959 at 149.

8. Page 465, para. 1 – "pretty big horse": Phillips to Bissell, December 22, 1959, UTA/A71-0011/33(03).

9. Page 465, para. 1 – "they must be limited": Phillips to Bissell, January 20, 1960, UTA/A71-0011/33(03).

10. Page 465, para. 1 – "from the original estimate": Bissell Diary, March 22, 1961.

11. Page 465, para. 1 – "too independent": Bissell to Phillips, December 18, 1959.

12. Page 465, para. 1 – "senior fellows who would run the college": Bissell to Phillips, January 3, 1961, UTA/A71-0011/44(08); Bissell, *Parnassus* at 61.

13. Page 465, para. 1 – "University's board of governors": Bissell, *Parnassus* at 61.

14. Page 465, para. 2 – "determinedly traditionalist": Bissell to Phillips, January 15, 1960, UTA/A71-0011/33(03).

15. Page 465, para. 2 – "strikingly modern in design": Robertson Davies, "The Grand Design for Massey College", *Varsity Graduate* (May, 1961) at 17-18.

16. Page 465, para. 2 – "concerned with every detail": Bissell to Phillips, January 15, 1960, UTA/A71-0011/33(03).

17. Page 465, para. 2 – "the first master": Bissell Diary, February 23, 1961.

18. Page 465, para. 2 – "Massey and Bissell": Bissell to Phillips, January 3, 1961.

19. Page 465, para. 2 – "distinction to the post": Ibid.

20. Page 465, para. 3 – "John Polanyi": "A College is Born", *Varsity Graduate* (December, 1963) at 14-15.

21. Page 465, para. 3 – "meetings and dinners": Bissell Diary, September 16, 1961.

22. Page 466, para. 1 – "no action was taken": Bissell Diary, January 13 and June 23, 1966; Claude Bissell, *The Imperial Canadian: Vincent Massey in Office* (University of Toronto Press, 1966) at 308-309.

23. Page 466, para. 1 – "Massey died in 1967": Bissell, *Imperial Canadian* at 311-312.

24. Page 466, para. 1 – "while he was master": *Fifth Business* was published in 1970, *The Manticore* in 1972, and *World of Wonders* in 1975: see Judith Skelton Grant, *Robertson Davies: Man of Myth* (Toronto: Viking Penguin, 1994) at 479, 481, 485, 502, 506, and 511.

25. Page 466, para. 1 – "spring review": "Hume to succeed Davies as master of Massey College", *University of Toronto Bulletin*, June 9, 1980.

26. Page 466, para. 1 – "drama centre at the University": "Saddlemyer, (Eleanor) Ann", *Canadian Who's Who 1997* at 1084-1085.

27. Page 466, para. 1 – "journalist and author": "Fraser, John Anderson", *Canadian Who's Who 1997* at 417-418.

28. Page 466, para. 1 – "graduate students each year": Massey Registrar to Charles Levi, February 9, 2000.

29. Page 466, para. 1 – "women as of 1974": "MASSEY COLLEGE: a new decade with *women* junior fellows arriving soon", *University of Toronto Graduate* (April, 1974) at 2.

30. Page 467, para. 1 – "Southam Fellows": "Raising the Potential", *Varsity Graduate* (December, 1963) at 6. The fellowships were arranged through the president of Southam, St. Clair Balfour: see Bissell Diary, December 16, 1960.

31. Page 467, para. 2 – "crucial administrative problem": Ernest Sirluck, *First Generation: An Autobiography* (University of Toronto Press, 1996) at 211.

32. Page 467, para. 2 – "to do graduate work": Sirluck, *First Generation* at 66 and 70.

33. Page 467, para. 2 – "a theory on most": Bissell, *Parnassus* at 75.

34. Page 467, para. 2 – "English at University College": Sirluck, *First Generation* at 211.

35. Page 467, para. 2 – "reputation principally depends": Ibid.; Bissell, *Parnassus* at 77; Bissell to Sirluck, June 13, 1961, UTA/A71-0011/51(01).

36. Page 467, para. 2 – "international quality": Sirluck, *First Generation* at 214.

37. Page 467, para. 3 – "dean of the graduate school": *President's Report, 1964/65* at 17 and 103.

38. Page 467, para. 3 – "humanities and social sciences": Sirluck, *First Generation* at 214.

39. Page 467, para. 3 – "election to membership": Ibid. at 233.

40. Page 468, para. 1 – "demand for university teachers": Ibid. at 211-212; see Chapter 31 (1958).

41. Page 468, para. 1 – "postgraduate work in Ontario": Sirluck, *First Generation* at 221-22; Bissell to Sirluck, June 14, 1962, UTA/A88-0050/10; Davis to Bissell, February 15, 1963, UTA/A71-0011/60(16).

42. Page 468, para. 1 – "humanities and social sciences": Sirluck, *First Generation* at 222.

43. Page 468, para. 1 – "to 1,645": Ibid. at 235.

44. Page 468, para. 1 – "over 2,000": *President's Report, 1965/66,* Part 2 at 46. The figures were 1,967 in 1964/65, 2,459 in 1965/66, and 2,925 in 1966/67.

45. Page 468, para. 1 – "Commonwealth": E.A. Corbett, *Sidney Earle Smith* (University of Toronto Press, 1961) at 65-66; Bissell Diary, June 10, 1959.

46. Page 468, para. 1 – "scholarship programs": "Fellowship Winners Choose Toronto", *Varsity Graduate* (December, 1961) at 15-16.

47. Page 468, para. 1 – "to study at Toronto": Ibid.; Bissell Diary, March 9, 1962.

48. Page 468, para. 2 – "about 60 students": Massey Registrar to Charles Levi, February 9, 2000.

49. Page 468, para. 2 – "was purchased, however,": Sirluck, *First Generation* at 263.

50. Page 468, para. 2 – "married students": Bissell Diary, August 21, 1968.

51. Page 468, para. 2 – "old observatory": Sirluck, *First Generation* at 221.

52. Page 468, para. 2 – "Oliver Mowat": Sirluck, *First Generation* at 235; www.waynecook.com/atoronto.html. Physical and Occupational Therapy, which had occupied temporary huts on the Massey site, were not as fortunate. They moved to the old 'Skulehouse', which was later torn down, and then to inelegant quarters on McCaul Street. As this is being written, however, they are about to move to a fine building at 500 University Avenue.

53. Page 468, para. 3 – "professional schools": Sirluck, *First Generation* at 246-247.

54. Page 469, para. 1 – "undergraduate department": Ibid. at 247.

55. Page 469, para. 1 – "professional faculties": Ibid.

56. Page 469, para. 1 – "School of Graduate Studies": Bissell to Woodside, September 19, 1963, UTA/A72-0026/001.

57. Page 469, para. 2 – "Laskin as its chair": Bissell, *Parnassus* at 80; Sirluck, *First Generation* at 249; Bissell to Laskin, October 30, 1963, UTA/A72-0026/001.

58. Page 469, para. 2 – "almost two years": Bissell, *Parnassus* at 80; Sirluck, *First Generation* at 249.

59. Page 469, para. 2 – "intellectual horizons": *Graduate Studies in the University of Toronto, Report of the President's Committee on the School of Graduate Studies 1964-1965* at 16; Bissell, *Parnassus* at 81.

60. Page 469, para. 2 – "unanimous report": *Graduate Studies* at vii.

61. Page 469, para. 2 – "written mainly by Laskin – stated": *Graduate Studies* at vii; Sirluck, *First Generation* at 249-50.

62. Page 469, para. 2 – "a centralist version": Sirluck, *First Generation* at 250-251.

63. Page 469, para. 2 – "selection of senior academics": Ibid. at 251.

64. Page 469, para. 2 – "blind centralism": *R.* v. *Wetmore Close,* [1983] 2 S.C.R. 284. The exact quotation from Dickson in his dissent is, "Blind centralism can be no answer".

65. Page 470, para. 1 – "did not take place": Frances Ireland oral interview Finding Aid, UTA/B86-0052 at 14.

66. Page 470, para. 1 – "Ontario Court of Appeal": "Laskin, Rt. Hon. Bora", *Canadian Who's Who 1983* at 642.

67. Page 470, para. 1 – "defence of the report": Sirluck, *First Generation* at 252; Bissell Diary, January 4, 1966.

68. Page 470, para. 1 – "report was approved": "Report of the Committee Appointed to Determine Whether a Restructuring of the Council of the School of Graduate Studies Along the Lines Suggested in the Laskin Report is Feasible and Desirable", UTA/A75-0021/010; Bissell Diary, May 27, 1966.

69. Page 470, para. 1 – "council was instituted": Sirluck, *First Generation* at 252-253.

70. Page 470, para. 2 – "establishing graduate programs": Ibid. at 238.

71. Page 470, para. 2 – "formula financing system": See Chapter 31 (1958).

72. Page 470, para. 2 – "numerous graduate programs": Sirluck, *First Generation* at 239 and 241.

73. Page 470, para. 2 – "study graduate programs": Paul Axelrod, *Scholars and Dollars: Politics, Economics and the Universities of Ontario 1945-1980* (University of Toronto Press, 1982) at 96; John B. Macdonald, *Chances and Choices: A Memoir* (Vancouver: UBC and UBC Alumni Association, 2000) at 161 et seq.

74. Page 471, para. 1 – "that of graduate studies": Quoted in Sirluck, *First Generation* at 238.

75. Page 471, para. 1 – "new programs be established": *Report to the Committee on University Affairs and the Committee of Presidents of Provincially-Assisted Universities of the Commission to Study the Development of Graduate Programmes in Ontario Universities* (Toronto, 1966) at 81; Axelrod, *Scholars and Dollars* at 98; Sirluck, *First Generation* at 241; Bissell, *Parnassus* at 85. The commission also included geographer Kenneth Hare and the former University of California graduate school dean Gustave Arlt. See Robert H. Blackburn, *Evolution of the Heart: A History of the University of Toronto Library up to 1981* (Toronto: University of Toronto Library, 1989) at 201.

76. Page 471, para. 1 – "University of California": Sirluck, *First Generation* at 240. The report also brought about the Advisory Committee on Academic Planning: see Sirluck, *First Generation* at 241 and Sirluck's letter to the author, February 17, 2000.

77. Page 471, para. 1 – "early 1967": Sirluck, *First Generation* at 241-266 and 268.

78. Page 471, para. 2 – "OISE": In 1966/67, OISE enrolled 675 graduate students, 17% of the total graduate enrollment. By 1969/70 OISE had 1,334 students, 21% of the total graduate enrollment. In both years, English was the next largest programme, with 341 students in 1966-7 and 427 in 1969/70: see *President's Report, 1966/67* at 442 and 459; *President's Report, 1969/70* at 76, 78, and 80. Out of a total of 10,000 graduate students at the University, OISE's projected enrollment for 1999/2000 was 1,360 students: see "Fast Facts About OISE/UT, www.oise.utoronto.ca/dean/positions/fastfacts.html.

79. Page 471, para. 2 – "degree-granting powers": *An Act to Establish the Ontario Institute for Studies in Education* (1965), sections 3(b) and 4. Section 3(b) of the act clearly lists as an objective of the Institute "to establish and conduct courses leading to certificates of standing and graduate degrees in education". Further, section 1(a) of the Draft Agreement between the Board of Governors and the Board of OISE states, "The Board [of OISE] will not, during the currency of this agreement, exercise its power of conferring graduate degrees in education": see *Draft agreement between the Board of Governors of the University of Toronto and the Board of Governors of the Ontario Institute for Studies in Education,* June, 1966, UTA/A75-0021/54. Michael Skolnik states in an e-mail to the author dated January 10, 2001, that it was believed at the time that the act gave OISE degree-granting powers and, indeed, they did grant an honorary degree to Bora Laskin, but the ministry took the position in the early 1980s that the Act was not wide enough to permit the granting of degrees. Skolnik states: "possibly if OISE had the power, events might have turned out differently, though perhaps not." Don Guthrie, the university's solicitor,

states that "The board was not given the power to grant degrees." and his remarks are concurred in by Dan Lang: see comments from Don Guthrie to Friedland, January, 2001, and comments from Dan Lang to Friedland, February 2, 2001.

80. Page 471, para. 2 – "promoted by Robin Harris": Jack Sword to author, October 12, 1998; Bissell Diary, November 2, 1962.

81. Page 471, para. 2 – "Alberta or the United States": E-mail from Michael Skolnik to the author, January 10, 2001.

82. Page 471, para. 3 – "OCE": Bissell noted in 1962 that the University would now enjoy more control over OCE: see Bissell Diary of Jan 23, 1962; see also Diary of December 4, 1964; and Chapter 21 (1909) describing OCE; "Copy of an Order-in-Council approved by His Honour the Lieutenant Governor, dated the 11th day of August, A.D. 1966", UTA/A75-0021/63; Dadson to Bissell, October 25, 1965 and February 4, 1966, UTA/A75-0021/32.

83. Page 471, para. 3 – "within the college": Dadson to Davis, January 18, 1965, UTA/A75-0021/54.

84. Page 471, para. 3 – "separate from OCE": Sirluck to Bissell, February 5, 1965, UTA/A75-0021/54; see also memo from Woodside to Bissell, October 7, 1964 and Fleming to Bissell, November 9, 1964, UTA/A75-0021/07.

85. Page 471, para. 3 – "the present institutional bases": Sirluck to Bissell, February 5, 1965.

86. Page 471, para. 3 – "membership in a university": Sirluck to Bissell, February 5, 1965; Bissell to Davis, May 13, 1965, UTA/A75-0021/34.

87. Page 471, para. 3 – "on almost any terms": Sirluck to Bissell, February 5, 1965.

88. Page 472, para. 1 – "with Toronto in 1966": "Tentative Agreement Reached on March 16, 1965 Between the Hon. W.G. Davis, Minister of Education and Minister of University Affairs and Dr. C.T. Bissell, President of the University of Toronto [and others]", UTA/A75-0021/54; *Draft agreement between the Board of Governors of the University of Toronto and the Board of Governors of the Ontario Institute for Studies in Education*, June, 1966, UTA/A75-0021/54; Sword to Bissell, June 10, 1966, UTA/A75-0021/54.

89. Page 472, para. 1 – "approved by the graduate school": Sword to Bissell, June 10, 1966; Sirluck, *First Generation* at 255.

90. Page 472, para. 1 – "following the Laskin report": Sirluck, *First Generation* at 251. This did not just apply to Ph.D.s, but also to the M.Ed. and Ed.D. degree. The Ed.D. degree had replaced the D.Paed. in 1952, and the M.Ed. was established the same year. Like the D.Paed., these degrees required a thesis: see UTA/A84-0028/011; *Graduate Studies* at 44.

91. Page 472, para. 1 – "award its own degrees": Draft affiliation agreement, 1966, section 1(a), which states: "The Board will not, during the currency of this agreement, exercise its power of conferring graduate degrees in education."

92. Page 472, para. 1 – "OISE's academic programs": Sirluck, *First Generation* at 255; Sword to Bissell, June 10, 1966.

93. Page 472, para. 1 – "on the OISE board": Sword to Bissell, June 10, 1966.

94. Page 472, para. 1 – "director of the institute": "Press Release Regarding the Ontario Institute for Studies in Education" (undated), UTA/A75-0021/54; "Jackson, Robert William Brierley", *Canadian Who's Who 1973-1975* at 507; Ireland finding aid at 9; Sirluck, *First Generation* at 255.

95. Page 472, para. 1 – "department of educational theory": Sirluck, *First Generation* at 255; "Flower, George Edward", *Canadian Who's Who 1983* at 372.

96. Page 472, para. 1 – "chair of the board": Sirluck, *First Generation* at 255-256.

97. Page 473, para. 1 – "north side of Bloor Street": W.G. Fleming, *Supporting institutions and services* (University of Toronto Press, 1971) at 227; plaque, OISE building and telephone conversation with OISE operator, February 8, 2000.

98. Page 473, para. 1 – "specifically for OISE": "Thirty Years", *OISE News* (October, 1995) at 2.

99. Page 473, para. 1 – "non-academic staff members": Fleming, *Supporting institutions* at 237.

100. Page 473, para. 1 – "known and well respected": "Thirty Years" at 7 and 16.

101. Page 473, para. 1 – "to the laughable": Sirluck, *First Generation* at 256.

102. Page 474, para. 1 – "control over their activities": E-mail from Michael Skolnik to author, July 14, 1998 at 3.

103. Page 474, para. 1 – "Scarborough College scenario": See Chapter 32 (1960).

104. Page 474, para. 1 – "series of reports": These were the Meincke task force, see *University of Toronto Bulletin*, January 12, 1973; the Mettrick committee, see *Bulletin*, June 11, 1979, and January 21, 1980; the Marsden-Skolnik committee, see report, October, 1983, printed in *Bulletin*; and other initiatives referred to in *Bulletin*, January 12, 1987, and November 7, 1988.

105. Page 474, para. 1 – "was unsuccessful": "SGS Council endorses Mettrick report", *Bulletin*, February 25, 1980. See also Chapter 39 (1980).

106. Page 474, para. 2 – "were joined together": The OCE became a faculty in 1972. See Sam Robinson, "Education at the University of Toronto" (Memorandum, July 6, 1998). For the merger, see *Bulletin*, August 22 and November 21, 1994, and July 22, 1996; and generally, J. Eastman and D. Lang, *Mergers in Higher Education: Lessons from Theory and Experience* (University of Toronto Press, forthcoming). Dan Lang points out that OCE was actually in existence until 1972. The government owned the building and the faculty were employees of OCE and were in the provincial pension plan for teachers. Until 1972, it was not part of U of T: see comments from Dan Lang to Friedland, February 2, 2001.

107. Page 474, para. 2 – "close to retirement": Skolnik e-mail at 4. See also Chapter 39 (1980).

108. Page 474, para. 2 – "head of both institutions": "Daniels, Fullan Appointed Deans", *Bulletin*, July 24, 1995.

109. Page 474, para. 2 – "dean of education": "Dean of FEUT appointed", *Bulletin*, June 29, 1987; "Fullan, Michael G.", *Canadian Who's Who 1997*. Fullan was a professor from 1968 to 1980 and an administrator thereafter.

110. Page 474, para. 2 – "too conspicuous": Skolnik e-mail at 5.

111. Page 474, para. 2 – "Angela Hildyard": Hildyard later became the principal of Woodsworth College and in 2001 became vice-president of human resources in the University.

112. Page 474, para. 2 – "rise to new heights": Or, as Michael Levin puts it, "OISE/UT will continue to... be as stimulating and creative as OISE has been over the past three decades": Both quotes in "Thirty Years" at 5.

113. Page 474, para. 3 – "increase in the number of graduate students": "The Ghost at the Feast", *Varsity Graduate* (March, 1963) at 14-15; Sirluck, *First Generation* at 223; Blackburn, *Evolution of the Heart* at 192.

114. Page 475, para. 1 – "his annual reports": *President's Report, 1965/66* at 9; Blackburn, *Evolution of the Heart* at 185.

115. Page 475, para. 1 – "extensive improvements": Blackburn, *Evolution of the Heart* at 176-77.

116. Page 475, para. 1 – "libraries in North America": Ibid. at 176.

117. Page 475, para. 1 – "Varsity Fund": Blackburn, *Evolution of the Heart* at 192-195; "The Ghost at the Feast", at 13, 15, and 23. The Varsity Fund was started in 1961: ibid. at 23.

118. Page 475, para. 1 – "the next million books": "The Ghost at the Feast" at 15 and 23.

119. Page 475, para. 2 – "two million books": Blackburn, *Evolution of the Heart* at 195.

120. Page 475, para. 2 – "other university library in Canada": "The Ghost at the Feast" at 26.

121. Page 475, para. 2 – "Pratt library in 1961": Blackburn, *Evolution of the Heart* at 189; "The Ghost at the Feast" at 36.

122. Page 475, para. 2 – "Laidlaw library a few years later": Ibid.

123. Page 475, para. 2 – "Larkin academic building was opened": "The Ghost at the Feast" at 38.

124. Page 475, para. 2 – "in Carr Hall": Ibid. at 39.

125. Page 475, para. 2 – "president of St. Michael's": Blackburn, *Evolution of the Heart* at 189. Kelly was President of St. Michael's College from 1958-1978: see *Canadian Who's Who 1980* at 511.

126. Page 475, para. 2 – "in library holdings": *Graduate Studies* at 107; Blackburn, *Evolution of the Heart* at 200.

127. Page 475, para. 3 – "university library facilities": Blackburn, *Evolution of the Heart* at 206; Bissell, *Parnassus* at 87.

128. Page 475, para. 3 – "old engineering building": Blackburn, *Evolution of the Heart* at 205; Bissell, *Parnassus* at 86.

129. Page 475, para. 3 – "rather than adopt a twenty-five-year horizon": Sirluck, *First Generation* at 223; Bissell, *Parnassus* at 86; Blackburn, *Evolution of the Heart* at 205.

130. Page 475, para. 3 – "site of the old library": Bissell Diary, January 11, 1963.

131. Page 475, para. 3 – "Hoskin Avenue": Bissell Diary, March 23, 1962, and January 11, 1963.

132. Page 475, para. 3 – "situating the library too far away": Blackburn, *Evolution of the Heart* at 179.

133. Page 475, para. 4 – "a major library": Bissell, *Parnassus* at 87; Bissell Diary, January 11, 1963, and January 17, 1963; Bissell to McCarthy, February 1, 1963, UTA/A71-0011/67.

134. Page 475, para. 4 – "province was sympathetic": Bissell Diary, April 25, 1963.

135. Page 476, para. 1 – "land north of Harbord was put in place": Bissell to Phillips, March 14, 1963, and Bissell to Frost, March 13, 1963, UTA/A71-0011/67; see Bissell Diary, December 10, 1964, referring to the expropriation of fraternity houses along St. George Street.

136. Page 476, para. 1 – "National Library in Ottawa": Bissell, *Parnassus* at 87.

137. Page 476, para. 1 – "major assignment on his own": Bissell to Henry Borden, February 25, 1965, UTA/A75-0021/20; Bissell Diary, February 24, 65; Blackburn, *Evolution of the Heart* at 206.

138. Page 476, para. 1 – "the other at Brown": Bissell Diary, May 6, 1965; Bissell, *Parnassus* at 87; Blackburn, *Evolution of the Heart* at 210. The firm was Warner, Burns, Toan and Lunde.

139. Page 476, para. 2 – "each of the private carrels": Blackburn, *Evolution of the Heart* at 211; Bissell Diary, November 19 and 29, 1965.

140. Page 476, para. 2 – "the triangular form": Bissell Diary, March 10, 1966.

141. Page 476, para. 2 – "Ontario College of Education": Bissell Diary, December 4, 1964; Bertha, Bassam, "The University of Toronto Faculty of Library Science and its Predecessors, 1911-1972", UTA/A83-0036/009 at 112; Pamela Cornell, "Collecting Yesterday", *The Graduate* (March/April 1983) at 17-19.

142. Page 476, para. 2 – "director of the school": "Land, Reginald Brian", *Canadian Who's Who 1983* at 632; Blackburn, *Evolution of the Heart* at 199; Bissell Diary, November 11, 1963, and January 17, 1964; *University of Toronto Graduate* (April, 1970) at 63.

143. Page 476, para. 2 – "400 students": Bissell, *Parnassus* at 88.

144. Page 476, para. 2 – "$40 million": Bissell to Blackburn, June 12, 1963, UTA/A71-0011/68; Bissell to Sirluck, July 13, 1966, UTA/A75-0021/62; Bissell Diary, May 4, 1966. At another intermediary stage, costs were estimated at $16 million: see Bissell, *Parnassus* at 87-88.

145. Page 476, para. 2 – "need for the library": Bissell Diary, March 31, 1966.

146. Page 476, para. 2 – "Canada Council account": Blackburn, *Evolution of the Heart* at 196; Bissell, *Parnassus* at 87.

147. Page 476, para. 3 – "library was almost lost": Blackburn, *Evolution of the Heart* at 201-02.

148. Page 476, para. 3 – "heart of the University": *Report to the Committee on University Affairs* at 54; Bissell, *Parnassus* at 85.

149. Page 476, para. 3 – "system be established": Blackburn, *Evolution of the Heart* at 202; see *Report to the Committee on University Affairs* at 70.

150. Page 476, para. 3 – "was left out": Ibid. The word 'system' was left out of recommendation 11 but not recommendation 16.

151. Page 476, para. 3 – "'Provincial University Library' was proposed": Ibid.

152. Page 476, para. 4 – "on neutral territory": Bissell to Sirluck, July 13, 1966; Bissell Diary, September 29, 1966, and November 14, 1966.

153. Page 476, para. 4 – "Spinks Commission had in mind": Bissell, *Parnassus* at 88.

154. Page 476, para. 4 – "Ontario Science Centre instead": Blackburn, *Evolution of the Heart* at 213-214; Bissell, *Parnassus* at 90-91; "University names its new library for the Hon. John P. Robarts", *University of Toronto Bulletin*, June 29, 1971.

155. Page 477, para. 1 – "serve provincial needs": Bissell, *Parnassus* at 89; Bissell to Sirluck, July 13, 1966 at 2.

156. Page 477, para. 1 – "happy to oblige": Bissell to Sirluck, July 13, 1966 at 2.

157. Page 477, para. 1 – "more floors were added to the plans": Blackburn, *Evolution of the Heart* at 214.

158. Page 477, para. 1 – "two underground floors": Ibid. at 324.

159. Page 477, para. 1 – "improve the hell out of it": Ibid. at 214.

160. Page 477, para. 2 – "further controversy would be avoided": Ibid. at 221. For informal sod-turning and corner-stone-laying ceremonies, see UTA/A95-0021.

161. Page 477, para. 2 – "Fort Book": Common knowledge.

162. Page 477, para. 2 – "access to the library stacks": See Chapter 36 (1967).

163. Page 477, para. 2 – "$40 million": Blackburn, *Evolution of the Heart* at 215, 223-224, and 324.

164. Page 477, para. 2 – "in the world": Ibid. at 225.

165. Page 478, para. 1 – "to goal post": Ibid. at 216; www.stadiumturf.com/canadian_football_field.htm. The dimensions of both Robarts and the football field are 100.61 metres.

166. Page 478, para. 1 – "at any one time": Blackburn, *Evolution of the Heart* at 325.

167. Page 478, para. 1 – "a faculty the following year": "A Handsome home for Library Science", *University of Toronto Graduate* (May, 1972) at 25.

168. Page 478, para. 1 – "largest in North America": "A home for Library Science", *University of Toronto Graduate* (April, 1970) at 61.

169. Page 478, para. 1 – "library science program": Bissell Diary, April 7, 1971; Bassam, "The University of Toronto Faculty of Library Science" at 152, 159, and 171.

170. Page 478, para. 2 – "British writers": Bissell, *Parnassus* at 91; Davies to Bissell, February 12, 1964, UTA/A71-0011/76.

171. Page 478, para. 2 – "balance to the structure": Blackburn, *Evolution of the Heart* at 220. In a letter to the author dated February 17, 2000, Sirluck states that the original plan called for the tower to have bells.

172. Page 478, para. 2 – "needed for its construction": Ibid.

173. Page 478, para. 2 – "St. George Street": E-mail from Richard Landon to the author, January 30, 2001.

174. Page 478, para. 3 – "John Robarts": Ibid. at 224; "University names its new library for the Hon. John P. Robarts", *Bulletin*, June 29, 71.

175. Page 478, para. 3 – "getting rid of the board of governors": See Chapter 36 (1967).

176. Page 478, para. 3 – "not have been built without it": Bissell, *Parnassus* at 91.

177. Page 478, para. 4 – "in North America": See e-mail from Carol Moore to the author of May 25, 2001, stating: "We just received the 1999-2000 rankings and we have moved up to #3 for that year". The ranking is based on five factors – volumes in library, volumes added yearly, current serials, permanent staff, and total expenditures: see *Chronicle of Higher Education*, September 17, 1999, and *Chronicle of Higher Education*, May 19, 2000. Blackburn, *Evolution of the Heart* at 326-327, gives the growth of holdings from 1849-1981.

178. Page 478, para. 4 – "taken for granted": Bissell, *Parnassus* at 91. The building has received negative reviews from architectural critics. See *Toronto Life*, November 1998 at 19, and John Bentley Mays, *Emerald City: Toronto visited.* Robert Fulford, one of the buildings early critics, admitted in a column of his on October 8, 1997, that he "fell in love, late in life, with the Robarts Library": see Fulford e-mail to Friedland, October 3, 1998.

CHAPTER 34 – 1963 – MULTIDISCIPLINARY ENDEAVOURS

1. Page 481, para. 1 – "programmes of research": *President's Report, 1961/62* at 2.

2. Page 481, para. 2 – "its first director": Ernest Sirluck, *First Generation: An Autobiography* (University of Toronto Press, 1996) at 227.

3. Page 481, para. 2 – "of his generation": J.M. Robson, "Bertie Wilkinson", *Proceedings of the Royal Society of Canada*, 4th Series, v. 20 (1982) at 153. Jack Robson was the son-in-law of Wilkinson.

4. Page 481, para. – 2 "Walter Goffart": Wilkinson to Kelly, January 2, 1963, and "Outline Proposal for the Establishment at the University of Toronto of a Graduate Centre for Mediaeval Studies", University of Saint Michael's College Archives, "President 1958 Letters O-R" at 8.

5. Page 481, para. 2 – "Natalie Zemon Davis in history": Natalie Davis was first appointed a part-time lecturer in History in July, 1963: see UTA/A73-0005/106. Note, however, that in her autobiographical speech, she says, "Then, with Chan's prison term behind him, a real break-through: he was offered a professorship at the University of Toronto and we moved in 1962 to Canada. Eventually I, too, obtained a post at the University of Toronto, first in the Department of Political Economy and in 1968 in the Department of History": see Natalie Zemon Davis, *A Life of Learning: Charles Homer Haskins Lecture for 1997* (American Council of Learned Societies Occasional Paper no. 39, 1997) at 12. See also Robert Bothwell, *Laying the Foundation: A Century of History at University of Toronto* (Toronto: Department of History, 1991) at 166.

6. Page 481, para. 2 – "Wilkinson as director in 1966": "Outline Proposal" at 9-10; "A Tough league", *Varsity Graduate* (June, 1966) at 47; Sirluck to Bissell, January 13, 1966, UTA/A75-0021/32.

7. Page 481, para. 2 – "Leonard Boyle": Wilkinson to Kelly, January 2, 1963, and "Outline-Proposal".

8. Page 481, para. 2 – "Vatican library": "Boyle, Leonard Eugene", *Canadian Who's Who 1994* at 131.

9. Page 481, para. 2 – "St. Michael's College": James Kelsey McConica c.v., UTA/A85-0009/15; "McConica, James K.", *Canadian Who's Who 1994* at 755.

10. Page 481, para. 2 – "more than 150 courses": "Outline-Proposal" at 3.

11. Page 481, para. 2 – "medieval studies in North America": Sirluck, *First Generation* at 228.

12. Page 481, para. 2 – "remains so to this day": Roberta Frank to author, February 7, 2000.

13. Page 481, para. 3 – "advocate for such a centre": Letter to Sirluck from 21 professors in the University, December 12, 1962, UTA/A85-0009/27.

14. Page 481, para. 3 – "*Canadian Journal of Linguistics*": E-mail from John Wevers to author, January 31, 2000; "Wevers, John William", *Canadian Who's Who 1994* at 1197; Wevers to author, January 27, 2000; Puhvel to Sirluck, April 26, 1966, UTA/A75-0021/32, refers to Wevers as the editor of the *Canadian Journal of Linguistics.*

15. Page 481, para. 3 – "Near Eastern Studies": Wevers e-mail.

16. Page 481, para. 3 – "get the centre approved": Sirluck, *First Generation* at 228.

17. Page 482, para. 1 – " nuclear fission": Sirluck to Bissell, December 31, 1963, UTA/A75-0021/32.

18. Page 482, para. 1 – "attracting a director": One leading American, Jaan Puhvel of Berkeley, had accepted and had

then backed out because some of the persons he had been counting on to build up the centre had left the University: see Puhvel to Sirluck, April 26, 1966.

19. Page 482, para. 1 – "their own research": Sirluck to Bissell, March 4, 1964, UTA/A75-0021/32.

20. Page 482, para. 1 – "from 1938 to 1942": Sirluck to Edey, January 18, 1967, UTA/A85-0009/27.

21. Page 482, para. 1 – "Hartford Seminary in the United states": Sirluck to Joos, September 5, 1967; Joos to Sirluck, October 24, 1967; Sirluck to Gleason, November 20, 1967 – all in UTA/A85-0009/27.

22. Page 482, para. 2 – "graduate centre was closed": Forster to Greene, April 3, 1974, UTA/A87-0021/32.

23. Page 482, para. 3 – "comparative literature": E-mail from Mario Valdes to Charles Levi, February 22, 2000.

24. Page 482, para. 3 – "Northrop Frye": *Centre for Comparative Literature: A Guide for the Perplexed* (January, 1996) at 2. In UTA/B86-0046/tape 5, Frye states that "the medieval and renaissance fields were already pre-empted by these institutes so that all the comparative literature department could take was romantics and modern and theory of criticism."

25. Page 482, para. 3 – "English department": Mueller to Sirluck, July 29, 1969 (document forwarded by Mario Valdes).

26. Page 482, para. 3 – "Valdés of Spanish": "Valdes, Mario James", *Canadian Who's Who 1994* at 1158.

27. Page 482, para. 3 – "German department took over": Hamlin was the chair from 1971 to 1976.

28. Page 482, para. 3 – "program's activities": "History of the Centre", 1982 (document forwarded by Mario Valdes) at 3.

29. Page 482, para. 3 – "Gadamer of Heidelberg": "Report on the Activities of the Graduate Programme in Comparative Literature", 1971-72.

30. Page 482, para. 3 – "comparative literature departments": "Hutcheon, Linda", *Canadian Who's Who 1994* at 545; "Appendix VI", annotated .

31. Page 482, para. 3 – "Valdes for Illinois": "History of the Centre" at 3.

32. Page 482, para. 3 – "designated a centre": Ibid. at 5.

33. Page 482, para. 3 – "Ted Chamberlin of English": J. Edward Chamberlin c.v. at 1; *Guide for the Perplexed* at 15.

34. Page 482, para. 3 – "Dolezel of Slavic literature": "Dolezel, Lubomir", *Canadian Who's Who 1994* at 301.

35. Page 484, para. 1 – "Gotlieb as its director": Sirluck, *First Generation* at 229.

36. Page 484, para. 1 – "about half the cost": "Fastest research 'brain' inaugurated at Varsity", *Varsity News* (December, 1962 at 2). The University also received a share of the proceeds of renting time to commercial enterprises – conversation with Gotlieb on August 13, 1998, in which he described that IBM wanted $2.5 million but accepted $1 million and a share of the money that the University got from renting out the computer; in the end it got the $2.5 million.

37. Page 484, para. 1 – "any computer the University then had": Kelly Gotlieb to author, August 13, 1998; "Fastest research 'brain'".

38. Page 484, para. 1 – "back to earth": Martha Hendriks, "An Institutional History of the Department of Computer Science at the University of Toronto 1948-1971" (January 6, 1992), Appendix 3.

39. Page 484, para. 1 – "history of the University": Gotlieb to author, August 13, 1998.

40. Page 484, para. 1 – "located in the physics building": See Hendriks, "Institutional History", Appendix 3, which mentions the conversion of the 7090 in 1964, the installation of the IBM 1460 in 1965 and the IBM 360 in 1967; "U of T Computer Centre orders new unit to increase capacity", *Bulletin*, October 21, 1971; "The Cray has arrived", *Bulletin*, September 15, 1986; "Cray too costly, Sevcik says", *Bulletin*, January 22, 1990.

41. Page 484, para. 1 – "the most powerful computer": Gotlieb to author, August 13, 1998.

42. Page 484, para. 1 – "laboratory at Dorval, Quebec": E-mail from Professor W.R. Peltier to author, November 16, 1999.

43. Page 484, para. 2 – "doctoral program in computer science": Hendriks, "Institutional History", Appendix 4.

44. Page 484, para. 2 – "took over as director": Hendriks, "Institutional History" at 15. Professor J.N.P. Hume replaced Hull in 1975 and served until 1980: see "Hume, James Nairn Patterson", *Canadian Who's Who 1994* at 540.

45. Page 484, para. 2 – "early in the 1970s": The undergraduate program in Computer Science was established in 1971: see Hendriks, "Institutional History", Appendix 4.

46. Page 484, para. 2 – "30 post-doctoral fellows": *University of Toronto Department of Computer Science* (1997) at 2.

47. Page 484, para. 2 – "Royal Society of London": "Cook, Hinton, Receive High Honour", *Bulletin*, September 28, 1998.

48. Page 484, para. 2 – "computational complexity": *Department of Computer Science* at 17.

49. Page 484, para. 2 – "strongest divisions": Ibid. at 21 and 31. Hinton was also one of eight members of the now-defunct Canadian Institute for Advanced Research's program on artificial intelligence.

50. Page 484, para. 2 – "graduates in these fields": "University to Double Computer Enrolments", *Bulletin*, November 30, 1998.

51. Page 484, para. 3 – "McLuhan at the University of Toronto": Bissell, *Halfway up Parnassus: A Personal Account of the University of Toronto 1932-1971* (University of Toronto Press, 1974) at 83.

52. Page 484, para. 3 – "development of his ideas": "Report of the Review Committee for the Centre for Culture and Technology" (May, 1980), UTA/B89-0031/008(05) at 4.

53. Page 485, para. 1 – "University of Pennsylvania": Bissell to Sirluck, October 9, 1962, UTA/A71-0011/60(16).

54. Page 485, para. 1 – "unlike some others": "Review Committee", Appendix x (Bissell to McCulloch, April 26, 1980).

55. Page 485, para. 1 – "occasionally send him": See McLuhan to Bissell November 7, 1960, March 5, 1962, and June 18, 1963 – all in UTA/B84-0036/002.

56. Page 485, para. 1 – "it's wrong!": McLuhan to Bissell, December 3, 1964, UTA/B84-0036/002.

57. Page 485, para. 2 – "taught English since 1946": Philip Marchand, *Marshall McLuhan: The Medium and the Messenger* (Toronto: Vintage Canada, 1998) at 87.

58. Page 485, para. 2 – "a convert to Roman Catholicism": Ibid. at 50-51.

59. Page 485, para. 2 – "remain in Toronto": Ibid. at 169; Bissell Diary, January 29, 1963.

60. Page 485, para. 2 – "Cambridge doctorate": McLuhan to Wallace, May 25, 1943, UTA/A87-0007/004.

61. Page 485, para. 2 – "at the University of Toronto": Marchand, *McLuhan* at 91. The quote relies on a paper by Thomas Dilworth of the University of Windsor at 296n6.

62. Page 485, para. 2 – "50 per cent teaching load": "Review Committee" at 3.

63. Page 486, para. 1 – "New York University": John Ayre, *Northrop Frye: A Biography* (Toronto: Random House, 1989) at 303; Bissell Diary, January 25, 1965.

64. Page 486, para. 1 – "only in the academic world": Ayre, *Frye* at 303 and 312. Frye was also given significant research support and an office in Massey College. Frye did not think much of McLuhan's ideas, as illustrated by the following entry in one of Frye's notebooks, edited by Robert Denham and to be published by University of Toronto Press as volume 13 of the *Collected Works of Northrop Frye.* Frye wrote: "Television is like a telescope, a new method of perception which tells us more, but also makes what it sees look cold, dead, and inconceivably remote. Global village my ass."

65. Page 486, para. 2 – "centre for McLuhan": Sword to Bissell, October 3, 1963; Sirluck to Bissell, October 3, 1963, both in UTA/A71-0011/77.

66. Page 486, para. 2 – "unorthodox probes": Bissell, *Parnassus* at 83.

67. Page 486, para. 2 – "media and society": "Review Committee", Appendix v.

68. Page 486, para. 2 – "Ford Foundation grant": Marchand, *McLuhan* at 126.

69. Page 486, para. 2 – "grant to any Canadian university": Sidney Smith referred to it as "the first investment they have made in Canadian scholarship": see W. Terrence Gordon, *Marshall McLuhan: Escape into Understanding* (Toronto: Stoddart Publishing, 1997) at 159.

70. Page 486, para. 2 – "was turned down": Ibid. at 165.

71. Page 486, para. 2 – "Jacqueline Tyrwhitt": Ibid. at 160.

72. Page 486, para. 2 – "*Explorations*": Bissell, *Parnassus* at 83.

73. Page 486, para. 2 – "*Understanding Media,* in 1964": Ibid.; Marshall McLuhan, *The Gutenberg Galaxy: The Making of Typographic Man* (University of Toronto Press, 1962); Marshall McLuhan, *Understanding Media: The Extensions of Man* (New York: McGraw-Hill, 1964).

74. Page 486, para. 3 – "in the fall of 1963": Board of Governors Minutes, October 24, 1963, UTA/A70-0024/20.

75. Page 486, para. 3 – "study them all": McLuhan to John L. Snyder, Jr., in Matie Molinaro et al., eds., *Letters of Marshall McLuhan* (Toronto: Oxford University Press, 1987) at 291.

76. Page 486, para. 3 – "a separate identity": Gordon, *McLuhan* at 195 and 402n10.

77. Page 486, para. 3 – "given to McLuhan": Ibid. at 232 and 234.

78. Page 487, para. 1 – "for a brain tumor": Ibid. at 229-230; Bissell diary, November 26, 1967.

79. Page 487, para. 1 – "creative years ahead": Carpenter to Bissell, March 21, 1968, UTA/A75-0021/96.

80. Page 487, para. 2 – "an obituary": Claude Bissell, "Herbert Marshall McLuhan", *Proceedings of the Royal Society of Canada*, 4th series, v. 19 (1981) at 138.

81. Page 487, para. 2 – "the Centre was Marshall McLuhan": "Review Committee" at 8.
82. Page 487, para. 2 – "the work of Marshall McLuhan": Ibid. at 9.

83. Page 487, para. 2 – "Tom Wolfe": Marchand, *McLuhan* at 284.

84. Page 487, para. 2 – "the change was made": "McLuhan program in culture and technology", *Bulletin*, June 23, 1980.

85. Page 487, para. 2 – "three-year grant": "McLuhan's work to be kept alive, carried forward, with help of Connaught grant", *Bulletin*, September 9, 1985.

86. Page 487, para. 2 – "secure funding since then": www.mcluhan.utoronto.ca/prog3.html.

87. Page 487, para. 2 – "technology on culture": www.mcluhan.utoronto.ca/prog.html.

88. Page 487, para. 2 – "children of Marshall McLuhan": Marchand, *McLuhan* at xiii.

89. Page 487, para. 3 – "established in 1965": Bissell, *Parnassus* at 82-85; Bissell Diary, May 26, 1965. It admitted its first students in 1966-67: see *President's Report, 1966/67* at 200.

90. Page 487, para. 3 – "theatres in Toronto": Bissell, *Parnassus* at 84.

91. Page 487, para. 3 – "rallies to the theatre": Ibid.

92. Page 488, para. 1 – "lighting was required": Robertson Davies, "A Report to the President Regarding Drama in the University", February 8, 1965, UTA/A75-0021/032 at 10.

93. Page 488, para. 1 – "drama should be instituted": Ibid. at 11.

94. Page 488, para. 1 – "now losing ground": Ibid. at 5.

95. Page 488, para. 1 – "better than Davies thought them": Bissell to Davies, February 12, 1965, UTA/A75-0021/32.

96. Page 488, para. 1 – "published academic work": Sirluck to Bissell, March 1, 1965, UTA/A75-0021/032; Sirluck to Bissell, March 10, 1965, UTA/A75-0021/032.

97. Page 488, para. 1 – "facilities at the University": John Brown of Birmingham to Winegard, June 10, 1966, UTA/A75-0021/032; Daniel Selzer of Harvard to Sirluck, October 1, 1966, UTA/A75-0021/064. Leach was the acting director of the centre: see Sirluck to Bissell, January 17, 1966, UTA/A75-0021/32.

98. Page 488, para. 2 – "to head the centre": Sirluck to Bissell, February 8, 1967, UTA/A75-0021/064; "Our new Men of the Theatre", *Varsity Graduate*, (June, 1967) at 89.

99. Page 488, para. 2 – "centre's theatre director": Sirluck to Major, February 8, 1967, UTA/A75-0021/064; "Our new Men" at 89-90.

100. Page 488, para. 2 – "who had not been well": Bissell to Gill, April 3, 1965, UTA/A75-0021/32.

101. Page 488, para. 2 – "in the graduate centre": Bissell to Davies, March 31, 1965, UTA/A75-0021/032.

102. Page 488, para. 2 – "resigned from the University": Sirluck to Parker, April 16, 1969, UTA/A77-0019/006; Parker to Sirluck, April 28, 1970, UTA/A82-0034/20.

103. Page 488, para. 2 – "Robarts Library": Brian Parker, "A flexible laboratory for the dramatic arts", *University of Toronto Graduate* (June, 1968) at 49.

104. Page 488, para. 2 – "perfect for the purpose": Ibid.; see *Varsity,* October 20, 1982 at 8.
105. Page 488, para. 2 – "low-budget productions": Parker to Bissell, January 6, 1970, UTA/A77-0019/20.

106. Page 488, para. 2 – "Parker as director in 1972": Safarian to Forster, February 10, 1972, UTA/A78-0028/19.

107. Page 488, para. 2 – "Augusta Gregory": Judith Knelman, "Ann Saddlemyer's Study of J.M. Synge", *University of Toronto Graduate* (May/June 1984) at 11.

108. Page 488, para. 3 – "Science and Technology": *Graduate Handbook for the Institute for the History and Philosophy of Science and Technology* (January, 1998) at 3-4. The Institute was founded in 1967 under the directorship of John W. Abrams, a professor of industrial engineering who believed in linking the science and the humanities: see Bruce Sinclair, "John W. Abrams", *Technology and Culture,* v. 22 (1982) at 527-529; Sirluck to Sword, January 29, 1968, UTA/A75-0021/96.

109. Page 488, para. 3 – "Renaissance Studies": The Centre for Renaissance and Reformation Studies was developed by a committee chaired by French scholar Victor Graham: see Sirluck letter, December 12, 1968, UTA/A85-0009/15.

110. Page 489, para. 1 – "Galileo's writings into English": William R. Shea, "Stillman Drake", *Nuncius* (1994) at 295.

111. Page 489, para. 1 – "Toronto in 1967": A.E. Safarian to Chairmen and Directors of Departments, Centres, and Institutes, October 31, 1972, UTA/A78-0028/048.

112. Page 489, para. 1 – "Fisher Library": Shea, "Drake" at 295-296. The collection was acquired through a combination of purchase and gift: see e-mail from Richard Landon to author, January 30, 2001.

113. Page 489, para. 2 – "Urban and Community Studies": The Centre was set up in 1964 to provide a forum for discussion, to encourage and facilitate multidisciplinary work, and to promote publication: see Sword to Milner, May 5, 1965, with attached constitution, UTA/A75-0021/008. After a search for a senior high-profile candidate failed, Stephen Dupré, who had joined the university in 1963, was selected as director: see, e.g., Milner to Bissell, April 26 and May 25, 1965, UTA/A75-0021/008, stating that Brian Berry of the University of Chicago geography department declined. See also, "Dupré, Joseph Stefan", *Canadian Who's Who 1994* at 322.

114. Page 489, para. 2 – "Centre for Industrial Relations": Industrial relations had started after the war as an interdisciplinary institute, with Vincent Bladen as its director. It was designed "to promote research and graduate instruction in the broad field of industrial relations". In 1964 the institute was converted into a graduate centre, with John Crispo of management studies as its first director. Like Urban and Community Studies, its mission was at first simply to promote interdisciplinary scholarly research, but in 1975 it introduced a Master of Industrial Relations program and in 1986 a Ph.D.: see "Institute of Industrial Relations", *University of Toronto Monthly,* v.46 at 168; V.W. Bladen, "The Institute of Industrial Relations", September 14, 1946, UTA/A83-036/009; Board of Governors Minutes, October 22, 1964, UTA/A70-0024/21; "Centre for Industrial Relations University of Toronto 1999-2000" at 2.

115. Page 489, para. 2 – "Institute for Policy Analysis": This was originally founded as the Institute for Quantitative Analysis of Social and Economic Policy in 1967, with economist Douglas Hartle as its first director. The current calendar states that its objective is "to develop and maintain a research program in economic and social policy that complements graduate studies in the social sciences, business and law": see *President's Report, 1967/68* at 123; "Hartle, Douglas Gordon", *Canadian Who's Who 1994* at 489; *University of Toronto Graduate Studies Calendar 1998-99* at 370.

116. Page 489, para. 3 – "Edwards as its director": Sirluck, *First Generation* at 229.

117. Page 489, para. 3 – "English Canada": John LL.J. Edwards, "Directing the Development of a University Centre of Criminology", in *Perspectives in Criminal Law: Essays in Honour of John LL.J. Edwards* (Aurora: Canada Law Book Inc., 1985) at 1. Montreal had already established a centre in 1960: see Département de Criminologie, Faculté des sciences sociales, économiques et politiques, Université de Montréal, *Annuaire 1969-70* at 1.
118. Page 489, para. 3 – "a research institute": Edwards, "Directing the Development" at 2; Sword to Bissell, October 24, 1962 and February 4, 1963, UTA/A71-0011/59(05).
119. Page 489, para. 3 – "prepared to have one": Sword to Bissell, December 11, 1962, UTA/A71-0011/59(05).
120. Page 489, para. 3 – "some other Ontario university": Ibid.
121. Page 489, para. 3 – "teaching at Dalhousie": "Edwards, John Llewelyn Jones", *Canadian Who's Who 1994* at 329.
122. Page 489, para. 4 – "contributions would originate": Edwards, "Directing the Development" at 3.
123. Page 489, para. 4 – "the correct one": Ibid.
124. Page 489, para. 4 – "John Beattie of history": Judith Knelman, "Criminal Interests", *University of Toronto Graduate* (Fall, 1987) at 13.
125. Page 489, para. 4 – "Peter Solomon of political science": For full list of faculty, see *School of Graduate Studies Calendar* (1988/89) at 105.
126. Page 490, para. 1 – "strong research centre": Edwards, "Directing the Development" at 4.
127. Page 490, para. 1 – "the research program": Edwards, "Directing the Development" at 8; Edwards to Bissell, March 26, 1970, UTA/A77-0019/26 at 2.
128. Page 490, para. 1 – "the federal government": Edwards, "Directing the Development" at 9-11; Edwards to Bissell, March 26, 1970 at 3; Bissell to Grossman, January 23, 1964, UTA/A71-0011/77.
129. Page 490, para. 1 – "research they were funding": Edwards, "Directing the Development" at 12-18.
130. Page 490, para. 1 – "policy of the University in this area": Ibid. at 15. Edwards wrote that he was actually reasserting long tradition and established principles.
131. Page 490, para. 1 – "veto on their publication": Ibid. at 14.
132. Page 490, para. 1 – "funding was established": Edwards to Bissell, March 26, 1970 at 1; Edwards, "Directing the Development" at 5; "Master's program in Criminology and our Indian-Eskimo project with Donner Foundation support", *Bulletin*, September 10, 1971, which also notes that the centre had sponsored an evening certificate course in criminology since 1965.
133. Page 490, para. 1 – "added in 1989": Telephone conversation between Charles Levi and Rita Donelan, February 5, 2001.
134. Page 490, para. 2 – "Skilling as its director": *President's Report, 1963/64* at 116; Bladen to Bissell, October 22, 1962, and Skilling to Bladen, December 21, 1962, both in UTA/B88-0007/002(44); Gordon Skilling, "Closing the Slav-Communist Gap", *Varsity Graduate* (May, 1963) at 7. See also H. Gordon Skilling, *The Education of a Canadian: My Life as a Scholar and Activist* (McGill-Queen's University Press, 2000).
135. Page 490, para. 2 – "Dartmouth College": "Skilling, H. Gordon", *Canadian Who's Who 1997* at 1028.
136. Page 490, para. 2 – "Nazis entered the country": UTA/Graduate Records/"Skilling, Harold Gordon"/UTA/A73-0026/422(57).

137. Page 490, para. 2 – "the CBC": "New Blood for Political Economy", *Varsity Graduate*, (May 1960) at 26.

138. Page 490, para. 2 – "Rockefeller Foundation": George Luckyj, "Department of Slavic Language and Literature", (1973) UTA/B88-007/002(042) at 1.

139. Page 490, para. 3 – "distinctive social order": Skilling to Innis, November 12, 1951, with "Memorandum on Russian Studies" at 1, UTA/B88-0007/002(042).

140. Page 490, para. 3 – "conflicts and their outcome": Ibid.

141. Page 490, para. 3 – "a similar approach": See Chapter 12 (1887).

142. Page 490, para. 3 – "training in Slavic Studies": Memo from Innis to Smith of March 23, 1952.

143. Page 491, para. 1 – "Slavic studies kept increasing": Shore to Smith, October 10, 1951, UTA/A68-0007/88(09).

144. Page 491, para. 1 – "Soviets in 1957": Luckyj, "Department" at 1.

145. Page 491, para. 1 – "interested in the field": "List of members and Associate Members of CREES" (1964), UTA/A75-0021/008.

146. Page 491, para. 1 – "Ukrainian literature": "Luckyj, George S.N.", *Canadian Who's Who 1997* at 756.

147. Page 491, para. 1 – "Soviet government": "List of members and Associate Members of CREES".

148. Page 491, para. 1 – "Russia and Eastern Europe at the University": *President's Report, 1964/65* at 137.

149. Page 491, para. 1 – "such as Ford and Mellon": Skilling to Howell, September 29, 1983, UTA/B88-0007/002(054) at 2; Robert E. Johnson, "Centre for Russian and East European Studies: Director's Five-Year Report 1989-93" (November, 1993) at 2.

150. Page 491, para. 2 – "courses in Russian": Skilling to Howell at 2.

151. Page 491, para. 2 – "with the Soviet Union": A diploma course was offered to those doing graduate work in other divisions of the University – *President's Report, 1963/64* at 117 – but this was not successful because it added an extra year to the student's program: see "Report of the Committee to Review the Centre for Russian and East European Studies" (May,1975), UTA/B88-0007/002(53) at 1.

152. Page 492, para. 1 – "cancelled the program": *Globe and Mail*, November 4, 1970; Bissell to Sharp, February 2, 1971; Skilling to Halstead, April 27, 1971; Skilling to Bazhanov, April 27, 1971 – all in UTA/A77-0019/045; "Centre for Russian and East European Studies Report of Activities 1963-1974" at 15-16.

153. Page 492, para. 1 – "meeting with dissidents": *President's Report, 1968/69* at 113.

154. Page 492, para. 2 – "student enrolments": E-mail from Ken Lantz to author, July 27, 1998.

155. Page 492, para. 2 – "have been launched": E-mail from Robert Johnson to Harvey Dyck, July 28, 2000, contained in e-mail from Dyck to Friedland, August 31, 2000.

156. Page 492, para. 2 – "Soviet authorities in 1929": E-mail from Dyck to Friedland, August 31, 2000.

157. Page 492, para. 2 – "teaching and research": E-mail from Peter Solomon to the author, December 7, 2000.

158. Page 492, para. 3 – "Canadian publisher": George Cook, "Scholarly Books as Best Sellers", *University of Toronto Magazine* (Summer, 1989) at 9.

159. Page 492, para. 3 – "300 new books": Marsh Jeanneret, *God and Mammon: Universities as Publishers* (Toronto: MacMillan of Canada, 1989) at 143.

160. Page 492, para. 4 – "A.S.P. Woodhouse": Jeanneret, *God and Mammon* at 31; Eleanor Harman, "Founding a University Press", UTA/A83-0036/020 at 32-33.

161. Page 492, para. 4 – "scholarship and letters": Cited in Jeanneret, *God and Mammon* at 34.

162. Page 492, para. 4 – "books since 1911": Jeanneret, *God and Mammon* at 22; Harman, "Founding a University Press" at 22.

163. Page 493, para. 1 – "100 books in print": Jeanneret, *God and Mammon* at 30.

164. Page 493, para. 1 – "scholarly publishing committee": Ibid. at 31.

165. Page 493, para. 2 – "university press in Canada": Cook, "Scholarly Books" at 9; Harman, "Founding a University Press" at 57. The French ones were the Editions d'Ottawa in 1936 and Laval in 1950.

166. Page 493, para. 2 – "throughout Canada": Harman, "Founding a University Press" at 38.

167. Page 493, para. 2 – "*The Vertical Mosaic*": Cook, "Scholarly Books" at 8; John A. Porter, *The Vertical Mosaic: an Analysis of Class and Social Power in Canada* (University of Toronto Press, 1965).

168. Page 493, para. 2 – "*Literary History of Canada*": Jeanneret, *God and Mammon* at 218; see also "One Hundred Most Influential Books Published by UTP", *University of Toronto Press Spring Summer 2001 Catalogue* at 32-33; Judy Stoffman, "Varsity printer bookmarked for success", *Toronto Star*, February 10, 2001; Francess Halpenny, "UTP's Many Masterpieces", *Press Notes*, March, 2001.

169. Page 493, para. 2 – "25 scholarly journals": *Spring Summer 1999 University of Toronto Press* at 74-75.

170. Page 493, para. 3 – "*Bias of Communication*": Harold Adams Innis, *The Bias of Communication* (University of Toronto Press, 1951); Cook, "Scholarly Books" at 8.

171. Page 493, para. 3 – "*Government of Canada*": Robert MacGregor Dawson, *The Government of Canada* (University of Toronto Press, 1947); Jeanneret, *God and Mammon* at 34. The press also published Dawson's *William Lyon Mackenzie King* in 1958.

172. Page 493, para. 3 – "*Gutenberg Galaxy*": Marshall McLuhan, *The Gutenberg Galaxy: The Making of Typographic Man* (University of Toronto Press, 1962); Jeanneret, *God and Mammon* at 153.

173. Page 493, para. 3 – "*No Mean City*": Eric Ross Arthur, *Toronto: No Mean City* (University of Toronto Press, 1965); Jeanneret, *God and Mammon* at 218 and 224.

174. Page 493, para. 3 – "*In Defence of Canada*": James George Eayrs, *In Defence of Canada* (University of Toronto Press, 1964-1983).

175. Page 493, para. 3 – "two authors from one department": Donald Grant Creighton, *John A. Macdonald* (Toronto: Macmillan, 1955-56); J.M.S. Careless, *Brown of The Globe* (Toronto: Macmillan, 1959-63).

176. Page 493, para. 3 – "*Portraits of Greatness*": Yousuf Karsh, *Portraits of Greatness* (University of Toronto Press, 1959); Jeanneret, *God and Mammon* at 156.

177. Page 493, para. 3 – "*Economic Atlas of Ontario*": W.G. Dean, *Economic Atlas of Ontario* (University of Toronto Press, 1969); "A Road Map for Industry", *Varsity Graduate* (April, 1965) at 72.

178. Page 493, para. 3 – "most beautiful book in the world": Jeanneret, *God and Mammon* at 246; "Economic Atlas of Ontario 'most beautiful book in the world'", *Bulletin*, September 24, 1970.

179. Page 493, para. 3 – "David Milne": David B. Silcox, *Painting Place: The Life and Work of David B. Milne* (University of Toronto Press, 1996) ; David Milne Jr. et al., *David B. Milne: Catalogue Raisonne of the Paintings* (University of Toronto Press, 1988).

180. Page 493, para. 3 – "*Historical Atlas*": *Historical Atlas of Canada*, v. 1 (*From the beginning to 1800*), v. 2 (*The land transformed 1800-1891*), v. 3 (*Addressing the twentieth century, 1891-1961*) (University of Toronto Press, 1987-1993); *Concise Historical Atlas of Canada* (University of Toronto Press, 1998); Cook, "Scholarly Books" at 8.

181. Page 493, para. 3 – "twenty-five-year period": Planning started in 1969: see "Atlas puts Canadians on the map", *Bulletin*, November 21, 1988.

182. Page 493, para. 3 – "research and production": "Historical atlas finds financial oasis", *Bulletin*, August 21, 1989.

183. Page 493, para. 4 – "King's College Circle": Jeanneret, *God and Mammon* at 135 and 232; Harman, "Founding a University Press" at 47; *Varsity Graduate* (December, 1958) at 179.

184. Page 493, para. 4 – "other side of University College": Jeanneret, *God and Mammon* at 29. It had acquired the Students' Book Department, a campus textbook store in 1933: see Cook, "Scholarly Books" at 9.

185. Page 493, para. 4 – "on St. George Street": Harman, "Founding a University Press" at 43 and 47.

186. Page 493, para. 4 – "Toronto reference library": Jeanneret, *God and Mammon* at 325-326; *University of Toronto Graduate* (September/October 1985) at 10-11.

187. Page 494, para. 1 – "St. Mary streets": 10 St. Mary Street: see http://www.utpress.utoronto.ca/editorial/reference.html. There is also a printing plant and distribution centre at Downsview in the north end of the city.

188. Page 494, para. 1 – "alumni and development purposes": http://www.dur.utoronto.ca/.

189. Page 494, para. 2 – "*Canadian Who's Who*": *The Canadian Who's Who 1999* (University of Toronto Press, 1999).

190. Page 494, para. 2 – "corporation in 1992": "University of Toronto Press Incorporation 1901-2001: A Short History", pamphlet in UTA/Current Subjects/"University of Toronto Press".

191. Page 494, para. 2 – "contributed to various projects": Such as Carnegie and Rockefeller: see Francess Halpenny, "The Ambience of Scholarly Publishing in Canada 1955-1975" (unpublished draft, 1998) at 9-10.

192. Page 494, para. 2 – "scholarly publishing program": Halpenny, "Ambience" at 24; Ford Foundation to Bissell, March 9, 1962, UTA/A71-0011/55(03); "$100,000 grant to U of T Press is to stimulate scholarly publishing", *Bulletin*, October 6, 1972; "Younger scholars will benefit from award to U of T Press", *Bulletin*, February 13, 1976.

193. Page 494, para. 2 – "Princeton University Press": The Bollingen Foundation was established in 1945 by Paul Mellon with an initial capital of $75,718.75 in stock and $25,000 in cash. As of 1963, the foundation had $16,500,000 available, of which $12,500,000 could be attributed to gifts from Mellon. The Foundation closed in 1969: see William McGuire, *Bollingen: An Adventure in Collecting the Past* (Princeton University Press, 1982) at 99 and 279; www.nga.xio.mellonpr.htm.

194. Page 494, para. 3 – "A.S.P. Woodhouse": "Robson, John Mercel", *Canadian Who's Who 1994* at 973. Robson acknowledges a "primary debt" to A.S.P. Woodhouse, in his first book, *The Improvement of Mankind* (University of Toronto Press, 1968) at xii; e-mail from Ann Robson to Friedland, February 12, 2000.

195. Page 494, para. 3 – "without success": Judith Knelman, "Robson on Mill", *University of Toronto Graduate* (September/October, 1985) at 14.

196. Page 494, para. 3 – "English department of University College": David Todd, "Mill Project Finished After 31 Years", *University of Toronto Bulletin,* June 10, 1991.

197. Page 494, para. 3 – "joined the Press in 1941": Jeanneret, *God and Mammon* at 64; "Halpenny, Francess Georgina", *Canadian Who's Who 1994* at 473.

198. Page 494, para. 3 – "receptive to the idea": Jeanneret, *God and Mammon* at 178-179.

199. Page 494, para. 3 – "Robson textual editor": Todd, "Mill Project"; Knelman, "Robson on Mill".

200. Page 494, para. 4 – "13 volumes": "Report on a Possible Collected Edition of the Works of John Stuart Mill", November 10, 1959, UTA/A71-0011/33(06) at 2.

201. Page 494, para. 4 – "published in 1991": Todd, "Mill Project".

202. Page 494, para. 4 – "textual editor": Jeanneret, *God and Mammon* at 181.

203. Page 494, para. 4 – "would have done": Ibid.

204. Page 494, para. 4 – "worse book": Todd, "Mill Project".

205. Page 494, para. 4 – "Bladen of political economy": John Stuart Mill, *Principles of Political Economy,* John M. Robson, ed., (University of Toronto Press, 1965), v. 2-3 of the Collected Mill Project.

206. Page 494, para. 4 – "Cairns of history": John Stuart Mill, *Essays on French History and Historians,* John M. Robson, ed., (University of Toronto Press, 1985), v. 20 of the Collected Mill Project.

207. Page 494, para. 4 – "Sparshott of philosophy": John Stuart Mill, *Essays on Philosophy and the Classics,* John M. Robson, ed., (University of Toronto Press, 1978), v. 11 of the Collected Mill Project.

208. Page 495, para. 1 – "Canadian scholarship": Jacqueline Swartz, "The Dictionary of Canadian Biography", *Bulletin,* April 7, 1980.

209. Page 495, para. 1 – "$350,000 to the University": "The Last Will and Testament of James Nicholson", *Varsity Graduate* (September, 1959) at 19-22; Jeanneret, *God and Mammon* at 38-39 and 167.

210. Page 495, para. 1 – "*Dictionary of National Biography*": Jeanneret, *God and Mammon* at 38.

211. Page 495, para. 1 – "honorary editor of the Press": Harman, "Founding a University Press" at 51. He was named editor in 1946: see *University of Toronto Monthly* (October, 1946) at 9.

212. Page 496, para. 1 – "hoped to undertake": Jeanneret, *God and Mammon* at 167.

213. Page 496, para. 1 – "Janie, died": Ibid.

214. Page 496, para. 1 – "raising the matter with her": Ibid. at 168.

215. Page 496, para. 1 – "for carrying it out": Ibid. at 167; G.W. Brown, "A Memorandum on a Dictionary of Canadian Biography" April 21, 1953, UTA/A71-0011/24(16). Smith to Brown, November 9, 1955, UTA/A71-0011/24(16), sets out the composition of the Editorial Preparatory Committee: Sidney Smith, chair, George Brown, vice-chair, and Blackburn, Woodside, Creighton, and Jeanneret.

216. Page 496, para. 1 – "during her lifetime": Jeanneret, *God and Mammon* at 171.

217. Page 496, para. 1 – "require from the estate": Ibid.

218. Page 496, para. 2 – "officially announced": Jeanneret to Bissell, April 1, 1959, UTA/A71-0011/24(16); Harman, "Founding a University Press" at 51; UTA/B88-0091, Claude Bissell Diaries, April 20, 1959.

219. Page 496, para. 2 – "within each volume": Jeanneret, *God and Mammon* at 170.

220. Page 496, para. 2 – "published in 1966": Ibid. at 175.

221. Page 496, para. 2 – "volume was in press": Ibid. at 282.

222. Page 496, para. 2 – "Mrs. Nicholson": Janie Elliot Dalton was born on February 28, 1876 in Toronto: see Public Archives of Ontario/Records of the Registrar General/RG80-2/1876-037812, on MS929, reel 27. She was a student at the University in 1894-95 and 1900-1901: see *University of Toronto Calendar*, 1895-1896, Appendix at 1 and *University of Toronto Calendar*, 1901-1902 at 4.

223. Page 496, para. 2 – "a copy of the volume": Bissell Diary, December 15, 1965.

224. Page 496, para. 3 – "*Dictionnaire biographique du Canada*": Jeanneret, God and Mammon at 173-175.

225. Page 496, para. 3 – "and then translated": Ibid. at 176; "Laval becomes full partner in enterprise", *Varsity Graduate* (May, 1961) at 19.

226. Page 496, para. 3 – "work of Quebec scholars": Jeanneret, *God and Mammon* at 176.

227. Page 496, para. 3 – "general editor in 1969": "Halpenny". David Hayne of the French department, who was in charge of the English translations, was the general editor in the interim between 1965 and 1969: see Jeanneret, *God and Mammon* at 176 and 282.

228. Page 496, para. 3 – "historian Ramsay Cook": "Consorting with the Humanities", *Bulletin*, November 21, 1988.

229. Page 496, para. 3 – "Research Council funding": "Canada Council Grant to Presses for Dictionary", *Bulletin*, June 8, 1973; Swartz, "Dictionary".

230. Page 496, para. 3 – "published in 1998": *Dictionary of Canadian Biography*, v. 14 (University of Toronto Press, 1998); see also Janet Wong, "The Past and Its People", *University of Toronto Bulletin*, October 16, 2000.

231. Page 497, para. 1 – "collected works of Erasmus": Ron Schoeffel and Prudence Tracy, "In Praise of Folly, or Life in the Underground", *Press Notes from the University of Toronto Press* (August-October, 1970, vol. XII numbers 8-10) at 1; J.K. McConica and R.M. Schoeffel, "The Collected Works of Erasmus", *Scholarly Publishing*, July, 1979) at 314; Robert Fulford, "Erasmus of Toronto", *Journal of Scholarly Publishing*, (April, 1999) at 124; Francess Halpenny, "Living a Project", *Scholarly Publishing*, (July 2001) at 264.

232. Page 497, para. 1 – "twenty years from now": Fulford, "Erasmus" at 125 and 130. There will be 86 volumes of Erasmus documents and three volumes on the contemporaries of Erasmus: see "Collected Works of Erasmus: Arrangement of Works by Volumes".

233. Page 497, para. 1 – "I cannot commend it enough": Hugh Trevor-Roper, "Master of the New Learning", *The Times Literary Supplement*, February 10, 1984 at 129.

234. Page 497, para. 1 – "never done before": McConica and Schoeffel, "Collected Works" at 315.

235. Page 497, para. 1 – "without success": Fulford, "Erasmus" at 124-125.

236. Page 497, para. 1 – "editors in the early years": James K. McConica, "Erasmus in Amsterdam and Toronto", in Erika Rummel, ed., *Editing Texts From the Age of Erasmus* (University of Toronto Press, 1996) at 98; "Schoeck, Richard J.", *Canadian Who's Who 1994* at 1019; J.H. Parker, "Beatrice Marion Corrigan", *Proceedings of the Royal Society of Canada*, 4th Series, v. 15 (1977) at 59.

237. Page 497, para. 1 – "throughout the world": McConica would be given the title "Chairman of the Editorial Board": see McConica, "Erasmus" at 100; McConica and Schoeffel, "Collected Works" at 321.

238. Page 497, para. 1 – "web of research and learning": Fulford, "Erasmus" at 126.

239. Page 497, para. 2 – "Renaissance studies": E-mail from Ron Schoeffel to author, January 21, 2000; *Classics, Medieval and Renaissance Books* (University of Toronto Press, 1998).

240. Page 497, para. 2 – "but there are others": See *The Centre for Medieval Studies Newsletter* (April 1999) at 7, referring to the 10th volume in the Toronto Old English Series, the 26th volume of the Toronto Medieval Latin Texts, Toronto Medieval Bibliographies, Toronto Medieval Texts and Translations, Corpus of British Medieval Library Catalogues, the British Library Studies in Medieval Culture, and the Jesuit Series. There is also a series of reprints of texts for teaching: see *Classics, Medieval and Renaissance Books* at 20-21.

241. Page 497, para. 2 – "closed the theatres": *Classics, Medieval and Renaissance Books* at 34.

242. Page 497, para. 2 – "English biblical drama": Alexandra F. Johnston, "Records of Early English Drama in Retrospect" in Gillian Fenwick, ed., *The Endangered Editor: Papers of the 34th annual Conference on Editorial Problems* (unpublished manuscript, no date) at 79-80.

243. Page 497, para. 2 – "published in 1999": Dorset/Cornwall Book Launch invitation, March 19, 1999; *Classics, Medieval and Renaissance Books* at 34 lists 13 other books; there is also a companion series on Studies in Early English Drama: ibid. at 33.

244. Page 497, para. 3 – "*Dictionary of Old English*": Temporary microfiches are being produced by the Pontifical Institute Press, but the books will be published by the U of T Press: conversation with Roberta Frank on February 7, 2000.

245. Page 498, para. 1 – "joined the University in 1968": "Angus Fraser Cameron", UTA/A87-0002/003 at 1 and 5; Constance B. Hieatt, "Angus Fraser Cameron", *Proceedings of the Royal Society of Canada*, 4th Series, v. 22 (1984) at 66.

246. Page 498, para. 1 – "Roberta Frank": "Frank, Roberta", *Canadian Who's Who 1994* at 382; see the 1973 document by Frank and Cameron, *A Plan for the Dictionary of Old English*, 1973, cited in "Cameron" at 13.

247. Page 498, para. 1 – "at the age of 42": "Cameron" at 1; *Globe and Mail*, May 28, 1983.

248. Page 498, para. 1 – "after teaching at Yale": Antoinette diPaolo Healey c.v.

249. Page 498, para. 1 – "the letter 'F'": *Globe and Mail*, January 10, 1998; *Centre for Medieval Studies Newsletter* at 7 states that "work is continuing on the letters F, G, and H".

250. Page 498, para. 1 – "in the fifteenth century": The *Globe and Mail* puts it at the early 16th century, but Roberta Frank says that there is now evidence that the word was used in the 15th century: conversation with Frank of February 7, 2000.

CHAPTER 35 – 1966 – ENGINEERING AND MEDICINE

1. Page 499, para. 1 – "old engineering building": "Engineers bid Schoolhouse farewell", *Varsity News* (December, 1966) at 8-9.

2. Page 499, para. 1 – "completed in 1878": C.R. Young, *Early Engineering Education at Toronto 1851-1919* (University of Toronto Press, 1958) at 59-62. This was the original building with the major addition: see Chapter 8 (1871).

3. Page 499, para. 1 – "opened in 1961": "The Galbraith Building", *Varsity Graduate*, (May, 1961) at 57; "The Galbraith Building", *University of Toronto Graduate* (December, 1967) at 43-44.

4. Page 499, para. 1 – "first year course": Richard White, *The Skule Story: The University of Toronto Faculty of Applied Science and Engineering 1873-2000* (University of Toronto Press, 2000) at 204. Computer programming was introduced for all first-year students: see White at 209.

5. Page 499, para. 2 – "over 5 years": Ford Foundation to Bissell, January 8, 1963, UTA/A73-0019/001; Bissell Diary, January 9, 1963, UTA/B88-0091/004(05); Gordon N. Patterson, *Pathway to Excellence: UTIAS – the first twenty-five years* (Toronto: Institute for Aerospace Studies, 1977) at 129-132; *Financial Post*, February 9, 1963; White, *The Skule Story* at 195-199. This was not the first time that Ford had assisted Toronto. In the early 1950s it had given the McLuhan seminar almost $50,000: see Chapter 34 (1963).

6. Page 499, para. 2 – "in the early 1920s": See Chapter 23 (1919).

7. Page 499, para. 2 – "created the same impact": This refers to Foundation grants and does not refer to important personal donations such as those of Dunlap, Wallberg, and Samuel: see Chapters 21 (1909), 26 (1931), and 33 (1962).

8. Page 500, para. 1 – "number of causes": The half billion accrued when the Foundation sold some of its holding of Ford stock: see Richard Magat, *The Ford Foundation at Work: Philanthropic Choices, Methods, and Styles* (New York: Plenum Press, 1979) at 166-167.

9. Page 500, para. 1 – "space satellite": Claude Bissell, *Halfway up Parnassus: A Personal Account of the University of Toronto 1932-1971* (University of Toronto Press, 1974) at 48.

10. Page 500, para. 1 – "science and technology": Paul Axelrod, *Scholars and Dollars: Politics, Economics, and the Universities of Ontario 1945-1980* (University of Toronto Press, 1982) at 24-26.

11. Page 500, para. 1 – "intensified the gloom": Bissell Diary, December 7, 1957, at 135. Bissell's spelling was actually 'sputnick'.

12. Page 500, para. 1 – "their graduate programs": In the 1950s and 60s, the Foundation seemed to concern itself with technology and the cold war: see Magat, *The Ford Foundation* at 112.

13. Page 500, para. 1 – "$10 million in 1959": Magat, *The Ford Foundation* at 179.

14. Page 500, para. 2 – "various faculty members": Trautman to McLaughlin, January 6, 1960, UTA/A78-0008/036; R.R. McLaughlin, "History of the Ford Foundation Grant to the Faculty of Applied Science and Engineering in the University of Toronto", April 25, 1963, UTA/A73-0019/001 at 1; Bissell Diary, January 18, 1960.

15. Page 501, para. 1 – "engineers to fill positions": Axelrod, *Scholars and Dollars* at 25-26.

16. Page 501, para. 1 – "time to think about it": McLaughlin, "History of the Ford Foundation Grant" at 2.

17. Page 501, para. 1 – "visiting professors": McLaughlin to Ford Foundation, March 30, 1962, UTA/A73-0019/001.

18. Page 501, para. 1 – "site on Dufferin Street": Patterson, *Pathway to Excellence* at 129-130; "Drawn, Quartered, Taken for a Ride: Our Sphere Will Breathe Again", *Varsity Graduate*, (December, 1963) at 66.

19. Page 501, para. 1 – "department of metallurgy": Ford Foundation to Bissell; White, *The Skule Story* at 198. The money was used to build an actual addition on the north-east corner of the building. Just one storey was built, but in the 1990s extra floors were added and the building was named the Pratt Building: White, *Skule Story* at 254-255.

20. Page 501, para. 2 – "250 doctoral students": There had been 132 graduate students in 1950: see White, *The Skule Story* at 180 and 199.

21. Page 501, para. 2 – "pursuing doctorates": Conversations with Michael Charles, February 25, 1998 and April 2001.

22. Page 501, para. 2 – "migrate to Toronto": Mawdsley to McLaughlin, February 18, 1963, UTA/A78-0008/36.

23. Page 501, para. 2 – "$3 million a year": White, *The Skule Story* at 198.

24. Page 501, para. 2 – "applied research throughout Canada": In 1957-58, the University had received almost half a million dollars from the NRC, but engineering received only about $20,000 of that amount: see White, *The Skule Story* at 180.

25. Page 502, para. 1 – "created or expanded": White, *The Skule Story* at 200.

26. Page 502, para. 1 – "Toronto and Queen's": Axelrod, *Scholars and Dollars* at 123.

27. Page 502, para. 1 – "perhaps 4,000": White, *The Skule Story* at 174 and 176.

28. Page 502, para. 1 – "in any given year": Ibid. at 188. By the early 1970s, it had risen to about 35: see James Ham, "Images of the Past and Future", in Robin S. Harris and Ian Montagnes, eds., *Cold Iron and Lady Godiva: Engineering Education at Toronto 1920-1972* (University of Toronto Press, 1973) at 157.

29. Page 502, para. 1 – "25 per cent of the class": "Engineering Attracts More Women", *Bulletin*, November 1, 1993; note from Michael Charles, April 2001.

30. Page 502, para. 1 – "risen to more than 50 per cent": For first year students, see ibid. Further, there were only 3 women members of the engineering faculty in the late 1960s: see Donald Forster to the chair of the Royal Commission on the status of Women in Canada, October 22, 1968, UTA/B83-0040/015. Today, there are about a dozen women faculty members: e-mail from Richard White, February 25, 2000.

31. Page 502, para. 2 – "at the end of the decade": White, *The Skule Story* at 200. Faculty had risen from 50 to 75 between 1955 and 1960: ibid. at 184.

32. Page 502, para. 2 – "20 hours per week": White, *The Skule Story* at 178.

33. Page 502, para. 2 – "nearly doubled": Ibid. at 40.

34. Page 502, para. 2 – "professional practice": Ibid. at 23 discusses professional practice in mining and civil engineering.

35. Page 502, para. 2 – "exceeded the output": Ibid. at 23.

36. Page 502, para. 3 – "a little too young": Woodside to Bissell, February 19, 1965, UTA/A75-0021/27.

37. Page 502, para. 3 – "technology in the early 1990s": "Winegard, Hon. William Charles", *Canadian Who's Who 1994* at 1217.

38. Page 502, para. 3 – "from the Faculty as a whole": Woodside to Bissell.

39. Page 503, para. 1 – "20 per cent of the engineering students": White, *The Skule Story* at 193-194.

40. Page 503, para. 1 – "chemistry had been added": Ibid.

41. Page 503, para. 1 – "succeed Ham as dean in 1973": "Etkin, Bernard", *Canadian Who's Who 1994* at 343. Ham had been given an unlimited term. The Haist Committee, that would recommend seven-year terms for deans – discussed in Chapters 31 (1958) and 37 (1971) – had not yet reported and the committee recommending Ham felt that "it would be invidious and even discouraging to set a time limit": see Woodside to Bissell.

42. Page 503, para. 1 – "later succeed Etkin as dean": "Slemon, Gordon R.", *Canadian Who's Who 1994* at 1055. The department would not change its name to electrical and computer engineering until 1992: see e-mail from Peter Boulton to Charles Levi, March 16, 2000.

43. Page 503, para. 2 – "a doctorate at Yale": "Michael Charles named chairman", *Bulletin*, January 10, 1975. Venetsanopoulos succeeded Charles as dean in 2001.

44. Page 504, para. 1 – "doctorate from UBC": "Salama, C.A.T.", *Canadian Who's Who 1997* at 1088. Salama, an expert on microchips, was the 1994 winner of the prestigious Killam Prize for a life-time achievement and contribution to engineering: see Karina Dahlin and Alfred Holden, "Simply the Best", *University of Toronto Magazine* (Summer, 1994) at 8.

45. Page 504, para. 1 – "a doctorate from Toronto": "Sedra, Adel", *Canadian Who's Who 1994* at 1026.

46. Page 504, para. 1 – "used by NASA": W. Murray Wonham c.v. Another appointment in electrical engineering was Richard Cobbold, who became the head of the Institute of Biomedical Engineering. He had graduated from Imperial College, London, and then received his doctorate from the University of Saskatchewan, joining the Toronto faculty in 1966: see "Cobbold, Richard Southwell Chevallier", *Canadian Who's Who 1994* at 217.

47. Page 504, para. 1 – "taught at the University of Colorado": Michael P. Collins c.v.

48. Page 504, para. 2 – "facilities on Dufferin Street": Patterson, *Pathway to Excellence* at 115; "The highways to the stars take shape on the ground", *Varsity Graduate* (November, 1959) at 20-22.

49. Page 504, para. 2 – "Aerophysics to Aerospace": Patterson, *Pathway to Excellence* at 133; Ben Etkin, "Beginnings", *Canadian Aeronautics and Space Journal*, v. 45, no. 2 (June, 1999) at 72.

50. Page 504, para. 2 – "satellite flight": *Varsity News*, (October 1957).

51. Page 504, para. 2 – "dynamics of space vehicles": Patterson, *Pathway to Excellence* at 122; J. Barry French to author, November 18, 1999; "Space-Age Achievements", *Varsity Graduate* (December, 1962) at 17.

52. Page 504, para. 2 – "upper atmosphere rare gases": Patterson, *Pathway to Excellence* at 125-126; "Dr. Jaap de Leeuw new director of Aerospace Studies Institute", *Bulletin*, January 25, 1974.

53. Page 504, para. 3 – "can sustain life": French to author, November 18, 1999.

54. Page 504, para. 3 – "other substances on earth": Jennifer Low, "The sweet smell of success", *University of Toronto Magazine* (Spring, 1995) at 6.

55. Page 504, para. 3 – "space robotics": T. Haasz, "Editorial", *Canadian Aeronautics and Space Journal*, v.45, no.2 (June, 1999) at 67.

56. Page 504, para. 3 – "flaps its wings": Ibid.; Karina Dahlin, "A Quest for Flapping Wings", *University of Toronto Magazine* (Summer, 1989) at 12.

57. Page 504, para. 3 – "return safely to earth": Patterson, *Pathway to Excellence* at 159; Grumman Aerospace to French, May 4, 1970.

58. Page 505, para. 1 – "its first director": "Moody, Norman F.", *Canadian Who's Who 1994* at 813; Henry O'Beirne, "History of the Institute of Biomedical Engineering 1962 to 1987" at 2; "Moody leaves Biomedical Engineering", *Bulletin*, June 17, 1977. Moody's interest in biomedical electronics was well known to Arthur Porter, who had been the dean of engineering at Saskatchewan before coming to Toronto in 1961 to head the department of industrial engineering. Porter had brought in Moody in 1958 to become part of what Porter called "the first true interfaculty bio-medical research unit ever to be established in the world": see R.H. Macdonald, *Thorough: An Illustrated History of the College of Engineering University of Saskatchewan 1912-1982* (Saskatoon: The College of Engineering, 1982) at 100 and 103-104.

59. Page 505, para. 1 – "separate studies in these fields": "Medicine's Marriage with Electronics is rich in promise", *Varsity Graduate* (December, 1964) at 73 and 78.

60. Page 505, para. 1 – "joined the institute": O'Beirne, "History of the Institute" at 3; "Medicine's Marriage" at 75. He was a pharmacologist.

61. Page 505, para. 1 – "biological adhesives": "Medicine's Marriage" at 77; *President's Report, 1969/70* at 97.

62. Page 505, para. 2 – "the word 'electronics'": O'Beirne, "History of the Institute" at 11. In 1971, for example, a mechanical engineer, David James, joined the group: see *President's Report, 1971/72* at 141.

63. Page 505, para. 2 – "design living systems themselves": E-mail from Hans Kunov to author, February 11, 2000; see also "Kunov, Hans", *Canadian Who's Who 1994* at 625-626.

64. Page 505, para. 2 – "synthetic hearts and pancreases": *Globe and Mail*, July 18, 1998; Michael Smith, "The New Body Builders", *University of Toronto Magazine* (Summer 1998) at 17; see also the work of Walter Zingg described in the *Bulletin* of February 25, 1980. The unit was renamed the Institute of Biomaterials and Biomedical Engineering when it merged with the Centre for Biomaterials on July 1, 1999: see e-mail from Anne Mitchell to Charles Levi, May 15, 2000. There were other institutes connected to engineering. For the Pulp and Paper Institute, see Chapter 28 (1944). The Great Lakes Institute was founded by Dr. George Langford in 1960: see "Lake Ontario uses heavy water to build a might wall from bottom to top", *Varsity Graduate* (June, 1967) at 113-116.

65. Page 505, para. 3 – "future development of the faculty": Bissell Diary, May 23, 1963; Henry Borden memoirs, National Archives of Canada MG30A86, v. 4 at 142.

66. Page 505, para. 3 – "report in May 1964": "Report of the Board of Governors' Special Committee on the Future Development of the Faculty of Medicine, May 1964", UTA/A86-0019/001.

67. Page 505, para. 3 – "head of pathology": "Hamilton, John Drenan", *Canadian Who's Who 1994* at 476.

68. Page 505, para. 3 – "Joseph Sullivan": "Future Development" at 2.

69. Page 505, para. 3 – "writing the report was John Evans": Frances Ireland Oral Interview Finding Aid, UTA/B86-0052 at 10.

70. Page 506, para. 1 – "research on cardiac diseases": "John Robert Evans", *Canadian Who's Who 1994* at 344.

71. Page 506, para. 1 – "nurtured academic medicine": Bissell, *Parnassus* at 104.

72. Page 506, para. 1 – "Boyd's on pathology": See Chapter 24 (1922).

73. Page 506, para. 2 – "surgeons in Canada": R.I. Harris, "William Edward Gallie 1882-1959: An Appreciation", *Canadian M.A.J.*, v. 81 (November 1, 1959) at 768.

74. Page 506, para. 2 – "part-time dean of medicine": He was succeeded by J.A. MacFarlane: see "New Dean of Medicine", *University of Toronto Monthly* (March, 1946) at 144.

75. Page 506, para. 2 – "pumps were introduced": Ronald J. Baird, "The story of heparin – as told by sketches from the lives of William Howell, Jay McLean, Charles Best, and Gordon Murray", Presidential Address at the Thirty-Seventh Scientific Meeting of the North American Chapter, International Society for Cardiovascular Surgery, New York, N.Y., June 19-20, 1989 at 4 and 13-16.

76. Page 506, para. 2 – "with spinal injuries": T.P. Morley, "Some Professional and Political Events in Canadian Neurosurgery", *Canadian Journal of Neurological Sciences*, v. 12 (1985) at 232.

77. Page 506, para. 2 – "before the Second World War": "W.G. Bigelow: A Surgeon's Life", *University of Toronto Magazine* (Winter, 1991) at 25.

78. Page 506, para. 2 – "cardiac pacemaker": "Research: What the Bigelow Team is Doing", *Varsity Graduate* (April, 1961) at 55; "W.G. Bigelow: A Surgeon's Life" at 25; W.G. Bigelow, *Cold Hearts; The Story of Hypothermia and the Pacemaker in Heart Surgery* (Toronto: McClelland and Stewart, 1984).

79. Page 506, para. 2 – "Mustard operation": Marilyn Dunlop, *Bill Mustard: Surgical Pioneer* (Toronto: Dundurn Press, 1989) at 8.

80. Page 506, para. 2 – "Salter operation": "Salter, Robert Bruce", *Canadian Who's Who 1994* at 1004; Robert B. Salter, *Disorders and Injuries of the Muscoskeletal System*, 3rd Edition (Baltimore: Williams and Wilkins, 1999) at xi.

81. Page 507, para. 1 – "expansion and reorganization": "Future Development" at 2.

82. Page 507, para. 1 – "experimental animals": Ibid.

83. Page 507, para. 2 – "Best Institute in 1953": Ibid. at 4.

84. Page 507, para. 2 – "20 per cent": Ibid. at 18.

85. Page 507, para. 2 – "heads of departments": Ibid.

86. Page 507, para. 2 – "clinical departments": Ibid. at 10.

87. Page 507, para. 2 – "training in Toronto": Chute memo, January 9, 1968, UTA/A73-0025/29(04) at 5; "Report from Consultants on Medical Education to Chairman of the Board of Governors, University of Toronto", May 1968, UTA/A75-0025/30(02) at 1.

88. Page 507, para. 2 – "degrees in clinical fields": "Future Development" at 9-10.

89. Page 507, para. 3 – "$7 million in 1964": Ibid. at 4.

90. Page 507, para. 3 – "full advantage of this funding": See generally, "Future Development".

91. Page 507, para. 3 – "of high calibre": "Future Development" at 5.

92. Page 508, para. 1 – "second school in Metropolitan Toronto": Ibid. at 27.

93. Page 508, para. 1 – "possibility of a medical school": See Chapter 32 (1960). Evans was interviewed by the chair of the York board on the issue of the development of a medical school at York: see John Evans Oral Interview, UTA/B86-0044, tape 6.

94. Page 508, para. 1 – "outlined in their report": "Future Development" at 27.

95. Page 508, para. 1 – "independent school in Metropolitan Toronto": Ibid. at iv and 27.

96. Page 508, para. 2 – "universal health care system": *Royal Commission on Health Services* (Ottawa: Roger Duhamel, 1964), vol. 1 at 70-71; *Globe and Mail*, June 20, 1964. These findings built on a paper by R.F. Farquharson's in 1961 and J.A. MacFarlane's study of Medical Education in Canada, published in 1964: see Axelrod, *Scholars and Dollars* at 118-119.

97. Page 508, para. 2 – "medical sciences building": Borden memoirs at 142-143.

98. Page 508, para. 2 – "chairman of the board earlier that year": Borden had taken over the chair from Phillips in March of 1964. Phillips stayed on the Board as Honorary Chairman until his death in December, 1964: see Chapter 32 (1960).

99. Page 508, para. 2 – "laboratory facilities": Borden memoirs at 142.

100. Page 508, para. 2 – "new university psychiatric hospital": Henry Borden Oral Interview, B87-0044 at 40-42.

101. Page 508, para. 2 – "on the medical program": Borden to Bissell, July 17, 1964, UTA/A75-0021/020.

102. Page 509, para. 1 – "McMaster University in Hamilton": Bissell Diary, October 29, 1964; Borden memoirs at 143; "Varsity to Graduate More M.D.'s", *Varsity News* (December 1964) at 1; Axelrod, *Scholars and Dollars* at 119.

103. Page 509, para. 2 – "used for teaching": "Future Development" at 8.

104. Page 509, para. 2 – "McCaul and Henry streets": Ibid. at 17.

105. Page 509, para. 3 – "south of College Street": The issue was discussed in the Bissell Diary, November 5 and 11, 1965.

106. Page 509, para. 3 – "new building and equipment": Bissell Diary, April 28 and May 19, 1966. The federal government's Health Resources Fund later contributed to the cost: see "A New Citadel for the Health Sciences", *University of Toronto Graduate* (April 1968) at 17.

107. Page 510, para. 1 – "site where it now stands": Board of Governors Property Committee Minutes, April 20, 1966, UTA/A70-0024/21.

108. Page 510, para. 1 – "laid in 1967": "Implementing the grand Design for Health Sciences at U of T", *University of Toronto Graduate* (February, 1968) at 12; "A New Citadel".

109. Page 510, para. 1 – "in late 1968": Hamilton to MacLeod, November 13, 1968, UTA/A75-0025/30(02) at 3.

110. Page 510, para. 1 – "take place until 1970": "Medical Sciences Building official opening and Convocation", *Bulletin*, October 15, 1970.

111. Page 510, para. 1 – "forty million dollars": Borden was especially proud of the work Canadian Bechtel did as project managers, outside of the standard property development hierarchy of the University: see Borden memoirs at 145-146; Bissell, *Parnassus* at 105.

112. Page 510, para. 1 – "field of medicine": Borden memoirs at 146.

113. Page 510, para. 2 – "teaching hospitals": Borden memoirs at 143-144; "Sunnybrook Medical Centre Development Programme", February 8, 1974, UTA/B79-0051/007 at 1.

114. Page 510, para. 2 – "veterans' hospital in Canada": Bissell Diary, March 12, 1964; Teillet to Borden of May 27, 1964.

115. Page 510, para. 2 –"chief of staff at Sunnybrook": Borden memoirs at 144.

116. Page 510, para. 2 –"not a training facility": John Evans to author, March 18, 1998 at 3.

117. Page 510, para. 2 –"a second medical school": Borden memoirs at 144; Bissell Diary, January 14 and March 18, 1964; John D. Hamilton Oral Interview Transcript, UTA/B87-0044 at 54-56. Sunnybrook is not mentioned in the Hamilton report, but it is surely Sunnybrook that is referred to when they state that "in the near future it may be desirable to establish relatively autonomous divisions of the faculty at suitable teaching hospitals remote from the University": report at 26. It is possible that they are also referring to Scarborough College then being planned. In a letter to Bissell of June 10, 1963, Carl Williams writes: "Were it to be considered desirable that a second medical school be established and located on the Scarborough campus, the committee would favour this possibility as strengthening the College": see Williams to Bissell, June 10, 1963, UTA/A72-0026/001.

118. Page 510, para. 3 –"I went on from there": Borden memoirs at 145.

119. Page 510, para. 3 –"for $1": January 19, 1965; The silver dollar is mentioned in "Sunnybrook is Key to More Doctors and Nurses", *Varsity Graduate* (February 1967) at 3.

120. Page 510, para. 3 –"controlled by the University": Arnold Aberman states, "Sunnybrook is not now and has never been 'owned' by the University of Toronto. The hospital is a non-profit corporation. The University of Toronto owns the land on which Sunnybrook is sited and recommends the appointment of a majority of the board. I think that 'controlled' is better than 'owned'": see e-mail from Aberman to author, January 20, 2001.

121. Page 510, para. 3 –"any university in Ontario": "Sunnybrook is Key" at 1; Borden to Sunnybrook staff, February 25, 1965, UTA/A75-0021/11.

122. Page 510, para. 3 –"full-time members of the University": Bissell, *Parnassus* at 106.

123. Page 511, para. 1 –"future expansion": Bissell Diary, January 24, 1963; Borden memoirs at 144.

124. Page 511, para. 1 –"obsession for months": Bissell Diary, January 19, 1965. Bissell also called it "Henry's great passion": see ibid., November 21, 1966.

125. Page 511, para. 1 –"180 acres at Sunnybrook": "Sunnybrook is Key" at 1 and 7.

126. Page 511, para. 1 –"entire St. George campus": According to the *University of Toronto News* (February, 1970) the latest developments in the 1970s would put the St. George grounds at 168 acres.

127. Page 511, para. 2 – "acquisition of Sunnybrook": Evans to author at 1.

128. Page 511, para. 2 – "while he was chairman": Borden memoirs at 146.

129. Page 512, para. 1 – "clearly they were both": Ibid. at 105; "Future Development" at 28.

130. Page 512, para. 1 – "came to my support": Ibid. at 106.

131. Page 512, para. 1 – "and this he did": Borden memoirs at 143.

132. Page 512, para. 2 – "a teaching hospital": "Future Development" at 28.

133. Page 512, para. 2 – "George Connell": "Connell, George E.", *Canadian Who's Who 1994* at 229.

134. Page 512, para. 2 – "Ronald Williams": Williams would later be the principal of Scarborough College: see "Williams, George Ronald", *Canadian Who's Who 1994* at 1209.

135. Page 512, para. 2 – "Fraser Mustard": "Mustard, James Fraser", *Canadian Who's Who 1994* at 835; Evans to author at 2; Evans oral interview, tape 6. The group also included physiologist Geza Hetenyi, later the vice-dean of health sciences at the University of Ottawa, and William Spaulding, who went to McMaster and "was one of the founders of what has been known and widely adopted as the 'McMaster approach' to medical education": *McMaster University Courier*, January 26, 1993.

136. Page 512, para. 2 – "University of London medical schools": Evans to author at 2.

137. Page 512, para. 2 – "own educational programme": Evans to Hamilton, May 4, 1965 with attached "Programme for the Development of Sunnybrook Hospital" and Hamilton to Bissell, May 5, 1965, all in UTA/A75-0021/011.

138. Page 512, para. 3 – "they were defeated": Evans to author at 2; also, notes of interview with Evans of February 26, 1998. Chute "vigorously opposed" the idea "as being even more divisive than the existing arrangement": see Chute memo at 4.

139. Page 512, para. 3 – "teaching hospitals": Evans to author at 2.

140. Page 512, para. 3 – "in 1972": "Evans".

141. Page 513, para. 1 – "Harvard medical school": "Dr. William Spaulding", *McMaster University Courier*, January 26, 1993, in William Spaulding papers, McMaster University Health Sciences Library Archives.

142. Page 513, para. 1 – "introduced at Toronto": Ibid.

143. Page 513, para. 1 – "specific hospitals": The academies began operation in 1994: e-mail from Richard Frecker to Patrick Okens, March 28, 2000. In 1993, enrolment of first-year medical students dropped back to 175 students and then in 2000 they went back up to 190: see "Province Expands Enrolment in Medical Schools", *University of Toronto Bulletin*, (September 11, 2000?).

144. Page 513, para. 2 – "Hamilton as dean": "Hamilton"; "Our new Dean of Medicine", *Varsity Graduate* (December, 1966) at 22.

145. Page 513, para. 2 – "for fifteen years": "Chute, Andrew Lawrence", *Canadian Who's Who 1994* at 206; "Hamilton".

146. Page 513, para. 2 – "decision-making in the Board": Bissell Diary, July 8, 1968.

147. Page 513, para. 2 – "pre-medical years": *President's Report, 1969/70* at 8; Thomson to Faculty Council, August, 1969, UTA/A77-0019/26.

148. Page 513, para. 2 – "about 600 members": Chute memo at 2-3.

149. Page 513, para. 2 – "Status of Women in Canada": Forster to chair of Royal Commission on the Status of Women. For a full discussion of the quota on women, see Jacalyn Duffin's presidential address to the Canadian Society for the History of Medicine, "'The Quota: 'An Equally Serious Problem' for Us All", May 26, 2001. See also R.D. Gidney and W.P.J. Millar, "'Medettes': Thriving or Just Surviving? Women Students in the Faculty of Medicine, University of Toronto 1910-1951", in Elizabeth Smyth et. all, eds., *Challenging Professions: Historical and Contemporary Perspectives on Women's Professional Work* (University of Toronto Press, 1999) at 217 and 227-228.

150. Page 513, para. 3 – "chaired by Borden": "Report from Consultants on Medical Education to Chairman of the Board of Governors, University of Toronto", May 1968, UTA/A75-0025/30(02); Hamilton to MacLeod, November 13, 1968, UTA/A75-0025/30(02); Borden to Chute, July 11, 1968, UTA/A73-0025/29(14).

151. Page 513, para. 3 – "controlling physicians' fees": "Report from Consultants" at 7.

152. Page 513, para. 3 – "teaching bodies": Hamilton to MacLeod.

153. Page 513, para. 3 – "for educational purposes": Ibid. at 2.

154. Page 514, para. 1 – "Toronto Western hospitals": "Report from Consultants" at 7, 9-10, and 12; Hamilton to MacLeod. See Bissell Diary, July 12, 1968, in which he says, 'The commission had recommended a concentration of hospital facilities in the General and the Western".

155. Page 514, para. 1 – "decline precipitously": Rieger to Borden, October 24, 1998, UTA/A73-0025/30(02); "Rieger, Budd Huntington", *Canadian Who's Who 1967-1969* at 929.

156. Page 514, para. 1 – "a teaching hospital": "Address to the Senate by the Vice President, Health Sciences, Dr. John Hamilton on Friday, March 10, 1967", UTA/A86-0019/001 at 4-5; Rieger to Borden.

157. Page 514, para. 1 – "funding for them": Implicit in Hamilton to MacLeod at 1; Hamilton to Chute, November 22, 1968, UTA/A73-0025/29(04).

158. Page 514, para. 1 – "St. Michael's Hospital": Irene McDonald, *For the Least of My Brethren: A Centenary History of St. Michael's Hospital* (Toronto: Dundurn Press, 1992) at 196-205.

159. Page 514, para. 1 – "Dr. Hamilton": Sullivan to Borden, November 21, 1968, UTA/A73-0025/30(02) at 2.

160. Page 514, para. 1 – "score a single goal": See Chapter 25 (1926) .

161. Page 514, para. 1 – "carried on as before": Borden to Chute; Hamilton to Bissell, December 6, 1968, UTA/A73-0025/30(02); Claringbold to Hamilton, December 13, 1968, UTA/A73-0025/30(02).

162. Page 514, para. 2 – "C.K. Clarke": "Charles Kirk Clarke", in Henry James Morgan, ed., *The Canadian Men and Women of the Time* (Toronto: William Briggs, 1912) at 237; see also Martin Friedland, *The Case of Valentine Shortis: a True Story of Crime and Politics in Canada,* (University of Toronto Press, 1986).

163. Page 514, para. 2 – "as teaching hospitals": "Future Development" at 5.

164. Page 514, para. 3 – "pathology": Discussions had started as early as 1957: see Leslie Marrus Barsky, *From Generation to Generation: A History of Toronto's Mount Sinai Hospital* (Toronto: McClelland and Stewart, 1998) at 100-103; Joseph Gollom, "Mount Sinai Hospital", UTA/A83-0026/012 at 7.

165. Page 515, para. 1 – "Elm Street": Plans called for 350 beds although the final building only had room for 337: see Barsky, *From Generation to Generation* at 53, 62, 66, and 128.

166. Page 515, para. 1 – "Toronto General Hospital": Ibid. at 116-117.

167. Page 515, para. 1 – "department of medicine": Ibid. at 116-17; Friedland conversation with Berris, August 11, 2000, in which Berris says he was told this by Jack Laidlaw. The first Jewish staff member at the Sick Children's was Bernard Laski in 1948: ibid. at 84.

168. Page 515, para. 1 – "at Mount Sinai": Ibid. at 117.

169. Page 515, para. 1 – "It was 6": letter from Berris dated August 6, 1998, containing a page from his memoirs. There were, however, referrals from other doctors in his own department. According to Barsky, *From Generation to Generation* at 116-117, Berris joined TGH in 1950 and MSH on July 1, 1964. The author had been told of the low referral rate by Charles Hollenberg in June, 1998.

170. Page 515, para. 2 – "beside the old one": Gollom, "Mount Sinai" at 10; Barsky, *From Generation to Generation* at 129.

171. Page 515, para. 2 – "flowed under the building": Barsky, *From Generation to Generation* at 129.

172. Page 515, para. 2 – "capital funding of hospitals": Ibid. at 130 and 132-133.

173. Page 515, para. 2 – "600-bed hospital": Ibid. at 134 and 148.

174. Page 515, para. 3 – "Banting and Best Department of Medical Research": "Fritz Research was Link in Tracing Muscle Disease", *Bulletin* March 11, 1996; "Fritz, Irving Bamdas", *Canadian Who's Who 1994* at 390-391; George Connell to author, December 31, 1998 at 2.

175. Page 515, para. 3 – "vice-dean of research": "Yip, Cecil C.", *Canadian Who's Who 1994* at 1236.

176. Page 515, para. 3 – "Royal Society of London": MacLennan replaced Fritz as the head of Banting and Best in 1993: see "MacLennan, David H.", *Canadian Who's Who 1994* at 714.

177. Page 515, para. 3 – "pruning and recruiting": Connell to author, December 31, 1998 at 2.

178. Page 516, para. 1 – "Ontario Cancer Institute": Ibid. at 2-3. The Institute was incorporated in 1952 under an act of the Ontario legislature which was revised in 1957: see Dr. and Mrs. H.E. Johns, "History of the Department of Medical Biophysics, University of Toronto" (November, 1973), UTA/A83-0036/011 at 1; Ernest McCulloch, "The Ontario Cancer Institute (OCI): A Brief Account" (undated manuscript) at 1. See generally, Edward Shorter, *A Century of Radiology in Toronto* (Toronto: Wall and Emerson, 1995).

179. Page 516, para. 1 – "Wellesley Hospital": Bissell Diary, September 25, 1958; Johns and Johns, "History of the Department" at 1; Dr. A.W. Ham to head new department", *Varsity News* (September, 1958) at 2.

180. Page 516, para. 1 – "the opposite was true": McCulloch, "Ontario Cancer Institute" at 4.

181. Page 516, para. 1 – "psychological damage": *Toronto Star*, October 3, 1993; R.J. Fitzpatrick, "In Memoriam M. Vera Peters", 1993 at 2; "Mildred Vera Peters", in Rose Sheinin and Alan Bakes, *Women and Medicine in Toronto Since 1883* (Toronto: Faculty of Medicine, 1987) at 77. See also Shorter, *A Century of Radiology*, Aditya Bharatha, "Mildred Vera Peters: A pioneering Radiotherapist" (unpublished paper presented at the U of Calgary History of Medicine Days 2001).

182. Page 516, para. 2 – "cancer institute": See Ham to Smith, April 17, 1946, UTA/A83-0036/019.

183. Page 516, para. 2 – "physics of radiology": "Johns, Harold Elford", *Canadian Who's Who 1994* at 570.

184. Page 516, para. 2 – "treatment of cancer": McCulloch, "Ontario Cancer Institute" at 11.

185. Page 516, para. 2 – "Victor Ling": "Siminovitch, Louis", *Canadian Who's Who 1994* at 1046; "Till, James Edgar", *Canadian Who's Who 1994* at 1137-1138; "McCulloch, Ernest Armstrong", *Canadian Who's Who 1994* at 757; "University Professors Named", *Bulletin*, May 10, 1993. As of the fall of 1999, Ling was the head of the BC cancer research centre and assistant dean, research, UBC faculty of medicine.

186. Page 516, para. 2 – "University Professors": Ling, who has left the University, is no longer listed; for the others, see undated list of university professors forwarded from the office of the V-P and Provost.

187. Page 518, para. 1 – "Nobel prizes": "Louis Siminovitch", in G.A. Kenney-Wallace et al., eds., I*n Celebration of Canadian Scientists: A Decade of Killam Laureates* (Ottawa, 1990) at 49.

188. Page 518, para. 1 – "biological problems": Ibid.

189. Page 518, para. 1 – "Connaught Laboratories": Ibid. at 50-51.

190. Page 518, para. 1 – "cancer problem": Ibid. at 51.

191. Page 518, para. 1 – "nobody was pressuring us": Ernest McCulloch oral interview with Hannah Institute: see e-mail from McCulloch to author of July 11, 2001.

192. Page 518, para. 1 – "60 papers together": McCulloch, "Ontario Cancer Institute" at 16-18; Ernest McCulloch to author, January 14, 2000.

193. Page 518, para. 2 – "work off campus": McCulloch, "Ontario Cancer Institute" at 5-6; McCulloch oral interview at 46; Johns and Johns, "History of the Department". George Connell has asserted that resistance came from Reginald Haist of physiology and Ken Fisher of Zoology: see Connell to author, December 31, 1998 at 2.

194. Page 518, para. 2 – "the graduate school": "Dr. A.W. Ham to head new department" at 2; Johns and Johns, "History of the Department" at 3-4.

195. Page 518, para. 2 – "for the next 10 years": Johns and Johns, "History of the Department" at 5.

196. Page 518, para. 2 – "in the late 1960s": Ibid. at 5-6.

197. Page 518, para. 3 – "Nobel prize": "Masui Wins Lasker", *University of Toronto Bulletin*, September 28, 1998; conversation with David MacLennan, February 21, 2001; see also *Science* (September 8, 2000) at 1716. Note, however, the letter to the *University of Toronto Bulletin* of October 29, 2001 from John Dirks, the president of the Gairdner Foundation, David MacLennan, and others, stating in part: "We write to highlight the many accomplishments of Professor Emeritus Yoshio Masui of the Department of Zoology. Although Dr. Masui was not included in the recently announced Nobel Prize in medicine and physiology awarded for discoveries in the cell cycle, he was a key founder of the field...Regrettably, the Nobel Prize rules stipulate no more than three joint winners per category and so Dr. Masui was excluded in what must have been a very close decision..'

198. Page 519, para. 1 – "clinical sciences": Connell to author, January 8, 1998.

199. Page 519, para. 1 – "clinical departments": *President's Report, 1968/69* at 137; Jennifer Jones memo, January 13, 2000 at 3; Connell to author, January 8, 1998. It does not include cellular and molecular pathology and clinical biochemistry: see Jones memo at 1.

200. Page 519, para. 1 – "funded by the government": McCulloch oral interview at 51.

201. Page 519, para. 1 – "clinical investigation unit": John Coleman Laidlaw c.v. at 1-2.

202. Page 519, para. 1 – "Lister Institute in London": McCulloch oral interview at 29.

203. Page 519, para. 1 – "clinical departments at Toronto": Jones memo at 2.

204. Page 519, para. 1 – "structure of a graduate program": McCulloch oral interview at 49.

205. Page 519, para. 1 –"strong supporter": Connell to author, January 8, 1998.

206. Page 520, para. 1 – "directly into the University": Bissell, *Parnassus* at 106.

207. Page 520, para. 1 – "high regard for Laidlaw": Ernest Sirluck to author, November 13, 1998.

208. Page 520, para. 1 – "had turned it down": Bissell Diary, April 29 and May 5, 1966.

209. Page 520, para. 2 – "graduate secretary": *President's Report, 1968/69* at 138.

210. Page 520, para. 2 – "dean of health sciences": Laidlaw c.v. at 2-3.

211. Page 520, para. 2 – "clinical departments": Connell to author, January 8, 1998.

212. Page 520, para. 2 – "graduate MDs": J.C. Laidlaw, "Institute of Medical Science" (1968), UTA/A76-0044/39 at 1.

213. Page 520, para. 2 – "20 students a year": *President's Report, 1968/69* at 138.

214. Page 520, para. 2 – "now have medical degrees": Jennifer Jones to author, January 14, 2000.

215. Page 520, para. 2 – "Mel Silverman": Jones memo at 5.

216. Page 520, para. 2 – "director of IMS": *University of Toronto School of Graduate Studies Calendar, 1997-1998* at 274.

217. Page 520, para. 2 – "graduate study at the University": Connell to author, January 8, 1998.

218. Page 520, para. 3 – "Toronto General Hospital": "Hollenberg, Charles H.", *Canadian Who's Who 1994* at 524.

219. Page 520, para. 3 – "looked at for a job": John Evans Oral Interview, UTA/B86-0044, tape 4.

220. Page 520, para. 3 – "head of medicine": Conversation with Hollenberg, June 1998; see Chapter 33 (1962). There is no document in the University records which makes the attempted discrimination explicit, except that there was a delay in the appointment to the Eaton chair and there is evidence that Duncan Graham, the first holder of the chair, felt that the two appointments could be given to separate individuals: see K.J.R. Wightman to John D. Hamilton, July 2, 1969, UTA/A76-0048/007.

221. Page 521, para. 1 – "Arnold Aberman": Barsky, *From Generation to Generation* at 163.

222. Page 521, para. 1 – "left McGill at that time": Lowy left for Ottawa in 1971 and arrived in Toronto in 1974: see "Lowy, Frederick Hans", *Canadian Who's Who 1994* at 690. Melvin Silverman, the chair of IMS left McGill for Toronto in 1971. Vivian Rakoff, who became chair of psychiatry, left McGill for Toronto in 1968: see "Rakoff, Vivian Morris", *Canadian Who's Who 1994* at 938.

CHAPTER 36 – 1967 – STUDENT ACTIVISM

1. Page 525, para. 1 – "premier of Ontario": "Rae, Robert Keith", *Canadian Who's Who 1998* at 1027.

2. Page 525, para. 1 – "member of parliament": "Langdon, Steven W.", *Canadian Who's Who 1994* at 642.

3. Page 525, para. 1 – "Trent University": E-mail from Andrew Wernick to Charles Levi, March 27, 2000.

4. Page 525, para. 1 – "National University of Ireland": "Schabas, William A.", *Canadian Who's Who 1998* at 1107. Schabas is on leave from the University of Quebec at Montreal: see letter from Ezra and Ann Schabas to the author, December 24, 2000.

5. Page 525, para. 1 – "more extreme students": Claude Bissell, *Halfway up Parnassus: A Personal Account of the University of Toronto* (University of Toronto Press, 1974) at 129.

6. Page 525, para. 1 – "disturbance in 1964": Michiel Horn, "Students and Academic Freedom in Canada", *Historical Studies in Education,* v.11, no. 1 at 25; Doug Owram, *Born at the Right Time: A History of the Baby Boom Generation* (University of Toronto Press, 1996) at 219; Cyril Levitt, *Children of Privilege: Student Revolt in the Sixties* (University of Toronto Press, 1984) at 45; see generally, Philip G. Altbach, ed., *Student Political Activism: An International Reference Handbook* (New York: Greenwood Press, 1989).

7. Page 525, para. 1 – "deep and irrational": Bissell Diary of March 8, 1965. In May, 1965 the University saw a small 'silent vigil' of faculty protesting the awarding of an honorary degree to Adlai Stevenson, the American representative to the United Nations: see Bissell, *Parnassus* at 124. Bissell was, after a meeting with students presidents that fall, "struck by the extent to which student radicalism has gone": see Bissell Diary, October 14, 1965.

8. Page 525, para. 2 – "civil rights movement played a part": Owram, *Born at the Right Time* at 166-167; Patricia Jasen, "In Pursuit of Human Values (or Laugh When You Say That)": The Student Critique of the Arts Curriculum in the 1960s", in Paul Axelrod and John G. Reid, *Youth, University, and Canadian Society: Essays in the Social History of Higher Education* (Montreal: McGill-Queen's University Press, 1989) at 252.

9. Page 525, para. 2 – "disarmament campaign": Michiel Horn, *Academic Freedom in Canada: A History* (University of Toronto Press, 1999) at 318; Owram, *Born at the Right Time* at 218.

10. Page 526, para. 1 – "most important factor": Jasen, "In Pursuit" at 252; Owram, *Born at the Right Time* at 219.

11. Page 526, para. 1 – "Vietnam war": Bob Rae, *From Protest to Power: Personal Reflections of a Life in Politics* (Toronto: Penguin Books, 1997) at 38-39.

12. Page 526, para. 1 – "from its influence": Horn, "Students" at 25; "Canadian Union of Students condemns 'corporate' universities", *University Affairs* (October, 1968) at 16.

13. Page 526, para. 1 – "atmosphere at universities": Kenneth McNaught, *Conscience and History: A Memoir* (University of Toronto Press, 1999) at 176. Some faculty came because of dissatisfaction with American policy: see e-mail from Chandler Davis to Friedland, January 4, 1998. See also UTA/Current People/"May, Kenneth"; UTA/Current People/"Kuerti, Anton"; and "Anatol Rapoport", *Canadian Who's Who 1994* at 941. See generally, John Hagan, *Northern Passage: American War Resisters in Canada* (Harvard University Press, 2001). Hagan, a University Professor at the University of Toronto, was a draft dodger who came to the University of Alberta in 1969 and then to the University of Toronto in 1974 (see ibid. at x). He describes the many Vietnam war resisters who came to Toronto (see ibid., chapter 3).

14. Page 526, para. 2 – "authoritarian institutions": Jasen, "In Pursuit" at 253; "Canadian Union of Students" at 16.

15. Page 526, para. 2 – "birth control pill": Horn, "Students" at 29; Owram, *Born at the Right Time* at 265-269.

16. Page 526, para. 2 – "drug culture": LSD figured prominently in the "Perception '67" festival at University College: see Charles Levi, "Where the Famous People Were? The Origins, Activities and Future Careers of Student Leaders at University College, Toronto 1854-1973" (Ph.D. Thesis, York University, 1998) at 481-486; Forster to Bissell, December 9, 1966, UTA/A75-0021/59; LePan to Bissell, February 13, 1967, UTA/A75-0021/59. Drugs were also prevalent at Rochdale College, contributing to the College's "exuberant weirdness" but also its "single greatest undoing": see Cynthia Macdonald, "Love it or loathe it, Rochdale College is hard to dismiss even 20 years after its closing", *University of Toronto Magazine* (Spring, 1995) at 38.

17. Page 526, para. 2 – "from the 'college'": Macdonald, "Love it or loathe it, Rochdale College is hard to dismiss"; Bissell, *Parnassus* at 63-64; Dennis Lee, "Getting to Rochdale", in Howard Adelman and Dennis Lee, eds., *The University Game* (Toronto: Anansi, 1968) at 69-94; David Sharpe, *Rochdale: The Runaway College* (Toronto: Anansi, 1987) at 15-22; see also Henry Mietkiewicz and Bob Mackowycz, *Dream Tower: The Life and Legacy of Rochdale College* (Toronto: McGraw-Hill Ryerson, 1988); Hagan, *Northern Passage: American War Resisters in Canada* at 71-74.

18. Page 527, para. 1 – "sexual diversity studies program at University College": *Varsity*, October 15 and November 5, 1969; e-mails from David Rayside to Friedland of November 10, 2000 and February 19, 2001; e-mail from Harold Averill to Friedland, February 18, 2001; http://webhome.idirect.com/~rbebout/oldbeep/concep.htm; Tom Warner, *Never Going Back: Lesbian and gay activism and organizing in Canada at the end of the 20th Century* (University of Toronto Press, forthcoming). Edith Rayside was David Rayside's great aunt: see Chapter 19 (1907).

19. Page 527, para. 2 – "supervision of the board of governors": Robin Ross, *The Short Road Down: A University Changes* (University of Toronto Press, 1984) at 93; Bissell to Borden, November 3, 1964, UTA/A73-0025/106(01).

20. Page 527, para. 2 – "student washrooms": Forster to Abols, February 18, 1970, UTA/B83-0040/18.

21. Page 527, para. 3 – "used in Vietnam": Ross, *Short Road Down* at 96; "A statement by John H. Sword, Acting President" (undated), UTA/A75-0021/147; Lawson to Westhead, December 7, 1967, UTA/A73-0025/106(04).

22. Page 527, para. 3 – "lying in front of the entrance": Lawson to Westhead at 2.

23. Page 527, para. 3 – "interviews on campus": "Statement by John H. Sword".

24. Page 527, para. 3 – "no action was taken": Lawson to Westhead at 1.

25. Page 527, para. 4 – "Revolution and Response": McNaught, *Conscience* at 176-179; "Teach-In Bulletin" and programme, UTA/A75-0021/39.

26. Page 528, para. 1 – "later married him": McNaught, *Conscience* at 177-178; conversation with Rosie Abella, October 11, 2000.

27. Page 528, para. 1 – "Varsity Arena": Donald Evans to Bissell, September 27, 1965, UTA/A75-0021/39.

28. Page 528, para. 1 – "session on Vietnam": McNaught, *Conscience* at 177; Bissell Diary, October 8 and 9, 1965.

29. Page 528, para. 1 – "an equal chance": *St. Louis Post Dispatch*, October 12, 1965, sent to Bissell, October 17, 1965, UTA/A75-0021/31.

30. Page 528, para. 1 – "religion and morality": Bissell, *Parnassus* at 125; Bob Rae, *From Protest* at 34; *Varsity*, October 17, 1966 and October 23, 1967. See also Catherine Gidney, "Rethinking the Sixties: Inter-generational Cooperation During the University of Toronto Teach-Ins, 1965-1968" (Unpublished paper, CHEA Conference, October, 2000).

31. Page 528, para. 2 – "governance of universities": Bissell, *Parnassus* at 117-120; Ross, *Short Road Down* at 34-35; Ernest Sirluck, *First Generation: An Autobiography* (University of Toronto Press) at 269-271.

32. Page 528, para. 2 – "boards of governors": Bissell, *Parnassus* at 118; *University Government in Canada: Report of a Commission Sponsored by the Canadian Association of University Teachers and the Association of Universities and Colleges in Canada* (University of Toronto Press, 1966) at 24 and 66-7.

33. Page 528, para. 2 – "to advise him": *University Government* at 25-26; Bissell, *Parnassus* at 119.

34. Page 528, para. 2 – "members of the board of governors": *University Government* at 25.

35. Page 528, para. 3 – "academic effects": Bissell, *Parnassus* at 120.

36. Page 529, para. 1 – "feasible proposal": *University Government* at 66.

37. Page 529, para. 1 – "decision-making bodies": Bissell, *Parnassus* at 135; *Varsity*, February 1, 1971.

38. Page 529, para. 1 – "two members of the board": Bissell, *Parnassus* at 132; Ross, *Short Road Down* at 41-42.

39. Page 529, para. 1 – "non-voting participants": Ross, *Short Road Down* at 42.

40. Page 529, para. 1 – "by the establishment": Ross to Bissell, September 13, 1968, UTA/A77-0019/17.

41. Page 529, para. 2 – "including the administration": Ross, *Short Road Down* at 42-43; see generally, Rae, *From Protest* at 39-40.

42. Page 529, para. 2 – "90 votes to 50": Bissell, *Parnassus* at 135; Sirluck, *First Generation* at 282-283. Sirluck was McNaught's brother-in-law, having married McNaught's sister. McNaught's "bitter experience" was otherwise known as the Crowe affair: see Horn, *Academic Freedom*, chapter 9; McNaught, *Conscience,* chapter 9.

43. Page 529, para. 3 – "resign the presidency": Sirluck, *First Generation* at 283.

44. Page 529, para. 3 – "was established": Ross, *Short Road Down* at 43; Bissell, *Parnassus* at 136.

45. Page 529, para. 3 – "political science student": Bissell, *Parnassus* at 162-163.

46. Page 530, para. 1 – "colonialism in Africa": Ibid. at 163.

47. Page 530, para. 1 – "held over the next year": The Commission reported that it "held over 145 meetings, in all parts of the university, and sat for nearly 400 hours": see *Toward Community in University Government: Report of the Commission on the Government of the University of Toronto* (University of Toronto Press, 1970) at 16.

48. Page 530, para. 1 – "published in 1970": Rae, *From Protest* at 40; *Toward Community in University Government: Report of the Commission on the Government of the University of Toronto* (University of Toronto Press, 1970).

49. Page 530, para. 1 – "*ex officio* members": *Toward Community in University Government* at 178.

50. Page 531, para. 1 – "concern to students": Or, as Patricia Jasen put it, "a major area of student discontent": see Jasen, "In Pursuit" at 248.

51. Page 531, para. 1 – "less than second class": Bissell, *Parnassus* at 184.

52. Page 531, para. 1 – "our largest faculty": Ibid. at 185.

53. Page 531, para. 1 – "in arts and science": "University professor emeritus C.B. Macpherson", *University of Toronto*

Bulletin, August 24, 1987; Frances Ireland Oral Interview, tape 9 at 325; Bissell Diary, January 21, 1966; A.D. Allen, "Arts and Science re-forms to face tomorrow's world", *University of Toronto Graduate* (March, 1969) at 4.

54. Page 531, para. 1 – "graduate student in economics": *Undergraduate Instruction in Arts and Science: Report of the Presidential Advisory Committee on Undergraduate Instruction in the Faculty of Arts and Science, University of Toronto* (University of Toronto Press, 1967) at 3-4; conversation between Frank Buck and Charles Levi, March, 2000.

55. Page 531, para. 1 – "were from students": 317 students submissions were made to the Committee, 237 from individual undergraduates. This can be compared to 114 faculty submissions, 86 from individual faculty members: see *Undergraduate Instruction* at 4.

56. Page 531, para. 1 – "unaware of his faults": Ibid. at 37.

57. Page 531, para. 2 – "reflection by the students": *Undergraduate Instruction* at 13-15.

58. Page 531, para. 2 – "appointments and promotions": Ibid. at 40.

59. Page 531, para. 2 – "should be encouraged": Ibid. at 45-46.

60. Page 531, para. 2 – "1965-6 academic year": Conversation with law professor Alan Brudner, March 2000; A.S. Brudner to Forster, December 9, 1965; Ian Drummond memorandum, January 25, 1966; and Richard J. Andrew to Forster, undated, UTA/B83-0040/010.

61. Page 531, para. 2 – "in 1966-7": *Undergraduate Instruction* at 45.

62. Page 531, para. 2 – "preparation of the forms": Ibid. at 45-46.

63. Page 531, para. 3 – "the general course": Ibid. at 54-61.

64. Page 532, para. 1 – "separate courses for each": Ibid. at 54-55. The separation of the curriculum began in the 1850s under President McCaul, but pass and honours courses were formally separated in 1877-8: see Chapter 7 (1860). For a discussion of the honour course system at the University of Toronto, see Patricia Jasen, "Educating an Elite: A History of the Honour Course System at the University of Toronto" *Ontario History*, Volume 81, December 1989 at 269.

65. Page 532, para. 1 – "thirty or so": Ibid. at 55.

66. Page 532, para. 1 – "after first year": Ibid. at 149.

67. Page 532, para. 1 – "Toronto was well known": Bissell Diary, September 30, 1968.

68. Page 532, para. 2 – "students who are not in them": *Undergraduate Instruction* at 54.

69. Page 532, para. 2 – "high specialization": Ibid. at 58.

70. Page 532, para. 2 – "general students the same": Ibid. at 60.

71. Page 533, para. 1 – "three-year general degree": Ibid. at 77.

72. Page 533, para. 1 – "between the disciplines": Jasen, "In Pursuit" at 248.

73. Page 533, para. 1 – "law": Author's personal knowledge.

74. Page 533, para. 1 – "engineering": "More elective freedom in Engineering curriculum", *University of Toronto Bulletin*, March 18, 1971.

75. Page 533, para. 1 – "honours system was adopted": "Arts and Science re-forms" at 4. Ramsay Cook states that this is not was the Macpherson committee had in mind. The "reforms", Cook states, abolished or "abandoned" the honours program as it had been known historically. "We wanted it maintained, opened to all students who could do it as either a 3 or 4 year programme." His disappointment was a factor in causing him to move to York University: see Cook to Friedland, February 14, 2001.

76. Page 533, para. 1 – "arts and science program": Not only did students want to select the subjects they wanted, but they wanted to take the courses at their own pace. Such a change would mean that students would not be judged by their performance over an entire year, but by individual courses, thereby introducing a credit system for arts and science. Before the adoption of the New Programme, students had to pass all their subjects but one in order to maintain standing, or else they had to repeat their year: see *University of Toronto Faculty of Arts and Science 1968-1969 Calendar* at 49 and 53. The New Programme allowed students to pass each course individually, and advance to second year after the completion of five first-year courses: see *University of Toronto Faculty of Arts and Science 1970-1971 Calendar* at 13. In the division of Extension, part-time students could be considered to have already been on the credit system, but if they took more than one course a year they could fail the year if they averaged less than 60% in the courses: see *University of Toronto Division of University Extension Degree Courses 1968-1969* at 26.

77. Page 533, para. 2 – " so many universities recently": Forster to Joliat, January 15, 1969, UTA/B83-0040/016. The Forster papers in the University of Toronto Archives were not open to the public when I started this project. Frank Felkai, one of Donald Forster's executors, obtained a judicial order from Justice Joseph Potts to allow me to inspect and use the papers for this history.

78. Page 533, para. 2 – "the revolutionaries": Ross, *Short Road Down* at 97; William H. Nelson, *The Search for Faculty Power* (Toronto: Canadian Scholar's Press, 1993) at 44.

79. Page 533, para. 2 – "opposed to the Vietnam war": Bissell, *Parnassus* at 139.

80. Page 533, para. 2 – "target of the far left": Alfbach, *Student Political Activism*, at 450; Adelman and Lee, "A Note on the Multiversity" in *The University Game* (Toronto: Anansi, 1968) at 173.

81. Page 533, para. 2 – "rise to haunt him": "Remember Berkeley?", undated pamphlet in UTA/A83-0012/001, underlining in original.

82. Page 534, para. 1 – "enraged the protesters": Bissell Diary, February 5, 1969.

83. Page 534, para. 1 – "added his views": Bissell, *Parnassus* at 141; "Resnick, Philip", *Canadian Who's Who 1998* at 1044-1045; www.shifty.com/twuc/resnick.htm.

84. Page 534, para. 1 – "'childish' and 'desperate'": Bissell Diary, February 5, 1969.

85. Page 535, para. 1 – "destroyed by student activists": Owram, *Born at the Right Time* at 286-287; Bissell Diary, February 13, 1969.

86. Page 535, para. 1 – "in the United States": Bissell, *Parnassus* at 142.

87. Page 535, para. 1 – "1969-70": Bissell Diary, March 24, 1969.

88. Page 535, para. 1 – "both documents": Bissell, *Parnassus* at 142-143.

89. Page 535, para. 1 – "Ralph Campbell": *Varsity*, September 26 and 29, 1969.

90. Page 535, para. 1 – "urged a sit-in": Bissell, *Parnassus* at 146-147.

91. Page 535, para. 2 – "occupied the front rows": Ross, *Short Road Down* at 98.

92. Page 535, para. 2 – "chair of the meeting": Bissell, *Parnassus* at 147.
93. Page 535, para. 2 – "give the president some support": Sirluck, *First Generation* at 291.
94. Page 535, para. 2 – "audience cheered": Bissell, *Parnassus* at 147; Bissell Diary, October 1, 1969; "Nine days in the life of a university president", *University of Toronto Graduate* (December, 1969) at 20.
95. Page 535, para. 2 – "where this audience stands": Bissell, *Parnassus* at 147; see also Ross, *Short Road Down* at 98.
96. Page 535, para. 2 – "a court jester": Bissell Diary, October 1, 1969. The court jester interpretation is the author's, who attended the meeting.
97. Page 535, para. 2 – "Bissell was elated": Bissell, *Parnassus* at 146-148; Bissell Diary, October 1, 1969.
98. Page 535, para. 3 – "day-care facilities at the University": Bissell, *Parnassus* at 148-154; Ross, *Short Road Down* at 98-100; Jill Ker Conway, *True North: A Memoir* (Toronto: Alfred A. Knopf, 1994) at 191-195; Sirluck, *First Generation* at 292-293.
99. Page 535, para. 3 – "a day-care centre": Donald Forster had been in correspondence on the issue as early as 1967: see Forster to Susan Mann, April 18, 1967, UTA/B83-0040/12 and Forster to Sue Russell, July 31, 1967, UTA/B83-0040/13.
100. Page 535, para. 3 – "for renovations": Bissell, *Parnassus* at 150. Conway says that it was taken over "illegally": see Conway, *True North* at 192.
101. Page 535, para. 3 – "Simcoe Hall was forthcoming": Sirluck, *First Generation* at 292, says that "a very reasonable request…was badly mishandled by middle management."
102. Page 537, para. 1 – "University campus": Conway, *True North* at 191.
103. Page 537, para. 1 – "Your Diapers": Sirluck, *First Generation* at 292; Conway, *True North* at 192.
104. Page 537, para. 2 – "in the senate chamber": Bissell, *Parnassus* at 152; Conway, *True North* at 194, states that "everyone showed a level of concentration and intellectual excitement I rarely saw in the classroom."
105. Page 537, para. 2 – "sweet smell of pot": Bissell, *Parnassus* at 152.
106. Page 537, para. 2 – "latest crisis was over": Ibid. at 153-154.
107. Page 537, para. 2 – "a court injunction": "Affidavit of Donald F. Forster", March 26, 1970, UTA/B83-0040/18.
108. Page 537, para. 2 – "leading the charge": Forster to Levine, April 29, 1970, UTA/B83-0040/18.
109. Page 537, para. 3 – "Robarts Library": Robert H. Blackburn, *Evolution of the Heart: A History of the University of Toronto Library up to 1981* (Toronto: University of Toronto Library, 1989) at 228; Ross, *Short Road Down* at 100-03; Bissell, *Parnassus* at 156-57.
110. Page 537, para. 3 – "not other students": Blackburn, *Evolution* at 228.
111. Page 537, para. 3 – "Graduate Students Union": Spencer to Sword, February 2, 1972, UTA/A78-0028/005.
112. Page 537, para. 3 – "signed and returned": "Council asks that 'access' be reviewed", *University of Toronto Bulletin*, February 4, 1972; "McQuaig, Linda Joy", *Canadian Who's Who 1998* at 856.

113. Page 538, para. 1 – "anyone who wants to use them": "Books for Whom? Books for What?" (undated pamphlet), UTA/A78-0028/005.

114. Page 538, para. 1 – "67 to 28": "Committee on Stack Access to the Robarts Library Report", February 29, 1972, UTA/A77-0035/19 at 8; "LIBRARY: what Heyworth Report means", *University of Toronto Bulletin*, March 9, 1972; Sword to "Colleague", March 15, 1972, UTA/A77-0035/19 at 2; Blackburn, *Evolution* at 234.

115. Page 538, para. 2 – "access to all undergraduates": Cassels Brock to Rickaby, March 15, 1972, UTA/A78-0028/005 at 2; "Police end 'the completely unnecessary occupation of Senate Chamber forced by small group of students'", *University of Toronto Bulletin*, March 13, 1972.

116. Page 538, para. 2 – "to get in": Cassels Brock to Rickaby at 3-5.

117. Page 538, para. 2 – "*Toronto Star*": "Walkom, Thomas Lawrence", *Canadian Who's Who 1998* at 1293.

118. Page 538, para. 2 – "such as assault": Three were charged with trespass and assault and one with trespass and obstructing police: see "Police end 'the completely unnecessary occupation'".

119. Page 538, para. 2 – "500 people": Cassels Brock to Rickaby at 6.

120. Page 538, para. 2 – "library administrators": "A message to the University Community from the Acting President", March 14, 1972, UTA/A77-0035/19.

121. Page 538, para. 2 – "proceed with the charges": Sword's proposed settlement had been approved by acting vice-president Don Forster, chairman of the board William Harris, graduate school dean Ed Safarian, Ben Etkin, the dean designate of engineering, and Peter Russell, the principal of Innis College: see "A message to the University Community"; Cassels Brock to Rickaby at 7-8.

122. Page 538, para. 3 – "against our own students": Sword to "Colleague" at 4.

123. Page 538, para. 3 – "14 to 3": Ross, *Short Road Down* at 103.

124. Page 538, para. 3 – "take time to heal": Forster to Redding, April 13, 1972, UTA/B83-0040/23.

125. Page 538, para. 3 – "three cases": Ross, *Short Road Down* at 102 – of the four charges of obstruction and assaulting police, one led to an acquittal, two to absolute discharges and the fourth to a conditional discharge.

126. Page 539, para. 1 – "of the library": Blackburn, *Evolution* at 236. The Heyworth revised rules were approved by the library council on April 5, 1972: see "Library Council approves revised rules", *University of Toronto Bulletin*, April 6, 1972. The Senate also approved them: see "Senate passes regulations for use of the libraries", *University of Toronto Bulletin*, April 19, 1972. A third occupation of Simcoe Hall took place following that meeting, in spite of assurances from the SAC that the meeting would be an orderly one, but the sit-in was quickly and voluntarily ended: see "Terms of Agreement with President of the SAC Concerning Proposed SAC Meeting on Monday, 20th March", UTA/A77-0035/19; *Globe and Mail*, March 21, 1972; Blackburn, *Evolution* at 236.

127. Page 539, para. 1 – "a university administrator": Ross, *Short Road Down* at 103.

128. Page 539, para. 1 – "given stack passes": Blackburn, *Evolution* at 237.

129. Page 539, para. 1 – "professional librarians": Ross, *Short Road Down* at 103.

130. Page 539, para. 1 – "might have been": Blackburn, *Evolution* at 237. Umberto Eco, however, has praised the openness of the Robarts stacks: see Robert Fulford, "Finding love among the bookshelves at the library", *Globe and Mail*, October 8, 1997.

131. Page 539, para. 2 – "Edward Banfield": Ross, *Short Road Down* at 103. *Varsity,* March 8, 1974.

132. Page 539, para. 2 – "the urban poor": See generally Ross, *Short Road Down* at 104-107; Nelson, *Faculty Power* at 86-89.

133. Page 539, para. 2 – "held at the University": Nelson, *Faculty Power* at 86.

134. Page 539, para. 2 – "prevented from speaking": "Dr. Evans outlines the background of the Banfield visit to campus", *University of Toronto Bulletin,* March 29, 1974.

135. Page 539, para. 2 – "radical student leaders": Their counsel at the appeal referred to them as communists: see "Notice of Appeal", September, 1974, UTA/A79-0051/93 at 4.

136. Page 539, para. 2 – "student in sociology": "CAPUT finds against Schabas, Leah, and suspends both", *University of Toronto Bulletin,* July 5, 1974.

137. Page 539, para. 2 – "library stacks affair": "18 charges are laid by police", *University of Toronto Bulletin,* March 13, 1972; Robin Ross, *Short Road Down* at 101, states that Schabas was also involved in the library issue.

138. Page 539, para. 2 – "doctorate in history": "Caput finds against Schabas, Leah".

139. Page 539, para. 2 – "day-care sit-in": "Affidavit of Donald F. Forster". Schabas was also involved in a sit-in by the worker-student alliance: see Bissell Diary, January 30, 1970.

140. Page 539, para. 2 – "prevent Banfield from speaking": "Dr. Evans outlines the background"; "Caput finds against Schabas, Leah".

141. Page 539, para. 2 – "adjourned the proceedings": *Globe and Mail,* May 28, 1974.

142. Page 539, para. 3 – "could deliver his lectures": See, for example, Rutherford, Bliss, and Bothwell to "Dear Sir", March 14, 1974, UTA/B95-0013/008(01).

143. Page 540, para. 1 – "likely to be trouble": Nelson, *Faculty Power* at 87.

144. Page 540, para. 1 – "academic purposes": "GC executive refers disruption to Caput", *University of Toronto Bulletin,* March 15, 1974.

145. Page 540, para. 1 – "free discussion": "UTFA council 'demands' action of safeguards for free discussion", *University of Toronto Bulletin,* March 20, 1974.

146. Page 540, para. 1 – "tone of his remarks": Forster to Evans, March 20, 1974.

147. Page 540, para. 1 – "by the disrupters": Conway, *True North* at 230.

148. Page 540, para. 2 – "life or property exists": Evans to "Colleague", March 14, 1974, UTA/B95-0013/008(01).

149. Page 540, para. 2 – "suitable environment": "On protection of freedom of speech – a statement by the President", *University of Toronto Bulletin,* March 29, 1974.

150. Page 540, para. 3 – "Leah and Schabas": "Dr. Evans outlines the background"; *Globe and Mail,* April 6, 1974. Note that another incident occurred at a governing council meeting on March 28, 1974: see "Council adopts the academic Code before interruption", *University of Toronto Bulletin,* March 29, 1974.

151. Page 540, para. 3 – "required reading list": "Governing Council hastily reconvened, completes Thursday's interrupted business", *University of Toronto Bulletin,* April 1, 1974. He also argued that SDS, which had been

suspended by the administration, should have its suspension revoked. The suspension was done without giving notice or a hearing: Ross, *Short Road Down* at 105.

152. Page 540, para. 3 – "disciplinary matters": "GC executive refers disruption to Caput".

153. Page 541, para. 1 – "nineteen-day hearing": *Toronto Star*, June 26, 1974, refers to a 19-day hearing; other documents say that the hearing was 22 days, but this includes the preliminary matters.

154. Page 541, para. 1 – "outside the University": Ross, *Short Road Down* at 104.

155. Page 541, para. 1 – "an American citizen"; "In Memoriam Albert S. Abel", *University of Toronto Law Journal*, v.28 (1978) at 367.

156. Page 541, para. 1 – "used his navy gavel": "Two students face Caput charges over Banfield", *University of Toronto Bulletin*, April 19, 1974; author's personal knowledge.

157. Page 541, para. 1 – "trying to restore order": Author's personal knowledge.

158. Page 541, para. 1 – "take the gavel away from him": *Globe and Mail*, June 18, 1974.

159. Page 541, para. 2 – "Charles Roach": "Two students face Caput charges".

160. Page 541, para. 2 – "start in May": Ibid.

161. Page 541, para. 2 – "members of the Caput": "Membership of Caput", *University of Toronto Bulletin*, April 19, 1974. The seven were Albert Abel, John Beckwith, Bernard Etkin, Goldwin French, Donald Ivey, Kathleen King, and Peter Russell: see "CAPUT finds against Schabas, Leah".

162. Page 541, para. 2 – "in the case of Schabas": "Caput finds against Schabas, Leah".

163. Page 541, para. 3 – "appealed to the governing council": *Globe and Mail*, March 5, 1975; "Schabas, Leah file their appeal", *University of Toronto Bulletin*, October 4, 1974.

164. Page 541, para. 3 – "have been effectively destroyed": "Caput finds against Schabas, Leah".

165. Page 541, para. 3 – "other human rights issues": "Schabas, William", *Canadian Who's Who 1998* at 1107-1108.

166. Page 541, para. 3 – "members of the Caput": Ivey to Harding, March 31, 1975, UTA/A79-0051/93.

167. Page 541, para. 3 – "Robin Ross": Ross, *Short Road Down* at 105.

168. Page 541, para. 3 – "two years' suspension": *Globe and Mail*, March 21, 1975.

169. Page 541, para. 3 – "less severe penalties": "Notice of Appeal" at 7; "Overturn Caput Suspensions", including excerpt from *Varsity*, September 30, 1974, UTA/A79-0051/93.

170. Page 541, para. 3 – "suspended sentences": "Overturn Caput Suspensions", including excerpt from *Varsity*, September 30,1974, UTA/A79-0051/93.

171. Page 541, para. 4 – "student activism": Horn, *Academic Freedom* at 321.

172. Page 541, para. 4 – "Bob Bossin in 1980": Jacqueline Swartz, "The Maturing of Militants", *University of Toronto Graduate* (May/June 1980) at 8.

173. Page 542, para. 1 – " support of the institution": Horn, *Academic Freedom* at 322.

CHAPTER 37 – 1971 – A NEW ACT

1. Page 543, para. 1 – "all well here": Telegram dated July 23, 1971, recorded in the Bissell Diary, May 16, 1971. In the last few months of 1971, Bissell stopped dating his diary entries and the actual date he made the entry is unknown.

2. Page 543, para. 1 – "July 1, 1972": Section 20 of the Act, which authorized the Board of Governors to call elections for Governing Council, was proclaimed on January 5, 1972. The remainder of the Act came into force on July 1, 1972: see *The Ontario Gazette*, vol. 105-6, February 5, 1972, at 299-300.

3. Page 543, para. 1 – "North America to do so": *Report of the President for 1972-73 and 1973-74* at 29; see "A Brief History and Description of the Governing Council", http://www.utoronto.ca/govcncl/tgc/history.htm.

4. Page 543, para. 2 – "June 30, 1971": Minutes of the Executive Committee of the Board of Governors, June 22, 1970, UTA/A78-0019/005.

5. Page 543, para. 2 – "fight through the changes": Bissell Diary, October 6-7, 1969.

6. Page 543, para. 2 – "thought that he should retire": Ibid, October 24, 1969.

7. Page 543, para. 2 – "strip it of power": Ibid.

8. Page 543, para. 2 – "changes in the governing structure": "Dr Bissell resigns Presidency to teach at U of T", *University of Toronto Bulletin*, July 2, 1970.

9. Page 544, para. 1 – "October 1969": "Six meeting to schedule CUG talks", *University of Toronto Bulletin*, November 6, 1969.

10. Page 544, para. 1 – "107 in all": *Toward Community in University Government: Report of the Commission on the Government of the University of Toronto* (University of Toronto Press, 1970) at 213; Robin Ross, *The Short Road Down: A University Changes* (University of Toronto Press, 1984) at 45.

11. Page 544, para. 1 – "and 6 others": *Toward Community* at 213-214.

12. Page 544, para. 1 – "to govern the University": See generally, Bissell Diaries during the 1960s.

13. Page 544, para. 1 – "of financial matters": Claude Bissell, *Halfway up Parnassus: A Personal Account of the University of Toronto 1932-1971* (University of Toronto Press, 1974) at 120; *Toward Community* at 173.

14. Page 544, para. 1 – "indisputable authority": *Toward Community* at 174; Bissell, *Parnassus* at 120.

15. Page 544, para. 2 – "It had worked": Henry Borden oral interview transcript, UTA/B87-0044 at 83.

16. Page 544, para. 2 – "commission's deliberations": McCutcheon died January 23, 1969. His last personal appearance was at the CUG meeting of January 21, and the meeting of January 24 passed a motion of sympathy and then adjourned: see UTA/Current People/"McCutcheon, Malcolm Wallace".

17. Page 544, para. 2 – "joined the board in 1968": "Copy of an Order-In-Council approved by his Honour the Lieutenant Governor, dated the 13th day of June, A.D. 1968", UTA/A70-0024/reel 3.

18. Page 544, para. 2 – "it was ridiculous": Sydney Hermant oral interview transcript, UTA/B78-0022 at 31.

19. Page 544, para. 3 – "CUG report": See generally, oral interview with William B. Harris, UTA/B86-0049; author's

conversation with John Tory on May 10, 2000. At the time, Tory had taken the position that some of the meetings of the governing council should be held in camera.

20. Page 544, para. 3 – "most did not": William Harris and Malim Harding probably accepted the report: see Ross, *Short Road Down* at 48.

21. Page 544, para. 3 – "board in 1945": "Copy of an Order-In-Council approved by The Honorable the Lieutenant-Governor, dated the 6th day of February, A.D. 1945", UTA/A70-0024/reel 3.

22. Page 544, para. 3 – "a member of the board": See Borden to Robarts, April 17, 1968, PAO/John P. Robarts fonds/Series 4-3/Box 12/"University of Toronto 1968-1970". Borden retired completely on June 30, 1971, having suffered two cerebral hemorrhages earlier that month: Borden memoirs at 146.

23. Page 544, para. 3 – "not a good chairman": Borden interview at 75.

24. Page 544, para. 3 – "conducted board meetings": Ibid.

25. Page 544, para. 3 – "literally": Hermant oral interview transcript at 30.

26. Page 545, para. 1 – "organizations on the campus": "Committee is being formed to organize discussions of report of governance", *Bulletin*, October 23, 1969; Ross, *Short Road Down* at 48.

27. Page 545, para. 1 – "Graduate Students' Union": Ross, *Short Road Down* at 48; Bissell, *Parnassus* at 172.

28. Page 545, para. 1 – "the *Varsity*": Ross, "Discussion of Governmental Structures", undated and unpublished document at 13.

29. Page 545, para. 1 – "preceding few months": Bissell, *Parnassus* at 172.

30. Page 545, para. 2 – "entire university community": The questionnaire was devised with the assistance of the sociology department: see Ross, *Short Road Down* at 48-49; "Questionnaire will help in planning a University-wide CUG Committee", *Bulletin*, January 23, 1970.

31. Page 545, para. 2 – "University-wide Committee (UWC)": About 45% of the faculty and 20% of the undergraduates responded to the questionnaire: see Ross, *Short Road Down* at 49.

32. Page 545, para. 2 – "end of the academic year": "CUG: nominations close March 31 for election of members to the University-Wide Committee", *Bulletin*, March 20, 1970; "Questionnaire indicates University-Wide Committee has 'substantial' support", *Bulletin*, April 2, 1970.

33. Page 545, para. 2 – "President's Council": Minutes of the President's Council, March 16, 1970, UTA/B98-0006.

34. Page 545, para. 2 – "general meeting of the association": William H. Nelson, *The Search for Faculty Power: The University of Toronto Faculty Association 1942-1992* (Toronto: Canadian Scholar's Press, 1993) at 49.

35. Page 545, para. 2 – "Macdonald Block": Bissell, *Parnassus* at 174-175.

36. Page 545, para. 2 – "struck in the University of Toronto": Ross, *Short Road Down* at 52.

37. Page 546, para. 1 – "worked out constituencies": Ibid. at 49.

38. Page 546, para. 1 – "refused to take part": Bissell, *Parnassus* at 176; Ross, *Short Road Down* at 50.

39. Page 546, para. 1 – "attended as observers": Harris to White, June 11, 1971, PAO/RG32-1-1/M298/File: Toronto, University of, Legislation, Comments (I) 1971.

40. Page 546, para. 1 – "involved with CUG": Bissell, *Parnassus* at 164-165.

41. Page 546, para. 1 – "took part in the deliberations": A.C.H. Hallett, "Summary of Proceedings of the University-Wide Committee June 1-3, 1970", UTA/A77-0019/061 at 1.

42. Page 546, para. 1 – "chaired the meetings": Ross, *Short Road Down* at 51; Bissell, *Parnassus* at 175-76.

43. Page 546, para. 1 – "vote of 111 to 15": Ross, *Short Road Down* at 51; Hallett, "Summary" at 2.

44. Page 546, para. 1 – "60 to 56": Hallett, "Summary" at 7. This was called a 'straw vote' preparatory to voting on the composition of the governing council. Ham noted that Hallett had to hold a 'straw vote' rather than a regular vote because any other type would preclude a final vote: see "UWC is re-visited: a cool call by a hard-pressed chairman", *University of Toronto News*, May, 1971.

45. Page 546, para. 1 – "unicameral governing body": Ross, *Short Road Down* at 51.

46. Page 546, para. 2 – "series of votes": Ibid.

47. Page 547, para. 1 – "10 students": Nelson, *Faculty Power* at 50-51.

48. Page 547, para. 1 – "support staff": Ross, *Short Road Down* at 51-52; Hallett, "Summary" at 9.

49. Page 547, para. 2 – "could be revisited": Bissell, *Parnassus* at 175; Ross, *Short Road Down* at 52; Hallett, "Summary" at 10; "Memorandum to the Members of the Steering Committee of the University-Wide Committee From the CUG Programming Committee", undated, UTA/B98-0006.

50. Page 547, para. 2 – "was ever prepared": Ross, *Short Road Down* at 52.

51. Page 547, para. 2 – "jubilation at the outcome": Bissell, *Parnassus* at 175.

52. Page 547, para. 3 – "board be established": "The President's Council accepts UWC report as the basis for new Act", *Bulletin*, June 25, 1970; Ross, *Short Road Down* at 53.

53. Page 547, para. 4 – "Board of Governors will follow": Report Number 49 of the Executive Committee of the Board of Governors, June 22, 1970, UTA/A78-0019/006.

54. Page 548, para. 1 – "revision of the University of Toronto Act": Board of Governors Minutes, October 22, 1970, UTA/A78-0019/006.

55. Page 548, para. 2 – "top governing body": "Statement of the Board of Governors University of Toronto on University Government", Appendix A of Board of Governors Minutes, November 26, 1970, UTA/A78-0019/006.

56. Page 548, para. 2 – "unicameral system": Bissell to heads of Divisions, December 3, 1970, UTA/B98-0006.

57. Page 548, para. 2 – "ferment in the university": Forster to Russell, March 8, 1971, UTA/B83-0040/020.

58. Page 548, para. 3 – "University-wide Committee": As minister of education, he had supported a unicameral system, but wanted a much stronger lay presence: Davis to Robarts of July 31, 1970, PAO/John P. Robarts Fonds/ Series 4-3/Box 12/"University of Toronto 1968-1970".

59. Page 548, para. 3 – "prepare the legislation": Bissell, *Parnassus* at 177.

60. Page 548, para. 3 – "become its vice-chair": "O.D. Vaughan retires June 30 as Chairman", *Bulletin*, June 29,

1971; "Copy of an Order-In-Council approved by His Honour the Lieutenant Governor, dated the 4th day of August, A.D. 1971", UTA/A85-0024/11; Harris oral interview, UTA/B86-0049, tape 1; "Vice-Chairman of the Board", *Bulletin*, November 11, 1971.

61. Page 548, para. 3 – "views of the board": "Statement of the Board of Governors University of Toronto on University Government".

62. Page 548, para. 3 – "members of the governing council": "Statement by the Minister of University Affairs", June 3, 1971, UTA/B98-0006.

63. Page 548, para. 3 – "recommended by the UWC": Davis had not worried about the size of the council, stating that "no new problems would seem to be created if that total were increased to eighty-four or ninety-six": see Davis to Robarts, July 31, 1970.

64. Page 548, para. 3 – "42-member council": "Alumni to elect Chancellor is among changes included in U of T Act revisions", *Bulletin*, June 29, 1971. Draft legislation tabled in early June would have resulted in a 40-member council – exposure bill; *Globe and Mail* of June 4, 1971; "'Exposure draft' of new University Act provides for Governing Council of 42", *Bulletin*, June 8, 1971.

65. Page 548, para. 3 – "50 members": *The University of Toronto Act, 1971*, Section 2.

66. Page 548, para. 4 – "NDP demanded parity": See, for example, speeches of Tim Reid, Walter Pitman, Robert Nixon, and Stephen Lewis, in *Debates and Proceedings of the Legislature of the Province of Ontario*, June 30 and July 5, 1971, at 3471-3473, 3517-3518, 3521-3522 and 3529-3530.

67. Page 548, para. 4 – "the number of faculty members": It was 60%. The bill as enacted had a composition of exactly 2/3rds: see *Debates and Proceedings*, July 22, 1971 at 4633. Faculty included academic administrators, except for the two presidential appointees who might be academic administrators.

68. Page 549, para. 1 – "eight days of hearings": White, in *Debates* at 4631, says 8 or 9 days.

69. Page 549, para. 1 – "UWC ratios": Bissell, *Parnassus* at 178; Ross, *Short Road Down* at 54.

70. Page 549, para. 1 – "18-year-olds would be voting": Davis introduced the legislation allowing 18-year olds to vote on July 18, 1971 and the first election at which they could vote was on October 21, 1971: see Claire Hoy, *Bill Davis: A Biography* (Toronto: Methuen Publications, 1985) at 92; Bissell, *Parnassus* at 177; Ross, *Short Road Down* at 54.

71. Page 549, para. 1 – "faculty and students together": J.B. Conacher to "Dear Colleague", July 9, 1971, UTA/B98-0006; *Debates and Proceedings*, July 22, 1971 at 4641; Nelson, *Faculty Power* at 52-53. A large file of correspondence and telegrams on the issue from campus and community persons alike can be found in PAO/RG32-1-1/ Ministry of Colleges and Universities – Central Registry – Legislation 1971-1972.

72. Page 549, para. 1 – "15 to 1": Conacher to "Dear Colleague", July 9, 1971.

73. Page 549, para. 1 – "adopted his proposal": *Debates and Proceedings*, July 22, 1971 at 4641.

74. Page 549, para. 1 – "the government majority": The vote was 51-36: ibid. at 4661.

75. Page 549, para. 1 – "passed by the assembly": Ibid. at 4692.

76. Page 549, para. 2 – "would be resolved": Minutes of the Executive Committee of the Board of Governors, June 22, 1970, UTA/A78-0019/005 ; "Dr Bissell Resigns", *Bulletin*, July 2, 1970.

77. Page 549, para. 2 – "rubber-stamped by the board": See Chapter 31 (1958).

78. Page 549, para. 2 – "such a committee": Bissell Diary, December 21, 1970.

79. Page 549, para. 2 – "put forward a proposal": Bissell Diary, October 14, 1970; "Recommend committee of 21 to nominate next President", *Bulletin*, October 29, 1970.

80. Page 549, para. 2 – "in October 1970": Bissell Diary, October 26, 1970. The faculty representatives argued for a composition similar to the UWC, but the council chose a parity model, ibid.; see also ibid. January 11, 1971.

81. Page 549, para. 2 – "a representative committee": Ibid., December 21, 1970.

82. Page 549, para. 2 – "Omond Solandt as chairman": Ibid.

83. Page 549, para. 2 – "early in 1971": "Nominations now open for election to Presidential Search Committee", *Bulletin*, January 14, 1971.

84. Page 549, para. 2 – "took place in February": Bissell Diary, February 8, 1971; "Committee of 14 invites suggestions for President", *Bulletin*, February 9, 1971.

85. Page 549, para. 2 – "somewhat 'conservative' slant": Forster to Russell, March 8, 1971.

86. Page 550, para. 1 – "recorded these in his diary": Bissell Diary, February 8, 1971.

87. Page 550, para. 2 – "dropped from the list": Author's conversations with Safarian and Schiff, May 2000.

88. Page 550, para. 2 – "supported Sirluck": Ernest Sirluck, *First Generation: An Autobiography* (University of Toronto Press, 1996) at 321-322; author's conversations with Safarian and Schiff.

89. Page 550, para. 2 – "to be put forward": Sirluck, *First Generation* at 322; but see also Bissell Diary, April 12, 1971, referring to events of May 17, 1971.

90. Page 550, para. 2 – "kept on the list": Sirluck, *First Generation* at 322.

91. Page 550, para. 2 – "Evans and Sirluck": Bissell Diary, March 20, 1971, referring to events of April 16, 1971.

92. Page 550, para. 2 – "Carrothers and Sirluck": Forster to Manfred Bienenfeld, May 10, 1971, UTA/B83-0040/020.

93. Page 550, para. 2 – "Sirluck's name": *Globe and Mail*, June 12, 1971.

94. Page 550, para. 2 – "he was not a candidate": Sirluck, *First Generation* at 322-323.

95. Page 550, para. 2 – "held out a larger promise": Bissell Diary, under the date of April 12, 1971, referring to events of May 17, 1971.

96. Page 550, para. 2 – "whether Carrothers would accept": Ibid., referring to events of May 23, 1971.

97. Page 550, para. 3 – "approved the recommendation": Bissell Diary, April 15, 1971, referring to events of May 27, 1971. The Board minutes, however, show no such recommendation being presented or accepted. The Executive Committee set up a committee in May to draft terms of appointment: see Minutes of the Executive Committee, May 10, 1971, UTA/A78-0019/007.

98. Page 550, para. 3 – "discuss a possible contract": Bissell Diary, April 15, 1971, referring to events of May 27, 1971; Harris oral interview, tape 2.

99. Page 550, para. 3 – "by the job": Bissell Diary, April 23, 1971, referring to events of June, 1971. Bill Harris recalled that both Carrothers and his wife were concerned about the size of the job: see Harris oral interview, tape 2.

100. Page 550, para. 3 – "dean of law there": Author's conversation with William Poole, May 10, 2000.

101. Page 550, para. 3 – "high salary, and so on": Bissell Diary, April 26, 1971, referring to events of June 24, 1971.

102. Page 550, para. 3 – "break off negotiations": Author's conversation with Poole, May 10, 2000.

103. Page 550, para. 3 – "University of British Columbia": "Carrothers, Alfred William Rooke", *Canadian Who's Who 1973-1975* at 167; *Globe and Mail*, September 25, 1998.

104. Page 551, para. 1 – "president there": Bissell noted that 'he is rumoured to be the choice of UBC for its new President': see Bissell Diary, April 12, 1971, referring to events of May 17, 1971. The University of British Columbia, however, did not choose a new President until 1975, when Douglas Kenny replaced Walter Gage. Gage had been President since 1968: see *The President's Report, 1974-1975* (Vancouver, British Columbia, 1975) at 3.

105. Page 551, para. 1 – "appointment to the board": Bissell Diary, April 26, 1971, referring to events of June 24, 1971. There is no record in the minutes of the Executive Committee or the Board of Governors that these actions were taken.

106. Page 551, para. 2 – "Sydney Hermant": Bissell Diary, April 27, 1971, referring to events of June 24, 1971. No such motion appears in the Board minutes of June 24, 1971.

107. Page 551, para. 2 – "member of the search committee": "Alumni President and Secretary are members of the Presidential Search Committee", *University of Toronto News*, March, 1971.

108. Page 551, para. 2 – "as a board member": Borden oral interview at 90. Borden resigned from the Board, effective June 30, 1971.

109. Page 551, para. 2 – "Carrothers as president": Borden oral interview at 88. No such motion or even discussion of the issue is noted in the Board minutes for June 24, 1971.

110. Page 551, para. 2 – "negotiating through a lawyer": Ibid. at 87-88; Bissell Diary, April 27, 1971, referring to events of June 24, 1971.

111. Page 551, para. 2 – "for the scholarship": Borden oral interview at 89.

112. Page 551, para. 2 – "offer was rescinded": Ibid. at 88; see generally Harris oral interview.

113. Page 551, para. 2 – "drink to it": Bissell Diary, April 27, 1971, referring to events of June 25, 1971.

114. Page 551, para. 2 – "easily selected Evans": Author's conversations with Safarian and Schiff, May, 2000; *Toronto Star*, December 24, 1971.

115. Page 551, para. 2 – "offering him the job": Harris oral interview.

116. Page 551, para. 2 – "Evans the position": Ibid.

117. Page 551, para. 2 – "on July 1, 1972": "Dr. John R. Evans becomes the President next July 1", *Bulletin*, November 24, 1971.

118. Page 551, para. 3 – "end of November 1971": Ibid.

119. Page 551, para. 3 – "provost Don Forster": Forster had been acting vice-president and provost from July 1, 1971: see minutes of the Executive Committee, May 26, 1971, UTA/A78-0019/07.

120. Page 551, para. 3 – "very low": Forster to Mrs. Joy Campbell, December 17, 1971, UTA/B83-0040/022.

121. Page 551, para. 3 – "within the University": John Evans Oral interview, UTA/B86-0044, tape 9.

122. Page 551, para. 3 – "attended the University of Toronto": "Dr John R. Evans".

123. Page 552, para. 1 – "management' and direction" Forster to Treleaven, May 26, 1972, UTA/B83-0040/23; conversation with Evans, August, 1998.

124. Page 552, para. 2 – "out of doors": "Our ninth President is officially installed", *Bulletin*, September 29, 1972.

125. Page 552, para. 2 – "lieutenant governor of Ontario": "McGibbon, Hon. Pauline M.", *Canadian Who's Who 1994* at 763.

126. Page 552, para. 2 – "under a clear sky": "Our ninth President".

127. Page 552, para. 2 – "repression of women": Ibid.

128. Page 553, para. 1 – "day-care controversy": *Globe and Mail*, September 29, 1972.

129. Page 553, para. 2 – "least certain about the future": "Address by Dr. Evans after his installation", *Bulletin*, September 29, 1972.

130. Page 553, para. 2 – "traditional college subjects": Ibid.

131. Page 553, para. 3 – "existing colleges, or both": Ibid.

132. Page 553, para. 3 – "political compromise": Ibid.

133. Page 553, para. 4 – "Evans was appointed": Evans oral interview, tape 9.

134. Page 553, para. 4 – "in the legislation": *University of Toronto Act, 1971*, sections 2 and 3.

135. Page 553, para. 4 – "secretary of the board, David Claringbold": Evans oral interview, tape 9; Harris oral interview, tape 2.

136. Page 554, para. 1 – "chair of the governing council": "C. Malim Harding 1911-1990", *Bulletin*, March 12, 1990.

137. Page 554, para. 1 – "Harris its vice-chair": Harris says that the province appointed him chairman and Harding the vice chairman, but he (Harris) got it switched: see Harris oral interview, tape 2.

138. Page 554, para. 1 – "governing council positions": "Count more than 10,000 valid ballots in election to staff and student seats", *Bulletin*, March 17, 1972.

139. Page 554, para. 2 – "the Italian community": Unsigned memorandum on stationary of the Chairman of the Board of Governors (attributed to Evans), April 6, 1972, UTA/A78-0028/34; Evans to Ireland, undated, UTA/A79-0042/005; Ireland memo on "ethnic names", May 5, 1972, UTA/A79-0042/005.

140. Page 554, para. 2 – "on July 4, 1972": "Five main areas await policy decisions Governing Council told at first meeting", *Bulletin*, July 5, 1972.

141. Page 554, para. 2 – "more manageable": Evans oral interview, tape 11.

142. Page 554, para. 3 – "five such committees": Ibid., tape 9.

143. Page 555, para. 1 – "day-care issue": See Chapter 37 (1967).

144. Page 555, para. 1 – "history of the University": Jill Ker Conway, *True North: A Memoir* (Toronto: Alfred A. Knopf Canada, 1994) at 207.

145. Page 555, para. 1 – "utterly dumbfounded": Ibid. at 203-204 and 206.

146. Page 555, para. 1 – "Smith College": *Bulletin*, July 5, 1974.

147. Page 555, para. 1 – "vice-president": "Prof Conway's successor will start at year's end, full-time July 1", *Bulletin*, October 25, 1974.

148. Page 555, para. 1 – "Paul Cadario": "Council selects its standing committees", *Bulletin*, July 21, 1972.

149. Page 555, para. 1 – "impressive community work": "Governing Council elects Marnie Paikin chairman", *Bulletin*, May 14, 1976.

150. Page 556, para. 1 – "standing committee": Walter J. MacNeill was its first chair: see "Council selects its standing committees". Norman James was the vice-president of external affairs: see UTA/Current People/"James, Norman".

151. Page 556, para. 1 – "it was dropped": Ross, *Short Road Down* at 76-77.

152. Page 556, para. 1 – "vice-president business affairs": "New administrative structure announced", *Bulletin*, June 19, 1972.

153. Page 556, para. 1 – "business affairs committee": "Council selects its standing committees".

154. Page 556, para. 1 – "Jack Sword": "Address by Dr. Evans", *Bulletin*, September 29, 1972.

155. Page 556, para. 1 – "standing committee": "Council selects its standing committees". Twaits was succeeded by W.J.D. Lewis: see Claringbold to Lewis, May 28, 1974, UTA/A94-0022/27.

156. Page 556, para. 2 – "vice-president and provost": "Council selects its standing committees"; "New administrative structure announced".

157. Page 556, para. 2 – "standing committee": *University of Toronto Act, 1971*, Section 2(14)(d).

158. Page 556, para. 2 – "a single vote": The arrangement was supported by Bill Harris, who stated that "it would contravene the unicameral principle of governance to delegate powers to any body that was dominated by one estate." Other former board members, however, such as Senator Daniel Lang and Sydney Hermant argued against its adoption, stating that to carry the principle into the committees would hamper the governance of the university: see "Academic Affairs Committee with 25 members is one of five in structure adopted by Council", *Bulletin*, July 14, 1972.

159. Page 556, para. 2 – "student members of council": Such as future Rhodes Scholars Paul Cadario and Brian Morgan: see "Two Student Councillors are Rhodes Scholars", *Bulletin*, December 15, 1972.

160. Page 556, para. 2 – "academic affairs committee": "Proposed Composition of the Academic Affairs Committee", August 14, 1978, UTA/A94-0022/026.

161. Page 556, para. 3 – “two persons to the council”: *University of Toronto Act, 1971*, Section 2(2)(b).

162. Page 556, para. 3 – “this was not enough”: See generally, Evans oral interview, tapes 9 and 10.

163. Page 556, para. 3 – “chaired by the provost”: Frances Ireland oral interview, UTA/B86-0052, tape 11 and Evans oral interview, tape 11.

164. Page 557, para. 2 – “ coming into force of the legislation”: *University of Toronto Act, 1971*, section 2(19); John B. Macdonald, “The Governing Council System of the University of Toronto 1972-1977: A Review of the Unicameral Experiment”, (December, 1977) at 1.

165. Page 557, para. 2 – “same as for the faculty”: Ross, *Short Road Down* at 67.

166. Page 557, para. 2 – “students and faculty”: Ibid. at 68; “Larger by 7 – 13 faculty – 11 students”, *Bulletin*, October 25, 1974.

167. Page 557, para. 2 – “reached by the Council”: Ross, *Short Road Down* at 68.

168. Page 558, para. 1 – “unionism will only accelerate”: Forster to Peter Salus, October 31, 1974, UTA/B83-0040/035.

169. Page 558, para. 1 – “should be solicited as well”: Nelson to Auld, December 12, 1974, UTA/A79-0051/111.

170. Page 558, para. 1 – “acted upon by the government”: Ross, *Short Road Down* at 69.

171. Page 558, para. 2 – “staff of the university”: “Report of the Special Study Group on the Role of the Teaching Staff in the Governance of the University of Toronto”, Appendix 1, UTA/A81-0058/019; Ross, *Short Road Down* at 69; Macdonald, “The Governing Council” at 1.

172. Page 558, para. 2 – “no major changes”: Macdonald, “The Governing Council” at 1.

173. Page 558, para. 2 – “five-year review”: Ross, *Short Road Down* at 72; “Dr. J.B. Macdonald to examine Council's effectiveness”, *Bulletin*, April 22, 1977.

174. Page 558, para. 2 – “end of 1977”: Ross, *Short Road Down* at 72; “Macdonald report produces mixed reaction in University community”, *Bulletin*, January 23, 1978.

175. Page 558, para. 2 – “initiate action”: Macdonald, “The Governing Council” at 9.

176. Page 558, para. 2 – “damaging conflict”: Ibid. at 14. John B. Macdonald states, “The University of Toronto had now five years experience with the new system and, whatever its weaknesses it was unlikely that the clock could be turned back. Almost certainly it would be unhelpful for me to offer such a solution. The task I saw, therefore, was to expose the problems and to offer solutions which would allow the system to function and restore confidence”: see John B. Macdonald, *Chances and Choices: A Memoir* (Vancouver: UBC and UBC Alumni Association, 2000) at 194.

177. Page 558, para. 3 – “constitute a majority”: Faculty members would have, in addition to their 7 elected places, 19 others on a 61-person committee – one elected by each division of the University not otherwise represented by an elected faculty member. Moreover, the committee would also include 7 senior academic administrators selected by the president: see Macdonald, “The Governing Council” at 14.

178. Page 558, para. 3 – “adopt the proposal”: Ross, *Short Road Down* at 76; “Majority principle rejected”, *Bulletin*, May 23, 1978; Jean Smith, the president of the faculty association, urged the governing council to adopt the report, without avail: see J.E. Smith to Paikin, February 10, 1978, UTA/A84-0026/122.

179. Page 558, para. 3 – “without a vote”: Ross, *Short Road Down* at 77.

180. Page 559, para. 1 – “more powerful”: Nelson, *Faculty Power* at 77-78; Ross, *Short Road Down* at 63.

181. Page 559, para. 1 – “Simcoe Circle”: Conway, *True North* at 212; Ireland oral interview, tape 11.

182. Page 559, para. 1 – “senior officials”: Ireland oral interview, tape 11.

183. Page 559, para. 1 – “issue of the moment”: Conway, *True North* at 212.

184. Page 559, para. 1 – “handpicked them”: Evans says he resisted the pressure to have them selected by a representative committee: see Evans oral interview, tape 11.

185. Page 559, para. 1 – “Simcoe Hall”: Forster to Randy Spence, April 3, 1973, UTA/B83-0040/027.

186. Page 559, para. 2 – “Reginald Haist”: Haist to Bissell, February 7, 1966; “Report on Academic Tenure Submitted by the Presidential Advisory Committee on Academic Appointments and Tenure”, UTA/A75-0021/079; Nelson, *Faculty Power* at 33.

187. Page 559, para. 2 – “completing their term”: Chairs were appointed on recommendation of a committee set up by the president and the dean of the faculty: see “Report on Academic Tenure Submitted by the Presidential Advisory Committee on Academic Appointments and Tenure, Part 1”, UTA/A75-0021/079.

188. Page 559, para. 2 – “administrators had had in the past”: Evans oral interview, tapes 9 and 1.

189. Page 559, para. 2 – “chairs in the system”: Ibid., tape 9.

190. Page 559, para. 2 – “changing the university”: Ibid.

CHAPTER 38 – 1975 – SLIDING DOWN PARNASSUS

1. Page 560, para. 1 – "Faculty Association (UTFA)": The association changed its name from the Association of Teaching Staff (ATS) to UTFA on July 1, 1971: see William H. Nelson, *The Search for Faculty Power* (Toronto: Canadian Scholar's Press, 1993) at 71.

2. Page 560, para. 1 – "by 25 per cent": Ibid. at 94.

3. Page 560, para. 1 – "value of salaries": Paul Axelrod, *Scholars and Dollars: Politics, Economics, and the University of Ontario 1945-1980* (University of Toronto Press, 1982) at 147.

4. Page 560, para. 1 – "becoming more militant": See Nelson, *Faculty Power* at 75 et seq.; "Dr. Bator Interview with Professor W.H. Nelson Finding Aid", UTA/B86-0082 at 3.

5. Page 560, para. 1 – "history of the association": Nelson, *Faculty Power* at 82.

6. Page 560, para. 1 – "other Canadian universities": Ibid. at 96-97; Axelrod, *Scholars and Dollars* at 204.

7. Page 560, para. 1 – "between 1973 and 1976": Nelson, *Faculty Power* at 168.

8. Page 560, para. 1 – "habitually trusted": Ibid. at 88.

9. Page 560, para. 2 – "offered 9 per cent instead": The administration finally imposed a 12% increase, significantly less than the 18% final offer by the faculty: see ibid. at 95.

10. Page 560, para. 2 – "keeping up with inflation": "University asked to propose substantial '75-'76 savings", *University of Toronto Bulletin*, January 10, 1975.

11. Page 561, para. 1 – "specifically for education": See Chapter 31 (1958).

12. Page 561, para. 1 – "universities in future years": Axelrod, *Scholars and Dollars* at 141-142.

13. Page 561, para. 1 – "more scholar for the dollar": Axelrod implies that the phrase was first quoted in the *Toronto Telegram*, March 8, 1971: see ibid. at 143-147 and 243n24. White used many formulations of the phrase, such as "more scholars per dollar": see *Debates and Proceedings of the Legislature of the Province of Ontario*, May 25, 1971 at 1953.

14. Page 561, para. 1 – "renovation of old buildings": "CUA hears University's reaction to capital freeze", *Bulletin*, December 1, 1972; "Address of Dr. J.R. Evans, President of the University of Toronto, to the Canadian Club, December 2, 1974", UTA/A79-0042/007 at 5; Axelrod, *Scholars and Dollars* at 164.

15. Page 561, para. 1 – "influence that public opinion": Forster to Scott Jolliffe, November 19, 1974, UTA/B83-0040/036.

16. Page 561, para. 2 – "last among Ontario universities": "Statement to the Governing Council, February 26th 1976 by President John R. Evans"; Chant to Evans, February 17, 1976, UTA/A81-0058(005). The year before, it was second last: see "Memorandum re Report of the President to the Governing Council, November 20th, 1975".

17. Page 561, para. 2 – "fixed pot of money": John Evans, "President's Statement in response to the Government's announcement of Financing", December 15, 1975. For a description of "global budgeting", see Axelrod, *Scholars and Dollars* at 167.

18. Page 561, para. 2 – "new growth was frozen": "Dr. Evans comments on the 76-77 grant", *Bulletin*, February 20,

1976; "Statement to the Governing Council, February 26th, 1976". The University wanted to control the temptation for expansion: see "President's report to the Governing Council, December 18th, 1975 Re: Government announcements about finance"; see also John B. Macdonald, *Chances and Choices: A Memoir* (Vancouver: UBC and UBC Alumni Association, 2000) at 165.

19. Page 561, para. 2 – "training of new professors": Axelrod, *Scholars and Dollars* at 150. Also the funds for graduate fellowships were reduced: ibid. at 162.

20. Page 561, para. 2 – "brought on real malnutrition": "Address of Dr. J.R. Evans... to the Canadian Club" at 5.

21. Page 561, para. 3 – "beginning of the decade": Evans to Editor, *Globe and Mail,* December 12, 1975, UTA/A79-0042/007.

22. Page 561, para. 3 – "Faculty has been reduced": Robert Greene to H. Parrott, January 3, 1977, UTA/A84-0026/070.

23. Page 562, para. 1 – "staff, hours, facilities": Jill Ker Conway, *True North: A Memoir* (Toronto: Alfred A. Knopf, 1994) at 232-233.

24. Page 562, para. 1 – "to a friend in late 1973": Forster to Steve Langdon, October 9, 1973, UTA/B83-0040/030.

25. Page 562, para. 1 – "surprisingly easy": Forster to Jolliffe, November 19, 1974.

26. Page 562, para. 1 – "incurring a deficit": "BUDGET: $4 million deficit", *Bulletin,* February 28, 1975; "'Little bit' will cut deficit, Dr. Evans says", *Bulletin,* May 9, 1975.

27. Page 562, para. 1 – "by the Government is a possibility": Norman James to Evans, November, 1974, and Evans to James, November 19, 1974, UTA/A79-0051/098; "Address of Dr. J.R. Evans... to the Canadian Club" at 11.

28. Page 562, para. 2 – "from the federal granting agencies": See generally, Evans to Donald Macdonald, June 28, 1976, UTA/A81-0058/002. Evans and faculty members had met with Macdonald on June 25, 1976 to discuss the plight of the University. Evans subsequently sent a letter to Trudeau.

29. Page 562, para. 2 – "warning in early 1972": Oral interview with William B. Harris, UTA/B86-0049, tape 2. For a discussion of the sale of Connaught, see Paul A. Bator, *Within Reach of Everyone: A History of the University of Toronto School of Hygiene and Connaught Laboratories Limited, Volume II 1955 to 1975, With an Update to the 1990s* (Toronto: Canadian Public Health Association, 1995) at 128-132.

30. Page 562, para. 2 – "remain in Canadian hands": "Work on agreement for sale of Connaught", *Bulletin,* May 12, 1972; "The University completes sale of Connaught Labs to the CDC", *Bulletin,* October 3, 1972; Minutes of the Meeting of the Board of Governors, May 4, 1972, May 25, 1972, and June 29, 1972, UTA/A78-0019/10. There were new construction costs and decreased earnings: see "Connaught Laboratories to erect new manufacturing building", *Bulletin,* December 2, 1971.

31. Page 562, para. 2 – "for the next ten years": University, Merieux come to terms", *Bulletin,* October 30, 1989; Connell memo to author, January 2, 2000 at 2-3. Donald Guthrie points out that the settlement was actually completed in July 1991 under Prichard although the essential elements of the deal were struck by Connell: see Guthrie comments to Friedland, February, 2001. At the time of writing the company is called Aventis Pasteur and in early 2000 gave the University $2 million to fund a chair in human immunology: see "Aventis Gift Benefits Vaccine Research", *Bulletin,* April 27, 2000.

32. Page 562, para. 3 – "about $2 million a year": "Connaught Awards are made: grants cover five research areas", *Bulletin,* October 4, 1974. It was higher later in the decade: see "The Connaught Fund", *Bulletin,* February 25, 1980.

33. Page 562, para. 3 – "research within the University": The terms of reference for the fund have been modified over the years to meet changing needs: see for example, "'Superstars' to get larger grants under proposed changes in Connaught fund", *Bulletin,* November 5, 1979.

34. Page 562, para. 3 – "establish research programs": "Connaught grants to new staff may be for junior level only", *Bulletin,* January 12, 1987.

35. Page 562, para. 3 – "interdisciplinary nature": See "Connaught Fund is under review terms of reference questioned", *Bulletin,* June 21, 1974; "The Connaught Fund 1998-99 Annual Report" (document forwarded by Jeannie Ing, July, 2000) at 6-7 and Appendix A.

36. Page 563, para. 1 – "a Connaught development grant": "Connaught Awards are made: grants cover five research areas".

37. Page 563, para. 1 – "Boris Stoicheff": Ibid.

38. Page 563, para. 2 – "undertaken in 1976": "'Update' campaign goal is $25 million", *Bulletin,* April 29, 1976.

39. Page 563, para. 2 – "Henry Borden": John Evans oral interview, UTA/B86-0044, tape 10.

40. Page 563, para. 2 – "campaign's success": Evans to Lee MacLaren, May 1, 1975, UTA/A79-0051/098.

41. Page 563, para. 2 – "campaign objectives": Ibid.; MacLaren to Evans, September 2, 1975, UTA/A82-0021/15.

42. Page 563, para. 2 – "Murray Koffler of Shoppers Drug Mart as vice-chairman": "'Update' campaign goal is $25 million"; "Format for Global T.V." (December, 1976), UTA/A84-0026/035; see also Frank Rasky, *Just a Simple Pharmacist* (Toronto: McClelland and Stewart, 1988).

43. Page 563, para. 3 – "John Wayne and Frank Shuster": Evans to Shuster, October 29, 1976, UTA/A84-0026/035.

44. Page 563, para. 3 – "Koffler Student Centre": *University of Toronto President's Report, 1974-1978* at 37; John Evans, "Update: Memo for file – re: Murray Koffler", January 11, 1978, UTA/A84-0026/089; "Koffler Centre opens with gala celebration", *Bulletin,* September 9, 1985 at 7; "Moving Experience", *University of Toronto Graduate* (September/October 1985) at 11.

45. Page 563, para. 3 – "earth sciences building": "$15 million earmarked for renovations", *Bulletin,* April 29, 1976; "Calling bids for athletic facility", *Bulletin,* December 19, 1975.

46. Page 563, para. 3 – "about $36 million": "The Update campaign for private support", *University of Toronto Bulletin,* January 25, 1982; "St. Clair Balfour elected Council chairman", *Bulletin,* April 9, 1984.

47. Page 563, para. 4 – "UTFA sought – negotiations": Nelson, *Faculty Power* at 94.

48. Page 564, para. 1 – "bring about this result": "Faculty union debated", *Bulletin,* November 14, 1975.

49. Page 564, para. 1 – "Labour Relations Act": Nelson, *Faculty Power* at 104.

50. Page 564, para. 1 – "voluntary agreement with the University": Ibid. at 105.

51. Page 564, para. 1 – "hard-edged underneath": Ibid.

52. Page 564, para. 1 – "Carole Moore": Carole Moore was Carole Weiss at the time, see ibid. at 105-106.

53. Page 565, para. 1 – "binding arbitration": Ibid. at 106.

54. Page 565, para. 1 – "an appeal process": "Academic appointments policy and procedure are recommended by the President's task force", *Bulletin,* September 7, 1973; Nelson, *Faculty Power* at 84. Forster did not wish to appear as the chairman, but he clearly was: see ibid. at 84; Frances Ireland oral interview, UTA/B86-0052, tape 12.

55. Page 565, para. 2 – "recommendations on tenure": There is no evidence the Board ever passed the rules. On November 18, 1966, they considered a text of a document entitled "Academic Tenure", suggested the deletion of three words and left the matter in the hands of the President, see Board of Governors Minutes, November 18, 1966, UTA/A70-0024/reel 22. Michiel Horn, *Academic Freedom in Canada: A History* (University of Toronto Press, 1999) at 305, cited Nelson, *Faculty Power* at 33, to the effect that the board adopted the rules. Exactly how these recommendations were adopted and implemented remains a mystery. For another aspect of the Haist rules, see Chapter 37 (1971).

56. Page 565, para. 2 – "following certain procedures": "Academic Tenure", UTA/B94-0004/007, section VIII(1). There is no document in the University of Toronto Archives which bears the title "The Haist Rules".

57. Page 565, para. 2 – "faculty-dominated committees": Ibid., section IX (6).

58. Page 565, para. 2 – "recently recognized": "An informal system for awarding tenured appointments existed prior to that time": see "Report of the Task Force on Academic Appointments", *Bulletin,* Supplement, September 7, 1973 at 1.

59. Page 565, para. 2 – "for fiscal reasons": See Nelson, *Faculty Power* at 84-85.

60. Page 565, para. 2 – "unlikely ever to happen": "Report of the Task Force on Academic Appointments" at 5.

61. Page 566, para. 1 – "in the hands of governing council": Nelson, *Faculty Power* at 107-108.

62. Page 566, para. 1 – "of the faculty members who voted": Ibid. at 108; see also "Failure of UTFA negotiations examined", *Bulletin,* March 18, 1977; "UTFA negotiating team receives strong support", *Bulletin,* April 15, 1977.

63. Page 566, para. 1 – "Smith in the *Bulletin*": "Failure of UTFA negotiations examined".

64. Page 566, para. 1 – "in favour of collective bargaining": Ibid.

65. Page 566, para. 2 – "UTFA and the governing council": The agreement was endorsed by 95% of the respondents. It was signed on May 17, 1977 and approved by the UTFA council without dissent and later by Governing Council: see Nelson, *Faculty Power* at 113; "Representatives sign Memorandum of Agreement", *Bulletin,* May 20, 1977 at 5. The Governing Council passed it June 16, 1977. No vote is recorded in the Governing Council Minutes.

66. Page 566, para. 2 – "rejected by the governing council": Nelson, *Faculty Power* at 109-110.

67. Page 566, para. 2 – "total University picture": Evans to Chant and Iacobucci, November 21, 1975, UTA/A82-0021/026; see also "President proposes alternative to collective bargaining", *Bulletin,* October 1, 1976.

68. Page 566, para. 3 – "consent of the faculty association": Nelson, *Faculty Power* at 109.

69. Page 566, para. 3 – "change them unilaterally": "Representatives sign Memorandum of Agreement".

70. Page 566, para. 3 – "reject the agreement": Ibid.

71. Page 567, para. 1 – "it has been workable": Chant to Ham, November 5, 1979, UTA/A86-0021/043. Roger Savory, the vice-president of UTFA, specifically warned Simcoe Hall about the consequences of rejection: "were this to happen next March, one can only speculate at this time on what the next step might be": see "UTFA clarifies terms of Memorandum of Agreement", *Bulletin,* October 22, 1979.

72. Page 567, para. 2 – " during his administration": Evans oral interview, tape 11.

73. Page 567, para. 2 – "were going into debt": Frances Ireland, "Memorandum on the Faculty of Arts and Science", December 22, 1971, UTA/A79-0051/071 at 3.

74. Page 567, para. 2 – "partial formula funding": Robin S. Harris, "Victoria in Federation with the University of Toronto", in *From Cobourg to Toronto: Victoria College in Retrospect* (Toronto: Chartres Books, 1986) at 43; Alexander Reford, "St. Michael's College at the University of Toronto 1958-1978: The Frustrations of Federation", *The Canadian Catholic Historical Association Historical Studies*, v.61 (1995) at 185-6.

75. Page 567, para. 2 – "Larry Lynch": Philip Marchand, *Marshall McLuhan: The Medium and the Messenger* (Toronto: Vintage Canada, 1990) at 88.

76. Page 568, para. 1 – "the rest to the University": See Chapter 10 (1883).

77. Page 568, para. 1 – "the social sciences": See generally, *Undergraduate Instruction in Arts and Science: Report of the Presidential Advisory Committee on Undergraduate Instruction in the Faculty of Arts and Science, University of Toronto* (University of Toronto Press, 1967) at 83 et seq.

78. Page 568, para. 1 – "transferred to University College": See Innis to Cody, October 28, 1943, UTA/A68-0006/62(08).

79. Page 568, para. 1 – "wanted to be university professors": See Chapter 10 (1883).

80. Page 568, para. 2 – "feeling of anonymity": "Memorandum of Understanding Relating to the Role of the Colleges in the Faculty of Arts and Science, University of Toronto", May, 1974, Trinity Archives/986-0095/004(10) at 4; John M. Robson to "Colleagues", November 2, 1971, UTA/A82-0040/005.

81. Page 568, para. 2 – "discontinued in the early 1970s": Some colleges allowed a substitute subject: see author's conversation with David Cook, June 5, 2000. Trinity required the course under the "old programme" but it vanished as a result of the Macpherson report: see "Report of the Committee to Review the Undergraduate Programme to the Dean of the Faculty of Arts & Science", *Bulletin*, May 5, 1979, at S-3.

82. Page 568, para. 2 – "Macpherson report": See Chapter 36 (1967).

83. Page 568, para. 2 – "Moffat Woodside": For a discussion of the Woodside report, see *Undergraduate Instruction in Arts and Science* at 86; see also Ireland, "Memorandum on the Faculty" at 3.

84. Page 568, para. 3 – "between the University and the colleges": "Proposing to teach college subjects in new University departments and foster distinctive instruction", *Bulletin*, May 3, 1974.

85. Page 569, para. 1 – "in which they have registered": "Memorandum of Understanding" (1974) at 4.

86. Page 569, para. 2 – "develop the college programs": "The Colleges: They Do a Better Job Than Their Critics Suppose", *Bulletin*, October 1, 1978; Arthur Kruger oral history transcript, UTA/B86-0062 at 20.

87. Page 569, para. 2 – "problems of morale were created": James McConica to Friedland, February 12, 2001

88. Page 569, para. 2 – "anxiety in the colleges": See, e.g., "The Teaching of Present College Subjects in the Proposed New University Departments: A Memorandum of Concern" (document prepared by University College chairs of departments, c. October, 1974), UTA/A82-0040/005.

89. Page 570, para. 1 – "classics faculties in North America": Fax from Kruger dated June 9, 1998; author's conversation with Paul Perron, June 6, 2000.

90. Page 570, para. 1 – "largest in the world": In terms of faculty members: author's conversation with Perron, June 6, 2000; Callaghan on June 8, 2000.

91. Page 570, para. 2 – "UC was *the* college": E-mail from Milton Israel to author, May 27, 2000.

92. Page 570, para. 2 – "memorandum of misunderstanding": Hallett to Robin Ross, November 26, 1975, UTA/A82-0021/003; James Ham, "Presidential Statement concerning the St. George Colleges and the Memorandum of Understanding", May 31, 1979, UTA/A87-0020/013.

93. Page 570, para. 2 – "where he had grown up": Evans oral interview, tape 11; "Hallett, Archibald Cameron Hollis", *Canadian Who's Who 1986* at 542.

94. Page 570, para. 3 – "criminology at Woodsworth": *University of Toronto Faculty of Arts and Science St. George Campus 2000-2001 Calendar* at 94, 219, 344, 398, 435, 443, and 447.

95. Page 570, para. 3 – "conflict studies at University College": "University College mounts peace studies program", *Bulletin,* March 10, 1986.

96. Page 570, para. 3 – "to mention only a few examples": *Arts and Science Calendar* at 268, 432, and 443.

97. Page 570, para. 3 – "the college in which they are given": Harris, "Victoria in Federation" at 50; Author's conversation with Roseann Runte on June 6, 2000.

98. Page 570, para. 4 – "taught in the college": Ignatieff to Israel, April 5, 1977, UTA/A84-0026/023.

99. Page 570, para. 4 – "gave rise to further reviews": See "Final Report of the Review Committee of the Collegiate Board, University of Toronto", November, 1979, UTA/A87-0020/013; see also "Report of the Presidential Working Group on the Academic Role of the Colleges on the St. George Campus" (chaired by Alexander Dalzell), March 9, 1983, St. Michael's College Archives/USMC President, 1978.

100. Page 570, para. 4 – "not just of understanding": "A Memorandum of Agreement Regarding the Institutional Relationships of the University of Toronto and the Federated Universities in the Faculty of Arts and Science", May 18, 1984; "Memorandum of agreement signed", *Bulletin,* September 10, 1984; Harris, "Victoria in Federation" at 43.

101. Page 570, para. 4 – "faculty of arts and science": "Report of the Presidential Working Group" at 6; Harris, "Victoria in Federation" at 50.

102. Page 570, para. 4 – "complement of faculty positions": "Memorandum of Agreement" (1984) at 5 and 10; see also "Final Report of the Review Committee of the Collegiate Board" at 8.

103. Page 570, para. 4 – "at their own expense": Harris, "Victoria in Federation" at 50; author's conversations with Peter Richardson on June 4, 2000 and David Cook on June 5, 2000; "Final Report of the Review Committee of the Collegiate Board" at 7.

104. Page 570, para. 4 – "conflict studies programs": See "Group raising funds for peace chair at UC", *Bulletin,* November 22, 1982; "UC peace chair endowment", *Bulletin,* May 25, 1987; author's conversation with Peter Richardson, June 4, 2000; see also "A Serious Celebrity", *University of Toronto Magazine,* (Winter, 1994) at 6. Kleber was appointed to comparative literature and Homer-Dixon to political science for the graduate components of their work: see e-mail from Paul Perron to Friedland, January 28, 2001.

105. Page 570, para. 4 – "made at other colleges": Author's conversation with Roseann Runte and Paul Perron on June 6, 2000, describing three appointments at Victoria College during this period.

106. Page 571, para. 1 – "for at least ten years": "A Memorandum of Agreement Regarding the Institutional Relation-

ships of the University of Toronto and the Federated Universities in the Faculty of Arts and Science", July 21, 1990 (copy forwarded by David Cook); "A Memorandum of Agreement between the University of Toronto and the Federated Universities", July 1, 1998 (forwarded by David Cook) at 14-15.

107. Page 571, para. 1 – "periodic external review": "A Memorandum of Agreement between the University of Toronto and the Federated Universities", July 1, 1998 at 3 and 5.

108. Page 571, para. 1 – "physical and health education": E-mail from Paul Perron, January 28, 2001.

109. Page 571, para. 1 – "quarters in college": Envisioned by the "Final Report of the Review Committee of the Collegiate Board" at 3.

110. Page 571, para. 1 – "Slavic studies in St. Michael's": Author's conversations with Peter Richardson on June 4, 2000; David Cook on June 5, 2000; Roseann Runte on June 6, 2000; Paul Perron on June 6, 2000; James McConica to Friedland, February 12, 2001.

111. Page 571, para. 2 – "students' choice of subjects": "Governing Council gives its approval to Kelly Report", *Bulletin,* April 21, 1980.

112. Page 571, para. 2 – "more structured curriculum": "Report of the Committee to Review the Undergraduate Programme", *Bulletin,* May 5, 1979 at S-4.

113. Page 571, para. 2 – "'cafeteria-style' program": "Governing Council gives its approval to Kelly Report".

114. Page 571, para. 2 – "even with colleges": "Report of the Committee to Review the Undergraduate Programme" at S-4.

115. Page 571, para. 2 – "after vigorous debate": See "The Kelly report: The debate begins", *Bulletin,* September 24, 1979 and "The Kelly report debate is over", *Bulletin,* December 3, 1979; "Governing Council gives its approval to Kelly Report"; see also "More Structure for Arts & Science", *Bulletin,* November 6, 1978.

116. Page 571, para. 2 – "prevent both extremes": "Report of the Committee to Review the Undergraduate Programme".

117. Page 571, para. 2 – "even more structure": "The Kelly report: The debate begins"; "The Kelly report debate is over".

118. Page 571, para. 2 – "own curriculum programme": Tamara Baggs to "Faculty Member of the General Committee", October 26, 1979, UTA/A86-0021/002.

119. Page 572, para. 1 – "to the general public": See Chapter 23 (1919).

120. Page 572, para. 2 – "introduced by President Falconer": "University of Toronto of the Air Series of Broadcasts Starts January 11", *University of Toronto Monthly,* v. 32 at 139; *Report of the President for the Year Ending June 30, 1932* at 5. The talks began in January, 1932. Another series was approved for the fall of 1932: see *Report of the President for the Year Ending June 30, 1933* at 83.

121. Page 572, para. 2 – "television series for the general public": "The Varsity Television Story", *University of Toronto Alumni Bulletin* (Autumn, 1954) at 29.

122. Page 572, para. 2 – "television script-writing": Ibid.

123. Page 572, para. 2 – "existence of the CBC": "Report of the University of Toronto Television Committee to the Advisory Planning Committee", June 14, 1957, UTA/A83-0036/017 at 5-8.

124. Page 572, para. 2 – "Banting Institute": "The Varsity Television Story" at 29.

125. Page 572, para. 2 – "the new medium": "Report by Dr. Harris on University Television Programmes", c. 1954, UTA/A83-0036/017 appendix at 4; Marchand, *Marshall McLuhan* at 134, mentions McLuhan's first experiment in television at the CBC studies in Toronto in the spring of 1954.

126. Page 572, para. 2 – "circumcision rites in Africa": "Report by Dr. Harris" appendix at 2.

127. Page 572, para. 2 – "the live productions": "Meeting of the Television Committee", January 30, 1953, UTA/A83-0036/017.

128. Page 572, para. 2 – "Donald Ivey": "'Live and Learn' returns on T.V.", *Varsity News* (September, 1958) at 3.

129. Page 572, para. 2 – "proved unsuccessful": See Chapter 32 (1960).

130. Page 572, para. 3 – "students kept growing": "Installation Address John R. Evans President, University of Toronto", September 28, 1972, UTA/A79-0042/005 at 8.

131. Page 572, para. 3 – "had poor teachers": "Report of the Presidential Advisory Committee on Extension", July, 1970 (Document forwarded by Bill Bateman) at 11-12; "Recollections", *Bulletin,* March 5, 1984; "Credible at last", *Bulletin,* November 10, 1978.

132. Page 573, para. 1 – "effective lobby for change": Arthur Kruger and Peter Silcox, "Woodsworth at Ten", *University of Toronto Graduate* (January/February 1984) at 16; "APUS is 20 years old this month", *Bulletin,* November 7, 1988.

133. Page 573, para. 1 – "for part-time students": "Part-time students' status and services should be raised, President is advised", *Bulletin,* November 5, 1970; "Advisory Committee on Extension" at 15 and 23.

134. Page 573, para. 2 – "their needs are met": "Advisory Committee on Extension" at 23.

135. Page 573, para. 2 – "College X": "A&S sub-committee recommends system for part-time undergraduate education", *Bulletin,* April 5, 1972; "'X College' for part-time students approved by General Committee", *Bulletin,* May 5, 1972.

136. Page 573, para. 2 – "newly arrived in Canada": "A Message from the President", 1977, UTA/A79-0042/007.

137. Page 574, para. 1 – "skill upgrading": E-mail from Mary Barrie to author, June 13, 2000; see also "A&S, SCS May Merge", *University of Toronto Bulletin,* January 10, 2000.

138. Page 574, para. 2 – "part-time students": For the steps that led up to this, see Norma Grindal, "The Six Years Before Woodsworth College", *The Arbor,* v. 4, (Winter, 1984) at 14-15; William Bateman to author, July 3, 1998.

139. Page 574, para. 2 – "its first principal": "Professor Arthur Kruger is appointed first Principal of College X", *Bulletin,* January 11, 1974. Kruger would leave to become the dean of arts and science but would return for a second term in 1984: see "Arthur Kruger back as principal of Woodsworth", *Bulletin,* January 9, 1984.

140. Page 574, para. 2 – "extension program over the years": "Professor Arthur Kruger is appointed"; *University of Toronto Graduate* (January, 1974) at 9; Arthur Kruger oral history transcript at 25-26.

141. Page 574, para. 2 – "to go to university": Kruger oral history transcript at 1.

142. Page 574, para. 2 – "at the usual stage": "Name for the College Established to Enrol Part-Time Students", UTA/A94-0022/12; "Woodsworth is the name adopted for 'College X'", *Bulletin,* January 25, 1974. Although Kenneth

McNaught had written extensively on Woodsworth, most prominently *A Prophet in Politics: A Biography of J.S. Woodsworth* (University of Toronto Press, 1959), no evidence has surfaced that he had any role in the selection of the name of the College or that he provided the wording that the Search Committee used in 1974.

143. Page 574, para. 3 – "member of the college": Mary Lawrence of psychology joined Kruger during his first term as principal: Kruger oral history transcript at 25-26.

144. Page 574, para. 3 – "York University": Kruger oral history transcript at 25-26; Bateman to author, July 3, 1998.

145. Page 574, para. 3 – "Alex Waugh": "Waugh and Woodsworth", *Bulletin,* May 15, 2000.

146. Page 574, para. 3 – "from its founding": "Woodsworth College announced the organization of its staff", *Bulletin,* February 22, 1974.

147. Page 574, para. 3 – "General Motors plant in Oshawa": Kruger oral history transcript at 25-26.

148. Page 574, para. 3 – "and Yorkdale shopping centre": "Woodsworth to offer courses in suburban shopping mall", *Bulletin,* September 15, 1986.

149. Page 574, para. 3 – "Guadalajara": "Waugh and Woodsworth"; "Update of the Strategic Plan" at 4.

150. Page 575, para. 1 – "usual academic credentials": "Senior Citizens' Program (documented forwarded by Noah Meltz, Principal of Woodsworth College); "Review of Woodsworth College" at 14.

151. Page 575, para. 2 – "enrolment has been decreasing": "Review of Woodsworth College", February, 1998 (document forwarded by Noah Meltz) at 3. Full-time students who reduce their load to part-time do not have to transfer to Woodsworth College from their original college.

152. Page 575, para. 2 – "students in Woodsworth": For a description of the program see Kruger to Evans, October 22, 1975, with enclosed memorandum, "In Defence of the Pre-University Course", July 8, 1975, UTA/A82-0021/004; "Students bloom in Woodsworth's pre-University program", *Bulletin,* October 23, 1978; "An Update of the Strategic Plan for Woodsworth College, 1998-2004 Submitted for Vice-President and Provost Professor Adel Sedra", November 4, 1997 (document forwarded by Noah Meltz) at 2-3.

153. Page 575, para. 2 – "visible minority communities": "In Defence of the Pre-University Course" at 2.

154. Page 575, para. 3 – "full-time students a year": "Updated Plan Transitional Year Programme University of Toronto" (November 6, 1997) at 1-2; "An Entry to Equity", *Bulletin,* April 27, 1992; "Transitional Year Program", *University of Toronto Magazine* (Autumn, 1998) at C23. It was taken over from a summer program organized by York University: see "TYP — a unique experiment", *Bulletin,* July 11, 1975.

155. Page 575, para. 3 – "other significant components": "Updated Plan Transitional Year Programme" at 2; author's conversation with Rona Abramovitch on June 9, 2000 and Keren Braithwaite, July 2000.

156. Page 575, para. 3 – "arts and science at the University": "Updated Plan Transitional Year Programme" at 2 says about 60%. Note, however, that the head of the program, Rona Abramovitch, says that this past year it was 80%: conversation with Abramovitch, June 9, 2000.

157. Page 575, para. 4 – "St. George Street": Douglas Richardson, ed., *The New Woodsworth College* (Woodsworth College, undated) at 4.

158. Page 575, para. 4 – "college's facilities": "Woodsworth College suddenly in the money", *Bulletin,* April 17, 1989; "The New Woodsworth College", *University of Toronto Magazine* (Summer 1992) at 37.

159. Page 575, para. 4 – "award-winning building": Richardson, ed., *The New Woodsworth College.*

160. Page 575, para. 4 – "officially opened in 1992": "The New Woodsworth College at 37; "More Than a Brush Stroke", *Bulletin,* February 24, 1992.

161. Page 575, para. 4 – "Woodsworth students": "Waugh and Woodsworth"; author's conversation with Bill Bateman on June 8, 2000.

162. Page 575, para. 4 – "a success story": "Review of Woodsworth College" at 22.

163. Page 575, para. 4 – "Rohinton Mistry (BA, 1982)": "Woodsworth College 'Distinguished Alumni' August 1995" (document forwarded by Noah Meltz).

164. Page 576, para. 1 – "in her hundredth year": "Student awarded honorary BA", *Bulletin,* March 26, 1990; also noteworthy is Manny Rotman, who received a B.A. in 1985 at the age of 76: see *Globe and Mail* web site, May 18, 1998.

165. Page 576, para. 2 – "School of Hygiene": Governing Council Minutes, December 20, 1973, UTA/A84-0033/015.

166. Page 576, para. 2 – "faculty of medicine": "Giving high priority to community health", *Bulletin,* April 19, 1974.

167. Page 576, para. 2 – "started in 1913": See Chapter 22 (1914).

168. Page 576, para. 2 – "food sciences in 1902": See Chapter 16 (1897).

169. Page 576, para. 2 – "not changed until 1962": "Recommends phasing out of the Faculty of Food Sciences", *Bulletin,* January 28, 1971.

170. Page 576, para. 2 – "closing hygiene": Evans oral interview, tape 11

171. Page 577, para. 1 – "food sciences in 1970": Claude Bissell, *Halfway Up Parnassus: A Personal Account of the University of Toronto 1932-1971* (University of Toronto Press, 1974) at 107-108; Bissell Diary, October 7, 1970; "Recommends phasing out"; e-mail from Milton Israel to Friedland, June 14, 2000.

172. Page 577, para. 1 – "offered similar programs": "Recommends phasing out".

173. Page 577, para. 1 – "stop further enrolment": 1,800 letters had been sent out: see "800 alumnae help to win reprieve for Food Sciences", *University of Toronto News* (May, 1971) at 6.

174. Page 577, para. 1 – "goal of structural reform": Bissell, *Parnassus* at 108.

175. Page 577, para. 2 – "rationalizing resources": Evans to Twaits, July 9, 1973, UTA/A79-0051/007(003).

176. Page 577, para. 2 – "reports was produced": For the Fisher report, see "A new image and new role urged for Food Sciences", *Bulletin,* June 14, 1972; "Implementation Committee on the Faculty of Food Sciences University of Toronto Final Report" (February 2, 1973), UTA/A79-0057/019; "Report to the Provost of the University of Toronto from the Programme Committee on Household Science" (November 1, 1974), UTA/A79-0057/022.

177. Page 577, para. 2 – "alumni kept up the attack": See, for example, the letter from W.O. Twaits to Lewis of June 29, 1973, UTA/A79-0051/007(03).

178. Page 577, para. 2 – "faculty's original benefactor": Janet Massey Horning to Evans, March 28, 1973, UTA/A79-0051/007(01).

179. Page 577, para. 2 – "enrolment was increasing": "Food Sciences merits right to continue, alumnae say", *Bulletin,*

November 16, 1973. The faculty also generated a surplus in 1972/73: see James H. Joyce to W.J.D. Lewis, May 23, 1973, UTA/A78-0028/045.

180. Page 577, para. 2 – "more students in the faculty": "Approval is given to the principle of separating resource centres and programming responsibilities", *Bulletin,* January 11, 1974; see also "The new Nutrition & Food Science", *Bulletin,* April 25, 1975. Individual faculty were moved into various departments and "the Faculty was closed down without any great bloodletting": see Israel to Friedland, June 14, 2000.

181. Page 577, para. 3 – "schools of public health": Bator, *Within Reach* at 138.

182. Page 577, para. 3 – "Faculty of Medicine": John Hamilton, "Problems of the School and University", December 10, 1973, UTA/A85-0044; see generally, W. Harding le Riche, "University of Toronto Medical School and School of Hygiene Historical Comments 1959-1980" (copy forwarded by Harding le Riche).

183. Page 577, para. 4 – "deteriorating facilities": Bator, *Within Reach* at 135.

184. Page 577, para. 4 – "the faculty of medicine": Hamilton, "Problems" at 5.

185. Page 578, para. 1 – "funds from Connaught": Bator, *Within Reach* at 134-136 and 164-165.

186. Page 578, para. 1 – "conquest of infectious disease": Hamilton, "Problems" at 3; but see also Bator, *Within Reach* at 164.

187. Page 579, para. 1 – "School of Hygiene be transferred there": "Major change is proposed for Hygiene", *Bulletin,* March 1, 1974; Bator, *Within Reach* at 140-41. There was an earlier report in 1973, chaired by Gordon Nikiforuk, the dean of dentistry: see Bator, *Within Reach* at 139 and "Presidential committee to study future of the School of Hygiene", *Bulletin,* April 14, 1972. For I.M.S., see Chapter 35 (1966).

188. Page 579, para. 1 – "health promotion": Bator, *Within Reach* at 140-141.

189. Page 579, para. 1 – "accepted by the governing council": "Giving high priority to community health"; "Medical Faculty may be home of new divisions", *Bulletin,* May 3, 1974.

190. Page 579, para. 1 – "John FitzGerald": "Now it's the FitzGerald building", *Bulletin,* May 30, 1975.

191. Page 579, para. 1 – "by the task force": Bator, *Within Reach* at 141.

192. Page 579, para. 1 – "rather than diplomas": Ibid. at 151-152.

193. Page 579, para. 1 – "the graduate school": Ibid. at 160.

194. Page 579, para. 1 – "cost of the division": Ibid. at 154-155.

195. Page 579, para. 2 – "John Hastings": Ibid. at 148-49; "John Hastings", *University of Toronto Graduate* (Spring 1989) at 27.

196. Page 579, para. 2 – "Eugene Vayda": Bator, *Within Reach* at 153.

197. Page 579, para. 2 – "other American universities": Author's conversation with McGill epidemiologist Barry Pless on June 11, 2000.

198. Page 579, para. 2 – "continued over the years": A decanal task force in 1987, chaired by William Hannah, the chair of obstetrics, decided by a majority of 10-7 to keep community health within medicine and a 1993 provostial task force, chaired by former graduate dean John Leyerle, agreed, although in its interim report several

months earlier it had recommended a separate faculty of population health and a grouping of health science faculties: see Bator, *Within Reach* at 156 and 161-162.

199. Page 579, para. 2 – "preventive medicine approach": Author's conversation with Connell on June 11, 2000.

200. Page 579, para. 2 – "School of Hygiene": Bator, *Within Reach* at 143.

201. Page 579, para. 3 – "given to the department": Harvey Skinner, *Public Health Sciences Update* (July, 1998).

202. Page 580, para. 1 – " epidemiologist": See "Naylor Appointed Dean of U of T Medical School", http://www.newsandevents.utoronto.ca/bin/19990630.asp.

203. Page 580, para. 2 – "for an extra year": *Ottawa Citizen*, September 6, 1977.

204. Page 580, para. 2 – "created in the 1960s": See Robin Matthews and James Steele, eds., *The Struggle for Canadian Universities* (Toronto: New Press, 1969) at 1; Nelson, *Faculty Power* at 85-86; Ireland oral interview, tape 12; John B. MacDonald, *Changes and Choices: A Memoir* (Vancouver: UBC Alumni House, 2000) at 159-160.

205. Page 580, para. 2 – "was gutted": "After the roof fell in, there wasn't much to save", *Bulletin*, February 25, 1977; "Planning and Resources examines plan for Sandford Fleming", *Bulletin*, October 31, 1977.

206. Page 580, para. 3 – "resignation of the finance minister, Donald Macdonald": The by-election was one of fifteen held on October 16, 1978: see Frank Feigert, *Canada Votes 1935-1988* (Durham, N.C.: Duke University Press, 1989) at 66-67; "Crombie, Hon. David Edward", *The Canadian Parliamentary Guide 1980*; *Globe and Mail*, February 7, 1978 and October 17, 1978 in UTA/Current People/"Crombie, David".

207. Page 580, para. 3 – "Pierre Trudeau's successor": *Toronto Star*, August 12, 1977.

208. Page 580, para. 3 – "organized by the University": *Ottawa Citizen*, September 6, 1977.

209. Page 580, para. 3 – "David Crombie": *Globe and Mail*, February 7, 1978, in Current People, "Crombie"; "Crombie, David Edward", *Canadian Who's Who 1986* at 289.

210. Page 580, para. 3 – "tiny perfect mayor": Jon Caulfield, *The Tiny Perfect Mayor* (Toronto: James Lorimer and Company, 1974).

211. Page 580, para. 3 – "85 per cent of the vote": *Globe and Mail*, March 14, 1978.

212. Page 580, para. 3 – "Evans lost": Crombie received 18,732 votes, or 58% of the popular vote. Evans' support was 31%, or 10,119 votes. The N.D.P. under Ron Thomson received 3,008 votes, or 9%, and other candidates received 471 votes: see Feigert, *Canada Votes* at 66-67; Current People, "Crombie".

CHAPTER 39 – 1980 – FINANCIAL AND OTHER CONCERNS

1. Page 581, para. 1 – "devoted to higher education": Paul Axelrod, *Scholars and Dollars: Politics, Economics and the University of Ontario 1945-1980* (University of Toronto Press, 1982) at 180-81; see also the previous chapter on financing.

2. Page 581, para. 1 – "last in provincial expenditure": "Ontario is in last place!", *University of Toronto Bulletin*, September 8, 1980.

3. Page 581, para. 1 – "average of all the provinces": James M. Ham, "A Strategic Assessment", *University of Toronto Graduate* (November/December 1982) at 12.

4. Page 581, para. 1 – "staff and acquisitions": "Proposed library cuts will reduce staff, hours, service", *University of Toronto Bulletin*, March 28, 1983.

5. Page 581, para. 1 – "for other administrative staff": "Excision of Arts & Science departments not planned but further budget cuts could force it, faculty says", *University of Toronto Bulletin*, April 11, 1983.

6. Page 581, para. 1 – "leaving the University": "Down to bare bone, lean flesh", *University of Toronto Bulletin*, September 24, 1979; "Survey ranks Ontario last in spending on universities – again", *University of Toronto Bulletin*, February 6, 1984; "It's a question of survival", *University of Toronto Bulletin*, November 5, 1979.

7. Page 581, para. 1 – "100 such appointments": James Ham Oral Interview, UTA/B90-0001, tape 12.

8. Page 581, para. 1 – "reduced by attrition": "Reduction quotas replace hiring freeze", *University of Toronto Bulletin*, September 20, 1982; "One of the harshest budgets U of T has faced", *University of Toronto Bulletin*, April 25, 1983; "Spelt report recommends reduction in teaching staff in arts and science", *University of Toronto Bulletin*, March 30, 1981.

9. Page 581, para. 2 – "universities be closed": "Increase funding or close some universities", *University of Toronto Bulletin*, August 24, 1981. The Fisher report also introduced the idea that universities in Ontario should be differentiated into "tiers", each of which would have an appropriate funding formula: comments from Dan Lang to Friedland, February 2, 2001. See the *Report of the Committee on the Future Role of Universities in Ontario* (Ontario Ministry of Colleges and Universities, 1981 (Fisher Report).

10. Page 581, para. 2 – "reduce enrolment": "1,000 fewer students next year", *University of Toronto Bulletin*, July 5, 1982; "First year enrolment reduced by 1,100", *University of Toronto Bulletin*, September 7, 1982.

11. Page 581, para. 2 – "leaner and tougher place": James Ham, "The University: A Strategic Statement", *University of Toronto Bulletin*, May 25, 1982 at S3; Ham, "A Strategic Assessment" at 13.

12. Page 581, para. 2 – "funding formula to be suspended": "U of T asks OCUA to recommend suspension of funding formula", *University of Toronto Bulletin*, February 21, 1983.

13. Page 581, para. 2 – "governing council in 1979": "Down to bare bone".

14. Page 582, para. 1 – "Marnie Paikin": "Committee for President", *University of Toronto Bulletin*, June 31, 1977; David Claringbold to Charles Hollenberg, May 11, 1977, UTA/A84-0008/18.

15. Page 582, para. 1 – "Five persons were interviewed": David Claringbold to members of the search committee, December 1, 1977, UTA/A84-0008/18.

16. Page 582, para. 1 – "later its president": "Naimark, Arnold", *Canadian Who's Who 1994* at 837.

17. Page 582, para. 1 – "Ontario Council on University Affairs": "Dupré, Joseph Stephen", *Canadian Who's Who 1994* at 322.

18. Page 582, para. 1 – "vice-president of research and planning": "Eastman, Harry Claude MacColl", *Canadian Who's Who 1987.*

19. Page 582, para. 1 – "Simon Fraser University": "Saywell, William George Gabriel", *Canadian Who's Who 1994* at 1013.

20. Page 582, para. 1 – "dean of the graduate school": "Ham, James Milton", *Canadian Who's Who 1994* at 474.

21. Page 582, para. 1 – "early January 1978" "A good man to know", *University of Toronto Graduate* (Spring, 1978) at 3.

22. Page 582, para. 2 – "serious contender from the beginning": Author's conversations with members of the search committee.

23. Page 583, para. 1 – "trust and affection": "Ham appointment welcomed by all University estates", *University of Toronto Bulletin,* January 16, 1978.

24. Page 583, para. 1 – "necessary cuts that were coming": "The President and the Years Ahead", *The Graduate* (March/April 1980) at 9.

25. Page 583, para. 2 – "her uniqueness": "The humanities define the shape of civilization, says new President James Milton Ham, reaffirming the University's commitment to undergraduate liberal education", *University of Toronto Bulletin,* October 10, 1978.

26. Page 583, para. 2 – "philosopher-engineer": *Financial Post,* January 28, 1978.

27. Page 583, para. 2 – "engineers make good philosophers": "A good man to know" at 3.

28. Page 583, para. 3 – "maze of abstractions": "The President and the Years Ahead" at 10-11.

29. Page 583, para. 3 – "later become its principal": "Morton, Desmond Dillon Paul", *Canadian Who's Who 1994* at 824.

30. Page 583, para. 3 – "its staff and students": "Wasn't implying suburban campuses be closed: President", *University of Toronto Bulletin,* June 7, 1982.

31. Page 583, para. 3 – "university is not about vocation": *Globe and Mail,* January 11 and 13, 1978; the *Financial Post,* January 28, 1978, noted that Ham claimed the words were taken out of context.

32. Page 583, para. 3 – "in the real world": *Globe and Mail,* January 13, 1978.

33. Page 584, para. 1 – "future facing the University": Ham Oral Interview, tape 14.

34. Page 584, para. 1 – "increased expenditures": William H. Nelson, *The Search for Faculty Power: The University of Toronto Faculty Association 1941-1992* (Toronto: Canadian Scholar's Press, 1993) at 125.

35. Page 584, para. 1 – "on the part of the government, Ham said": "It's a question of survival".

36. Page 584, para. 2 – "declining resources": See generally, Nelson, *Faculty Power,* chapter 7.

37. Page 584, para. 2 – "binding supplication": Nelson, *Faculty Power* at 122.

38. Page 584, para. 2 – "acceptable to the council": Ibid.

39. Page 584, para. 2 – "the administration's position": "Mediator recommends 9.1% salary increase for faculty", *University of Toronto Bulletin*, February 23, 1981; Nelson, *Faculty Power* at 121; "UTFA wants arbitration board", *University of Toronto Bulletin*, September 8, 1981.

40. Page 584, para. 2 – "increase in the cost of living": Nelson, *Faculty Power* at 121-122.

41. Page 584, para. 2 – "by the government to the University": "Faculty members are not a greedy bunch", *University of Toronto Bulletin*, April 13, 1981.

42. Page 584, para. 2 – "85 per cent of those voting": Nelson, *Faculty Power* at 122.

43. Page 584, para. 3 – "of nearly 1,000 cast": Nelson, *Faculty Power* at 123; "Faculty members are not a greedy bunch".

44. Page 584, para. 3 – "binding arbitration": "Proposed agreement to amend Article 6 negotiated by the administration and faculty association", *University of Toronto Bulletin*, December 21, 1981.

45. Page 584, para. 3 – "Ham opposed": Nelson, *Faculty Power* at 125.

46. Page 584, para. 3 – "certifying as a union": Ham Oral Interview, tape 14.

47. Page 584, para. 3 – "rejected binding arbitration": Nelson, *Faculty Power* at 125; author's conversation with Dyck on July 7, 2000.

48. Page 584, para. 3 – "did not want certification": "Faculty members are not a greedy bunch"; author's conversation with Dyck.

49. Page 584, para. 3 – "support the faculty's position": Author's conversation with Dyck.

50. Page 584, para. 3 – "allies in the governing council": He was helped by Jean Smith, the chair of the academic affairs committee: see "Decision-making in Simcoe Hall, reduced deficit, changes to Memorandum of Agreement", *University of Toronto Bulletin*, September 21, 1981; author's conversation with Dyck. A Governing Council committee headed by the vice-chair of the council, Noranda executive Kendal Cork, put forward an alternate proposal – binding arbitration would be by the Governing Council itself: see "Report of the Advisory Committee on the Memorandum of Agreement with the University of Toronto Faculty Association", *University of Toronto Bulletin*, December 7, 1981. This was not, however, taken seriously by the council of the faculty association, which unanimously rejected the committee's report: see Nelson, *Faculty Power* at 127 and "Administration, UTFA negotiate directly", *University of Toronto Bulletin*, December 7, 1981. A meeting of principals, deans, directors, and chairs also strongly advised the president not to accept it: see author's conversation with Cork of June 26, 2000. See also K.G. McNeill to Wardrop, December 3, 1981, UTA/A89-0016/014, which says that the chairmen's views have been "scathing"; see also "Proposed agreement to amend Article 6". The meeting of principals, deans, directors, and chairs, according to David Strangway in a letter to author of January 23, 2001, was the first meeting at which chairs joined the body and the meeting "overwhelmingly supported making the deal" with the faculty association.

51. Page 585, para. 1 – "negotiating an agreement": "Administration, UTFA negotiate directly"; Nelson, *Faculty Power* at 127.

52. Page 585, para. 1 – "drive would be launched": Nelson, *Faculty Power* at 129.

53. Page 585, para. 1 – "neutral territory": Author's conversation with Dyck, who adds that earlier in the year, Ham had given him a "dressing down" in his office on a faculty association matter.

54. Page 585, para. 1 – "subsequent negotiations": Author's conversation with Dyck.

55. Page 585, para. 1 – "immense personal strain": Ham Oral Interview, tape 14.

56. Page 585, para. 1 – "the next nine days": "President Ham endorses binding arbitration", *University of Toronto Bulletin,* December 21, 1981.

57. Page 585, para. 1 – "in a downtown hotel": "Proposed agreement to amend Article 6"; author's conversation with Dyck.

58. Page 585, para. 1 – "a two-year agreement": "Proposed agreement to amend Article 6".

59. Page 585, para. 1 – "approved quickly by the faculty association": The vote was 39 to 2: see Nelson, *Faculty Power* at 131.

60. Page 585, para. 2 – "the President will resign": "Binding arbitration approved in principle by narrow margin at Governing Council", *University of Toronto Bulletin,* January 25, 1982.

61. Page 585, para. 2 – "would be the outcome": Author's conversation with vice-chair at the time, Kendall Cork, June 26, 2000.

62. Page 585, para. 2 – "23 votes to 20": "Binding arbitration approved in principle".

63. Page 585, para. 2 – "binding arbitration": Author's conversation with Kendall Cork, June 26, 2000; John Whitten, June 28, 2000.

64. Page 585, para. 3 – "Burkett was undertaken": "UTFA asking for 30% salary increase", *University of Toronto Bulletin,* March 29, 1982.

65. Page 585, para. 3 – "had asked for": "First U of T Salary award under binding arbitration", *University of Toronto Bulletin,* June 21, 1982; Nelson, *Faculty Power* at 132. The Burkett award is set out in "In the Matter of an Arbitration Between the University of Toronto and the University of Toronto Faculty Association", *University of Toronto Bulletin,* June 7, 1982. It might have been even higher, except that he also accepted the administration's argument that 'ability to pay' should be taken into account: see "In the Matter of an Arbitration" at S6.

66. Page 586, para. 1 – "faculty and staff salaries": "University moves quickly to find $$$", *University of Toronto Bulletin,* June 21, 1982.

67. Page 586, para. 1 – "salaries of administrative staff": "Binding arbitration approved in principle".

68. Page 586, para. 1 – "hirings were frozen": "University moves quickly".

69. Page 586, para. 1 – "under provost David Strangway": "University moves quickly"; "Report of the Presidential Advisory Committee on Institutional Strategy", *University of Toronto Bulletin,* June 20, 1983.

70. Page 586, para. 1 – "were 'traumatic'": "University moves quickly".

71. Page 586, para. 1 – "led to binding arbitration": "Fiscal responsibility means limiting diversity", *University of Toronto Bulletin,* July 5, 1982.

72. Page 586, para. 1 – "some of its best faculty members": One consequence was that Christie Biscuits executive John Whitten, who had been opposed to binding arbitration, defeated Terrence Wardrop in the subsequent

election for chair of the Governing Council: see "Binding arbitration approved in principle". Further, Dr. Bette Stephenson, the minister of colleges and universities, wrote to Whitten expressing her concern about the award – "a most disturbing development which could influence subsequent settlements and hamper the bargaining flexibility of other institutions": see Bette Stephenson to John Whitten, August 10, 1982, UTA/A89-0016/038. Moreover, she said, "there will be no additional funding for institutions which incur unmanageable deficits". The Ontario government subsequently brought in wage restraint for universities and other public sector institutions: see Nelson, *Faculty Power* at 135; see also Finlayson e-mail to the author, March 29, 1998, which states that "it is widely believed that there was a relationship between the Burkett award and the legislation".

73. Page 586, para. 2 – "further term as president": "The President has decided – no extension", *University of Toronto Bulletin*, May 25, 1982.

74. Page 586, para. 2 – "search committee had already been established": "Interim budget approved, but Council defers decision on advisory bureau", *University of Toronto Bulletin*, April 26, 1982.

75. Page 586, para. 2 – "not under any circumstances": Author's conversation with John Whitten, June 26, 2000.

76. Page 586, para. 3 – "Warren Stevens": "Something New, Something Old, As University of Toronto's Multi-Million Dollar Athletic and Physical Education Centre Opens" (Press release, September, 1979), UTA/A93-0007/001; "Dust off your sneakers and get ready to sweat!", *University of Toronto Bulletin*, September 10, 1979.

77. Page 586, para. 3 – "spark demonstrations": Iacobucci to A.J. Fraser, March 14, 1977, A93-0007/001.

78. Page 587, para. 1 – "almost $10 million": "Sandford Fleming – five years after the fire", *University of Toronto Bulletin*, June 7, 1982; Richard White, *The Skule Story: The University of Toronto Faculty of Applied Science and Engineering 1873-2000* (University of Toronto Press, 2000) at 235-237.

79. Page 587, para. 1 – "$400,000 in a student levy": Author's conversation with Joan Foley, July 6, 2000; Ham Oral Interview, tape 15; "$2.7 million library for Scarborough", *University of Toronto Bulletin*, June 23, 1980.

80. Page 587, para. 1 – "Press bookstore": "Design work set to begin on $9 million renovation of 214 College St.", *University of Toronto Bulletin*, May 25, 1982; "Student services centre to be named in honour of donor and fundraiser Murray Koffler", *University of Toronto Bulletin*, June 20, 1983.

81. Page 587, para. 1 – "the *Varsity*": As late as 1985, Downtown Legal Services, U of T Radio, the *Varsity*, and the Women's Centre were petitioning for space in the Centre: see McKee to Lang, November 26, 1985, UTA/A92-0023/004.

82. Page 587, para. 2 – "Adam Zimmerman": "Construction could begin in '84 on Natural Resources Centre", *University of Toronto Bulletin*, April 26, 1982; "After 'six years of non stop pressure' Gov't gives go-ahead for natural resources centre", *University of Toronto Bulletin*, June 6, 1983; Ham Oral Interview, tape 12. David Strangway spent six or seven years doing the planning for the earth sciences building and can claim much of the credit for the provincial funding: see letter from Strangway to Friedland, January 23, 2001.

83. Page 587, para. 2 – "environmental studies": "Construction could begin".

84. Page 587, para. 2 – "opened officially until 1989": "March move-in planned for Earth Sciences Centre", *University of Toronto Bulletin*, September 26, 1988.

85. Page 588, para. 1 – "close to Lake Ontario": Ham Oral Interview, tape 16. David Strangway states in a letter to the author of January 23, 2001, that when he was president he also had a meeting with Davis who had his eye on Varsity Stadium for a new sports stadium. The U of T could be partial owners of the two hotels planned. "I told him", Strangway writes, "we were not interested and to his credit he said he would not raise the subject with U of T again". In the 1990s, entrepreneur Steve Stavro made a concerted effort to convince the University to sell him the same grounds for his planned hockey/basketball arena. Robert Prichard turned him down and the Air Canada

Centre was built elsewhere: see e-mail from Bruce Kidd to University of Toronto History Project, August 24, 2000.

86. Page 588, para. 2 – "Korean studies at the University": "Our realism is winning alumni and corporate support", *University of Toronto Bulletin*, May 24, 1983.

87. Page 588, para. 2 – "Falconer's tenure": See Chapter 19 (1907).

88. Page 588, para. 2 – "made continuing involvement difficult": See Chapter 26 (1931).

89. Page 588, para. 2 – "Norman Bethune": See Chapters 22 (1914) and 26 (1931).

90. Page 588, para. 2 – "a welcome participant": "The U of T - China connection", *University of Toronto Bulletin*, September 22, 1980; "Our Chinese Connection", *University of Toronto Alumni Magazine* (Autumn 1986).

91. Page 588, para. 2 – "York University": "Our realism". The Joint Centre on Modern East Asia (to use its proper name) was established in the early 1970s. Its annual report for 1980/81, in UTA/A89-0016/006, refers to its "seventh year of operation".

92. Page 588, para. 2 – "South Asian studies": "Our realism". Governing Council approved the centre on June 19, 1980, its first acting director was appointed July 1, 1980, and its first permanent director was appointed July 1, 1981: see documents from UTA/A87-0020/009.

93. Page 588, para. 3 – "settling in the Toronto area": "The beauty queen, the tai chi master, the power brokers, the patrons, the activists, the ladies who lunch: who's who in the Chinese community", *Toronto Life* (July, 1997) at 69.

94. Page 588, para. 3 – "by the mid 1970s": James W. St. G. Walker, "Defining Human Rights in Canada: What is the Question?" (Paper presented at Canadian Historical Association Conference, May 29, 2000) at 23.

95. Page 588, para. 3 – "about one-half of that number": *Globe and Mail*, February 18, 1998.

96. Page 588, para. 3 – "considered themselves 'white'": "Ethnic Mix Changes Student Body", *University of Toronto Bulletin*, March 14, 1994; "Race and Ethnicity Comparison", Office of the Vice-President and Provost, June, 1995 (forwarded from Simcoe Hall).

97. Page 588, para. 4 – "gathering information": Author's conversation with John Whitten, June 26, 2000; "How they picked a president", *University of Toronto Bulletin*, January 24, 1983.

98. Page 588, para. 4 – "names were assembled": "How they picked".

99. Page 588, para. 4 – "Canadian university presidents": Author's conversations with various members of the search committee.

100. Page 588, para. 4 – "was selected": "How they picked"; "Forster's career", *University of Toronto Bulletin*, January 24, 1983; author's conversations with various members of the search committee. Forster would be Toronto's first bachelor president: see Judith Knelman, "Donald Forster", *The Graduate* (March/April 1983) at 13. See also e-mail from Frank Felkai to the author on December 7, 2001: "In the summer of 1983, he was under a lot of stress, determined to lead U. of Guelph till the end of August, but also looking forward, receiving requests from U of T interest groups, even accepting a few meetings, so he could have a running start (an oxymoron in his case) on September 1. I have personal knowledge – I had dinner with him, the last..., the night before."

101. Page 589, para. 1 – "praised the appointment": "He loves a challenge – and he's found one", *University of Toronto Bulletin*, January 24, 1983.

102. Page 589, para. 1 – "respected by the faculty association": "U of T reacts with shock, disappointment to death of Donald Forster", *University of Toronto Bulletin*, August 22, 1983.

103. Page 589, para. 1 – "mood of optimism": "He loves a challenge".

104. Page 589, para. 1 – "planned for September 21": George Ignatieff to Principals, Deans, Directors and Chairmen, May 31, 1983 (document forwarded by Frank Felkai); "Sept. 21 Dinner for U of T's President-Elect Cancelled" (Press Release, August 12, 1983), UTA/A90-0021/025; "Dinner cancelled, memorial fund to be established", *University of Toronto Bulletin*, August 22, 1983.

105. Page 589, para. 1 – "great disappointment": "U of T reacts with shock".

106. Page 589, para. 2 – "new president took office": "Approval, Relief, for Strangway Appointment", *The Graduate* (November/December 1983); "Governing Council appoints David Strangway president", *University of Toronto Bulletin*, September 6, 1983.

107. Page 589, para. 2 – "members of the earlier committee": "Presidential search committee, Simcoe Hall reorganization approved at Council", *University of Toronto Bulletin*, October 24, 1983; "Presidential search committee approved at Council", *University of Toronto Bulletin*, November 21, 1983.

108. Page 589, para. 2 – "who the faculty members of the committee would be": Author's conversations with Whitten and Cork.

109. Page 590, para. 1 – "clear-cut choice": Author's conversations with various members of the search committee; see also "Search committee for president not ready to report", *University of Toronto Bulletin*, May 7, 1984.

110. Page 590, para. 1 – "geology at the University": "Approval, Relief".

111. Page 590, para. 1 – "the support of the committee": Author's conversations with various members of the committee.

112. Page 590, para. 1 – "after the Burkett": "PACIS' approach unwarranted and self defeating", *University of Toronto Bulletin*, June 20, 1983.

113. Page 590, para. 1 – "University Teachers": Harvey Dyck wrote that it was 'so perverse, unworkable and deeply flawed that the entire report must be rejected without qualification': see ibid. As well as the comments about dismissal for lack of promotion, the report recommended that outside candidates be permitted to compete with internal tenure-stream candidates for tenure positions: see "Tightening tenure procedures, lobbying to improve government support": *University of Toronto Bulletin*, June 20, 1983.

114. Page 590, para. 1 – "being renegotiated": Nelson, *Faculty Power* at 136 and 141.

115. Page 591, para. 1 – "vice-president of research and planning": "Connell, George E.", *Canadian Who's Who 1994* at 229; "Appointment in Medicine", *University of Toronto Bulletin*, March 20, 1972; "Dr. George E. Connell is to become vice-president, planning, July 1", *University of Toronto Bulletin*, February, 2, 1974.

116. Page 591, para. 1 – "did not let his name stand": Author's conversations with various members of the search committee.

117. Page 591, para. 1 – "his experience and ability": "Former U of T student, teacher, VP George Connell to return as president", *University of Toronto Bulletin*, June 25, 1984; author's conversation with Whitten on June 26, 2000 and Connell on June 30, 2000.

118. Page 591, para. 1 – "Toronto needs you": Author's conversation with Connell, June 30, 2000.

119. Page 591, para. 1 – "October 1, 1984": "Former U of T student, teacher" ; "Connell takes over October 1", *University of Toronto Bulletin*, July 23, 1984.

120. Page 591, para. 2 – "new moons to conquer": "Thank you, Dave", *University of Toronto Bulletin*, September 24, 1984.

121. Page 591, para. 2 – "president of U of T": Author's conversations with various members of the search committee.

122. Page 591, para. 2 – "president of Western": "Pedersen, K. George", *Canadian Who's Who 1994* at 891.

123. Page 591, para. 2 – "the presidency of UBC": "Strangway to head UBC", *University of Toronto Bulletin*, July 22, 1985.

124. Page 591, para. 3 – "Lois Reimer": "Lois Reimer named status of women officer", *University of Toronto Bulletin*, August 20, 1984.

125. Page 591, para. 3 – "in 1981 for financial reasons": Ronald de Sousa et al. to Ham, March 25, 1981, and SAC Women's Commission to Ham, April 9, 1981, both in A87-0020/015.

126. Page 591, para. 3 – "University College in 1884": Anne Rochon Ford, *A Path Not Strewn With Roses: One Hundred Years of Women at the University of Toronto 1884-1984* (University of Toronto Press, 1985) at 6; "U of T women plan celebration of 100th anniversary of admission of women", *University of Toronto Bulletin*, November 7, 1983.

127. Page 591, para. 3 – "and early 1980s": See Connell's Renewal document at 11; George Connell, "Matters of Equality and Human Rights", *University of Toronto Graduate* (March/April 1985) at 19.

128. Page 591, para. 3 – "admitted to Hart House in 1972": "Hart House membership open to women students", *University of Toronto Bulletin*, January 25, 1972.

129. Page 591, para. 3 – "Massey College in 1974": See Chapter 33 (1962).

130. Page 591, para. 3 – "Pauline McGibbon": Ford, *Path* at 87; "Pauline McGibbon elected Chancellor of the University", *University of Toronto Bulletin*, April 27, 1971.

131. Page 591, para. 3 – "Eva Macdonald": "The Chancellor-elect", *University of Toronto Bulletin*, June 21, 1974.

132. Page 591, para. 3 – "the first vice-president": See Chapter 37 (1971); Ford, *Path* at 87.

133. Page 591, para. 3 – "first chair of the governing council": Ford, *Path* at 88-89.

134. Page 591, para. 3 – "Natalie Davis": Val Ross, "The Not-So-Quiet Revolution", *University of Toronto Magazine* (Spring 1997) at 18-19; Ceta Ramkhalawansingh, "We have studied money... we have studied the moon – now we are well into Women's Studies", *University of Toronto Graduate* (April 1975). A college program in women's studies was later offered by New College: see Chapter 38 (1975).

135. Page 592, para. 1 – "full-time faculty positions": Jill Ker Conway, *True North: A Memoir* (Toronto: Alfred A. Knopf, 1994) at 217-218; "Report announces increases for full-time faculty women", *University of Toronto Bulletin*, April 26, 1974. The seven per cent figure was for full-time only: see "Only 15% of U of T academic staff are women, Commission is told", *University of Toronto Bulletin*, May 5, 1972.

136. Page 592, para. 1 – "latter part of the 1980s": Nelson, *Faculty Power* at 153.

137. Page 592, para. 1 – "maternity leave": "Task force delivers on maternity leave", *University of Toronto Bulletin*, July 23, 1984.

138. Page 592, para. 1 – "day care": See Chapter 36 (1967).

139. Page 592, para. 1 – "safety on campus": "Lighting improved on Philosopher's Walk", *University of Toronto Bulletin*, March 9, 1981; see also Lynn Walsworth to Ham, November 5, 1979, John Dimond to Ham, November 8, 1979, and Ham to Walsworth, November 9, 1979, all in UTA/A86-0021/014.

140. Page 592, para. 1 – "250 cases a year": Letter from Lois Reimer to author of April 4, 2001. See also Gay Abbate, "Sexual Harassment: A Question of Fairness", *University of Toronto Magazine* (Summer, 1991) at 31; Nelson, *Faculty Power* at 152; Dafoe to Ham, December 11, 1980, UTA/A87-0020/016; Robert F. Brown to Ham, February 12, 1981, UTAA87-0020/018; Connell and Fred Wilson to the editor, *Maclean's*, April 14, 1989, UTA/A98-0008/035; "Harassment policy passes", *University of Toronto Bulletin*, May 25, 1987.

141. Page 592, para. 1 – "in the Hart House pool": The charge was "prolonged and intense staring". "Appeal Board upholds Hummel conviction", (Press Release, December 8, 1989), UTA/A98-0008/058; "Hummel to appeal charge", *University of Toronto Bulletin*, April 3, 1989; "Hummel harassment hearing set for July 24, 1989", *University of Toronto Bulletin*, May 1, 1989.

142. Page 592, para. 2 – "in the mid-1980s": Reimer to Connell, June 16, 1987, UTA/A94-0013/032.

143. Page 592, para. 2 – "50 per cent of the student body": Ford, *Path* at 77.

144. Page 593, para. 1 – "demonstrably better": Nelson, *Faculty Power* at 153-154.

145. Page 593, para. 1 – "academic performance and potential": Michael Marrus, "Gender and Hiring: A Flawed Policy", *University of Toronto Bulletin*, September 14, 1987.

146. Page 593, para. 1 – "to serve as role models": "Graduate students need female role models for careers", *University of Toronto Bulletin*, September 28, 1987.

147. Page 593, para. 1 – "to the male candidates": Joan Foley, "Moving towards equity in faculty hiring", *University of Toronto Bulletin*, December 7, 1987.

148. Page 593, para. 1 – "reasoned and thoughtful": "Foley's response is worthy of backing", *University of Toronto Bulletin*, December 7, 1987.

149. Page 593, para. 2 – "humour publication": See Richard White, *The Skule Story* at 252-253.

150. Page 593, para. 2 – "a good laugh!": Luis Alegre to Connell, February 27, 1986, UTA/A94-0013/017.

151. Page 593, para. 2 – "what might rub off": Reimer to Connell, June 12, 1986, UTA/A94-0013/017.

152. Page 593, para. 3 – "continued to be a problem": "Connell warns of decline unless funding improves", *University of Toronto Bulletin*, May 5, 1986.

153. Page 593, para. 3 – "rewarded growth": George E. Connell, "Notes for Review by the University Historian", July 11, 1998 at 5-6.

154. Page 593, para. 3 – "would have helped Toronto": "Money for faculty, buildings, research, libraries", *University of Toronto Bulletin*, January 21, 1985. The terms of reference for the Bovey Commission are set out in "Bovey commission terms of reference", *University of Toronto Bulletin*, February 6, 1984. For a discussion of the Bovey report, see the comments to the author by Dan Lang on February 2, 2001, in which he points out that in addition to extra funding for research infrastructure allocated on the basis of research intensity, the formula would have a "corridor" in which there would be no sensitivity to enrolment fluctuation. The Bovey report that had been commissioned by the Conservatives and the above two ideas were later taken up by the Liberal government. Lang

points out that the Research Overhead and Infrastructure Fund (ROIF) was introduced in 1983 and corridors were introduced in 1987.

155. Page 593, para. 3 – "bottom of the hamster cage": "U of T too big, cold and crowded: students", *University of Toronto Bulletin,* March 5, 1984.

156. Page 594, para. 1 – "not beyond our reach": "The opportunities are boundless – and not beyond our reach" (installation address of George E. Connell), *University of Toronto Bulletin,* November 19, 1984.

157. Page 594, para. 2 – "in mid-November 1984": "Celebration of Warmth", *University of Toronto Alumni Magazine* (January/February 1985) at 11.

158. Page 594, para. 2 – "binding arbitrations": "UTFA prepares for certification drive", *University of Toronto Bulletin,* August 20, 1984; "Provision for binding arbitration a price worth paying, Connell tells Council", *University of Toronto Bulletin,* November 19, 1984.

159. Page 594, para. 2 – "were unionized": "10 Ont. faculty associations have certified since 1975", *University of Toronto Bulletin,* November 5, 1984.

160. Page 594, para. 2 – "had expired": There was an issue, however, over whether it had expired in the light of the government wage restraint legislation the previous year: see "Long night's negotiations end months of uncertainty", *University of Toronto Bulletin,* November 19, 1984.

161. Page 594, para. 2 – " previous ten months": "Long night's negotiations".

162. Page 594, para. 3 – "the following day": Ibid.

163. Page 594, para. 3 – "faculty association council": Nelson, *Faculty Power* at 141-142.

164. Page 594, para. 3 – "governing council a few days later": "Provision for binding arbitration". Dyck and Sedra, however, were opposed to the agreement, claiming that it would unduly influence the arbitrator to bring in an award that would not be rejected by Governing Council: see Nelson, *Faculty Power* at 141-142.

165. Page 594, para. 3 – "without arbitration": Connell to Friedland, July 4, 1998 at 2; Nelson, *Faculty Power* at 142.

166. Page 594, para. 3 – "accepted by the governing council": Nelson, *Faculty Power* at 142.

167. Page 594, para. 4 – "one presidential regime to the next": Connell, "Notes for review" at 2.

168. Page 594, para. 4 – "overlooking a parking lot": "Presidential offices move to first floor of Simcoe Hall", *University of Toronto Bulletin,* November 25, 1985. Dan Lang points out in his comments to the author of February 2, 2001, that the reason for the move of Connell's office was "to restructure the senior administration so that vice-presidents were functionally part of the president's office... Initially the vice-presidents agreed, and then one-by-one (there was no organized cabal) they withdrew".

169. Page 594, para. 4 – "one mistake Connell had made": *University of Toronto Magazine* (Spring 2000) at 12

170. Page 595, para. 1 – "could be paid out": Connell, "Notes for review" at 5.

171. Page 595, para. 1 – "improvements to the plan": Nelson, *Faculty Power* at 155. In retrospect, the deal was a good one for the University and an unwise one for the faculty association. At the time, however, this was less clear. Connell had to be talked into it by Alex Pathy and others: author's conversation with Robert Prichard, July 18, 2000. At the time of writing, retired professors and librarians have formed an association, "Retired Academics and Librarians of the University of Toronto" (RALUT), which, along with the faculty association (UTFA), is seeking to obtain better pensions. They claim that the University unduly benefited from the 1987 arrangement: see letter

from Michael Finlayson to persons affected, April 23, 2001, and *University of Toronto Bulletin,* May 27, 2001. See generally, the various issues of the *Ralut Reporter* and the association's website www.ralut.ca.

172. Page 595, para. 1 – "student scholarships": Connell, "Notes for review" at 8.

173. Page 595, para. 2 – "Library Automation Systems": See Connell, "Notes for review" at 11, which describes the cancellation of a contract entered into by Strangway that would "destroy any possibility of selling UTLAS": see William Broadhurst's concerns, noted in "Concern about UTLAS loan voiced at Council", *University of Toronto Bulletin,* September 19, 1983.

174. Page 595, para. 2 – "drain on university resources : "New CEO appointed at UTLAS", *University of Toronto Bulletin,* February 22, 1982; "Council approves $3 1/2 million more for UTLAS", *University of Toronto Bulletin,* June 21, 1982; Pathy to Whitten, November 30, 1983, UTA/A90-0021/032. Pathy noted that "much of the $12.2 million advanced has no practical value today", see Pathy to Business Affairs Committee, March 20, 1984, UTA/A92-0024/019 at 4.

175. Page 595, para. 2 – "sum of $1 million": "University negotiating with Thomson company for sale of UTLAS, Connell tells Council", *University of Toronto Bulletin,* January 7, 1985; "University hopes to recover $12 million UTLAS investment over long term", *University of Toronto Bulletin,* February 4, 1985.

176. Page 595, para. 2 – "share in future profits": Pathy to Business Affairs Committee, January 9, 1985, UTA/A92-0024/019 at 2-3.

177. Page 595, para. 2 – "its successor companies": E-mail from Carole Moore to Friedland, July 17, 2000.

178. Page 595, para. 3 – "Cray supercomputer": Connell to Members of Governing Council, May 1, 1985, UTA/A92-0024/012; "U of T's supercomputer on its way – installation set for June", *University of Toronto Bulletin,* March 24, 1986.

179. Page 595, para. 3 – "supported its acquisition": John Bossons et al., "The University of Toronto in the Supercomputer Age", *University of Toronto Bulletin,* January 20, 1986; "Supercomputer fans turn out for open hearing", *University of Toronto Bulletin,* February 3, 1986; "Research board endorses supercomputer proposal but asks for assurances of sufficient funding", *University of Toronto Bulletin,* February 24, 1986.

180. Page 595, para. 3 – "exercise was viable": "Supercomputer proposal raises cost concerns", *University of Toronto Bulletin,* January 6, 1986; George J. Luste, "A CRAY supercomputer at any price?", *University of Toronto Bulletin,* January 20, 1986.

181. Page 595, para. 3 – "certain disaster": George J. Luste, "A Prescription for Disaster", March 17, 1986, summary, in UTA/A94-0013/004.

182. Page 595, para. 3 – "commercial operation": Connell to A.K. Adlington, August 5, 1987, UTA/A98-0008/003.

183. Page 595, para. 3 – "use was disappointing" Neil Dobbs to Balfour, June 22, 1987, and Pathy to Adlington, June 23, 1987, both in UTA/A94-0013/023.

184. Page 596, para. 1 – "review of the Cray operation": Wilson to Connell, November 20, 1987, UTA/A98-0008/003.

185. Page 596, para. 1 – "another $8 million": Thomas A. Brzustowski to Connell, October 26, 1987, UTA/A98-0008/003; "New deal soon on supercomputer", *University of Toronto Bulletin,* November 23, 1987; "New deal for supercomputer", *University of Toronto Bulletin,* December 7, 1987.

186. Page 596, para. 1 – "in Pittsburgh": Sadleir to Prichard, April 22, 1992, and Sadleir to Keffer, April 24, 1992, both in UTA/A98-0008/098.

187. Page 596, para. 1 – "less expensive computers": See chapter 34 (1963).

188. Page 596, para. 1 – "physics building in June 1992": Sadleir to Prichard, July 29, 1992, UTA/A98-0008/098.

189. Page 596, para. 2 – "concern about South Africa": Connell, "Notes for review" at 10.

190. Page 596, para. 2 – "debate had to be cancelled": Eric A. McKee to Marvi Ricker, November 18, 1985, with draft statement to Governing Council, UTA/A92-0023/002; Arthur Kaptainis, "A Matter for Debate", *The Graduate* (March/April, 1986) at 18.

191. Page 596, para. 2 – "in the history of the University": Burchell to Connell, November 21, 1985, UTA/A94-0013/016.

192. Page 596, para. 3 – "talk had been disrupted": "U of T apologizes to S. African ambassador, issues a general invitation to return", *University of Toronto Bulletin*, November 25, 1985.

193. Page 596, para. 3 – "everyone without reservation": "Administration will continue to oppose attempts to block Babb from speaking: Connell", *University of Toronto Bulletin*, January 20, 1986.

194. Page 596, para. 3 – "completely dismantled": "Improper to invite South African ambassador", *University of Toronto Bulletin*, January 20, 1986.

195. Page 596, para. 3 – "Tony Clement": David Cameron to Clement, February 5, 1986, UTA/A92-0023/002.

196. Page 596, para. 3 – "the debate took place": "Media spotlight turned on Babb debate", *University of Toronto Bulletin*, February 3, 1986; "University has no further obligation to South African ambassador, President tells Council", *University of Toronto Bulletin*, February 24, 1986.

197. Page 597, para. 1 – "visit the U of T campus in a decade": "A Matter for Debate" at 16.

198. Page 597, para. 2 – "dealings with that country": At the time about 15% of its endowment funds: see "Connell recommends against divestment – accepts finding that South African holdings not socially injurious", *University of Toronto Bulletin*, June 24, 1985.

199. Page 597, para. 2 – "Strangway's presidency": Virginia Green and Ava Szurko to Strangway, October 12, 1983, UTA/A90-0021/025.

200. Page 597, para. 2 – "divestiture by the University": "A Matter for Debate" at 16; "Advisory Board to study divestment issue", *University of Toronto Bulletin*, December 3, 1984.

201. Page 597, para. 2 – "supporting that cause": It would be different, he conceded, if a corporation contributed directly or indirectly to any form of persecution: see "Divestment would be possible course of action if corporations contributed to repression", *University of Toronto Bulletin*, August 19, 1985.

202. Page 597, para. 2 – "passed by 32 to 8": "A Matter for Debate" at 17; Connell, "Notes for review" at 10.

203. Page 597, para. 2 – "he should resign": "Appalled by position on divestment", *University of Toronto Bulletin*, March 9, 1987.

204. Page 598, para. 1 – "250 demonstrators": "Anti-apartheid protestor disrupt Council meeting", *University of Toronto Bulletin*, March 9, 1987.

205. Page 598, para. 1 – "business in South Africa": "Divestment urged in Thornton report", *University of Toronto Bulletin*, December 7, 1987; Connell, "Notes for review" at 10.

206. Page 598, para. 1 – "approved by the governing council": By a vote of 30-12: see "U of T dumps South African holdings, *University of Toronto Bulletin,* January 25, 1988. The policy was extended to pension funds after Ontario legislation made this possible: see "President hopes for pension divestment", *University of Toronto Bulletin,* February 12, 1990. It was, of course, abandoned when the Apartheid regime was overturned: see "Divestment Policy Rescinded", *University of Toronto Bulletin,* December 13, 1993.

207. Page 598, para. 2 – "U of T's faculty of education": Connell, "Notes for review" at 7.

208. Page 598, para. 2 – "elected Liberal government": David Peterson became premier of Ontario on June 26, 1985, after a negotiated deal with the NDP following the provincial election of May 2, 1985: see Georgette Gagnon and Dan Rath, *Not Without Cause: David Peterson's Fall From Grace* (Toronto: Harper Collins, 1991) at 25-26.

209. Page 598, para. 2 – "faculty of education": "Preliminary negotiations under way for faculty of education, OISE merger", *University of Toronto Bulletin,* October 21, 1985; Connell to Shapiro, June 18, 1985, and Shapiro to Connell, June 19, 1985, both in UTA/A94-0013/014.

210. Page 598, para. 2 – "worked well together": Dan Lang's comments to Friedland, February 2, 2001.

211. Page 598, para. 2 – "Ontario Institute for Studies in Education to the University of Toronto": *Hansard Official Report of Debates, Legislative Assembly of Ontario* (October 24, 1985) at 1060.

212. Page 598, para. 3 – "for future development": Connell to Shapiro, October 24, 1985, UTA/A94-0013/014.

213. Page 598, para. 3 – "members of the legislature": Guttman to OISEFA, October 31, 1985, UTA/A94-0013/014. There was some opposition: see memo from a number of faculty members to "All Faculty", February 13, 1986, UTA/A94-0013/014.

214. Page 598, para. 3 – "joined the protest": "OISE faculty to fight transfer to U of T", *University of Toronto Bulletin,* November 25, 1986.

215. Page 598, para. 3 – "the city of Toronto": City Clerk to Connell, May 27, 1986, UTA/A94-0013/014.

216. Page 598, para. 3 – "and others": "OISE-U of T negotiations suspended", *University of Toronto Bulletin,* January 20, 1986.

217. Page 598, para. 3 – "negotiations with the University on the issue": Ibid.; Connell to Adlington, December 19, 1985, UTA/A94-0013/014.

218. Page 598, para. 3 – "non University of Toronto options": Fullan to Connell, December 13, 1985, UTA/A94-0013/014.

219. Page 598, para. 3 – "OISE degree-granting powers": Bernard J. Shapiro, "Statement for the General Government Committee of the Ontario Legislature", April 13, 1986, UTA/A94-0013/014 at 2.

220. Page 598, para. 3 – "would finally come about": "OISE Merger Approved", *University of Toronto Bulletin,* November 21, 1994.

221. Page 598, para. 4 – "in early 1986": "Recommendation for closure of the Faculty of Architecture and Landscape Architecture", February 20, 1986, published in *University of Toronto Bulletin,* February 24, 1986; "Architecture Soon to Close?", *The Graduate* (March/April 1986) at 31. For an analysis of the importance of the issue of the closure of architecture on the future of planning at the University, see comments by Dan Lang to Friedland, February 2, 2001. See also comments by Joan Foley to Friedland, February 4, 2001.

222. Page 598, para. 4 – "housed in inadequate quarters": "Recommendation for closure"; see also "Friedland commit-

tee, Spelt clash over review of Architecture problems", *University of Toronto Bulletin*, July 23, 1984. Closure had been contemplated in the 1970s but was not proceeded with by Evans, who had his hands full with other matters: see "Architecture as a faculty is approaching its end", *University of Toronto Bulletin*, May 9, 1975.

223. Page 599, para. 1 – "it could survive": "Joint meetings to consider future of architecture", *University of Toronto Bulletin*, February 3, 1986.

224. Page 599, para. 1 – "others joined in opposition": "Architecture debate at academic affairs this week", *University of Toronto Bulletin*, April 7, 1986; see also Larry Grossman to Connell, April 1986, UTA/A94-0013/001.

225. Page 599, para. 1 – "faculty into a school": "Provost ready with plan for school of architecture", *University of Toronto Bulletin*, December 8, 1986; "School of Architecture gets final approval", *University of Toronto Bulletin*, January 26, 1987; see also "Report outlines options for architecture", *University of Toronto Bulletin*, July 21, 1986.

226. Page 599, para. 1 – "discontinued its graduate program": *1998 Architectural Program Report University of Toronto* (document forwarded by John Knechsel, Dean of Architecture, Landscape and Design, 1999) at 23.

227. Page 599, para. 1 – "got me to take this job": *Toronto Star*, February 19, 1991.

228. Page 599, para. 1 – "seven years as dean": Comments from Foley to Friedland, February 4, 2001.

229. Page 599, para. 1 – "new life into the institution": *1998 Architectural Program* at 14-15.

230. Page 599, para. 1 – "again became a faculty": "Architecture faculty has new name", *University of Toronto Bulletin*, June 22, 1998.

CHAPTER 40 – 1986 – MOVING FORWARD

1. Page 603, para. 1 – "thirty years earlier": "John Polanyi the toast of U of T", *University of Toronto Bulletin,* October 27, 1986; Lydia Dotto, "Nobel Brings Obligations", *University of Toronto Alumni Magazine* (Winter 1986) at 8; *Globe and Mail,* October 16, 1986; George Connell, "A Memorandum of the Events at the University of Toronto October 15-18, 1986", UTA/A86-0051 at 4.

2. Page 603, para. 1 – "unexpected news": Dotto, "Nobel" at 8.

3. Page 603, para. 1 – "chemistry at the University of Toronto": "Polanyi, John Charles", *Canadian Who's Who 1994* at 916.

4. Page 603, para. 1 – "at the age of 33": Ibid.

5. Page 603, para. 1 – "University Professor": "John Polanyi University Professor first scientist to be so honoured", *University of Toronto Bulletin,* February 15, 1974.

6. Page 603, para. 2 – "brought him the prize": Connell, "Memorandum of Events" at 4-5.

7. Page 603, para. 2 – "creation of molecules": Dotto, "Nobel" at 9; *Globe and Mail,* October 16, 1986.

8. Page 604, para. 1 – "the chemical laser": "John Polanyi the toast of U of T".

9. Page 604, para. 1 – "Ken Cashion": Cashion received his Ph.D. in 1960 for "Infrared Chemilunescence": Judy Mills and Irene Dombra, *University of Toronto Doctoral Theses (1897-1967)* (University of Toronto Press, 1968) at 35). He then worked at Madison, Berkeley, Harvard, and IBM before taking a position in 1968 at University of Wisconsin – Parkside in Kenosha, Wisconsin, where he is now Emeritus Professor of Chemistry: see www.uwp.edu/academic/chemistry/chemfac/cashion.html.

10. Page 604, para. 1 – "Bladen had told him": Dotto, "Nobel" at 10.

11. Page 604, para. 2 – "post-secondary institutions": Connell, "Memorandum of Events" at 3 and 6.

12. Page 604, para. 2 – "outside the building": Ibid. at 6; "Rally sends message of solidarity", *University of Toronto Bulletin,* October 27, 1986.

13. Page 605, para. 1 – "standing ovation": Connell, "Memorandum of Events" at 7; George Connell, "Illumination of an Intellectual Tradition", *University of Toronto Alumni Magazine* (Spring, 1987) at 19.

14. Page 605, para. 1 – "must have been immense": Connell, "Memorandum of Events" at 7.

15. Page 605, para. 1 – "funding of Ontario universities": Ibid. at 8-9. The memo makes clear, however, that the universities were hoping for more.

16. Page 605, para. 2 – "come to fruition": "Federal funding program bad for research: Polanyi", *University of Toronto Bulletin,* December 8, 1986.

17. Page 605, para. 2 – "suggest they go abroad": John C. Polanyi, "Scientists and the world they live in" (speech to the joint meeting of Empire and Canadian Clubs, November 27, 1986), *University of Toronto Bulletin,* December 8, 1986.

18. Page 605, para. 3 – "history of the University": Connell, "Memorandum of Events" at 9.

19. Page 605, para. 3 – "psychological depression": See below.

20. Page 605, para. 3 – "finish the document": Author's conversation with Connell on Friday, June 30, 2000.

21. Page 605, para. 4 – "*Renewal 1987*": George E. Connell, Renewal 1987: a discussion paper on the nature and role of the University of Toronto (March, 1987).

22. Page 605, para. 4 – "within the University community": "Undergraduate reform tops renewal agenda", *University of Toronto Bulletin*, March 23, 1987; "Divisions welcome renewal paper, begin preparing responses", *University of Toronto Bulletin*, April 6, 1987; "Renewal 1987", *University of Toronto Alumni Magazine* (Summer 1987) at 8. It continued to be influential throughout the 1990s: see "Decade of the Dynamo", *University of Toronto Magazine* (Summer, 2000), at www.magazine.utoronto.ca.

23. Page 605, para. 4 – "for some ten months": *Renewal* at ix; "Time for a review, Connell tells Council", *University of Toronto Bulletin*, June 23, 1986.

24. Page 605, para. 4 – "achieving its full potential": *Renewal* at vii.

25. Page 605, para. 4 – "to prepare a report": Connell to Foley et al., April 29, 1986 at 2 (document forwarded from Connell).

26. Page 606, para. 1 – "he himself should undertake the task": Author's conversation with Prichard on July 18, 2000.

27. Page 606, para. 1 – "conform to those goals": *Renewal* at vii; "pinnacle of Parnassus" is quoted in "University renewal: Directions for change", *University of Toronto Bulletin*, March 23, 1987.

28. Page 606, para. 1 – "characterized the 1960s": *Renewal* at 10.

29. Page 606, para. 2 – "many issues raised by the paper": "Divisions welcome renewal paper"; J.E. Foley, "Renewal Retreat 23-24 June, 1987", May 28, 1987, UTA/A94-0013/046; Robin Armstrong to Connell, July 7, 1987, UTA/A98-0008/001; "Presidential advisory committee considers ways and means of renewal", *University of Toronto Bulletin*, August 24, 1987.

30. Page 606, para. 2 – "*Time* magazine": "Supernova celebration to be held April 24, 1987; *University of Toronto Bulletin*, April 6, 1987; "Shelton to describe discovery at supernova celebration", *University of Toronto Bulletin*, April 20, 1987; "Shelton shares meaning of discovery", *University of Toronto Bulletin*, May 4, 1987.

31. Page 607, para. 1 – "to remain in Toronto": "Polanyi anxious to return to lab", *University of Toronto Bulletin*, January 12, 1987.

32. Page 607, para. 2 – "education had to be improved": *Renewal* at 31.

33. Page 607, para. 2 – "Waterloo": Ibid. at 29-30 and 71; conversation with Arnold Weinrib, chair of U of T Law School's admission committee for at least 25 years, September 13, 2000.

34. Page 607, para. 2 – "Classrooms were crowded": Ibid. at 29-30; "Classrooms bulging as students return", *University of Toronto Bulletin*, September 14, 1987.

35. Page 607, para. 2 – "improved funding": "Undergraduate reform"; *Renewal* at 31.

36. Page 607, para. 3 – "arts and science degree": "Undergraduate reform"; *Renewal* at 34.

37. Page 607, para. 3 – "fifteen years later": "Three-year degree to be phased out", *University of Toronto News and Events*, April 10, 2000 at www.newsandevents.utoronto.ca; Stacey Gibson, "1 degree - 20 credits", *University of Toronto Magazine* (Summer 2000). Joan Foley points out that the motion was approved for the faculty of arts and

science only, so did not include Scarborough, but she states that "by moving towards having a majority of students in co-op programs, which require completion of a four-year degree, Scarborough foresees a drop in demand for the three-year degree, and will then presumably move to terminate it": see e-mail from Foley to Friedland, February 4, 2001.

38. Page 607, para. 3 – "full-time undergraduate students": *Renewal* at 40.

39. Page 607, para. 3 – "outside Canada": Ibid. at 63.

40. Page 608, para. 1 – "outside Ontario": Ibid. at 44.

41. Page 608, para. 1 – "for 6 or so students a year": The first National Scholar was actually admitted in 1986: see "First National Scholar", *University of Toronto Bulletin,* October 27, 1986. Five were to be admitted in 1987, but the actual terms of the award were not finalized until late in 1987: see "Award Record: The U of T National Scholarship Award Fund" (October 22, 1987), document forwarded from Merike Remmel, Office of Admissions and Awards, September 13, 2000. Of the twenty finalists in the first year, seven were selected National Scholars and admitted in 1988: see Karel Swift to Peter Harris, April 22, 1988, UTA/A94-0002/002. It was also hoped that admitting students in first year directly to streams within the Faculty of Arts and Science would encourage applications from students from outside Metropolitan Toronto. The first students were admitted under this policy in September, 1992. The three streams were Economics and Commerce, Science, and Humanities, and Social Sciences (other than Economics): see Darlene Frampton to Carol Allen et al., August 23, 1990, UTA/A94-0002/001. The original term was "programme cluster": see Armstrong to Connell, April 11, 1988, UTA/A98-0008/001; see also *Renewal* at 36; Connell to Foley, September 15, 1987; UTA/A98-0008/001; see also *Curriculum Renewal Committee: Report to the Dean, Faculty of Arts and Science, University of Toronto* (April, 1989), UTA/A98-0008/021 at 16. It must be noted, however, that the percentage of students from outside the GTA has not increased. *Renewal* at 68 stated that 68% of all full-time students in 1985/86 were from the Metro Region including Peel county, while the University of Toronto Performance Indicators in the 1990s gave the figures for the GTA as 79% in 1995/96, 78% in 1996/97, and 76% in 1997/98: see www.utoronto.ca/provost/perf98/demand.html. Recruiting efforts, however, continue: see Peter Silcox, "Recruiting the Best", *University of Toronto Bulletin,* October 2, 1995; "Student Recruitment Assumes Higher Priority", *University of Toronto Bulletin,* November 6, 1995; "Recruitment Efforts Impress Students", *University of Toronto Bulletin,* June 24, 1996; *Toronto Star,* January 12, 1998.

42. Page 608, para. 1 – "20 scholarships a year": The current number of awards are fifteen National Scholars and five Arbor Scholars: see www.utaps.utoronto.ca/financial_aid/resources/awards_programs.htm.

43. Page 608, para. 2 – "promotion decisions": "Tenure and Teaching Excellence Take Centre Stage", *University of Toronto Bulletin,* November 18, 1991.

44. Page 608, para. 2 – "faculty of arts and science": "An Advocate for Undergraduates".

45. Page 608, para. 2 – "School of Continuing Studies": "Teaching development", *University of Toronto Bulletin,* November 12, 1990.

46. Page 608, para. 2 – "for PhD candidates": The course is called "Teaching in Higher Education": see www.wdw.utoronto.ca/current/the.html. It was first offered in 1994: *University of Toronto Bulletin,* July 25, 1994.

47. Page 608, para. 2 – "undergraduate education": Foley to Principals, Deans, and Directors, February 7, 1989, UTA/A98-0008/030; "Kirkness new adviser of undergraduates", *University of Toronto Bulletin,* February 27, 1989. Kirkness had been involved in similar work earlier in the decade, but it had been curtailed for financial reasons: see "Kirkness appointed director of educational development", *University of Toronto Bulletin,* March 24, 1980. Medicine continued its teaching development program under Richard Tiberius: see *Renewal* at 26. See also "The found art of teaching", *The Graduate* (Winter, 1979) at 3.

48. Page 608, para. 2 – "outstanding instructors": "An Advocate for Undergraduates".

49. Page 608, para. 2 – "link teaching and research": "The Idea Is to Take Students on a Research Journey", *University of Toronto Bulletin*, June 24, 1996.

50. Page 609, para. 1 – "particular interest to the professor": Ibid.; *University of Toronto the Faculty of Arts and Science St. George Campus 2000-2001 Calendar* at 42.

51. Page 609, para. 2 – "about twenty students": "An Advocate for Undergraduates"; *St. George Campus 2000-2001 Calendar* at 42.

52. Page 609, para. 2 – "previous twenty years": Author's personal knowledge.

53. Page 609, para. 2 – "connect with other students": Quoted in George Cook, "The Discovery University", *University of Toronto Magazine* (Fall, 1994) at 14-15.

54. Page 609, para. 2 – "Convocation Hall": "Teaching Big", *University of Toronto Alumni Magazine* (Winter, 1987) at 24; "Gilmore named top prof", *University of Toronto Bulletin*, September 14, 1987; "Enter Talking, Stage Left", *University of Toronto Bulletin*, October 21, 1991.

55. Page 609, para. 3 – "diversity of its graduate programs": *Renewal* at 44.

56. Page 609, para. 3 – "other English-speaking university in Canada": Ibid. at 66.

57. Page 609, para. 3 – "were unique in Canada": Ibid. at 45.

58. Page 609, para. 3 – "with a few more than 1,200": Ibid. at 44 and 66.

59. Page 609, para. 3 – "research streams": Ibid. at 47.

60. Page 609, para. 3 – "500 students": Ibid. at 48; "Renewal 1987" at 11; "Divisions welcome renewal".

61. Page 609, para. 4 – "absolute value was decreasing": *Renewal* at 46-49.

62. Page 610, para. 1 – "cannot afford this success": Ibid. at 53.

63. Page 610, para. 1 – "long-term strategy": Ibid. at 48-49.

64. Page 610, para. 1 – "University at the time": Ibid. at 52; A.W. Johnson, *Giving greater point and purpose to the federal financing of post-secondary education and research* (Ottawa, Ontario: Department of Secretary of State, 1985). Johnson was professor of political science at the University from 1983 to 1989: see "Johnson, Albert Wesley", *Canadian Who's Who 1994* at 571.

65. Page 610, para. 2 – "appropriate funding": *Hansard Official Report of Debates, Legislative Assembly of Ontario*, April 22, 1986 at 7; *Renewal* at 12. See generally, Daniel Lang, University Finance in Ontario (Winnipeg: Canadian Society for the Study of Higher Education, forthcoming) at 12 et seq. of draft. See also David Wolfe, "Harnessing the Region: Changing Perspectives on Innovation Policy in Ontario" in T. Barnes and M. Gertler, eds., *Reorganizing Economic Geography* (London: Routledge, 1999) at 127-54.

66. Page 610, para. 2 – "based on excellence": *House of Commons Journals*, October 1, 1986 at 17; *Renewal* at 12-13.

67. Page 610, para. 2 – "over the next five years": *Renewal* at 13.

68. Page 610, para. 2 – "over five years": George Connell, "Centres of Excellence", *University of Toronto Alumni Magazine* (Winter, 1987) at 15; *Renewal* at 57. The centres were part of the government's $1 billion technology fund: see "Cabinet to consider future of centres", *University of Toronto Bulletin*, January 21, 1991; Richard White,

The Skule Story: The University of Toronto Faculty of Applied Science and Engineering 1873-2000 (University of Toronto Press, 2000) at 246.

69. Page 610, para. 3 – "research relationships": *Ontario Universities: Options and Futures: The Commission on the Future Development of the Universities of Ontario* (December, 1984) at 27; White, *The Skule Story* at 245.

70. Page 610, para. 3 – "faculties of engineering": White, *The Skule Story* at 246.

71. Page 610, para. 3 – "Michael Charles as its first incumbent": Ibid. at 248.

72. Page 610, para. 3 – "an industrial partner": Ibid. at 249.

73. Page 610, para. 3 – "400 per cent": Ibid.

74. Page 611, para. 1 – "lightwave research": "Five centres of excellence for U of T", *University of Toronto Bulletin*, June 29, 1987. The seven centres were reduced to four in 1997-98: see Lang, *University Finances in Ontario* at 15 of draft.

75. Page 611, para. 1 – "exclusively a U of T operation": Ibid.; "New laser centre opens", *University of Toronto Bulletin*, November 7, 1988.

76. Page 611, para. 1 – "a further five years": "Cabinet to consider future"; "Centres of Excellence Receive Support", *University of Toronto Bulletin*, December 16, 1991; "Centres Receive $216M", *University of Toronto Bulletin*, August 24, 1992.

77. Page 611, para. 1 – "flowed to the University of Toronto for research": $11 million was received in 1990-91: see "Centres of Excellence Receive Support". Connell estimated in 1987 that at least $60 million would come to the U of T in the five year period: see Connell, "Centres of Excellence" at 15.

78. Page 611, para. 1 – "indirect overhead costs": "Benefits of the Ontario excellence program", *University of Toronto Bulletin*, July 24, 1989.

79. Page 611, para. 1 – "new faculty members": Ibid.

80. Page 611, para. 2 – "Salama of electrical engineering": "Andre Salama to lead electronics network", *University of Toronto Bulletin*, October 30, 1989; www.vrg.utoronto.ca.

81. Page 611, para. 2 – "participating in all the centres": E-mail from Peter Munsche to Friedland, August 14, 2000.

82. Page 611, para. 2 – "11 private companies": "More Industry Support Needed", *University of Toronto Bulletin*, April 11, 1994.

83. Page 611, para. 2 – "sociologist in the faculty of medicine": Ibid.; "Marshall, Victor", *Canadian Who's Who 1994* at 736; Victor Marshall, "Into the Age of Aging", *University of Toronto Bulletin*, February 18, 1991.

84. Page 611, para. 2 – "equate with small returns": "More Industry Support Needed"

85. Page 611, para. 3 – "encourage its development": E-mail from Munsche to Friedland, August 14, 2000. The technology transfer office and the Innovations Foundation have joined forces "to create Utech Services to help researchers protect – and better profit from – their research": see Althea Blackburn-Evans, "Researchers to Profit from New Tech Office", *University of Toronto Bulletin*, October 16, 2000.

86. Page 611, para. 3 – "Innovations Foundation": The Innovations Foundation was founded in 1980: see "The Innovations Foundation", *University of Toronto Bulletin*, January 7, 2000; Michael Smith, "Marketing Ingenuity",

University of Toronto Magazine (Spring, 1995) at 10; Michael Smith, "Did Someone Say Eureka?", *University of Toronto Magazine* (Summer, 2000) at 29-32.

87. Page 611, para. 3 – "$5 million in royalties": Conversation with David MacLennan, September 7, 2000; Munsche to Friedland, August 14, 2000; Munsche to Friedland, August 16, 2000.

88. Page 611, para. 3 – "pork industry": Conversation with MacLennan; e-mail from Munsche to Friedland, August 30, 2000.

89. Page 611, para. 3 – "about five a year": Munsche to Friedland, August 14, 2000; Mary Magri to Friedland, August 31, 2000. Some of the spin-off companies are GlycoDesign, Polyphalt, Sciex, and Innova: see www.appliedbiosystems.com; www.polyphalt.com; www.glycodesign.com; www.inovatech.com.

90. Page 612, para. 1 – "during the 1980s": Author's conversations with Charles Hollenberg on July 15, 1998, and August 4, 2000.

91. Page 612, para. 1 – "insecurity in Quebec": See Chapter 35 (1966).

92. Page 612, para. 1 – "research funding and productivity": Ibid.

93. Page 612, para. 1 – "heparin at the Toronto General": See Chapters 24 (1922) and 35 (1966).

94. Page 612, para. 1 – "Pablum at the Sick Children's": Max Braithwaite, *Sick Kids: The Story of the Hospital for Sick Children in Toronto* (Toronto: McClelland and Stewart, 1974) at 90-91.

95. Page 612, para. 2 – "established a research institute": Ibid. at 128

96. Page 612, para. 2 – "reputation for research": Author's conversations with Hollenberg; "Rothstein", *University of Toronto Bulletin,* November 24, 1980.

97. Page 612, para. 2 – "might as well not be done": "Rothstein".

98. Page 612, para. 2 – "more than 500 persons": Ibid. The $10 million figure did not include overhead, and the staff complement included clinicians: author's conversation with Rothstein, August 11, 2000.

99. Page 612, para. 2 – "Louis Siminovitch": Louis Siminovitch, "Louis Siminovitch", in G.A. Kenney-Wallace et al., *In Celebration of Canadian Scientists: A Decade of Killam Laureates* (Winnipeg: The Charles Babbage Research Centre, 1990) at 57; Lesley Marrus Barsky, *From Generation to Generation: A History of Toronto's Mount Sinai Hospital* (Toronto: McClelland and Stewart, 1998) at 181; "Siminovitch, Louis", *Canadian Who's Who 1994* at 1046.

100. Page 612, para. 2 – "cystic fibrosis": "Six Appointed to University's Highest Rank", *University of Toronto Bulletin,* May 30, 1994.

101. Page 612, para. 2 – "funding categories": E-mail from David Naylor, August 17, 2000.

102. Page 612, para. 3 – "Mount Sinai Research Institute": He was appointed in 1983: see Barsky, *From Generation to Generation* at 183-184.

103. Page 612, para. 3 – "Samuel Lunenfeld": Ibid. at 189-190; "Bernstein, Alan", *Canadian Who's Who 1994* at 93; "Three Win Medals from Royal Society", *University of Toronto Bulletin,* May 6, 1996; Barsky, *From Generation to Generation* at 184 and 236.

104. Page 612, para. 3 – "came from Queen's": Ibid. at 185-186; Barsky, *From Generation to Generation* at 185.

105. Page 612, para. 3 – "four divisions of the institute": "Bernstein, Alan", *Canadian Who's Who 1994* at 93; "Three Win Medals from Royal Society", *University of Toronto Bulletin,* May 6, 1996; Barsky, *From Generation to Generation* at 184 and 236.

106. Page 612, para. 3 – "Tony Pawson from UBC": "Professor Anthony James Pawson" (undated press release about Pawson's appointment as University Professor, c. July, 1998); "Three named to highest rank", *University of Toronto Bulletin,* October 13, 1998. Some predict that Pawson will someday win a Nobel Prize: author's conversations with Hollenberg and with Yip on August 8, 2000.

107. Page 613, para. 1 – "genetic basis of disease": Barsky, *From Generation to Generation* at 185.

108. Page 613, para. 1 – "Pharmaceutical Research Institute": "Centre for Genetics Receives $5 Million", *University of Toronto Bulletin,* February 6, 1995; Barsky, *From Generation to Generation* at 239.

109. Page 613, para. 1 – "$5 million for research": *Mount Sinai Hospital Annual Report 1998-1999,* located on Mount Sinai website at www.mtsinai.on.ca/foundation/AnnualReport9899/chairs.html.

110. Page 613, para. 1 – "$75 million in three years": Barsky, *From Generation to Generation* at 229.

111. Page 613, para. 2 – "Tak Mak": Another potential Nobel laureate: e-mail from David Naylor, August 17, 2000; "Professor Tak Mak" (undated press release about Pawson's appointment as University Professor, c. July, 1997); "U of T Honours Four", *University of Toronto Bulletin,* October 14, 1997; "Tak Mak Wins Sloan Prize for Cancer Research", *University of Toronto Bulletin,* June 24, 1996.

112. Page 613, para. 2 – "Joseph Penninger": "Penninger, Joseph", *Canadian Who's Who 2000* at 993; "Woodgett, James Robert", *Canadian Who's Who 2000* at 1364; author's conversations with Hollenberg; *Globe and Mail,* February 26, 1999.

113. Page 614, para. 1 – "ask for help and you get it": *Globe and Mail,* August 24, 2000.

114. Page 614, para. 2 – "trauma research": Author's conversations with various individuals, including Hollenberg and Yip.

115. Page 614, para. 2 – "cardiovascular disease": *ICES Annual Report 1998-99,* on website at www.ices.on.ca/docs/icesinfo.html; see also author's conversation with Cecil Yip on August 8, 2000; e-mail from David Naylor, August 17, 2000.

116. Page 614, para. 3 – "hospital institutes' access to research funds or flexibility in recruiting": Author's conversations with Hollenberg and others.

117. Page 614, para. 3 – "thalassaemia": See "Sick Kids Investigation Prompts Policy Review", *University of Toronto Bulletin,* December 4, 1998; the 1998 report by Arnold Naimark; "University Working to Ensure Olivieri Can Continue Research", *University of Toronto Bulletin,* January 25, 1999; "President Brokers Olivieri Deal", *University of Toronto Bulletin,* February 8, 1999; *Varsity,* January 26, 1999; T*he Olivieri Report…commissioned by the Canadian Association of University* Teachers (Toronto: Lorimer, 2001 (Jon Thompson, chair, Patricia Baird, and Jocelyn Downie); *University of Toronto Bulletin,* October 29, 2001. Martin Friedland, it should be pointed out, was involved in one aspect of the controversy involving an allegation by Olivieri of research misconduct by an associate: see *Varsity,* January 26, 1999.

118. Page 615, para. 1 – "in the area of drug trials": *Toronto Star,* January 28, 1999; "Prichard Reports on Olivieri Case", *University of Toronto Bulletin,* October 25, 1999. See also Bernard Dickens, "Harmonization of Research Policies and Procedures between the University of Toronto and its Affiliated Teaching Hospitals,' 1999. Charles Hollenberg was appointed to help harmonize the policies: *University of Toronto Bulletin,* June 26, 2000. See also John Furedy, "A Price too High", *University of Toronto Bulletin,* March 27, 2000; Manuel Buchwald, "Policies at

Sick Kids Among the Best", *University of Toronto Bulletin*, April 10, 2000. Harmonization was later achieved: see "Hospitals, U of T Harmonize Research Policies", *University of Toronto Bulletin*, March 26, 2001.

119. Page 615, para. 2 – "built up by other hospitals": Author's conversation with Yip on August 8, 2000.

120. Page 615, para. 2 – "interdisciplinary collaboration": Alan Bernstein, "Virtual Transformation", *University of Toronto Bulletin*, October 16, 2000; author's conversations with Hollenberg; author's discussion with Yip, August 8, 2000; e-mail from David Naylor, August 17, 2000.

121. Page 615, para. 3 – "an American consulting firm": "$100 million a possible campaign target, study says", *University of Toronto Bulletin*, September 15, 1986.

122. Page 615, para. 3 – "University to govern itself": Marts and Lundy, "Feasibility Study Report Prepared for the University of Toronto, Toronto, Ontario, Canada", July, 1986 (document forwarded by Marts and Lundy, New Jersey, August, 2000) at 12-13.

123. Page 615, para. 3 – "University's endowment": Ibid. at 9-10.

124. Page 615, para. 3 – "staff would have to be added": Ibid. at 41.

125. Page 615, para. 3 – "well-conceived projects": "$10 million success", *University of Toronto Bulletin*, April 6, 1987.

126. Page 615, para. 3 – "several-fold increase was possible": *Renewal* at 104.

127. Page 615, para. 4 – "was begun in late 1987": "Campaign goal $100 million", *University of Toronto Bulletin*, December 7, 1987; George E. Connell, "Dollars & Donors Break All Records", *University of Toronto Alumni Magazine* (Autumn, 1987) at 34.

128. Page 615, para. 4 – "CJRT radio station": *Breakthrough* (undated campaign brochure).

129. Page 615, para. 4 – "chair the campaign": Author's conversation with Prichard on July 18, 2000. Don Fullerton of the CIBC had been the chair of the campaign planning committee but did not go on to head the campaign: see "Broad-based campaign would meet need for ongoing support: Cameron", *University of Toronto Bulletin*, May 25, 1987.

130. Page 615, para. 4 – "six-year period": George E. Connell, "Notes for Review by the University Historian", July 11, 1998 at 6.

131. Page 616, para. 1 – "the development team": "President's Priorities Linked", *University of Toronto Alumni Magazine* (Fall, 1988).

132. Page 616, para. 1 – "about $135 million": Connell, "Notes for Review" at 6.

133. Page 616, para. 1 – "featured goals of the campaign": Polanyi dinner and lecture, G.E. Connell remarks, 25 October, 1987 (document forwarded by Connell).

134. Page 617, para. 1 – "additional $8.5 million": "Centre established for study of neurodegenerative disease", *University of Toronto Bulletin*, July 20, 1987. Other major gifts in the campaign included the Pratt Building and the Kaneff Centre at Erindale: see "Erindale tops $3 million", *University of Toronto Bulletin*, June 11, 1990; "Breakthrough Campaign News", *University of Toronto Magazine* (Summer, 1990) at 22-4. The Koffler Institute for Pharmacy Management was a gift of the friends of Murray Koffler in 1995 and completed with campaign funds: see D.W. Lang to Planning and Resources Committee, April 4, 1986, UTA/A94-0013/004; Janice Oliver to Business Affairs Committee, April 10, 1987, UTA/A94-0013/023.

135. Page 617, para. 1 – "more than 50 researchers": "Fight for the Mind", *University of Toronto Magazine* (Summer, 1994) at 26-27.

136. Page 617, para. 1 – "Alzheimer's disease": "Familial Alzheimer's Gene Identified", *University of Toronto Magazine* (Autumn, 1995) at 4; "Protein Discovery May Lead to New Alzheimer's Drugs", *University of Toronto Bulletin*, September 11, 2000.

137. Page 617, para. 2 – "south-west campus": "October Means U of T Day", *University of Toronto Magazine* (Fall, 1989) at 9.

138. Page 617, para. 2 – "for more than ten years": "Consultants Interim Report on the South-West Campus – A Centre for Resource and Environmental Studies", *University of Toronto Bulletin*, November 5, 1979.

139. Page 617, para. 2 – "taken inflation into account": Connell comments to Friedland, December 29, 2000; Connell, "Notes for Review" at 4; see also Connell to Sorbara, June 16, 1986, UTA/A94-0013/018; "Earth Sciences Centre goes ahead", *University of Toronto Bulletin*, August 25, 1986.

140. Page 617, para. 2 – "serious cost overruns": Janice Oliver to Pathy, April 8, 1988, UTA/A98-0008/002.

141. Page 617, para. 2 – "disaster of the first magnitude": Connell, "Notes for Review" at 4.

142. Page 617, para. 2 – "to complete the project": *Breakthrough.*

143. Page 617, para. 2 – "effect of the campaign": Connell to Cressy, May 24, 1988, UTA/A98-0008/030.

144. Page 617, para. 2 – "geology": "October Means U of T Day".

145. Page 617, para. 2 – "Institute for Environmental Studies": IES moved into the building in September, 1995: see e-mail from Roger Hansell to University of Toronto History Project, August 25, 2000.

146. Page 617, para. 2 – "on St. George Street": Lang to Foley; November 30, 1988, UTA/A98-0008/024. Social geography remained at Sidney Smith Hall with social anthropology. Physical anthropology moved to the Borden building: see e-mail from Elizabeth Sisam to Friedland, February 5, 2001.

147. Page 617, para. 2 – "Prichard's tenure as president": Connell, "Notes for Review" at 4. The building was paid off from the Long-term Adjustment fund that Connell had set up from savings in contributions to the pension plan: comments by Dan Lang to Friedland, February 2, 2001.

148. Page 617, para. 3 – " unicameral governing structure": "McGill Professor will study views on unicameral gov't", *University of Toronto Bulletin*, January 12, 1987; see also "Opinions sought on unicameral system", *University of Toronto Bulletin*, December 8, 1986; Stansbury to Friedland, January 19, 1987, UTA/B98-0006.

149. Page 617, para. 3 – "list of complaints": Edward J. Stansbury, "Report on the Unicameral Governing Structure of the University of Toronto", March 10, 1987, UTA/A94-0013/027; "Governance report urges major changes", *University of Toronto Bulletin*, March 23, 1987.

150. Page 618, para. 1 – "governance at the University of Toronto": Finlayson to Balfour, May 1, 1987, UTA/A98-0008/007; see also W.H. Nelson, "From double innocence to double ignorance", *University of Toronto Bulletin*, November 24, 1986.

151. Page 618, para. 1 – "about the system as Stansbury": "Governance Report".

152. Page 618, para. 1 – "including the budget": Connell to Friedland, July 4, 1998 at 4.

153. Page 618, para. 1 – "changes in the system of government": *Renewal* at 14 et seq.

154. Page 618, para. 2 – "governance issue settled": "President's Priorities Linked". The fundraising consultants' report had influenced his decision to draft the document: see "Development & Renewal", *University of Toronto Bulletin*, May 28, 1990.

155. Page 618, para. 2 – "the rest will be more difficult": "Governance reform considered", *University of Toronto Bulletin*, April 6, 1987.

156. Page 618, para. 2 – "special meetings of the council were held": "Special Council meetings planned to consider governance", *University of Toronto Bulletin*, August 24, 1987; "Special meeting of Council airs views of governance", *University of Toronto Bulletin*, September 28, 1987; "Council asked to consider reform", *University of Toronto Bulletin*, October 26, 1987; "Significant changes to unicameralism approved in principle by Council", *University of Toronto Bulletin*, December 7, 1987.

157. Page 618, para. 3 – "more fundamental change": "Council asked to consider reform"; "Tempers Intrude on Industrious Peace", *University of Toronto Alumni Magazine* (Spring, 1988) at 21.

158. Page 618, para. 3 – "reformed unicameral structure": "Special meeting of Council".

159. Page 618, para. 3 – "Michael Uzumeri": Minutes of the Governing Council, December 3, 1987.

160. Page 618, para. 3 – "fund-raising campaign": "Significant changes to unicameralism approved"; "Campaign goal $100 million".

161. Page 618, para. 4 – "Provost Foley": "Faculty votes to censure U of T president, provost", *Globe and Mail*, December 1, 1987; "Tempers Intrude on Industrious Peace" at 19.

162. Page 618, para. 4 – "hand-delivered to the *Globe*": "Procedure of negotiating at issue: Connell", *University of Toronto Bulletin*, December 7, 1987.

163. Page 618, para. 4 – "previous academic year": The agreement had involved requiring the possibility of an appeal to the grievance review panel of a negative pre-tenure review at the three-year period: see "Procedure of negotiating at issue". In a conversation with the author on August 10, 2000, Foley pointed out that the administration negotiator David Cook was going on leave abroad and so there was not adequate time for the administration to do the necessary consultation; see also e-mail from David Cook to Friedland, September 11, 2000. The censure issue has been one of the most difficult in the entire manuscript to pin down, although discussions have been held in the fall of 2000 with most of the principal participants – Joan Foley, David Cook, George Connell, Fred Wilson, Bill Nelson, Bill Graham, and others. I have also gone through the records of UTFA and the relevant provostial records. Recollections of the event differ widely. William H. Nelson, *The Search for Faculty Power: The University of Toronto Faculty Association 1942-1992* (Toronto: The University of Toronto Faculty Association, 1993) at 157, suggests that there was a difference of opinion on whether it was an agreement, as UTFA thought, or only negotiations. This author believes that there was an agreement: see Cook to Friedland, September 11, 2000, stating, in part: "The time pressure meant that we worked in too much isolation but it spurred us on to agreement. That is, basically the Provost's office and the UTFA came to an agreement that included the three year review".

164. Page 619, para. 1 – "disputed by the administration": See "Procedure of negotiating at issue". A committee was set up under law professor Richard Risk to look into procedures: see Risk to Connell, February 17, 1989, UTA/A98-0001/031.

165. Page 619, para. 2 – "bewilderment in Simcoe Hall": See Connell, "Notes for Review" at 3; "Tempers Intrude on Industrious Peace" at 19.

166. Page 619, para. 2 – "explosion of public rage": *Globe and Mail*, December 3, 1987; "Tempers Intrude on Industrious Peace" at 20.

167. Page 619, para. 2 – "unreasonable and shrill": "Connell, Wilson will meet to discuss differences", *University of Toronto Bulletin*, December 7, 1987.

168. Page 619, para. 3 – "proposal for pay equity for women": E-mails from Fred Wilson to Friedland, August 11 and 27, 2000; "Critics of policy on employment equity are missing the point: UTFA president", *University of Toronto Bulletin*, November 9, 1987; Joan Foley, "Moving towards equity in faculty hiring", *University of Toronto Bulletin*, December 7, 1987; "Things *should* be done properly: Wilson", *University of Toronto Bulletin*, January 25, 1988; *UTFA Newsletter*, November 18, 1987; see generally, Chapter 39 (1980).

169. Page 619, para. 3 – "change in those policies": See Chapter 37 (1971)

170. Page 619, para. 3 – "under the University of Toronto Act": *Renewal* at 17. "I hoped", Connell later reminisced, "that we would bring into being an academic arm of the council so strong and well-respected that Article 2 would be unnecessary, and that the role of UTFA could be confined to the special interests" of faculty – salary, benefits and grievances: see Connell to Friedland, July 4, 1998 at 4-5. Fred Wilson later made it clear that a change in the governing structure would not necessarily result in a change in the memorandum of agreement: see "Tempers Intrude on Industrious Peace" at 21.

171. Page 619, para. 3 – "in the restructuring process": Carol Nash and Fred Wilson, "Joint Response to the October 22nd Proposal on University Governance Submitted to the Executive Committee of Governing Council", November 17, 1987, UTA/A98-0008/007 at 4.

172. Page 619, para. 3 – "was not to be written off": It may also be that some who wanted certification thought that provoking the administration might lead to a reaction by the administration that would lead to certification: conversation with Yip on August 8, 2000.

173. Page 619, para. 4 – "academic administrators": "Significant changes to unicameralism approved". This had previously been suggested by the Macdonald report: see Chapter 37 (1971). The rule which prohibited any estate from having a majority on a committee was a governing council rule that did not require a change in legislation: see Chapter 37 (1971).

174. Page 620, para. 1 – "resigned to the proposals": *Varsity*, December 3, 1987.

175. Page 620, para. 1 – "supported the changes": *Varsity*, November 26, 1987.

176. Page 620, para. 1 – "flesh out the plan ": "Report of the Chairman's Advisory Committee on Governance", May 3, 1988, UTA/A98-0008/007; "Significant changes to unicameralism approved"; "Draft report details Governing Council reform", *University of Toronto Bulletin*, March 21, 1988. The group was moderated by David Meen of the consulting firm McKinsey and Co.: see Connell comments to Friedland, December 29, 2000.

177. Page 620, para. 1 – "matter on to the governing council": Dimond to Balfour, October 19, 1987, UTA/A98-0008/007.

178. Page 620, para. 1 – "council and its committees": "Significant changes to unicameralism approved".

179. Page 620, para. 1 – "of whom 16 would be students": "Major changes to governance approved by Governing Council", *University of Toronto Bulletin*, May 24, 1988; "Report of the Chairman's Advisory Committee on Governance" at 41.

180. Page 620, para. 1 – "majority of governing council members": "Major changes to governance approved".

181. Page 620, para. 2 – "often to the minute": E-mail from Marrus to Friedland, May 20, 1998.

182. Page 620, para. 2 – "and has remained so": Ibid. Prichard's opinion was that "when the next history of the

University of Toronto is written, I believe it will judge that you, more than any other individual, reasserted and revitalized collegial decision-making for the faculty of the University of Toronto": see Prichard to Marrus, June 3, 1996.

183. Page 620, para. 2 – "Roger Beck": "Beck and Waugh chair boards", *University of Toronto Bulletin*, July 22, 1996.

184. Page 620, para. 2 – "worked extraordinarily well": Beck to Friedland, July 27, 1998.

185. Page 621, para. 1 – "bring them on board now": "Mellon Foundation awards U of T challenge grant for bridging appointments in humanities", *University of Toronto Bulletin*, April 12, 1982.

186. Page 621, para. 1 – "permitting new hirings": "Early retirement scheme approved in principle", *University of Toronto Bulletin*, June 20, 1983.

187. Page 621, para. 2 – "came into force in April 1985": "Mandatory retirement stays for now", *University of Toronto Bulletin*, March 25, 1985; "Mandatory retirement upheld by court", *University of Toronto Bulletin*, October 27, 1986.

188. Page 621, para. 2 – "employment past age 65": Connell, "Notes for Review" at 3.

189. Page 621, para. 2 – "would win the case": Ibid.

190. Page 621, para. 2 – "It did": "Mandatory retirement upheld by court"; "Court upholds mandatory retirement", *University of Toronto Bulletin*, December 10, 1990; see *McKinney* v. *University of Guelph*, [1990] 3 *S.C.R.* 229.

191. Page 621, para. 2 – "other universities could not": See generally, *Renewal* at 94. York University, for example, had made an arrangement with its faculty to allow employment past 65: see Connell, "Notes for Review" at 3. Universities in some other provinces, such as Quebec and Manitoba, could not introduce mandatory retirement at age 65 because it would violate provincial law. The Ontario Human Rights Code permitted mandatory retirement at age 65, and so the plaintiffs had to strike down that provision as well as the specific university policy: see the *Ontario Human Rights Code*, in *Revised Statutes of Ontario 1980*, chapter 340, Part V, section 26a.

192. Page 621, para. 2 – "forced into retirement": Departments were entitled to keep faculty members on staff for another three years on year-to-year appointments, but the faculty association insisted that they not have a reduction in pay and the departments were therefore reluctant to keep persons on under those conditions. They could usually get two junior faculty members for the same price.

193. Page 621, para. 2 – "law and engineering": E-mail from Richard White to Friedland, January 29, 2001.

194. Page 621, para. 3 – "financial equilibrium": Connell to President's Advisory Committee, March 23, 1989 (document forwarded by Connell: copy can also be found in UTA/A98-0008/054).

195. Page 621, para. 3 – "change drastically from year to year": Connell to Members of the Academic Board, January 11, 1990, UTA/A98-0008/054; "Long-Range Budget Guidelines, 1990-91 to 1995-1996", UTA/A98-0008/054; Governing Council adopted the guidelines February 8, 1990, see Irene Birrell to M. England, February 13, 1990, UTA/A98-0008/054.

196. Page 621, para. 3 – "planning at the University": Connell comments to Friedland, December 29, 2000.

197. Page 622, para. 1 – "circumstances or personalities": "Draft 6", attached to Lang to Tony Melcher, April 10, 1989, UTA/A98-0008/028.

198. Page 622, para. 2 – "support during that period": The assumptions and thus the budget would change as circumstances changed: see "Long Range Budget Guidelines 1990-91 to 1995-96" at 31-32. Divisional planning had also been enhanced by another policy that had been introduced in 1977, which allowed a carry forward of

unspent operating budget funds into the ensuing fiscal (and budget) year. As R.G. White, the university's chief financial officer, stated to the author in an e-mail of February 3, 2001: "It was very significant because it was the beginning of real delegation in its truest form for financial management throughout the University. No longer was it necessary to spend out one's budget to avoid 'losing' one's money at fiscal year end. Under the new policy a dean could manage his/her funds to bridge from one year to the next and help to accommodate the inevitable budget cuts that continued from year to year unabated. Our philosophy was that once a budget was struck for a faculty for a given year then 'let the dean manage within that allotment without Simcoe Hall (head office) looking over one's shoulder".

199. Page 622, para. 2 – "nearly $30 million": Connell to Prichard, June 29, 1990, UTA/A98-0008/054.

200. Page 622, para. 3 – "second term in office": "Renewal 1987" at 12. *Renewal* was released to the University community March 19, 1987: see "Undergraduate reform".

201. Page 622, para. 3 – "six at Toronto": "Connell, George E.", *Canadian Who's Who 1994* at 229.

202. Page 622, para. 3 – "established in January 1989": "Presidential search committee", *University of Toronto Bulletin*, January 9, 1989; "Presidential Search Committee Appointed", *University of Toronto Magazine* (Spring, 1989) at 27. Robert McGavin took over as chair of governing council on July 1, 1989 and as chair of the search committee, but Joan Randall stayed on as a member of the committee: see conversation with Joan Randall, February 19, 2001.

203. Page 622, para. 3 – "William Saywell of Simon Fraser": "Downey, James", *Canadian Who's Who 1994* at 309; "Naimark, Arnold", *Canadian Who's Who 1994* at 837; "Saywell, William George Gabriel", *Canadian Who's Who 1994* at 1013.

204. Page 622, para. 3 – "were interviewed": Author's conversations with a number of persons involved in the process.

205. Page 622, para. 3 – "allergic to failure": "Prichard appointment gets optimistic response", *University of Toronto Bulletin*, October 30, 1989.

206. Page 622, para. 4 – "relied heavily on his advice": Author's various conversations with Connell.

207. Page 622, para. 4 – "negotiations with the faculty association": Author's conversation with Prichard, July 18, 2000.

208. Page 623, para. 1 – "self-fulfilling prophecy": Prichard to Connell, March 20, 1989 (document forwarded by Connell).

CHAPTER 41 – 1994 – RAISING THE SIGHTS

1. Page 624, para. 1 – "Connell had had six": J. Robert S. Prichard, "Efficiency for New Knowledge", *University of Toronto Magazine* (Autumn, 1995) at 3.

2. Page 624, para. 1 – "best vice-presidents in Canada": Martin Friedland, "Notes on Lunch with Rob Prichard on December 22, 1998" at 3.

3. Page 624, para. 2 – "human resources in 1994": Following vice-president (business affairs) Bryan Davies' departure to the Royal Bank in May 1994: see "Davies to Join Royal Bank", *University of Toronto Bulletin*, April 11, 1994; "Administration Reorganizes – Vice-Presidents Down to Four", *University of Toronto Bulletin*, November 7, 1994. The position has now been split: see "Business VP Position Created", *University of Toronto Bulletin*, November 27, 2000.

4. Page 624, para. 2 – "taken on in 1991": "Michael Finlayson V-P Human Resources", *University of Toronto Magazine* (Summer 1991) at 40; "A Shift in Perspective", *University of Toronto Bulletin*, September 23, 1991.

5. Page 624, para. 2 – "for a two-year period": "Michael Finlayson V-P".

6. Page 624, para. 2 – "on only one occasion": Conversation with Finlayson, September 5, 2000.

7. Page 624, para. 3 – "binding arbitration in the early 1980s": "Budget Chair Appointed Provost", *University of Toronto Bulletin*, February 8, 1993.

8. Page 625, para. 1 – "board's budget committee": Conversation with Sedra, August 25, 2000.

9. Page 625, para. 1 – "appointment as provost": "Budget Chair Appointed Provost".

10. Page 625, para. 2 – "dean of social work since 1989": "Munroe-Blum Appointed", *University of Toronto Bulletin*, May 10, 1993.

11. Page 625, para. 2 – "making change happen": "Refocusing, Renewal, and Research", *University of Toronto Bulletin*, March 14, 1994. Quote has been slightly altered from original: see Munroe-Blum to Friedland, October 10, 2000.

12. Page 626, para. 1 – "chief development officer": "Dellandrea New VP", *University of Toronto Bulletin*, January 31, 1994.

13. Page 626, para. 1 – "university development": Undated list of OISE degrees on higher education sent to the author by Glen Jones of the higher education group at OISE.

14. Page 626, para. 1 – "defensive positions": Dellandrea to Friedland, June 6, 2000.

15. Page 626, para. 1 – "$86 million": Ibid.

16. Page 626, para. 2 – "at Jay's side": Jack Batten, "Decade of the Dynamo", *University of Toronto Magazine* (Summer 2000) at 17.

17. Page 626, para. 2 – "head of neurology": "Tracking Prichard's rise", *University of Toronto Bulletin*, October 30, 1989.

18. Page 626, para. 2 – "reported with pride": Batten, "Decade of the Dynamo" at 17.

19. Page 626, para. 3 – "in October 1990": "Images of the Installation", *University of Toronto Bulletin*, October 22, 1990.

20. Page 626, para. 3 – "it is being lost": "The installation address of J. Robert S. Prichard", *University of Toronto Bulletin*, October 22, 1990.

21. Page 626, para. 3 – "law school at the same time": Rae entered in September of 1974, Prichard's third year: Bob Rae, *From Protest to Power: Personal Reflections of a Life in Politics* (Toronto: Penguin Books, 1997) at 53.

22. Page 626, para. 3 – "did not improve": See e.g., "Meager Transfer Payments Mean University Must Develop New Strategy, Says Prichard", *University of Toronto Bulletin*, January 27, 1992; "University Faces Drastic Cuts in Budget", *University of Toronto Bulletin*, February 10, 1992; "Deeper Budget Reductions Could Affect Administrative Activities, President Says", *University of Toronto Bulletin*, March 23, 1992; "University Adheres to Financial Strategy with Cuts Totaling $9 Million", *University of Toronto Bulletin*, May 11, 1992; "Staff Take Salary Freeze", *University of Toronto Bulletin*, March 15, 1993; "Universities Take Big Hit", *University of Toronto Bulletin*, April 26, 1993.

23. Page 626, para. 3 – "inadequate funding": "Continue Attack on Cutbacks, Says Prichard", *University of Toronto Bulletin*, October 21, 1991.

24. Page 626, para. 3 – "reduced from 8,000 to 6,500": Conversation with Finlayson, September 5, 2000.

25. Page 627, para. 1 – "women's ice hockey": "Alternatives to Blues' Blues Contemplated", *University of Toronto Bulletin*, December 14, 1992. See also e-mail from Bruce Kidd to author of May 18, 2001.

26. Page 627, para. 1 – "pay more for it": "Alumni Offers Sports Support", *University of Toronto Bulletin*, February 8, 1993.

27. Page 627, para. 1 – "Calgary Dinosaurs 37-34": "VARSITY VICTORY!", *University of Toronto Bulletin*, November 22, 1993. For women's hockey, see e-mail from Bruce Kidd to author of May 18, 2001.

28. Page 628, para. 1 – "open to tremendous criticism": "Athletic Department Vows Equal Funding", *University of Toronto Bulletin*, March 14, 1994.

29. Page 628, para. 1 – "equal facilities for women": "Women's Locker Plan Approved", *University of Toronto Bulletin*, December 8, 1997.

30. Page 628, para. 1 – "to break even": "Up to 12 Hart House Positions Lost", *University of Toronto Bulletin*, December 14, 1992.

31. Page 628, para. 2 – "$3 million a year": "Medicine Moves to Fill Dean's Vacated Position", *University of Toronto Bulletin*, December 2, 1991.

32. Page 628, para. 2 – "had not been properly followed": Ibid.; "An Open Letter From the President", *University of Toronto Bulletin*, November 18, 1991.

33. Page 628, para. 2 – "errors made by Simcoe Hall": "An Open Letter From the President"; "President's Report on Medicine Looks to the Future", *University of Toronto Bulletin*, February 10, 1992.

34. Page 628, para. 2 – "divisive debate": "Medicine Moves to Fill Dean's Vacated Position".

35. Page 628, para. 2 – "problem-based learning to the medical school": E-mail from John Dirks to Friedland, February 19, 2001.

36. Page 628, para. 2 – "achievements in the medical field": "Dirks, John Herbert", *Canadian Who's Who 2000* at 343; *The Gairdner Foundation International Awards* (Willowdale: The Gairdner Foundation, 1997).

37. Page 628, para. 2 – "subsequently became dean": "Aberman Appointed Dean of Medicine", *University of Toronto Bulletin*, November 9, 1992.

38. Page 628, para. 2 – "through an associate dean": Conversation with Sedra, August 25, 2000. Aberman had stated during the crisis: "As the slogan goes: nothing disinfects like sunlight": see "Restoring Trust is Priority", *University of Toronto Bulletin*, December 2, 1991.

39. Page 628, para. 2 – "rapidly to those received": Personal knowledge of author, whose spouse was the chair of occupational therapy during this period.

40. Page 628, para. 3 – "during his administration": See for example the Apotex letter: "Prichard Apologizes to Council", *University of Toronto Bulletin*, September 27, 1999; *Globe and Mail*, September 16, 1999.

41. Page 628, para. 3 – "learn from the experience"; "An Open Letter from the President"; "President's Report on Medicine Looks to the Future"; "President Will Define Roles", *University of Toronto Bulletin*, February 24, 1992.

42. Page 629, para. 1 – "supported the dismissals": "Administration Support Layoffs, Dirks Says", *University of Toronto Bulletin*, February 10, 1992.

43. Page 629, para. 1 – "never come before PVP": "President's Report Will Examine Events at Medical Faculty", *University of Toronto Bulletin*, January 13, 1992.

44. Page 629, para. 1 – "including academic planning": Munroe-Blum to Friedland, October 10, 2000.

45. Page 629, para. 1 – "a vice-provost": Aberman became Vice-Provost, Relations with Health Care Institutions, effective July 1, 1994: see www.library.utoronto.ca/cre/abermanad.htm. In a conversation with the author on February 27, 2001, Aberman says he asked to become a vice-provost.

46. Page 629, para. 2 – "racism had to be dealt with": For the Cannizzo affair, see "Disruption unacceptable", *University of Toronto Bulletin*, October 22, 1990; Michiel Horn, *Academic Freedom in Canada: A History* (University of Toronto Press, 1999) at 330.

47. Page 629, para. 2 – "improve the racial climate": "Freedoms defended, racism rejected", *University of Toronto Bulletin*, October 22, 1990. UCAR was founded after the Students' Administrative Council announced the ejection of the African and Caribbean Student Association (ACSA) from their offices at 44 St. George Street. SAC claimed that they needed the space for other purposes and denied any racist intentions. ACSA and its supporters disrupted several SAC meetings before the Office of Student Affairs allocated to them other space at 44 St. George. The ACSA incident convinced many students on campus that further pressure on issues of race relations was necessary. One of UCAR's first events was a protest rally at U of T day in October of 1989. UCAR held a successful teach-in against racism at Hart House the Friday after Martin Luther King day in January, 1992, but classes were not cancelled: see *Varsity*, October 23, 1989, January 23, 1992, January 27, 1992; *the newspaper*, January 24, 1992.

48. Page 629, para. 2 – "some catching up to do": "Statement by President J. Robert S. Prichard to Governing Council on the Report of the Presidential Advisors on Ethno-cultural Groups and Visible Minorities at the University of Toronto December 20, 1990", *University of Toronto Bulletin*, January 7, 1991.

49. Page 629, para. 2 – "committee on race relations": A suggestion for greater outreach activities was not immediately adopted: see "Initiating Means to Fight Racism", *University of Toronto Magazine* (Spring 1991) at 29; "Five measures announced", *University of Toronto Bulletin*, January 7, 1991.

50. Page 629, para. 2 – "anti-racism": A permanent office of Race Relations and Anti-Racism Initiatives was estab-

lished in January, 1993, "to ensure that all members of the University are afforded the right to work and study in an environment in which the individual, regardless of race, ancestry, colour, creed, citizenship or ethnic origin, is guaranteed treatment which is dignified, respectful, and free of biases based on these attributes": see www.library.utoronto.ca/equity/rrr/htm.

51. Page 629, para. 3 – "non-white": See Chapter 42 (1997).

52. Page 629, para. 3 – "remained relatively low": Chandrakant Shah and Tomislav Svoboda, "A Question of Fairness", *University of Toronto Bulletin*, January 11, 2000; *Varsity*, January 11, 2000.

53. Page 630, para. 1 – "equal academically": "Report recommends rights code", *University of Toronto Bulletin*, January 7, 1991.

54. Page 630, para. 1 – "new appointments by the end of the decade": *Toronto Star*, January 10, 2000.

55. Page 630, para. 1 – "consisted of members of visible minority groups": "A Question of Fairness".

56. Page 630, para. 1 – "an expert on China": "Six Appointed to University's Highest Rank", *University of Toronto Bulletin*, May 30, 1994.

57. Page 630, para. 1 – "3 per cent of the tenured faculty was Chinese": "More Minority Faculty Hiring Essential", *University of Toronto Bulletin*, January 24, 2000.

58. Page 630, para. 2 – "characterize the faculty as well": *Raising Our Sights: The Next Cycle of White Paper Planning Key Priorities for 2000-2004* January 6, 1999, *University of Toronto Bulletin*, January 18, 1999 at S3.

59. Page 630, para. 2 – "representation in the pool": E-mail from Carolyn Tuohy to Friedland, November 21, 2000; Sedra to Principals, Deans, Directors and Chairs, July 29, 1999; Sedra to Principals, Deans, Directors, and Chairs, November 7, 2000; "Proactive Faculty Recruitment" (undated memo forwarded from the provost's office).

60. Page 630, para. 3 – "occasions during that period": *Toronto Star*, July 27, 2000.

61. Page 630, para. 3 – "researcher in the department": "President Addresses Chun Procedures", *University of Toronto Bulletin*, September 15, 1997.

62. Page 630, para. 4 – " had to move to another location": "Protest May Lead to Change in Meetings", *University of Toronto Bulletin*, March 2, 1998; see also "President Addresses Chun Procedures".

63. Page 630, para. 4 – "Chun supporters": *Varsity*, March 22, 1999.

64. Page 631, para. 1 – "board of inquiry be established": *Globe and Mail*, February 7, 2000.

65. Page 631, para. 1 – "claim of racism": *Toronto Star*, July 27, 2000; "U of T Rejects Call for Chun Inquiry", *University of Toronto Bulletin*, April 10, 2000.

66. Page 631, para. 1 – "qualified to apply for": "U of T and Chun Reach Agreement", *University of Toronto Bulletin*, September 11, 2000; *Globe and Mail*, September 9, 2000; "An Open Letter to the University Community", *University of Toronto Bulletin*, September 25, 2000; "Physics Department Strives to Increase Diversity", *University of Toronto Bulletin*, February 28, 2000. The agreement created some controversy in the physics department: see, e.g., "Chun Agreement a Mistake", *University of Toronto Bulletin*, September 25, 2000.

67. Page 631, para. 1 – "ambiguities of Chun's appointment": E-mail from Cecil Yip to Friedland, January 26, 2001; e-mail from Paul Gooch to Friedland, February 19, 2001. The policy is called "Policies, Procedures and Terms and Conditions of Appointment for Research Associates (Limited Term) and Senior Research Associates" and was adopted by the Business Board on February 26, 1996.

68. Page 631, para. 2 – "all the estates are at the table": Friedland, "Notes on Lunch with Rob Prichard" at 1.

69. Page 631, para. 2 – "as good a relationship as possible"; "Seasoned negotiator assumes presidency", *University of Toronto Bulletin*, March 26, 1990. Bill Graham took over as president in 1992: see "Graham Acclaimed as UTFA President", *University of Toronto Bulletin*, March 23, 1992.

70. Page 631, para. 3 – "agreement entered into in 1977": See Chapter 38 (1975).

71. Page 631, para. 3 – "unionized faculties": Friedland, "Notes on Lunch with Rob Prichard" at 5; conversation with Prichard, July 18, 2000.

72. Page 631, para. 3 – "agreed to by the association": "Conflict of Interest Policies Welcomed", *University of Toronto Bulletin*, June 27, 1994. The author's report on the subject was commissioned by the president in the spring of 1991: see "President names Friedland to study conflict of interest", *University of Toronto Bulletin*, April 15, 1991. The report was made public in early 1992: see "University of Toronto Presidential Commission on Conflicts of Interest December, 1991", *University of Toronto Bulletin*, January 13, 1992.

73. Page 631, para. 3 – "just in one of the categories": E-mails from Cecil Yip to Friedland, January 26 and February 5, 2001; "Proposed Policy and Procedures on Academic Appointments Submitted by the Drafting Committee Academic Board University of Toronto May 28, 1992" (document supplied by Charles Levi) at 24-27. The committee was chaired by Cecil Yip: see Marrus to Academic Board, November 8, 1991 (document supplied by Charles Levi). A contentious issue dealing with tutors was, however, not enacted: see William H. Nelson, *The Search for Faculty Power: The University of Toronto Faculty Association 1942-1992* (Toronto: Canadian Scholar's Press, 1993) at 158-160; "Discussion Begins on Yip Report", *University of Toronto Bulletin*, November 4, 1991; Sandra Alston et al. to Academic Board, December 4, 1991 (document supplied by Charles Levi); *Tutors and Senior Tutors at the University of Toronto: Five Perspectives* (University of Toronto Faculty Association, 1991: document supplied by Charles Levi); conversation with Sedra, August 25, 2000; "Tenure Restricts, Business Board Says", *University of Toronto Bulletin*, January 11, 1993.

74. Page 631, para. 4 – "tenure was necessary": "Business Board Questions Tenure", *University of Toronto Bulletin*, November 9, 1992; "Tenure Restricts, Business Board Says", *University of Toronto Bulletin*, January 11, 1993.

75. Page 631, para. 4 – "institution of tenure itself": "Business Board Questions Tenure".

76. Page 632, para. 1 – "uncomfortable the ideas may be": Stephen Waddams, "In Defence of Tenure", *University of Toronto Bulletin*, January 11, 1993.

77. Page 632, para. 1 – "nobody would look at us": "Business Board Questions Tenure".

78. Page 632, para. 2 – "great public research universities": "Tenure is Centrepiece of University's Mission", *University of Toronto Bulletin*, October 15, 1996. Prichard also defended free speech on a number of occasions. For Canizzo, see "Disruptions unacceptable", *University of Toronto Bulletin*, October 22, 1990; see also Carol Tator et al., *Challenging Racism in the Arts: Case Studies of Controversy and Conflict* (University of Toronto Press, 1998) at 36-62; see also David Icke incident in *Varsity*, October 12, 1999. Prichard's support of free speech dated back to the Babb controversy of 1986: see Chapter 39 (1980).

79. Page 632, para. 2 – "through the chair of the committee": Conversation with Sedra, August 25, 2000.

80. Page 632, para. 3 – "appointment of academic administrators": "Boards Plan 1991-92 Debates", *University of Toronto Bulletin*, October 7, 1991.

81. Page 632, para. 3 – "recommended the changes": See Perron to Marrus, December 17, 1991 (document supplied by Charles Levi); "Report Number 38 of the Academic Board March 26th and April 2nd 1992" (document supplied by Charles Levi); conversation with Sedra, August 25, 2000.

82. Page 632, para. 3 – "not to discuss specific names": Simcoe Hall took far less interest in the appointment of chairs, leaving those appointments primarily to the deans: conversation with Sedra, August 25, 2000.

83. Page 633, para. 1 – "first budget in November": *Globe and Mail*, June 9 and November 30, 1995; see also "Quality, Selectivity in, Across-the-Board Cuts Out", *University of Toronto Bulletin*, November 20, 1995. See generally, Daniel Lang, *University Finance in Ontario* (Winnipeg: Canadian Society for the Study of Education, forthcoming in 2001) at 15 et seq. of draft.

84. Page 633, para. 1 – "operating support per student": J. Robert S. Prichard, "On Course", *University of Toronto Magazine* (Spring 1996) at 3.

85. Page 633, para. 1 – "in operating support": Ibid.

86. Page 633, para. 1 – " great public research universities": Ibid.

87. Page 633, para. 1 – "had been introduced by Connell": See Chapter 40 (1986).

88. Page 633, para. 1 – "Prichard and Sedra": Conversation with Prichard, July 18, 2000, and with Sedra, August 25, 2000.

89. Page 633, para. 2 – "staff salaries were rolled back": Conversation with Finlayson, September 5, 2000; "3% Cut, Days Off Proposed for Staff", *University of Toronto Bulletin*, February 5, 1996; "Three percent rollback for senior staff", *University of Toronto Bulletin*, April 8, 1996.

90. Page 633, para. 2 – "administrative staff were not part of one": "New Union Hopes for Speedy Agreement", *University of Toronto Bulletin*, December 14, 1998.

91. Page 633, para. 2 – "eligible voters": "Union bid fails; UTSA consults", *University of Toronto Bulletin*, November 12, 1990.

92. Page 633, para. 2 – "turned out for the vote": About 600 senior administrators with significant managerial responsibilities had been excluded: see "New Union Hopes"; Michael Finlayson to PDAC and C et al., December 8, 1998 (internal document in possession of the author).

93. Page 633, para. 3 – "interested in academic planning": Conversation with Sedra, August 25, 2000.

94. Page 633, para. 3 – "in the early 1990s": He also had been at the university when the school of hygiene and the faculty of food sciences had been closed: see Chapter 38 (1975). For forestry, see "Forestry Prepares for Cuts", *University of Toronto Bulletin*, January 11, 1993; "Decision on Forestry Postponed", *University of Toronto Bulletin*, January 25, 1993.

95. Page 633, para. 3 – "rationalizing academic resources": Conversation with Sedra, August 25, 2000.

96. Page 633, para. 3 – "*Planning for 2000*": *Planning for 2000: A Provostial White Paper on University Objectives University of Toronto*, February 14, 1994, *University of Toronto Bulletin*, February 21, 1994 at S3; "Vision of the Future", *University of Toronto Bulletin*, February 28, 1994.

97. Page 633, para. 3 – "decline into mediocrity": George Cook, "The Discovery University", *University of Toronto Magazine* (Fall 1994) at 12.

98. Page 633, para. 4 – "governing council in March 1994": Ibid.; see also "Vision 2000", *University of Toronto Magazine* (Summer 1994) at 2.

99. Page 633, para. 4 – "twenty-first century": *Planning for 2000* at S3.

100. Page 634, para. 1 – "restructuring areas of study": Ibid. at S2.

101. Page 634, para. 1 – "sole program of its type in Ontario": Ibid. at S13.

102. Page 634, para. 2 – "academic priorities fund": Discussions with Prichard and Sedra. Dan Lang points out that the practice of "taxing back" a percentage of divisional budgets was in the 1989-90 budgeting and planning process: "What was new about the Academic Priorities Fund was that it was not necessarily fully allocated in the year that it was generated and, usually, was used to underwrite overall divisional plans instead of individual items. This approach encouraged longer term, more comprehensive planning", see Lang comments to Friedland, February 2, 2001.

103. Page 635, para. 1 – "concentrate on graduate work": Conversation with Sedra, August 25, 2000.

104. Page 635, para. 2 – "from 2000 to 2004": *Raising Our Sights: The Next Cycle of White Paper Planning Key Priorities for 2000-2004*, January 6, 1999, *University of Toronto Bulletin*, January 18, 1999; "More Planning Ahead", *University of Toronto Bulletin*, October 26, 1998.

105. Page 635, para. 2 – "planning at the University of Toronto": *Raising Our Sights* at S3.

106. Page 635, para. 2 – "strengthening academic programs": Ibid. at S10.

107. Page 635, para. 2 – "significant research university": *Planning for 2000* at S3.

108. Page 635, para. 2 – "universities of the world": *Raising Our Sights* at S3. The University's Statement on Institutional Purpose, approved in 1992 and unchanged since, contains the mission statement, "The University of Toronto is committed to being an internationally significant research university, with undergraduate and professional programs of excellent quality": see "University of Toronto Governing Council Statement of Institutional Purpose, October 15, 1992", www.utoronto.ca/govcncl. In *Planning for 2000* in 1994 the mission of the university was in quotes, in *Raising our Sights* it was not. As Susan Bloch-Nevitte has commented, "the mission still stands as originally written; however this office – and I suspect a fair number of folks in Simcoe Hall, ultimately felt that it was too vague and didn't reflect the ambitions of the institution": see Bloch-Nevitte comments to Friedland, September 25, 2000. Carolyn Tuohy points out to the author in an e-mail of February 26, 2001 that objective 2.2 and 2.8 in the *Planning for 2000* document used something like these words in relation to undergraduate and graduate education.

109. Page 635, para. 2 – "approved by the governing council": Governing Council approved the document, February, 1999.

110. Page 635, para. 3 – "campaign were set": Dellandrea to Friedland, June 6, 2000.

111. Page 635, para. 3 – "word of mouth at every turn": Peter Herrndorf to Business Board, May 17, 1991, UTA/A98-0008/076.

112. Page 635, para. 3 – "upper year research experience": *Raising Our Sights* at S13; see also Chapter 39 (1980). Both 299 and 399 research courses are currently available.

113. Page 635, para. 4 – "raise $300 million": Discussion with Prichard July 18, 2000.

114. Page 635, para. 4 – "publication of the white paper": "The Campaign of Campaigns", *University of Toronto Magazine* (Autumn, 1998) at C2.

115. Page 636, para. 1 – "chair of the campaign": "Comper Chairs U of T Campaign", *University of Toronto Bulletin*, October 28, 1996.

116. Page 636, para. 1 – "$400 million": "The Campaign Kicks Off", *University of Toronto Bulletin*, September 29, 1997.

117. Page 636, para. 1 – "$575 million": Conversation with Prichard of July 18, 2000.

118. Page 636, para. 1 – "year 2004": Conversation with Prichard of July 18, 2000; "New Goal: U of T to Raise $1 Billion", *University of Toronto Bulletin*, October 16, 2000.

119. Page 636, para. 2 – "rather than physical facilities": Dellandrea to Friedland, June 6, 2000.

120. Page 636, para. 2 – "occupants of the chairs": Friedland, "Notes on Lunch with Rob Prichard" at 5. Batten, "Decade of the Dynamo" at 16, notes that only seven of the 14 were "permanently" endowed.

121. Page 636, para. 2 – "160 such chairs": Conversation with Prichard, July 18, 2000.

122. Page 636, para. 2 – "endowed adjustment fund": Conversation with Prichard, July 18, 2000; see Chapter 39 (1980).

123. Page 636, para. 2 – "senior faculty positions": Conversation with Prichard, July 18, 2000.

124. Page 636, para. 2 – "chairs in civil engineering": "U of T Matches $2.5 Million Gift to Civil Engineering", *University of Toronto Bulletin*, November 21, 1994; conversation with Sedra, August 25, 2000 at 7. The Tanenbaum family was also responsible for providing air conditioning in Convocation Hall: see "Keeping Cool at Convocation", *Campaign Quarterly* (Summer 1998). Anne Tanenbaum further gave $10 million for chairs in biomedical research: see "$10 Million Gives Boost to Biomedical Research", *University of Toronto Bulletin*, October 23, 1995.

125. Page 636, para. 2 – "AGF mutual funds": "U of T Established 100th Chair", *University of Toronto Bulletin*, May 10, 1999; "Update on the Campaign", *U.C. Magazine* (Winter 1998) at 3.

126. Page 636, para. 2 – "lawyer Ann Wilson": E-mail from Ron Daniels, June 30, 2000. The chair will formally be known as the Prichard-Wilson Chair in Law and Public Policy: see e-mail from Bloch-Nevitte to Friedland, September 26, 2000.

127. Page 636, para. 3 – "going to the humanities": See for example, "100 Chairs and Counting", *University of Toronto Magazine* (Summer 1999) at 18-19.

128. Page 637, para. 1 – "$3 million each": "U of T to Create $30 Million Research Fund", *University of Toronto Bulletin*, August 17, 1998; Dellandrea to Friedland, June 6, 2000.

129. Page 637, para. 1 – "Holocaust studies": Marrus Named to Holocaust Chair, *University of Toronto Bulletin*, November 27, 2000.

130. Page 637, para. 1 – "Chinese civilization": "Studying Chinese thought and culture at the University of Toronto", *Campaign Quarterly* (Spring 1998) at 2.

131. Page 637, para. 1 – "St. Michael's College": Another chair in Christianity and Culture was funded by the Roman Catholic Archdiocese of Toronto: see "Two chairs for Christianity and culture", *Campaign Quarterly* (Summer, 1999) at 3.

132. Page 637, para. 2 – "and the University": Micah Raynor, "Good Chemistry", *University of Toronto Magazine* (Winter 1997) at 18-19; "Great chemistry", *Campaign Quarterly* (Winter 1997) at 1 and 8.

133. Page 637, para. 2 – "for a student loan fund": Claude Bissell Diary, June 5, 1969.

134. Page 637, para. 2 – "David Dunlap Observatory": See Chapter 26 (1931).

135. Page 637, para. 2 – "Wallberg Memorial Building": See Chapter 28 (1944).

136. Page 637, para. 2 – "Lash Miller Chemical Laboratories": "Great chemistry"; Dellandrea to Friedland, June 6, 2000.

137. Page 638, para. 1 – "computer engineering in 1987": "Making Contact", *University of Toronto Bulletin,* July 26, 1999; *Globe and Mail,* July 8, 1999.

138. Page 639, para. 1 – "Centre for Information Technology": Dellandrea to Friedland, June 6, 2000.

139. Page 640, para. 1 – "$20,000 per year": *Globe and Mail,* June 23, 2000; "$25-Million Gift Honours Radio Pioneer", *University of Toronto Bulletin,* June 26, 2000. Rogers also gave $2.5 million for the John Graham Library of Trinity College: see "Trinity Receives $2.5 Million Gift", *University of Toronto Bulletin,* September 29, 1997.

140. Page 640, para. 2 – "Koffler Centre": "$25-Million Gift Honours Radio Pioneer".

141. Page 640, para. 2 – "department of computer science": The two departments had been together in the Sanford Fleming building since it was rebuilt after the fire. Richard White points out that "new labs and equipment will bring them closer together": see White e-mail to Friedland, January 29, 2001.

142. Page 640, para. 2 – "where disciplines converge": "Bahen, Skoll gifts boost information technology programs at U of T", *Campaign Quarterly* (Autumn, 1999) at 1.

143. Page 640, para. 3 – "cellular and biomolecular research": "Landmark gift for U of T", *Campaign Quarterly* (Summer, 2000) at 1.

144. Page 640, para. 3 – "Let's wrap it up then": "$150 M Centre Catapults U of T into Global Ranks of Medical Research", *University of Toronto Bulletin,* June 12, 2000.

145. Page 640, para. 3 – "remaining funds": Some money went to other universities, such as $10 million to the University of Ottawa: see Bloch-Nevitte comments to Friedland, September 25, 2000.

146. Page 640, para. 3 – "by the Ontario government": The Ontario Innovation trust matched the donation: see "$150 M Centre Catapults U of T Into Global Ranks of Medical Research".

147. Page 640, para. 3 – "$150 million": Ibid.; *Globe and Mail,* June 6, 2000; "Landmark gift for U of T".

148. Page 640, para. 3 – "other surrounding buildings": Conversation with Munroe-Blum, September 5, 2000. Elizabeth Sisam states that the Centre for Cellular and Biomolecular Research will link the Rosebrugh, the medical sciences building, the Fitzgerald building, the Tanz Centre, and the new pharmacy building: see e-mail from Sisam to Friedland, February 5, 2001.

149. Page 640, para. 3 – "with this initiative": *Globe and Mail,* June 6, 2000.

150. Page 641, para. 1 – "student in the 1950s": See Chapter 29 (1950).

151. Page 641, para. 1 – "Margaret (1952)": "Bahen, Skoll gifts". Margaret was a graduate in physical and occupational therapy.

152. Page 641, para. 1 – "Jackman (1953)": "Jackman Gift Creates $15 Million Fund for Humanities Chairs", *University of Toronto Bulletin,* November 30, 1998.

153. Page 641, para. 1 – "Rogers (1956)": "$25-Million Gift Honours Radio Pioneer".

154. Page 641, para. 1 – "Tanenbaum (1955)": "U of T Matches $2.5 Million Gift".

155. Page 641, para. 1 – "Queen's Park and College Street": "Pharmacy Grad's Prescription: $8 million for U of T", *University of Toronto Bulletin,* June 12, 2000.

156. Page 641, para. 1 – "Trinity College": "Bringing the World to U of T", *Campaign Quarterly* (Spring, 1998).

157. Page 641, para. 1 – "international studies": *University of Toronto Munk Centre for International Studies at Trinity College Newsletter,* September 2000 at 1. See also Brendan Howley, "World Stage", *University of Toronto Magazine* (Spring 1998) at 25. The Centre was officially opened in August 2000, Munk stating: "I am proud that my name is attached to a centre that will allow Canadians to know what globalization is all about", see "A World of Difference", *University of Toronto Bulletin,* September 11, 2000.

158. Page 642, para. 1 – "on St. George Street": "Rotman Donates $3 Million", *University of Toronto Bulletin,* December 14, 1992; "Enhanced Programs, Endowed Chairs Planned by Management", *University of Toronto Bulletin,* January 20, 1997. Avie Bennett, who entered the University of Toronto much earlier, in 1944-45, gave a majority interest in his publishing company, McClelland and Stewart to the University: see "U of T to Safeguard M&S", *University of Toronto Bulletin,* July 24, 2000; student record for Avram J. Bennett, A89-0011/reel 6.

159. Page 642, para. 1 – "from 1991 to 1997": "A Passionate Commitment to U of T", *University of Toronto Bulletin,* May 21, 1991; "Noble Ambassador", *University of Toronto Bulletin,* June 30, 1997.

160. Page 642, para. 1 – "Mount Sinai Hospital": See Chapter 40 (1986).

161. Page 642, para. 2 – "employ our graduates": *Report on Business Magazine* (June 1998) at 38.

162. Page 642, para. 2 – "Corporatism and the University": Bill Graham, "Corporatism in the University - Part 1", *UTFA Newsletter,* February 9, 1998; Bill Graham, "Corporatism in the University - Part 2", *UTFA Newsletter,* February 25, 1998.

163. Page 642, para. 2 – "purpose of the University": Graham, "Part 1".

164. Page 642, para. 2 – "on these issues": See, e.g., *Varsity,* November 24, 1997, January 12, 1998, and January, 1998. Others pointed to the "rigid, uncompromising and destructive scrutiny" of this criticism: see *the newspaper,* January 21, 1998.

165. Page 642, para. 2 – "doubts about the wisdom of it all": *Globe and Mail,* November 21, 1997. John McMurtry of Guelph University further noted "the current supremacy of this perspective is undermining ecological and social well-being, particularly when public institutions are being influenced by corporations": see *Varsity,* September 25, 1998. Neil Tudiver has made similar points in his *Universities for Sale*: see Donald Fisher, "Commercialization Threatens the University's Mission", *CAUT Bulletin,* January, 2000 at 6.

166. Page 642, para. 3 – "management and of law": See generally, Graham, "Part 2". A further controversy was raised by the Bell Emergis gift to establish the Bell University Laboratories: see www.bul.mie.utoronto.ca; see also *Varsity,* October 18, 1999; see also "Bell Commits to Research Network", *University of Toronto Bulletin,* February 16, 1998.

167. Page 642, para. 3 – "relevant medical departments": See Chapter 23 (1919).

168. Page 643, para. 1 – "selected by the two deans": Graham, "Part 2" at 4.

169. Page 643, para. 1 – "consultation with Nortel": Ibid.

170. Page 643, para. 1 – "receptive thereto": Ibid. at 3.
171. Page 643, para. 1 – "policies was scary": Ibid.

172. Page 643, para. 1 – "Board's advice" Ibid.

173. Page 643, para. 1 – "Munk gift": Ibid.

174. Page 643, para. 1 – "Rotman's": *Globe and Mail*, November 21, 1997.

175. Page 643, para. 1 – "progress made": Graham, "Part 2" at 3; *Globe and Mail*, November 21, 1997.

176. Page 643, para. 2 – "outside influence": *Report on Business Magazine* (June, 1998) at 42.

177. Page 643, para. 2 – "freedom of its members" "Commitment to Academic Freedom Reaffirmed", *University of Toronto Bulletin*, December 8, 1997.

178. Page 643, para. 2 – "academic unit or units": Ibid.; "The Provost's Guidelines on Donations", Revised April 30, 1998 (document forwarded from Office of the V-P and Provost); "The Provost's Statement on the Role of Advisory Bodies", Revised April 30, 1998 (document forwarded from Office of the V-P and Provost).

179. Page 643, para. 2 – "which was nothing": "Gift Guidelines Brought Forward", *University of Toronto Bulletin*, April 6, 1998.

180. Page 643, para. 2 – "driving influence": *Report on Business Magazine* (June 1998) at 37.

181. Page 644, para. 1 – "Munk's interests": Ibid. at 35; "Bush Receives Degree", *University of Toronto Bulletin*, November 24, 1997.

182. Page 644, para. 1 – "Vietnam war": Bruce Rolston, "Just Seems Like Yesterday", *University of Toronto Bulletin*, November 24, 1997.

183. Page 644, para. 1 – "Memory and Reconciliation": "Desmond Tutu to receive honorary degrees", *University of Toronto News and Events*, February 16, 2000.

184. Page 644, para. 2 – "as it hoped to do": "Holding the Line", *University of Toronto Bulletin*, March 28, 1994.

185. Page 644, para. 2 – "became a double match": "Province Announces Student Aid, Tax Credits", *University of Toronto Bulletin*, May 21, 1996; Bloch-Nevitte paraphrasing remarks of Rivi Frankle in comments to Friedland, September 25, 2000; e-mail from Dan Lang to Charles Levi, November 24, 2000; Dan Lang to Planning and Budget Committee, October 3, 1995 (document forwarded by Dan Lang); "Matching Funds for Student Support", July 30, 1996 (document forwarded by Dan Lang).

186. Page 644, para. 3 – "$100 million of that sum": Prichard to Friedland, March 1, 2000 at 3.

187. Page 644, para. 3 – "half a billion dollars": Conversation with Prichard, July 18, 2000.

188. Page 644, para. 3 – "$1.2 billion": Prichard to Friedland at 3; "U of T Endowment Surpasses $1 Billion", *University of Toronto Bulletin*, June 14, 1999.

189. Page 644, para. 3 – "$200 million in 1990": *Toronto Star*, June 17, 1999.

190. Page 644, para. 3 – "Alberta is not far behind": Prichard to Friedland at 3.

191. Page 644, para. 3 – "$300,000 per student": "U of T Endowment Surpasses $1 Billion"; http://web.mit.edu/accreditation/overview/standard9.html.

192. Page 645, para. 1 – "completely deregulated": Dan Lang points out that it was not complete deregulation but an

increase in the level of discretion that the universities would now have in these fields: see Lang comments to Friedland, February 2, 2001.

193. Page 645, para. 1 – "doctoral programs": "Tuition Schedule Approved", *University of Toronto Bulletin,* May 19, 1998. Graduate student fees increased from $3,077 in 1995 to $4,701 in 2000: see www.toronto.edu/gsunion/tuitionfees.html; www.library.utoronto.ca/president/tuition_fee_schedule.

194. Page 645, para. 1 – "regulated programs": See, e.g., "Announcement Surprises Some", *University of Toronto Bulletin,* March 28, 1994.

195. Page 645, para. 1 – "more than doubled": "Student Financial Aid Guarantee Working", *University of Toronto Bulletin,* October 16, 2000.

196. Page 645, para. 1 – "from that source": Prichard to Friedland at 3.

197. Page 645, para. 1 – "$200 million at the end": Friedland, "Notes on Lunch with Rob Prichard" at 2.

198. Page 645, para. 2 – "Derek McCammond": *Report of the Provost's Task Force on Tuition and Student Financial Support,* in *University of Toronto Bulletin,* February 16, 1998.

199. Page 645, para. 2 – "over their course of study": "Students Need Fees Guarantee: Report", *University of Toronto Bulletin,* February 3, 1998; "Guarantee financial aid, says task force", *University of Toronto Magazine* (Spring 1988) at 7.

200. Page 645, para. 2 – "resources necessary to get here": "Board, Committees Pleased with Task Force Recommendations", *University of Toronto Bulletin,* March 2, 1998.

201. Page 645, para. 2 – "Canadian universities": The policy of Student Financial Support was approved by governing council on April 30, 1998: see e-mail from Carolyn Tuohy to Friedland, February 21, 2001.

202. Page 645, para. 2 – "financial means": Ibid. Tuohy states, "Using the needs assessment formula of the provincial government's Ontario Student Assistance Program (OSAP), the policy provided that need in excess of that covered by government loans would be met by the University – through grants in the case of first-entry programs such as Arts and Science and Engineering, and through a mix of grants and preferred-access loans in the case of second-entry programs such as Law and Medicine".

203. Page 645, para. 3 – "excess of $50 million": "A guarantee of success", *University of Toronto Magazine* (Autumn, 1999) at 5.

204. Page 645, para. 3 – "useless research we have ever seen": *Varsity,* February 5, 1998. Dan Lang points out that the research based on student postal codes was really research based on census tracts: see Lang comments to Friedland, February 2, 2001.

205. Page 645, para. 3 – "increased tuition": "Report of the Vice-Provost, Students, on Student Financial Support 1999-2000". See generally, Daniel Lang, *University Finance in Ontario.* Lang states in the introduction: "It was not possible to address the impact of tuition increases in student accessibility since the increases had not been in place long enough to support statistically reliable observations and conclusions". Note, however, Lang states, at 166 of the draft manuscript, that tuition increases may affect student decisions on where to study: "there is an indication, at least based on a longitudinal analysis of admission surveys, that some students are increasingly interested in attending a university close to home, and that the academic reputation of a university is decreasing in importance in terms of influencing a student's decision on which university to attend". Lang also notes, at 18 et seq. and 63, that the overall increase in tuition fees at the University of Toronto between 1993 and 1998 was 106.7 per cent.

206. Page 645, para. 3 – "in the 1890s": See Chapter 15 (1895).

CHAPTER 42 – 1997 – MOVING UP PARNASSUS

1. Page 646, para. 2 – "Toronto's basic operating funds": Ontario government support started in the early part of the 20th century. At the turn of the century it was only $7,000 a year: see Chapter 17 (1901).

2. Page 646, para. 2 – "down to 60 per cent": Prichard to Friedland, March 1, 2000 at 3. Dan Lang states in an e-mail to the author of February 23, 2001: "going back to 1957, the highest percentage that I can find for government operating grants is 81% and the lowest percentage for tuition fees is 15%. So, in terms of your draft, the figures that would make the most sense would be 85 and 15, leaving out the three or four points for other income".

3. Page 646, para. 2 – "operating budget of over a billion dollars": Prichard to Friedland, March 1, 2000; see also J. Stephen Dupré, "Far Removed from the 1970's: Canadian Universities and their Government Relations at the Fin de Siecle" (An Address to the National Association of University Board Chairs and Secretaries, Montreal, May 1, 1998) at 18.

4. Page 646, para. 2 – "roughly $350 million": Munroe-Blum to Birgeneau, Spring 2000 at 4.

5. Page 646, para. 2 – "below that of every other province": *University of Toronto National Report 1999* at 17.

6. Page 646, para. 3 – "Centres of Excellence program started in the 1980s": See Chapter 40 (1986).

7. Page 647, para. 1 – "Future Directions for Postsecondary Education": *Excellence Accessibility Responsibility: Report of the Advisory Panel on Future Directions for Postsecondary Education*, www.edu.gov.on.ca/eng/document/reports/futuree.html; "Correct Serious Inadequacies in Funding, Says Panel", *University of Toronto Bulletin*, January 6, 1997.

8. Page 647, para. 1 – "in Canada in the last 25 years": "Report Gets it Right", *University of Toronto Bulletin*, January 9, 1997.

9. Page 647, para. 1 – "contributes greatly to our economic competitiveness": *Excellence Accessibility Responsibility* at 27.

10. Page 647, para. 1 – "cuts for universities and community colleges": "Report Gets it Right".

11. Page 647, para. 1 – " the basis of measures of quality": *Excellence Accessibility Responsibility* at 7.

12. Page 647, para. 2 – "almost half of these awards": Munroe-Blum to Birgeneau, Spring 2000 at 4.

13. Page 647, para. 2 – "$15 million": "Energenius, U of T Create Centre for Advanced Robotics, Mechatronics, and Intelligent Systems", *University of Toronto Campaign News*, v. 3, no. 5 at 4; *Toronto Star*, April 8, 1998.

14. Page 647, para. 2 – "$12 million": "Bell Commits to Research Network", *University of Toronto Bulletin*, February 16, 1998; "U of T Receives Almost $30 Million for Research", *University of Toronto Bulletin*, April 12, 1999.

15. Page 647, para. 2 – "$9 million": "Nortel, University Establish Institute", *University of Toronto Bulletin*, February 17, 1997.

16. Page 647, para. 2 – "silicon chip through chemical reactions": "More Support for Researchers", *University of Toronto Bulletin*, May 10, 1999.

17. Page 647, para. 3 – "faculty members who win awards": Munroe-Blum to Birgeneau, Spring 2000 at 4-5; "Budget Benefits Students, Research", *University of Toronto Bulletin*, March 15, 2000

18. Page 647, para. 3 – "expansion of student enrolment and for research": "Provincial Budget Encouraging: Prichard", *University of Toronto Bulletin*, May 10, 1999; Munroe-Blum to Birgeneau, Spring 2000 at 5.

19. Page 648, para. 1 – "Sheridan College ($27 million)": "University to Double Computer Enrolments", *University of Toronto Bulletin*, November 30, 1998; "Super U of T: Three Projects Funded by SuperBuild", *University of Toronto Bulletin*, February 28, 2000; "U of T Gets $5.7 M More for Buildings", *University of Toronto Bulletin*, July 24, 2000; *Globe and Mail*, February 23, 2000. The total cost of the Bahen centre is now over $100 million: see "Construction Costs of Bahen Centre Rise", *University of Toronto Bulletin*, October 16, 2000. On increases in enrolment in engineering and computer science, see Daniel Lang, *University Finance in Ontario* (Winnipeg: Canadian Society for the Study of Higher Education, forthcoming in 2001) at 13 of draft.

20. Page 648, para. 1 – "provincial report on university research by vice-president Heather Munroe-Blum": Heather Munroe-Blum et al., *Growing Ontario's Innovation System: The Strategic Role of University Research* (December, 1999); "Munroe-Blum Urges Action on Innovation", *University of Toronto Bulletin*, December 13, 1999; "Analysis of the 2000 Ontario Budget in Relation to the Munroe-Blum Report", May 3, 2000 (document forwarded from office of Heather Munroe-Blum); conversation with Munroe-Blum, September 5, 2000.

21. Page 648, para. 1 – "direct costs of the projects": Conversation with Munroe-Blum, September 5, 2000; "Budget Delivers More Student Aid", *University of Toronto Bulletin*, June 12, 2000. The province also established an Ontario Science and Innovation Council: see Dianne Cunningham to Munroe-Blum, December 14, 1999 (document forwarded from office of Heather Munroe-Blum).

22. Page 648, para. 2 – "Canadian Foundation for Innovation (CFI)": Prichard to Friedland at 2; "$53M to U of T Research", *University of Toronto Bulletin*, April 10, 2000.

23. Page 648, para. 2 – "major infrastructure developments": Munroe-Blum to Birgeneau, Spring 2000 at 2.

24. Page 648, para. 2 – "8 per cent of Canada's university faculty": *University of Toronto National Report 2000* at 9; e-mail from Corrine Pask-Aubé to Charles Levi, December 8, 2000; www.aucc.ca/en/research/fac_inst98.htm.

25. Page 648, para. 3 – "launched in 1997": "Budget Confirms Federal Role in Research", *University of Toronto Bulletin*, March 3, 1997; "Evans-sent", *University of Toronto Magazine* (Summer 1997) at 11.

26. Page 649, para. 1 – "Department of Medical Research": "Great Minds No Walls", *Edge: Research and Discovery at the University of Toronto* (Winter 2000).

27. Page 649, para. 1 – "Donald Stuss": "Research at U of T Nets $54 Million", *University of Toronto Bulletin*, June 28, 1999; "Stuss, Donald T.", *Canadian Who's Who 1994* at 1103.

28. Page 649, para. 1 – "Lash Miller Chemical Laboratories": Ibid.

29. Page 649, para. 1 – "Mississauga's Centre for Applied Biosciences and Biotechnology": "$31 Million Boost for U of T Infrastructure", *University of Toronto Bulletin*, August 21, 2000.

30. Page 649, para. 1 – "medicine, engineering, and science": The social sciences at Toronto (as well as those at York and Ryerson) are, in collaboration with Statistics Canada, to get one of the six research data centres that will be set up across the country. The centre will be located in the Robarts Library: see conversation with Munroe-Blum, September 5, 2000; "CFI injects new funds into research support", *University of Toronto News and Events*, July 27, 2000.

31. Page 649, para. 1 – "the Ontario government": Comments by Heather Munroe-Blum on draft 1997 chapter, undated.

32. Page 649, para. 1 – "another billion dollars added to the pot": "$31 Million Boost for U of T Infrastructure". In the November 2000 election, the Liberals promised to continue the CFI: see "Educating Politicians", *University of Toronto Bulletin*, November 27, 2000.

33. Page 649, para. 1 – "John Polanyi's path-breaking work in the 1950s": See Chapter 40 (1986).

34. Page 649, para. 2 – "the new millennium": "New Chairs Program Welcomed", *University of Toronto Bulletin*, October 25, 1999; "Feds Fund 'Ideas, Innovation'", *University of Toronto Bulletin*, March 13, 2000.

35. Page 649, para. 2 – "Driving Canada's economic growth": *National Post*, August 10, 2000. David Strangway notes that "The Canada Research Chairs program was not a recommendation from the Advisory Council of Science and Technology": see Strangway to Friedland, January 23, 2001.

36. Page 649, para. 2 – "the loss of leading scholars": *University of Alberta Folio*, May 26, 2000.

37. Page 649, para. 2 – "Sedra told the press": *Globe and Mail*, November 5, 1998.

38. Page 649, para. 2 – "Paul Martin": *Toronto Star*, September 25, 1999.

39. Page 649, para. 2 – "the best from across Canada": "Martin, Hon. Paul", *Canadian Who's Who 2000* at 823.

40. Page 649, para. 2 – "Canada's research capacity": *Globe and Mail*, February 29, 2000.

41. Page 649, para. 3 – "federal granting agencies": "New Chairs Program Welcomed".

42. Page 649, para. 3 – "council for health research": Munroe-Blum to Birgeneau, Spring 2000 at 3; *UTFA Newsletter*, June 24, 2000.

43. Page 649, para. 3 – "funds of these councils": Prichard to Friedland at 1; "$37 Million for Health Research", *University of Toronto Bulletin*, September 11, 2000; "Health Research Receives Big Boost from MRC", *University of Toronto Bulletin*, February 28, 2000.

44. Page 650, para. 1 – "chairs will be allocated to it": *University of Toronto National Report 1999* at 12; *University of Toronto National Report 2000* at 9.

45. Page 650, para. 1 – "University of British Columbia, with 160": Prichard to Friedland at 1 says Toronto will get 14% of the 2,000 chairs, which would mean 280 chairs. The 250 figure may go up somewhat depending on the future success with the granting councils: see "A Framework for Allocating Canada Research Chairs at the University of Toronto: Discussion Paper, June 1, 2000" (document in possession of the author) at 4.

46. Page 650, para. 1 – "$40 million a year in perpetuity": Munroe-Blum to Birgeneau, Spring 2000 at 3 suggests that the University will get 285 chairs at an average cost of $150,000 a year.

47. Page 650, para. 1 – "a billion dollars in endowment funds": Munroe-Blum to Birgeneau, Spring 2000 at 3 assumes that the total allocation across Canada is the equivalent of a $6 billion dollar endowment and that Toronto will get 15% of that amount, which would be $0.9 billion.

48. Page 650, para. 1 – "research strength": "A Framework for Allocating" at 5.

49. Page 650, para. 1 – "began in June 2000": Sedra and Munroe-Blum to Principals and Deans, June 1, 2000 (document in possession of the author); "Canada Research Chairs Strategic Research Plan (SRP) For the University of Toronto and Its Formal Affiliates", undated (forwarded by Paul J. Fraumeni).

50. Page 650, para. 2 – "each year for ten years": "Prime Minister Announces New Scholarship Program", *University of Toronto Bulletin*, September 29, 1997; *Globe and Mail*, February 25, 1998.

51. Page 650, para. 2 – "growth of the university system": See Chapter 31 (1958).

52. Page 651, para. 1 – "medicine, the natural sciences, and engineering": *UTFA Newsletter*, June 24, 2000 at 2.

53. Page 651, para. 1 – "corporate take-over of our University": Ibid. at 3-4; *UTFA Newsletter*, August 4, 2000 at 2; Rhonda Love, "Musical Chairs", *University of Toronto Bulletin*, September 25, 2000.

54. Page 651, para. 2 – "funds that can then be reallocated internally": Conversations with Prichard, Sedra, and Munroe-Blum.

55. Page 651, para. 2 – "over $60 million": Conversation with Munroe-Blum, September 5, 2000. See e-mail from Marty England of the provost's office to the author of February 25 and 26, 2001 and e-mail from Carole Moore of May 25, 2001. In addition, over $4 million is spent each year by federated and affiliated libraries.

56. Page 651, para. 2 – "university libraries in North America": "Due Praise", *University of Toronto Bulletin*, November 8, 1999; "U of T Library tops in North America", *University of Toronto Bulletin*, October 16, 2000. See e-mail from Carole Moore to the author of May 25, 2001: "We just received the 1999-2000 ranking and we have moved up to #3 for that year."

57. Page 651, para. 2 – "any public university on the continent": "U of T Library tops". See also the *University of Toronto Bulletin*, October 9, 2001, "U of T Measures Up."

58. Page 651, para. 3 – "variety of sources of funding": Prichard to Friedland at 4.

59. Page 651, para. 3 – "diversification of risks": Ibid.

60. Page 651, para. 3 – "private donations": Ibid.

61. Page 652, para. 1 – "forced upon the university system": Ibid. at 4-5.

62. Page 652, para. 2 – "the 'great divide,' as it has been known": Alfred Holden, "A Friendly Place Where People Gather", *University of Toronto Magazine* (Spring 1995) at 44.

63. Page 652, para. 2 – "widened to four lanes in the 1940s": "St. George Slays a Dragon", *University of Toronto Bulletin*, June 24, 1996.

64. Page 652, para. 2 – "free flow of motor traffic": "Students press on with campaign to unify the St. George Campus", *Varsity News* (December 1966) at 2.

65. Page 652, para. 2 – "no single perfect vision surfaced": Holden, "A Friendly Place" at 44-45. Traffic calming had been suggested as early as 1992: see "Street Closure Rejected", *University of Toronto Bulletin*, November 9, 1992.

66. Page 652, para. 3 – "Toronto's old city hall": Robert Fulford, "The resurrection of St. George", *Toronto Life* (May 1996) at 45.

67. Page 652, para. 3 – "hired outside planners": E-mail from Elizabeth Sisam to Friedland, February 5, 2001.

68. Page 652, para. 3 – "narrowed by 8 feet": "Celebrating a $4 Million Makeover", *Campaign News*, v.1, no. 8 at 2; John Barber, "No Mean Street", *University of Toronto Magazine* (Winter 1996) at 12.

69. Page 652, para. 3 – "remodelled street": "St. George Street Wins Award", *University of Toronto Bulletin*, September 29, 1997.

70. Page 652, para. 3 – "quite a different street": "One of the Best Streets in the City", *University of Toronto Bulletin*, October 28, 1996.

71. Page 652, para. 4 – "open spaces of the University": Conversation with Prichard, December 28, 1998.

72. Page 653, para. 1 – "140 acres of downtown land": "University of Toronto Open Space Plan", *University of Toronto Bulletin*, April 12, 1999.

73. Page 653, para. 1 – "Toronto's version": *Globe and Mail*, May 12, 2000. Some would consider the 399 acre High Park in the west end of the city to be Toronto's central park.

74. Page 653, para. 1 – "open space plan": The selection committee was chaired by Alex Waugh, the vice-principal of Woodsworth College: "Open Space Consultants Selected", *University of Toronto Bulletin*, June 1, 1998.

75. Page 653, para. 1 – "importance of pedestrians": "University of Toronto Open Space Plan"; e-mail from Judy Matthews to Friedland, February 12, 2001.

76. Page 653, para. 1 – "under Jon Dellandrea": E-mail from Sisam to Friedland, February 5, 2001.

77. Page 653, para. 2 – "given new life": This and the following material are found in "Open Space Master Plan"; Bruce Rolston, "A Grand Plan", *University of Toronto Bulletin*, January 11, 1999; *Globe and Mail*, May 10, 1999; *Toronto Star*, April 10, 1999; *Varsity*, March 4, 1999; see also *University of Toronto Open Space Master Plan Working Report October 1998*.

78. Page 653, para. 2 – "surface on the campus": Ian Montagnes, "Taddle Tale", *The Graduate* (September/October 1979) at 13; Alfred Holden, "Taddle Creek", *University of Toronto Magazine* (Winter 1995) at 42; "Resurrecting Taddle Creek", *University of Toronto Bulletin*, December 8, 1997; *Varsity*, March 12, 1998.

79. Page 653, para. 2 – "buried as a sewer in the 1880s": See Chapter 6 (1856).

80. Page 654, para. 1 – "unfulfilled hope over the years": See Chapter 30 (1955).

81. Page 654, para. 1 – "carrying us forward": Rolston, "A Grand Plan".

82. Page 654, para. 2 – "the fabric of the university": *Globe and Mail*, May 12, 2000.

83. Page 654, para. 2 – "the fund-raising campaign": "Open Space Gets Go-Ahead", *University of Toronto Bulletin*, March 27, 2000.

84. Page 654, para. 2 – "safer pedestrian access": *Globe and Mail*, May 12, 2000.

85. Page 654, para. 2 – "develop the first stage": Conversation with Finlayson, September 11, 2000; "Firm Chosen for Campus Design", *University of Toronto Bulletin*, October 16, 2000. See generally on the open space plan an e-mail from Judy Matthews to Friedland, February 12, 2001.

86. Page 654, para. 3 – "part of their buildings": Michael Marrus, "PDDAC Report to Governing Council June 22, 1998" (document forwarded by Elizabeth Sisam) at 2.

87. Page 654, para. 3 – "Malcove collection": Lisa Balfour Brown, "A Fine Balance", *University of Toronto Magazine* (Winter 1996) at 16. Funds for the Centre were from the proceeds plus interest from the sale of the Delta Gamma woman's fraternity house when the fraternity ceased operations: see Don Guthrie comments to Friedland, February, 2001.

88. Page 654, para. 3 – "Galbraith Building": Other works have since been added. See also *University of Toronto Bulletin*, November 22, 1982.

89. Page 655, para. 1 – "medieval Christian art": University of Toronto Art Centre brochure, November, 1996; Pamela Cornell, "The Malcove Collection", *The Graduate* (September/October 1983) at 14.

90. Page 655, para. 1 – "left her collection to the University of Toronto": Cornell, "The Malcove Collection" at 14.

91. Page 655, para. 1 – "the Art Centre": Until it was moved to University College, the Malcove Collection was inadequately housed in the Pontifical Institute of Mediaeval Studies: see Brown, "A Fine Balance" at 17.

92. Page 655, para. 2 – "Barnicke Gallery": "Hart House gets a state of the art gallery", *University of Toronto Bulletin*, February 21, 1983.

93. Page 655, para. 2 – "Scarborough and Mississauga campuses": "Hiring of art curator recommended", *University of Toronto Bulletin*, February 8, 1982. Light and humidity were having their effects, and thefts of and damage to art in the University were becoming more common: see "Security stepped up at University after paintings stolen", *University of Toronto Bulletin*, May 10, 1982.

94. Page 656, para. 1 – "the private sector": Lovat Dickson, *The Museum Makers: The Story of the Royal Ontario Museum* (Toronto: The Royal Ontario Museum, 1986) at 140-145.

95. Page 656, para. 2 – "donor in 1997": Peg McKlevey, "Prospects for the Future Become Plans for the Present – Celebrating the First Anniversary of the U of T Art Centre", *UC Magazine* (Winter 1998) at 12.

96. Page 656, para. 2 – "double its size in University College": "Art Centre to Double in Size", *Partners: A Newsletter for Friends of the University of Toronto Art Centre* (Spring 1998) at 1; "The Art of Change", *University of Toronto Magazine* (Summer 2000) at 33.

97. Page 656, para. 2 – "spring of 2000": Invitation to Gallery re-opening, April 7, 2000.

98. Page 656, para. 2 – "David Milne": "Silcox, David Phillips", *Canadian Who's Who 2000* at 1158. In 2001, Silcox left as director to take a position with Sotheby's (Canada).

99. Page 656, para. 2 – "support teaching and scholarship": "The Art of Change"; David Silcox, "The Art of Learning", *University of Toronto Bulletin*, April 10, 2000.

100. Page 656, para. 2 – "second president": Undated University Art Centre brochure, supposedly from 2000.

101. Page 656, para. 2 – "J.M.W. Turner": For Turner, see Chapter 6 (1856); see also Marinell Ash, "Daniel Wilson: The Early Years", in Elizabeth Hulse, ed., *Thinking with Both Hands: Sir Daniel Wilson in the Old World and the New* (University of Toronto Press, 1999) at 12-13.

102. Page 656, para. 3 – "athletic centre": See Chapter 39 (1980).

103. Page 656, para. 3 – "downtown campus": "City of Toronto Approves Campus Plan", *University of Toronto Bulletin*, April 7, 1997. *University of Toronto Area*, Document 3, February 1, 1997 at 113, lists 27 sites. Of these, one belonged to Trinity, one to the Royal Conservatory of Music, two to the Royal Ontario Museum, one to the Sisters of St. Joseph, and one to the Christian Brothers, see e-mail from Elizabeth Sisam to Charles Levi, February 9, 2001; see also *University of Toronto Campus Master Plan Discussion Draft*, 1991 (document forwarded by Elizabeth Sisam); "City Discusses Plan for U of T", *University of Toronto Bulletin*, October 28, 1996. Elizabeth Sisam states, "The official plan has provision for the University to increase the number of development sites as long as appropriate procedures are maintained. The acceptance of this plan is significant because the last series of discussions regarding the Official Plan and resulting changes to zoning by-laws ended with the University opposing the City at the Ontario Municipal Board (1978). A Liaison Committee meets with representatives of community groups on a regular basis about four or five times each year": see e-mail from Sisam to Friedland, February 5, 2001. Dan Lang states, "The agreement has attracted a great deal of world-wide attention. The Department of Geography and the Faculty of Management have both used it as a case study. I am still receiving inquiries from many US universities and municipalities about it": see comments from Lang to Friedland, February 2, 2001.

104. Page 656, para. 3 – "heritage sites": "City of Toronto Approves Campus Plan".

105. Page 656, para. 3 – "conform to certain guidelines": These guidelines are spelled out in *University of Toronto Area*, Document 3; see also comments by Dan Lang to Friedland, February 2, 2001.

106. Page 657, para. 1 – "Harbord Street": See *University of Toronto Area,* Document 3.

107. Page 657, para. 2 – "future university buildings": "Committee Will Oversee Campus Building Design", *University of Toronto Bulletin,* May 12, 1997.

108. Page 657, para. 2 – "visual excellence to the campus": Alan Waterhouse, "Reign of the Bland and Dreary", *University of Toronto Bulletin,* May 12, 1997.

109. Page 657, para. 2 – "campus to look good": "Committee will Oversee Campus Building Design", Marrus, "PPDAC Report" at 1.

110. Page 657, para. 3 – "student housing": "New Future for Stadium", *University of Toronto Bulletin,* September 27, 1999.

111. Page 657, para. 3 – "indoor skating rink": *The Independent,* March 2, 2000; e-mail from Michael Finlayson to Friedland, February 6, 2001.

112. Page 657, para. 3 – "power of the little people": *Varsity,* September 21, 1999.

113. Page 657, para. 4 – "students who seek places": J. Robert S. Prichard, "A place for people and ideas", *University of Toronto Magazine* (Spring 2000) at 5; "New Future for Stadium"

114. Page 657, para. 4 – "would have to be constructed": "Plan for Residences Approved", *University of Toronto Bulletin,* November 8, 1999.

115. Page 657, para. 4 – "Spadina Avenue and Harbord Street": "Home Away from Home", *University of Toronto Bulletin,* December 8, 1997; *Toronto Star,* November 29, 1997 and November 20, 1999; "New Grad Residence Open, Finally", *University of Toronto Bulletin,* September 11, 2000. The building won the award of excellence of the Los Angeles chapter of the Institute of Architects: see "SGS Residence receives excellence award", *University of Toronto Bulletin,* November 30, 1998.

116. Page 657, para. 4 – "athletic centre was planned": See Chapter 30 (1955). Bill Davis announced that the Spadina Expressway project would be stopped on June 3, 1971: see Claire Hoy, *Bill Davis* (Toronto: Methuen, 1985) at 89.

117. Page 658, para. 1 – "width of Harbord Street": "Concerns Over Sign Raised", *University of Toronto Bulletin,* October 25, 1999.

118. Page 658, para. 1 – "I liked that part of it a lot": *Globe and Mail,* January 8, 2000; *Globe and Mail,* November 22, 2000; see also "Eye Sore or Subtle Beauty", *University of Toronto Bulletin,* November 27, 2000.

119. Page 658, para. 1 – "residences are being planned": "Plan for Residences Approved".

120. Page 658, para. 2 – "study student needs": *The Independent,* September 3-9, 1998; "Task Force Recommends New Student Centre", *University of Toronto Bulletin,* April 12, 1999.

121. Page 659, para. 1 – "close to your classroom": "Task Force Recommends New Student Centre".

122. Page 659, para. 2 – "changes to its design": *Varsity,* November 4, November 9, and November 18, 1999.

123. Page 659, para. 2 – "but not the other two": "Heritage Board Puts Obstacle in Way of New Technology Centre", *University of Toronto Bulletin,* October 25, 1999. In fact, 44 St. George Street is not at the corner because Sir Daniel Wilson's house was at the corner, but was torn down many years earlier: see e-mail from Harold Averill to Friedland, February 18, 2001.

124. Page 659, para. 2 – "incorporated into the centre": *Varsity*, November 9, 2000.

125. Page 659, para. 2 – "Sussex Avenue and Huron Street": *Varsity*, September 28, 2000.

126. Page 659, para. 3 – "demand for university places": "Academic Board OK's Expansion Framework", *University of Toronto Bulletin*, March 13, 2000; *A Framework for Enrolment Expansion at the University of Toronto*, *University of Toronto Bulletin*, March 13, 2000; "Discussion Paper on Enrolment Expansion at the University of Toronto", *University of Toronto Bulletin*, December 13, 1999; J. Robert S. Prichard, "Plans for Growth", *University of Toronto Magazine* (Summer 1999) at 5; *Globe and Mail*, March 10, 2000; "U of T Considers Suburban Expansion", *University of Toronto Bulletin*, November 29, 1999.

127. Page 659, para. 3 – "post-war baby boomers": David K. Foot with Daniel Stoffman, *Boom Bust & Echo 2000: Profiting from the Demographic Shift in the New Millenium* (Toronto: Macfarlane Walter & Ross, 1998) at 214; *Globe and Mail*, February 22, 2000. David Foot notes, "we are closing in on 350,000 copies... not bad for a Canadian popular (i.e. non-text) book eh?": see e-mail from David Foot to Friedland, November 27, 2000.

128. Page 659, para. 3 – "so many copies in so short a time. Ever.": *Globe and Mail*, February 7, 1998.

129. Page 659, para. 3 – "upgrade their skills": "Huge Enrolments Loom: Report", *University of Toronto Bulletin*, April 12, 1999; Foot, *Boom* at 215.

130. Page 659, para. 3 – "40 per cent": "Huge Enrolments Loom"; "Academic Board OK's Expansion Framework"; *Toronto Star*, November 1, 1999; *Excellence Accessibility Responsibility: Report of the Advisory Panel on Future Directions for Postsecondary Education* at 44; see also comments by Dan Lang to Friedland, February 2, 2001.

131. Page 659, para. 3 – "in the year 2003": *Toronto Star*, October 5, 1998.

132. Page 659, para. 4 – "50 per cent on each campus": "Academic Board OK's Expansion Framework"; *A Framework for Enrolment Expansion*; Susan Bloch-Nevitte, "Enrolment Predictions Drop", *University of Toronto Bulletin*, November 13, 2000.

133. Page 659, para. 4 – "mixes of work and study": *Toronto Star*, November 25, 1999.

134. Page 659, para. 4 – "half the students in such programs": *A Framework for Enrolment Expansion at the University of Toronto* at S3; e-mail from Joan Foley to Friedland, February 18, 2001.

135. Page 660, para. 1 – "culture and information technology": Ibid. Mississauga, headed by scientist Robert McNutt, would continue developing its strength in science and technology: see "McMaster Dean Joins Erindale as Principal", *University of Toronto Bulletin*, February 20, 1995; see also "Pharmaceutical Company Helps Establish New Chairs", *University of Toronto Bulletin*, November 9, 1998; "Erindale Plan Builds on Academic Strengths", *University of Toronto Bulletin*, November 21, 1994; "University of Toronto at Mississauga", *University of Toronto Magazine* (Autumn 1998) at C29.

136. Page 660, para. 2 – "directly from high school": "Academic Board OK's Expansion Framework"; *A Framework for Enrolment Expansion* at S2.

137. Page 660, para. 2 – "architecture": "Architecture School to Emphasize Graduate Education", *University of Toronto Bulletin*, September 15, 1997.

138. Page 660, para. 2 – "nursing": "Nursing Program Becomes Second Entry", *University of Toronto Bulletin*, May 12, 1997. Beginning in 2005 all nurses must have a four-year bachelor's degree in order to practice in Ontario: see "Nursing Funding Benefits U of T", *University of Toronto Bulletin*, April 24, 2000.

139. Page 660, para. 2 – "became second-entry": Conversation with Adel Sedra, August 25, 2000.

140. Page 660, para. 2 – "entry from high school": Conversation with Sedra.

141. Page 660, para. 2 – "doctoral-stream programs": *A Framework for Enrolment Expansion.*

142. Page 660, para. 2 – "into the regular programs": Foot, *Boom* at 212.

143. Page 660, para. 3 – "given greater support": *Report of the Task Force on Graduate Student Support May 31, 2000*, in *University of Toronto Bulletin*, September 11, 2000; "Provost Endorses Grad Student Aid Report", *University of Toronto Bulletin*, November 11, 2000.

144. Page 660, para. 3 – "teaching assistants in 1999": *University of Toronto News and Events*, December 13, 1999; *Varsity*, January 11, 2000.

145. Page 660, para. 3 – "national and international students": Michael Marrus states, "We haven't quite delivered on the promise yet. And indeed it will still be some time before we do so for OISE/UT": see e-mail from Marrus to Friedland, December 16, 2000. See also, "U of T Assures PhD Funding," *University of Toronto Bulletin*, August 20, 2001: 'The support package, which is being rolled out in almost all faculties this September, starts at a minimum of $12,000 plus tuition and fees...and will be available for up to five years of study."

146. Page 660, para. 3 – "not good for anybody": "Provost Endorses Grad Student Aid Report".

147. Page 660, para. 3 – "graduate school dean, Jon Cohen": "Changes Suggested for Graduate Studies", *University of Toronto Bulletin*, May 8, 1995; "Report of the Task Force on Restructuring The School of Graduate Studies", April 1996 (document forwarded by Michael Marrus).

148. Page 660, para. 3 – "'bureaucratic tendencies' of the graduate school": E-mail from Marrus to Friedland, July 9, 1998 and December 16, 2000; conversation with Sedra, August 25, 2000.

149. Page 661, para. 1 – "high standards across the divisions": E-mail from Marrus to Friedland, December 16, 2000.

150. Page 661, para. 2 – "decided to step down": Prichard to Cecil-Cockwell, December 1, 1998 (document forwarded from Robert Prichard).

151. Page 661, para. 2 – "wanted to return to teaching, he stated": Ibid.; "President to Return to Law", *University of Toronto Bulletin*, January 11, 1999; *Toronto Star*, December 17, 1998. After a year teaching at Harvard Law School, Prichard accepted an offer in the spring of 2001 to head the Toronto Star organization: *University of Toronto Bulletin*, May 28, 2001.

152. Page 661, para. 2 – "fundamentally good shape": Prichard to Cecil-Cockwell.

153. Page 661, para. 2 – "prospects may have never been better": J. Robert S. Prichard, "A good time to say goodbye", *University of Toronto Magazine* (Summer 2000) at 5.

154. Page 661, para. 3 – "in acquisitions": *UTLibrary News* (Summer 1998) at 1.

155. Page 661, para. 3 – "grants and awards per faculty member": *University of Toronto National Report 2000* at 9.

156. Page 661, para. 3 – "genetics and microbiology": "Six big awards", *University of Toronto Magazine* (Summer 2000) at 10. In 1994-95, Toronto had won all three of the Killam prizes awarded – to André Salama of computer engineering, Adrian Brook of chemistry, and Endel Tulving of psychology: see "U of T Wins all Three Killams", *University of Toronto Bulletin*, March 28, 1994.

157. Page 661, para. 3 – "chemist Ian Manners": *University of Toronto News and Events*, December 18, 2000. The three others were J.M. Xu of Electrical and Computer Engineering in 1995, S. John of Physics in 1996, and L.E. Kay of Biochemistry in 1999: see www.sao.nrc.ca/steacie/past_e.html.

158. Page 661, para. 3 – "Royal Society of Canada and other bodies": Since 1995, for example, University of Toronto professors have received half of the Molson prizes awarded by the Canada Council in the humanities and social sciences, the most recent being to philosopher Ian Hacking.

159. Page 661, para. 4 – "*Maclean's* magazine": "Maclean's Ranks U of T Tops", *University of Toronto Bulletin*, November 8, 1999; Prichard to Friends of the University of Toronto, December, 1999; "Tops Again: U of T Retains *Maclean's* Ranking", *University of Toronto Bulletin*, November 13, 2000; *Maclean's*, November 20, 2000.

160. Page 661, para. 4 – "the participating universities": "U of T Ranks Fourth in Survey", *University of Toronto Bulletin*, October 21, 1991. For the U of T's involvement with the survey, see UTA/A98-0008/109.

161. Page 663, para. 1 – "research university group": "Maclean's Ranks U of T Second", *University of Toronto Bulletin*, November 9, 1992.

162. Page 663, para. 1 – "McGill and Queen's": "U of T Ranks Third", *University of Toronto Bulletin*, November 22, 1993; *Maclean's*, November 15, 1993.

163. Page 663, para. 1 – "Toronto topped the list": *Maclean's*, November 15, 1994.

164. Page 663, para. 1 – "academic administrators, and others": "For the 6th consecutive year... U of T is No. 1" (glossy document from U of T). U of T in 2000 ranked in the top reputationally overall for "leaders of tomorrow" and second overall for "most innovative" and "highest quality": see "Tops Again".

165. Page 663, para. 1 – "best overall": "Maclean's Ranks U of T Tops"; *Maclean's*, November 15, 1999.

166. Page 663, para. 1 – "the most innovative": "For the 6th consecutive year... U of T is No. 1"; *Maclean's*, November 15, 1999.

167. Page 663, para. 2 – "a new president in March 1999": "Presidential Search Begins", *University of Toronto Bulletin*, March 29, 1999; "New U of T President Named by December", *University of Toronto Bulletin*, September 27, 1999.

168. Page 663, para. 2 – "Massachusetts Institute of Technology": "Birgeneau, Robert J.", *Canadian Who's Who 2000* at 117.

169. Page 663, para. 2 – "seven-year term": The term is renewable to ten years: see "Birgeneau Charts Course for Presidency", *University of Toronto Bulletin*, December 13, 1999.

170. Page 663, para. 2 – "November 1999": See generally, "Birgeneau Charts Course for Presidency"; "Robert J. Birgeneau Named University of Toronto's 14th President" (University of Toronto Press release, November 30, 1999); *Globe and Mail*, November 30 and December 1, 1999; *Varsity*, December 2, 1999; *The Independent*, December 2, 1999.

171. Page 663, para. 2 – "into the next century": "Robert J. Birgeneau Named University of Toronto's 14th President".

172. Page 663, para. 3 – "University of Toronto Act": *The University of Toronto Act, 1971 as amended by 1978, Chapter 88*, section 5(2).

173. Page 663, para. 3 – "graduated in 1963: "Birgeneau Charts Course".

174. Page 663, para. 3 – "other North American teams": The team was given an "honourable mention": see H.S.M. Coxeter, "Achievement in Maths", *Varsity Graduate* (April, 1966) at 15. Also while at University, Birgeneau led Toronto's effort in the Canadian Association of Physicists National Prize competition: see e-mail from Birgeneau to Friedland, October 2, 2000.

175. Page 663, para. 3 – "graduate in English": "Robert J. Birgeneau Named University of Toronto's 14th President".

176. Page 663, para. 3 – "first day of law school": Jack Batten, "Decade of the Dynamo", *University of Toronto Magazine* (Summer 2000) at 17.

177. Page 663, para. 3 – "first day of university": *Globe and Mail*, December 1, 1999.

178. Page 663, para. 3 – "dean of science": "Robert J. Birgeneau Named University of Toronto's 14th President"; "Birgeneau Charts Course".

179. Page 663, para. 4 – "correcting inequalities": Biologist Mary-Lou Pardue: see *Toronto Star*, January 3, 2000.

180. Page 663, para. 4 – "New Haven's black community": "Birgeneau Charts Course".

181. Page 663, para. 4 – "black college in South Carolina": "Robert J. Birgeneau U of T's New president", *University of Toronto News and Events*, November 30, 1999.

182. Page 665, para. 1 – "if people didn't act": "Birgeneau Charts Course".

183. Page 665, para. 1 – "community that it serves": "Birgeneau Charts Course"; "Robert J. Birgeneau Named University of Toronto's 14th President". Birgeneau said on several occasions that he expects administrators to share his views on diversity and if they do not, "they may as well step down": see *Toronto Star*, January 3, 2000. Psychologist John Furedy publicly worried about the "future chilling effect on my university if the new president really intends to apply this sort of radical social-engineering litmus test to our administrators and leaders": see "Birgeneau a Social Engineer?", *University of Toronto Bulletin*, February 28, 2000. See also Susan Bloch-Nevitte, "Themes for a New Presidency: Excellence, Equity, Outreach", *University of Toronto Bulletin*, October 16, 2000; "The Installation Address of Robert J. Birgeneau", *University of Toronto Bulletin*, October 30, 2000.

184. Page 665, para. 2 – "took over on July 1, 2000": "Birgeneau Charts Course".

185. Page 665, para. 2 – "in number of students": *Toronto Star*, December 17, 1998; *University of Toronto National Report 2000* at 11.

186. Page 665, para. 2 – "full-time and part-time students": Marty England states, "With a headcount of 54,000 we're the largest university. However, a footnote is warranted. We have 12,000 at Scarborough and Mississauga, and 42,000 on St. George. The St. George campus on its own is about sixth largest". The figures count part-time students the same as full-time students. In terms of FTEs, Ohio State, which has fewer part-time students than Toronto, was, according to England, first amongst the American Association of Universities in 1999 with 44,707 FTE students and Toronto was second with 44,584: see e-mail from England to Friedland, February 21, 2001.

187. Page 665, para. 2 – "greater number of staff positions": *Toronto Star*, December 17, 1998. In 1999/2000, total student enrolment was 54,132: see *University of Toronto National Report 2000* at 16; *University of Toronto Facts and Figures 2000*. Marty England states, "At present we have 1,710 full-time tenure stream professoriate. When you take account of all of the academic staff, regardless of rank or tenure stream status, there are 2,955 FTEs funded through the operating budget. This includes 950 FTEs in the faculty of medicine, many of whom are clinicians on partial budgetary appointments. The figures do not include other hospital staff or contract positions throughout the University paid for from research grants": see e-mail from England to Friedland, February 21, 2001.

188. Page 665, para. 2 – "prediction on his appointment": "Robert J. Birgeneau Named University of Toronto's 14th President".

EPILOGUE – 2000 – A WALK THROUGH THE CAMPUS

1. Page 667, para. 2 – “diversity of the student body”: See Chapter 41 (1994).

2. Page 667, para. 3 – “chair of medicine”: See Chapter 23 (1919).

3. Page 667, para. 3 – “now The Bay”: See Chapter 18 (1905).

4. Page 668, para. 1 – “board of governors of the University”: See Chapter 37 (1971).

5. Page 668, para. 1 – “dispute involving Queen's Park land”: See Chapter 11 (1887).

6. Page 668, para. 2 – “twelve strokes of midnight”: See Chapter 17 (1901).

7. Page 668, para. 2 – “influence on the architecture of the city”: See Chapter 30 (1955).

8. Page 668, para. 3 – “‘godless’ University of Toronto”: See Chapter 3 (1849)

9. Page 668, para. 3 – “eventually was accorded in 1957”: See Chapter 31 (1958).

10. Page 668, para. 4 – “present legislative building”: See Chapter 2 (1842).

11. Page 668, para. 4 – “George IV in 1827”: See Chapter 1 (1826).

12. Page 668, para. 4 – “to witness the ceremony”: See Chapter 2 (1842).

13. Page 668, para. 4 – “the present legislative building”: See generally, Roger Hall, *A Century to Celebrate/Un Centenaire à fêter, 1893-1993* (Toronto: Dundurn Press, 1993).

14. Page 669, para. 1 – “of which Englishmen are proud”: See Chapter 1 (1826).

15. Page 669, para. 1 – “a force in the determination of Canadian culture”: See Chapter 31 (1958).

16. Page 669, para. 1 –“prevent American cultural domination of Canada”: See Chapter 25 (1926).

17. Page 669, para. 2 – “Toronto General Hospital across the street”: See Chapter 35 (1966).

18. Page 669, para. 2 – “directly from Mount Sinai”: E-mail from Eliot Phillipson to Charles Levi, December 11, 2000.

19. Page 669, para. 2 – “Taddle Creek ran under it”: See Chapter 35 (1966).

20. Page 669, para. 2 – “a source of delight for the University”: See Chapter 6 (1856).

21. Page 669, para. 2 – “First Nations people”: See John Borrows, “Buried Spirits”, *University of Toronto Bulletin*, March 3, 1997; Borrows, *Recovering Canada: The Resurgence of Indigenous Law* (U of T Press, forthcoming), Introduction; *Toronto Life*, January 2000.

22. Page 669, para. 2 – “buried below ground in 1884”: See Chapter 6 (1856).

23. Page 669, para. 2 – “parts of the creek”: See Chapter 42 (1997).

24. Page 669, para. 3 – “cancer research and treatment”: See Chapters 35 (1966) and 40 (1986).

25. Page 669, para. 3 – "before the First World War": See Chapter 21 (1909).

26. Page 669, para. 3 – "as an emergency hospital": See Chapter 21 (1909).

27. Page 670, para. 1 – "bring fame to the University": See Chapter 24 (1922).

28. Page 670, para. 2 – "around the park": See Chapter 12 (1887).

29. Page 670, para. 2 – "later the school of nursing": See Chapters 18 (1905) and 26 (1931).

30. Page 670, para. 2 – "part of St. Michael's": See Chapter 19 (1907).

31. Page 670, para. 2 – "jewels in Toronto's crown": U of T Directory.

32. Page 670, para. 3 – "old Botany Building": Botany moved to the new Earth Sciences Building: see Chapter 40 (1986).

33. Page 670, para. 3 – "Leslie Dan pharmacy building": See Chapter 41 (1994).

34. Page 670, para. 3 – "bloom every hundred years": www.scienceu.com/library/articles/flowers/agave.html; e-mail from Bruce Hall to Charles Levi, December 4, 2000, stating that, in fact, it takes roughly 25-35 years for the plant to reach maturity and bloom; see also e-mail from Elizabeth Sisam to Friedland, February 5, 2001.

35. Page 670, para. 3 – "significant contributions to the University": See Chapter 41 (1994).

36. Page 670, para. 3 – "played only the piano": See Chapter 31 (1958).

37. Page 670, para. 3 – "the School of Hygiene": See Chapter 22 (1914).

38. Page 670, para. 3 – "lobbied the government to finance": See Chapter 17 (1901).

39. Page 670, para. 4 – "1,000 graduate students": See Chapter 35 (1966).

40. Page 670, para. 4 – "other side of St. George Street": See Chapter 42 (1997).

41. Page 671, para. 1 – "very little green space": See Chapter 30 (1955).

42. Page 671, para. 1 – "on account of the city": See Chapter 18 (1905).

43. Page 671, para. 1 – "more suitable location than Ajax": See Chapter 28 (1944).

44. Page 671, para. 2 – "completed in 1859": See Chapter 6 (1856).

45. Page 671, para. 2 – "facing in any other direction than south": See Chapter 6 (1856).

46. Page 671, para. 2 – "non-denominational University of Toronto established": See Chapter 3 (1849).

47. Page 671, para. 2 – "became president of the University of Toronto": See Chapter 4 (1850).

48. Page 671, para. 2 – "Trinity College on Queen Street West": See Chapter 3 (1849).

49. Page 671, para. 2 – "Henry Croft": See Chapter 6 (1856).

50. Page 671, para. 2 – "connected with University College": Douglas Richardson, *A Not Unsightly Building: University College and Its History* (Toronto: Mosaic Press, 1990) at 111.

51. Page 671, para. 2 – "John Tyndall, who applied for positions in the 1850s": See Chapter 5 (1853).

52. Page 671, para. 3 – "a fondness for him": See Chapter 5 (1853).

53. Page 671, para. 3 – "south from College Street": Eric Arthur, *Toronto: No Mean City* (University of Toronto Press, 1986) at 285.

54. Page 671, para. 3 – "a house in the residence": See Chapter 18 (1905).

55. Page 671, para. 4 – "a gift from the alumni": See Chapter 17 (1901).

56. Page 671, para. 4 – "student activism of the 1960s": See Chapter 36 (1967).

57. Page 672, para. 1 – "Northrop Frye in 1981": The text is incorrect in stating that the memorial service for Northrop Frye was in 1981. It was in 1991. It is strange that I did not spot this typo because Northrop Frye was one of the contributors to the author's collection, *Rough Justice: Essays on Crime and Literature*, published by University of Toronto Press in 1991.

58. Page 672, para. 1 – "the University Act of 1906": See Chapter 19 (1907).

59. Page 672, para. 1 – "the more I liked him": See Chapter 19 (1907).

60. Page 672, para. 1 – "Second World War": See Chapters 26 (1931), 27 (1939), and 28 (1944).

61. Page 672, para. 2 – "'Skulehouse', built in 1878": See Chapter 8 (1871).

62. Page 672, para. 2 – "old medical school, constructed in 1903": See Chapter 12 (1887).

63. Page 672, para. 2 – "new Medical Sciences Building": See Chapter 35 (1966).

64. Page 672, para. 2 – "name the medical school after him": See Chapter 12 (1887).

65. Page 672, para. 3 – "Gerstein Science Information Centre": See Chapter 14 (1890).

66. Page 672, para. 3 – "Robarts Library": See Chapter 33 (1962).

67. Page 672, para. 4 – "Students' Administrative Council": See Chapter 20 (1908).

68. Page 672, para. 4 – "saying 'hands off'": See Chapter 17 (1901).

69. Page 673, para. 1 – "after 3 o'clock in the afternoon': See Chapter 29 (1950).

70. Page 673, para. 1 – "George Wrong, and others": See Chapter 22 (1914).

71. Page 673, para. 1 – "executed in Buchenwald": See Chapter 27 (1939).

72. Page 673, para. 2 – "tying its tail to the bell": See Chapter 6 (1856).

73. Page 673, para. 2 – "admission to the college in the early 1880s": See Chapter 9 (1880).

74. Page 673, para. 2 – "gutted much of the college": See Chapter 14 (1890).

75. Page 673, para. 2 – "student strike of 1895": See Chapter 15 (1895).

76. Page 673, para. 2 – "it would surely have been on this day": See Chapter 6 (1856).

77. Page 673, para. 3 – "University Act of 1906": See Chapter 18 (1905).

78. Page 673, para. 3 – "Robarts Library": See Chapter 33 (1962).

79. Page 673, para. 3 – "the age of 100": See Chapters 10 (1883), 12 (1887), and 28 (1944),

80. Page 673, para. 4 – "women's sport at the University": Conversations with Bruce Kidd in February 2001 and e-mail to the author of February 23, 2001.

81. Page 674, para. 1 – "royal charter in 1827": See Chapter 2 (1842).

82. Page 674, para. 1 – "the residence was built anyway": See Chapter 18 (1905).

83. Page 674, para. 1 – "John Graham Library of Trinity College": See Chapter 41 (1994).

84. Page 674, para. 2 – "opened in 1963": See Chapter 33 (1962).

85. Page 674, para. 2 – "household science building": See Chapters 16 (1897) and 18 (1905).

86. Page 674, para. 2 – "Annesley Hall": See Chapter 9 (1880).

87. Page 674, para. 2 – "Burwash Hall": See Chapter 10 (1883).

88. Page 674, para. 2 – "Hart House": See Chapter 23 (1919).

89. Page 674, para. 2 – "Queen Street Site in the 1920s": See Chapter 23 (1919).

90. Page 674, para. 3 – "Flavelle's grand house": See Chapter 31 (1958).

91. Page 674, para. 3 – "the music man": See Chapter 31 (1958).

92. Page 674, para. 4 – "in the early 1890s": See Chapter 10 (1883).

93. Page 674, para. 4 – "the University's fortunes": See Chapter 10 (1883).

94. Page 675, para. 1 – "constructed behind the main building": *Campaign News*, September, 1998; *University of Toronto Bulletin*, March 12, 2001; *Globe and Mail*, February 23, 2001.

95. Page 675, para. 2 – "Institute of Mediaeval Studies": See Chapter 24 (1922).

96. Page 675, para. 2 – "Marshall McLuhan": See Chapter 34 (1963).

97. Page 675, para. 2 – "Pierre Trudeau's house in Montreal": James McConica to Friedland, February 12, 2001.

98. Page 675, para. 2 – "still standing in their original location": See Chapter 4 (1850).

99. Page 675, para. 3 – "*Collected Works of Erasmus*": See generally, Chapter 34 (1963).

100. Page 675, para. 4 – "as an endowment": See Chapter 29 (1950).

101. Page 675, para. 4 – "corner of Bloor and Queen's Park": See Chapters 16 (1897) and 19 (1907).

102. Page 675, para. 4 – "Annie Laird – worked there": See Chapter 16 (1897)

103. Page 676, para. 1 – "the museum might not have been built": See Chapters 21 (1909), 26 (1931), and 42 (1997).

104. Page 676, para. 1 – "the tomb was outside the building": See Chapter 26 (1931).

105. Page 676, para. 1 – "widened after the second World War": E-mail from Harold Averill to Friedland, February 18, 2001.

106. Page 676, para. 1 – "a visit of royalty in 1901": The Duke and Duchess of Cornwall and York: see *Torontonensis 1902.*

107. Page 676, para. 2 – "McMaster University": See Chapter 10 (1883).

108. Page 676, para. 2 – "department of political economy": See Chapter 24 (1922).

109. Page 676, para. 2 – "before the Second World War": See Chapter 27 (1939).

110. Page 676, para. 2 – "Royal Conservatory of Music": See Chapter 31 (1958).

111. Page 676, para. 2 – "new residences and athletic facilities": See Chapter 42 (1997).

112. Page 676, para. 2 – "spectator team sports at the University": See Chapters 25 (1926) and 29 (1950).

113. Page 676, para. 2 – "undefeated and unscored-against": See Chapter 25 (1926).

114. Page 676, para. 3 – "pleased with its growth": See Chapter 31 (1958).

115. Page 676, para. 3 – "benefit of both institutions": See Chapters 33 (1962) and 39 (1980).

116. Page 676, para. 4 – "governors made many of the key decisions for the University": See Chapters 33 (1962) and 35 (1966).

117. Page 677, para. 1 – "became president in 1972": See Chapter 37 (1971).

118. Page 677, para. 1 – "Simcoe Circle": See Chapter 39 (1971).

119. Page 677, para. 1 – "turning point in the University's history": See Chapter 39 (1971).

120. Page 677, para. 2 – "an important need in the community": See Chapter 38 (1975).

121. Page 677, para. 2 – "now taken for granted": See Chapter 36 (1967).

122. Page 677, para. 2 – "gift for its redevelopment: See Chapter 42 (1997).

123. Page 677, para. 3 – "learned to like it": See Chapter 33 (1962).

124. Page 677, para. 3 – "growth of the University in the 1960s": See Chapter 33 (1962).

125. Page 677 para. 4 – "Rotman School of Management": See Chapters 31 (1958) and 41 (1994).

126. Page 677, para. 4 – "Harold Innis": See Chapters 30 (1955) and 32 (1960).

127. Page 677, para. 4 – "women's and men's buildings now united": See Chapters 39 (1980) and 41 (1994).

128. Page 677, para. 4 – "stretching out over Harbord Street": See Chapter 42 (1994).

129. Page 678, para. 1 – "as some hoped it would": See Chapter 39 (1980).

130. Page 678, para. 2 – "using the existing street pattern": See Chapter 30 (1955).

131. Page 678, para. 2 – "Nobel prize for his work": See Chapters 16 (1897), 22 (1914), 24 (1922), and 31 (1958).

132. Page 678, para. 2 – "University's sixth president": See Chapters 30 (1955) and 31 (1958).

133. Page 678, para. 2 – "built since University College": See Chapter 32 (1960).

134. Page 678, para. 2 – "did not like what the sculptor produced.": See Chapter 31 (1958).

135. Page 678, para. 2 – "complicated simplicity": See Chapter 30 (1955).

136. Page 678, para. 3 – "government funds through competitions": See Chapters 41 (1994) and 42 (1997).

137. Page 678, para. 3 – "John and Margaret Bahen": See Chapter 41 (1994).

138. Page 678, para. 3 – "David Strangway": See Chapters 38 (1975), 39 (1980), and 40 (1986).

139. Page 678, para. 4 – "Earth Sciences Centre": See Chapters 39 (1980) and 40 (1986).

140. Page 678, para. 4 – "Spadina Circle": See Chapter 42 (1997).

141. Page 678, para. 4 – "'infirmary' over the side door": See Chapter 13 (1889).

142. Page 679, para. 2 – "dean of medicine": See Chapters 21 (1909) and 35 (1966).

143. Page 679, para. 2 – "Toronto reference library": See Chapters 38 (1975) and 39 (1980).

144. Page 679, para. 2 – "Fields Institute of Mathematics": "Provost's Fund to Assist Institute", *University of Toronto Bulletin*, October 18, 1993; "U of T Likely Site for Fields Math Institute", *University of Toronto Bulletin*, May 25, 1993; "Academic Board Approves Fields", *University of Toronto Bulletin*, November 22, 1993; "Fields on Fast Track", *University of Toronto Bulletin*, January 10, 1994; "Trees Move Out, Crews In for Mathematical Institute", *University of Toronto Bulletin*, April 25, 1994; "Fields Institute Delayed", *University of Toronto Bulletin*, June 27, 1994.

145. Page 679, para. 2 – "Johns Hopkins University in the nineteenth century": See Chapter 11 (1887).

146. Page 679, para. 2 – "Student mathematicians in the 1940s": See Chapter 27 (1939).

147. Page 679, para. 2 – "maths and physics student at the University in the 1960s": See Chapter 42 (1997).

148. Page 679, para. 3 – "engineering, and medicine": See Chapters 41 (1994) and 42 (1997).

149. Page 679, para. 3 – "technology or knowledge": See Chapter 41 (1994).

150. Page 679, para. 3 – "take-over of our University": See Chapters 41 (1994) and (1997).

151. Page 679, para. 3 – "maintaining accessibility will remain a challenge": See Chapter 42 (1997).

152. Page 679, para. 4 – "public research universities of the world": See Chapter 41 (1994).

153. Page 680, para. 1 – "productive periods in the university's history": See Chapter 42 (1997).

154. Page 680, para. 1 – "truly international stature": See Chapter 42 (1997).

www.ingramcontent.com/pod-product-compliance
Lightning Source LLC
LaVergne TN
LVHW082157080826
844660LV00046B/1261